COMPARATIVE POLITICS 91/92

Ninth Edition

Annual Editions
A Library of Information from the Public Press

Editor

Christian Soe
California State University, Long Beach

Christian Soe was born in Denmark, studied in Canada and the United States, and received his doctoral degree in political science from the Free University in Berlin. He is a political science professor at California State University, Long Beach. Dr. Soe teaches a wide range of courses in comparative politics and contemporary political theory, and actively participates in professional symposiums in the United States and abroad. He founded and continues to direct the Pacific Workshop on German Affairs, and his research deals primarily with developments in contemporary German politics. As an observer of the first free election in East Germany in March 1990, he gathered fresh data on the reemergence of political pluralism in that part of the country. In November and December 1990 he returned as an observer of the first Bundestag election after Germany's unification.

At present Dr. Soe is writing a short study of the Free Democratic Party in the enlarged Federal Republic, and is co-editor of a planned book, *The Germans and Their Neighbors,* that will examine foreign reactions to the emergence of a larger and more powerful Germany.

Cover illustration

D1402333

The Dushkin Publishing Group, Inc.
Sluice Dock, Guilford, Connecticut 06437

The Annual Editions Series

Annual Editions is a series of over fifty volumes designed to provide the reader with convenient, low-cost access to a wide range of current, carefully selected articles from some of the most important magazines, newspapers, and journals published today. Annual Editions are updated on an annual basis through a continuous monitoring of over 200 periodical sources. All Annual Editions have a number of features designed to make them particularly useful, including topic guides, annotated tables of contents, unit overviews, and indexes. For the teacher using Annual Editions in the classroom, an Instructor's Resource Guide with test questions is available for each volume.

VOLUMES AVAILABLE

Africa
Aging
American Government
American History, Pre-Civil War
American History, Post-Civil War
Anthropology
Biology
Business and Management
Business Ethics
Canadian Politics
China
Comparative Politics
Computers in Education
Computers in Business
Computers in Society
Criminal Justice
Drugs, Society, and Behavior
Early Childhood Education
Economics
Educating Exceptional Children
Education
Educational Psychology
Environment
Geography
Global Issues
Health
Human Development
Human Resources
Human Sexuality

Latin America
Macroeconomics
Management
Marketing
Marriage and Family
Microeconomics
Middle East and the Islamic World
Money and Banking
Nutrition
Personal Growth and Behavior
Psychology
Public Administration
Race and Ethnic Relations
Social Problems
Sociology
Soviet Union and Eastern Europe
State and Local Government
Third World
Urban Society
Violence and Terrorism
Western Civilization, Pre-Reformation
Western Civilization, Post-Reformation
Western Europe
World History, Pre-Modern
World History, Modern
World Politics

Library of Congress Cataloging in Publication Data
Main entry under title: Annual Editions: Comparative Politics. 1991/92.
1. World politics—Addresses, essays, lectures—Periodicals. 2. Politics, Practical—Addresses, essays, lectures—Periodicals. I. Soe, Christian, comp. II. Title: Comparative Politics.
ISBN 1–56134–015–4   909'.05   83–647654

Ninth Edition

Manufactured by The Banta Company, Harrisonburg, Virginia 22801

Editors/ Advisory Board

To the Reader

In publishing ANNUAL EDITIONS we recognize the enormous role played by the magazines, newspapers, and journals of the *public press* in providing current, first-rate educational information in a broad spectrum of interest areas. Within the articles, the best scientists, practitioners, researchers, and commentators draw issues into new perspective as accepted theories and viewpoints are called into account by new events, recent discoveries change old facts, and fresh debate breaks out over important controversies.

Many of the articles resulting from this enormous editorial effort are appropriate for students, researchers, and professionals seeking accurate, current material to help bridge the gap between principles and theories and the real world. These articles, however, become more useful for study when those of lasting value are carefully *collected, organized, indexed,* and *reproduced* in a *low-cost format*, which provides easy and permanent access when the material is needed. That is the role played by *Annual Editions*. Under the direction of each volume's *Editor*, who is an expert in the subject area, and with the guidance of an *Advisory Board*, we seek each year to provide in each ANNUAL EDITION a current, well-balanced, carefully selected collection of the best of the public press for your study and enjoyment. We think you'll find this volume useful, and we hope you'll take a moment to let us know what you think.

This collection of readings brings together many recent articles to help you understand the politics of distant, foreign lands. You will soon discover that studying politics from a comparative perspective not only opens up a fascinating world beyond our borders, it also leads to greater insights into yourself and your social and political situation.

The articles in unit one cover Britain, Germany, France, and Japan in a serial manner. Each of these modern societies has developed its own governmental institutions, defined its own political agenda, and found its own dynamic balance of continuity and change. Nevertheless, as the readings of unit two show, it is possible to point to some common denominators to make useful cross-national comparisons among these and other representative democracies. Unit three goes one step further by discussing the impact of two major changes that are rapidly transforming the political map of Europe—the growth of the European Community (EC) and the collapse of communism in much of Central and Eastern Europe.

The continuing political importance of Europe has been underscored by these two developments. While the integration of the European Community has been a process of several decades, it accelerated markedly in the latter part of the 1980s with the passage and implementation of the Single Europe Act. By contrast, there was little advance warning of the recent upheaval that has weakened or toppled the Communist regimes imposed in the countries of Central and Eastern Europe after World War II. The result is nothing less than a major revolution, as these nations attempt to replace one-party rule and socialist state planning with multi-party democracy and market economics.

Unit four deals with the Soviet Union and China. These two giants are still dominated by the Communist parties that carried through revolutions and took power in 1917 and 1949 respectively. However, now there are serious challenges to the long-established rulers and their policies in both countries. Similar to other Communist powerholders, they have also functioned as development regimes in countries that had failed to modernize on their own. The politics of development in the so-called Third World is examined further in unit five. Here the emphasis is on the diversity of the many countries that are struggling to overcome traditional obstacles to development.

There has rarely been so interesting and important a time for the study of comparative politics as now. We can already see that the political earthquake of 1989–1990 has altered the political landscape with consequences that will be felt and studied for many years to come. But even in a time of such major political transformation, there are important patterns of continuity as well. We must be careful to look for both as we seek to gain a comparative understanding of the politics of other countries and peoples.

This is the ninth edition of *Annual Editions: Comparative Politics.* It includes many new articles that reflect the changes discussed above. The basic format has also been adjusted to take into account the revolutionary developments that have created a post–cold war world.

I am grateful to members of the advisory board and The Dushkin Publishing Group as well as to many readers who have made useful comments on past selections and suggested new ones. My own students also keep me posted on concerns and needs that this anthology must address. Susan B. Mason, who recently received her master's degree in political science at my university, has been a superb research assistant over the past few years. A special note of thanks to Harmon Zeigler and his students, who have provided this volume with a statistical appendix that is both attractive and useful. I ask you all to help me improve future editions of this anthology by keeping me informed of your reactions and suggestions for change. Please complete and return the article rating form in the back of the book.

Christian Soe
Editor

Contents

Unit 1

Pluralist Democracies: Country Studies

Nineteen selections examine the current state of politics in the United Kingdom, Germany, France, and Japan.

The concepts in bold italics are developed in the article. For further expansion please refer to the Topic Guide and the Index.

The concepts in bold italics are developed in the article. For further expansion please refer to the Topic Guide and the Index.

Unit 2

Modern Pluralist Democracies: Elements in the Political Process

Twelve selections examine the functioning of Western European democracies with regard to political ideas and participation, the role of women in politics, electoral laws, Parliament, and heads of state.

The concepts in bold italics are developed in the article. For further expansion please refer to the Topic Guide and the Index.

Unit 3

Politics in a New Europe: Countries and a Continent in Transformation

Eleven articles discuss the challenges facing a new Europe: developing institutions, essential policy problems, and the dynamics of a post-Communist Eastern Europe.

The concepts in bold italics are developed in the article. For further expansion please refer to the Topic Guide and the Index.

Unit 4

The Soviet Union and China: Two Communist Giants and the Dilemma of Reform

Seven selections examine the incredible political and economic changes in the Soviet Union and China.

Unit 5

The Third World: Diversity in Development

Nine selections review Third World economic and political developments in Latin America, Africa, the Middle East, and Asia.

The concepts in bold italics are developed in the article. For further expansion please refer to the Topic Guide and the Index.

Topic Guide

This topic guide suggests how the selections in this book relate to topics of traditional concern to students and professionals involved with the study of comparative politics. It is very useful in locating articles that relate to each other for reading and research. The guide is arranged alphabetically according to topic. Articles may, of course, treat topics that do not appear in the topic guide. In turn, entries in the topic guide do not necessarily constitute a comprehensive listing of all the contents of each selection.

TOPIC AREA	TREATED IN:	TOPIC AREA	TREATED IN:
Administrative Elites	16. Quiet Revolt in Corridors of Power	Environment and Politics	9. East German Disaster 22. Squabbling German Greens
Africa	52. Africa's Great Black Hope 53. South Africa's Constitutional Cry 54. Apartheid's Laws Are Dismantled	Ethnicity and Politics	5. Scots Who Want to Be Alone 6. Two Irelands Struggle to Recover 15. France Questions Its Identity
British Government and Politics	Articles 1 through 6 25. What We Know About Women Voters 26. Women in Parliament 27. Europe's Women 29. Parliament and Congress 30. Presidents and Prime Ministers 31. With All Her Faults, She Is My Country Still 34. German Unification		24. Europe's Extremes 43. Gorbachev's Gathering Storm 44. Russian Character 45. Soviet Politics 52. Africa's Great Black Hope 53. South Africa's Constitutional Cry 54. Apartheid's Laws 55. Islam's New Political Face 57. Turmoil Erodes Nehru Legacy 58. Just Changing the Guard Can't Save India
Central and Eastern Europe	40. Eastern Europe I 41. Dustbin of Economics 42. Dilemmas of Freedom	European Community	1. 1990: A Europe Transformed 14. France Faces the New Europe Articles 32 through 39
Chinese Government and Politics	48. Ominous Embers From Fires of 1989 49. China: The Coming Changes	The Executive	3. Margaret Thatcher 4. John Major 7. Reunited Germany 12. France's Fifth Republic 14. France Faces the New Europe 28. We the Peoples 30. Presidents and Prime Ministers 37. Six EC Institutions 38. Tackling the Democratic Deficit 43. Gorbachev's Gathering Storm 45. Soviet Politics 46. Gorbachev Lines Up New System 51. Salinas Takes a Gamble 57. Turmoil Erodes Nehru Legacy 58. Just Changing the Guard Can't Save India
Christian Democrats	7. Reunited Germany 8. German Elections and National Unity 23. Europe's Christian Democrats		
Civil Service	See Administrative Elites		
Communists in Western Europe	8. German Elections and National Unity 12. France's Fifth Republic 13. End of French Exceptionalism 14. France Faces the New Europe 24. Europe's Extremes		
Conservative Party in Britain	Articles 1 through 6	Federal and Unitary Systems	5. Scots Who Want to Be Alone 6. Two Irelands Struggle to Recover 10. Federalism and Federal Republic 11. New Federalists 31. With All Her Faults, She Is My Country Still 45. Soviet Politics 46. Gorbachev Lines Up New System 52. Africa's Great Black Hope 53. South Africa's Constitutional Cry 58. Just Changing the Guard Can't Save India
Constitutions	5. Scots Who Want to Be Alone 6. Two Irelands Struggle to Recover 7. Reunited Germany 10. Federalism and Federal Republic 11. New Federalists 12. France's Fifth Republic 28. We the Peoples 45. Soviet Politics 46. Gorbachev Lines Up New System 53. South Africa's Constitutional Cry		
Democratic Left	1. 1990: A Europe Transformed 2. British Politics in Post-Collectivist Era 7. Reunited Germany 8. German Elections and National Unity 12. France's Fifth Republic 13. End of French Exceptionalism 20. Reflections 21. Interview With Michel Rocard 22. Squabbling German Greens	French Government and Politics	Articles 12 through 16 21. Interview With Michel Rocard 23. Europe's Christian Democrats 24. Europe's Extremes 25. What We Know About Women Voters 26. Women in Parliament 27. Europe's Women 30. Presidents and Prime Ministers 31. With All Her Faults, She Is My Country Still 34. German Unification
Eastern Europe	See Central and Eastern Europe	German Government and Politics	Articles 7 through 11 22. Squabbling German Greens 23. Europe's Christian Democrats 24. Europe's Extremes 25. What We Know About Women Voters 26. Women in Parliament 27. Europe's Women 32. Predicting the New Europe 33. Euro Future 34. German Unification
Electoral Systems	7. Reunited Germany 8. German Elections and National Unity 19. Giving Hostages to Electoral Fortune 26. Women in Parliament 56. Israel: The Deadlock Persists		

Pluralist Democracies: Country Studies

The United Kingdom, Germany, and France rank among the most prominent industrial societies in Western Europe. Although their modern political histories differ sharply, they have all become stable pluralist democracies with competitive party systems and representative governments. Japan is far less pluralist in sociocultural terms, but it occupies a similar position of primacy among the few industrial democracies in Asia. A study of comparative government can usefully begin by examining the politics of these countries more closely through the articles in this and the following two units.

The first article reviews the recent political earthquake in Europe, whose aftershocks will be felt for a long time to come. But it also serves to remind us that along with the radical discontinuities, as represented by the unification of Germany and the emergence of post-Communist governments in Eastern Europe, we should also pay attention to the record of more moderate change or continuity in European politics such as the occasional change of government or the holding of routine elections.

Britain has long been regarded as a model of parliamentary government and majoritarian party politics. In the 1960s and 1970s, however, the country became better known for its apparent governing crisis. Anthony King, Richard Rose, and other political scientists in the 1970s defined the British problem as one of governmental *overload*, resulting from economic and social pressures that resulted in a severe condition of what they sometimes called *ungovernability*. A second but related explanation of the governing crisis in Britain focused on the unusually sharp *adversarial* character of the country's party politics, symbolized by the sharp confrontation of government and opposition parties in the House of Commons. Still other interpreters explained Britain's *relative decline* in terms of a varying mixture of economic, social, cultural, and ideological factors that kept the country from keeping up with some of its European neighbors.

As if to defy such pessimistic analyses, Britain by the mid-1980s began to pull ahead of other Western European countries in its annual economic growth. This apparent economic turnabout was associated with the rule of Prime Minister Margaret Thatcher, who had come to power in May of 1979 and introduced a drastic change in economic and social policy for the country. Her radical rhetoric and somewhat less drastic policy changes spawned yet another debate about what came to be called the *Thatcher Revolution* and its social and political consequences. By the late 1980s, the pragmatic argument in favor of Thatcher's approach lost some of its force when the country slipped back into *stagflation*, or sluggish economic performance coupled with high inflation.

Thus the concern about "ungovernability," which dominated discussions about British politics in the 1970s, gave way in the 1980s to quite different questions about the consequences of Thatcher's economic and social policies. The debate also shifted to new concerns about the government's efforts to tighten central controls over education at all levels, its introduction of cost controls into the popular National Health Service, its privatization of electricity and water industries as well as its inroads upon what had long been considered established rights in such areas as local government powers and civil liberties. Moreover, Thatcher was a staunch defender of national sovereignty who distrusted the drive toward monetary and eventual political union in the European Community. She became known throughout the continent for her unusually sharp attacks on what she regarded as tendencies toward undemocratic statism or technocratic socialism in Brussels. There were critics in her own party who regarded her position as untenable because it isolated Britain and deprived it of possible influence on questions of strategic planning for the EC's future. Her stepped-up attacks on closer European union finally led the deputy prime minister, Sir Geoffrey Howe, to resign on November 1, 1990 with a sharp public rebuke of the party leader's attitude to Europe. This step triggered the leadership struggle in the Conservative party that ended with Thatcher's own resignation toward the end of the month.

For the mass electorate, however, nothing seems to have been so upsetting as the introduction of the *community charge*, a tax on each adult citizen that would replace the local property tax or rates as a means of financing local public services. Although this so-called *poll tax* was very unpopular in Scotland, where it had been introduced a year earlier, Thatcher resisted all pressure to abandon the tax and its planned introduction into England and Wales in April 1990. Not only did such a tax appear inequitable or regressive, as compared to one based on property values, it also turned out to be set much higher by local governments than the national government originally had estimated. Many voters were up in arms, and by the spring of 1990 some observers correctly anticipated that the tax rebellion would undermine Thatcher's position in her own party and become her political Waterloo.

By this time Labour was in a better position to capitalize on the growing electoral disenchantment with the Conservative government. As the main opposition party, it was no longer dogged by the social democratic or social liberal alternatives that had fragmented the non-Conservative camp in the elections of 1983 and 1987. Under its leader, Neil Kinnock, Labour had moved back toward its traditional center-left position and now again presented itself as a politically moderate and socially caring reform party. It was far ahead of the Conservatives in some opinion polls, and it won some impressive victories in by-elections to the House of Commons.

Not surprisingly, these same developments led to an increasingly outspoken criticism of the prime minister in her own party and from its electoral supporters. This is the essential background for understanding how by November Michael Heseltine, a longtime critic of Thatcher, could mobilize considerable support among Conservative members of Parliament for his challenge to her leadership. In a vote among Tory M.P.'s she received far less support than her supporters had expected in early tallies: 204 votes for Thatcher to 152 for Heseltine, with only 16 abstentions. Politically, if not arithmetically, it was a defeat for Margaret Thatcher—but not a victory for her challenger. Her resignation was followed by the Conservative party's election of John Major, long regarded as one of her closest cabinet supporters, rather than Heseltine, to succeed her as party leader.

Although his economic views do not differ sharply from those of Thatcher, Major is identified with a far less controversial governing style. He appears to be more flexible on questions regarding European integration and has already indicated that he will modify if not entirely abolish the hated poll tax. In the spring of 1991, it was generally estimated that the Conservative party had a very good chance to recover in time for the next general election that must be held no later than the early summer of 1992.

However one reacts to Thatcher's style and policies, it seems certain by now that her long tenure as head of government will be looked back upon as an era that brought fundamental change to Britain. Most of the articles on Britain deal in some way with her record and legacy. In the first, Professor Anthony Messina gives a balanced assessment of the political results of the Thatcher years, emphasizing the social and ideological changes that have brought a *post-collectivist* era in British politics. He stresses that this is not a propitious setting for traditional Labour party politics. Next follows an assessment of the rise and fall of Margaret Thatcher by Hugo Young, the author of what is widely considered to be the best political biography we have of Prime Minister Thatcher. Another article gives reasons for concluding that John Major is no carbon copy of Margaret Thatcher. Two final pieces remind us that the ethnic factor is still of importance in British politics, as far as Scotland and Northern Ireland are concerned.

Germany was united in 1990, when the eastern German Democratic Republic was merged with the western Federal Republic of Germany. The two German states had been established in 1949, four years after the total defeat of the German Reich in World War II. During the next 40 years, rival elites and ideologies set the tone in each of the two successor states. *East Germany* was created on the territory of the former Soviet Occupation Zone of Germany. Its one-party rule and centrally planned economy reflected the power monopoly of the Communist party on which the state rested. By contrast, *West Germany*, based on the former American, British, and French zones of postwar occupation, developed a pluralist democracy and a flourishing market economy. When the two states were getting ready to celebrate their fortieth anniversaries in 1989, no leading politician was on record as having foreseen that the German division was about to come to an end.

The East German state had been widely regarded as the most successful economy in the Communist-ruled part of Europe, but it always lacked democratic legitimacy. This was demonstrated unforgettably when many East Germans used the chance to "vote with their feet" after the opening of the Hungarian border in the summer of 1989. The hard-line Communist regime was embarassed by this massive defection to the west, and that in turn encouraged many who remained in East Germany to join in demonstrations for reform that grew into mass protests by October and November. Giving way to popular pressure, the Communist rulers finally decided to ease the restrictions on travel to the west. As the German writer Peter Schneider ironically observed, they opened the Berlin Wall in November 1989 for the same reason they had put it up in 1961—to keep East Germans from leaving the country permanently. But this gesture was clearly a desperate move by a Communist government that had lost its will to power. It only encouraged protesters to make stronger demands, ending in public calls for unification with West Germany.

Such popular demands only had a chance of having results because of two major developments. First, the Soviet leader, Mikhail Gorbachev, had abandoned the so-called Brezhnev Doctrine, according to which the Soviets claimed the right of intervention on behalf of the established Communist regimes in central and eastern Europe. And second, the imposed Communist regimes of these countries turned out to have lost the will or ability to hold on to their power monopoly. As Alexis de Tocqueville had observed a century and a half earlier, no popular revolution can succeed until the latter condition has been fulfilled.

It was not that the East German Communists gave up without trying to hold on to power. But in the end, they refrained from resorting to a violent repression of the protesters. In October 1989, they unceremoniously replaced their long-time leader, Erich Honecker, with a more pliable top functionary, Egon Krenz. The latter never managed to gain popular trust despite some concessions to public pressure that would have been unthinkable a few months earlier. After a little more than a month in office, he was succeeded by Hans Modrow, a fairly popular and respected Communist reformer, as the head of government, while the party chose a new leader, a new program, and a new name (the Party of Democratic Socialism) to emphasize its own dissociation from what was now conveniently disparaged as a Stalinist past.

Prime Minister Modrow in turn introduced a form of "power sharing" with non-Communist groups and parties in East Germany. It was agreed to seek democratic legitimation through a free election in May of 1990—the first truly free election in this part of Germany since November 1932, shortly before Hitler's rise to power. But this prospect could no longer appease the impatient population. The flight of thousands of East Germans to the west continued to have devastating consequences for the economy, and the election date was eventually moved up to March 18.

By the time of the March election, it was clear even to the East German Communists that the pressure for national unification could no longer be stemmed. The issue was no longer *whether* but had become *how* and *how quickly*. The question was settled when an alliance of Christian Democrats, largely identified with and supported by Chancellor Kohl's party in West Germany, won a surprisingly decisive victory, with 48 percent of the vote. It advocated a short, quick route to unification, beginning with an early monetary union in the summer and a political union by the fall of 1990. This also meant that the new East German government, headed by Lothar de Maziere, followed the short route to a merger with the Federal Republic, under Article 23 of the West German Basic Law. The electoral result for the SPD was only 22 percent of the vote. That also meant a defeat for its alternative strategy for unification that would have involved the protracted negotiation of a new German constitution, as envisaged by Article 146 of the Basic Law.

During the summer and fall of 1990, the governments of the two German states and the four former occupying powers completed their so-called two-plus-four negotiations that resulted in mutual agreement on the German unification process. A monetary union in July was followed by a political merger in October. In advance of unification, Bonn was able to negotiate an agreement with Moscow in which the latter accepted the gradual withdrawal of Soviet troops from eastern Germany and the membership of the united country in NATO, in return for considerable German economic support for the Soviet Union. The result was a major shift in both the domestic and international balance of power.

The Christian Democrats repeated their electoral success in

the contest for the parliaments of the five new (or revived) states of eastern Germany in October. They won again in the first Bundestag election for united Germany in early December of 1990, even though their share of the vote in western Germany dipped slightly. The only Bundestag party to increase its share of the vote was the FDP, the small liberal coalition party that has been a majority maker in West German politics for years. The Greens failed to get the required minimum of 5 percent of the vote in western Germany and dropped out of the Bundestag.

The composition of the Bundestag was affected by the provision that for this election only, the two parts of united Germany operated as separate electoral entities as far as the 5 percent threshold was concerned. That made it possible for another Green grouping, in electoral coalition with left-wing reformers calling themselves Alliance 90, to win enough votes in eastern Germany to get a small foothold in the Bundestag. The special electoral conditions for 1990 also enabled the former ruling party, in its new identity as Party of Democratic Socialism, to gain representation in the Bundestag by winning about 10 percent of the vote in eastern Germany. It appealed to a number of groups that feared social displacement and ideological alienation in a market economy, including many former privileged party members but also some rural workers and young people. Ironically, the party was weakest among the wage workers for whom it claimed to speak.

The election results raise the question of how the unification will eventually affect the German party system, since the special electoral arrangement will have been lifted by the next Bundestag election. If the eastern and western Greens had been united in 1990, their total winnings would have been just enough to meet a 5 percent threshold for united Germany, but the reform Communists would have fallen considerably below this minimum because of their negligible support in western Germany. However, it is misleading to project the 1990 results into the future, for it is already becoming apparent that new and important economic, social, and cultural conflicts will characterize the politics of the enlarged Federal Republic. There will be a significant impact on the party system and the balance of power within Germany, even though it cannot at this point be predicted which actors or strategies will stand to gain or lose. Anyone interested in political development will want to keep a close eye on the difficult transition period in Germany. Simon Head's article on the East German socioeconomic disaster underlines the enormous challenge that faces the country.

The articles on Germany include a balance sheet drawn up by Stephen Szabo in the fall of 1990. There follow short studies of the three main elections in March, October, and December of that year. Each gives a short description of the main issues and analyzes the results as they affect the balance of power among the parties and the resultant government strategies. A follow-up article shows that only three months after the electoral victory of early December, Helmut Kohl and his party have plummeted in popularity among German voters, particularly in the east.

Arthur Gunlicks's article on the peculiarities of German federalism has gained additional interest in view of the movement toward some form of federal or confederal union of East and West Germany. It is already clear that the West German structures, which have worked quite well for over four decades, will serve in some way as role model for the united country. However, there are some serious problems in adding five and a half new states to the federal system. The new or revived states are relatively poor in resources, including competent administrative and legal personnel. They will be a heavy drain on the limited

resources of the rest, and the ideal solution might have been a reconstitution of the state boundaries, as the *Economist* suggests.

The bicentennial of the French Revolution was duly celebrated in France in 1989. It served as an occasion for public ceremonies and a revival of historical-political debate about the costs and benefits of that great exercise in the radical transformation of a society. Ironically, however, there has for some years been evidence that the ideological cleavages that marked French politics for much of the nineteenth and twentieth centuries are losing much of their significance. Instead, there is now emerging a more pragmatic, pluralist form of accommodation in French public life. To be sure, this deradicalization and depolarization of political discourse is by no means complete in France. If the Communists have been weakened and become ideologically confused, Le Pen's National Front on the right has had some success with a xenophobic rhetoric directed primarily against the many residents of Arab origin in the country.

The first article in this subsection deals with French party politics in the 1980s, with particular attention to the developments after the French Socialists lost their majority in the National Assembly in 1986. This political setback could have led to the early resignation of the socialist president, François Mitterrand, whose seven-year term officially lasted until 1988. Instead, he decided to bridge the gap by entering a two-year period of *cohabitation* with a conservative prime minister, Jacques Chirac, who represented the new center-right majority in the National Assembly. There had been no precedent for such a party division in the dual executive built into the constitution of the Fifth Republic by Charles de Gaulle. Thus the following two years became a veritable test of the system's adaptability to new circumstances. In effect, a modus vivendi was found through a pragmatic division of labor between the two executives. Prime Minister Chirac and his cabinet largely determined the course of domestic policy, while President Mitterrand retained an important hand in foreign and defense matters.

Inevitably, the period of "cohabitation" resulted in some friction and conflict within the dual executive. Whether the new division of responsibilities would be more than a temporary interlude in the history of the Fifth Republic depended at least in part on the outcome of the presidential election of 1988. In this contest, the socialist and conservative executive officeholders ran against each other, and Mitterrand was able to defeat Chirac decisively in the run-off. As he had done after his first victory in 1981, the president then proceeded to dissolve the National Assembly, whose five-year term would not have ended until 1991. His hope was clearly that new elections would change the parliamentary balance of power in favor of the Socialists. They did improve their position markedly, but there was no clear-cut majority for either Left or Right in the 1988 election. As a result, the new prime minister, the moderate Socialist Michel Rocard, must seek support among centrist deputies when building parliamentary majorities.

The presidency seems to have regained some of its primacy within the Fifth Republic since 1988, but some observers think that the period of cohabitation left an institutional legacy by shifting the balance of power within the executive somewhat toward the prime minister and away from the president. Others suggest caution in drawing such conclusions. An aging Mitterrand may simply have decided in his second term to partially withdraw from some of the domestic responsibilities that used to involve him more in the earlier years of his presidency. If this interpretation is correct, Mitterrand's personal example of a somewhat reduced presidential role may not be followed by his successor, and we may expect a reassertion of strong leadership from that office in the future.

Claude Imbert explores the waning of the sharp ideological struggle between the Left and Right in France. In his view, France has ceased being exceptional or strikingly different from most other Western democracies in this regard. But he does not neglect to point out that his country has some serious social problems that can fuel political indignation or sustain an extremist movement as Le Pen's National Front. And he agrees with other observers who find the civil service elite to be an obstacle to much-needed practical reforms. Another article points out that this privileged political class, whose supposed influence used to be summarized with the formula l'ENArchie, or rule by graduates of the Ecole Nationale d'Administration, may finally be weakened by economic developments in France. It now appears that private business opportunities have begun to draw some of the most talented administrators away from the traditional path of state service.

There may well be a sense of loss among some French intellectuals who still prefer the political battle to have apocalyptic implications. They will find it hard to accept that the grand battle between Left and Right has been replaced by a more moderate and seemingly more mundane party politics of competition among groups that are closely clustered near the center of the political spectrum. To be sure, they may discover that what they regard as a tedious political competition between those promising a "little more" or a "little less" may have considerable practical consequences in terms of "who gets what and how." Moreover, such incremental politics need not be without dramatic conflict, since new issues, events, or leaders often emerge to sharpen the differences and increase the apparent stakes of politics. At this particular juncture, leadership succession is a major issue in each of the larger political parties of France. It will have to be resolved well in advance of the next scheduled parliamentary elections in 1993.

Still, the loss of the great ideological alternatives may help account for the mood of political malaise that Alan Riding finds widely discussed in contemporary France. But the French search for identity, which is also addressed by Stephen Philip Kramer's article, has another major origin as well. The sudden emergence of a larger and potentially more powerful Germany next door cannot but have a disquieting effect upon France, even though opinion polls show a strong support for the right of the Germans to choose national unification. French elites now face the troubling question of redefining their country's role in a post–cold war world, in which the Soviet Union has lost in power and influence while Germany has gained in both. Kramer suggests that we may expect a major new cleavage in French politics between those who favor a reassertion of the traditional French nation-state ideal—a kind of "Gaullism" found on both the Left and Right—and those who want the country to accept a new European order, in which the sovereignty of both the French and German nation-states would be diluted or contained by a network of international obligations within the larger European framework.

Japan, the fourth country in this study of representative governments of industrial societies, has long been an object of fascination to students of politics and society. After World War II, a representative democracy was installed in Japan under American supervision. This political system has acquired indigenous Japanese characteristics that set it off from the other major democracies examined here. James Fallows explores some of

these differences, arguing that it is both a mistake and a presumption to believe that Japan is becoming a pluralist Western society. Two American reporters, who have just ended a longer stay in Japan, conclude that it is very difficult to generalize about the country in this period of social and economic change. But they stress that there is still a strong and sometimes stifling social discipline in Japan that contrasts sharply with American norms.

The Japanese political system has long been headed by the Liberal Democratic Party, which as the saying goes is "neither liberal, nor democratic, nor a party." It is essentially a conservative political force, comprising several delicately balanced factions. These are often personal followerships identified and headed by political bosses who stake out factional claims to benefits of office. In the summer of 1989, the LDP seemed to be reeling from successive scandals that felled Prime Ministers Noboru Takeshita and Sosuke Uno in quick succession. The LDP lost its majority in the upper house of the legislature, and for a while the Socialist Party seemed to be headed for a political breakthrough.

The political establishment in Japan proved to be more resilient than many foreign journalists had led their readers to expect. In the February 1990 election of the lower house, the LDP won a decisive victory that left it in charge of government under Toshiki Kaifu, a somewhat younger and relatively unknown politician. He had become prime minister some months earlier, when he apparently was pushed forward by his party's heavyweights as a seat-warmer until the scandals died down enough for one of the usual factional leaders to take over. But Kaifu's larger than expected victory may make it harder for the old-timers to replace him with one of their own. If so, another Japanese tradition would appear to have been weakened. In any case, the Japanese government faces a number of problems in addition to such potential leadership wrangles. In the absence of a majority in the upper house, it must continue to build coalitions there. Trade talks with the United States and other major trade partners will become increasingly difficult, and the Japanese electorate cannot be expected to be as quiescent as in the past even if the LDP can still mobilize a majority with its campaign of "no experiments."

Looking Ahead: Challenge Questions

Why was Britain once called "the sick man of Europe?" How did Margaret Thatcher differ in her perception of the British problems and her determination to do something about them? Will her resignation significantly affect the post-collectivist character of British politics? How is John Major likely to be different? What are some important recent developments in British regional politics, with particular attention to Scotland and Northern Ireland?

Would you agree that the democratic order in West Germany has long been sound and stable?

What is meant by France's exceptionalism, and what is the evidence that it is coming to an end?

In what significant ways does Japan differ from the sociopolitical pluralism of a Western society?

1990: A Europe Transformed

Wayne C. Thompson

Wayne C. Thompson is professor of political science at the Virginia Military Institute.

Not since the 1815 Congress of Vienna redrew Europe's map in the aftermath of the Napoleonic Wars have Europeans, joined by the U.S. and Canada, gone so far to replace conflict with cooperation. On 19 November 1990 the thirty-four members of the Conference on Security and Cooperation in Europe (CSCE), meeting in Paris, declared an end to "the era of confrontation and division in Europe" and welcomed "a new era of democracy, peace and unity." French President François Mitterrand noted a significant difference from the Congress of Vienna: "There are no winners and no losers sitting around this table."

> **On 19 November 1990 the thirty-four members of the Conference on Security and Cooperation in Europe (CSCE), meeting in Paris, declared an end to "the era of confrontation and division in Europe" and welcomed "a new era of democracy, peace and unity."**

In many ways, the agreements merely ratified and codified far-reaching developments already underway since Mikhail Gorbachev had declared the end of the Soviet empire in Eastern Europe, for which he was awarded the 1990 Nobel Peace Prize. In the absence of a threat from the Soviet Union, defense budgets were being cut everywhere in Europe. The Warsaw Pact had become moribund, and the dismantling of its military structure is possible in 1991. The newly democratic Eastern European countries have already negotiated the gradual withdrawal of all Red Army forces from their territory. A freshly united Germany is not only diminishing its Bundeswehr to 370,000 troops in 1992, but is being slowly relieved of most of the foreign troops and weapons on its soil since 1945.

Soviet nuclear arms have been taken out of the eastern part of Germany, leaving a *de facto* nuclear-free zone; the 380,000 strong Red Army contingent is scheduled to follow by 1994. The U.S. began withdrawing 50,000 troops and hundreds of its best tanks and equipment from Germany for use in Saudi Arabia, a prelude to further troop cuts. Its nuclear weapons in Europe had sunk from 6,500 to fewer than 3,500, with a further 1,200 nuclear artillery shells slated for removal. Its artillery shells filled with poison gas had been removed in September for destruction on an isolated Pacific island. France, Britain, The Netherlands, Belgium and Canada were also drawing up plans for bringing their forces home from a much-changed Germany.

The CSCE nations pledged to refrain from using or even threatening force against each other. Reiterating an earlier NATO announcement that the Soviet Union was no longer an enemy, they declared that "they are no longer adversaries, will build new partnerships and extend to each other the hand of friendship." While ceilings on troop levels will be worked out in 1991, they agreed to destroy a quarter million conventional arms in what the *Economist* called "the biggest scrap-metal deal in history." Neither side will be permitted to have more than 20,000 tanks, 20,000 artillery pieces, 30,000 armored combat vehicles, 6,800 combat aircraft, and 2,000 attack helicopters from the Atlantic to the Urals. Since the Warsaw Pact countries had an overwhelming quantitative advantage, they will have to make more than 90 percent of the reductions. Thanks to a complicated monitoring and verification system, a surprise attack will be impossible. A conflict prevention center was established in Vienna.

Americans have misgivings about the CSCE gaining an institutional structure that could one day replace NATO, in which the U.S. still assumes the lead. However, many Europeans wish to see a stronger CSCE in order to ensure that the USSR and Eastern Europe will not be excluded from economic and political advancements in Western Europe. As a compromise, a small CSCE secretariat was created in Prague, and annual foreign minister meetings are to be held in a new CSCE Council. The agreements bind the signatories to respect free elections, free markets and human rights.

Reprinted from *Freedom Review*, Vol. 22, No. 1, 1990, pp. 46-51.

The new harmony and the extent of American-Soviet cooperation were reflected in the common action supporting U.N. and U.S. efforts to confront Iraq's 2 August invasion of Kuwait.

GERMAN UNIFICATION

The meeting crowned a development that Chancellor Helmut Kohl had said in Moscow two years earlier he would never see in his own lifetime: German unity. Since 1945 many observers had come to regard a divided Germany as essential to a stable and peaceful Europe. But on 9 November 1989, the Berlin Wall tumbled down, and in December and March, the last two Communist governments, led by Egon Krenz and Hans Modrow, collapsed. East Germans conducted the only successful revolution in German history, and it was a bloodless one. On 18 March East German voters handed the conservative "Alliance for Germany," led by Kohl's Christian Democrats, a stunning victory in their first free election since 1932. As in 1949, Germans turned to the CDU as the party of prosperity and assured democracy.

The train was speeding toward unity, and the best the Bonn government could do was to make it an orderly, legal process. There was no time for a transition, no pause to "study the problems." A breathless Kohl, seeing a unique opportunity, announced in February: "We are jumping with a single leap!" He waved aside Social Democrats' call for a more deliberate process and the demand of many intellectuals for a "better" East Germany treading a "third path" between capitalism and socialism.

The next steps toward unity on 3 October were taken with dizzying rapidity. On 1 July the West German mark was introduced in the GDR in a currency reform without precedence on such a large scale. In a stunning diplomatic breakthrough, Kohl went to the Soviet Union 14–16 July to get Gorbachev's assurances that he would not stand in the way of Germany unity and that a united Germany could decide "freely and by itself if, and in which alliance, it desires membership"; in other words Germany would not have to leave NATO in order to be united. Returning to Moscow on 12 September, Bonn's leaders joined GDR Chancellor Lothar de Maizière and the foreign ministers of the four Allied Powers to sign the "two plus four" treaty granting full sovereignty to Germany and suspending the four powers' rights. The CSCE endorsed this agreement in New York on 1 October. It went into effect at midnight on 2 October.

Unity left unsettled business for a part of Germany in which the economy had to be privatized and in which the secret police, *Stasi*, supported by 85,000 officers and over a half million informants, had penetrated every niche of GDR society and maintained files on 6 million persons. Germans must wrestle with the problem of what to do with such files, which were assembled with a complete disregard for the individual's privacy. The files hold many of the keys to rooting out and punishing those persons who suppressed citizens' freedom, but their misuse could again endanger that freedom. They shed light on the GDR's extensive contacts with terrorist organizations and the sheltering of eight fugitive West German Red Army Faction killers. They also can help Bonn uncover spies who had infiltrated the FRG more thoroughly than had ever been imagined. Revelations were made almost daily. The biggest catch was Klaus Kuron, a senior West German counterintelligence officer in charge of converting East German spies into double agents. Gabriele Gast, who helped prepare a top-secret intelligence summary for Chancellor Kohl, had passed copies to East Berlin for six years. Former GDR citizens must confront their own troubled past.

The campaign for the first free all-German election in almost six decades was marred by bloodshed, as SPD chancellor candidate, Oskar Lafontaine, and CDU interior minister and exported heir to Kohl's party leadership, Wolfgang Schäuble, were seriously wounded by deranged assassins. Other political figures were attacked by terrorists, making it dangerous for public servants to face their people. The prelude for the 2

The train was speeding toward German unity, and the best the Bonn government could do was to make it an orderly, legal process. A breathless Kohl, seeing a unique opportunity, announced: "We are jumping with a single leap!"

December federal elections were state elections in the five newly recreated lands in the former GDR on 14 October; the CDU won in four of them. Therefore, few observers were surprised to see the CDU/FDP coalition win a resounding victory in December and Chancellor Kohl reap the electoral reward for presiding over the mending of Germany's division.

Columbia University historian Fritz Stern noted that "Germany has been given something uncommon: another chance. The century is ending as it began, with a major German lead in Europe based on economic clout, technological advance, and human efficiency and performance . . . [but] under much more favorable circumstances than in the pre-1914 age of rough-hewn nationalism." There were few signs that unification would make Germany more assertive; a survey taken by *Der Spiegel* in October indicated that only 23 percent of German respondents thought Germany should be a major power in Europe, versus 47 percent who opposed it.

Kohl and Foreign Minister Hans-Dietrich Genscher knew that while no European country wanted to thwart German unity, there was uneasiness about the possibility that an economically powerful Germany, 43 percent larger than before and more populous than any country West of Russia, would dominate Europe. Most European leaders were too polite to express these fears publicly, but they had a lively private existence.

To minimize these fears, Germany maintained its low diplomatic profile, eschewing all suggestions of having a permanent seat on the U.N. Security Council, signing landmark treaties with the USSR and Poland, and, above all, continuing to push for European unity. On 9 November it signed a friendship treaty with the Soviet Union that amounted to the closest links the Soviets had with any major Western nation. It contains a section affirming that both nations "will refrain from any threat or use of force which is directed against the territorial integrity or political independence of the other side." Neither country would aid an aggressor against the other. The French had avoided such a far-reaching nonaggression statement in the treaty of cooperation it had signed with the Soviet Union in October. But Bonn officials insist that their agreement was aimed at forging a new relationship with the USSR in a way consistent with Germany's obligation with NATO, which is a defensive alliance.

The ink was hardly dry when Germany signed a treaty with Poland on 14 November fixing their mutual border along the Oder-Neisse Line. The formerly German land to the East of this line constituted a third of Poland's territory. Genscher stated bluntly that "we Germans are aware that the treaty does not surrender anything that was not lost long ago as the result of a criminal war and a criminal system." But he also admitted that settling this last major dispute of the war hurt: "For those who have lost their homelands, who suffered expulsion [after 1945], it is an especially painful one."

THE MARCH TOWARD EUROPEAN UNITY

The most important German reassurance is its press for further European unity. President Mitterrand and EC President Jacques Delors were especially determined to dilute German power by binding it more tightly into Europe. In April, they extracted a promise from Kohl to step up European integration and accept European Monetary Union (EMU) by the end of the decade. The FRG's central bank, which has had its hands full operating the present European Monetary System (EMS) and keeping the mark stable after the currency union with the GDR in July, is not pleased.

However, the *Bundesbank's* objections are technical, whereas those of Britain's then prime minister, Margaret Thatcher, were rooted in principle. "In my view, we have surrendered enough." Her foot-dragging on European unity proved to be her undoing.

The willingness of France and Germany to relinquish more sovereignty to Europe widened the chasm between the U.K. and its continental partners. This was at exactly the time that French and British workers were burrowing their way toward each other under the English Channel, opening the path for completion of the "Chunnel" in mid-1993. Thatcher's cabinet had been rocked by high-level resignations stemming from disagreements over Europe: In 1986 Michael Heseltine stormed out because he wanted a European consortium, not one from the U.S., to purchase a British helicopter company. In 1989 Nigel Lawson left because he wanted to include the pound in EMS. The fatal resignation—and the catalyst for her downfall—was that of Sir Geoffrey Howe, the last surviving member of her original 1979 cabinet and an architect of "Thatcherism." He charged in parliament that her obstruction in Europe carried "serious risks for our nation."

This devastating speech led to a successful challenge to her leadership in late November. After a historic eleven-year rule, the longest prime ministership since the Victorian era and the longest consecutive one since the Napoleonic age, Thatcher resigned. The events leading to her downfall related to Europe, but the

---

The secret police had penetrated every niche of GDR society and maintained files on 6 million persons. Germans must wrestle with the problem of what to do with such files, which were assembled with a complete disregard for the individual's privacy.

---

reason why 45 percent of her parliamentary party colleagues voted against her was that she was leading her party toward defeat in the next election scheduled for mid-1992. For eighteen months her party had trailed in the polls a Labour Party that has become more moderate and friendlier toward the EC. The Britain which she had changed irreversibly was again experiencing 11 percent inflation, the highest of any major industrial country, a growing trade deficit, a slow-down in economic growth, and intense domestic opposition to her poll tax for local governments. With her passing, the U.K. entered a period under John Major, Britain's youngest prime minister this century. Since he was the Iron Lady's protege and hand-picked successor, Thatcherism will survive, albeit in a less strident form.

Another woman's star rose across the Irish Sea. Mary Robinson, endorsed by the minority Labour Party, was elected president of the Irish republic. For years she has opposed Catholic positions on contraception, divorce and homosexuality. Although her hard-won post is largely ceremonial in Ireland's parliamentary democracy, her election signals a potentially important change from traditional social attitudes. The fact that she is married to a Protestant manifests tolerance on this religiously torn island. The IRA failed to get the message, though, as it crossed another grisly threshold in its effort to murder the British out of Ireland: It forced innocent drivers, whose families were held hostage, to drive explosive-laden vans into British check-points in Northern Ireland. Such disregard for life helped prompt the pope to appoint Bishop Cahal B. Daly, a fierce critic of IRA terrorism, as Ireland's primate.

The irresistible logic of European unity has affected countries all over the continent. Austria, Malta and Cyprus have formally applied to the EC, and interest has quickened in the Nordic countries, even though the EC announced that it would accept no more applications for full membership until 1993. Sweden faces debilitating economic problems, which include high inflation and current-account deficit and low productivity. This caused Ingvar Carlsson's Social Democratic [party] to fall briefly in 1990 and to rethink Sweden's position toward the EC. The jolt of competition that membership would bring could lift Sweden out of the doldrums. Therefore, Foreign Minister Sven Andersson recommended that Sweden, Norway and Finland should jointly negotiate.

With the Cold War over, the Soviet Union no longer opposes their entry, and neutrality ceases to be the obstacle it once was. The new attitude was shown by the leader of the coruling Conservative party (KOK) in Finland, Ilkka Suoninen: "If the world changes from confrontation to more cooperation, then where does neutrality lie?" Finland's entire approach to foreign affairs, which has centered on not provoking the Soviet Union in any way, is drifting toward formal ties with the West. The same applies to Switzerland, where interest in EC membership is rising. It submitted its applications to the International Monetary Fund (IMF) and World Bank and, for the first time ever, it joined an economic embargo, supporting U.N. policy against Iraq.

It was controversy over European policy that caused the collapse of the Conservative-led coalition in Norway, led by Jan Syse. Norway had negotiated EC membership in 1972, but its voters rejected it, fearing

adverse cosmopolitan effects on Norwegian society. In 1990 public opinion polls showed that citizens now favor membership. During talks between the EC and the six European Free Trade Association countries (EFTA) aiming at a link with the EC known as the European Economic Area (EEA), the Center party objected to allowing foreign firms to operate in Norway without government permission and therefore scuttled the coalition. This left Gro Harlem Brundtland and her Labor party to form yet another minority government. In an effort to obtain authority to reform Denmark's system of taxes, which range from 52 percent to 68 percent of personal income, Europe's second-highest rate after Sweden, the Conservative Prime Minister Poul Schlüter called early elections in December 1990.

IMMIGRATION: POLITICAL DYNAMITE FOR EUROPE

People flee from collapsing empires and economies. The peace settlement after the First World War left a quarter of Eastern Europeans as minorities under alien rule, and each of the USSR's fifteen republics is a patchwork of ethnic groups. Communism's released grip, the break-up of the Soviet Union and its Eastern European empire, and the potential splintering of multi-national states such as Yugoslavia, have unleashed a westward migration which could become a flood. Economic distress and population explosions in northern and western Africa have sent millions of Arabs and blacks northward. Such a massive influx threatens to overwhelm welfare systems, exacerbate social unrest in Western Europe, and make the EC's plans for the free flow of goods, capital, and people by

---

After a historic eleven-year rule, the longest British prime ministership since the Victorian era and the longest consecutive one since the Napoleonic age, Margaret Thatcher resigned.

1993 a dangerous pipe-dream. In this century massive migrations in Europe have sparked ethnic massacres and pogroms. This time it is causing domestic backlashes and fueling the rise of xenophobic right-wing parties, despite the fact that foreigners are needed in many countries to compensate for low birth rates and that prosperous Europeans want others to do their dirty and dangerous work.

Germany tightened its asylum laws, but still accepts

ethnic Germans from the East, who have numbered 700,000 since the Berlin Wall fell. According to 1990 polls, two-thirds of respondents believe that immigrants have unfairly taken advantage of the welfare system. Polish street vendors and Romanian Gypsies are blamed for rising crime and have been attacked by rowdy youths. Even more embarrassing for a country with Germany's past was Bonn's decision to halt Jewish immigration from the Soviet Union; 4,000 had entered Germany in the summer of 1990, and the government concluded that too many wanted to resettle in Germany. This incensed some members of Germany's 40,000-strong Jewish community. While others are debating whether to encourage Bonn to accept more Soviet Jews, one German Jewish leader admitted that "it's the old internal conflict between German Jews and Jews from the East. They are different from us and much more different from the Germans. We get along well with the Germans."

In September, Austria, which had helped spark the fall of the GDR by opening its border in the summer of 1989, began requiring entry visas for Poles. It sent 1,500 soldiers to its border with Hungary to prevent Romanians from sneaking in through the woods. In October, the anti-immigrant backlash was visible in parliamentary elections. Led by the youthful and charismatic Jörg Haider, the far-right Freedom Party (FPÖ) increased its share of the vote from 10 percent to 17 percent, at the expense of the Christian Democrats (ÖVP), which fell from 41 percent to 32 percent. FPÖ posters saying "Don't Let Vienna Turn into Chicago!" found a receptive audience. Despite scandals within the Social Democratic Party, the SPÖ, led by Chancellor Franz Vranitsky, emerged the big winner, garnering 43 percent of the votes.

The ÖVP must bear the onus that one of its members, President Kurt Waldheim, remains an international outcast because of his part in Nazi atrocities in the Balkans. In July, for the first time since he became president in 1986, he was visited by a Western head of state, Cypriot President George Vassiliou. His hopes that the international boycott was being permanently broken by visits from Presidents Václav Havel of Czechoslovakia and Richard von Weizäcker of Germany were dashed when Havel said in his presence that "whoever fears to look his past in the face must necessarily fear what is to come. Lies cannot save us from lies."

RACISM

Racism was the main domestic political problem in France, which is particularly vulnerable: it has 4.5 million legal immigrants, half of whom are Arabs and a fourth black. This represents over 7 percent of its population and does not include illegals or their children born in France, who therefore automatically become citizens. A government survey in 1990 revealed that three-fourths of respondents thought there were too many Arabs in France, and almost half believed there were too many blacks. Arabs are the targets of attacks and harassment, and conflict in the Middle East heightens the tensions even further. Earlier immigrant groups are often among the opponents of the new arrivals. Portuguese- and Spanish-born workers in the Marseilles area are among Jean-Marie Le Pen's most fervent supporters. His right-wing National Front consistently rides the xenophobic crest to win almost 15 percent of the votes in any election.

Jacques Chirac, former prime minister and leader of the Gaullist Rally for the Republic (RPR) party, noted that "today's racism is the result of exasperation with too many foreigners who make life unbearable for the native French." Worse, France experienced another outbreak of anti-Semitism, which manifested itself in appalling desecrations of Jewish grave sites. In the words of Socialist Prime Minister Michel Rocard, the government has tried in vain to "stop the gangrene from spreading." As in many other Western European countries, some inner-city schools have non-French majorities, which are blamed for rising crime and lower educational standards. At the same time, many of the student protesters demanding tighter security in schools, more teachers, smaller classes and better facilities were themselves immigrant children, who saw their chances for advancement being curbed by inadequate educational opportunities.

The Socialist government, held responsible for the 9 percent unemployment, faced strikes from other sectors as well. In June and October, hundreds of judges, prosecutors and prison wardens protested a lack of equipment and funding. They also retaliated against a controversial amnesty law which rescued party officials from prosecution for illicit campaign financing. Nevertheless, the popular prime minister survives with his minority government, despite serious feuding within the Socialist Party (PS) over who should succeed Mitterrand as presidential candidate in 1995. In November Rocard narrowly defeated the ninth vote of no-confidence in the National Assembly leveled against his cabinet, which contains only twenty-two Socialists among forty-eight ministers. His opponents were not only the badly divided conservative parties, but also the Communists, whose decline continues. Rocard might be the first prime minister in the history of the Fifth Republic to survive the full five years of a parliamentary term.

ITALY AS A BRIDGE

Until recently Italy was a land of emigration, but its long coastline facing North Africa has made it a natural bridge between the burgeoning populations of Africa and the rich nations of Europe. Not wishing to damage its good relations with its Arab neighbors on the other side of the Mediterranean, Italy has not wanted to impose quotas. To encourage its growing number of illegal residents to register with the authorities, it offered its generous welfare benefits to non-EC citizens, but this merely stimulated even greater immigration. In a country which thought it was above racism, daily headlines now report racial strife. Nowhere was that more visible than in Florence, where the presence of hundreds of North African street vendors sparked a protest march in February to decry the influx. Gangs of white rowdies set upon the newcomers with baseball bats and iron bars. Unable to agree with his Communist allies on how to deal with this problem,

---

A massive influx of immigrants threatens to overwhelm welfare systems, exacerbate social unrest in Western Europe, and make the EC's plans for the free flow of goods, capital and people by 1993 a dangerous pipe-dream.

Socialist mayor Georgio Morales resigned, declaring that "not even God could resolve the present situation in Florence!"

In Northern Italy competition between African immigrants and southern Italians for blue collar and other low-paying jobs has sparked outbreaks of violence. Profiting from the tensions are several regional autonomy parties, especially the Lombard League, which rocketed to 19 percent of the vote in that region's elections. They have capitalized on local dissatisfaction against what they see as misrule by Rome, which does not seem to act vigorously enough to stem the wave of immigrants and to reverse Northern Italy's subsidizing of the South. They charge that too much of those funds end up in the pockets of Mafia contractors. Indeed, the Neopolitan Camorra and Calabrian 'Ndrangheta families were believed to have been behind the killing of nine candidates or outgoing members of municipal and regional assemblies during local election campaigns in Campania and Calabria; other candidates were threatened or shot in the legs. This was an obvious underworld effort to influence the vote. In Sicily, 100 judges and magistrates threatened to resign if more state protection were not offered them. The murder of the eighth judge in eleven years by the increasingly violent organized crime networks prompted President Francesco Cossiga to order special measures against organized crime.

Sensing that the term "Communist" now connotes failure, Italian Communists changed the name of their party to the "Democratic Party of the Left" and their insignia to a spreading tree, with the hammer-and-sickle practically hidden in the roots. The party has seen its vote decline from 34 percent in 1976 to only 24 percent in local elections in May. Not to be outmaneuvered, the rising Socialist Party, led by Bettino Craxi, changed its own name to Socialist Unity. Craxi hopes to unify the left so that it can challenge the Christian Democrats' (DC) stranglehold on power. The DC suffered a mild embarrassment when Prime Minister Giulio Andreotti admitted that in 1956 the government, aided by the U.S. Central Intelligence Agency, had set up a clandestine paramilitary network (code name: *Gladio*, Latin for "sword") to resist a possible Communist occupation. Weapons and explosives were hidden in 139 caches. A national scandal ensued when suspicions were aired that renegade *Gladio* agents might have used some of the explosives to make right-wing terrorist attacks in the 1960s and 1970s, a charge that the government vehemently denied. The revelations also stirred debate in Belgium, on the suspicion that right-wing terrorists there might have gotten their weapons from similar caches.

After two parliamentary elections in 1989 had failed to produce a majority, Greek voters finally realized that continued "nongovernment" was hurting them, domestically and internationally. Therefore, in elections on 8 April 1990, the conservative New Democracy party won a razor-thin majority. A delegate from the Independent Right joined with it to form a government under Constantine Mitsotakis. PASOK, the former ruling party, was left on the sidelines struggling against charges of financial impropriety and mismanaging the ship of state after winning power in 1981.

Mitsotakis granted full diplomatic recognition to Israel, thus ending Greece's role as the only EC member without such ties. He also moved to fulfill one of his main foreign policy planks, "the full normalization of relations with the U.S.," after the acrimonious Papandreou years. Negotiations were resumed with Washington on a defense cooperation agreement that would include U.S. bases in Greece, which had been the target of considerable nationalist ire. They ratified Washington's prior unilateral decision at the beginning of the year to relinquish its two bases on the Greek mainland, reduce its troop presence, and retain only two bases in Crete, whose leases were extended to eight years. Greeks' traditional good feelings toward America were hurt when Atlanta was picked over Athens as the site of the 1996 centennial of the modern Olympic games. A doubly stung Melina Mercouri, whose bid to become Athens' mayor was defeated in October, exclaimed: "Coca-Cola has prevailed over the Parthenon!"

British Politics in the Post-Collectivist Era

". . . in the short term, the Labour party finds itself uncomfortably suspended between past and future. It is too recently Socialist for many British voters yet not very different in any important sense from a Conservative party that over the past 11 years has shaped the economic and political environment to its own electoral advantage."

ANTHONY M. MESSINA
Associate Professor of Political Science, Tufts University

Anthony M. Messina is the author of *Race and Party Competition in Britain* (Oxford: Oxford University Press, 1989) and many articles on British politics; he is a coeditor of *Ethnic and Racial Minorities in the Advanced Industrial Societies* (New York: Greenwood Press, forthcoming).

THE period since June, 1989, has not been a happy time for British Prime Minister Margaret Thatcher or her ruling Conservative party. Starting with the loss of 13 seats and an erosion of 8.6 percent of the Conservative party vote in the elections to the European parliament of June, 1989 — the worst showing of the Conservative party in a nationwide election in this century — Thatcher's government and her party have suffered numerous political and economic setbacks.

Consider the scope and magnitude of some of these difficulties. Following the defeat of the Labour party in the elections to the European parliament, anti-Thatcher sentiment within the Conservative party visibly boiled over, culminating in a challenge to her leadership in December, 1989, by a relatively obscure backbench member of Parliament (MP), Sir Anthony Meyer. Although Meyer was defeated easily, a politically embarrassing 57 Conservative MP's either voted against Thatcher or spoiled their ballots. In March, 1990, the Conservative party lost a parliamentary by-election to Labour in the constituency of Mid Staffordshire, a Conservative political bastion.

In May, 1990, the Conservative party suffered one of its worst-ever poll performances in a series of local elections held simultaneously across the country. The distribution of the vote nationwide implied an 8 percent lead for the Labour party heading into the next general election.[1]

In July, 1990, Nicholas Ridley, a close ideological ally of Thatcher's, was forced to resign as the secretary of state for trade and industry after making provocative statements about the alleged intention of German leaders to dominate contemporary Europe. Although Ridley "unreservedly" withdrew his remarks immediately after they were published, they nevertheless embarrassed Thatcher's government across West Europe. Moreover, since June, 1989, public opinion has shifted considerably toward the Labour party. Opinion surveys taken during this period indicate that the electorate either supports the two major parties almost evenly or, at the peak of the unpopularity of the Conservative party in the spring of 1990, that it overwhelmingly prefers Labour. At various points in time, Labour's lead over the Conservative party in the opinion polls has exceeded 20 percent.

All these negative political developments for Thatcher and her party have occurred in the context of, or have been precipitated by, a slumping national economy. The national balance of payments, for example, was in deficit by £14.5 billion (about $23.6 billion) in 1988 and an estimated £20 billion (about $32.6 billion) in 1989. On the basis of rather rosy projections, the government expects the deficit to shrink to £15 billion (about $24.4 billion) in 1990.[2] Real personal disposable income is expected to grow by only 1.5 percent this year, compared with an average growth rate of 4.5 percent during the previous four years. Annual inflation in 1990 is inching toward 10 percent, while real interest rates (and, hence, home mortgage rates) remain relatively high in a depressed national housing market. In June, 1990, consumer confidence was lower than it was at the nadir of the 1980–1982 recession.[3]

Compounding these difficulties has been the sporadic eruption of street demonstrations over the government's recent introduction of the local community charge (or poll tax, as it is commonly known), the escalation of terrorist violence on the British mainland by the Irish Republican Army (IRA) and the continuing political conflict between Thatcher and European Community (EC) leaders over issues related to the future of the EC. On this last score, Thatcher's tepid endorsement or outright opposition to European monetary union, rapid German unification, expanding the membership of the EC, maintaining economic sanctions against South Africa and extending considerable financial assistance to the Soviet Union have isolated Britain from its EC partners and alienated a significant fraction of the British electorate. In the latter context, there is probably no issue that divides the contemporary Conservative party more and that is seen by the British public to divide the party more than the future of the European Community. Unfortunately for Thatcher, most Conservatives outside Parliament oppose her broad policy toward the EC.[4]

One would have to go back to the dreary economic and political environment in Britain before the Falklands war to recall a gloomier period for the Conservative party since it assumed the reins of government in 1979. Yet many observers, including this writer, believe that the Conservative party will either win the next general election, which will probably be called in June or October, 1991, or will emerge from it as the largest parliamentary party in a no-majority or "hung" Parliament. Given the current difficulties of the Conservative party, why the guarded optimism about its electoral chances in the next general election?

The most obvious reason is that the Conservative party currently finds itself in an unusually favorable electoral position by the standards of postwar British politics. With the recent collapse of David Owen's Social Democratic party (SDP) and the poor performance of the Social and Liberal Democratic party (SLD) in the 1989 European and the 1990 local elections, the Labour party at present is the only viable political alternative to the Conservatives. Yet in the run-up to the next general election Labour faces a monumental electoral hurdle. Before Labour can win power, the Conservative party must forfeit it. The traditional adage, "oppositions don't win elections, governments lose them," still reflects the empirical reality of British electoral politics. There is little question that the current difficulties of the Conservative party will have to con-

tinue or worsen to give Labour an outside chance of forming the next British government; even if they do, the Conservative party could still probably win the election without difficulty if it replaced the increasingly unpopular Thatcher with another leader.[5]

Moreover, in order for Labour to emerge from the next election with a parliamentary majority, the party will have to gain an additional 97 seats over its 1987 general election total, a feat requiring an 8.5 percent vote swing from the Conservative party to Labour.[6] Such a large vote gain would not only be difficult for the Labour party to achieve, it would be unprecedented in the post-1945 history of British elections. Even a greater than normal swing of 4.5 percent from the Conservatives to Labour would not deny the Conservative party a parliamentary majority.

Labour's uphill electoral struggle only begins to explain why the Conservative party is likely to remain in government for the foreseeable future. The greatest political advantage of the Conservative party derives from the erosion of the postwar collectivist sentiment in Britain and the partial construction since 1979 of a conservative project to replace it.[7] What are the central features or goals of this proposal? Although scholars are sharply divided on this question,[8] there is a consensus that the political goals of the conservative project in Britain include undermining the social base of the Labour party and constructing a durable anti-Socialist electoral coalition; encouraging the emergence of an alternative "enterprise" party within the British party system; and dismantling or intellectually discrediting the institutions in British society that have a vested interest in a collectivist system. The broad intent of these interrelated goals is to eradicate all vestiges of economic and political socialism in Britain.[9] If these objectives are ultimately realized, conservatism will be established as the hegemonic political ideology and the Conservative party as the dominant political actor in Britain.

THE CONSERVATIVE POLITICAL PROJECT

Although none of the political goals of the conservative project have as yet been accomplished, all three have been advanced by explicit political design during the past 11 years of Conservative party government. Consider, for example, how Thatcher's three governments have substantially altered Britain's social structure to the political advantage of the Conservative party since 1979. In 1980, there were only 3 million individual shareholders in Britain. As a result of the government's privatization of British Telecom (1984), the Trustee Savings Bank (1986), British Gas (1986), British Airways (1987) and other state-owned assets, as well as the creation of various incentives to encourage employee share-ownership, the number of individual shareholders is now 9 million, or 20 percent of the adult population.[10]

In 1979, there were 13.3 million trade union members, representing 54 percent of all British workers. As a direct consequence of the government-engineered recession of 1980–1982 and its continuous legal assaults on the power of the trade unions, union membership has declined by 2.8 million, with the heaviest losses concentrated in the unions most closely affiliated with the Labour party. Trade unionists currently constitute less than 47 percent of the labor force. Similarly, in 1979, 55 percent of all residential properties in Britain were owner-occupied. As a result of the Conservative government's "right to buy" law of 1980, 1.25 million council houses have been sold at below market value to their predominantly working-class tenants, helping to swell home ownership to 65 percent.

In each of these as well as other areas of public policy, successive Conservative governments since 1979 have sought to erode the electoral support of the Labour party among the working and lower middle classes by detaching the individual from the state and by cultivating the growth of an anti-Socialist, "enterprise society." In such a society, British voters have increasingly less incentive to support a Labour party that intends to expand social welfare services and the fiscal responsibilities of government.

It is, of course, too early to evaluate the ultimate electoral consequences of the new trends in share and home ownership and trade union membership. These changes are relatively recent and they cannot be expected to alter significantly the electoral balance between the Conservatives and Labour in the short term. Nevertheless, the preliminary evidence is not encouraging for the Labour party. In the 1987 general election, 36 percent of all manual workers voted for the Conservatives, the highest level of support for the party in this constituency since 1945. Moreover, the Conservative party outpolled Labour 44 percent to 32 percent among working-class homeowners and 42 percent to 31 percent among those who had purchased council houses. Among first-time share buyers in the newly privatized industries, of whom half were manual workers, the Conservatives garnered 51 percent of the vote.[11]

Although these results may not be permanent, they signal that an anti-Labour electoral alliance exists among a sizable fraction of Britain's working class, especially "affluent" workers, and the middle and upper class constituencies that have traditionally supported the Conservative party. The Conservatives have won three consecutive general elections on the back of this cross-class alliance. Unhappily for the Labour party, this electoral coalition will broaden and deepen if the recent changes in Britain's social structure have the expected political impact.

On the second front of the conservative project, the emergence of an alternative enterprise party within the party system, the Conservative party by all appearances has been less successful during the past decade. Despite the sporadic efforts of Thatcher and her Conservative colleagues to "talk up" the prospects of a realignment on the political left and the possibility that the Liberal Democrats will replace Labour as the Conservative party's primary electoral opponent, the SLD has not gained a secure place in the British party system. Nevertheless, the failure of the SDP and the SLD to displace Labour should not be interpreted as a permanent setback for the conservative project. Indeed, if the recent embrace of pro-market economic policies by the Labour party endures, then the second political objective of the conservative project is very close to fruition.

PROSPECTS FOR LABOUR

Labour's recent metamorphosis was effected by Social Democrats in the party, including current leader Neil Kinnock, who interpreted Labour's electoral debacles of 1983 and 1987 as the British electorate's rejection of the party's traditional Socialist policies. Operating on this assumption, the leaders of the Labour party initiated a comprehensive "policy review" in 1987 that, on its completion in 1989, committed the party to a macroeconomic strategy emphasizing the importance of market forces. Expunged from the current platform of the Labour party is the promise of old-style nationalization; emphasized in the new policy review are the rights of consumers. Under a future Labour government, British industry and the peak financial interests in the City (London) could expect accommodating policies that provide considerable continuity with the economic strategy pursued by Conservative governments during the past decade. Indeed, the economic policies of the Labour party now embrace market forces so thoroughly that in a recent survey of prominent British economists and representatives of the City, 51 percent agreed that a Labour government would benefit the economy and a plurality believed that Labour's shadow chancellor, John Smith, would make a better chancellor of the exchequer than the current Conservative chancellor. Moreover, an astonishing 62 percent of those surveyed approved of Labour's moderately redistributive tax proposals.[12]

Labour's recent embrace of the market undoubtedly improves its electoral position at the margins. So long as the party was widely perceived to be antagonistic to the Conservatives' new political economy, it could not make electoral inroads into the various constituency groups, including affluent workers, who have profitted from this economy. However, questions must be raised about the extent to which Labour's metamorphosis improves its electoral position and, specifically, whether the new economic orientation of the party will help it win the next general election.

There is at least one reason to doubt that it will. By allowing its economic policies to converge substantially with those of its political opponent, Labour risks being viewed by millions of British voters, especially in affluent southern England where its electoral support has significantly declined since the 1970's, as politically opportunistic and comparatively less committed to the ideological principles of the new political economy. Barring a major economic slump, much of the electorate will continue to support the architects of the new political economy, the Conservatives, rather than defect to Labour, a recent convert.

Moreover, Labour's apparent abandonment of socialism has undermined morale among many of its hardcore activists, an important intra-party faction that routinely mobilizes the vote and raises some financial resources for the party. Given Labour's historical difficulties in raising revenue and, at least since the 1960's, recruiting activists to canvass during general election campaigns, any loss of party workers will handicap its short-term electoral efforts. Nationwide, Labour has an enormous vote gap that it will not successfully bridge in the next general election without the support of substantial numbers of highly committed activists.

In contrast to the first two goals of the Conservative project, Conservative governments have not pursued the third goal primarily for partisan advantage. In dismantling or intellectually discrediting many of Britain's prominent intermediate institutions, the past three Conservative governments have often offended important constituencies in the Conservative party, especially during the government's well-publicized disputes with the Church of England, the Confederation of British Industry, the British Medical Association and the Bar.[13] However, on balance, the decade-long campaign to strengthen the state at the expense of civil society has injured the Labour party far more than its political opposition. In particular, the sustained assaults of Conservative governments on the political and industrial power of the trade unions and on the autonomy of local government have adversely affected Labour.

DECLINE OF TRADE UNIONS

The organizational decline of the trade unions since 1979 has already been noted. Apart from its negative effects on Labour's social base, declining union membership imperils the financial foundations of the party, as the unions have historically funded a very large percentage of Labour's annual operating budget and its general election expenses. It is fair to assume that Labour could not operate and compete as a modern political party without substantial financial contributions from the trade union movement. To date, however, the steep decline in union membership and the Conservative government's legislation in 1984, which obligates the trade unions to hold a ballot of their members every ten years on the question of maintaining a political fund, do not appear to be seriously hampering the ability of the unions to support Labour. The affiliation fees that the trade unions deliver annually to Labour's central headquarters increased between 1984 and 1987 from £2.9 million to £4.2 million. In the 1987 general election, the trade unions donated £3.8 million to Labour's national campaign, a 50 percent rise from the previous election in 1983.[14] Although generous, this level of assistance from the unions has not eroded the comparative financial advantage that the Conservative party has historically enjoyed. Labour was outspent two to one by its political opposition in the 1987 national campaign, a slight increase in the financial gap between the two major parties over the previous general election.

Like its assault on the trade unions, the attacks by successive Conservative governments on the economic and political autonomy of local government have not undercut the electoral position of the Labour party in the short term.[15] Indeed, if anything, Thatcher's hostility toward local government has probably stimulated higher levels of support for Labour in recent local elections. However, the decade-long strategy of Conservative governments to divest local government of significant economic and political functions, especially in the areas of education, finance, housing, land use and essential social services, and to reallocate these functions to appointed boards or to the market have diminished the prospects of Labour coming to power nationally on the basis of an alternative economic and political program. To a considerable degree, local economic and political infrastructure that supported collectivist politics during the postwar period and that helped Labour dominate national politics in Britain between 1964 and 1979 has all but disappeared.

Perhaps the most important change in local-national government relations during the past decade is the incremental usurpation by the central government of the powers of local authorities to tax and to set expenditure. As a result of the abolition by Conservative governments of the domestic rates, introduction of a regressive poll tax and a centrally determined business rate, and the establishment of annual ceilings on local poll tax charges and the size of local authority budgets, local government in Britain has been transformed into a virtual agent of central government and made dependent on it for approximately 80 percent of local funding.[16]

This constitutional change in central-local government relations has had a negative impact on the Labour party in at least two ways. First, the severe restrictions on local government's expenditure penalize primarily the large, big-spending, urban councils that, not coincidentally, are predominantly Labour-controlled.[17] Fiscal constraints imposed from above prevent these local authorities from providing the breadth and depth of social services that Labour voters traditionally expect from their party. The result is an incremental erosion in the incentive among Labour-inclined voters to support Labour or to participate in local elections. Second, by stripping local government of much of its traditional economic and political authority, the last three Conservative governments have made local politics less relevant and, hence, a less effective arena for mobilizing either pro-Labour or anti-Conservative sentiment. Insofar as pro-Labour activism and political opposition to the Conservative party have been strongest since the mid-1970's at the local level, the decline of local politics in Britain has undermined an important political base for Labour.[18]

The considerable advance of the conservative project's political goals since 1979, indeed, has undercut both the ability of the Labour party to win general elections and, if and when the party does assume office, to implement a coherent economic and political program that significantly deviates from the record of the previous three Conservative governments. Recognizing this reality, the leaders of the Labour party have recently adopted comprehensive policy changes in the electoral platform of the party that all but formally abandon the Labour party's historic promise to establish socialism in Britain.

If the party continues on its present course and does not resume its habitual slide toward disunity and internal policy disputes, Labour's metamorphosis can and probably will yield electoral success eventually. However, in the short term, the Labour party finds itself uncomfortably suspended between past and future. It is too recently Socialist for many British voters yet not very different in any important sense from a Conservative party that over the past 11 years has shaped the economic and political environment to its own electoral advantage.

CHANGE IN EAST EUROPE

Like politics elsewhere, British party politics is continuously being influenced by external events and trends. Apart from the influence of the 1992 project and the EC's ongoing drive toward greater economic and political integration, perhaps the most salient external events shaping the trajectory of British politics in the post-collectivist era are the political liberalization of East Europe and the associated decline of cold war tensions. The ultimate impact of these events is not yet fully apparent. However, for the present, they appear to be exerting conflicting pressures on British politics.

On the one hand, political liberalization in the formerly Communist polities of East Europe and the apparent victory of the West in the cold war legitimize the ideological premises of the political and economic goals of the conservative project in Britain.[19] With its preference for market over collectivist policies, its celebration of individual over class or corporate interests and its rejection of socialism in favor of economic liberalism and political and social conservatism, the conservative project is, and is probably seen by most of the British electorate to be, fundamentally compatible with the desirable changes taking place in East Europe and elsewhere in the postwar Communist world. As such, the direction of change in East Europe works to the political advantage of the Conservative party, which, in recent months, has initiated a public relations campaign to assume partial credit for the liberalization in East Europe and to emphasize Thatcher's good personal relations with Soviet President Mikhail Gorbachev.[20]

On the other hand, liberalization in East Europe and the end of the cold war politically benefit the Labour party in two ways. First, these events diminish the salience of defense and security issues in domestic British politics. This outcome is advantageous to Labour because the party has been judged historically by the British electorate as less competent than the Conservatives to defend Britain against external aggression, less willing to use nuclear weapons in a military conflict and less committed to maintaining adequate armed forces and defense expenditures. In particular, Labour's periodic advocacy since the late 1950's of British unilateral nuclear disarmament and its loose association with the Campaign for Nuclear Disarmament have unambiguously cost the party votes. Confusion and disunity within the party on defense issues especially undermined Labour's electoral efforts in the general election campaigns of 1983 and 1987.[21] The partial removal of these issues from public political debate allows Labour to avoid them and gives the party greater opportunity to influence the political agenda to its electoral advantage.

Second, the eclipse of Socialist politics in East Europe discredits, perhaps unfairly, socialism everywhere, including domestic British socialism. In so doing, it strengthens the political hand of the group of Labour party leaders who are currently attempting to realign their ideologically heterogeneous party around pragmatic and nonsocialist policies. The most important implication of this outcome is that it enhances the prospects for enduring cohesion within the Labour party, which has often been penalized by British voters — especially during the 1980's — for being internally divided. Greater cohesion within the Labour party improves, however modestly, its electoral position vis-à-vis the Conservative party, which is becoming increasingly fragmented over the economic and political future of Europe.

[1] *The Economist,* May 12, 1990, p. 59.

[2] *British Politics Group Newsletter,* no. 60 (Spring, 1990), p. 5.

[3] *The Economist,* June 16, 1990, p. 63.

[4] *The Economist,* June 24, 1989, pp. 55–56.

[5] *British Politics Group Newsletter,* no. 60 (Spring, 1990), p. 4.

[6] *British Politics Group Newsletter,* no. 58 (Fall, 1989), p. 9.

[7] See Peter Hall, *Governing the Economy: The Politics of State Intervention in Britain and France* (New York: Oxford University Press, 1986); and Dennis Kavanagh, *Thatcherism and British Politics: The End of Consensus?* (Oxford: Oxford University Press, 1987).

[8] See, for example, Andrew Gamble, *The Free Economy and the Strong State: The Politics of Thatcherism* (London: Macmillan Education Ltd., 1989); Stuart Hall and Martin Jacques, eds., *The Politics of Thatcherism* (London: Lawrence and Wishart, 1983); and Bob Jessop et al., *Thatcherism* (Oxford: Basil Blackwell, 1988).

[9] Peter Jenkins, *Mrs. Thatcher's Revolution: The Ending of the Socialist Era* (Cambridge: Harvard University Press, 1988).

[10] Pippa Norris, "Thatcher's Enterprise Society and Electoral Change," *West European Politics,* vol. 13, no. 1 (January, 1990).

[11] Ivor Crewe, "What's Left for Labour: An Analysis of Thatcher's Victory," *Public Opinion,* vol. 10, no. 2 (July–August, 1987).

[12] *The Economist,* April 14, 1990, pp. 61–62.

[13] *The Economist,* December 9, 1989, p. 54.

[14] Michael Pinto-Duschinsky, "Financing the British General Election of 1987," in Ivor Crewe and Martin Harrop, eds., *Political Communications: The General Election Campaign of 1987* (New York: Cambridge University Press, 1989).

[15] For an account of how far the powers of local government have eroded, see George W. Jones, "The Crisis in British Central-Local Government Relationships," *Governance: An International Journal of Policy Administration,* vol. 1, no. 2 (April, 1988).

[16] Ibid.

[17] *The Economist,* April 7, 1990, pp. 65–66.

[18] R.J. Johnson et al., *A Nation Dividing? The Electoral Map of Great Britain 1979–1987* (London: Longman, 1988), pp. 327–328.

[19] For a concise account of the economic goals of the Conservative project, see Paulette Kurzer, "A Decade of Thatcherism: The Debate on the Left," *Comparative Political Studies,* vol. 23, no. 2 (July, 1990), pp. 257–277.

[20] *The Economist,* June 2, 1990, pp. 63–64.

[21] David Butler and Dennis Kavanagh, *The British General Election of 1987* (London: Macmillan Press, 1988), pp. 103–105.

Margaret Thatcher— brought down by her own strengths

Hugo Young

She died as she had lived, in battle. It was a quite extraordinary end, but it was in keeping with everything important that had gone before. There was a continuity, not only in the texture of these events but in the circumstances of her long life and swift demise. Just as her triumphs were often rooted in her zest for combat, her refusal to listen to advice and her unwillingness to admit that she could be wrong, so were these the sources of her last predicament. Until last Thursday, when all three habits were finally broken.

It is a shocking way to go. Having lost no vote either in the Commons or in the country, she was yet disposed of by the unaccountable will of fewer than 400 politicians. There has been nothing like it in the democratic era: no verdict apparently so perverse and unprovoked delivered by a governing party against a leader upon whom it had grown fat for so many years. Many Conservatives will be thunderstruck by what they accomplished last week; some, even among those who did the deed, will be ashamed. For the first time in her prime ministership she provoked, while not requesting it, the human sympathy reserved for a helpless creature at bay.

The symmetry between the life and the death was nonetheless compelling. She was a leader of lurid style and risky habits, especially in the field of personal relations. Aggressive to a fault, she spent years scorning not only consensual policies but the consensual demeanour. With nerveless indifference, she was prepared to see the larger portion of her friends as well as enemies in high places depart the scene as a direct result of her behaviour. A kind of rough justice therefore now prevails, its chemistry precipitated by the most enduring victim of these gross habits, Geoffrey Howe. She who lived by fire and insult cannot wholly complain when the ultimate insult repays her.

These have, however, been years which will not be forgotten. The Callaghan era might never have happened, for all that history makes of it. This is less true of the periods to which Harold Wilson and Ted Heath attach their names, but what lingers from them is notoriety more than fame. The Thatcher Era will be different, and nowhere more so than in the evidence it offers that personality can be the single most potent contributor to the pattern of events. For better or for worse, this will truly and for ever be called the Thatcher Era.

She was a creature of her times. Although as a minister under Heath she showed an opportunist's capacity to find different times congenial enough, from the mid-Seventies she rode the tide of liberal economics and anti-state politics with missionary aplomb. All reformers need circumstances to coincide with destiny. But character matters more. There were things that happened which would, I think, have happened quite differently without her.

The first was the Falklands War. It was a prime example of ignorance lending pellucid clarity to her judgment. Surrounded by ministers who knew what war was and dithered at its prospect, she understood what the soldiers wanted and shirked neither the military consequences nor the huge political risk. This quality of leadership was justly rewarded. She was, in fact, especially decisive in war. But for her it is also certain that American bombers would not have been allowed to bomb Libya from British bases in April 1986.

Second, the conduct of economic policy in the early Eighties owed almost everything to her moral fibre. It may have been a failed policy, but it was hers. She was committed to an economic theory and committed against caring about unemployment. When Lord Hailsham told her, in July 1981, that she would destroy the Conservative Party as surely as Herbert Hoover led the Republicans to oblivion in 1932, she spat in his eye. Blood on the streets did not alarm her, any more than the self-starvation of Irish republicans. She worried not about the jobless masses but the looted shopkeepers: a priority which, nine years later, no longer seems odd.

Third, and for similar reasons, the dethroning of trade union power would have taken a different course without her. She acted out with utmost seriousness the anti-union prejudice which most other Tories shared but which many of them had not dared to deploy. Public sector strife, culminating with the 1984 coal strike, was permitted to drag out as ministers watched with almost sadistic fascination. But without the gimlet eye of their leader upon them, their record suggests that they would have lost their nerve well before the desired "demonstration effect", which always mattered more than the money, was achieved.

With Mrs Thatcher's fourth irreplaceable mark, we reach more contentious territory: the region, in fact, where hubris and nemesis met, to ultimately catastrophic effect. Few qualified observers doubt that her stand against the European Community achieved a British advantage in the early days, which was unavailable by other means. By asking reasonable questions in a wholly unreasonable manner, she secured more of "our money" from Brussels. A decade's combative diplomacy made for a quite different British presence. Arguably, we counted for more in Europe, in a constructive as well as critical role, in 1985 than in 1975.

Reprinted by permission from *The Manchester Guardian Weekly*, December 2, 1990, pp. 3-4.

But here came the first source of her trouble. The mark in Brussels became a kind of curse at home. Her elemental convictions about nationhood and sovereignty were not accompanied by sufficient sensitivity to the opposite feelings of significant colleagues. The issue became an emblem of the style as well as the content at the heart of her difficulties. It showed the falsity of this distinction. With this leader the style *was* the woman.

In modified form, this was also a key to her fifth uniquely personal policy, the poll tax. It is the only tax in the western world to have grown more out of character than reason. Reason, expressed by Nigel Lawson and the Treasury, said that it would be unjust, unworkable, and insupportably expensive. Character, sticking blindly with a Thatcher commitment dating from 1974, insisted that it must go forward and enlisted—another consistent trait of these years—the incautious support of enough meekly compliant ministers for the blame to be spread.

Policies alone, however, do not define the place she will take in the annals. The intangibles are perhaps more important, and may ensure her name a longer life. Thatcherism embodies a style and a set of values that will take a long time to disappear from British policies. At the least, they may be the model of what to avoid: a memory studiously honoured in the breach. More likely, they will endure as an example others cannot neglect.

As a leader, she developed abrasiveness into an art form. She despised, above all, consensus: the goal of most other leaders but not her. She inveighed against it with as much vigour in November 1990 as she did before she became Prime Minister. As a leader, also, she needed to know everything and often seemed to do so. There never has been a leader better briefed, with readier riposte, more scornfully deployed against her ignorant enemies. This most formidable capacity was some kind of answer to those who charged her, accurately, with an insatiable desire to interfere in every minister's business. Hardly anything moved in Whitehall without her approval; but for hardly anything that happened did she fail to have a detailed justification.

As well as this ambiguous virtue, however, she had a plainer one. She did not want to be liked. The least likeable of all leaders, according to consistent opinion poll findings, she nonetheless won three elections. In this she was wholly admirable. She did not pander to the people. They often remarked on how much they hated her, even as they admitted to a grudging respect. This quality, often described as a flaw, did much for the moral calibre of our politics. No other leader in our time, I guess, will be so easily willing to resist the desire to please.

She used this harshness to establish a more prominent British presence in the world. Of all the people bewildered by what has happened, none flounder in deeper astonishment than foreigners from all over. For most of them, Margaret Thatcher has given a passable imitation of the Britannia whom, during the Falklands crisis, she shamelessly sought to personify. Before her, a series of faceless men, usually in grey suits, trod the global stage pretending to an influence that depended on past glories some of them could almost remember. They rarely said or did anything worthy of report on an inside page of the New York Times.

In the Thatcher era, the image has been different. During the Reagan years, moreover, image proclaimed more than mere appearance. Through their shared ideology, they formed a society for the mutual support of leaders determined to abolish the post-war consensus. Mrs Thatcher visited Washington often, was invariably feted and, if an election year loomed, notionally drafted for the presidency. She had a very special relationship with Mr Reagan and, as the interlocutor with Mr Gorbachev, a special role in the dialogues that led to the ending of the Cold War. When that ice age broke up, moreover, it was to the Thatcher model that many of the newly free countries consciously turned for guidance on the modalities of the free market. All this was due to her personal charisma.

Evangelism and showmanship captured the east, beginning in the Soviet Union shortly before the 1987 election. Some might say that the influence thereby attained was a little illusory. How could a weak country like Britain aspire to change the world, especially when Germany was becoming so manifestly the dominant power in Europe? But that only serves to reinforce the Thatcherite point: without her peculiar quality of conviction, proclaimed by her flamboyant personality, Britain would have continued to take its proper place as an increasingly obscure island off the shore of north-west Europe. It is a destination her successor will have the greatest difficulty in avoiding.

So this defiance of historic inevitability may not last long. There were signs of it waning well before she fell. Developments in both east and west were beginning to relegate Britain back into the second division. What the lady spoke for at home, on the other hand, could expect a longer shelf-life. It was here that her legacy had best chance of surviving, if only because some of it has been seized by her opponents.

She spoke, as no one else did, for business Britain. Not just for big business but, rather more, for small. Detached from her party, she could easily have been a latterday Poujadist, expressing the economic but also the social philosophy of little-England shop-keeping, the world from which she sprang. In entrepreneurship, in profit-making, in market-place success she saw the unalterable foundations of a successful society. She never deviated from this philosophy, and never tired of reiterating its principles as a guide to human conduct. Doubted and even despised during the Seventies, these at last became conventional wisdom in the Eighties.

Nowhere was this more apparent than in the Labour Party. Arguably, the new model Labour Party was one of her most important creations. She often vowed not to leave politics until socialism had been scorched off the face of Britain. One more term, she thought, would finally disabuse the country as well as Labour that the politics of the left had any future. A pseudo-socialist Labour Party has outlived her, which she will deeply regret.

But the pseudery is significant. In Labour rhetoric, the virtues of private property and market economics have replaced ancient promises to dismantle the integument of the capitalist system. By departing, Mrs Thatcher may have removed Mr Kinnock's favoured electoral target: but she leaves an Opposition more anxious to retain than remove a fair amount of what she has done.

She also leaves an economy which, for all their railings, is stronger than it was. Maybe the most history will be able to say is that the Thatcher years decelerated British decline. Certainly the wondrous miracle, which many of her former colleagues were pointing to in their tributes this week, takes its reality only from an assumption about where we might have been without the medicine she administered in the early Eighties. Even so, if we grant that all political careers can be said to end in failure, with their grand promises never fully achieved, this career can nonetheless be deemed less of a failure than many.

There were failures, however. And of many candidates for consideration, two strike me as reaching close to the heart of the Thatcher experience. Just as there were positive events unattainable without her, so were there the negative: specific and peculiar to her person.

The first concerned her attitude to government itself, and in particular the role of the state. She came into power determined to reduce it. Most Tory leaders have said as much, but she was the first who announced a conscious mission to abandon parternalist aspirations and get government, even benign government, off the people's backs.

This was conspicuously accomplished in only one department, that of state ownership. The privatising of productive business will never be reversed, and even the utilities are likely, under Labour, to remain outside the public sector. Selling council houses and cheap shares in gas switched a few million people from being clients of Labour, as the party of public ownership, to being clients of the capitalist party.

But elsewhere, Mrs Thatcher's relations with the state ended in confusion, futility, and contradiction. One of her famous axioms was that no such thing as society existed: which postulated a dismantling of the collective institutions that propped society up. This did not happen. Her sentiment was widely regarded with ridicule and incomprehension, even among her own supporters. Society at large showed no inclination to assume its disintegrating role. Quite the opposite. Every test of public opinion showed that in her didactic task, of persuading people that the state could not be benign, she failed.

But her actions, also, countermanded her ambition. In the Thatcher years, there were many ways in which the central state grew more—not less—powerful. In finance, in education, in health services, the edicts of the centre overrode those of the locality, as local government was substantially undermined. She was aware of this paradox. In schools and hospitals, a species of market choice was supposed to stand substitute for local democracy. But in the end the gentlemen, and un-gentlewoman, in Whitehall knew best. We were told that this would be temporary.

But a government of different temper will find a lot of new instruments in place, the tools of Mrs Thatcher's rage for action, conveniently ready for use.

Add to this the curtailments of civil liberties, notably concerning free expression, and the Thatcher era will go down as one in which state powers increased. All Tory leaders have been vigilant in defence of the state's policing power. But a special edge was given this trait by this prime minister. Her own experience with terrorism, always an underrated aspect of her psyche, made her an unyielding proponent of media curbs which touched upon it. She was in favour of freedom as long as it could be paid for: a less reliable defender of the intangible liberties of man.

The second failure concerned, in the end, her view of what political leaders were meant to be and do. She had the vices of her virtues. This was what finally engulfed her.

She was strong, but put excessive weight on strength. She accumulated more personal power than any peacetime prime minister in history; and in that guise will interest the constitutional historians for many years. But she saw too little value in the art of compromise. Leadership, for her, was equated too often with the satisfaction of her will. How often, when challenged with being overmighty, did she deride the notion of a leader who gave precedence to other virtues than strength. She was a conviction politician, but too often scorned the reasoned statement of different convictions, sometimes by her closest colleagues. Argument she relished, as long as she won, but persuasion she neglected. Give-and-take and the other techniques of sweet reason were alien to her nature. This made for abrasive and often decisive government, but it was fatally disabling for any kind of collective leadership. For surprisingly many years, it wrought no lasting damage.

The collective was willing to put up with its uncomradely supremo because, essentially, it was persuaded that she was going in the right direction: and in any case she kept on winning elections.

But at the end, over Europe, the one issue on which the Conservative Party was prepared to concede that it is most seriously divided, the obedience of the collective—beginning with Nigel Lawson and ending with Geoffrey Howe, and not forgetting the destruction wrought by Nicholas Ridley in between—collapsed.

Behind Mrs Thatcher's political method lay a vision of Britain but, perhaps more importantly, also a vision of herself. Although insecurity was never entirely missing from her makeup, it coexisted with even less confidence in the ability of anyone else to do what she was doing.

For many years she thought she was irreplaceable, a judgment which grew not out of simple vanity so much as an assessment of Britain's plight and what she could contribute to it. When the tumbrils began to roll three weeks ago, she still could not credit that this verdict was being revised. Nor could many other people. Some still cannot. Having broken the rules and beaten the system often in the past, she seemed capable of doing it again. It was almost an offence against nature to suppose that she could not.

But finally the system, which says that this is cabinet and not prime ministerial government, reacted. There was a point beyond which it declined to be flouted. This point was identified by an age-old reflex: the perception that an election was about to be lost and power surrendered to the other side. No fear exceeds that of politicians faced with the loss of office, not even fear of the avenging virago across the table. So in the end, in a drama whose outlandishness aptly reflected the years before, she went.

John Major
More than a tedious talent

Some think he will be a poor man's Thatcher-in-trousers. Not those who have worked with him on his way up

WHO is the new prime minister? A surprising number of Mr John Major's ministers are unsure. Can he be as ordinary as he seems? Has he got the physical and mental stamina to dominate a job so complex it can crumple the merely ordinary? Does he have the fire to lead a nation?

Nothing annoys Mr Major more than the insistent repetition that he is "grey". Yet he rose through grey behind-the-scenes jobs—in the whips' office; as parliamentary under-secretary and then minister for social security; and as chief secretary to the Treasury. Good jobs. Important jobs. But grey jobs. Until he was catapulted into the job of foreign secretary, few people beyond the Westminster village had noticed him. He rose with a self-deprecating smile on his face, and a misleading air of diffidence.

A paid-up, card-carrying member of the human race, Mr Major has an engaging talent for bathos. At the moment of his triumph this week, he looked thoughtful, then remarked: "It is a very exciting thing to become leader of the Conservative party."

He starts his prime-ministership under a shadow; the huge one cast by the reputation of his predecessor and patron, Mrs Margaret Thatcher. It is extraordinary that the admirers of someone who has just become his nation's leader should feel it necessary to assert that "John is his own man". His bold cabinet reshuffle was designed above all to establish his independence.

The first misconception about Mr Major is that he is Son of Thatcher. Many of the radical right-wingers who campaigned for him knew perfectly well he was not "one of us". The only member of his cabinet to have drawn unemployment pay and to have known real hardship, he was considered a Tory left-winger in his younger days. He is a liberal on many social issues—he is firmly opposed, for instance, to racism and to capital punishment.

His guiding economic principles are the Thatcherite trio of free markets, sound money and low public expenditure. But he was far more worried about the run-down of the manufacturing sector in the early 1980s than was Mrs. Thatcher. One of the least-educated of modern prime ministers, having left school at 16 with only two O-levels (rather like the much-mocked Princess of Wales), he is happy to admit that he does

Getting there

THE storming campaign waged by Mr Major for the Tory leadership enabled him, in just five days, to sweep past the man who had been campaigning for the job for the past five years. So runs the conventional wisdom. Before it becomes history, here is a mild corrective.

Mr Major was talked about as a future Tory leader almost from the moment he arrived in the Commons in the first Thatcher wave of 1979. His colleagues saw something different in him, a steely determination masked by an engagingly modest manner. Mrs Thatcher, who started taking a close interest in him after he stood up to her during a dinner-party row at Downing Street, promoted him with dizzying speed. While Mr Heseltine was impressing local Tory workers, Mr Major was impressing senior ministers.

During Mrs Thatcher's resignation crisis, Mr Major was mostly out of sight, recovering at home from a wisdom-tooth operation. But once she had gone, making clear that he was "her" candidate, he quickly got the support of a clutch of the younger cabinet ministers and a strong team of young, ambitious Tories. They put together a formidable campaign machine and worked ferocious hours.

After Mrs Thatcher withdrew on Thursday, November 22nd, all three candidates launched a telephone blitz on their colleagues. Then followed a whirlwind of television, press and radio interviews, with Mr Heseltine clearly outperforming the others. But opinion polls showed that the party insider, Mr Major, could be as effective an election-winner as the outsider, Mr Heseltine.

On Monday, November 26th, the candidates turned to private meetings with MPs. Mr Major and Mr Hurd sat in their Commons rooms, letting supporters shepherd undecided colleagues to them for 20-minute chats. Mrs Thatcher started telephoning around for Mr Major, and gave right-wing Heseltine supporters an earful at a private lunch. Mr Heseltine worked the Commons lobbies like a door-to-door evangelist.

By then, Mr Major and Mr Heseltine were level-pegging. On Tuesday, as voting got under way, Mr Major's team started the rumour that Mr Hurd's support was collapsing—only their man could stop Mr Heseltine. MPs love to back a winner, and they started flocking towards Mr Major. He won 185 votes against Mr Heseltine's 131 and Mr Hurd's 56. When the losers swiftly and graciously conceded defeat, the party dispensed with the formality of a third ballot. Mr Major had confirmed eleven years of predictions.

He's got class

SO MARX was right after all. "The class struggle," he wrote, "necessarily leads to the dictatorship of the proletariat." After a leadership battle in which the class issue was played to death, victory went to the only man with any claim to membership of Marx's illustrious club.

Class came to the fore partly because the candidates were distressingly gentlemanly and the press needed its fun. So Mr Douglas Hurd was driven to protest that he was running for the leadership of the Conservative party, not of a Marxist organisation, while Lord Whitelaw complained about discrimination against public schoolboys.

But class is rather like sex: the jokes surrounding the business divert attention from its importance. The issue did matter. The Tory party is concerned to keep the working-class vote it has won during the Thatcher years. In 1987 the Tories got 40% of the votes of skilled manual workers, compared with Labour's 36%. The battle for the wavering, over-mortgaged sales-rep is vital, too. Tory MPs worried that a toff might put these people off.

Politicians have changed as well as the voters. In Mrs Thatcher's first cabinet there were six Etonians; in her last, three—Mr Hurd, Mr William Waldegrave and Lord Belstead. The posher public schools had lost out to minor ones, while five ministers (Mrs Thatcher, Mr Major, Mr Kenneth Clarke, Mr Cecil Parkinson and Mr Michael Howard) came from state schools. The same has happened in the civil service. More than half of the permanent secretaries come from minor public schools; a third are from the state sector.

Britain's boardrooms have gone the same way during the 1980s. According to Professor Leslie Hannah, at the London School of Economics, in 1979, 18 of the chairmen of the top 50 companies came from state schools; by 1989, the count was up to 35. The change in the 1980s was greater than that during 1900-1980.

So does the rise of the meritocracy herald a classless era? No, for several reasons. Eton and Cambridge (or the Guards) may no longer run politics and the civil service, but the people in charge still come from the fee-paying schools that educate a mere 7% of the population.

Again, today's state-sector meritocrats came up through the grammar schools, abolished by a Labour party keener on equality than on opportunity. Comprehensive pupils have yet to prove that they can scale the walls of the establishment. They may be less successful than their predecessors: the proportion of Oxford students coming from state schools fell from 49% in 1980 to 46% in 1988.

And money has stuck to the old rich. According to a *Sunday Times* list of the 200 richest people in the country, 57% inherited their dosh. Tax cuts and the boom in the stockmarket have more than made up for the falling value of land.

Certainly, the 1980s made new people rich. But what did they do with their money? They copied the old rich. Green wellingtons, Barbour jackets, Range Rovers (or their Japanese equivalents) all imply country estates and shooting weekends; yet they have all been taken up by City slickers whose closest experience of game is *faisan à la normande*.

Anyway, the British are too attached to class prejudices to give them up. As John Betjeman, bard of Britishness, wrote:

Think of what our nation stands for,
Books from Boots and country lanes,
Free speech, free passes, class distinction,
Democracy and proper drains.

not understand bits of received economic wisdom and often demands that they be explained in detail.

Although he knows the English-speaking world far better than continental Europe, he is not, as Mrs Thatcher is, a visceral Euro-sceptic. She seized on his "hard ecu" proposal as a political dodge to help block a single European currency. Mr Major became committed to it as a route to a single currency. He believes that an anti-inflationary hard ecu could quickly push weaker currencies out. If the pound was one of them, this ex-banker would lose little sleep.

But Mr Major, while no fundamentalist, needs no reminding of the political traps for the Conservative party in the Delors plan: he knows that if he allowed the plan to be rammed through at the coming Rome intergovernmental conferences, he could split his party. So, like Mrs Thatcher, he will be looking for a fudge, or a get-out clause. Unlike her, he will relish the hunt and try to charm his way to success.

What he does share with Mrs Thatcher is a self-made man's contempt for the Britain of the old boy network, the free lunch and the stuffy class distinction. This is a matter of his background (modest), age (youngish) and personality (open) as much as a philosophy. His shirt-sleeved style of business did not amuse the more uptight of his officials at the Foreign Office, where his time was unhappy and short.

A surer guide to the style of government he may now bring to Number 10 is provided by his time as chancellor. After the intellectual gymnastics of Mr Nigel Lawson, Mr Major came as quite a shock. He asked for huge wodges of briefing material, subjecting ideas to two practical questions: will it work and, if so, how can we implement it? He started meetings by asking everybody to present their thoughts and lay out the options. Nobody quite knew what he wanted to be told, as they generally had known with Mr Lawson. After listening to the discussion, Mr Major would seize on somebody else's idea and turn it into his pet policy.

He disliked Mrs Thatcher's habit of second-guessing the civil service, and is not at home in the hot-house world of think tanks. At the Treasury, he was most at home with top civil servants, relying little on special advisers or outside academics; his special advisers never got to know him in the way they get to know many cabinet ministers. Instead, he would pick a couple of civil servants he felt he could trust and take them into his confidence.

So expect Mr Major, in his new job, to listen less to the political theoreticians and gurus beloved of Mrs Thatcher and to rely instead on career civil servants he admires, such as Mr Michael Scholar, the Treasury man in charge of monetary policy. His will not be policy by think-tank, but by civil service cabal. And by cabinet: Mr Major has a good reputation already as a chairman of cabinet committees. His colleagues find him good at listening, good at boiling down arguments to their essentials, and excellent at then taking a decision and sticking by it. Cabinet meetings could ring again with the sound of a debate.

His style will be different in other ways, too. One of the first acts of the new regime was to announce that the prime minister's wife Norma would not be taking up residence with their two children in Downing Street, but will try to lead a semi-normal life at their Huntingdonshire home, coming to London only for essential functions. This is a determinedly normal family, fighting desperately to stay so.

Again, Mr Gus O'Donnell, the new Number 10 press officer in place of Mr Bernard Ingham, is a gentler, more open and less combative soul than his predecessor. It is hard to imagine him unattributably rubbishing cabinet ministers at private lobby meetings—and hard, at this stage anyway, to imagine Mr Major wanting him to.

The Tories have taken a small risk in opting for Mr Major. Grey? So are many Britons, and proud of it. Dull? If so, let no one worry overmuch. Mr Major may take comfort from the words of Walter Bagehot on "Dull Government":

Dullness is our line, as cleverness is that of the French. Woe to the English people if they ever forget that, all through their history, heavy topics and tedious talents have awakened the admiration and engrossed the time of their Parliament and their country.

The Scots who want to be alone

The campaign for a separate parliament north of the border is gaining pace, writes **James Buxton**

This Friday, while in London a new prime minister gets ready to form a government, a gathering in Glasgow will make what is being called the greatest ever challenge to the British constitution. The Scottish constitutional convention will ceremoniously issue its blueprint for a separate Scottish parliament.

The St Andrew's Day meeting was arranged months before the events that are certain to drive it out of the news. But it is a serious business: the convention, which first met in early 1989, is strongly backed by the Labour party, and Mr John Smith, the shadow chancellor, will be a star participant. He will pledge Labour to introduce a Scottish parliament along the lines of the convention's scheme within a year of coming to power.

The convention's blueprint, worked out over the past year and a half, is an expression of the dissatisfaction in Scotland with its 1707 union with England. Another manifestation is the bolder policy, proclaimed separately by the Scottish National party, that would have Scotland become a distinct, independent member of the European Community. Opinion polls show that only about 20 per cent of Scots favour the status quo: about 45 per cent say they want a separate Scottish parliament and 35 per cent outright independence.

Dissatisfaction in Scotland with the working of the union swelled after the 1987 election when the Conservatives, left with only 10 of the 72 Scottish parliamentary seats, imposed unpopular policies such as the poll tax (launched north of the border a year earlier than in England). The Scots' intense dislike of Mrs Thatcher, who was widely seen as an overbearing product of the arrogant south of England, revived a sense of Scotland's separate identity, reminding Scots how different many of their attitudes are from those of the English. These feelings may well subside now that Mrs Thatcher has gone.

The opinion polls have always shown that although most Scots want constitutional change, it ranks well down their list of concerns, which is headed by the poll tax and unemployment. But the drive for a Scottish parliament is still important and could have a big effect on the rest of Britain. The convention, supported by Labour and the Liberal Democrats but boycotted by the Tories and the SNP, has produced a highly ambitious scheme. A Scottish parliament would have power over virtually all Scotland's internal affairs, leaving Westminster to deal with defence, foreign policy, central economic and taxation issues, and social security policy.

It would be much more than the devolved Scottish assembly devised by the last Labour government and rejected in a referendum in 1979: just as the term "assembly" has been replaced by "parliament", the term "devolution" is rejected. According to Canon Kenyon Wright, the eloquent episcopalian clergyman who chairs the convention's executive committee: "Enoch Powell used to say that power devolved was power retained. The powers of a Scottish parliament would be entrenched so that Westminster could never take them back."

The parliament would have powers of strategic planning over industry, the ability to nationalise companies and to operate a Scottish monopolies and mergers policy to limit takeovers of Scottish companies.

It would be funded from three sources: first, it would receive all income tax and Vat raised in Scotland; second, it would enjoy the right to levy a small supplementary income tax of 2p to 3p in the pound; and third, Westminster would still make extra revenue contributions because of Scotland's supposed extra needs.

But critics such as Mr Malcolm Rifkind, the Scottish secretary, believe that the convention has done the easy work of agreeing what powers a Scottish parliament would have without tackling the hard issues. He says it is unrealistic

to propose that with its own parliament Scotland could still expect England and Wales to contribute to a level of public spending which is about 25 per cent higher than south of the border. English and Welsh taxpayers would, after all, have no say in how the money was spent.

It is also implausible, he says, that Scotland would still be allowed to send all 72 of its MPs to Westminster with the right to vote on matters affecting, say, East Anglia. East Anglian MPs would have no say on internal matters in Scotland.

Conservatives are not alone in saying it is unrealistic to imagine that a Labour government, even with a working majority, could ever get such a scheme through the House of Commons – even though it would eventually be offering its backbenchers from other parts of Britain their own less powerful regional assemblies.

If parliament did make such a big transfer of power to Scotland a future Conservative government would be likely to reduce the number of Scottish MPs at Westminster or prevent them voting on some English issues. That would have particularly dire consequences for Labour, which currently supplies 49 of the 72 Scottish MPs, and could reduce its chances of forming a UK government.

Canon Wright says the blueprint is internally consistent

and gives Scotland enough power to avoid wrangles with Westminster that would lead to demands for outright independence (the so-called "slippery slope" argument).

But an elaborate parliament (meeting five days a week in Edinburgh, elected by proportional representation and with crèches for members' children) seems to some people a disproportionate response to the current defects of the union. If Scotland wants that much power over its own affairs, why not go the whole hog and become independent? they say.

"What the convention is doing is out of place and out of time," says Mr Jim Sillars, an SNP MP. "It's provincialisation, not independence. You'd be setting up a parliament to decide whether a hospital should go on one side or the other of Falkirk."

Mr Sillars and the SNP say Scotland, as an independent state in the EC, would be no smaller in population than Denmark and would have North Sea oil revenues to help make it economically self-sufficient. By severing the tie with England Scots would have "to face up to responsibility for what happened in their own country, rather than blaming England," he says.

People such as Mr Michael Heseltine argue that other EC countries such as Spain, France and Italy would be reluctant to allow Scotland to join as a separate country, fearful about secession of their own minorities. But Mr Sillars says all these problems could be overcome: "Our opponents don't really contest the merits of our case, they only say it wouldn't be in our interests."

Some Scottish businessmen say, almost always privately, that they like the idea of independence, now that the EC is becoming more integrated and the threat of Scotland sailing off into a kind of Albanian isolation in the North Atlantic has gone.

They can see the large Scottish financial services sector benefiting in the absence of rules designed for the City of London. More generally they see independence as an end to political uncertainty, away from the socialism that pervades Scottish politics, including those of the SNP. But only one or two leading figures in the business community, the most notable being Sir Iain Noble, chairman of the merchant bank Noble & Co, and a leading Scottish financier, ever say this in public.

Canon Wright says that the convention's solution meets the spirit of the times. "Europe is moving away from nation states to a Europe of the people. Why set up all the paraphernalia of embassies, armies and navies?"

But as he launches on Friday a campaign to proclaim the case for a Scottish parliament to people outside the ranks of political activists he will have to answer the point made by Mr Hamish Morrison, who runs the Scottish Council Development and Industry, a widely representative Scottish economic pressure group.

"The constitutional differences with England only amount to an irritant, far down most peoples' priorities. If we sat down with the English and reviewed all aspects of our relations we'd find we agreed on most points. For the rest, a revision of the treaty of union would be enough."

History as Plague: Two Irelands Struggle to Recover

History: Ireland—and Britain—too long relied on 19th-Century institutions and a sense of history. Justice has not been served.

Michael Elliott

Michael Elliott is the Washington bureau chief for the Economist.

WASHINGTON

Easter weekend in Ireland was sufficiently full of the sad symbols of that divided island to provoke the usual sighs. In the North, there were the funerals of three Catholics, victims of the latest sectarian murders. These were ostensibly carried out in reprisal for the shooting, a few weeks earlier, of a Protestant policeman's widow. In Dublin, the Republic's capital, the 75th anniversary of the Easter Rebellion of 1916 was marked by parades and speeches. And, as usual, no comment on them was possible without a quotation from William Butler Yeats—usually his sense that after the rebellion all was "changed, changed utterly: a terrible beauty is born."

Yet from afar—and even though hopes have been raised many times before, only to be dashed on the rocks of obduracy and fear—it looked as if something had changed this year. In Northern Ireland, the leaders of all the political parties save for Sinn Fein—the political wing of the Irish Republican Army—had agreed to take part in talks designed to lead to power sharing between the majority Protestant and minority Catholic communities. In Dublin, the Easter celebrations were markedly subdued, not triumphant. It was as if the Republic's leaders, led by Mary Robinson, its new, charismatic president, had decided that appeals to a glorious history were of little help in forging a livable future for the island's two communities.

Let's hope so. If any place in the world can be said to suffer from the effects of too much history, it is Ireland. In the North, Protestants march each July to celebrate the Battle of the Boyne, when Protestant King William III defeated the army of catholic James II. The battle took place in 1690.

In the South, as in Irish expatriate bars around the world, not just the Easter Rebellion is celebrated as if it had happened yesterday, but every British slight and Irish act of heroism since Oliver Cromwell sacked Drogheda—less than three decades after the Mayflower landed on Plymouth Rock.

Myth and tradition are grand things. They can provide a sort of social glue for a nation. But in Ireland, for 300 years, each community's myth and tradition has been defined in terms of opposition to the other. In Ireland, history does not bring Catholic and Protestant, North and South, Scottish and Irish stock together—it serves to remind each community of what keeps them apart.

The casualties of the abiding sense of history are numberless. Since the last episode of the Troubles started in Northern Ireland 22 years ago, thousands have died in sectarian violence. The only sensible test of any political initiative—by British politicians or Irish—is whether it reduces that violence. Everything else is secondary.

Yet, for some, one of the secondary reasons for praying for an end to history in Ireland, and a reconciliation of the island's two communities, is nonetheless important. For Ireland's divisions, especially as manifested in the Troubles in the North, have done terrible things to the reputation of British justice. In March, six men were set free after more than 16 years in British prisons for murders they did not commit. These men are the Birmingham Six, named after the city where IRA bombings killed more than 20 people—the crime for which they were wrongly convicted. They now join others who can testify that the scales of British justice are not always fairly balanced. In 1989, three men and a woman—the Guildford Four, named after another site of IRA atrocities—were freed after 14 years of another wrongful sentence.

In both cases, everything was done by the book. Juries found the defendants guilty; courts of appeal reviewed the convictions; successive home secretaries had looked at the cases and let them stand. Yet still a great injustice was done.

The book of British justice was not good enough. Once the police fabricated evidence—as they did in both cases—a terrible snowball started rolling: The juries would not disbelieve the police; the appeal-court judges would not meddle with a jury verdict; the home secretaries would not second-guess the appeal-court judges. Over both sorry affairs hung the palpable feeling that, faced with terrorist threats, civil liberties take a back seat.

Britain now hums, just as it did after the Guildford Four were released, with plans to change the criminal justice system so that such injustices will not happen again. But a tweak here or there is not all that will be required. In the length of time it took to reverse the Guildford and Birmingham cases, in the amount of effort it took from an honorable roll-call of journalists, retired judges and Cardinal Basil Hume to get the 10 free, Britain comes face-to-face with an awkward truth.

That truth is that Britain, too, is trapped by its history. Of all the rich countries, only the United States has a form of government older than Britain's. (Dating Britain's modern form of government from the Reform Act of 1832.) Most European countries have had great ruptures in their modern history—defeats in wars, occupations, revolutions, regicide. Britain has not—which means its government institutions are much as they were in the early 19th Century.

At that time, it was possible to argue a "sovereign" parliament, made up of men with an independent cast of mind, unconstrained by party whips or the search for office, was a bulwark of liberty. Now it is not. Parliament's main role is to provide a permanent body of support for the government of the day, no more than that.

Lacking a Supreme Court, or any constitution against which the actions of government can be measured against timeless principle, Britain lacks the institutions that give formal underpinning to a commitment to civil liberties. And so—as in the Birmingham and Guildford cases—those liberties too often go by default.

In an ideal world, Britain would give itself a Bill of Rights; not because such a document would be a panacea, but because it would breathe life into a culture of liberty, of rights against the state. And if such a culture were to come into being, the long, uphill struggle to prove the innocence of those imprisoned after Birmingham and Guildford would not have been attended with the suspicion that it was, in fact, greeted with by the powers-that-be.

A Bill of Rights is a long way off. Still there are signs of change. Increasingly, the European Convention on Human Rights, a 40-year old treaty, is turned to by those who wish to challenge British justice. The European Commission and Court of Human Rights in Strasbourg are increasingly the arenas were the actions of British governments are tested against general principles.

If, as may be the case, the wholehearted identification of Britain—and, for that matter of Ireland too—with a European destiny is happening, this grafting on of constitutionalism is likely to be one of its most important consequences. It will not bring about a reconciliation of the two traditions in Ireland—other initiatives must do that—but it will ameliorate at least one of the ways in which the divisions in Ireland have been so disastrous for Britain itself.

Reunited Germany

". . .the future of European security and of Germany's role in it provides grounds for optimism. German unification is likely to be a stabilizing factor. . . . Unlike the post-Versailles era, the Germans will have a constructive leadership role in the new Europe."

STEPHEN F. SZABO

Associate Dean for Academic Affairs, School of Advanced International Studies, Johns Hopkins University

Stephen F. Szabo teaches European studies at the Paul H. Nitze School of Advanced International Studies, Johns Hopkins University. He is the author of *The Changing Politics of German Security* (New York: St. Martin's Press, 1990), and editor of *The Bundeswehr and Western Security* (New York: St. Martin's Press, 1990).

WHILE the revolutions of 1989 produced new regimes with the overthrow of communism, they also produced a new Germany in the heart of Europe. The collapse of the former German Democratic Republic (GDR) in East Germany and its incorporation into the Federal Republic of Germany (FRG) mean more than just the addition of five new states and a unified Berlin to the West German federation.* It means the enlargement of the population of Germany by almost one-fourth and its geography by more than one-third. Internally, it raises fundamental questions about the impact on German politics and political culture of the inclusion of a large number of people who have not experienced democracy for almost six decades. Externally, it opens a new era in European security, politics and economics.

The constitutional structure of the new Germany appears clear. The West German Basic Law (or constitution) provided for the unification of East Germany with West Germany in two ways. The two German states could have pursued the Philadelphia-style Constitutional Convention route under Article 146 of the Basic Law.[1] Under this provision, the two Germanys would have held a constitutional convention and drawn up a new German constitution. Under the Article 23 option, however, the East German state (or federal states) could simply apply for membership in the West German federation, much as a territory would apply for statehood under the American constitution.[2] Unlike the American model, however, the West German Parliament (the lower house Bundestag and the upper house Bundesrat) does not have the option of denying the application of these states. This is because the West German Basic Law states clearly in its preamble that it is a provisional constitution until the unification of the nation and that West Germany, which claims to be the legal successor to the Third Reich, is committed to the unification of the nation.

When the East German parliamentary election of March 18, 1990, produced a government led by close allies of West German Chancellor Helmut Kohl and his Christian Democratic party, the new East German Prime Minister, Lothar de Maizière, decided on the Article 23 route. He chose this method in close consultation with Kohl because he was faced with the imminent collapse of East Germany, and the preference of East Germans for unity as quickly as possible was clear. De Maizière and his alliance of Christian Democrats and Free Democrats ran on an election platform of rapid political and economic unity; their main opponents, the Social Democrats, favored the slower route of Article 146. The decisive victory of the conservatives on March 18 answered the constitutional and political questions.[3]

The entry of East Germany into the Federal Republic means that the political rules of the game as they were played in West Germany will continue to guide the politics of a unified Germany. On July 22, the East German Parliament (Volkskammer) reconstituted the five federal states that had been abolished by the Communists in 1952 and scheduled state legislative elections for October 14, 1990. These five states, along with the city-state of Berlin, and the ten West German states, will constitute the new German Republic that will have its capital in Berlin.

---

*On August 22, the East German Parliament voted to reunify with West Germany on October 3; the treaty was signed August 31.

Reprinted with permission from *Current History* magazine, November 1990, pp. 357-360, 388-390. Copyright © 1990 by Current History, Inc.

There may be some redrawing of state borders and a consolidation of the 16 states to a smaller, more manageable polity early in the life of the new Republic, but overall the constitutional system is likely to operate much as did that of West Germany. This means a decentralized federal system in which the states will continue to have important autonomy in administration, cultural policies and law enforcement. Given the divergence of East Germany from West Germany for over four decades, the new constitution is likely to be even more decentralized than the Basic Law. Important disputes over social policy as illustrated by an impasse over abortion law are likely to be settled by allowing the states a great deal of leeway in dealing with these issues.

A more uncertain aspect concerns the impact on the German political culture of the inclusion of 16 million people with no real democratic experience. The practice followed by West Germany of offering a haven to East German dissidents (including payment in West German marks to the East German government for their emigration) deprived the East Germans of a democratic political opposition and of charismatic leaders like Vaclav Havel of Czechoslovakia and Lech Walesa of Poland. This lack of political experience and leadership has been painfully apparent in the well-intentioned but ineffectual de Maizière government, a loose and unmanageable coalition that began to dissolve in July, 1990. The result has been a unification almost entirely managed by West German politicians.

Effective political parties will have to be developed in East Germany and professionalism in political leadership and administration will have to be nurtured. Like people in the other former Communist states of Central Europe, the Germans will have to co-opt many people who collaborated with or were integral parts of the old regime. This was, of course, also true in West Germany when many former Nazi party members and collaborators participated in the transition to democracy.

Another aspect of the democratization problem goes deeper. The last free election in East Germany was held in 1933 and at least two generations have been socialized in one of the most pervasive and efficient police states in Europe. Yet the early signs have been encouraging. Almost all East Germans watched democracy operate via West German television for years, and the German revolution of 1989 was restrained and democratic. It was a revolution from below and a peaceful one as well. In addition, the parliamentary election of March, 1990, produced a 93 percent voter turnout and a broad majority for democratic parties. The election may have been about a desire for prosperity and materialism, but there was also a strong democratic

desire and joy. To East Germans, unification is about the deutsche mark and democracy. Merging into the mature democracy of West Germany means added insurance against any return of the secret police (the Stasi) and the police state.

Yet this new democracy, like the others in East Europe, will be severely tested in its early years. Unemployment, which had been officially non-existent, soared by August, 1990, to one million people, either out of work or expecting to be laid off shortly (one out of every nine in the workforce) and may rise to three million before topping out. Anywhere from 30 percent to 75 percent of East German firms are likely to fail.[4] The general expectation among economists and business leaders in West Germany is that the former East Germany will take off economically within three to five years, but the politicians worry about the short-term effect on the upcoming all-German election. The bill for the West Germans for unification is also likely to be higher than most current estimates, which already amount to hundreds of billions of deutsche marks.

Will the bleak short-term economic effect of unification lead voters to shift their support to more radical parties on both the left and the right? Possibly, although the stability of West German institutions and parties is likely to contain these tendencies. Yet the future of the party system in the new unified Germany needs to be considered more closely.

THE NEW GERMAN PARTY SYSTEM

One of the keys to the success of democracy in West Germany has been the stability of its system of political parties. Unlike the failed democracy of the Weimar Republic, which was undermined by an unstable multiparty system dominated by extremist antidemocratic parties, in the West German party system, centrist, democratic parties have dominated. There has been a tendency toward a concentration of the system as well toward a three- or four-party system in which the centrist Free Democratic party (the FDP) has held the balance of power. This stable coalition system has produced majority centrist governments that have been able to govern effectively.

Will the addition of 12 million new voters to a West German electorate of 45 million swing the political balance away from the center or, alternatively, fragment the party system by adding new and undemocratic parties? Probably not. The electoral system adopted for the new German Republic (after much haggling and a coalition crisis in East Germany) will be, in effect, the system that has operated in West Germany since 1949. This is in essence a proportional representation system that requires a party to obtain at least five percent of the national vote in order to enter Parliament, a hurdle that has proved to be an effective barrier against small extremist parties and is likely to remain so.

A look at the elections held in East Germany for the national Parliament in March, 1990, and for local councils in May, 1990, shows little support for nondemocratic parties. The former Communist party (now called the party of Democratic Socialism, PDS) was the only exception, gaining the support of 1.8 million voters, or 16.3 percent of the East German electorate, in March. Yet the PDS is unlikely to gain 5 percent nationally in the all-German election scheduled for December 2, 1990. In order to do so, it would have to win about 20 percent of the vote in the former East Germany, because it will find little support in West Germany. The PDS, however, is likely further to split a left already divided between the Greens and the Social Democrats; thereby it will enhance the conservative percentage of parliamentary seats.

Although the election of 1990 will probably be the most unpredictable one since the first Bundestag election in 1949, most surveys taken in West Germany at the end of the summer of 1990 indicated that the Christian Democratic Union (CDU) under the leadership of Chancellor Kohl had a strong lead and was the favorite to win the parliamentary elections.[5] Kohl was running as the Chancellor of reunification and the symbol of a revived Germany. He also benefitted from a strong economy, from optimism about the economic future, and from the public's view that his party was united while those of his opponents were not.

On the negative side, as a German commentator noted, "Kohl and de Maizière want to invite voters to the ballot box before they invite them to the teller's window to pay the bills."[6] The Kohl-led rush to unification and the impending economic collapse of East Germany provided incentives for Kohl to push for an early election as he and de Maizière attempted unsuccessfully in August to advance the date of the election from December 2 to October 14, 1990.

The Social Democrats, as they have so often done in the past, have stressed social issues rather than the national issue. Led by the mercurial young politician Oskar LaFontaine, the Social Democratic party (SPD) in its campaign played heavily on the costs of rapid unification for both Germanys. LaFontaine reminded voters in the East of the social dislocations they were likely to face and voters in the West of the bill they would have to pay, especially in terms of new taxes. The Social Democratic candidate for Chancellor, who had opposed the economic and monetary union engineered by Kohl in July, consistently argued for a slower pace toward unification; thus he divided his party over the na-

tional issue. The SPD leader in the Bundestag, Hans Jochen Vogel, helped reverse LaFontaine's opposition to the state treaty with East Germany that ratified monetary union, because he feared that the SPD would miss the boat on the national issue once again.

LaFontaine represents a major generational break within the party and in society at large. Like many West Germans of the postwar generations, LaFontaine is post-national in his views of Germany and of Europe. His concerns about rapid reunification went beyond the social and economic costs to worries about a revival of German nationalism. This distinguished him from the generations that had experienced a unified Germany and were committed to overcoming its division, a generation symbolized by figures like former Chancellor Willy Brandt.

The result has been a divided party and a divided message to the electorate. The SPD campaign in the East German election of March proved to be a forerunner of the all-German campaign, with Brandt and the old guard stressing the unification of the two Germanys while LaFontaine and many younger party leaders emphasized the costs and dangers of unification. The main beneficiary appeared to be Chancellor Kohl.

While the left was perhaps more divided than at any time since the founding of the Federal Republic, the right was relatively stable and cohesive. The fear that the new party on the right, the Republican party (Republikaner or Reps), which soared to prominence in state and local elections in 1989, might split the right in a manner similar to the Green split on the left, proved to be unfounded. The Reps were similar in appeal and leadership style to the National Front of Jean-Marie Le Pen in France. As was true in the case of Le Pen, the Reps mixed appeals to anti-Semitism, resentment against immigrants from the third world, nationalism and anti-Europeanism with the charismatic allure of their leader, Franz Schoenhuber.

The party faded quickly in early 1990 when Chancellor Kohl captured the national issue, although at the price of stirring up anxieties for a few months about the future of the Polish-German border. Once assured that the Republicans were no longer a significant threat and faced with pressure from inside and outside the Federal Republic, Kohl finally agreed to the binding nature of the current Oder-Neisse line as the final Polish-German border.** Although they may find some resonance among voters in East Germany with their nationalist and antiforeign appeals, the Republikaner are given little chance to pass the five percent barrier in the all-German election.

**The border drawn after World War II granting Poland the area east of the Oder and Neisse rivers.

The other conservative party, the Bavarian Christian Social Union (CSU), and its sister party in East Germany, the German Social Union (DSU), appear to be headed for smaller roles in the future. A Catholic and regional party, the CSU apparently lacks a constituency in Protestant Prussian and Saxon eastern Germany.

THE FREE DEMOCRATS

Finally, the Free Democrats are apparently entrenched as the center party in a future coalition with the CDU-CSU. Their titular leader, Foreign Minister Hans-Dietrich Genscher, remains by far the most popular politician in West Germany and is well known and respected in East Germany, especially in his native region of Halle.[7]

All this implies that the new German party system is likely to look a good deal like the old one. It will probably remain a four-party system (CDU-CSU, FDP, SPD and the Greens) although small groupings in East Germany may form alliances and survive briefly. The left faces the prospect of emerging even more divided than it was in West Germany, while the CDU will probably be the largest party in the system, marginally larger than it was in West Germany.

Will the election of 1990 be similar to the election of 1949? That crucial election was won by Konrad Adenauer, who established a CDU era of 20 years' duration. Then the Christian Democrats appealed to broad desires for materialism and security. In 1990, the CDU is likely to win on similar issues and will probably snatch the national issue as well. Its image as the party best able to provide peace and prosperity may prove to be decisive. If East Germany begins to experience an Eastern Economic Miracle before the next national election in 1994, a new CDU era will be in the offing. If, however, the implosion of East Germany is not slowed and if its reconstruction begins to drag significantly on the economy in West Germany, then the SPD may be able to return to power.

In any case, one of the German Questions of the twentieth century, the question of why Germany failed to sustain a liberal democracy,[8] seems to have been set to rest. While German democracy faces enormous challenges, it has a solid foundation in a mature democratic political system. The German party system and its political and economic institutions are flexible and stable. It should not take long for these democratic roots to be transplanted and to flourish in East Germany.

THE EXTERNAL DIMENSION

The other German Question concerns the role of a united Germany in a new Europe.[9] Besides the problem of building a stable democracy, the major German problem of this century has been fitting this dynamic and powerful state into the larger European state system while preserving an equilibrium. The Federal Republic of Germany fit well into postwar Europe. In terms of population it was roughly the same size as Britain, France and Italy. While its economy was the strongest in Europe, it was not dominant. West Germany was a medium-size state with limited political ambitions and a broadly European rather than a national approach.

In terms of population and economic power, the new Germany will be the largest state in Europe. Its population of 78 million will eclipse the population of its major European partners (France, Britain and Italy all have populations around 55 million). Its trillion-dollar economy will make up about 35 percent of the gross national product (GNP) of the European Community (EC). While it may not be a superpower, given its limited military capabilities, it (along with Japan and the United States) will be one of the three key global economic centers. Clearly, its perspective will change.

This raises questions about the role Germany will play in Europe. Will a unified Germany remain a cooperative partner in the European enterprise or will it become a hegemonic power with revanchist pretensions in the east? Will the price of unification be the end of the Atlantic Alliance and a Europe without a defense force to counteract residual or even resurgent Soviet pressure? Will the Germans form an economic and political partnership with the Soviet Union, creating a Central European Co-Prosperity Sphere?[10] Or is what is happening in Germany a precursor of a new type of political and security system that will replace the balance of power that has characterized European security since the rise of the nation-state?

ECONOMIC POWER

It seems probable that Germany will be a trading state rather than a military power and will base its influence on the economic dimensions of power. As a trading state that depends on exports, Germany will have strong incentives to work in an interdependent manner with its trading partners and will continue to be sensitive to their views and interests. A strong emphasis on military power would set off counter-alliances and confront Germany once again with its old problem of encirclement by hostile powers.

In addition to these broad considerations, the new Germany will operate under external constraints. These constraints were accepted in the "Two plus Four" talks between the two Germanys and the four Allied powers of World War II (Great Britain, France, the United States and the Soviet Union), consultations within the North Atlantic Treaty Organization (NATO) and the important Soviet-German agreement reached by Chancellor Kohl and Soviet President Mikhail Gorbachev in the Caucasus Mountains in July, 1990.

Soviet forces will be removed from East Germany by the end of 1994 at the latest, and Allied forces in West Germany will probably be dramatically reduced as well and combined into multinational corps. German forces (the Bundeswehr) will not exceed 370,000 men (the combined total of East and West German forces at the beginning of 1990 was about 600,000) and Germany will remain a non-nuclear power.

The result of these negotiations will mean that the new Germany will remain a member of NATO but that NATO will become "kinder and gentler" in its force structure and strategy. NATO forces are not likely to be deployed on the territory of the former East Germany, and the alliance has begun restructuring its nuclear and conventional doctrine in order to reduce its reliance on the threatened first use of nuclear weapons.

Germany will play an important role in assisting the Soviet Union in its economic restructuring. Before unification, the two Germanys were the Soviet Union's largest trading partners, and the new Germany will not only expand this relationship but will also provide substantial credits and other payments to the Soviet Union.

The new Germany will also have a new geography. It will no longer be a front-line state with little strategic depth. The Inner-German Border (IGB) will vanish and the new defense line will move 200 kilometers east from the Elbe to the Oder-Neisse line and 1,000 kilometers to the western border of the Soviet Union. The new Germany will have a greater strategic depth than the old Federal Republic. The thin waist of 225 kilometers will now be expanded to 600 kilometers (as measured to the Oder-Neisse). In West Germany, about one-third of the population and the industrial base was within 100 kilometers of the IGB. This will be greatly reduced, because East Germany is not so densely populated nor so industrialized as the eastern part of West Germany.

This new geography, combined with the removal of Soviet forces 1,000 kilometers eastward, will make the new state less dependent on its NATO allies for defense. It will no longer require large numbers of foreign forces on its territory, nor will it rely on a doctrine that emphasizes early use of nuclear weapons.

All this will add up to a new structure of political, economic and security relations in Europe. While NATO will continue to exist and the Warsaw Pact will probably disappear, the Germans will increasingly emphasize cooperative security over deterrence and will look to European institutions like the EC and the Conference on Security and Cooperation in Europe (CSCE) as the primary pillars of a new European architecture. They will certainly try to make the CSCE more than the series of floating conversations it is currently, by giving it a bureaucracy and headquarters and strengthening its role in confidence building and collective security.[11]

German unification, plus the eventual withdrawal of Soviet forces from Central Europe, will dramatically change the strategic culture of a unified Germany and the calculus for the new Bundeswehr. Key elements of continuity will remain. The Soviet Union is likely to remain the most important potential military threat to Germany. In addition, a Western alliance will continue to be required both to reassure Germany's neighbors and to provide for the element of deterrence that Germany, a non-nuclear state, will not be able to provide for itself.

Yet the future of nuclear deterrence could become a contentious issue between Germany and its nuclear allies, the United States, Great Britain and France. In the new Germany, antinuclear pressures will probably increase from a population that is unlikely to see a credible threat to justify the deployment of nuclear weapons under foreign control and that will be increasingly sensitive to environmental concerns. The Social Democrats, the Greens and the Free Democrats will continue to press for a Germany without nuclear weapons on its soil. If this leads to a withdrawal of all United States forces because of an American unwillingness to station troops without nuclear weapons, then Germany will face a crisis in its security policy.

A NEW GERMANY AND A NEW EUROPE

With these key questions in mind, the future of European security and of Germany's role in it provides grounds for optimism. German unification is likely to be a stabilizing factor in the new Europe for a number of reasons.

First, the experience of two world wars has left a deep impression on the collective memories of all Europeans, especially the Germans. The existence of nuclear weapons and the destructiveness of even a conventional war with modern technology in a densely populated urbanized environment is likely to reinforce the new strategic culture and to continue to deter the use of military force in Europe. War as a realistic option of state policy in Europe seems anachronistic to most Europeans.

Second, the development of the EC offers a successful working structure for a post-national Europe. It has already made the thought of war between its members almost obsolete. The role of the new Germany within the EC, while creating many new questions and problems, is likely to be very positive. West Europe will probably remain the major market for German exports. Chancellor Kohl has continued to press for a deepening of the EC toward monetary and political union and has seen reunification as an impetus rather than a hindrance to the building of a more unified Europe. He and future German leaders will press to strengthen the EC and to widen it to include Central Europe, at first by means of associate membership and then, perhaps by the end of the decade, by full membership. Unlike the post-Versailles era, the Germans will have a constructive leadership role in the new Europe.

Third, Germany is a stable democracy in a democratic Europe. The foreign and defense policies of democracies toward other democracies rely on diplomatic and political negotiations rather than aggression. The German militarism of the first half of this century would have been controlled by an effective democracy. The democratic record of West Germany and of the Bundeswehr has been impressive. In this sense, the two German Questions with regard to democracy and security have both been solved to the benefit of Germans and all Europeans.

---

[1] Article 146 states, "This Basic Law shall cease to be in force on the day on which a constitution adopted by a free discussion of the German people comes into force."

[2] After stating that the Basic Law applied to all the states of the Federal Republic and listing them, Article 23 states, "In other parts of Germany it shall be put into force on their accession."

[3] The results of the March 18, 1990, Volkskammer elections were Alliance for Germany (Christian Democrats, the German Social Union and the Democratic Departure), 48.2 percent; Social Democratic party, 21.8 percent; party of Democratic Socialism (Communists), 16.3 percent; Free Democrats, 5.3 percent; with smaller parties picking up the remaining 13 percent of the vote. *Der Fischer Welt Almanach: Sonderband DDR* (Frankfurt: Fischer Taschenbuch Verlag, 1990), p. 258.

[4] Marc Fisher, "East Germany Appeals for October Union, Vote," *Washington Post,* August 9, 1990, p. A16. By the end of June, 1990, the number of unemployed had risen to 142,000, up 47,300 from the previous month. See Miriam Neubert and Theo Moench-Tegeder, "Wie tief liegt die Talsole?" *Rheinischer Merkur,* July 20, 1990, p. 11. See also Marc Fisher, "Two Ger-

manys' Leaders Call for Unification in October," *Washington Post,* August 4, 1990, p. A18.

[5] A monthly poll commissioned by the weekly newsmagazine *Der Spiegel,* for example, found that in July, 1990, 43 percent of West German voters surveyed said that if the election were held that week they would vote for the CDU or its Bavarian affiliate the Christian Social Union (CSU), while 38 percent picked the SPD, 9 percent the FDP, 8 percent the Greens and 2 percent the new right Republicans. With the exception of the Republicans, who did not run, these results are almost identical to those of the last Bundestag election of March, 1987. They reflect, however, a surge of support for both Chancellor Kohl and his party following his summer successes in obtaining international approval for reunification. About three-quarters of those questioned believed that the Kohl government would win the coming national election. See "Nur jeder vierte glaubt an Wechsel," *Der Spiegel,* no. 31, July 30, 1990, p. 33.

[6] Dieter Schroeder of the *Süddeutsche Zeitung* as quoted in David Binder, "German Unity Drive Mired in Politics," *The New York Times,* August 6, 1990.

[7] While the East German Free Democrats received 5.3 percent of the national vote in the March election, they received 10 percent in Halle.

[8] See David Calleo, *The German Question Reconsidered: Germany and the World Order: 1870 to the Present* (Cambridge: Cambridge University Press, 1987), pp. 1–7.

[9] As Stanley Hoffmann has observed, ". . . the most serious concern is likely to be the prospect of a Germany, even harnessed inside a 'tight' European Community, that yields to the 'arrogance of power' that has been a characteristic of so many major states in history. Under these circumstances, Germany might behave less like a wise 'hegemon,' understanding the need to take account of the interests of lesser powers, than like a selfish player concerned above all with relative gains and insensitive to the claims and fears of others." "Reflections on 'the German Question,' " *Survival,* vol. 32, no. 4 (July–August 1990), pp. 295–296.

[10] A.M. Rosenthal, "Nobody Tells the Truth," *The New York Times,* May 2, 1989.

[11] The shape of this package emerged from a series of discussions that took place between the key international and domestic actors over the first half of 1990. A good short summary of the key elements can be found in Thomas L. Friedman, "U.S. Will Press the Soviets To Accept Plan on Germany," *The New York Times,* June 5, 1990. See also Friedman, "NATO May Offer Moscow Specific Limit for Future German Army," *The New York Times,* June 23, 1990; "Text of the Declaration after the NATO Talks," *The New York Times,* July 7, 1990 (for excerpts, see *Current History,* October, 1990); and "Excerpts from Kohl-Gorbachev News Conference," *The New York Times,* July 17, 1990 (for excerpts, see "World Documents" on page 382 in this issue).

German Elections and National Unity in 1990

FUNNY THING, DEMOCRACY

From our Bonn correspondent

The first, and almost certainly the last, free election in a separate East German state was a decidedly odd affair. The Social Democrats were expected to emerge on top thanks to traditional backing from workers in the industrial south. Instead, the conservative-led Alliance for Germany (Christian Democrats, German Social Union and Democratic Awakening) grabbed nearly 60% of the workers' vote and won easily overall. Why?

Largely because the Alliance, especially its weightiest backer, Mr Helmut Kohl, clearly drummed home that it aimed for quick German unity, with D-marks in the East "within months." Quite a lot of white-collar workers and farmers were ready to wait on unity a bit, as Social Democrats and other leftist parties proposed. But the "industrial proletariat," sick of rotten working conditions and low pay in Ostmarks, rallied to the conservative call. What would Marx have thought?

Hardly less surprising was the strong showing of the Party of Democratic Socialism, as the communists now call themselves. You might have thought almost no one would back the successor to an organisation that collapsed in disgrace only months ago after 40 years of misrule. In fact, 1.9m East Germans gave them their votes.

The party won the support of people who fear change and apparatchiks who have most to lose from it—hence the thumping 30% the party won in East Berlin. The new-model communists

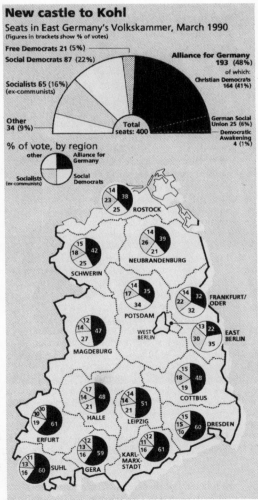

New castle to Kohl

Seats in East Germany's Volkskammer, March 1990
(figures in brackets show % of votes)

Free Democrats 21 (5%)
Social Democrats 87 (22%)
Socialists 65 (16%) (ex-communists)
Other 34 (9%)
Total seats: 400
Alliance for Germany 193 (48%) of which: Christian Democrats 164 (41%)
German Social Union 25 (6%)
Democratic Awakening 4 (1%)

% of vote, by region
other / Alliance for Germany / Socialists (ex-communists) / Social Democrats

had as their standard-bearer Mr Hans Modrow, the prime minister widely judged (rightly or wrongly) a pretty honest chap. And it had the most money of its own to spend on the election campaign, though unlike many of the other parties it got no western aid.

In the days when the communists dominated the rubber-stamp Volkskammer, the Christian Democrats were their loyal vassals. It is ironic to think that, if the ex-communist Socialists and the revived Christian Democrats joined forces now, they still would have an easy parliamentary majority. By sad contrast, the people who led the bloodless revolution last autumn—many of them artists, writers, musicians and teachers—were eclipsed at the polls. Alliance 90, bringing together leading opposition groups including New Forum, scored less than 3%. Yesterday's heroes ran an amateurish campaign and, in the main, are no fans of quick unity.

One last oddity. The East German economics minister-designate is Mr Elmar Pieroth, until recently a leading West German Christian Democrat. He now recommends that East Germany stay in Comecon and fulfill its commitments to the Soviet Union and other eastern partners. That, he reckons, will keep a lot of East Germans in jobs while they learn western ways. Small wonder that only four months after the Berlin Wall came down East German satirists are finding it hard not to be outdone by reality.

Kohl's country

FROM OUR BONN CORRESPONDENT

IS THE German general election in six weeks' time all over bar the voting? It looks that way after polling to choose the governments of six *Länder* (federal states) on October 14th. The six could hardly have gone better for the chancellor, Mr Helmut Kohl.

In four of the five states of former East Germany, reunited with the west since October 3rd, Mr Kohl's Christian Democratic Union easily won the most votes. In the fifth state, Brandenburg, the Social Democrats emerged on top but may yet have to form a coalition with the Christian Democrats. The alternative would be a shaky-looking alliance with the Greens and Bündnis 90 (Alliance 90), one of the little groups that emerged from last winter's bloodless revolution. A lot of Social Democrats would prefer that, but it would do little to encourage investment in Brandenburg, one of the poorest bits of the ramshackle east.

In Bavaria, part of what used to be West Germany, the Christian Social Union surprised even itself by winning 54.9% of the vote. True, it did even better in the previous state election four years ago, but then it was led by the late Franz Josef Strauss, a dynamic vote-catcher invincible on his home ground.

Now the Christian Social Union, sister party to Mr Kohl's Christian Democrats, has achieved a Strauss-sized result without Strauss. That is lovely for Mr Kohl, who was often at odds with Strauss but gets on with the new top Bavarians: Mr Theo Waigel, the party leader and federal finance minister, and Mr Max Streibl, Bavaria's premier.

The Social Democrats have tried to put a brave face on things. After all, didn't they improve their showing in the east compared with the results in the Volkskammer (East German parliament) election in March? They did (see table). But that still leaves them far behind the Christian Democrats, who also raised their vote a bit and tightened their grip on what are normally thought of as Social Democratic strongholds. For instance, compared with March, the Christian Democratic share of the vote rose by 11.3 points in towns with more than 200,000 people, whereas the Social Democrats managed only an extra 0.6 points. In Bavaria the Social Democratic vote dropped to a post-1945 low of 26%. The party there seems to have neither the local leaders nor the structure to offer a serious challenge to the conservatives for many years to come.

This was a dismal showing. On the face of it, the Social Democrats ought to have profited from these state elections in two ways. The voters in the eastern part of the country, it might have been assumed, would be shocked by soaring unemployment (2.2m people there are now either jobless or on short time). And Bavarians would be grousing over the cost of unity, which many people think will mean higher taxes, though Mr Kohl claims it need not.

In the event, East Germans went in droves to Mr Kohl as the "architect of unity" (no surprise to those who have seen the fervour with which Mr Kohl is greeted on his campaign stomps in the east). And they went for his party as the one most likely to pull them out of the economic slough that unity has revealed. The Social Democratic candidate for the chancellorship, Mr Oskar Lafontaine, cautioned voters that quick unity would be a nasty, costly business. But since he seemed to offer no clearly workable alternative, he is winning few plaudits now for being proved right.

The truth is that the Social Democrats were caught on the hop by German unification. They took too long to decide whether they liked the idea or not and, despite visible effort, Mr Lafontaine still fails to convey much enthusiasm for it. Without the unity issue he might well have run Mr Kohl close on December 2nd. Now few people, even in his own party, give him much of a chance.

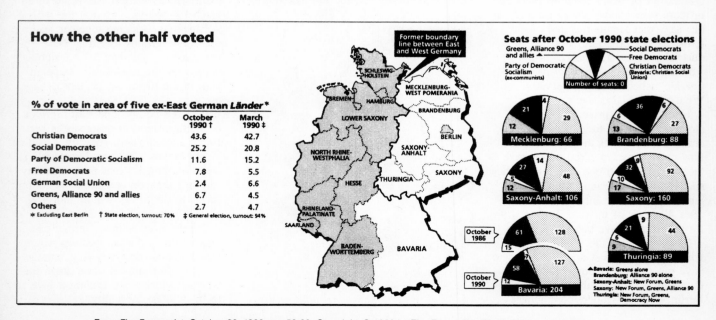

How the other half voted

% of vote in area of five ex-East German *Länder* *

	October 1990 †	March 1990 ‡
Christian Democrats	43.6	42.7
Social Democrats	25.2	20.8
Party of Democratic Socialism	11.6	15.2
Free Democrats	7.8	5.5
German Social Union	2.4	6.6
Greens, Alliance 90 and allies	6.7	4.5
Others	2.7	4.7

* Excluding East Berlin † State election, turnout: 70% ‡ General election, turnout: 94%

Former boundary line between East and West Germany

SCHLESWIG-HOLSTEIN
MECKLENBURG-WEST POMERANIA
BREMEN
HAMBURG
BRANDENBURG
LOWER SAXONY
BERLIN
NORTH RHINE-WESTPHALIA
SAXONY-ANHALT
SAXONY
THURINGIA
HESSE
RHINELAND-PALATINATE
SAARLAND
BADEN-WÜRTTEMBERG
BAVARIA

Seats after October 1990 state elections

Greens, Alliance 90 and allies ▲ — Social Democrats
Free Democrats
Party of Democratic Socialism (ex-communists) — Christian Democrats (Bavaria: Christian Social Union)
Number of seats: 0

Mecklenburg: 66 — 21, 4, 12, 29
Brandenburg: 88 — 36, 6, 13, 27
Saxony-Anhalt: 106 — 27, 14, 5, 12, 48
Saxony: 160 — 32, 9, 10, 17, 92
October 1986 — 61, 128, 15, 7
Thuringia: 89 — 21, 9, 6, 9, 44
October 1990 — 58, 127, 12
Bavaria: 204

▲ Bavaria: Greens alone
Brandenburg: Alliance 90 alone
Saxony-Anhalt: New Forum, Greens
Saxony: New Forum, Greens, Alliance 90
Thuringia: New Forum, Greens, Democracy Now

That seems to leave Mr Kohl stronger than any chancellor since West Germany's first, Konrad Adenauer. But he is far from all-powerful. Adenauer once won an absolute majority in a general election, in 1957. Even now, with the unity bonus, Mr Kohl is unlikely to do the same. The latest opinion poll by the Allensbach Institute, made public on October 17th, gives the conservatives 45.3% of the all-German vote and the Social Democrats 33%. The Free Democrats (liberals) have 8.8% and the Greens-Alliance 90 partnership has 8.5%. That points to another four years of centre-right coalition government.

Even the victories in four of the five eastern *Länder* do not, as some claim, automatically give Mr Kohl's men undisputed sway over the Bundesrat, the second chamber of the German parliament, in which the *Länder* representatives sit. For one thing it is still not clear just what government coalitions will emerge in the states of Brandenburg and Mecklenburg; the outcome will do much to decide the way the states vote in the Bundesrat. For another the five *Länder* in the east may regularly vote together in the Bundesrat across party lines. It is some comfort to Mr Kohl that the previous clear Social Democratic majority in the Bundesrat has been removed. But, in practice, it may not help him much.

The other main thing the voters of the six *Länder* did was to reject, by and large, extremist parties. True, the Party of Democratic Socialism, the former East German communist party, is still getting more than 10% of the eastern vote, and will probably have seats in the next German parliament. It has also been strong in Berlin, which did not take part in the *Länder* polls now but will hold its own local vote on the sidelines of the December 2nd election. Even so, it is losing ground fast.

On the far right the Republicans, fading since their spectacular successes of a year ago, failed even in Bavaria, the home of their leader, Mr Franz Schönhuber, to get the 5% of the votes needed to win any parliamentary seats. On the other hand the Free Democrats won seats in all six state parliaments, including for the first time in years in Bavaria.

The attempt on October 12th to assassinate Mr Wolfgang Schäuble, the interior minister, cast a pall over the voting. Although apparently the act of a lone, unbalanced gunman, it reawakened memories of other recent attacks on public figures, two of them by terrorists of the wild left. These things make it all the more comforting that the great majority of Germans continue to support the political centre.

Germany takes on the world

FROM OUR BONN CORRESPONDENT

WITH his third general-election victory behind him, Mr Helmut Kohl now has to forge a world role for his newly united nation. Squeezed between mounting foreign cries for aid and fears of an all-too-pushy Germany, he faces a challenge that would have daunted even Bismarck.

The demands on Mr Kohl at the start of his new four-year term as chancellor come from all sides. The Soviet Union and Eastern Europe look to Germany for money, food and blueprints for an economic miracle. West Europeans hope (some may fear) that Germany will lead the drive for greater EC integration. The Americans urge the Germans to come out of their post-1945 shell and take on more of the burden of world policing.

Mr Kohl badly needs to set priorities, but that is easier said than done. He feels committed to helping President Mikhail Gorbachev, not just out of gratitude for cooperation over German unity but for fear that still greater chaos in the Soviet Union could bring a flood of refugees to Germany. That danger is treated seriously in Bonn, although officials talk little about it in public. Hence the current drive to send food to Russia and the readiness to put up still more state-backed credits, even though the Germans are dismally aware that their efforts may not change much.

The Soviet Union is a special case, but then so is Hungary. Mr Kohl is deeply grateful to the Hungarians for opening their border to Austria last year, letting East Germans flee west and precipitating the collapse of the Honecker regime in East Berlin. Czechoslovakia is also special, thanks to the outspokenly pro-German-unity stance taken from the start by President Vaclav Havel. So is Poland, because of the particularly painful legacy of Polish-German history. Every talk between the chancellor and a visiting East European leader, runs a joke doing the rounds, costs the finance minister, Mr Theo Waigel, DM500m ($330m).

That comes on top of the costs of German unity which seem to be, literally, incalculable. Every time the government makes an estimate, it turns out too low. It now reckons that, mainly because of unity, net public borrowing next year will jump to DM140 billion, or more than 5% of GNP. Even that figure is based on the assumption that Mr Kohl's coalition will be able to chop an unprecedented DM25 billion-worth of subsidies and tax breaks in 1991 alone.

The government argues that unity-induced deficit spending helps keep German economic growth high and sucks in more imports. It does. But the jump in borrowing, sharply attacked by the independent Bundesbank, also forces up German interest rates and keeps rates elsewhere in Europe higher too. Hence the snarls, especially from the French, that the Germans are financing unity on the backs of their partners.

Mr Kohl could have saved himself some stick from abroad (though hardly at home) if he had raised taxes a bit to help pay the unity bill. But he hopes to silence accusations about "go-it-alone Germany" by pressing for more integration in the European Community.

Mr Kohl has his gaze set on three events in 1994. First, the start of "stage two" of EC economic and monetary union, clearing the way for a Bank of Europe and a single currency; second, elections to the European Parliament, which he hopes will by then have been given much stronger powers; third, his own reelection for a fourth term. Mr Kohl also wants European defence revamped, though less is heard now about his old idea for a "European army", and there is more talk about multinational forces including the Americans (but not necessarily led by them).

It is a formidable agenda. For one thing, the Germans, having just regained their national sovereignty, are being asked to embed it irrevocably in European institutions. But Mr Kohl believes that unity makes the task of "Europeanising" Germany more urgent, and that only thus can fears be removed of a newly expansionist Germany breaking free of its western moorings. For another thing, the Germans have differences with the French on all three elements—defence, political union, even EMU—and still more with the British on the las two, though the atmosphere of Anglo-German contacts will improve now that Mrs Thatcher has gone.

Mr Kohl will also be working under two domestic constraints. First, the relative weight of the Free Democrats (liberals) in Mr Kohl's coalition has grown as a result of the December 2nd election (see box on next page). There is likely to be more tension between the liberals and Mr Kohl's conservatives in what is already, after eight years of coalition, a far from friction-free alliance.

That goes not least for foreign policy. Mr Kohl and the Free Democratic foreign minister, Mr Hans-Dietrich Genscher,

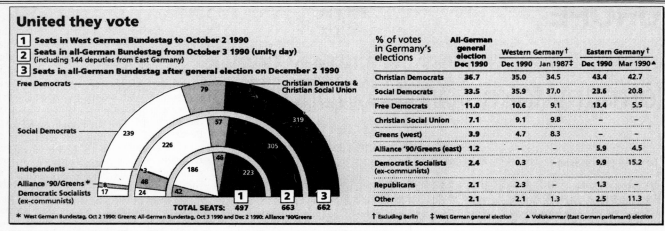

United they vote

[1] Seats in West German Bundestag to October 2 1990
[2] Seats in all-German Bundestag from October 3 1990 (unity day)
(including 144 deputies from East Germany)
[3] Seats in all-German Bundestag after general election on December 2 1990

Free Democrats — 79 — Christian Democrats & Christian Social Union
57
319
Social Democrats — 239 — 226 — 305
186 — 46 — 223
Independents —
Alliance '90/Greens * — 8 — 48 — 3
Democratic Socialists (ex-communists) — 17 — 24 — 42

TOTAL SEATS: [1] 497 [2] 663 [3] 662

* West German Bundestag, Oct 2 1990: Greens; All-German Bundestag, Oct 3 1990 and Dec 2 1990: Alliance '90/Greens

% of votes in Germany's elections	All-German general election Dec 1990	Western Germany †		Eastern Germany †	
		Dec 1990	Jan 1987‡	Dec 1990	Mar 1990▲
Christian Democrats	36.7	35.0	34.5	43.4	42.7
Social Democrats	33.5	35.9	37.0	23.6	20.8
Free Democrats	11.0	10.6	9.1	13.4	5.5
Christian Social Union	7.1	9.1	9.8	–	–
Greens (west)	3.9	4.7	8.3	–	–
Alliance '90/Greens (east)	1.2	–	–	5.9	4.5
Democratic Socialists (ex-communists)	2.4	0.3	–	9.9	15.2
Republicans	2.1	2.3	–	1.3	–
Other	2.1	2.1	1.3	2.5	11.3

† Excluding Berlin ‡ West German general election ▲ Volkskammer (East German parliament) election

Variegated winners, red-green losers

FROM OUR BONN CORRESPONDENT

GERMAN voters have made sure that Mr Helmut Kohl stays chancellor but they have not given him a free hand. In the first free all-German election since 1932, Mr Kohl's Christian Democrats and their Bavarian allies in the Christian Social Union won only 43.8% of the votes, fewer than they have won in any West German election since 1949.

Why? Mr Kohl has deftly handled the tricky problems on the way to unity over the past year. He has gained a lot in popularity and stature. The economy in western Germany is booming and looks set to pick up next year in the east too (at least, polls show that most eastern voters think it will). These are all reasons, on the face of it, why Mr Kohl might have sailed to an absolute majority—achieved only once in West German history, by Konrad Adenauer in 1957.

Mr Kohl lost some backing because Germans, probably rightly, distrust his "no tax rise to pay for unity" pledge. Some 330,000 conservative voters, many disgusted by Mr Kohl's decision to recognise the Oder-Neisse line as Poland's western border, slipped away to the far-right Republicans (who even so failed to gain the 5% of the votes needed to win parliamentary seats.)

Above all, the Free Democrats (liberals), now the second biggest party in Mr Kohl's centre-right coalition, ran a clever campaign stressing the danger of a lurch to the right if Mr Kohl got more than 50%. They also picked up bags of support, especially in the east, because of the popularity of Mr Hans-Dietrich Genscher, the Free Democratic foreign minister (who

Number of eligible voters and % turnout in German general election

BERLIN 2.5m 81.0%
EASTERN GERMANY 11.3m 74.5%
WESTERN GERMANY 46.5m 78.5%

was born in Halle in eastern Germany). The outcome was their best result in a general election since 1961, and more weight in government.

The left flopped. The Social Democrats paid the price for having Mr Oskar Lafontaine a leader at best lukewarm about German unity. They mustered only 33.5%, their worst result since 1957 and their third successive general-election defeat. Even Mr Lafontaine's claim to have won the youth vote is suspect. True, the Social Democrats got the backing of 38% of 18-to-24-year-olds in the west (but much less in the east). That is a bit better than the Christian Democrats' showing in the west, but far below the 50% or so of young voters the Social Democrats used to draw under their former chancellors, Mr Willy Brandt and Mr Helmut Schmidt.

The Social Democrats now need a new chairman to replace Mr Hans-Jochen Vogel, who plans to step down (Mr Lafontaine has wisely refused the job). They also need to ask themselves where they are going.

The biggest surprise was the collapse of the western Greens. After seven years in the Bundestag they plunged to below 5%, and hence won no seats. This was partly because Mr Lafontaine, seen as a green-minded Social Democrat, pinched 600,000 Green voters (though he lost far more voters to the other parties); partly because the Greens were even more sceptical about German unity than Mr Lafontaine; but also because the Christian Democrats and Free Democrats also stressed green themes, further cutting the special attractions of the Green party.

There will now be only eight Green-ish deputies in the Bundestag. They are members of the coalition in the east between Greens and Alliance '90. This group jumped the 5% hurdle in the east, which for this election alone was treated as a separate voting area.

In a final blow, the former coalition of Social Democrats and Greens in Berlin, where an election for the local parliament was also held on December 2nd, was trounced after less than two years in office. The Christian Democrats, with 40.3% of the vote, emerged as easily the strongest party, ahead of the Social Democrats with 30.5%. The next Berlin government (all-Berlin now that the Wall has been scrapped) looks set to be a "grand coalition" between the two big parties. It will begin work with a disappointment. Mr Kohl let slip on election night that the federal government will not move from Bonn to Berlin after all—at best (or worst, depending on your view), only bits of it. Bismarck would have shuddered.

A tale of one city

Seats in Berlin's parliament after the city's election on December 2 1990

Social Democrats — 76 — Free Democrats
18 — Christian Democrats
Alliance '90/Greens — 11 — 100
Greens — 12
Democratic Socialists (ex-communists) — 23

TOTAL SEATS: 240

% of votes in Berlin's elections	United Berlin Dec 1990	West Berlin		East Berlin	
		Dec 1990	Jan 1989*	Dec 1990	May 1990†
Christian Democrats	40.3	48.5	37.7	25.0	18.6
Social Democrats	30.5	29.5	37.3	32.1	34.1
Democratic Socialists (ex-communists)	9.2	1.1	–	23.6	30.0
Free Democrats	7.1	7.9	3.9	5.6	2.2
Greens (west)	5.0	6.9	11.8	1.7	–
Alliance '90/Greens (east)	4.4	1.4	–	9.7	9.9
Republicans	3.1	3.7	7.5	1.9	–
Other	0.4	1.0	1.8	0.4	5.2

* West Berlin state election † East Berlin local election

broadly share the same aims but they are treading more often on one another's toes. After a slow start eight years ago in foreign affairs, Mr Kohl made up for lost time, failed to inform Mr Genscher of some of his initiatives, and built up his personal aide, Mr Horst Teltschik, as a kind of joint foreign minister. Mr Teltschik is now leaving for a business job, but Mr Kohl still aims to keep the foreign-policy reins, thanks not least to his close ties with Presidents Bush, Gorbachev and Mitterrand.

Mr Genscher, strengthened by an election victory in which his personal popularity played a big role, is not a man to see his empire eroded. So stand by for more rows between chancellery and foreign ministry. They will not mean an early coalition break, because the Free Democrats have no other available partner. But they could make a split more likely after the election in 1994.

Second, to push through some of his main foreign-policy plans, such as devolving power to the European Parliament and letting German forces take part in action outside the NATO area, Mr Kohl needs changes to the constitution. These are possible only through a two-thirds majority in the Bundestag—which requires the backing of the opposition Social Democrats, demoralised and almost leaderless after their election drubbing. Partly with an eye on this problem, Mr Kohl has already been giving Social Democrats some top jobs (such as head of the intelligence service) and has been cultivating Mr Willy Brandt, their still-influential honorary chairman. Even so, success is not certain, especially on German troops outside Europe, where the Americans want action because of the Gulf confrontation.

Perhaps the danger is not so much that the Germans will use sharp elbows on their neighbours, as that they will overstretch even their considerable resources and come a cropper. Mr Kohl proudly noted recently that a united Germany has no enemies. True; but having so many needy friends can be an awful strain.

The weight on Kohl's mind

FROM OUR BONN CORRESPONDENT

ONLY months after his triumphs in German unity year, Helmut Kohl is on the defensive again. Under attack from allies abroad for foot-dragging over the Gulf war and at home for mishandling the economic side of unity, Wunderkohl suddenly looks sadly like the Blunderkohl of old. As the jobless total soars and more demonstrators take to the streets in the east, Mr Kohl's foes mutter about a crisis, demanding a new election or even a "grand coalition" government (without Mr Kohl as chancellor).

Forget the mutterers. Mr Kohl has a firm majority, despite incessant sniping among the parties in his centre-right coalition. And his critics are forgetting as usual that the moment Mr Kohl looks weakest is usually the moment before he rebounds to biff them harder than before. This does not mean, however, that Mr Kohl had no errors to muse over as he sweated off surplus kilos over Easter at an Austrian spa.

The biggest is that he underestimated the cost of unity and reckoned tax rises would not be needed to help pay for it. That does not amount to the "tax lie" for election purposes of which he is widely accused. Mr Kohl holds fast to the notion that high taxes are bad for economic growth (hence the steady cuts since he came to power in 1982). He thought that, after a boost in aid from western Germany, the take-off in the east would soon be self-sustaining and largely self-financing. So he did not raise taxes a year ago, when Germans in their brief early euphoria over unity would have been less unhappy to pay. He has been obliged to do so now, on the mainly spurious and certainly unpopular ground that the cash is needed to help pay for the Gulf war.

Mr Kohl was also rash to tell easterners time after time last year that "no one will be worse off" after unity. True, all of them have freedoms undreamt of 18 months ago: to travel, to elect whom they please, to buy and read what they like. But rents, energy and transport costs are soaring. Scores of firms are going out of business, unable to cope with competition from the west and the collapse of what used to be the Comecon market to the east. An EMNID poll reports that only 2% of easterners feel their economic situation is good (compared with 66% in the west) and that nearly 90% feel like second-class citizens.

Mr Kohl could have helped his case by visiting the east regularly since the December election, pinning the blame on four decades of communism and arguing, justifiably, that help was on the way. But, unfathomably, he has not once been east (apart from a visit to east Berlin for a foreign-policy speech), leaving it to his political foes to show ostentatious solidarity with easterners on the march. His aides say he was either worn out or busy but is planning a series of trips east soon. Coming so late, they will be all the tougher.

Yet Mr Kohl feels time is working in his favour, and he is probably right. The tax pill has been swallowed (albeit late). Huge amounts of aid have been earmarked for the east; after a new increase agreed upon in February, the federal government alone is now ploughing about DM100 billion into the east this year, roughly half of it for investment. Private investment is picking up too and should be encouraged by the government's improved (but still far from perfect) guidelines on handling disputed property ownership. A building boom also seems in the offing.

That still leaves plenty of big obstacles, above all the lack of qualified westerners ready to help out with business and administration in the east. Hence the special sense of loss caused by the murder on April 1st of one of the very best of those who did volunteer, Detlev Rohwedder, boss of the Treuhandanstalt in Berlin. But with luck the economy in the east should be through the worst this year, albeit with plenty of trials to come. Mr Kohl's talk of a "flourishing" eastern Germany in maybe three years (when another general election is due), or in five years at the latest, does not seem far-fetched.

Even assuming the best, won't these huge efforts mean that for years the Germans will be largely occupied with their own affairs? If so, that would mean little or no progress on European integration (which might please Britain but not most of Germany's other EC partners). It would probably also mean no readiness to shoulder a military burden outside NATO, or even much of one inside it. The sleepy reaction of Germany's leaders to the Gulf war might seem like evidence of a trend to navel-gazing in Bonn.

Don't bet on it. It is certainly not what Mr Kohl has in mind. He may fail, of course, but that foreign-policy speech in February in Berlin shows he is going to fight. The speech was little noted at the time, maybe because Mr Kohl's asides were more revealing than his printed text.

He made three main points. First, the Gulf experience showed that in future united Germany had to play a full role in international peacekeeping, for instance, in a UN military force and a stronger Western European Union. A "minimal solution", such as taking part only in UN "blue helmet" operations (the maximum concession the opposition Social Democrats are ready to accept for the present), was not enough.

Second, Mr Kohl stuck firmly to his promised schedule for European union. This runs as follows: completion by the end of this year of the two EC inter-governmental conferences, on political union and economic and monetary union; ratification of the results of both conferences by all EC parliaments before the end of 1993; start of the second of the three stages to EMU in 1994, followed by an independent European central bank (preferably based in Germany) and a single currency, with luck, soon after 1997.

Third, Mr Kohl insisted that for him a far-reaching agreement on political integration, including much more power for the European Parliament, and an agreement on economic union were indivisible. He would present neither treaty for the Bundestag to ratify without the other.

Some listeners judged that Mr Kohl may have insisted on both in the expectation that he will as a result get neither. Germany could then get on with its own agenda. Nothing so Machiavellian, say those who know him. Mr Kohl, they explain, really believes that after the achievement of German unity at the start of the decade, European union can emerge (more or less) by the end of it. He feels as committed to this second union as he did to the first, and believes he may still be chancellor when it happens.

That, incidentally, implies that he would pass (in 1996) Konrad Adenauer's record as modern Germany's longest-serving leader. These are big ambitions for a man who at present is on the defensive; but they are not intrinsically absurd.

The East German Disaster

Das Deutsche Wagnis
by Klaus von Dohnanyi.
Droemer Knaur, 326 pp., DM 36

Simon Head

Helmut Kohl's victory on December 2 was among the most decisive in the forty-one-year history of the newly enlarged *Bundesrepublik*, but there is a fragility about his triumph that the voting statistics do not reveal. Kohl campaigned as the architect of unification and, as the opinion polls suggested, this was the achievement that carried him to victory.[1] But Kohl also ran as the candidate who could best deal with the one big task of unification still remaining: the rehabilitation of the East German economy. Since the two German economies united in July 1990 Kohl has been consistently upbeat about the economic prospects for eastern Germany. "We must," he said in October, "do everything we can to transform the five new *Länder* (states) into blooming landscapes within three, four, five years," and he has never expressed doubt that this could be done.[2]

It was a measure of Kohl's strength that many voters were willing to accept these assurances despite the flood of bad economic news from eastern Germany. If one counts as unemployed the workers who are today put in government-subsidized "short work" programs (*Kurzarbeit*) but who are in fact not working, East German unemployment increased eleven-fold between June and November, and industrial production has been cut in half during the last year. West German businessmen are still reluctant to invest in the former GDR, and East Germans are still leaving for West Germany in large numbers. Now that he has been reelected on a platform of economic optimism, Kohl is under strong pressure to reverse these trends, or risk suffering the fate of a politician who arouses expectations among the voters which he cannot fulfill. The economic problems of the five new eastern *Länder* are therefore likely to be among Kohl's chief preoccupations during the lifetime of his new government.

With 40 percent of its work force employed in industry, East Germany is one of the most industrialized regions in Europe. Despite East Germany's small domestic market of 16 million, the leaders of the East German Communist regime were determined that the GDR's economy should be comparable to West Germany's in the diversity and sophistication of its industrial base. East Germany therefore has a considerable variety of manufacturing industries, including mechanical and electrical engineering, optics, electronics, automobiles, chemicals, textiles. Every large East German city is an industrial center. Shipbuilding is concentrated in Rostock, chemicals in Halle, textiles in Chemnitz (formerly Karl Marx Stadt), and engineering in Leipzig, Dresden, Magdeburg, and East Berlin. The industrial heartland of East Germany between Halle, Chemnitz, and Dresden resembles the old Ruhr of the 1930s and such declining Midwestern industrial centers as Youngstown, Ohio, in the vastness and ugliness of its industrial landscape, although its pollution is far worse.

The Honecker regime used to boast that the GDR economy was strong even by Western standards, and some West German politicians accepted such claims, partly it seems out of a sense of national pride, partly in order to keep up friendly relations with the East German leaders. But when the Wall came down and West German entrepreneurs and consultants were able to enter East German factories and look around, they were depressed by what they saw. Herbert Henzler of the McKinsey management consulting company, whose firm advises East German companies and who has himself probably visited more East German factories than any other West German, has estimated that only between 20 and 30 percent of East German companies were even worth considering as candidates for Western investment.[3] The West Germans found

that the GDR had a huge but mostly obsolescent engineering industry that was adapted to selling in the Soviet market but would not be able to compete elsewhere, and a large but primitive chemicals industry, which was inflicting colossal damage on the environment. The state companies producing consumer goods suffered from the traditional Stalinist bias in favor of heavy industry, and their ouput was often shoddy.

Those weaknesses were revealed to be even worse than had been expected when, at the beginning of July, the two German economies were merged and the West German deutsche mark became the currency of East Germany. Exposed overnight to West German competition, eastern Germany's loss of industrial production has far exceeded that of Poland, the only other Eastern-bloc economy to have introduced comparable economic reforms. The UN Economic Commission for Europe estimates that during the first nine months of 1990 industrial production in Poland fell by 27 percent.[4] But by August 1990 East German industrial output was 50 percent below the level of August 1989, and the German Finance Ministry estimates that East German output will fall by another 10 to 15 percent in 1991. Allowing for a conservative 5 percent decline in output between September and December of this year, East German industry may, by the fall of next year, have lost between 65 and 70 percent of its output over a two-year period. East German unemployment has risen from 130,000 in June 1990 to 1.5 million in November, an increase of 270,000 a month.[5]

Kohl's strategy for reviving the East German economy has always relied on the willingness of West German and foreign companies to invest there—whether in existing East German plants or in creating new factories. The currency union and the establishment of a market economy in East Germany were meant to encourage this investment to take place. As the former economics minister Helmut Haussmann proclaimed this September, "The trough is now full, now the horses must drink."[6] Of the two forms of investment anticipated by Kohl and Haussmann, future growth will depend mainly on new industries coming to East Germany. Only a relatively small number of weakened East German companies seem likely to survive the current industrial depression.

The most informative discussion I have seen of the difficulties facing new industry in East Germany is in *Das Deutsche Wagnis* ("The German Venture"), the recent book by Klaus von Dohnanyi, the former Social Democratic mayor of Hamburg who is now on the supervisory board of a large engineering company in Leipzig. As chief executive of one of the federal *Länder* (a status Hamburg was given in recognition of its Hanseatic past), Dohnanyi did much to attract new industry to his city, and his recent experience in Leipzig has made him a discerning observer of the East German economy. (He is also the grandson of the Hungarian composer Ernst von Dohnanyi and his brother is the conductor of the Cleveland Orchestra.) In the autumn of 1986, I attended an election rally in Hamburg where Dohnanyi and Willy Brandt were greeted by a howling audience of anarchists and extreme leftists. Brandt shouted back at them, antagonizing them further; the tall and elegant Dohnanyi coolly reminded his listeners of the importance of free speech and of the price the Germans had paid in the past for ignoring it.

Klaus von Dohnanyi's analysis of eastern Germany's economic prospects reflects his sense of the changes within West Germany itself, where during the last thirty years economic power has shifted away from the traditional centers of industry such as the Ruhr, the Saar, and Hamburg, to the southern states of Hesse, Baden-Württemberg, and Bavaria. Today the most dynamic industrial cities in Germany are Stuttgart and Munich. A comparable migration has taken place in the United States, as the industrial Midwest has declined and Southern California and the San Francisco Bay area have prospered. Both migrations have taken place for much the same reasons. The advanced engineering and electronics companies that have the most potential

for growth favor cities free of the disadvantages of declining smokestack industries whose workers lack high-tech skills and whose factories and neighborhoods are decaying.

German companies, Dohnanyi says, want to establish branches in places where there are "other enterprises in the same line of work, as well as leading scientific institutions, a high quality of life, and competent and cooperative public administrations"—in short, the qualities that make Silicon Valley more desirable than Gary, Indiana. One big difference between the US and western Germany is that the less favored German regions have been more successful in competing with the newly prosperous regions than their American equivalents such as Cleveland and Detroit. For example, the SPD minister-president of North Rhine Westphalia, Johannes Rau, has cleaned up most of the industrial wasteland of the Ruhr Valley. Hardly a week goes by without *Der Spiegel* or the magazine supplement of the *Frankfurter Allgemeine Zeitung* carrying a two-page advertisement portraying the *Ruhrgebiet* as a rural paradise. Dohnanyi has himself helped to restore Hamburg as one of Europe's most prosperous cities, and it now has the highest income per person of all the West German *Länder*. He helped to offset the decline of shipbuilding, for example, by attracting major investment in electronics and aerospace.

With unification the governments of the new East German *Länder* have to compete for new industry with the advanced industrial regions in the West. As Dohnanyi puts it, "Saxony is pitted against Baden-Württemberg, Sachsen-Anhalt against the *Ruhrgebiet*, Thuringia against Bavaria, Mecklenburg against Lower Saxony." In this competition, moreover, politicians of the West German *Länder* cannot, in Dohnanyi's view, be expected to be particularly generous:

Anyone who thinks that they will subordinate their own interests in favor of the reconstruction of East Germany does not understand the fierce competitive pressures to which West German politicians are subject. No *Bürgermeister* or minister-president will improve his chances for re-election by saying that he has given away the chance of a...company or a factory in favor of some city or *Länder* in eastern Germany.

West German companies will be equally ruthless in choosing where to go:

Patriotism is not a capitalist concept. Western capital will therefore judge eastern Germany as a location without sentimentality, using the same profit and loss calculations which it might apply to all other locations.

Dohnanyi believes that in this rough competition "the advantages of the East German region as a location for industry are not very convincing," notwithstanding Kohl's optimism. It is true that Mercedes Benz and Volkswagen will build new factories in eastern Germany, Mercedes at Ludwigsfelde, south of Berlin, VW at Zwickau in Saxony, the center of the East German automobile industry. But most German companies are not following their examples, particularly the large- and medium-sized engineering companies that have been central to the success of the West German economy. Here eastern Germany's disadvantages as a location for investment are having an effect. Many West German companies are, for example, finding that the East German market is not large enough to justify setting up an entire new factory in the former GDR.

In the words of Franz Steinkühler, president of the Metalworkers Union and the most powerful union leader in Germany:

The business leadership said loudly and clearly that they were going to invest in the east but they hadn't taken the exact measure of the ex-GDR, a region which after all has only 16 million inhabitants, the equivalent of the population of North Rhine Westphalia. That has dampened their enthusiasm. For North Rhine Westphalia one does not build a new factory, one puts on a third working shift to maximize profits. I now have the impression that all the statements of the business leaders about poor conditions in the ex-GDR are simple ways of disguising their unwillingness to make good their previous commitments.[7]

However these "poor conditions in the ex-GDR" to which Steinkühler refers are all too real. Eastern Germany's industrial reputation has been badly damaged by such horrors as the chemical plants at Halle and Bitterfeld, where the land and rivers are drenched in poisonous wastes, where pollution turns sunlight a sickly yellow, and thousands of children have developed respiratory diseases.

Even the less contaminated East German industrial cities like Chemnitz and Magdeburg still have a bleak, postwar feeling about them, with their oppressive smell of brown coal, the dispiriting presence of modern "socialist" public buildings in the town centers, and, beyond them, the grim world of crumbling apartment blocks, decaying factories, and dimly lit streets. The Kohl government is about to undertake the huge task of cleaning up East Germany's industrial communities; but in Dohnanyi's view it will be at least a decade before they can reach the standards of even the less prosperous West German cities.[8]

Dohnanyi touches on another obstacle to West German investment in the East, which has grown in importance since he finished his book: the rising uncertainty about the ownership of land and property. West German businesses wanting to buy land or buildings from the state often cannot be sure that these assets won't eventually be claimed by their former owners. German officials have disclosed that just under half the land and property in East Germany has been claimed by former owners, with a total of more than a million claims. In November, the *Financial Times* reported that East German municipal governments alone had filed 14,500 claims involving an astonishing 750,000 items of property and land. Two hundred fifty thousand claims have been made by citizens in the *land* of Thuringia, 150,000 by citizens in Berlin.[9] The unification treaty between the two German states signed last October was supposed to resolve this problem of disputed property, at least in cases where land and buildings were needed for industrial development. In such cases former owners were to receive financial compensation, but not the return of the property itself. However this clause of the treaty is now being challenged as unconstitutional, and a ruling from the German Supreme Court is not expected until the middle of 1991.[10]

The loss of East German production, the failure of foreign investment to replace it, and the rapid rise in unemployment—these three troubling developments are linked to a fourth: the migration (*Ubersiedlerstrom*) of East German labor, and particularly skilled labor, to West Germany. Of all the market forces unleashed by German economic union, those that lure East German workers westward toward more plentiful jobs at higher wages are among the most powerful. In 1990, for example, the West German economy grew by 4.5 percent and created 800,000 new jobs, while the East German economy contracted by 33 percent, with a loss of 1.1 million jobs.[11] This migration is damaging to both economies. In West Germany it overburdens health and social welfare services, adds to the housing shortage, and, by slowing the growth of wages, creates tensions between established and newly arriving workers. For the East German economy emigration is much more damaging. It deprives the region of its skilled labor, leaving the East with an aging and unproductive population. It also undermines its ability to attract new investment, so intensifying the economic inequalities between the two parts of Germany.

The exodus of East Germans through Hungary and Czechoslovakia in the late summer and autumn of 1989 contributed to Honecker's fall and led directly to the opening of the Wall by his successor, Egon Krenz. Krenz hoped that the opening of the GDR's borders would reduce the *Ubersiedlerstrom,* and for a few weeks in November and December 1989 this indeed happened. But in January and February 1990 emigration rose to two thousand a day, forcing Kohl to accelerate the pace of economic and political union. As Kohl said, "We had to move fast or the people in the GDR would have fled."[12] But despite the establishment of East Germany's first democratically elected government in March, despite economic union in July, and political union in October, emigration has remained heavy during 1990. Between the beginning of March and the end of September East Germans migrated westward at a rate of just under a thousand a day. At the end of November the Labor Ministry in North Rhine Westphalia estimated that each month between 15,000 and 20,000 East Germans were settling in that one *Land*. Helmut Kohl's council of economic advisers estimates that about a thousand people a day will continue to emigrate in 1991.[13] If East Germans keep moving at this rate eastern Germany will lose between 4 and 5 percent of its work force each year.

Many of the East Germans who left the GDR in the summer and fall of 1989 were still fleeing the oppression of Honecker and the Stasi. By the fall of 1990, with Honecker long out of power, and with unification in prospect, those who are leaving have to be classified as economic migrants looking for a better life. As long as Eastern Germany's economic decline continues, the *Ubersiedlerstrom* is likely to continue with it. In a recent *Der Spiegel* poll 12 percent of those responding said that they definitely or probably were going to emigrate.[14] Among an East German work force of 9.3 million, 12 percent would represent a potential *Ubersiedlerstrom* of just over a million. After visiting the industrial *Länder* of Saxony and Sachsen-Anhalt in October I suspect that the potential emigration is even higher, particularly among young skilled workers.

My visit coincided with the *Länder* elections in eastern Germany, and I was able to talk to several dozen young workers attending campaign rallies for CDU and SPD candidates. Most of the forty-odd workers I interviewed had worked for years in engineering plants turning out machinery for the Soviet market, and their lives had been affected by the East German economic depression. Seven of them had lost their jobs, a dozen were classified as working "short time," and most of their wages were paid for by the government. The rest still had regular jobs but most said that their companies had fewer orders now because their mainly Soviet customers would soon have to start paying for their machinery in deutsche marks.

Most of the workers I talked to seemed very well informed about conditions in West Germany and the prospects that would be open to them there. The West German TV programs they see every day work against the interests of the Kohl government just as they worked against Honecker's. The Communist regime's efforts to create a separate "GDR consciousness" were constantly frustrated by the images of West German prosperity carried into East German living rooms by West German TV. Now the same images lure East German workers westward. Particularly telling are the frequent stories carried by TV and newspapers about young East Germans who left the GDR in the first wave of *Ubersiedler* last fall and are already enjoying West German comforts; a job paying 2,500 or 3,000 DM a month (two and a half and three times the East German industrial wage) with a good chance for promotion; an apartment in a solid neighborhood of Dortmund or Hanover, with a new VW parked outside; even vacations in France and Spain.

Still, the proportion of young workers who told me they would emigrate was no greater than the 12 percent who gave the same answer in the *Der Spiegel* poll, although about half of them said they would consider leaving unless their salaries and working conditions improved in eighteen months to two years. Some of the workers in Saxony told me that their wives and families had lived near Dresden and Leipzig for hundreds of years and that they would much prefer to stay there if only they could count on reasonable wages and better prospects. And who or what, I asked, might bring such improvements about? Most of the young men, it turned out, put their hopes in Helmut Kohl, and were ready to vote for him now as they had in the past. In industrial Saxony, the CDU won over 50 percent of the blue-collar vote both in the *Länder* elections in October and in the Bundestag elections in December.[15]

The readiness of blue-collar voters to support a conservative party does not, in my view, represent an endorsement of the free-market principles of the CDU against the more interventionist tradition of the SDP; it reflects instead a conviction that Helmut Kohl will use his power to improve life for East Germans. A young machinist in Leipzig said, "Kohl has told us that he'll help us, and we believe him. We never trusted Oskar Lafontaine." Down-to-earth and *bürgerlich*, with the easy optimism of a salesman, Kohl has managed to convince the East Germans that he can be trusted to make life better. After fifty years of dictatorship, belief in the *Führerprinzip* is not yet dead in East Germany.

But can Helmut Kohl now fulfill the expectations he has aroused? With East German unemployment climbing toward 25 percent, the rate at which workers are being laid off from collapsing industries far exceeds the capacity of new industries to absorb them. If Klaus von Dohnanyi's analysis is correct, and the evidence so far supports it, high unemployment may continue for years. To relieve it the German government will have to rely on the kind of public

works programs to create jobs that were put into effect during the New Deal in the US. A DM 10 billion ($6.6 billion) program for renovating housing has already been announced, and other labor-intensive programs for improving the environment will follow, for example building new houses, and repairing the road and rail network. David C. Roche of Morgan Stanley International estimates that during the 1990s the German government may spend between DM 130 and DM 160 billion a year (between $87 and $107 billion) to improve roads, rail transport, telecommunications, and other parts of the infrastructure.[16]

However the capacity of such expenditures to create new employment in eastern Germany may be quite limited. In April the leading private institute specializing in the East German economy, the Deutsche Institut für Wirtschaftsforschung (DIW), estimated that public and private expenditure could in the short term boost employment in the East German construction industry by 100,000 (in April the DIW was also estimating a loss of one million jobs in industry and mining).[17] However, economists at the DIW now believe that this estimate was over-optimistic. Investment in housing has declined by 40 percent during 1990 and employment in the construction industry therefore also has fallen. It seems inevitable that eastern Germany will have high levels of unemployment during the early 1990s and that the gap in living standards between the two German economies will not be closed within the five-year period envisaged by Helmut Kohl or, earlier, by Alfred Herrhausen, the president of the Deutsche Bank who was assassinated in November 1989.[18]

The Kohl government will not find it easy to head off the *Ubersiedlerstrom* during these years of continuing economic inequality between the two parts of Germany. The collapse of East German industry will force large numbers of workers to move to public works projects during the early 1990s. Some of these workers may return to industrial employment in the later 1990s, as the damaged infrastructure is renovated and new industrial investment flows in. But many workers may prefer to cut short this public works phase of employment and seek better paying, skilled jobs in western Germany. Working on the railroad or on a polluted site in Halle or Leipzig may have less appeal to young workers today than did com-

parable jobs in the 1930s. If such disaffection happens on a large enough scale the drastic decline of industry in East Germany would become more and more difficult to reverse. Western industrialists would be encouraged to follow the *Ubersiedlerstrom* westward, avoiding eastern Germany as a region increasingly barren of population and skills. Despite Kohl's success and his promise of a bright future for the former GDR, eastern Germany could remain a stagnant and damaged region for years to come.

[1]See for example the monthly poll appearing in *Der Spiegel* between June and November 1990. The CDU's lead over the SPD (and Helmut Kohl's over Oskar Lafontaine) widened with the approach and attainment of unification.

[2]Interview with *Süddeutsche Zeitung*, October 11, 1990.

[3]Interview with *Der Spiegel*, August 13, 1990.

[4]*Financial Times*, November 28, 1990. For a discussion of the Polish economy see "Eastern Europe and Democracy; the Case of Poland," Institute for East-West Security Studies (1990).

[5]*Frankfurter Allgemeine Zeitung*, June 21, 1990; *International Herald Tribune*, October 19, 1990; *Die Welt*, December 6, 1990.

[6]Quoted in *Das Deutsche Wagnis*, p. 193.

[7]Interview with Luc Rosenzweig, *Le Monde*, November 27, 1990.

[8]Interview with the author, December 5, 1990.

[9]*Financial Times*, November 1 and November 22, 1990.

[10]*Financial Times*, November 22, 1990.

[11]*Frankfurter Allgemeine Zeitung*, December 5, 1990.

[12]Kohl's press conference in Washington, DC, May 17, 1990.

[13]ZDF (German TV Channel 2) October 12, 1990; *The Guardian*, December 1, 1990; *Frankfurter Allgemeine Zeitung*, November 16, 1990.

[14]*Der Spiegel*, October 29, 1990.

[15]ARD (German TV Channel 1), October 14, 1990; *Die Welt*, December 4, 1990.

[16]*Der Spiegel*, October 29, 1990.

[17]*Deutsches Institut für Wirtschaftsforschung*, Wochenbericht 17/90, "Quantitative Aspekte einer Reform von Wirtschaft und Finanzen in der DDR," April 26, 1990.

[18]*International Herald Tribune*, November 8, 1990.

Some Thoughts on Federalism and the Federal Republic

Arthur B. Gunlicks

University of Richmond

While a number of countries in Western Europe, including Great Britain, Spain, Italy and Belgium, have certain federal features, only three are commonly recognized as federal systems. For reasons peculiar to their respective historical and geographical circumstances, all three are German-speaking or predominantly German-speaking states. In spite of numerous similarities, each of these federal states is different from the other in certain key respects, and they are sometimes ranked on an imaginary scale of federalism from "strong" to "weak." (While the criteria for such a ranking are often vague and uncertain, they usually try to capture some concept of regional autonomy.) According to the criteria selected, Switzerland invariably ends up as the "strongest," Austria as the "weakest" federal system. But given its size, population, geography, economic strength, and influence in the European Community in particular and in world affairs in general, the Federal Republic of Germany offers the most interesting model of a functioning federal system for international comparison. One might also speculate on the role of federalism in explaining the relative success of West Germany in maintaining political stability in a society as free and open as any other in Europe, in achieving economic growth, and in retaining a reputation for efficient and effective administration.

Not all Germans are persuaded that federalism is appropriate for a country about the size of the state of Oregon, with no significant ethnic or linguistic differences comparable to those in Switzerland. They sometimes complain that federalism was "imposed" on them by the Allies, especially the Americans, but ignore the tradition of federalism in Germany and the general agreement among the founding fathers of the Bonn Republic that federalism was desirable for a postwar German state. The complaint, however, usually turns on the argument that federalism is conservative if not reactionary, that it is an obstacle to the achievement of a more equal society, e.g., with respect to educational standards or the constitutional goal of achieving "uniform living conditions" throughout the country, or that it is simply too costly, inefficient, irrelevant, and unnecessary. There are also those who, like their American counterparts, accept federalism as a vague abstraction but invariably support the national government in almost any conflict between it and the regional and local governments over public policy and financing. Finally, there is a less ideological perspective that argues that as desirable as federalism was and perhaps still is, it has been undermined by growing pressures toward centralization. The welfare state in particular and the nationalization of so much public policy, together with public expectations, are said to have led to a "unitary federal state" characterized by a loss of real autonomy by the Länder and the local governments.

In spite of the critics and doubters, the case for federalism in Germany is strong, both as an institutional prescription and as a crucial element in any description of the actual functioning of the political system. This is not to deny that there are powerful forces that challenge German federalism; however, the reports of the demise of federalism in Germany are both premature and exaggerated.

Prescriptive Case for Federalism

Arguments that Germany should be a federal state because of particularistic values in the different regions of the country and historically rooted political units were severely weakened by the results of World War II and developments since then. Millions of refugees from the Eastern territories; the formation of new and artificially created Länder except for Hamburg, Bremen, and Bavaria; a decline in religiosity; and the growing importance of a national welfare system, a national (and international) market, and national standards for all kinds of activities undermined much of the objective case that could be made for federalism in the past.

And yet it seems that federalism has served West Germany well in numerous and important ways, and that the German federal state can certainly stand comparison with the other midsized states in Europe. A traditionally strong system of local government has been preserved in its diversity by the eight territorial Länder. German municipalities and the Länder have been able to experiment with numerous policies that were sometimes adopted elsewhere, but other times were opposed by other regions. The traditional focus on administration even of most national laws by the Länder and local governments has preserved important responsibilities for regional and local politicians and officials and has probably reduced the bureaucratic "overload" alleged by many to exist in the highly developed welfare—and mostly unitary—states of Europe.

The existence of Land parliaments has provided voters with an additional opportunity to influence policies and personalities through regional elections and multiplied many times the number of politicians who were successful in participating in politics above the local level but did not or could not serve in the Bundestag. Land cabinets as well as leadership positions in the Land parliaments have provided politicians with practical political and administrative/managerial experience above the local level and with a base of operations not found in unitary states. The unique institution of the Bundesrat makes it possible for regional leaders to participate even in national affairs, since the Bundesrat considers all national legislation with the right of either a suspensive or an absolute veto. Indeed, today the Bundesrat has an absolute veto over more than 60 percent of all national legislation, i.e., those bills that affect the Länder in ways that permit the application of the absolute veto.

Regional leadership opportunities have contributed to the quantity and quality of political leaders available for national office. The existence of regional as well as local bases of political operations has also made it possible to create and maintain a noncentralized party system with regional leaders not infrequently willing to challenge the national leader or leaders. The most recent example of this reality was the demand by Lower Saxony's CDU Minister-President, Ernst Albrecht, that the federal government share the exploding costs for the social welfare grants (*Sozialhilfe*) provided by municipalities when unemployment benefits have been exhausted, a demand that has been resisted not only by the Christian Democratic-dominated federal government but also by the Christian Democratic Minister-Presidents of Baden-Württemberg (Lothar Späth) and Bavaria (the late Franz-Josef Strauss). Federalism probably made it possible for some parties to come into existence (the Greens), for others to remain in existence (the FDP), and for the major parties to lick their wounds and regenerate themselves (the CDU from 1969 to 1982 and the SPD since 1983). Thus federalism has served to promote and sustain party competition in ways that are not available to the British or French parties, for example.

German and American Federalism and Administration: Some Problems of Semantics

In almost any discussion of American federalism, reference is made to the concept of "dual federalism" that prevailed in American political thinking until about the New Deal. The idea behind the concept is that the national government has one set of functional responsibilities, the states and their local governments another. The federal government as well as the state governments legislate, execute, and adjudicate their own laws. Each level is responsible for financing its own public policies. There is little overlap; however, in case of conflict in an area of concurrent powers, federal law is supreme. The system of dual federalism, while never in existence in a pure form, prevailed until federal policies identified mostly with the New Deal brought the federal government into areas previously considered to be the responsibility of the states or, in the view of some critics, to be outside the area of any government's responsibility. Many of these policies called for some form of cooperation, for example, through shared financing, between the federal and state/local governments, which led to what came to be called cooperative federalism. Lyndon Johnson's Great Society programs brought about a dramatic increase in cooperative policies in which the national, state, and local governments shared in numerous ways the administrative and fiscal responsibility for most public services and activities. Since then the network of complex interrelationships among governments in the United States has been frequently referred to as intergovernmental relations and has led to demands, such as those reflected in the "sorting out" or "swap" proposals of Ronald Reagan's "new federalism," that efforts be undertaken to return to something more like the old dual federalism.

German scholars also sometimes refer to the traditional German system of federalism as "dual federalism," but here the concept can mean something quite different from the American term. What Germans usually mean is that federalism in the German tradition is characterized by policy making in most areas at the national level and policy implementation at the state (since 1919, Land) level. The Länder are not, however, mere administrative subdivisions of the national government. They enjoy a large degree of autonomy in their administration of national policies. In addition, municipalities—in contrast to the *ultra vires* tradition in the Anglo-Saxon countries that restricts local governments to the activities permitted them in their charters—have enjoyed considerable discretionary powers since the early nineteenth century, that is, the right to engage in any activity that does not violate national or Land law.

German federalism has also differed from the American model in the adherence to continental European practice of "unity of command" (*Einheit der Verwaltung*). In theory, at least, this concept requires that the administration of all laws and regulations be combined in each subnational territorial unit. Thus, in addition to administering its own laws, each Land is responsible for administering all federal laws and regulations delegated to it. Because most of these national and Land laws are then turned over to the local governments for administration, the local units become responsible for the administration of national, Land and local laws, regulations and ordinances within their respective territorial boundaries. This territorial or "spatial" system of administration contrasts sharply with the intergovernmentalized and highly dispersed and fragmented "functional" administration (e.g., independent regulatory commissions, special districts) characteristic of American public administration.

Unfortunately, some German scholars also describe German federalism and administration as "functional." By this they mean, again, that the national government has the function of legislating, while the Länder have the function of administering most national laws.

However, the late Frido Wagener, a leading scholar of German public administration, insisted that functional administration—whether in a federal or a unitary system—is administration by task, examples of which would be the American system of "picket fence" federalism and government by special districts or, in Great Britain, administration by "quangos." He sometimes referred to this as "vertical administration." Other authors, for example, Arnold Brecht, have referred to American dual federalism as a "vertical" division of power between the nation and the states, which is a narrower but related application of Wagener's use of vertical administration. Gordon Smith makes use of the term "dual administration," which seems to be the same thing as Wagener's general concept of functional administration. Just to confuse matters further, some American textbook authors use the term vertical in a wholly atheoretical sense of merely describing relations among the national, state, and local governments.

Territorial or spatial administration that results from the continental system of unity of command makes the chief administrative officer of each level of administration (whether in a unitary or federal system) legally responsible for all of the public services and activities, whether delegated, mandated, or self-generated, within his territory (e.g., the former French prefects). In the Federal Republic, even units of administration that are roughly similar to American special districts, e.g., *Zweckverbände*, fall under the administrative responsibility of the chief administrative officer, e.g., county manager (Landrat), of a territorial, general purpose unit of administration. This is what Gordon Smith refers to as "fused administration," though it is more frequently called horizontal administration. Frido Wagener and other authors, including Arnold Brecht, used this term to distinguish territorial or spatial administration from vertical or functional administration. But horizontal administration, too, is sometimes used atheoretically by American textbook authors to describe relationships among administrative structures within one level of government.

In practice, both models of administration, the functional and the spatial, have been moving toward each other in a mixed system of intergovernmental relations. In the United States, numerous nationally inspired programs have been turned over to the states and/or local governments for partial administration, sometimes with very loose federal supervision, while "picket fence" federalism, involving functional experts at the national, state, and local levels, continues as well. Functional relationships among experts at different levels (*Fachbrüderschaften*) also exist in German federalism, especially since the finance reform of 1969. Whether characterized by a system of functional administration (Great Britain, United States) or spatial administration (France, Germany), and regardless of their unitary (Great Britain, France) or federal (United States, Germany) organization, Western European countries and the United States have been moving toward a highly complex system of shared powers, or intergovernmental relations that challenges the older, more standard descriptive concepts.

Decline Of Federalism?

While German federalism has been characterized since the Bismarck Reich by the delegation of national laws to the regional and then local governments for administration, the Bonn Basic Law did provide for some dualism in the American sense. For example, cultural affairs, including all aspects of education, police and administration of justice, local government law, and the administration of their own and national laws on their own responsibility are Land functions. The original idea was also to have separate tax systems for the national and Land governments.

Since 1949 there have been thirty-five amendments to the Basic Law, more than twenty of which have concerned federalism in some manner. In no case did the Länder gain any new powers, let alone gain authority at the expense of the federal government. With the finance reforms of 1969 and changes in the Basic Law providing for an elaborate system of shared taxes and "joint tasks" (*Gemeinschaftsaufgaben*) that called for federal/Land cooperation in areas previously reserved for the Länder alone (e.g., education), it became increasingly difficult (as in the United States, for that matter) to identify any public policy area as belonging solely to the federal, Land, or local level. Instead, national policy making, Land and local administration, shared taxes, joint tasks and joint planning led to a complex system of shared powers and responsibilities (*Politikverflechtung*).

This is not to say that the Länder have been left out of the decision-making process. Since the Länder administer most national laws, since the most important taxes are shared, and since the joint tasks involve the Länder by definition, the role of the Bundesrat has actually increased over the past decades. This provides opposition parties control of Land governments and even dissenting minister-presidents associated with the governing coalition in Bonn, e.g., the late Franz-Josef Strauss, with additional opportunities to influence national decisions. But the Bundesrat's participation in decision making is by Land governments, not parliaments, which are frequently left with the responsibility of merely ratifying actions of the Bundesrat.

Pressures toward centralization or uniformity have had many sources: changes in national and international markets and the goods and services produced; a growing welfare state; provisions of the Basic Law calling for "uniformity of living conditions" (Article 72.2, or Article 104a.4); an almost naive faith in the 1970s in social and economic planning under national guidance; a perceived need in the 1970s for significant reforms in education and other policy areas requiring more national uniformity. In the 1980s, however, the general enthusiasm for more federal involvement in virtually all areas of government has waned for a series of reasons. The planning and the administration of many joint activities have been disappointing in their effects and administrative costs have been high. Tendencies toward increasing bureaucratization still persist; Land autonomy in the setting of priorities has been weakened and Land parliaments have been ignored in decision-making processes. Finally, accountability for programs and actions has become increasingly difficult to assign. It should not be surprising that counter pressures not unlike some of the reactions in the United States have emerged.

One can note tendencies in recent years toward a removal of the national government from certain activities. Some activities involving shared financing (*Mischfinanzierung*) by the national government and Länder have been turned over to the Länder (e.g., educational grants and hospital financing), and joint educational planning involving the national government has been discontinued. Regulations concerning urban renewal have been made the responsibility of the Länder, although the federal government may still provide grant aid. In other areas the federal government has encouraged the Länder to regulate certain activities while resisting the temptation to act itself.

Unfortunately, most Länder are not in a financial position to assume many new responsibilities. The growing gap between the economic health of the Länder in the North and those in the South led to a complaint in the mid-1980s before the Federal Constitutional Court over fiscal equalization measures among the Länder. The Court decided in June 1986 that the measures required change, but the new legislation passed in December 1987 did not satisfy the SPD-governed Länder in general, and Hamburg and Bremen in particular. The former Lord Mayor of Hamburg, Klaus von Dohnanyi, has revived the debate in the 1970s over a redrawing of Land boundaries, suggesting that a new *Nordstaat* be created. It is hardly clear, however, whether combining "poor states" into larger units would do much to solve current fiscal problems. The political problems involved in a reordering of the Länder would also be formidable.

Assessment

Some authors began to use the term "unitary federal state" to describe the centralizing tendencies of recent decades, while others have noted that the increased focus on the Länder and local governments as administrative agents of the national government have created a system of "administrative federalism" (*Verwaltungsföderalismus*).

In spite of the numerous arguments that can be made about the decline of federalism and trends toward increasing centralization (which will not disappear), a strong case also can be made that German federalism, like other federal systems (including the American), is constantly changing, and that this change is not in any consistent direction. One must also use care in describing what is happening in German federalism, because the choice of terms is important.

While it is generally true that the national government has assumed ever greater powers at the expense of the Länder and local governments, it is also important to remember that all levels are bound in joint activities involving mostly policy initiative by the federal cabinet, debate and passage of bills by the Bundestag and Bundesrat, and administration by Land and local elected officials and bureaucrats. As Peter Katzenstein has noted, the "state is only semi-sovereign in this political process, because numerous private and quasi-public groups may also be involved in various ways. The "problem" then is not really centralization *per se* so much as a nationalized system of joint policy making and administration involving public and private actors at different levels of government who cannot easily be held accountable for their actions, since they only share responsibility with others in making and executing policy. It should also be pointed out that joint decision making is found in various forms in other political systems. As suggested earlier, intergovernmental relations appear to be a characteristic of modern political systems. Three main features continue to distinguish the Federal Republic from most of its neighbors: (1) a Bundesrat that offers leading regional politicians of the major parties opportunities to influence national policy; (2) Land cabinets and parliaments that in spite of much criticism continue to attract numerous talented political activists and provide them with valuable training and experience; and (3) a focus on administration at the regional and local levels that gives considerable responsibility to politicians and officials at those levels and frees the national government from some of the criticism of bureaucratic "overload." All of this adds up to conditions encouraging competitive political parties and interest groups, more citizen influence in the political process, and a more pluralistic, open society. These are no small accomplishments.

Germany

New Federalists

FROM OUR BONN CORRESPONDENT

AFTER toasting the death on October 3rd of their dismal country, the people of the late German Democratic Republic have another treat in store. On October 14th they will elect parliaments in the five newly-born *Länder* (federal states) which the communists dissolved in 1952.

Three cheers for that, surely. In what was West Germany the federal system has worked well in the main. It has encouraged regional pride and devolved political power, tapping (to the relief of non-Germans too) a tradition which long preceded Hitler. The *Länder* have acted both as shock absorbers of local unrest and as springboards for national careers (the chancellor, Mr Helmut Kohl, made his name nationally via the premiership of Rhineland-Palatinate).

The Germans in the east have extra reasons to be keen federalists. After decades of rule by communists from the centre, they want the same local control that the western states enjoy over the police, cultural affairs and finance. And although they welcome unity, they face strange western ways and one economic blow after another. The re-emerging *Länder* of Saxony, Saxony-Anhalt, Thuringia, Brandenburg and Mecklenburg offer people a sense of stability, of *Heimat*, at a time of disorientation.

Yet there is a catch. According to the constitution (hitherto West German but now applying to all Germans), states are to have a "size and capacity" so that they are able "effectively to fulfil the functions incumbent upon them." Even in West Germany with its 11 states (including West Ber-

lin) this ideal was never achieved. Some are big and rich like Baden-Württemberg, others are small and poor like Bremen and the Saarland. Under a complex system, the rich states have paid to bail out the others, with "topping up" from the federal government. Despite irritation and appeals to the constitutional court, the system has worked.

The arrival of the "pfennigless five" makes things a lot worse. All the newcomers are small. The southern state of Saxony, the biggest in eastern Germany with close to 5m people, is only number six on the all-German scale (see map on next page). All are poor. Mecklenburg in the north accounts for less than 1% of all-German GNP. Brandenburg next door is little better off if you exclude united Berlin (the new German capital which may become a *Land* in its own right) in the middle. Industry is in ruins, pollution is endemic, local administration is generally chaotic. Even with big improvements in the next year or two, will five states for 16m people (compared with 11 for 61m in the west) make economic and political sense?

The outgoing East German government thought not, but decided not to meddle. Mergers? Unthinkable, say the people of Thuringia, a state boasting extensive forests (albeit half dead from pollution) and packed with history (Wartburg castle, the Weimar of Goethe, and so on). Intolerable, snort the Mecklenburgers, deeply attached to their land of lakes and meadows and unready to climb into bed with the snooty Brandenburgers next

door. Saxony feels safe anyway, with its relatively strong economy—nearly one-third of East German industrial production—and the fine though scarred cities of Dresden and Leipzig.

More *Länder* will make decision-taking harder in the Bundesrat, the second chamber of the federal parliament which groups states' representatives and has a veto on tax legislation. Even with 11 states, Bundesrat wheeling and dealing made for cumbersome government. Now there will be five more, armed with four votes apiece. As a precaution against being outvoted by the small and poor, the four big western states (those with at least 7m people each) have recently won six Bundesrat seats apiece instead of five. That gives them the edge in a combined onslaught by the easterners, but not if the latter can find an ally or two.

Potentially more far-reaching is the finance deal the western states have managed to prise out of the federal government. Under it the westerners will not have to make what would have been whopping transfers to the east for a few years. Instead they have pledged a modest contribution to the DM115 billion ($75 billion) German Unity Fund and are smirking over getting off the hook so easily. They may be laughing too soon. If the federal government is forced to pay most of the bill for the east now, it will insist in the long run on a bigger say over the doings of states (not just eastern ones) which cannot pay their way.

The best guarantee against that would

1. COUNTRY STUDIES: Germany

be to revamp the whole system, creating fewer, stronger *Länder*. Prospects are not good. The principle has often been endorsed in the west, but local pride and Bundesrat politics get in the way.

At present the Social Democrats, in opposition to Mr Kohl's centre-right coalition government in Bonn, have a clear majority in the Bundesrat because of their success in regional elections. Now Mr Kohl has a chance to narrow the gap. Polls indicate the Social Democrats may win outright only in Brandenburg in the October 14th elections.

Western politicians are trying to use

German Länder	Population m	Seats in the Bundesrat after (before) unification
North Rhine-Westphalia	16.7	6 (5)
Bavaria	10.9	6 (5)
Baden-Württemberg	9.3	6 (5)
Lower Saxony	7.2	6 (5)
Hesse	5.5	4 (4)
Saxony	5.0	4 (0)
Rhineland-Palatinate	3.6	4 (4)
Berlin	3.3	4 (4)
Saxony-Anhalt	3.0	4 (0)
Brandenburg	2.7	4 (0)
Schleswig-Holstein	2.6	4 (4)
Thuringia	2.5	4 (0)
Mecklenburg-West Pomerania	2.1	4 (0)
Hamburg	1.6	3 (3)
Saarland	1.1	3 (3)
Bremen	0.7	3 (3)
TOTAL	77.7	69 (45)

those elections to rise higher. For instance, Mr Kurt Biedenkopf, an old rival of Mr Kohl's in the Christian Democratic party (west), is fighting to become premier of Saxony. His opponent is Mrs Anka Fuchs, general secretary of the Social Democrats (west) and one of her party's most experienced campaigners. Westerners are seeking the premierships in Thuringia and Mecklenburg too. All that suggests there are already a lot of vested interests in maintaining the status quo. More *Länder* may complicate federalism, but they also mean more jobs for the boys and girls.

FRANCE'S FIFTH REPUBLIC
Sure-footed

This month brings the 30th anniversary of France's Fifth Republic. It has coped with the political strains of the past few years far better than most observers expected. But it may soon be ripe for some changes

THE Fifth Republic used to be famous for its clarity. To two basic questions asked of any political system, France gave shiningly simple answers. What distinguishes the main parties? The old divide between left and right. Who's in charge? The president.

These sharp outlines have softened with middle age—not so odd a term if you remember that 30 years is more than twice the average length of France's 15 constitutions or regimes since 1791. Party lines have blurred. Power has become more diffuse. Does this mean France is slipping into muddle-through habits ill-adapted to the economic and defence challenges facing Western Europe? Or are these changes signs of a suppleness that promises constitutional long life?

During this year's elections, anybody hoping for an obvious clash of left and right would have been disappointed. Socialists and conservatives hid behind a cloud of shared generalities about schools, Europe and human values. Nor does France's president seem as regal as he used to. In 1986-88, President François Mitterrand, a Socialist, shared power with a conservative government led by Mr Jacques Chirac. The presidential election in May this year gave Mr Mitterrand another seven-year term in the Elysée. But the general election in June denied the new Socialist government under Mr Michel Rocard a clear majority in parliament.

Besides making French politics harder to follow, this blurring of lines has led some puzzled France-watchers to think the system itself needs an overhaul. Party divisions, on this view, ought to be re-drawn to reflect new alliances, and the constitution changed to prevent president and government getting out of line again. A more relaxed view, favoured in this article, is that, apart from some friction points in need of oil, a flexible constitution is giving many French voters what they want: a lessening of policy swings between left and right, and a counter-balancing of executive power, whichever party is in charge. Written for Charles de Gaulle,

the constitution has proved its worth under three successors, Georges Pompidou, Mr Valéry Giscard d'Estaing and Mr Mitterrand, who used to be one of the system's harshest critics.

The constitution was written in a scramble during the turbulent summer of 1958. None of its main authors quite saw eye to eye. De Gaulle, taking a soldier's view, wanted above all to insulate foreign affairs and defence from, as he saw it, the party carousel in parliament. These responsibilities became the president's "reserve". The constitution made clear that the president named a prime minister and could dissolve parliament, but that parliament could not overturn him.

Mr Michel Debré, de Gaulle's first prime minister, was keen to stop governments falling every time a few votes changed sides in parliament. He insisted on including the cunning devices making it hard for governments to lose confidence votes in the National Assembly. Civil servants strove, successfully, to keep the powers of the permanent administration. The mainspring of the system, the popular election of the president, was added only as an afterthought in 1962.

That an improvised document worked so well was a bit of a surprise. Yet, by the standards of France's neighbours or of France's own past, work it has. Part of the answer may lie in the half-joking words of a wise French constitutional lawyer: "A mistake to avoid is to think that we have a French constitution. We have a British one, where what matters is how the rules are applied in practice."

Those puzzling elections

A democratic constitution provides for effective, accountable government. To stay attuned to voters, politicians need to read elections well. Recent ones in France have been a puzzle. What do French voters want? The results suggest there is no stable voting majority in France either for all-out free-market liberalism, or for tight government-led management of the economy.

The 1986 general election brought conservatives to power. A lot of votes were against the ins rather than for the outs. Many people wanted to punish the Socialists for their economic management in the early 1980s, when inflation and unemployment were high. Some also wanted to reward the Socialists for their anti-inflationary change of heart in 1983. The punishment was accordingly light: the conservatives won a majority of three seats.

The pattern was similar this year. Voters in the general election tempered Mr Mitterrand's sweeping 54% presidential victory. A majority preferred Mr Mitterrand's steady, avuncular style to Mr Chirac's off-putting mixture of tough talk and often flabby action. But a lot of Mr Mitterrand's supporters would not vote Socialist in the parliamentary elections. Although Mr Mitterrand and Mr Rocard cannot have believed the wilder polls, they campaigned against a Socialist landslide. "It is not healthy for just one party to govern," said Mr Mitterrand in a memorable "vote-for-our-opponents" piece of campaign advice.

Voters took him at his word. The Socialists won 275 seats in the 577-seat National Assembly, 14 less than an outright majority, 13 more than the conservative opposition. Mr Rocard was able to carry on as prime minister at the head of a mainly Socialist government thanks to Mr Debré's fears of 30 years ago: to overturn a government, parliament must find a majority of deputies to vote against it on a vote of confidence. An unlikely combination of Communists and conservatives could upset Mr Rocard; failing that, he was safe.

The search for a centre

The widely reported message of this double result was that voters wanted middle-of-the-road government. But what did this really mean? Sometimes it seems France-watchers need as much energy to find the "centre" of French politics as physicists do looking for sub-atomic particles. At least physicists have theories to predict their quarries' existence. The search for a centre seems to rest by contrast on a confusion. Government at the centre, which many French voters are getting, need not be government of the Centre, which is certainly elusive and perhaps not there at all.

One of the odder commonplaces in this bicentennial period is, as if it were news, that the French Revolution is over. Nobody talks a better middle-of-the-road line than Mr Rocard. He promised an "opening to the centre". He told his ministers to give the opposition its due and to listen to "civil society", in other words not just to party politicians, particularly Socialist ones.

Noble sentiments. But Mr Rocard's muffled overture to centre-right politicians this summer butted up against the facts of party life. Despite tensions and disagreements, politicians of the centre-right were allies of the other main group of mainstream conservatives, the neo-Gaullists. For centre-right politicians openly to have backed, let alone joined, a new Socialist government would have been to admit that this conservative alliance was dead. Though ailing, this alliance's life-signs were strong enough to deter all but a few minor centre-right politicians from deserting.

Socialists, too, grumbled about Mr Rocard's "overture". They disapproved of his readiness to share *fromages*—patronage jobs—with non-Socialists, and of his government's right-wing drift. Some Socialists argue, with force, that one-time Communist voters have not become centre-minded yuppies simply because they have given up on a rigid, old-fashioned party and that Socialists should address their concerns. Of 275 Socialist deputies, some 115 have been teachers. Perhaps another 50 are from other parts of the public sector. Here is a state-spending lobby with which any Socialist prime minister must reckon.

It is no great surprise that by this autumn's local elections, more classic party lines were forming once more. The main parties in France have a tolerable agreement about how much real manoeuvring room either left or right have once in power. But left and right continue to exist, with their own patronage networks, rituals and loyalties. Both agree France needs anti-inflationary policies. But most French conservatives want to go on privatising banks and industry. The Socialists do not. Non-economic questions—immigration, civil rights, culture, press and broadcasting—also divide the two main groups.

The big divide

Consensus government can work with competitive parties. A swing party at the centre is not necessary. Some day, one might emerge in France. But two-round, first-past-the-post constituency voting tends to work against small parties. If they exist at all, they do so courtesy of larger ones.

So France could be developing a party system in which distinct centre-right and centre-left parties alternate in government, each getting a turn at public jobs. At the

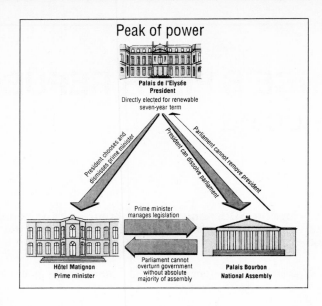

Peak of power

Palais de l'Elysée
President
Directly elected for renewable seven-year term

President chooses and dismisses prime minister

President can dissolve parliament

Parliament cannot remove president

Hôtel Matignon
Prime minister

Prime minister manages legislation

Parliament cannot overturn government without absolute majority of assembly

Palais Bourbon
National Assembly

same time, they both agree enough about economic and foreign-policy ground rules to make swapping power more of a handover than an upheaval.

As Communist support has collapsed to around 12% of the parliamentary vote, the Socialists are now the main force on the left. This corrects a fault of the early Fifth Republic when a divided left allowed, in effect, 23 years of conservative rule until Mr Mitterrand's victory in 1981.

The awkwardness is that the mainstream right risks splitting up. France may not, as is often said, have "the stupidest right in the world." But it surely has one of the most fractious. The neo-Gaullists, with 132 seats in parliament, are split. Some are right-wing populists who might work with an extreme right shorn of its overt racialism. Some are economic liberals, close to the centre-right. A dwindling few are old Gaullist barons. Mr Chirac bridged these groups. He was terribly battered by his defeat. Younger politicians such as Mr Alain Juppé and Mr **Pierre Seguin are already elbowing for his succession.**

Today's centre-right is an even odder group. It has no single party. The biggest is the Republican party, started by Mr Giscard d'Estaing. Waiting still for his comeback, the ex-president would like to lead a united conservative group in "constructive opposition" to the Socialists. But the old Christian Democrats, led by Mr Pierre Méhaignerie, have split away to form their own parliamentary group. Both men must reckon also with a third centre-right leader, Mr Raymond Barre. A law to himself, this ex-prime minister and defeated presidential candidate continues to play Puck one day and national saviour the next.

Fractious as they are, even the wettest conservatives are still likelier to hold on to Nurse for fear of finding something worse. A test will come during next spring's local elections, which cover small towns right through to the biggest cities. Before the summer, Mr Mitterrand's people spoke of these local elections as a chance for alliances between Socialists and politicians of the centre-right. Now few expect more than rare exceptions to the usual pattern: Communists and Socialists on one side, centre-right and neo-Gaullists on the other.

Not all voters in France want fudge and compromise. Though down, the Communist party is not out. The racialist far-right got 14% of the vote in the first round of the presidential election. A protest vote, many said, but still depressingly high. In the general election, 34% of voters abstained, a record. A system in which lots of people feel unheard is not healthy.

Some say France has too many elections: hence the high abstention rate. This is debatable. The calendar is over-charged: 1986, a one-round general election; 1988, a two-round presidential and a two-round general election, cantonal elections in many departments this week (with a record-low turnout), a referendum on New Caledonia; 1989, two-round local-council elections and a proportional election for the European parliament in June; 1991, more cantonals; 1992, regional elections; 1993, another general election, if parliament lasts till then. Bunching some of these would be a good idea, if the parties can agree on a neutral moment to pass the necessary laws—perhaps 1990, when no elections are scheduled.

Cohabitation clockwork

A different calendar problem is the hoary question of preventing "cohabitation" by a president of one party with a parliamentary majority of another. Presidents have seven-year terms, a carry-over from the Third Republic. Parliament's normal life is five years, though it can be less if the president dissolves it prematurely. In such a system, presi-

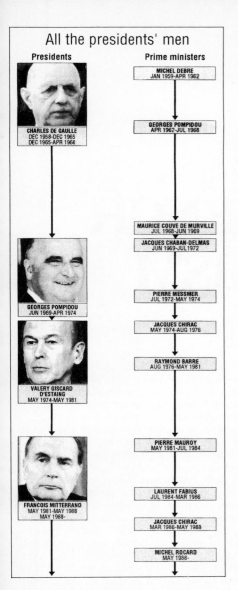

All the presidents' men

Presidents	Prime ministers
	MICHEL DEBRE JAN 1959-APR 1962
CHARLES DE GAULLE DEC 1958-DEC 1965 DEC 1965-APR 1968	GEORGES POMPIDOU APR 1962-JUL 1968
	MAURICE COUVE DE MURVILLE JUL 1968-JUN 1969
	JACQUES CHABAN-DELMAS JUN 1969-JUL 1972
GEORGES POMPIDOU JUN 1969-APR 1974	PIERRE MESSMER JUL 1972-MAY 1974
	JACQUES CHIRAC MAY 1974-AUG 1976
VALERY GISCARD D'ESTAING MAY 1974-MAY 1981	RAYMOND BARRE AUG 1976-MAY 1981
	PIERRE MAUROY MAY 1981-JUL 1984
FRANCOIS MITTERRAND MAY 1981-MAY 1988 MAY 1988-	LAURENT FABIUS JUL 1984-MAR 1986
	JACQUES CHIRAC MAR 1986-MAY 1988
	MICHEL ROCARD MAY 1988-

dential and parliamentary majorities can get out of line. France lived with this in 1986-88. It came off better than many predicted, but also with more wear-and-tear on Mr Mitterrand and Mr Chirac than showed at the time. Could the terms of president and prime minister be better aligned? Could their lines of responsibility be made clearer? Is either change necessary?

There are three basic ways to impose Gallic clarity on this Anglo-Saxon muddle. One would be to make the job of France's president, though not his election, more like Italy's or West Germany's. He would be a popular figurehead—a head of state who represented France ceremonially to the rest of the world. A second route would be somehow to write into the constitution that the president directs the government, and make the link between parliament and president more direct. It is unclear how this could be done without weakening the president.

Either way would wreck the clever compromise that has evolved under the Fifth Republic. France's president, in some guises, represents the nation. In others, he represents his own, usually the majority, party. This makes the president both figurehead and executive with real power. He is both von Weizsäcker and Thatcher. Playing both parts well takes a fine ear for public opinion. If played badly, the likely price is defeat after one term.

The third, most modest, course is to argue that seven years is too long for a modern president. Shortening it to five years would make the president more accountable—and it would lower, though not remove, the risk of cohabitation. Giving parliament and the president fixed five-year terms would virtually rule out cohabitation. But that would disturb the balance of the system by taking away a president's power to dissolve parliament.

Paper change is not what really matters. "De Gaulle would have governed the way he did whether he had a Swiss or a Chinese constitution," according to one seasoned expert. Modern practice in France accepts that the clash between a popularly elected president and parliament cannot be too great. Had Mr Chirac won by 50 parliamentary seats in 1986, would Mr Mitterrand really have stayed on? The constitution says he could have done. The odds are he would have resigned. Again, in 1981 and 1988, Mr Mitterrand called a general election immediately after his presidential victory. This was to get backing in parliament. Though not called for in the constitution, this is becoming normal practice.

Some tension between president and prime minister is built into any two-headed executive, even when, as now, both heads belong to the same party. Mr Rocard is a Protestant who makes a virtue of speaking his mind and has no hang-ups about the creation of wealth. Mr Mitterrand is a Catholic who favours hidden manoeuvre and who distrusts economics. Mr Rocard was once his junior rival. The two profess old scores now settled. Not everyone believes them.

Counterweight needed

Tempered as it may be, the hitting-power of France's executive branch remains strong. This makes fears of government paralysis look exaggerated. Rather than trying to close doors to future cohabitation, reformers would do better to foster counterweights to executive power.

The little-noticed strength of France's Constitutional Council is a step in this direction. Since 1974 it has required only 60 senators or deputies to send it a bill for a constitutional vetting. Much major legislation now routinely passes before the Council, which does not hesitate to strike down what is unconstitutional. The Council could be bolder in broadening its remit to protecting citizens against civil-rights abuses. Few Americans thought the Supreme Court could strike down acts of Congress until Chief Justice Marshall said it could.

The president of the National Assembly, Mr Laurent Fabius, wants to make parliament less of a doormat. He proposes committee hearings in public, more speaking time for the opposition, and more questioning of ministers. Deputies ought to have more time for this now that they are being restricted to holding only two elected offices. But parliament, too, could be bolder in demanding more grilling of ministers and officials, more follow-up on how laws are applied and money spent.

Another welcome change would be the gradual disappearance of a modern French allergy to independent commissions. France has one, in theory, for broadcasting. It was used in such a crudely partisan way by the previous government that Mr Rocard's government is replacing it with a new one. It would be a pity for the Socialists to repeat the mistake. Another is the Competition Council, set up under the conservatives. Like most of France's financial and economic overseers, this is still, in practice, too closely tied to the Treasury.

The beginning of this article deliberately blurred a distinction. It lumped together as examples of French "muddle through" three different things: a certain narrowing of the gap between parties, a greater balance between different constitutional forces, and a putting off of tough economic and defence choices facing France. It is wrong to think that the first two need encourage the third. Bringing France's parties into better balance and making the system more democratic ought to make facing up to France's challenges easier. If politicians duck France's European choices, it will not be the system that is to blame.

THE END OF FRENCH EXCEPTIONALISM

Claude Imbert

Claude Imbert is editor of *Le Point.*

In this year of 1989, France has been celebrating the bicentennial of its revolution at a time when the myth attached to that event is in the process of dying out among the public at large. The French have spent the past two centuries building a dream of their revolution, either to damn it or to exalt it.

During the nineteenth century the dominant attitude was one of condemnation; in this century the event has become definitively sanctified. So much so that the dominant ideology up to this point in the twentieth century has seen the revolution as a kind of "legend of saints." One Marxist school of historical thought, which holds the revolution to be unfinished, has seen the event as a kind of happy precursor of the Bolshevik Revolution of 1917. From this point of view, the terror was a cruel but essential stage in the human race's long march of progress. For the past century this perspective colored not only the opinions of the French left, but also that of most teaching in state schools. It is this myth that has given French politics its singularly lyrical quality, making Paris for so long the center of theatrical ideological debate.

At the present time that particularly French passion which leads intellectuals and politicians to want to build society according to theoretical constructs is coming to an end. It was born from a revolutionary mythology and it is dying at a time when that mythology is fading away. The current phrase in France is that "the revolution is over," which means that modern historians have blown to pieces its legendary dimension, and that above all, the long ideological furrow plowed by the country's history through two centuries is coming to an end. Thus, the bicentennial marks the end of a historical cycle.

The French people are proud to have given the world the Declaration of the Rights of Man. But they are no longer one bit proud to have invented the guillotine in 1793, and along with it a theory of political violence that would claim Lenin as one of its later disciples. The French are proud to have been among the first countries to have laid down the sovereignty of the people as a basic principle of their republican constitution. But at the same time the French are conscious that six of the 12 European Community countries remain monarchies, and that the citizens of those lands are no less free than they.

The French are proud to have played a leading role in the history of the West in 1789, but they no longer believe that their model is unique. They have since learned, in their schools, on films and TV, that both England and the United States had preceded and inspired their revolution. They are even pretty well convinced today that the process that pushed events toward revolutionary terror also ushered in, after the dictatorship of Napoleon, a long period of political and economic stagnation that cost their country the leadership which it had enjoyed on the eve of 1789, both in terms of population growth and industrial creativity. Asked recently to pronounce a new sentence on King Louis XVI, after a television dramatization of his trial, French viewers voted against execution; they would have preferred to send him off to quiet exile—to Monaco, perhaps.

II

This change in the political mentality of the French marks the end of a certain dissonance in the concert of Western nations. And it is only the latest in a series of rapid changes. France has no doubt seen more of such developments than any other European country, the most traumatic of them being the defeat of 1940. For although they may pretend to have forgotten all about it, the French know in their heart of hearts that their country collapsed in humiliating conditions, even if later de Gaulle, the Resistance and above all the Allies allowed France to scramble onto the bandwagon of victory.

But then in 1945 the rise of the strategic power of the United States and the Soviet Union and the internationalization of the world economy were to sound the death knell of France's status as an imperial power. For the next 25 years, until 1970, France was to spend a good part of its political energy on one of the most delicate operations in its history: the decolonization of its vast African empire and the repatriation of some two million of its citizens from Morocco, Algeria and Tunisia. The Fourth Republic (1945–58) was to start the process in sub-Saharan Africa and in Morocco and Tunisia. But de Gaulle had to return to power in 1958 to realize the hardest part: the inde-

Reprinted by permission of *Foreign Affairs,* Vol. 68, No. 4, Fall 1989, pp. 48-60. Copyright © 1989 by the Council on Foreign Relations, Inc.

pendence of Algeria, which the local French settlers and some of the army were refusing.

Throughout that difficult period one man, General de Gaulle, applied his prestige and historic authority to the much needed liquidation of long-standing national traditions. Not only did he crush the military revolt, but at the same time he ended the French right's resistance to change and its nostalgia for nationalistic causes. And then, 25 years later, it was the turn of General de Gaulle's main opponent, François Mitterrand, a representative of the doctrinaire socialism of the left, to end the "exile" of his own political current, which had channeled itself away into a Marxist ideological ghetto.

The convergent paths of those two irreconcilable adversaries highlights the mysterious, roundabout ways in which French history works. Just as de Gaulle started out with the support of the right and the Algerian settlers, only to prod them gradually, using both cunning and teaching, toward acceptance of a historical necessity, so Mitterrand in 1981 became the presidential candidate of a Socialist movement that claimed to break with capitalism, and which was to have the upper hand in France until 1983. But Mitterrand had taken care to avoid a split with either the Atlantic alliance or with Europe. He was soon to realize the unsustainable contradictions between his international commitments and his Socialist project; his adherence to the system of the market economy was seen to be inconsistent with his national utopia. By 1983 the obvious failure of French-style socialism (nationalization, increased spending on social programs and accelerated cuts in working hours) had painted the government into a corner; Mitterrand opted abruptly for a return to economic and monetary rigor.

In fact, and without admitting it, on the day in March 1983 that French socialism decided not to leave the European Monetary System in order to pursue a more traditionally leftist economic policy it was making the same radical switch that had pushed West Germany's Social Democrats to reject Marxism at their 1959 Bad Godesberg congress. The French Communist Party speeded up even further its impressive decline: from 28.3 percent of the vote in 1946, it slid to only 11.3 percent in the 1988 parliamentary elections, and 7.7 percent in the European Community (EC) poll of 1989. Since 1983 the French left, led by Mitterrand, who was reelected to the presidency in 1988, has quietly brought an end to the ideological war that had split the country's public opinion for a century. A strong majority consensus has now formed around the principles of a market economy, and a political system similar to that of the other major Western democracies.

The outcome of all this has been that in less than half a century an essentially traditionalist and elitist right has accepted modernity and democracy in social life, while an egalitarian and protectionist left has thrown in its lot with the selective laws of the market and free trade.

As a result power has passed from the right to the left and back again three times in seven years—in 1981, 1986 and 1988—without the slightest disorder. And we have even seen a left-wing president cohabiting with a right-wing prime minister. It is true that the latter episode does not stand out as a model of strong and coherent government, but at least the acceptance of political institutions won out, perhaps for the first time, over age-old passions.

It should not be concluded from the above that the political scene has ceased to be characterized by conflict. The Communist Party remains on the scene as a small but determined electoral rallying point for the discontented, while Socialist activism remains tinged by backward-looking ideological beliefs that may yet have a last fling. But overall, and in spite of spells of egalitarian demagogy during election campaigns, the general drift sees the extremes withering away.

This change in French political life, which in fact has taken place with relatively little upheaval, has only reflected the accelerated tearing-away of civil society from the past, perhaps

the most abrupt change that France has experienced in all of its long history. In forty years, the number of French people living in cities has grown from 20 million to 40 million, while the ranks of the farming population have shrunk from 7.5 million to 1.5 million in 1985. The number of non-salaried workers—farmers, shopkeepers, craftsmen and so forth—has been cut by half, while that of white-collar executive staff has doubled.

When one considers how many French political traditions had their roots in rural culture and individualistic economic activity, and remembers that even in the nineteenth century France was already falling behind England and Germany in terms of industrialization—if one thinks of what the transformation means for French lifestyle, ideas and behavior—one realizes that France has been through perhaps the most profound economic, social and cultural changes of any country in Western Europe. The strong wind of modernization has blown like a tornado through the old France of dreaming spires and peasant lots. True, it has not yet worn down the centralizing Jacobinism of Paris, but the new era has seen the renaissance of several large regional cities whose economic interests have suddenly spilled over France's borders: Toulouse and Montpellier now look toward Barcelona, Lyons toward Geneva and Milan, Lille toward London, Brussels and Amsterdam.

Meanwhile the educational system and television have in two generations succeeded in unifying a language that less than 50 years ago was still characterized by defiant regional dialects. A society formerly rooted in the earth, in provincial tastes and self-sufficiency, divided by well-marked ideological frontiers between Christians and non-believers and between clannish left and right political factions, has been tumbled and turned and mixed up as never before. The result is that a political consensus, previously so elusive, has been built upon the ruins of France's old order.

III

This consensus can now be found, more or less explicitly expressed, on the three key foundations of the French state: its institutional arrangements, foreign policy and defense.

France's current institutions, those of the Fifth Republic, were the result of General de Gaulle's determination to create a strong executive. This was required in order to cure the country of the instability of the Fourth Republic, in which the party system had led to precarious and ever-shifting majorities: between 1946 and 1958 there were no less than 22 governments, of which 11 lasted less than six months.

The bedrock of the current system is the election every seven years, by universal suffrage, of a president who appoints the prime minister, and who has the power to dissolve the National Assembly and call new elections. It was an institutional system strongly and consistently criticized by François Mitterrand during the rule of de Gaulle. But then once he was elected, Mitterrand slid easily, and with apparent pleasure, into a mold that he had formerly found so hateful. And although he continues to say, without insisting too much, that the system is imperfect, he has not so far chosen to change it. Whatever the imperfections of the system—the main one is that it favors a drift toward a type of "monarchical" government—public opinion has taken to it without any major problems. The most one can expect is that the seven-year term of what is in essence a "republican monarch," a concept so well adapted to the French mentality, might one day be shortened.

It is true that Mitterrand's reelection in 1988 to a second term raises questions about the wisdom of concentrating power in the same hands for 14 long years. And although it seems out of the question that the constitution would be reformed in its basic principles, one may see a growing demand for either a term of five years, renewable once, or for a non-renewable term of six years. If things start to get difficult for the current president toward the end of his second term, he may decide to give himself some breathing-space by proposing such a reform. But the basic point is that up to now the institutions of the Fifth Republic have been well accepted by the population as a whole.

The same progressive movement toward consensus can be seen at work in the field of foreign policy. Here it is the Gaullist right that has gone through the biggest changes. Its often stormy nationalism has been relaxed; above all it has progressively shed its objections to the European Community. And the European Parliament elections of June 1989 saw the Gaullist party of Jacques Chirac throwing its weight behind the centrist and very pro-European list headed by former President Valéry Giscard d'Estaing.

On the question of Europe, and the idea that France and West Germany should form the basic tandem pulling the rest of the European Community along in its wake, Giscard and Mitterrand have very few quarrels. Unlike Britain's Prime Minister Margaret Thatcher, both are in favor of pushing for the quickest possible progress toward a shared EC currency. And neither is against giving up certain aspects of national sovereignty to Community mechanisms. When the integrated economic foundations of the EC have been laid, both favor building a political Europe, a project that for the moment is only opposed by minority extremes in the Communist Party and a small far-right group that is not currently represented in parliament.

On other fronts, Mitterrand is pursuing the same policies as his predecessors with respect to the Arab and African worlds. Even though his "Third-Worldist" tendencies are more pronounced—witness his support for reducing the debt burdens of various poor countries—and in spite of the divergences he has expressed in the past from U.S. views on Latin America, continuity has been the keynote of his foreign policy. It has caused absolutely no major divisions in public opinion.

On East-West relations, France has for a long time shown more prudence than its European partners concerning the progress of disarmament. In fact the views of France's public and its president are today much more in tune with the careful approach of President George Bush than they were with the idealistic policies of the Reagan Administration at the time of Reykjavik summit. It has to be added that the proven popularity of Soviet leader Mikhail Gorbachev has never sparked the same enthusiasm it has in "Gorbymaniacal" West Germany.

On the third and last point, that of defense, Mitterrand dropped his hostility toward France's independent nuclear deterrent even while he was still in the opposition. And since he has been in power he has cast himself as the heir to the Gaullist tradition, the vigilant defender of France's nuclear industry, both in the military and civilian fields.

IV

Such impressive changes in the French political landscape could not have taken place without leaving scars. Although the political scene today appears calm, civil society has been deeply affected by its various upheavals. The most spectacular of these has been the decline of Christianity. In fifty years the country that liked to call itself "the Roman Church's eldest daughter" has seen the decline of the political, moral and social authority of Catholicism, with spectacular effects.

Consider that for centuries the Christian system was the major source of inspiration and unification of the French nation, that it inspired French law along with both individual and collective morality, and you will get some idea of the hole left behind by its decline. For a time the socialist ideology, with its promise of a heaven on earth, provided a kind of substitute religion, a secular source of hope for those on the left. That too has now collapsed. And the psychodrama of the failed student mini-revolution of 1968, with its quickly extinguished fireworks, brought the demise, more cultural than political, of an old social and psychological order, that of authoritarian

social relations in the school and workplace. It also hastened the advent of more permissive sexual mores, which have now become general throughout the West.

The economic crisis, the huge industrial transformation that has accompanied the decline of such old sectors as steel making, coal mining and textiles, has left ten percent of the active population out of work. The phenomenon of unemployment persists, and is today much worse than in Britain or West Germany. In spite of a welfare system that makes it less explosive, unemployment increases the isolation of hundreds of thousands of people and has given birth to forms of delinquency and insecurity that are worrying to a people who in spite of their individualism are great lovers of public order.

Finally, an immigrant population estimated at around 4.5 million, of whom some two million are of North African origin, sparks feelings of alienation and exasperation in areas in which thresholds of acceptability are exceeded. The French people, themselves the result of some twenty centuries of racial mixing, have a well-established ability to assimilate newcomers. But through its size the influx of Arab Muslim immigrants is proving much more difficult to integrate than was that of Italians, Poles and Spaniards at the start of the century. The current immigration, amplified by a difficult-to-control phenomenon of illegal entry, is a key question in determining the future of France; it could become an advantage, if it does not get out of control, in bolstering France's birthrate. The French fertility rate of 1.8, though one of the highest in Europe, is nevertheless insufficient to ensure renewal of the population. On the other hand, immigration could also present risks if the rate of integration falls and if schooling and professional training for the newcomers are inadequate. Then Islamic and North African ghettos within France could reach a flash point.

None of these upheavals have so far resulted in any civil disorder. On the contrary, social change has been peacefully managed. But it has nevertheless created points of tension, and stiffened the resolve of the conservative resistance.

The most spectacular and most talked-about phenomenon has been the emergence of a far-right movement under Jean-Marie Le Pen. From 1983 to the presidential election of 1988, when its vote peaked at 14.3 percent, the success of Le Pen's National Front party has mainly been built on fear of change.

Contrary to what has often been said, and in spite of the racist tendencies of some of its activists, Le Pen's party is not "fascist" in the true meaning of the word. It is the product of the shock caused by modernization; it attracts voters from outside the regular parties, who have suffered from the effects of the economic crisis. Its influence spreads among working-class people who are in contact with immigrants. Like the recently emerged West German far-right party, the so-called "Republicans," Le Pen targets fears of AIDS, of homosexuals, outcasts and all other kinds of "differences." But his basic political platform, for tradition and order, is not very different from that of the old-fashioned right in many Western democracies. In France, however, the right-wing parties that take part in government, be they Gaullist or not, have now become centrist and modernist, and have no time for the simplistic messages demanded by a part of their working-class electorate, who seek a return to the past and the defense of traditional moral values and patriotism.

Le Pen therefore fills a need; he is to the right what the Communist Party, or rather the remains of the Communist Party, is to the left. But his influence today is weak; in the last parliamentary elections in June 1988, held under an electoral system which admittedly worked against him, he lost two million voters—i.e., the equivalent of half of the people who had voted for him for the first time in the preceding month's presidential tally—to win only one seat. In the Euro-elections of June 1989 he took 11.73 percent of the vote and will send 10 of France's 81 members to the EC Assembly in Strasbourg.

A second effect of the great upheaval in French ways of

thinking has been a certain political listlessness among the public. A turning-away from collective interests has occurred in several Western democracies; in France it appears more marked than elsewhere. And as elsewhere, it has gone hand in hand with a strong trend toward individualism, even narcissism, a desire for personal well-being and "making it." The recent appearance on the scene of several private TV channels, where previously there was only the state broadcasting monopoly, has resulted in a huge increase in exposure to advertising, sharpening the French passion for "keeping up with the Durands." The media explosion has replaced the idea of success through ability with that of success for the sake of success, at a time when critical thought has been devalued by the vanishing of France's traditional intellectual authorities, and the collapse of the influence of academics.

The decline of political passions has weakened even the French people's image of their own nation, so that politics is now viewed with irony, disillusion and skepticism by many people. The result is that no less than 34.3 percent of eligible voters stayed away from the last parliamentary elections, an unprecedented development for France. And in the June 1989 Euro-elections only one voter in two went to the polls, although it has to be admitted that the issues to be decided in that vote did not strike most people as being very clear.

At the same time France's political parties are recruiting fewer and fewer new members. In fact, France has a lower proportion of card-carrying members of political parties—less than two percent—than any other nation in the EC. As for the trade unions, which have always attracted fewer recruits than elsewhere in Europe, they are experiencing a new and impressive decline, losing around half their members over the past decade. Only around ten percent of salaried workers are now members of unions.

v

The transformation of French society is running into two major types of resistance. The first is caused by the high burden of spending on social programs. Over the past thirty years successive French governments have sought to ease the pain of modernization by continually broadening the scope of state aid to various categories of people. The left did it out of conviction, and from what remained of its ideology. But the French right was for a long time also a big spender on social programs, beating even Social Democratic governments in other European states. Ninety-nine percent of French people are now protected by a health insurance system that is both the most protective and the most ruinously expensive of any in the West. The unemployment benefit system is the most generous in Europe. French companies have of course played their part, a very onerous one, in financing this increase in costs. But the result is that the level of all types of statutory deductions from earnings—taxes plus health insurance and other social programs—is one of the highest on the continent.

President Mitterrand, during his socialist utopian period from 1981 to 1983, piled on further pressure, in particular by reductions in the retirement age which have proved so expensive, and which are now slowly and painfully inching back. But even under the liberal governments of the Giscard d'Estaing presidency, from 1974 to 1981, France had a more "socialist" economic structure than did West Germany under the Social Democrat Helmut Schmidt. The coming to power of the Socialists under Mitterrand in 1981 inevitably accentuated the process. Since 1983 the Socialists have mended their costly ways, but commitments already made in the fields of health, unemployment benefits and retirement rights have already had a ratchet effect, making it difficult to turn back.

The resulting situation is a serious handicap for France at a time when the mechanisms of EC integration require that the 12 member nations harmonize their tax systems in order to lay the groundwork for monetary union. France may well try to persuade its partners to bring their systems closer to its own, but many European countries—and not only Thatcher's Britain—will refuse, considering such a course of action to be harmful. Which means that, to start with, France will be obliged to cut its indirect taxes, and in particular its value-added tax rates, thereby slashing state revenue. And as the 12 have agreed that from July 1, 1990, capital must be allowed to circulate freely among them, France is going to run into a new difficulty. If it tries to make up the shortfall by a new wealth tax, as some observers have suggested, money will immediately flow out toward other member states that tax capital income at lower levels.

Although France's economic outlook is fairly good, with growth at 3.7 percent in 1988, up from the previous year's 1.9 percent, unemployment remains at around ten percent. The risk of a new wave of social unrest arising from this situation cannot be ruled out.

The second major handicap for France is the state's own resistance to change. Thanks to the decline of ideology, the state has lost much of the historical prestige it inherited from the Jacobins. It nevertheless continues to be a heavyweight machine, too much so for a modern economy founded on liberal principles. The privatizations carried out by the government of Prime Minister Jacques Chirac stripped off a bit of the excess weight, and the present Socialist government has not threatened to turn the clock back. But the rate of state spending as a proportion of total national income still remains one of the highest in Europe. It is true that the French state can claim some clear technological successes, such as a space program, nuclear power, high-speed trains and an aeronautical industry that includes such projects as the Airbus passenger plane. But at the same time the state's inherent growth, which equals or exceeds that of the economy as a whole, has turned it into an obese, insatiable monster employing no fewer than 4.5 million civil servants.

And the more the state grows, the poorer its parts become. The teaching profession, for example, with its mass of one million badly paid employees, has been described as "the biggest army in Europe after the Red Army." It has become a giant, difficult to administer and even more difficult to reform. Meanwhile, the budget of the Justice Ministry is no longer big enough to cover necessary expenses.

To sum up, reform of the state system, a break-up of civil service pay scales and the modernization of an old-fashioned tax system that still affects to ignore the principle of deduction at source have become urgent necessities for France.

In a system that has been through such profound renewal, the bloated state apparatus has become the last refuge of the sclerosis that used to be called "the French disease." It is the only sector that has so far escaped reform. Above all, the culture of the sovereign state maintains a system which is unique among the major democracies, that of a top-level administrative elite, a caste whose members not only occupy the key state posts but also hold the reins of the political parties (of the left and right), of state-run industries and often of major private companies to boot.

In this field the "French exception" is by no means a thing of the past. The same old state aristocracy still holds the reins of power. Although technically competent, its political efficacy is low, and in general the mistakes it makes are only the ones that really count. Nine of the ten prime ministers who have served under the Fifth Republic have been members of the caste, and its members at present hold two-thirds of all cabinet posts. Meanwhile only three percent of members of parliament come from the ranks of salaried employees, even though that category accounts for two-thirds of the nation's earned income.

The problems posed by this caste system from the point of view of democracy are obvious: politics has become the business of civil servants, and at the same time civil servants have become politicized. And above all, the concentration of various types of power in the hands of a small elite, with a Parisian outlook and training, acts as a brake on the circulation of ideas and the interaction of the diverse outlooks of different professions, regions and social circles. The system therefore militates against the variety and political representation needed to run a modern democracy.

VI

If one takes a step back to get a clear view of the French situation, one sees a former great power with a long history, which in less than half a century has succeeded in carrying through rapid change without going through a major upheaval.

However, France's modernization crisis is not yet over. In many respects, its people are still in a state of shock from the rapid transition. The legitimacy of the state is now accepted, but the nation's identity has become less clear-cut. The French as a people are less sure of themselves, less "patriotic"; they are looking for a new course and think they have found it in Europe, even though that avenue contains risks as well as opportunities. The main opportunity is for a collective future capable of giving back to the French people their former ambition and desire for historic challenges. The risk lies in having to submit to Community constraints that are likely to prove tough indeed for a country which has a heavier and more thoroughly socialistic state structure than its partners.

In this Cartesian country which likes clarity of thought, the processes of change seem often obscure and disconcerting. But that is one of the paradoxes of France. For even three hundred years ago, Cardinal Richelieu expressed wonder at the fact that a country "which is so incapable of adhering to goodness finds it so easy to pull itself out of evil."

France Faces the New Europe

*Some observers argue that "the old left-right cleavages in French politics based on socioeco-
nomic and class differences are being replaced by a new distinction between those struggling to
defend the national ideal and the nation-state, and those who want France to adapt to a new
European and international reality, in which the nation-state will be less important."*

STEVEN PHILIP KRAMER

Steven Philip Kramer is the author of *Abel Gance*
(Boston: Twayne Publishers, 1978), and *Socialism in
Western Europe: The Experience of a Generation* (Boul-
der, Col.: Westview Press, 1984). He has served in
the United States State Department, Bureau of In-
teramerican Affairs, Office of Policy Planning; and
at the Carnegie Endowment for International
Peace.

WHAT matters to France today?* For its
political elites, the answer is clear—
France's role in a post-cold war world in
which there is no longer a Soviet bloc but in which
there is a reunified Germany. France may not have
as decisive a role in affecting the architecture of the
new Europe as it would like, but it will have some
influence. Just how much will depend in part on
knowing what it wants. Its influence will be max-
imized by the fact that France is much less divided
today than it has been for a long time and that the
institutions of the Fifth Republic, now universally
accepted, allow the President of the Republic great
latitude in formulating and executing French defense, foreign and European policy.

What matters to France—at least from the point
of view of the political elite—may not be what matters to most French people. Other issues, like racism and immigration, are on their minds—issues
that make the established parties uncomfortable.
This has allowed the virulent Front National to set
the domestic political agenda. What is the connection between the apparent "end of ideology" that
seems to characterize establishment politics in recent years and the Front National, which wants to
shatter the relative political peace that France has
acquired? How serious a threat is the Front to the

system? Could it weaken President François Mitterrand's hand in international affairs? As President
Charles de Gaulle remarked on February 4, 1965:

> Assuredly, the success of so vast and difficult an enter-
> prise [German unification] implies many conditions.
> Russia must evolve in such a way as no longer to con-
> ceive its future in totalitarian constraint imposed at
> home and abroad, but in progress accomplished in
> common by men and free peoples. Its satellites must
> play their role in a renewed Europe. It must be recog-
> nized, above all, by Germany, that the settlement of
> which it would be the object would necessarily include
> its frontiers and armaments in agreement with all its
> neighbors, East and West. The six states that, let us
> hope, are in the process of establishing the West Euro-
> pean economic community must succeed in organiz-
> ing themselves in the political and defense domain in
> order to make possible a new equilibrium of our conti-
> nent. Europe, the mother of modern civilization,
> must be established from the Atlantic to the Urals in
> concord and cooperation to develop its immense re-
> sources and to play, together with its daughter, Amer-
> ica, the appropriate role in the progress of two billion
> people who badly need it. What a role Germany could
> play in this worldwide ambition of the rejuvenated
> Old Continent!

President Charles de Gaulle's inheritors are witnessing the fulfillment of one of his greatest hopes,
the dissolution of the Soviet and American blocs.
Naturally, they welcomed the transformation of the
Soviet system and the democratic revolutions that
swept East Europe. But the French, like everyone
else, were caught off guard when the unlikely prospect of German unification suddenly became a fact.
When they discovered the limits of their
power—they could not arrest or even slow down the
process of unification—there was a moment of
panic. Taken aback by West German Chancellor
Helmut Kohl's announcement of a ten-point plan
for German reunification without prior consultation, Mitterrand went on a previously scheduled

*I would like to thank Paul Manuel and Josef W. Konvitz for
their comments on this article. Some of the material herein
derives from Josef W. Konvitz and Steven P. Kramer, "Mitterrand Is Europe's Middleman," *Los Angeles Times*, January 14,
1990.

trip to East Germany on December 20–22, 1989, where he seemed anxious to prop up East Germany as a separate entity. A December 6 visit to Soviet President Mikhail Gorbachev in Kiev had seemed like a forlorn effort to enlist Soviet cooperation in blocking German unification. Fortunately, France and Germany soon adopted a more cooperative approach. The German question would be solved within a European framework.

The French decision to seek a solution to German unification within the structure of Europe is fully consistent with 40 years of postwar French policy. Therefore, France is striving to anchor Germany ever more firmly to the European Community, hoping that there will still be room for French political and military leadership in Europe even with an economically powerful Germany. At the same time, French leaders are reassessing some of the contradictions of Gaullism.

To understand the significance for France of the reopening of the German question, we must briefly examine its historic context. From the age of Louis XIV to the battle of Waterloo, France, the most powerful, prosperous and populous nation in West Europe, tried repeatedly to attain hegemony in Europe. In 1648, at the Treaty of Westphalia, France was only too happy to keep Germany splintered into hundreds of ministates without a strong central authority. Napoleon Bonaparte's humiliation of Prussia helped arouse a spirit of German nationalism. In 1815, at the Congress of Vienna, French leaders shared the European consensus — maintaining the status quo of a divided Germany.

Between 1815 and 1870, however, France lost most of its comparative economic and demographic advantage. The political incompetence of Napoleon III allowed Prussia a free hand in gaining domination in north Germany. In 1870, France fought Prussia in what was in effect a last-ditch effort to prevent German unification, despite France's manifest lack of preparation. Following the debacle of the Franco-Prussian War, France was no longer perceived as the paramount land power in West Europe; it became a weak state whose survival would be threatened in the event of another conflict with Germany.

A widening economic and demographic gap and France's political isolation aggravated this situation between 1870 and 1890; after 1890, France tended toward dependence on its allies, especially Great Britain. It sought security, not dominance. In 1919, at Versailles, the French endeavored to cripple a Germany more powerful than France. If they could not dismember Germany, an idea to which their allies would not agree, they could at least make sure that Germany would be shackled, demilitarized and weighed down with reparations. This policy,

however, only undermined the economic basis of peace and encouraged rightist extremists in Germany, including Adolf Hitler, who did exactly what the French feared. (In all fairness, France did follow a much more conciliatory policy after 1924, but it did not succeed.)

After World War II, the French initially returned to their hard-line vision of 1919. After all, the case could be made that the problem of the Versailles settlement was that it had been too soft. But the advent of the cold war made France's Western allies regard Germany as an indispensable part of Western defense against Soviet communism; persistence in a hard-line policy threatened to make France, not Germany, into a pariah, an unacceptable situation when French economic survival was dependent on American aid.

Finally, in 1950, diplomat and political economist Jean Monnet inspired and Foreign Minister Robert Schuman carried out the Schuman Plan, which became the model for a new vision of Europe. Economic rivalry and French claims over German resources were resolved by Europeanizing coal and steel within the European Coal and Steel Community. Later expanded into the Common Market, this approach received American support but lacked British involvement. West German Chancellor Konrad Adenauer and Schuman worked together to bring about European economic integration as a step toward political integration. A United States of Europe would constitute the solution to historic European conflicts.

The process toward integration was thrown into disarray, however, with the failure of the French National Assembly in 1954 to adopt a French-designed proposal for a European Defense Community (EDC). After the outbreak of the Korean War in 1950, the Americans had insisted on a greater European contribution to defense, which presupposed a German military role. By arming Germans within a common European army rather than rearming Germany, the European Defense Community was intended to palliate fears of German militarism and to move forward plans for European unification under French leadership.

This badly timed effort to make a virtue of necessity was fought by those in France who opposed German rearmament as well as by those who opposed abandoning French control over its national defense. After some confusion, the movement toward European integration was carried forward in the economic realm, with the signing of the Treaty of Rome in 1956 and the establishment of the European Community (EC).

De Gaulle, who opposed the Monnet vision of European supranational institutions, an Atlanticist Europe, and the EDC, returned to power in 1958, after the Fourth Republic collapsed as a result of the Algerian War. De Gaulle was no less concerned about Franco-German relations and European construction, but his model was different. He believed that the basic unit in politics is the nation; thus he refused to subjugate France to any supranational authority. "A so-called integrated Europe, which would have no policies, would come to depend on someone outside; and that someone [a clear reference to the United States] would have a policy of its own," he declared in a press conference on May 15, 1962.

Contrary to the fears of the Europeanists, he did not withdraw France from the EC, but the Luxembourg compromise of 1966 froze community development, preventing the emergence of a true common market and blocking the introduction of majority voting and other measures that would have increased supranational authority. De Gaulle also vetoed British membership, on the grounds that the British were not yet truly European and would be a Trojan horse for the Americans. Thus he helped to usher in the era of Eurosclerosis.

At the same time, de Gaulle opposed Anglo-American domination of the North Atlantic Treaty Organization (NATO). When his efforts to increase the French role were rejected, he withdrew France from the NATO integrated military command and evicted NATO forces from France; France, however, remained within the Alliance. To give substance to French claims to defense independence, de Gaulle developed a French nuclear force.

De Gaulle was not anti-European, but he wanted a Europe founded on states and led by France. His efforts to create greater European unity through a mechanism of state consultations, the so-called Christian Fouchet Plan of 1962, was rejected by Benelux leaders who thought it would undermine the EC.** So de Gaulle turned to Franco-German rapprochement. He wanted to establish a special Franco-German relationship that would enable France to lay claim to European leadership. Adenauer was attracted to aspects of the Gaullist program. In 1963, the Elysée Treaty was signed, providing for Franco-German military cooperation. The German Bundestag ratified the treaty but attached a preamble explaining that cooperation should take place within the framework of NATO. This essentially negated the treaty, which was not put into effect. If asked to choose between France and the United States, the Germans would not abandon the American nuclear umbrella. Nor, for that matter, were they prepared to abandon the

European ideal. The French veto of British membership in the Common Market, Adenauer's retirement and French withdrawal from NATO's integrated military command initiated a period of deteriorating Franco-German relations.

After de Gaulle's departure in 1969, the Gaullist legacy underwent a sea change. President Georges Pompidou ended the veto of British membership in the Common Market. Presidents Valéry Giscard d'Estaing and François Mitterrand, while continuing to affirm defense independence, moved closer to NATO and the United States. Rather than wanting to confront the United States, the French came to see the American nuclear umbrella as compatible with, even essential to, an independent French policy. At the same time, concerns about the danger of a German drift away from NATO toward neutralism mounted in the early 1980's. Germany had to be anchored firmly in NATO and Europe. In 1983, Mitterrand virtually campaigned against his brother Socialists in West Germany because they were soft on the Intermediate-Range Nuclear Forces (INF) treaty.

Both Giscard and Mitterrand seemed anxious to open up the prospects of closer Franco-German military cooperation; even the possibility that French nuclear sanctuary would be enlarged to include Germany was raised. In 1982, Mitterrand and German Chancellor Helmut Schmidt reactivated the Elysée Treaty; in 1984, a modified Western European Union (WEU) was put into effect. France wanted to reinforce the European pillar of the Alliance, perhaps through the WEU, but it certainly did not want the United States to leave Europe. France continued to balance its two historical fears of the postwar era: American hegemony and American abandonment. The latter was now feared more strongly.

By the 1980's, the French were also ready to join the Germans in bringing Eurosclerosis to an end. Resuming their historic role as the locomotive of the European Community, the two states formulated the Single European Act. The EC moved toward becoming a true common market. The French finally accepted qualified majority voting on many kinds of issues and supported monetary integration. Meanwhile, the British, under Prime Minister Margaret Thatcher, fought a rearguard action on behalf of the national state.

The sea change referred to above did not, however, constitute the equivalent of a reversal of fundamental Gaullist defense positions. France has not been willing to return to the NATO integrated military command. French defense continues to be national and independent. Enlarged sanctuary has not meant joint decision making; cooperation and consultation meant no more than that. However

---

**Benelux consists of Belgium, the Netherlands and Luxembourg.

much Mitterrand's inner heart may have remained Atlanticist—and there is no way to know—it was politically necessary that his defense policy remain more or less in the Gaullist tradition. It was the position that divided France least and that divided the ruling Parti Socialiste (PS) least as well.

The emergence of German unification in 1989 accelerated French efforts to moor Germany to Europe by deepening the EC. On April 19, 1990, Mitterrand and Kohl jointly advocated a European political and security union. The question remained: would the French desire to moor Germany in West Europe prove stronger than traditional French fears of supranational authority? It is increasingly obvious that Mitterrand has answered in the affirmative. In the spring and summer of 1990, Mitterrand and Kohl issued a series of joint declarations on matters ranging from Lithuania to aid to the Soviet Union, a demonstration of their commitment to work closely together. Even more striking, Mitterrand used the term "federalism" to describe his goals for Europe, and federalism is not a Gaullist word.

Much harder to assess is the question of French attitudes toward new security arrangements in Europe. The reason may be the delicacy of the situation. If the French had their own way, they would probably opt to maintain the status quo, that is to say, retaining a military not a political NATO, with a continued American military presence in Europe and an American nuclear umbrella. They would also move toward creating a European pillar in the Alliance.

But the French are doubtful that the Americans will remain in Europe and that in any case Germany will continue to accept their presence indefinitely. If that is true, then it is even more important to create a European security system including Germany before the Americans leave. But it is equally essential that the attempt to create such a system not prejudice the maintenance of an American presence.

At the same time, the ambiguity and precariousness of the present situation can be construed as justifying de Gaulle's belief that, in the final analysis, France needs to maintain its own defense capability. But will a purely French national defense prove ultimately compatible with a genuinely European security system? The French are also concerned about the possibility of NATO's abandonment of nuclear deterrence for conventional defense—after all, France's defense policy is fundamentally based on the concept of nuclear deterrence.

The French have been remarkably discreet in discussing future security options; the President's utterances have often been sibylline. This has led to conjecture that Mitterrand lacks the vision to create a model for European defense cooperation and a new NATO, that France is missing a historical opportunity to do what de Gaulle wanted, namely, to take the leadership of Europe. Yet Mitterrand's leadership on Community matters indicates that he has a vision for Europe that involves giving priority to Community questions (which is one reason he is so frustrated with Thatcher). He has always proceeded carefully and masterfully behind the scenes. Does he believe that the security issue is so complex that he wants to move slowly and privately, that the moment to raise new options has not yet arrived? In any case, Mitterrand has proved that France still remains capable of exerting leadership in the European arena.

PRESIDENTIAL AUTHORITY

Fortunately, France is in a relatively good position to cope with the new European situation. Today, there is a broad agreement among all major parties on matters of defense and foreign policy. Furthermore, the constitution of the Fifth Republic and the present political situation give the President almost complete authority in this domain.

This is a significant change. The curse of French political life since the Revolution of 1789 has been political instability. Instability contributed to France's decline as a great power in the nineteenth century. In the 1930's, polarization between the left and the right reached such extremes that agreement on the definition of national interest was lost, leading to the debacle of 1940. The Fourth Republic, created in 1946, also failed to create consensus and collapsed 12 years later. Even the Fifth Republic initially divided the French people, although in the long run its strong executive-dominated institutions proved well suited to contemporary needs.

In recent years, however, the ideological fervor and the insurmountable differences separating right and left seem to have come to an end. After decades in opposition, the Socialists finally came to power in 1981, determined to make a "break" with capitalism. This effort failed in 1981–1983; the Socialists then moved back toward the center. Faced with popular opposition, the right's efforts to roll back most of the Socialist legislation soon ground to a halt. Cohabitation between a Socialist President and a conservative parliamentary majority in 1986–1988 was decisive in producing an "end to ideology." The voters reelected Mitterrand because he appeared less divisive than his Gaullist rival, Prime Minister Jacques Chirac. Party politics did not come to an end, but simply became less ideological—more the struggle of "outs" versus "ins."

Michel Rocard, Prime Minister since 1988, has pursued a reassuring centrist policy line, which has been well received by the business community but has been regarded somewhat less favorably by the left of the Parti Socialiste, which feels that not enough is being done to promote the interests of the left's traditional electorate. But economic indicators show high growth, very low inflation, a strong franc and improvement in both employment and the trade deficit. France has become a basically modern society; it approaches 1992 with a growing sense of confidence.

With general agreement on the basics and with most of society more attuned to consumerism than ideology, the political debate between the center-right Union pour la Démocratie Française (UDF) and the Gaullist Rassemblement pour la République (RPR), on the one hand, and the Socialists on the other, has virtually dried up. So party politics has been mostly posturing in view of future elections (parliamentary by 1993, presidential in 1995) too far away to interest most of the French. Only party militants and political junkies concern themselves with the rivalries between the parties and the internal struggles within them. But the prospect that real ideological issues might no longer divide the French has been set back by the rise and persistent appeal of Jean-Marie Le Pen's Front National (FN).

There was nothing surprising in the rise of the Front National. Extremist right movements often go from latency to activity when the left comes to power or when economic conditions decline. Both occurred in 1981. The Front has the characteristics of the many antisystem protest movements of the far right that have cropped up over the past century. It is racist and xenophobic. Its nationalism is not based on an inclusive Jacobin ideal but on an exclusionary message of "France for the French."

Its values and leadership style are both authoritarian. It is antiparliamentary and thrives on political scandals, like the recent amnesty of those involved in dubious campaign financing. Although anti-Semitism may be counterproductive to a broad electoral appeal, it is intrinsic to the intellectual tradition of the extreme right and is embodied in the Front's leadership. Yet it was anti-Semitism rather than anti-Arab sentiment that provoked the strongest reaction against the Front at the time of the desecration of the historic Jewish cemetery of Carpentras on May 10, 1990.

The Front's basic message, however, is anti-immigrant, in particular, anti-Arab immigrant. Immigrants are blamed for France's current woes, especially for unemployment and crime. The Front takes advantage of the perception that Arab immigrants are not willing to assimilate. Each manifestation of Islamic fundamentalism abroad (the Rushdie affair, the victory of fundamentalists in the Algerian municipal elections) or Muslim ethnocentricity in France (the affair of the head scarves) is grist for its mill.[†]

The most striking thing about the FN is not that it came into existence, but that unlike so many movements of the extreme right, it has survived so long. Improved economic conditions have not undercut its popularity. How can we account for that? First, while all three major parties seem decidedly proestablishment and technocratic and the Parti Communiste Français (PCF) is moribund, only the Front National seems willing to take strong ideological positions.

Second, it has a receptive audience of "forgotten men" who have been or see themselves as victims of France's modernization, not just temporarily affected by the economic cycle. Many of these people live in proximity to Arab immigrants and compete with them for jobs, services and education. To the extent that Le Pen's clientele consider themselves victims of the "system," actions taken by that system to prosecute Le Pen seem like persecution.

Third, Le Pen is charismatic and entertaining, and most of his mainstream political opponents are not. Fourth, the Front National is much better organized than previous protest movements. Finally, the FN is the only party bluntly opposing Europe in the name of the traditional concept of the nation. Because the Front National's clientele is by its very nature circumscribed, the movement does not constitute a genuine threat to the political system. In fact, it is the exception that proves the rule of the end of ideology.

But if the FN does not constitute a threat to the political system, it does constitute a threat to the traditional right. The left, although it may well deplore the impact of the Front on the higher level of principle, has been its political beneficiary. The FN puts the RPR and the UDF on the horns of an intractable dilemma: if the right cooperates with the FN, it will be tarred with extremism; if it stalwartly opposes the FN, it loses votes on the right and perpetuates the FN's existence.

Such a situation divides each of the rightist parties over philosophy, strategy and tactics. It leads to a variety of prescriptions, including talk of unity or confederation. In June, 1990, the UDF and the RPR created a Union for France, which will pre-

----

[†]In 1989, Iranian Muslim fundamentalists issued a death threat against Salman Rushdie for publishing a novel they considered blasphemous; the same year, Muslim schoolgirls in France insisted on wearing head scarves in accordance with religious proscriptions, but in contravention of school dress codes.

sumably hold an indirect presidential primary in 1995. Since the parties of the right tend to be vehicles for the personal ambition of their leaders (who blame each other for losing the last two presidential elections), nothing is more divisive to the right than plans for unity. Whether current plans for right-wing unity survive the next parliamentary, let alone presidential, elections remains to be seen. In the meantime, thanks to the FN, the Socialists can govern with minority electoral support. The danger to the Socialists is that the FN will actually succeed in unifying the traditional right; the danger to the nation is that the FN will promote serious social and political instability and undermine the Republic. Neither seems very likely.

The FN has forced its agenda on the political world. The government has made it clear that France will not accept new immigrants (it has not been doing so for some time) and will act more stringently to keep illegal aliens out. It will also do more to promote the integration of existing immigrants into French society and to fight racism. Especially since the Carpentras incident, the government has tried to take the high road, holding an all-parties roundtable to hammer out a common policy. The opposition attended, but refused to cooperate further. Admittedly, taking the high road can be good politics.

If the Socialists can tar the right with being soft on radical right extremism, the traditional right, on the other hand, can hardly accuse the PS of being soft on communism, for French communism is in a state of putrescent decay. For those who still remember the French Communist party of the 1960's, stubbornly defying the capitalist world and being rewarded with nearly one-fourth of the votes for doing so, it it hard to understand how dramatically the PCF decomposed.

The decline of its major constituencies — especially the industrial working class — was certainly a factor. But even more important was the disintegration of the myth that the PCF was the party of the revolution (before the very word "revolution" lost its luster). The party leadership failed to follow the Italian Communist party (PCI) in loyally adopting Eurocommunism; it maintained Stalinist controls against an increasingly restive membership.

The decline of its mystique as a revolutionary party began in 1968, when it clearly worked to sabotage the May revolution. In 1978, it betrayed the left's hope for a Socialist-Communist electoral victory. It would have done likewise in 1981, but its tepid endorsement of Mitterrand on the second ballot did not deter Communist voters from rallying to Mitterrand. By preaching the solidarity of the left, Mitterrand walked off with a large part of the Communist electorate and held on to this sector. Since that time, the PCF has paid for secretary general Georges Marchais's tortuous tactics, but Marchais continues to hold the tiller of this modern-day raft of the Medusa.

With the decline of the PCF, the PS has been liberated from a half-century of Communist demagoguery. It has the opportunity to become the governing party of France. Its main problem is that it lacks a distinctive ideology and program, because much of its historic orientation was swept away after the failure of the Socialist programs of 1981–1983. It has not been exempt from the in-fighting that has plagued the right. The party congress at Rennes in March, 1990, saw, not the traditional confrontation of ideas and ideologies, but a naked and premature struggle for control over the party organization by former Prime Minister Laurent Fabius and Minister of Education Lionel Jospin, who were planning the next presidential elections.

The spectacle was embarrassing to the party and damaging to the protagonists; its real beneficiaries may have been Prime Minister Rocard and Jacques Delors, president of the European Commission, who stayed conspicuously out of the fray. Interestingly enough, a recent poll of business executives shows Delors and Rocard to be their preferred Socialist presidential candidates in 1993, with the liberal mayor of Lyons, Michel Noir, at the top of the list on the right.

In a recent article, sociologist Alain Touraine argued persuasively that the old left-right cleavages in French politics based on socioeconomic and class differences are being replaced by a new distinction between those struggling to defend the national ideal and the nation-state, and those who want France to adapt to a new European and international reality, in which the nation-state will be less important. The French left and right are both divided on this question. Touraine concludes:

> It seems logical that one day or another the Socialists and liberals, who both belong to the party of movement, will join together, while a great party of the right will be formed, organized around the defense of national identity and capable of absorbing most of the electorate of the National Front.[1]

As France becomes part of a new European reality and as a new generation takes over French political life, this vision becomes increasingly persuasive.

[1]Alain Touraine, "Identité, la question nationale et la politique française," *Le Monde*, March 13, 1990.

France Questions Its Identity As It Sinks Into 'Le Malaise'

ALAN RIDING
Special to The New York Times

PARIS — As if stubbornly ignoring good reasons to feel cheered by the end of the cold war, the rapid integration of Europe and the fruits of recent economic growth, France today seems consumed by gloom, unsure where it is heading or even where it wants to go.

The popular diagnosis is "le malaise français," a sort of national liverache that somehow explains everything from strikes by judges and protests by high school students to provincial irritation with Parisian haughtiness and growing intolerance of nonwhite immigration.

Yet the problem seems to run deeper, with a country that was long guided by such reassuring concepts as "grand design" and "national destiny" suddenly thrown off course by the unexpected nature and pace of change at home and abroad over the last 18 months.

In the eyes of many Frenchmen, the leading pillars of traditional French society appear to be threatened — the country's status in the world, the strong national identity of its citizens, the paternalism of a highly centralized state and the solidly bourgeois quality of daily life.

Such is the evidence of public anxiety that the Government's own Planning Secretariat recently published a 265-page study of what it called "the future of the French identity," an analysis of why the French, from individuals to society as a whole, now view tomorrow with fear.

"We have the impression that many Frenchmen have doubts about the capacity of their country to meet successfully the dangers, opportunities and uncertainties which the future holds," the study, which was prepared by a group of prominent intellectuals, noted.

The "malaise" theme became the talk of France in early December when Michel Noir, the ambitious young mayor of Lyons, resigned noisily from the neo-Gaullist Rally for the Republic party, arguing that the country was tired of the parties and politicians that have long been at the helm here.

The French Sickness

"France is sick," Mr. Noir said, "sick of seeing politicians of all colors dedicated to their favorite game of internecine battles for power, sick of crises in justice, education, safety and health, sick that France no longer holds its historic role on the international stage."

A few days later, 11 socialist deputies attributed France's troubles to its "progressive Americanization," which they described as growing individualism, the impoverishment of the state, the omnipotence of television, untempered consumer spending and the emerging power of lobbies.

Many conservatives, of course, are quick to blame President François Mitterrand, now in his 10th year in office, for adopting a de Gaulle-like aloofness and losing touch with the population. Yet others, like Mr. Noir, argue that the opposition, including the Rally for the Republic, has done no better in offering an alternative vision.

With their image muddied by a series of corruption scandals, politi-

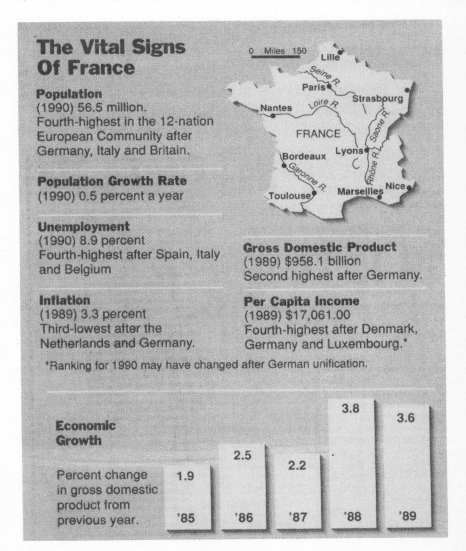

The Vital Signs Of France

Population
(1990) 56.5 million.
Fourth-highest in the 12-nation European Community after Germany, Italy and Britain.

Population Growth Rate
(1990) 0.5 percent a year

Unemployment
(1990) 8.9 percent
Fourth-highest after Spain, Italy and Belgium

Inflation
(1989) 3.3 percent
Third-lowest after the Netherlands and Germany.

Gross Domestic Product
(1989) $958.1 billion
Second highest after Germany.

Per Capita Income
(1989) $17,061.00
Fourth-highest after Denmark, Germany and Luxembourg.*

*Ranking for 1990 may have changed after German unification.

0   Miles   150

Lille
Seine R.
Paris
Strasbourg
Nantes
Loire R.
FRANCE
Saône R.
Bordeaux
Lyons
Rhône R.
Garonne R.
Nice
Toulouse
Marseilles

Economic Growth

Percent change in gross domestic product from previous year.

'85	'86	'87	'88	'89
1.9	2.5	2.2	3.8	3.6

cians as a whole now seem to be deeply distrusted. "For the first time, when people have recently asked me my profession, I have not dared to reply, deputy," said François Hollande, a Socialist member of the National Assembly.

Three Dominant Politicians

The perception of an unchanging political scene is reinforced by the fact that the same three men have dominated the political stage for more than 15 years — and that all three have worked assiduously to insure that no natural successor to their share of power emerges.

Mr. Mitterrand was the long-time leader of the Socialist Party before he became President in 1981; Valéry Giscard d'Estaing was his predecessor as President and now heads the Union for French Democracy; and Jacques Chirac, a former Prime Minister and current mayor of Paris, has led the Rally for the Republic since its foundation in 1974.

A fourth figure, the Communist leader, Georges Marchais, has seen support for his party evaporate. And with all traditional parties being torn apart from infighting, the principal beneficiary has been Jean-Marie Le Pen, whose far-right National Front presents itself as the last refuge of true patriots.

The wide gap between the political class and the population has been well illustrated over the last year by their contrasting reactions to German unification, a prospect that caused alarm among top echelons of the Government and opposition and one that was welcomed as natural by most Frenchmen.

Threat of Germany

For the country's leadership, a powerful united Germany was a threat to France's privileged position in Europe, a position that had enabled it to play a role of political leadership within the 12-nation European Community as well as to underline its independence from Washington.

But with Germany suddenly the center of power in a new undivided Europe, France visibly shrank in importance. In response, the Mitterrand Administration decided to gamble on speeding up the economic and political integration of the European Community as a counterweight to German might.

While eager to maintain what is known here as the Paris-Bonn axis, Mr. Mitterrand even told Chancellor Helmut Kohl during a visit to Munich in September that in the new Europe "there will be no lack of conflicts, rivalries and misunderstandings." He then added acidly, "I don't know why I speak in the future tense."

In two other regions, the influence of France also appears to be on the wane.

Its traditional role as a power-broker in the Middle East was badly hurt when its closest regional ally, Iraq, invaded Kuwait on Aug. 2, while its early moves to try to settle the Persian Gulf crisis on its own angered its Western allies.

Former African Colonies

And in Africa, where France has long sustained one-party rule in many of its former colonies, it is now bending to international pressure to allow democracy to flower. In early December, for example, French troops stationed in Chad stood by as rebels ousted President Hissen Habré, who in the past had often been saved by France.

But while politicians struggle to find a new role for France in Europe and beyond, experiencing a crisis of national identity in the broadest sense of the phrase, ordinary citizens seem concerned with a different kind of identity crisis, one that relates much more to the quality of their lives.

In part, this is a question of economics. While the economy has grown steadily over the last three years, the visible prosperity of Paris and other large cities, including Lyons, does not accurately mirror the state of most ordinary households and urban areas.

Yet the Government was caught off guard in November when protests over a rape at a high school in a Paris suburb suddenly escalated into a huge nationwide protest movement over insufficient teachers and overcrowded classrooms at many of France's high schools.

Anger and Vandalism

When one huge march in Paris was disrupted by unemployed youths from depressed outlying districts of the capital, who set about looting stores, burning cars and attacking police, France as a whole was then shocked by the explosion of anger and vandalism.

The Government promptly pledged $1 billion more to rescue the high school system. In early December, it began a new program to improve living conditions in 400 urban communities where homelessness, violence and drug abuse are on the rise.

In many of these communities, though, an important part of the population is made up of immigrants from Algeria, Morocco, Tunisia and other parts of Africa. And even when parents are employed, their French-born children are increasingly leaving school without much hope of a job.

With simmering xenophobia and occasional incidents of racist violence already reflecting France's own difficulties in coexisting with a growing non-white population, the mounting frustration of children of immigrants is now adding a dangerous new element of tension to urban life.

"One has the impression that some-

thing is breaking apart, that society is decomposing and no one has caught onto its decomposition," said Pierre-André Wiltzer, an opposition deputy.

The new debate about France's future, though, implies growing awareness that something must be done. In a article entitled, "The Moral Disintegration of French Society," Maurice Allais, a prominent economist, wrote that France still did not understand "the economic and ethical conditions necessary to sustain a humanistic and liberal society."

For other sociologists, the current "malaise" reflects the crisis of a highly centralized state that for generations concentrated power and decision-making in relatively few hands and that today is being increasingly challenged by demands for greater grassroots democracy.

Mood of Pessimism

For example, even the National Assembly complains that it is largely impotent because of the enormous power given to the Presidency under the Gaullist constitution of the Fifth Republic. "Parliament exercises no control over the Executive," Jean-Pierre Balligand, a socialist deputy, said.

As internal and external change shakes France, then, the distance between state and society seems to be growing. The current mood of pessimism mirrors "a disarray of the national identity at the same time as a loss of legitimacy of a state which traditionally had responsibility for mobilizing national energies," the Planning Secretariat's study said.

Thus, while politicians offer to bring change through elections, the population seems less convinced. Voters must wait until 1993 for the next parliamentary elections and until 1995 for a chance to pick Mr. Mitterrand's successor. Even then, they will probably face familiar choices.

Mr. Le Pen plans to carry the ultra-nationalist flag, Mr. Giscard d'Estaing and Mr. Chirac are already preparing new bids for the Presidency, Mr. Noir may run as an independent candidate and Michel Rocard, currently Mr. Mitterrand's Prime Minister, is front-runner to become the socialist nominee in 1995. Another household name, Jacques Delors, currently President of the European Community's executive commission, may also join the race.

Yet if anything France today appears to be less disillusioned with the Government as such than it is with the shortcomings of the state as a whole.

"The postwar society is falling apart," Jean-Christophe Cambadelis, a socialist deputy, argued, echoing the sentiments of many Frenchmen. "All the institutions built over the past 40 years are in crisis and are therefore incapable of responding."

Quiet revolt in the corridors of power

The civil service is losing out as more of France's elite turn to industry, writes **William Dawkins**

A quiet but revealing change is taking place among the discreet networks of highly educated civil servants and businessmen who run the French economy.

A largely male elite, dominated by Parisians with a background in public administration, is becoming more open and attuned to entrepreneurial virtues, as the state loses some of its considerable grip on the business world. It provides a rare insight into how the establishment is yielding to the influence of free market thinking and the internationalisation of business. The effect has been to make the French business sector more flexible, at the expense of some traditional social and intellectual values.

"There was a time when senior civil servants could guarantee they would take the place of honour at the right of the hostess at dinner. Now they will have to compete against someone like Mr Bernard Tapie," jokes Mr Michel de Rosen, a typical example of the new generation of the French elite.

Mr de Rosen began a brilliant public service career in the fast stream at the Treasury, moving on to become a diplomat in Washington, before becoming chief adviser to a former French industry minister. He then hopped back into business and is now running the FFr16bn turnover fibres division of Rhône-Poulenc, the state-owned chemicals giant, at the age of only 39.

The difference is that he started all this by first going to business school to train as a manager, a move seen only recently as an eccentric move for an aspiring star. "Some members of my family thought I was sick," he says.

It used to be that the cream of France's intelligentsia followed careers in the civil service, capped by a top job in state-owned industry in their 40s or 50s. But now they are more likely to depart in their 30s or even straight after graduation at one of the prestigious public administration colleges through which every self-respecting high flyer must pass.

Moreover, they are just as likely to go to the private sector as into state industry. Business schools all over France are reporting a huge increase in attendances. Groups as diverse as Bouygues in construction, Rossignol in skis and Peat Marwick in accountancy now boast young civil service stars in their senior ranks.

"I am pretty certain that out of all my private staff, only one will be left in public administration in five years," says Mr Roger Fauroux, industry minister and another classic product of the establishment. "It's not only a question of salary, for they have always been able to get more in the private sector. It is that nowadays there is more prestige working for a company. It is a reflection of our growing economic liberalism . . . business is chic."

The traditional networks are based on contacts built at one of the better known of the more than 300 *grandes écoles*, state-sponsored colleges which prepare university graduates for professional life, usually in the civil service. Ecole Nationale d'Administration (Ena), one of the most respected of them – including among its 4,000 or so alumni three prime ministers and most of France's brightest industry chiefs – is uneasy at the number of its alumni who leave for private sector jobs early in their civil service careers. "A young person doesn't feel he is betraying the public interest by going into the private sector. He might have done a few years ago," mourns Mr René Lenoir, director of Ena.

Founded after the Second World War to groom bright youngsters to rebuild a shattered public administration, Ena takes less than 100 graduates per year, for which it usually receives at least 10 times as many applications.

Enarques – Ena graduates – must promise to work in the civil service for at least 10 years. If they leave early, as an increasing number do, they are fined. Few pay the penalty and the chances are that their prospective employers are only too happy to pay.

Mr Lenoir is pressing for an end to the current system under which Enarques are guaranteed their former public service jobs should they wish to return. "I am all for the free circulation of our elite, but I am against letting them go without risk," he says.

The top Enarques feed into one of the top *"grands corps"* of public administration – the elite professional training colleges. The most highly regarded of these is the inspectorate of finances, the fast track to the summit in the treasury, open to only a handful of pupils each year. This qualification – held by Mr de Rosen – identifies the holder as one of the couple of dozen or so brightest people of his generation.

An even more venerable but larger taking-off point for high flyers is the Ecole Polytechnique, a science college used by Napoleon to train engineers for his army. Most people call it X, pronounced eeks. There are around 350 'X' graduates a year, the top handful of which move on to one of the top four industrial *corps*. Depending on the *corps* they choose, alumni might identify themselves as X-Ponts or X-Mines – jargon essential to understanding the flight path of a French business star.

Enarques and Polytechniciens are often hunted by companies just as much for the content of their address books as for their formidable brains. For they have the unspoken right to contact almost any fellow alumnus, though this is used with discretion.

As a mark of how the public administration's senior men dominate business, only two of France's top 25 companies have been run consistently by career managers over the past 20 years, according to a recent survey carried out for the financial newspaper Les Echos. In some cases specific jobs are even reserved for certain *corps*, a far more structured old boy network than its Oxbridge counterpart in the UK, or Harvard and Yale in the US.

The top people at Electricité de France, the state power utility, and at Seita, the state tobacco group, for example, have traditionally come from the Ecole Polytechnique. The chairmanship of Elf Aquitaine, the state-controlled oil group was reserved for X-Mines until recently, when the government raised eyebrows by appointing a graduate of the Grenoble National Polytechnic Institute, Mr Loïk Le Floch-Prigent — though this socialist does have a public service background as a former chief adviser at the ministry of industry.

These networks would not operate so efficiently without the existence of several string-pulling godfather figures, like Mr Roger Martin (X-Mines), a former chairman of Saint-Gobain, the privatised glass and packaging group. During his long period in the Saint-Gobain throne, he hired a brilliant youngster every three or four years, to be groomed for a top job in state-owned industry.

The best known Martin protégés include Mr Fauroux himself (another former chairman of Saint-Gobain) Mr Alain Gomez, the head of the Thomson state-controlled defence and consumer electronic group; Mr Francis Mer, head of the Usinor Sacilor state-owned steelmaker and Mr Jean-Louis Beffa, current head of Saint-Gobain.

Mr Ambroise Roux is another industrial godfather to be reckoned with. As head of the powerful but almost invisible Association Française des Entreprises Privées, he is cred-ited with exercising a discreet steering influence on the growth of economic liberalism in the socialist government.

Mr Roux's star is on the wane since his recent retirement from the chairmanship of Générale Occidentale, the publishing group. His protégés include Mr Pierre Suard (like Roux, an X-Ponts), chairman of CGE, the telecommunications and engineering group and Mr Alain Minc — a former Saint-Gobain finance director — who now runs Cerus, Mr Carlo De Benedetti's French holding group.

In the financial world, probably the most distinguished godfather is Mr Antoine Bernheim, senior partner of Lazard Frères, the investment bank. Some of France's best known new entrepreneurs depend on Lazard's discerning support, like Bernard Arnault, the former Polytechnique student who last spring won a bitterly contested battle for control of LVMH, the champagne-to-handbags luxury products group, or like Vincent Bolloré, the brilliant young founder of the industrial group which bears his name.

Just how far the change has gone is open to debate. The French establishment is still seen by some people as too rigid, still too much in the grip of the *grands corps*.

"This so-called French elite creates a bottleneck," says Rhône-Poulenc's Mr de Rosen. "Of course it's a good thing that we all understand each other very clearly, but the problem is that we don't have enough self-made men. I am sure there are thousands of people with talent who don't get near the top because they didn't have the opportunity to come through the top educational and social system." Even so, he and others agree that the road to the top in France is becoming just a little more open.

The Real Japan

James Fallows

The Enigma of Japanese Power:
People and Politics in.a Stateless Nation
by Karel van Wolferen.
Knopf, 496 pp., $24.95

Trading Places: How We
Allowed Japan to Take the Lead
by Clyde V. Prestowitz, Jr.
Basic Books, 365 pp., $19.95

Karel van Wolferen's *The Enigma of Japanese Power* is the subject of much controversy and has been generally vilified in Japan, even though it has not been officially published there, is written in a language most Japanese cannot read, and does much to explain the roots of the political crisis that has preoccupied Japan for most of the last year. The book would be important for non-Japanese readers even if it had evoked no reaction whatever from the Japanese. *The Enigma of Japanese Power* will, I think, stand with other classic attempts by foreigners to interpret Japanese society and institutions, including Ruth Benedict's *The Chrysanthemum and the Sword* and Chalmers Johnson's *MITI and the Japanese Miracle*. Like those books, this one will change the course of subsequent debate about Japan; it will be very hard for anyone to discuss the Japanese political system without responding to Van Wolferen's argument. The intensity of the Japanese reaction against the book underscores the significance of the messages Van Wolferen is trying to convey.

The furor began three years ago, when "The Japan Problem," a précis of some of the arguments Van Wolferen has developed in his book, was published in *Foreign Affairs*. The article advanced a view that the subsequent twists of Japanese politics would seem to have borne out: that there is not a clear center of power in the Japanese government, but that the "buck" is circulating constantly and does not stop on anyone's desk. The Japanese government is extremely influential, Van Wolferen said, if one considers the cumulative effects of its various parts, but it is not centrally directed or controlled. A variety of Balkanized ministries exercise very strong supervision of trade policy, the schools, public works, prisons, banks, the medical and legal systems, et cetera, but no one stands above the separate organizations, with the authority or power to steer the entire system in a new direction. The best parallel in the American government would be the Pentagon, with its strong but very independent bureaucracies (the ship-building faction of the navy, the long-range bombing faction of the air force, the research-and-development faction, and so on) that fiercely resist the attempts of any president or defense secretary to coordinate them.

Van Wolferen was saying, in short, that Japan may seem structurally and legally a typical liberal democracy, but in practice its politics work differently from those of most other democratic states. One basic difference is that Japan's is effectively a one-party system. Since 1955, when the ruling LDP was formed, the party has constantly dominated the Diet and therefore the prime minister's office and the bureaucracy. (In English it is more appropriate to use the neutral acronym LDP than the full name "Liberal Democratic Party," which is the direct translation of the Japanese name, *Jiyuminshuto*. The *Jiminto*, as it is colloquially known, was created from the merger of Japan's main conservative parties, and the role it plays is exactly the opposite of what Americans think when they hear the words "Liberal Democratic.")

The peculiarities of Japan's electoral system strengthen the LDP's hold and illustrate Van Wolferen's point about the differences between Japan's political behavior and that of other advanced democracies. Japan's version of "one man, one vote" is "one man, three votes"—Supreme Court decisions permit a three-to-one disparity between the most and least populated Diet districts and in reality the disparity is now almost five to one. This gives farmers a hugely disproportionate role in Japanese politics and is much of the reason why Japan's urban consumers and industrial workers have had so little voice in the nation's policy.

The farmers and the LDP are locked together in a kind of "agricultural-electoral complex" that is at least as strong as the "military-industrial complex" is in the United States and is probably more destructive to the nation's overall welfare. For example, the Diet, under the control of the LDP, refuses to let imported rice into the country, even though Japanese rice, grown on tiny plots, costs 600 to 800 percent as much as rice from the vast flatlands of Thailand, Australia, California, or Arkansas. The rice-import ban and other farm quotas force Japanese consumers to pay 30 percent of their income for food, while Americans pay about 15 percent, and the policy indirectly compels them to live in tiny, expensive quarters, since about half of Japan's scarce nonmountainous land is used for these grossly inefficient farms. The farmers, nonetheless, are pleased and grateful, and they recirculate some of their profits into substantial contributions to the LDP.

According to an opinion poll conducted last December by the prime minister's office, only one quarter of the Japanese public feels that government policy reflects the best interests of the public; two thirds feel that, on the contrary, the Japanese government acts against the "popular will." Since "government policy" really means LDP policy, this would seem to be a devastating indictment of the ruling party, and because of year-long bribery scandals, the LDP will probably suffer significant losses in the elections from the Upper House of the Diet in July. But almost no one expects the LDP to lose its control of the government.

A further peculiarity, amplifying Van Wolferen's themes, is that even though the LDP dominates Japanese policy, policy and issues play almost no part in the workings of the LDP. Under the Japanese "multimember district" system, individual LDP members have to run against each other in the same district, a problem that US congressmen face only when redistricting pits two incumbents against each other. Most election campaigns turn into sheer name-recognition contests—more than half the members of the Diet are the sons of former Diet members, riding in on their fathers' established names. Within the Diet, LDP politicians ally themselves with *habatsu*, or "factions" that compete for power the way Republicans and Democrats do in the United States. But while the difference between Democratic and Republican policies sometimes seems slim, there are no differences over policy whatever between the LDP factions. The factions are known by the name of the strong-man who leads them (the Takeshita faction, the Nakasone faction, and so on) and they compete only for political "market share," much as Toshiba does against the electronics conglomerate NEC. In fact, the real opposition party in Japanese politics is the United States. The LDP prides itself on maintaining a smooth relationship with the Americans, but constant pressure from American politicians and trade negotiators serves the function that an opposition party does in other countries, that of pushing policy in a different direction. There is very little push from within.

At about the time Van Wolferen's *Foreign Affairs* article was published, Yasuhiro Nakasone was going into eclipse, in a way that conformed to Van Wolferen's thesis. Nakasone seemed the exception to the general rule of Japanese politics that no one leader becomes dominant: he was a prime minister who tried to behave like a president rather than a committee chairman, and to impose his views on the government. One of Nakasone's goals was to increase Japan's military spending and generally have Japan viewed as a mature world power. Another was to reduce the trade surplus that is America's chronic grievance

against Japan. His military plan succeeded: he pushed military spending above the informal limit of 1 percent of Japan's GNP without making China, Korea, and the Philippines worry about being invaded again. But he failed in his attempt to redefine the prime minister's job. Nakasone's attempts to change Japan's policy seemed too pushy to the Japanese bureaucracy—and too feeble to other world leaders, who doubted Japan's ability to carry out commitments Nakasone had made.

The most powerful illustration was the Maekawa Commission Report, a major study by a panel appointed by Nakasone. This report, which was issued just before the Tokyo Economic Summit meeting in 1986, said that the time had come to transform Japan from an export machine, with long working hours and high prices, into a more relaxed, balanced state with more emphasis on imports. Nakasone put his authority behind the report and offered it to other leaders at the summit as an indication that Japan's trade policy was about to change. But all the entrenched power of the Japanese bureaucracy was against him, and by the time he left office the Maekawa recommendations were moribund. The episode fit the pattern Van Wolferen described:

> If Japan seems to be in the world but not of it, this is because its prime minister and other power-holders are incapable of delivering on political promises they may make concerning commercial or other matters requiring important adjustments [in .domestic power arrangements]. The field of domestic power normally leaves no room for an accommodation to foreign wishes or demands.

What has happened since Nakasone left office even more vividly illustrates Van Wolferen's themes. Nakasone's successor, the luckless Noboru Takeshita, came to office through a whimsical, nondemocratic process whose closest US counterpart is the way an American presidential candidate chooses his vice-presidential running mate. Through the summer of 1987, Nakasone showily deliberated about the personal merits of the "new leaders," three veteran politicians in their sixties who had waited for their turn in line. He settled on Takeshita as the country's next prime minister, largely because of Takeshita's reputation as a backstage deal-maker and a proven money-raiser.

In office, Takeshita used his skills to push through two highly unpopular measures, a new consumption tax and an increase in beef and citrus imports from the United States. But he spent the last year watching his cabinet fall apart because of the complex "Recruit Cosmos" scandal. One ambitious parvenu businessman, Hiromasa Ezoe, was shown to have illegally given money and shares in his Recruit company to virtually every prominent figure in the LDP, and leaders of most of the non-Communist opposition parties as well. In some cases the donations were bribes for specific favors from the government; in other cases, Ezoe seemed mainly to be investing in future good will. Ezoe was arrested early this year, and by this spring forty-two politicians or bureaucrats had resigned, fourteen had been arrested, and Takeshita himself had had to admit that Recruit had secretly contributed hundreds of thousands of dollars to his political campaigns.

Early in April, opinion polls showed that approval of Takeshita's government had sunk to a ludicrously low 3.9 percent, or one eighth as much support as Richard Nixon had on the day that he resigned. A week after this poll was published, Takeshita announced that he too would resign—but two months later, he was still in office, mainly because the LDP could not find any plausible replacement who was not also tainted by Recruit. The most prominent politician of the LDP who was not implicated in the scandal, the seventy-five-year-old Masayoshi Itoh, refused to take the job unless there were also sweeping reforms in the political fund-raising system typified by the secret payoffs of the Recruit company. "He didn't hear a word I said," Itoh was quoted as saying after a meeting with Takeshita in which he discussed political reforms. "I could just as well have been a clown."

Early in June, Takeshita and a handful of party elders startled the nation by presenting Sosuke Uno as the LDP's savior. Uno is reputedly an intelligent if prickly man, who was serving at the time of his elevation as Takeshita's foreign minister—but the widespread joke was that the only reason he'd escaped the Recruit scandal is that no one considered him important enough to bribe. (Joking became even more widespread a few days later, when a semirespectable weekly magazine carried a geisha's claims that Uno had paid her $25,000 for sexual favors over a several-month period three and a half years ago. As with Nakasone's "minority groups have low IQs" comment three years ago, the Japanese newspapers did not mention the story until an American newspaper, in this case *The Washington Post*, publicized it in the US. Uno now says it is a "private matter" not fit for public comment.) About the time Uno was selected, Nakasone announced that he would "resign" his connection with the LDP (though he would keep his seat in the Diet), Uno's approval rating "soared" to 32 percent, and the public prosecutor's office conveniently declared the Recruit case closed.

This brings us back to Karel van Wolferen, who might have predicted that the scandal would have ended with something less than a full, cleansing investigation of the Recruit case or the "money-politics" system it exemplified. No one part of Japan's recent political saga is unique to Japan. Uno will probably be a mere caretaker leader, but the US has had caretakers too, Gerald Ford, for example. Some American presidents have had trouble carrying out their international commitments, as Jimmy Carter demonstrated with the SALT treaty and Woodrow Wilson long before him with the League of Nations. But the combination of recent traits in Japanese politics is unusual: the near-total unimportance of public opinion, the sequence of prime ministers personally choosing their successors, the disgrace of virtually all prominent politicians in one big scandal, the intervention of one of the ministries to stop the scandal from going further. The combination is also consistent with what Van Wolferen called the "Japan problem."

But when his original article was read in Japan, Van Wolferen became the object of bitter attack—one prominent magazine ran an issue containing half a dozen articles taking him to task. With the publication of Van Wolferen's book, the criticism has become even more personal. In Japanese newspapers, his book is routinely cited as a harbinger of a new, inexplicably hostile attitude to Japan in the US. In my own talks with Japanese journalists, government officials, and businessmen, I've never heard a kind word for Van Wolferen and rarely heard any serious discussion of his argument. Instead I've heard countless times that Van Wolferen, a Dutchman who has lived in Japan for twenty-five years, must simply detest the country and its culture, that his animus against Japan must be

racially biased. (Many Japanese intellectuals and officials instinctively see criticism of the Japanese political/economic system as a challenge to the achievements, dignity, and equality of the Japanese "race." Such sensitivity may be understandable, in view of the history of anti-Asian prejudice in the US and Europe, but it is a real barrier to serious discussion of Japan's economic policies.)

Why has one relatively complicated book made so many people so mad? Part of the explanation is no doubt a spillover from other frustrations Japan is encountering just now. In the good old days of the postwar economic miracle, Japan could concentrate on smooth relations with the US and otherwise forget about foreign policy. Now it is besieged by countries that want more Japanese aid, want more—or less—Japanese investment, and in general are unhappy about how Japan is using its wealth. Also, Van Wolferen's rhetorical style is exactly the opposite from the one most Japanese intellectuals prefer. Van Wolferen likes to push every argument to its logical extreme and state everything as bluntly as possible. This makes his book lively to read but violates the Japanese tradition of half-specific, half-vague discourse. "Japanese are treated by their school system and their superiors in the way a landscape gardener treats a hedge; protruding parts of the personality are regularly snipped off," Van Wolferen says. Many Japanese have used this line to illustrate what they see as a contemptuous tone. But it also demonstrates the power, the directness and clarity of the book—and no one who has seen the Japanese schools or corporate-training programs can argue that what he says is wrong.

Because Van Wolferen pushes every point to its limit, inevitably in a few cases he overstates. For instance, I think Japan is not as helplessly dependent on American good will for its security as Van Wolferen says it is. (The US military is more visibly fearful about losing its bases in Japan than most Japanese are about losing US military protection.) Also, Van Wolferen typically contrasts troublesome Japanese practices with an idealized description of how things are done in "the West," where Van Wolferen, after all, has not actually lived for many years. But the book's excesses are only occasional, and the heart of Van Wolferen's argument is strongly argued, original, and important.

The power and originality of his argument are, finally, the real reasons for Japanese outrage at Van Wolferen's book. *The Enigma of Japanese Power* presents a theory of the "differentness" of Japan that is completely at odds with the version that most Japanese believe in, and that Japanese spokesmen have propagated to outsiders. The notion that Japan is different is the starting point for almost every discussion of Japan's place in the world. The explanations of its differentness, even uniqueness, take many forms. Japan is different because it is better run than other societies (universal literacy, scant crime); because it is so fragile and vulnerable (no natural resources, constant threat of earthquakes); because of its tradition of harmony and consensus; because it has uniquely suffered the atomic bomb. The cartoon version of this concept shows up in *nihonjinron*, the "study of Japaneseness," which includes the familiar assertions by Japanese writers that Japanese intestines, brains, snow, and soil are different from those found elsewhere in the world.

Some theories work along the margins between science and crackpottery. For instance, a Japanese government researcher recently wrote that Japanese/Shinto traditions of purity gave Japan a crucial edge in the semiconductor business. (The explanation was that Japan's instinct for purity allowed factories to reduce ambient dust to levels unattainable in the West; in a cleaner environment the percentage of perfect chips was higher.)

Van Wolferen says that Japan is, indeed, different from other advanced societies, but not for biological or mystical or hazily traditional reasons. The crucial difference, he says, lies in the intellectual and practical foundation of Japan's political system, which produces behavior and values unlike those in most of the West. The political phenomenon Van Wolferen is discussing is comparable to the differentness in Japan's economic goals that Clyde Prestowitz analyzed in his carefully reasoned book *Trading Places*, which was published last year.

Americans often complain that Japan's trading practices are "unfair," Prestowitz said, but such objections completely miss the point. To call Japanese practices "unfair," as the US government did last month under the "Super 301" trade law, assumes that Japan's goals are the same as America's and that Japan is taking shortcuts to reach them. In fact, Prestowitz said, Japan's trade and economic policies represent consistent and impeccably "fair" efforts to reach an entirely different set of goals. The United States mainly wanted to improve the individual consumer's standard of living, and therefore it usually permitted imports unless some powerful lobby, such as the beet-sugar growers, stood in the way. Japan mainly wanted to develop industries within its own territory, and therefore it usually resisted imports of high-value products it could make on its own.

The significant fact about Japan's trade patterns is not that it exports so much—West Germany and many other countries export proportionately more—but that it imports so few manufactured goods. In 1986 Germany imported 37 percent of all the manufactured goods it consumed; Japan, 4.4 percent. As Chalmers Johnson of the University of California has recently pointed out, "Japan's imports, particularly of manufactured goods, are between 25 and 45 percent below what would be expected of a country with Japan's economic attributes."[1] The "Four Tigers"—South Korea, Taiwan, Hong Kong, and Singapore—have a combined gross national product only one eighth as large as Japan's, but their combined imports are greater.

Most developed economies have a very high "specialization ratio"—an economic term of art which means that countries both import and export within the same product category. Automobiles, for instance, are a leading export and a leading import for Germany. The United States exports a tremendous amount of food but imports even more. Japan is the only developed country with a very low "specialization ratio."[2] If it can make a certain item for itself, it generally does not buy from abroad.

Americans are often frustrated in their trade negotiations with Japan, Prestowitz writes, because they fail to imagine how different Japan's goals might be from their own. American politicians and negotiators continually say that Japan must "open" its markets, "but the

[1] From "The Problem of Japan in an Era of Structural Change," a speech at the International House of Japan (June 2, 1989).

[2] "Analysis of the US-Japan Trade Problem," Report of the Advisory Committee for Trade Policy and Negotiations, report to Carla Hills, US Trade Representative (February 1989).

Japanese had no conception of what the Americans meant by *open*." In the American economic and political system, "openness" meant that anything not specifically forbidden should be permitted; in the Japanese regulatory scheme, "opening" the market meant allowing foreign competitors in one by one. Rather than whine about Japan's failure to pursue the same goals in the same way that America does, Prestowitz argues, Americans should accept Japan for what it is and adjust their policies so as to coexist with it.

In the case of Japan's political system, Van Wolferen says that the difference lies in the essential source of political legitimacy. Western politics, in the slightly idealized version that Van Wolferen outlines, turns on a constant tension between the power of the state and the loyalties that reach beyond the state—to religious values, to ideas of the universal rights of man. In Japan, he says, the forces that offset the power of the state are extremely weak. This, he says, is

> the characteristic that, in the final analysis, is the most crucial factor determining Japan's socio-political reality, a factor bred into Japanese intellectual life over centuries of political suppression. It is the near absence of any idea that there can be truths, rules, principles or morals that always apply, no matter what the circumstances.

Japanese Shinto religion, Van Wolferen says, lacks a strong ideology or even a set of scriptures. LDP-dominated politics rarely turn on issues, which is why the change from one prime minister to another makes so little difference to the outside world. Even the codes of behavior and personal morality that are taught to Japanese youth stress needs springing from different situations, such as duty to friends and family or loyalty to superiors, rather than abstract principles. "Japanese are not expected to take their cues from an inner voice that reminds them of moral absolutes they came to embrace while growing up," he says.

> They cannot appeal to any principle or ideal with which to justify their behaviour in the eyes of their neighbors, fellow workers or superiors. To understand this moral world one must imagine a situation in which good behaviour is constantly deter-

mined by individuals' views of how others expect them to behave.

Van Wolferen's argument that the Japanese have "no absolute truths" has been infuriating to many people in Japan, but not for the reason most outsiders might suspect. The concept itself has not been the main concern of Van Wolferen's critics, partly because so many Japanese theorists have claimed that Japan's ethics are more flexible and "situational" than those of the rule-bound West. It is, instead, Van Wolferen's tone that has stung many Japanese, who see in it raw contempt for Japan and a continuation of the age-old struggle to show the white man's superiority over the devious yellow man. ("How could he have stayed here so long if he hates us so much?" an official of the Japanese foreign ministry asked me after he'd read Van Wolferen's book.)

This reaction, I think, misreads Van Wolferen's intentions, and in a serious way. Van Wolferen clearly prefers the legal and intellectual world of the West to that of Japan, but he is not condemning the Japanese system so much as he is trying to explain it clearly. Similarly, Clyde Prestowitz is renowned in Japan as a "Japan-basher"; yet his book, far from demanding that Japan change its trading practices, merely asked foreigners to understand the practices for what they are. The phrase *wakatte kudasai*—"please understand"—is used frequently by Japanese negotiators. It represents a request to recognize the peculiarities of Japanese politics or society and accept them without criticism. This is the rule that Van Wolferen has violated. His argument about the absence of consistently applicable values could be wrong, but his book leaves the burden of proof on the other side.

Van Wolferen explains one other political difference, which is of much greater practical significance to outsiders dealing with Japan. Japanese spokesmen like to say, and Americans and Europeans seem willing to believe, that Japan's distinctive social traits somehow come naturally to its people. After all the millennia of living in close quarters, the Japanese, it is said, have learned to work well in groups. Because of some instinctive sense of the collective good, Japanese employees are loyal to their companies, and the companies are said to be willing to look past short-term profitability and invest for the long haul. Japanese students concentrate harder on their work; Japanese factory hands devote themselves to making the best possible product.

No doubt there are some basic behavioral differences between the average Japanese citizen and the average American or Frenchman. Japan's idea that it is monoracial makes it easier to generate a feeling of national unity. (The idea of racial unity, which was propagated during the Meiji era and again in the buildup to World War II, is the important trait, since the Japanese population itself is less homogeneous than, say, Korea's.) For a variety of reasons, Japanese blue-collar workers seem on the whole more diligent than their counterparts in the US or Europe. But for American readers, the most startling part of Van Wolferen's book will be his extensive demonstration that most of these "innate" traits are actually the results of the deliberate use of political and economic power.

The "loyalty" of white-collar workers to their company, in contrast to the constant movement of employees in other countries, is one clear example. Van Wolferen points out that the major corporations tacitly agree never to hire someone who has left another firm. Japanese children are studious in large part because admission to the University of Tokyo, which is based on examination scores, is essentially their only hope for having an influential place in society. In the higher reaches of the US civil service, 11 percent of appointees have some connection to Harvard. In Japan's extremely powerful Ministry of Finance, 88 percent of the senior officials are from the University of Tokyo, as are most of the officials in other agencies.

Japanese are "nonlitigious," not just because of their alleged love of consensus but also because of the acute shortage of lawyers. The Ministry of Justice controls the Legal Training and Research Institute, where future lawyers and judges must train, and it admits only 2 percent of those who apply. (Of the 23,855 who took the entrance examination in 1985, 486 were admitted.) "The widespread idea that the Japanese are reluctant to enter the legal profession is pure myth," Van Wolferen says.

As one specialist has pointed out, the number of Japanese, relative to the total population, who took the judicial examination in 1975 was slightly higher than the figure for Americans taking a bar examination.

Most criminals arrested by the police confess partly out of a sense of remorse but also because they know what a trial would mean: in 99 percent of criminal trials, the verdict is guilty.

Japanese salarymen devote eighteen hours a day to the company partly out of dedication but also because they feel they have no choice. "The phenomenon of a middle class deprived to a large extent of men functioning as husbands and fathers is of relatively recent origin," Van Wolferen says. He quotes an academic study: "If Japanese 'naturally'—because of cultural preconditioning—were prepared to give up their egos to a large organisation, the organisation would not have to work so hard to instill loyalty and identification." That is, the quasi-compulsory morning exercises and company songs that are common in Japanese companies may not indicate how "naturally" the Japanese conform but rather how unnatural the overwhelming emphasis on teamwork is.

A less benign effort to instill the team spirit is now being contemplated. The *monbusho*, or Ministry of Education, has long been one of the most conservative and pig-headedly nationalistic of all Japanese bureaucracies. Every year or two, the *monbusho* provokes outrage throughout Asia when it considers new history texts that gloss over Japan's role in China before and during World War II. Predictably, the Chinese and Korean governments lodge bitter protests, and predictably the *monbusho* is forced to back off. It also typically meets resistance from the *Nikkyoso*, or national teacher's union, which is the main source of organized left-wing sentiment in the country. Early this year, the *monbusho* announced plans for a new emphasis on national pride in Japan's public school curriculum, which is centrally controlled from Tokyo. (In every corner of the country, students cover the same subjects with the same books in the same weeks of the year, as directed by the *monbusho*.)

Japan's schools are already heavily directed toward developing the character traits that have made the Japanese productive system strong. Children go to school six days a week, for instance, even though the academic courses they take could easily be fitted into five days, because the six-day schedule teaches them the value of perseverance and hard work. Onto this existing pattern the *monbusho* proposes to add a stronger emphasis on the narrowly nationalistic glories of Japan: children will learn more about Japan's military heroes and spend more time hearing the national anthem and seeing the flag. It's to be expected that schools will cultivate national pride but there's hardly a shortage of it in Japan. For several years, Japanese diplomats, government spokesmen, and conference-goers have been assuring foreigners that Japan's new motto is *kokusaika*—"internationalization," to reduce the spiritual and psychological barriers between Japan and the rest of the world. Apparently the Japanese school system has not gotten the news.

To point out the remaining factors that make Japan unusual, as Prestowitz and now Van Wolferen have done, is not to foment hostility toward Japan. If anything, it is the best way to ensure smoother relations in the future. In the long run, the greatest source of hostility toward Japan is the myth of *kokusaika*—the idea that, any minute now, Japan's economy and its political system will be just like those in the United States or Western Europe, and that trade imbalances and other misunderstandings will therefore naturally melt away. The Japanese system is not about to transform itself, and it is presumptuous for outsiders to say that it should. Japan has been very successful doing things its own way. It has virtually no street crime, drugs, homeless families, or single parents. Its savings rate is high, and the literacy rate is nearly 100 percent. Every hour of every day, its foreign assets increase by $10 million.

This society does not seem to its leaders such a total failure. And if foreigners like Van Wolferen do not like the social contract on which the success is built, well, no one is asking them to become Japanese. The rest of the world will have no trouble getting along with this society, including its trading practices, if outsiders take Japan's system for what it is, not as some midway point en route to becoming just like the United States. Prestowitz's description of Japan's economy and Van Wolferen's analysis of its political system do more than any other books in many years to encourage a healthy realism about Japan.

The Two Faces of Japan:

Most of What You've Heard Is True

But then, so is the contrary

By Fred Hiatt and Margaret Shapiro

Fred Hiatt and Margaret Shapiro completed their assignment in Japan this summer.

TOKYO—After living here three years we've discovered it's easy to dump on Japan.

For a start, Japanese can be rigid, officious, humorless, sexist, narrow-minded, clannish, conformist, uncharitable, xenophobic and smug.

Their love of nature? Take a look at their cemented-over coastline and riverbanks, littered with beer cans, plastic bags and cigarette butts. Their vaunted politesse? Just don't stand in the way of that little old lady angling for a subway seat—and don't expect anyone to give you a seat even if you're sick, crippled, pregnant or a little old lady yourself.

Their free-thinking democracy? Tell it to the schoolgirl with natural red highlights who was forced to dye her hair black by school officials, or to the Nagasaki mayor who was shot and wounded by a rightist after he dared suggest that Emperor Hirohito bore some responsibility for World War II.

Their free-market triumph? Listen to the Foreign Ministry official admitting, in an unguarded moment, that Japan will always rather produce something itself than buy it overseas. Or talk to one of Tokyo's rare discount retailers about how he gets blacklisted by Japan's giant manufacturers if he drops his prices too low.

It's no wonder that, as Japanese influence grows around the world, a common reaction is, "We admire them, but we don't like them."

We've felt that way, too. But something always happens the next day to make us see things differently.

A stranger at a sushi bar strikes up a conversation over still-squirming shrimp and, by the second cup of tea, has invited us to a family picnic on the weekend. A kimono-clad grandmother working at a Japanese inn sweeps our toddler daughter into her arms and carries her off into the kitchen. This is

Japan, so we have no worries for her safety, and she returns a half hour later with a big smile and a fistful of chocolates.

A group of Japan Peace Corps volunteers who have stepped off the corporate ladder head for Tonga, the Solomon Islands and China, not with any grand American visions of changing the world but with modest hopes of helping a few people in need. A worldly journalist friend levels far more incisive criticism against his own society than that by any foreign Japan-basher these days.

When our beat-up Nissan Bluebird blows a tire near the prime minister's house, a half-dozen riot policemen jog over, suspicion melting into sympathy as they notice our children in the back. They take charge, change our tire and send us on the way with salutes far snappier than our jalopy.

This is the quandary of Japan, one we found ourselves grappling with for three years. It is a quandary that on another level helps explain Washington's official schizophrenia—is Japan a threat or an ally?—and it is one that seems to deepen, not be resolved, with increasing exposure to the country.

The greatest experts are often the most confounded, and conflicted. A U.S. diplomat, who has spent a career defending the Japanese, muses at lunch about how unlovable, and at times infuriating, they can be; an academic extols their incredible accomplishments and bemoans their towering arrogance, almost in the same breath.

There's no question that this society works in ways that often astonish Americans. People are diligent. Students study, workers work, no one begs and no one slouches. Drive into a gas station, and four or five employees swoop down on your car with enthusiasm, as if they have never filled a tank or washed a windshield before.

Late one night, the clang of metal dustpans echoing on our darkened street brings us to our window; a group of elderly volunteers in hardhats is sweeping its way down the street, removing gum wrappers and soda cans.

Leave your wallet in one of Tokyo's sparkling taxis, and the white-gloved driver will

spend hours tracking you down to give it back.

The civility and small considerations often accorded others—these can relax and refresh the spirit. Men may not hold doors for women, but someone exiting an elevator presses the "Close Door" button as a courtesy to those left behind. In subways, no one would dream of playing loud music or sullying the seat with muddy shoes or wet umbrellas. To walk down a dark street alone without fear, to leave one's car doors unlocked or department store merchandise unguarded—these are freedoms Americans have almost forgotten.

But the civility extended to each other, and to white foreigners, often is withheld from Filipino babysitters, Pakistani day laborers and other darker-skinned visitors, who live in fear of Japanese police and with the open contempt of many Japanese civilians.

Nor does the civility extend to international business competition, where Japan's take-no-prisoners approach is often seen as less than fair and honorable.

Nor does everything here hum along as efficiently as a Honda Accord engine. Tokyo's international airport, Narita, is a nightmare of poor planning. Some traffic-clogged roads resemble parking lots more than freeways. Many homes still have no indoor plumbing, with even some Tokyo residents still using outhouses.

Subways crisscrossing the capital deep underground usually provide no air conditioning, and few elevators or escalators; handicapped people are expected to stay out of sight. Paying bills can often mean an ordeal of trooping from bank to bank, with each taking a healthy cut along the way, since checks and credit cards remain underused.

More serious, the social pressures and ingrained restraints that make Japan work also inevitably limit individualism and diversity. After some time in Japan, an American breathes a sigh of relief upon reaching Hong Kong or Seoul, where women laugh heartily and without demurely covering their mouths, where people wear bright colors,

" There's no question that this society works in ways that often astonish Americans. "

where an acquaintance will poke you in the chest, look you in the eye and tell you what's really on his mind.

Many Japanese feel stifled, too, but their system is so demanding and tightly woven that it is virtually impossible to opt only half-way out. From cram schools for kindergartners to lifetime employment demanding more devotion to company than family, Japanese accept that to get ahead means to buckle under. Thus when our friend, a government bureaucrat, was told by his boss that he needed a wife by year's end to qualify for his next promotion, he booked a wedding hall for Dec. 29. Then, through a go-between, he found a wife.

A Japanese reporter based in Washington recently begged his editors for an extension of his three-year tour. His children had spent so much time in the United States that there was no chance they could reenter the Japanese educational system and be accepted; their only hope was to finish American schooling and enter an "international" university in Japan.

It is easy to criticize the irritating conformity, the somewhat frightening willingness to obey uncritically dictates from above, and many foreigners do. Many Japanese who remember the poverty and hunger of a few decades ago view the sacrifices demanded by the system as a reasonable price to pay for the prosperity, security and relative equality of today's society.

But increasing numbers of Japanese too are becoming critical, chafing against the cradle-to-grave gridlock of their society. Those sent overseas, a rapidly growing contingent, revel in the freedom there and swear they won't return to the strictures of the past. We heard that time and again from our Japanese friends in the United States. But somehow, once they hit Narita their resolve withered.

The politician's son, wild and crazy owner of a Trans-Am in the United States who was determined to escape his destiny, now dutifully spends nights and weekends attending constituent weddings and funerals.

A young Japanese banker spent a summer month agonizing over whether to leave his company for a more exciting, high-paying and, of course, risky job with an American competitor. In the end he stayed with what he knew, even though he felt he had somehow given in.

This is why it is so hard to say whether Japan is changing—and how quickly. On the one hand, more Japanese are traveling, more women are working, more young people are committing the previously unpardonable sins of job-hopping and demanding weekends off for time with their families. On the other hand, a recent survey showed that Tokyoites are working longer and spending more time commuting than they did 10 years ago.

In some ways Japan is becoming more rigid, more Japanese, as it moves further away from the shakeups imposed by the U.S. postwar occupation: School rules have become stricter, the establishment more hereditary and less meritocratic.

Is Japan an ally or a threat? Our answer still depends on whether we're coming from the sushi shop or Narita airport. But three years have left us with no doubt about the ferocity of the Japanese economic challenge and what appears from overseas to be a dangerous lack of resolve in the United States about getting its own house in order.

Whether one likes the Japanese or not, whether they are changing or not, they clearly will continue working hard, and well. And all the Japan-bashing in Washington is not going to change that.

Japan's LDP has won again but will have to look more carefully to its base of support, reports **Stefan Wagstyl**

Giving hostages to electoral fortune

On the face if it, the result of the Japanese general election looks like an unqualified mandate for the governing Liberal Democratic Party to continue the one-party rule of the past 35 years.

The sight of Mr Yasuhiro Nakasone, the former prime minister claiming triumphantly that victory has freed him from the taint of the Recruit scandal, makes it appear that the course of Japanese politics has not changed at all in the turmoil of the past year.

But in reality it has changed. Voters backed the LDP in Sunday's elections to the lower house of the Diet (Parliament) in the knowledge that they had already punished the party by inflicting last year its biggest-ever defeat in upper house elections.

"We still have LDP Government," Mr Rei Shiratori, a professor of politics at Tokai University, said yesterday. "But it is not the LDP Government of the time before 1989."

LDP leaders will in future have to take more notice of public opinion and of the opposition parties which control the upper house, including the Japan Socialist Party, which scored big gains under the flamboyant leadership of Miss Takako Doi.

Foreign governments, which have had to wait patiently for more than a year while Japan's politicians were preoccupied with their domestic crisis, may find the next 12 months as frustrating as the last 12.

The ruling party made election promises to voters which will restrict its room for manoeuvre in trade talks, pledging repeatedly to oppose the liberalisation of the rice trade, for example. Japan could be more belligerent and less accommodating—just at the time when Washington is pressing for concessions from Tokyo in negotiations over the Structural Impediments Initiative, the bilateral talks aimed at finding ways to cut Japan's trade surplus with the US. The first signs of post-election LDP views could emerge in these talks in Tokyo this week.

Moreover, in the past, trade problems were largely settled by bureaucrats from increasingly-internationally minded ministries led by the Ministry for International Trade and Industry (Miti). The issues of the future—including further liberalisation in agriculture and reform of the distribution system—are ones which politicians cannot ignore.

Never the less, the scale of the LDP's victory at least gives the party more confidence in facing these difficulties than it had before the poll. "We should make further efforts to expand domestic demand and imports," Mr Toshiki Kaifu, the prime minister, said yesterday.

The ruling party made election promises which will restrict its room for manoeuvre in trade talks

In the poll on Sunday, the LDP secured 275 seats to the 512-seat lower house—comfortably above the top of the range of most forecasts and only 20 seats short of the record 295 won by it in 1986.

The main reason for the party's success was the voters' willingness to give the LDP full credit for the peace and prosperity which they have enjoyed since the liberal democrats took office in 1955. Voters were prepared to put aside the concerns of the last two years—the Recruit scandal, unpopular moves to liberalise agricultural imports and a controversial 3 per cent consumption tax.

The LDP owed much to the inability of the opposition parties to portray themselves as a realistic alternative government. Miss Doi performed wonders on the hustings but she could not persuade her own party leaders to discard their ideological baggage. While voters were ready to accept Miss Doi as prime minister, according to opinion polls, the rest of her potential cabinet were beyond the pale.

Moreover, the LDP made great efforts to win back public confidence—in particular by promoting a reform of the hated consumption tax and bringing new leaders into office, notably Mr Kaifu, whose youthful looks and clean image proved surprisingly popular with the public though he lacked a party power base.

In the election itself, LDP candidates fought unprecedentedly energetic campaigns to compensate for years of electoral neglect. Mr Nakasone, who was heavily implicated in the Recruit affair, toured his mountainous electoral district in Gumma, near Tokyo, bowing so low to his constituents that people said he resembled a first-time candidate. Meanwhile members of the Keidanren, the employers' federation, were so worried about the possibility of an LDP defeat that they handed over a war chest worth Y30bn—the biggest-ever—to fund the campaign. Mr Eishiro Saito, chairman of the Keidanren, said: "I'm relieved we can now see a stable political situation ahead."

All this support was more than enough for victory, given the unequal distribution of seats in Japan in favour of the countryside where the LDP is strong. It made its majority with 46 per cent of the vote, slightly down from the 49 per cent in 1986.

Not everything went the way of the LDP. Mr Sadanori Yamanaka, the 68-year-old chairman of the party's tax research committee, lost his seat because of his role in creating the consumption tax. So did Mr Hisao Horinouchi, a former agriculture minister, who paid the price for declaring last year that Mrs Thatcher apart, women were useless in politics. Altogether 40 sitting LDP members lost their seats—far more than usual—often to first-time LDP candidates competing against them in multi-seat constituencies.

The Recruit affair effected the result in a roundabout way. Only one out of six men implicated in the scandal failed to win his seat. Nevertheless, Mr Nakasone, who was in office when the events which led to the scandal took place, suffered the indignity of seeing his intra-party faction lose 10 of its 60 lower house members—the biggest defeat for any of the factions which comprise the LDP.

The Socialist party increased its tally from 83 seats to 136, thanks to the support of many women voters who stayed loyal from the time of last year's upper house poll. Across Japan the JSP won seats in LDP strongholds which had never, or not for many years, returned a Socialist. In rural Niigata, for example, a Socialist topped the poll in the constituency once held by Mr Kakuei Tanaka, a former prime minister and the godfather of modern LDP politics. However, by fielding only 149 candidates, the most it could muster because of its organisational weakness and lack of suitable candidates emerging in time, the JSP never looked like posing a serious threat to the LDP.

Following the election, three issues top the political agenda: the LDP's internal wrangles over the party leadership, its search for political allies in the opposition camp and the future of the country's international relations.

• Within the LDP, the main issue is how long Mr Kaifu will survive as prime minister. He was chosen last summer by party elders for his clean record and youth to restore the LDP's public image. But he carries little weight inside the party because he comes from the smallest of the factions which comprise the LDP.

The real power in the party is Mr Noboru Takeshita, himself once prime minister, who is the de facto leader of the largest faction. Mr Takeshita is under pressure from Mr Shintaro Abe, head of the second-largest faction, to smooth the way for Mr Abe, who is 65, to take office. But to dump Mr Kaifu too quickly after an election victory would be a snub to voters. So Mr Abe must wait; but he has been ill and wants his turn soon.

Moreover, Mr Abe has younger men snapping at his heels. The undoubted intra-party victor of the election was Mr Ichiro Ozawa, the 47-year-old secretary-general of the LDP. His beaming face dominated television coverage of the election count. Mr Ozawa is credited with masterminding the LDP's success, handling the crucial task of securing campaign funds from industry and then disbursing the money to candidates. Mr Ozawa and others his age will not wait

for ever for Mr Takeshita's generation to retire gracefully—they may decide to seize power for themselves as Mr Takeshita once did, when he broke away from his mentor Mr Kauei Tanaka, though it seems too early for such a shake-up.

• The party needs a strong leader to forge a workable alliance with one or more opposition parties. In Mr Takeshita's view "a partial coalition" is needed—meaning that the LDP is prepared to give its partners a say in policy formation.

Despite its victory in the lower house, the LDP's Parliamentary forces are paralysed unless it finds a way of passing legislation through the upper house. It can only force through budget bills—almost anything else requires the upper house's agreement. In particular, the LDP cannot secure the passage of its planned reforms to the consumption tax as long as the opposition insists on its abolition.

Publicly, the LDP is wooing the Socialists. But Miss Doi is not interested. The ruling party is more likely to find a partner in Komeito, the centrist clean government party. Komeito, with its roots in a conservative religious movement, has always been a reluctant member of the JSP-dominated coalition of opposition parties which now controls the upper house. With Komeito's help the LDP would have an upper house majority.

• The greatest difficulties lie in handling foreign policy, especially trade relations with the US. Washington has made no secret of the fact that it wants action from Tokyo on the Structural Impediments Initiative. The Democrats intend to make US-Japan relations the heart of their campaign in the autumn mid-term elections. Republicans will put President Bush under pressure to act tough.

On the Japanese side, government bureaucrats are increasingly willing to do what they can to avoid a trade war. In the past three years, they have decided a measure of appeasement is in Japan's interest. "We used to see Miti as the enemy. Now we think they're an ally," says one senior western diplomat in Tokyo.

But the problem is that while bureaucrats can solve non-political disputes—

such as a current argument between the US and Japan over American access to the Japanese satellite market—the biggest issues are increasingly political.

The LDP is not ready to start making concessions abroad, if they cost votes at home. It allowed itself to be bullied two years ago by the US into easing restrictions on imports of beef and oranges. In last year's election and in those last Sunday some of its biggest losses were in farm areas most affected by these moves. In this election the LDP has wooed the farmers' vote by swearing to maintain the ban on rice imports—even though it has already agreed to refer the issue to the Uruguay Round of Gatt.

The employers' federation is relieved to see 'stable political situation ahead'

Similarly, the party is most unlikely to support reform in the law restricting the opening of large stores and supermarkets. The small shopkeepers are the bedrock of LDP support in towns and cities—and a constituency avidly wooed by the Socialists. It will be left to Miti to try to satisfy the Americans by re-interpreting the existing regulations without offending the shopkeepers.

Mr James Vaughn, director of the California Office of Trade and Investment in Tokyo, says "the LDP is going to find it more and more difficult to respond to increasing demands from the US and Europe because it is more indebted than ever to special interests which supported its campaign."

The main consolation for western governments is that dealing with a divided coalition of opposition parties, each with its own supporters to satisfy, would undoubtedly be worse. The LDO is a broad organisation with plenty of talented members able to see that Japan's best interests lie in good relations with its trade partners. But in the wake of the upheaval of the last year, these people will have to voice their opinions more carefully than they did before.

Modern Pluralist Democracies: Elements in the Political Process

- **Ideas, Movements, Parties (Articles 20–24)**
- **Women and Politics (Articles 25–27)**
- **Parliament, Prime Minister, and Cabinet (Articles 28–30)**
- **Nation and State (Article 31)**

Observers of Western industrial societies frequently refer to the emergence of a new politics in these countries. They are not always very clear about what is supposedly novel within the political process or how it is of significance. Although few would doubt that some major changes have taken place in both political attitudes and behavior in recent years, it is very difficult to establish clear patterns of transformation or gauge their endurance and impact. Yet making sense of continuities and changes in political values and behavior must be one of the central tasks of a comparative study of government.

None of this should be mistaken for a return to the political patterns of the past, nor is it to be confused with either traditional conservatism or a libertarian rejection of the welfare state. Instead, we may be witnessing the emergence of a new mix of materialist and post-materialist orientations. The first five articles in this unit deal with a variety of political ideas, movements, and parties that have little else in common than the attempt to establish a more clearly defined political identity and a more solid political base for themselves.

In the area of political ideas, traditional socialism seems to have fallen on hard days in the advanced industrial world. The ambiguity is reflected in the article by Robert Heilbroner, who for many decades argued that business civilization based on advanced capitalism suffered from a terminal illness. Like many thinkers of the Left, he has now concluded that centralized planning under state socialism has been an economic and political disaster as compared to practices associated with market economies. Yet he still finds room for the reform demands of the Left, since capitalism will continue to engender its own social problems and dissatisfactions.

In the next article, an interview with the Socialist prime minister of France, Michel Rocard also reflects upon the lessons that the democratic Left can draw from the collapse of state socialism in much of Central and Eastern Europe. For him, to be on the Left means to be committed to such ideals as more justice, more equality, more democracy, more pluralism. It also means the effort to create a public power that will promote such values while reducing the arbitrariness in society. At the same time, Rocard stresses that the democratic Left must recognize that competition has socially beneficial results and must be maintained if not promoted.

The Greens of the western part of Germany are going through a similar soul-searching at the present time. After their unprecedented parliamentary success in the past decade, they failed to return to the Bundestag in the recent German election. The problems faced by the Greens are at least as much internal as external.

On the center-Right, the Christian Democrats have been the most successful political movement in Europe since 1945. Yet here too there is something of a political identity crisis, as idealists who subscribe to the social teachings of the Church find themselves deprived of much influence in parties run by non-visionary technocrats and political managers, like Giulio Andreotti in Italy and Helmut Kohl in Germany. The latter seem to reflect little of the original ideals of personalism, solidarity, and subsidiarity that originally set the Christian Democrats off from

liberals and conservatives. An article from *The Economist* outlines some further differences between the idealists and the pragmatists in the Christian Democrats and suggests that their argument will determine the future of the movement. A major issue is whether the Christian Democrats should line up in Europe with other nonsocialist but secular parties, such as the British Conservatives and French Gaullists.

The final article on political parties, by Jeffrey Gedmin, looks at the far Left and the ultra-Right parties in Western Europe. The Communists are in deep political trouble, stemming from the erosion of their ideology, the loss of members and voters, and, in some cases such as France, the rigid unwillingness to reform. But even the Italian Communist party, by far the most popular and reform-oriented in Western Europe, appears unable to revitalize itself despite recent changes of name, symbolism, and program that all intend to emphasize its commitment to democratic socialism.

If the far Left has lost in strength, there are signs that parties of the far Right may find at least a marginal support among some socially alienated voters in Italy, France, and possibly Germany. The recent decline of the new right-wing party of *Republikaner* in Germany, after its widely discussed initial success (7.1 percent of the vote) in the European elections of 1989, suggests that this right-wing protest party may have no solid base in that country, at least for the time being. But the picture could change again as a result of the social and cultural conflicts engendered during the unification process and compounded by the fear of a large-scale flight of economic refugees into Germany from eastern Europe. In France, where Jean-Marie Le Pen's National Front for a long time got away with being more explicitly xenophobic, racist, and anti-Semitic than appears to be either legally or socially acceptable in today's Germany, the National Assembly recently approved a bill that would outlaw the incitement of ethnic hatred.

Women in politics is the concern of the second section in this unit. There continues to be a strong pattern of underrepresentation of women in positions of political leadership practically everywhere. Yet there are some notable differences from country to country, as well as from party to party. Generally speaking, the parties of the Left have been readier to place women in positions of authority, although there are some remarkable exceptions, as the center-right cases of Margaret Thatcher in Britain and Simone Weil in France illustrate. On the whole, the system of proportional representation gives parties both a tool and an added incentive to place female candidates in positions where they will be elected. But here too, there can be exceptions, as in the case of France in 1986 when women did not benefit from the one-time use of proportional representation in the parliamentary elections. Clearly it is not enough to have a relatively simple means, such as proportional representation, for promoting women in politics: There must also be a will among decisionmakers to use the available means for such a purpose.

The Scandinavian countries illustrate the prevailing pattern. There is a markedly higher representation of women in the parliaments of Denmark, Finland, Iceland, Norway, and Sweden, where the political spectrum is somewhat to the Left and proportional representation makes it possible to set up party lists that are more representative of the population as a whole. It is of some interest that Iceland now has a special feminist party with parliamentary representation, but it is more important that women are found in leading positions within most of the parties of the other Scandinavian countries. It is indicative that in contrast to Margaret Thatcher, who included no women in her cabinet, Norway's first female prime minister, Dr. Gro Harlem Brundtland, used that position to advance the number of women in ministerial positions (8 of 18 cabinet posts). She stepped down after her party's defeat in the 1989 election, but Norway remains among the world's leaders in the representation of women in high governmental posts. Recently, Gro Harlem Brundtland regained the prime ministership, while Margaret Thatcher stepped down. In another widely reported sign of change, the relatively conservative Republic of Ireland has just chosen Mary Robinson as its president. It is a largely ceremonial post, but it has a symbolic potential that Mary Robinson, an outspoken advocate of liberal reform in her country, is likely to be willing to use on behalf of social change.

There is undoubtedly a growing awareness of the pattern of discrimination in most Western countries. It seems likely that there will be a significant improvement in this situation over the course of the next decade if the pressure for change is maintained. At one time there used to be a considerably lower voter turnout among women, but this gender gap has been practically eliminated in recent decades. Similarly, the tendency for women to be somewhat more conservative in party and candidate preferences has given way to a more liberal disposition among women in foreign and social policy than among men. These are aggregate differences, of course, and Nancy Walker's comparative article is important also because it reminds us that women, no more than men, do not represent a monolithic bloc in political attitudes or behavior.

Nevertheless, there are some very important policy issues that affect women as a group. The article on women in the paid labor force of Europe offers statistical evidence to support three widely shared impressions: (1) there has been a considerable increase in the number and relative proportion of women who take up paid jobs, (2) these jobs are more often unskilled and/or part-time than in the case of men, and (3) women generally receive less pay and less social protection than men in similar positions. By showing that there are considerable differences among Western European countries in the relative position of female workers, the article also supports the argument that political intervention in the form of legislation can do something to improve upon the situation—not only by training women better for advancement in the labor market but also, and importantly, by changing the conditions of the labor market to provide them with better conditions and opportunities than hitherto.

In the third section of this unit, the authors make some comparisons among democratic constitutions, as well as between parliamentary and presidential systems of government. Robert Goldwin reminds us that most of the world's constitutions have been very short-lived. There has been a flurry of constitution-writing after the collapse of dictatorships in several parts of the world, and he suggests that the products may turn out to be more lasting if some basic questions are considered carefully by the drafters. Above all, the constitution writers must remember to take into account the peculiarities of their own society. They can learn much that is useful from the experience of other countries, but they will find no valid universal formula for a good constitution. They would, in any case, court disaster if they ignored their own history by trying to begin with a completely clean slate.

Gregory Mahler focuses on the legislative-executive relationship of parliamentary and congressional systems, by drawing upon the British, Canadian, and American examples. He avoids the trap of idealizing one or the other way of organizing the functions of representative government. That is also true for Richard Rose, who compares the governmental leadership and systems of checks and balances found in the United States, Britain, and France. He finds that each system has its own constraints upon arbitrary rule, which can easily become obstacles to prompt, clear-cut decisions. One could add that the authors of *The Federalist* would not have been surprised.

In the final and somewhat controversial article of this unit, the author argues that the nation-state is a very recent political phenomenon, but that it may turn out to be more tenacious and possibly more flexible and useful than some reformers and critics concede. It surveys the arguments made by world integrationists and concludes that the goal of greatly reducing limits on the freedom of movement is not incompatible with a system of strong states. What really matters is the effective size of the governing units and the principles on which they operate. Compared with the alternatives of the infranationalist breakdown of existing states into smaller tribal regions, as may happen in Yugoslavia, or their supranationalist collection into larger units ruled by distant bureaucrats, as some plans for European political integration may imply, the author concludes that the present national setup is likely to last for decades to come.

Looking Ahead: Challenge Questions

How has capitalism managed to convince even socialists, like Robert Heilbroner, that it is a more attractive and satisfactory way of organizing economic affairs than centralized socialist planning?

What is socialist in Michel Rocard's articulation of the ideals of the Left? Where does he differ outright with a widespread socialist assumption about capitalism or market economies?

With all their differences, both the Greens and the Christian Democrats seem to be torn between an idealist and pragmatic wing. Explain. Where do idealist Christian Democrats differ from secular conservatives or classical liberals?

Why have the Communists in Western Europe had such a drastic political decline, and how are they trying to reverse the process?

Why are women so poorly represented in Parliament and other positions of political leadership? How do institutional arrangements, such as election systems, sometimes help or hinder an improvement in this situation? Which parties and countries tend to have a better record of female representation? Why? Are there similar differences in social policy for women in the paid labor force?

What are some of the major arguments made in favor of the parliamentary system of government? How does it differ from America's congressional system? What features of the British system are not shared by other parliamentary governments? How does the dual executive of the French system operate?

If the nation-state is such a recent phenomenon, how can it be argued that it will prove to be a tenacious and useful unit in a world committed to greater freedom in movement for people, goods, and capital? Do you find the argument convincing?

REFLECTIONS

THE TRIUMPH OF CAPITALISM

Robert Heilbroner

LESS than seventy-five years after it officially began, the contest between capitalism and socialism is over: capitalism has won. The Soviet Union, China, and Eastern Europe have given us the clearest possible proof that capitalism organizes the material affairs of humankind more satisfactorily than socialism: that however inequitably or irresponsibly the marketplace may distribute goods, it does so better than the queues of a planned economy; however mindless the culture of commercialism, it is more attractive than state moralism; and however deceptive the ideology of a business civilization, it is more believable than that of a socialist one. Indeed, it is difficult to observe the changes taking place in the world today and not conclude that the nose of the capitalist camel has been pushed so far under the socialist tent that the great question now seems how rapid will be the transformation of socialism into capitalism, and not the other way around, as things looked only a half century ago.

Yet I doubt whether the historic drama will conclude, like a great morality play, in the unequivocal victory of one side and the ignominious defeat of the other. The economic enemy of capitalism has always been its own self-generated dynamics, not the presence of an alternative economic system. Socialism, in its embodiments in the Soviet Union and, to a lesser degree, China, has been a military and political competitor but never an economic threat. Thus, despite the rout of cen-

tralized planning—to judge by the stories coming from Moscow, it has the proportions of a rout—one would have to be very incautious to assume that capitalism will now find itself rid of its propensity to generate both inflation and recession, cured of its intermittent speculative fevers, or free of threatening international economic problems. Nevertheless, in one very important respect the triumph of capitalism alters the manner in which we must assess its prospects. The old question "Can capitalism work?," to which endless doubting answers have been given by its critics, becomes "Can capitalism work well enough?," which is quite another thing.

Even such hedged speculations are regarded with suspicion by most of the members of my profession. Modern-day economists sedulously avoid scenarios of long-term capitalist development—a caution that was not shared by the great economists of the past, virtually all of whom wrote boldly about prospects for the system. What is perhaps more surprising is that, although they disagreed about many things, those economic thinkers were near-unanimous in depicting the prospects as gloomy. Adam Smith, for example, believed that the society of his time, which had not yet been named capitalism, would have a long run but would end up in decline. Marx, of course, expected the demise of the system, but so did John Stuart Mill, whose "Principles of Political Economy" was published in 1848, the year

of Marx's "Manifesto." The most important Victorian economist, Alfred Marshall, warned against socialism and unconsidered changes, but his very Victorianism—he called for "economic chivalry"—makes us squirm a little as we read the exhortative concluding words of his "Principles." His pupil and protégé, John Maynard Keynes, was of a different mind. Only a "somewhat comprehensive socialization" of investment, he wrote, would rescue the system from intolerable levels of unemployment. Even Joseph Schumpeter, the most conservative (and the least publicly known) of these magisterial economists, asked in his famous "Capitalism, Socialism and Democracy," in 1942, "Can capitalism survive?" and answered, "No. I do not think it can."

THUS, I imagine that the great economic prophets would be taken aback by the present turn of events. No doubt it is possible to conclude from these failed predictions that present-day economists are right in shunning long-run prognoses. I think, however, that a more useful lesson can be learned by asking why the worldly philosophers were wide of the mark. Three general answers can be given to that question. One of them, of which we still hear echoes, has to do with the limited expansive possibilities for the economy. From Smith on, many observers have depicted the process of capitalist growth as that of occupying a given territory of opportunity. This view was certainly visible in "The Wealth of Nations," which speaks of the long ascent's coming to an end when a country has finally attained "that full complement of riches" to which "the nature of its soil and climate" and "its situation with respect to other countries" entitled it. What Smith had in mind was a condition of market saturation. In the opening pages of the "Wealth" he presents a vivid description of a ten-man pin manufactory whose improving productivity formed the basis for the improving well-being of the larger society. It is entirely reasonable to foresee a future in which the market would be flooded with pins, to the extinction of any incentive to continue the process of productive betterment. With the benefit of hindsight, it is also very clear that such a view rests on a static conception of economic growth. Smith did not see that his petty manufacturers were corporals with field marshals' batons in their knapsacks, who would transform and vastly extend the economic opportunities before them—that ten-man pin factories would give way to thousand-man iron foundries and ten-thousand-man steel complexes. Keynes was similarly bemused by a bounded conception of the nature of economic opportunities: "Two pyramids, two masses for the dead are twice as good as one," he wrote in 1936, "but not so two railways from London to York." He did not foresee that capitalism would generate the computer, nuclear energy, and the jet plane within thirty years of his likening its prospects to those of building a redundant railway.

The fear of exhausted opportunities is still sometimes voiced by economists seeking to project the gross national products of the United States or the Organization for Economic Coöperation and Development nations during the next few years. One need only extrapolate the production of cars or personal computers a few years ahead to depict a world drowning in these goods, as Smith's world seemed about to drown in pins. Yet the lesson of the past is assuredly that market saturation is a transient, not a permanent, condition of the system, both because its driving impulse has continually extended the technological frontiers of the economy and because the special province of capitalism has always been finding ways of expanding its commodity frontiers by moving activities from the sphere of personal life into that of profitable business. Particularly in modern times, every generation has extricated itself from satiety by reinventing its own "standard" of life. Even Marx, who was keenly alive to capitalism's capacity for generating outlets for expansion, would have been nonplussed by the extent to which such once wholly noneconomic pursuits as family entertainment, meal preparation, housework, and exercise have been "commodified" by TV, precooked foods, detergents, and running shoes.

In addition, the increasing reliance of business on research and development has made scientific inquiry itself part of the life process of the system. Thus, fears that capitalism will run out of things to do appear much less plausible than they did in the past. There is no doubt that important markets may become saturated—there is a limit to the number of cars the world can accommodate, as there is to the number of pins it needs—but the long-term process of expansion has bypassed saturation by discovering or creating new commodities, and that process does not suffer from the same fixed capacities for absorption that limit the demand for specific goods. Steel reaches its peak, but plastics and ceramics take its place; the market for cars is clogged, but that for high-speed rail transport begins to open; the Sony Walkman has shown how even strolling along can be put to profitable use. God knows what profitable invasions of our remaining privacy await us. In this never-ending search for overlooked crevices in which capitalism might grow, or for wholly new endeavors it might undertake, there is no doubt that individual nations will fare differently—some neglecting and some encouraging the research or education that opens the technological frontier, some aggressive and some defensive about opening up the commodity frontier. But by all indications we live in a period of extremely rapid scientific advance, part of which will very likely result in new commodity possibilities; and the rout of socialism itself opens up virgin territory to the extension of capitalist enterprise.

SHEER physical saturation has, however, played only a minor role in the dour forecasts of the economic philosophers. Keynes, despite his rather unfortunate railway analogy, based his prognosis not on material limitations of the system but on economic ones—not on the intrinsic lack of any need for a second line from London to York but on the lack of enough purchasing power to buy all the tickets on the first line and thereby establish a possible demand for a second. Quixotically, this lack of purchasing power was itself the result of a failure on the part of business to undertake enough investment projects—railways and others. A pessimistic appraisal of the investment outlook led to insufficient employment on investment projects; and this, in turn, resulted in an insufficiency of the purchasing power needed to make such projects profitable. Given this catch-22, which is one of Keynes' enduring contributions to economic theory, it is not surprising that he looked to the "socialization" of investment as necessary to avoid economic stagnation.

Marx's scenario was not hobbled by a static view of the capacity of the system for inventing new technologies and developing new commodity wants, but it, too, had its catch-22s. These were based on inherent conflicts—contradictions, Marx called them—between the needs of individual enterprises and the working requirements for the system as a whole. One of them was the tendency of capitalism to undercut the buying power of the working class by the continuous introduction of labor-saving machinery, to which business was driven by the pressures of competition. Each enterprise thereby sought to steal a march on its competitors, but instead all enterprises found themselves facing a condition of underconsumption. It is summed up in the perhaps apocryphal story of Henry Ford II walking through a newly automated engine factory with Walter Reuther, the legendary organizing figure of the United Automobile Workers, and asking, "Walter, how are you going to organize these machines?"—to which Reuther is supposed to have answered, "Henry, how are you going to sell them cars?" Another contradiction foreseen by Marx was the erosion of profit rates—not purchasing power—which stemmed from this same substitution of machinery for labor. According to Marx's analysis, labor power was the goose that laid the golden eggs of profits, because employers were able to extract more value from their workers than they paid out as wages. The replacement of living labor by machinery constricted the base from which profit arose, and thus ultimately reduced the rate of return on capital. And well before Marx, Thomas Robert Malthus (whose fame as a demographer has obscured the fact that he was the first "professional" economist, employed by the East India Company) worried about the possibility of a general glut—a general insufficiency of purchasing power. From the moment Malthus's fears were voiced, they were the subject of refutation and ridicule and, because they were not very cogently put, were easily dismissed. But every time a depression has come, the spectre of a general glut has reëmerged. Indeed, it can be argued, I think, that the lurking question of economics, certainly during the present century, has been whether a capitalist economy will experience general gluts, under whatever name.

An immense body of theory has been built on, about, and against the master theories of Marx and Keynes and their distant predecessor Malthus, and a vast amount of research has sought to produce evidence that profit rates have indeed fallen or that inadequate purchasing power has acted as an undertow against growth. It is fair to say that the debate remains unsettled. Keynes' skepticism, like Marx's more precisely structured doubts, remains a matter of contention, as vigorously denied by conservative theorists as it is maintained by more radical ones. Nor does an appeal to the facts entirely resolve the matter. On one side we have the powerful demonstration that the march of capitalist performance has been upward for two centuries. According to the calculations of the economic historian W. W. Rostow, manufacturing output has increased at an average rate of 2.8 per cent per year—not a terribly impressive figure until one realizes that it has multiplied production more than seventeen hundredfold during that period. On the opposite side is the succession of interruptions to that march, the worst of which, in the nineteen-thirties, threatened to bring the system to a halt, and possibly to bring it down. Fifty years of research has not definitely established

that the rate of profit does fall or doesn't fall. In the more recent past, too, there are contradictory signs. The last seven years have been a period of steady economic expansion in the United States—perhaps the longest uninterrupted such period in its peacetime history—but they have also been a period of rising and intractable unemployment in Europe and of worsening poverty and increasingly ill-distributed income at home: the economist Robert Hamrin has recently pointed out that in 1986 the top twenty per cent of all American households received 46.1 per cent of all pretax and pretransfer income, while the bottom twenty per cent received 3.8 per cent—income before taxes and transfers being the best way to show how raw market forces work. Thus our much-touted boom is also the period in which we have set an all-time American record for disparity of income.

One can hence review the record and conclude that our present condition is either a prelude to much worse or evidence of how well we have avoided the ominous-seeming prospects of the past. That ambiguity of interpretation leads me once again to introduce the distinction between "working" and "working well enough." Adam Smith wrote that there is a great deal of "ruin" in a nation, meaning that its capacity for enduring misfortune was much greater than its critics often supposed. That worldly-wise point of view may be on the ascendant. Most economists on the left today claim that capitalism is working badly, but I do not think that many of them would venture to say that the system is about to collapse. On the conservative side, many economists believe that the intrusion of government impairs capitalism's inherent capacity for growth, but I do not think that even the most pessimistic of them expects the system to fail even if government does its worst.

THIS retreat from the generally more apocalyptic views of the not so distant past emphasizes an aspect of the future to which economists often fail to pay sufficient heed. It is that the decisive factor in determining the fate of capitalism must be political, not economic. Schumpeter, for example, expected capitalism to disappear, but not because of any strictly economic diffi-

culties. The stumbling block was cultural. "Capitalism," he wrote, "creates a critical frame of mind which, after having destroyed the moral authority of so many other institutions, in the end turns against its own; the bourgeois finds to his amazement that the rationalist attitude does not stop at the credentials of kings and popes but goes on to attack private property and the whole scheme of bourgeois values." Schumpeter anticipated a painless metamorphosis of capitalism into socialism, by which he meant a presumably democratic, planned economy run by the former managers of capitalism. Marx would have scoffed at Schumpeter's low appraisal of capitalism's self-esteem, but he, too, laid its ultimate downfall on the doorstep of political, not economic, events. Capitalism would be progressively weakened by its economic crises, but, in the famous words of "Capital," the "knell of capitalist private property" would not sound or the "expropriators" be "expropriated" until the working class arose to take things into its own hands.

Schumpeter obviously did not anticipate the present-day resurgence of conservative self-confidence, nor did Marx expect that working-class attitudes and politics would become middle class. Despite their recognition of the importance of mustering and holding the faith of its participants, neither man fully grasped the capacity of the system to do so. This is so, I believe, because neither sufficiently appreciated that capitalism is a social order built upon a deeply embedded and widely believed principle expressed in the actions and beliefs of its most important representatives. From such a viewpoint it is comparable to imperial or aristocratic or Communist regimes, with their universally accepted principle of kingship or aristocracy or socialism, embodied in the personages of monarchs or lords or sacred texts. Capitalism is not normally thought of as possessing such a principle, but its largely uncritical worship of the idea of economic growth is as central to its nature as the similar veneration of the idea of divine kingship or blue blood or doctrinal orthodoxy has been for other regimes. Suggesting that capitalism can be likened to a "regime" rubs our sensibilities the wrong way, but the word is useful in forcing us to consider capitalism as an order of social life, with distinctive hierarchies, imperatives, loyalties, and beliefs. It is this regimelike aspect of capitalism that turns Schumpeter's feared rational skepticism of its privileges into a rationalization of its rights, and makes the working class, far from the opposition that Marx hoped it would become, into stalwart supporters.

The idea of a regime also illumines the nature of its central, dominant, "ruling" class. Immanuel Wallerstein, one of the most influential modern economic historians, has suggested that regimes are, save in moments of convulsion, characterized by the presence of one standard-bearing, "universal" class. I have always pictured such a class as regarded by all, including itself, as the living and legitimate embodiment of the aims and sentiments of the entire society. Thus, it is not only lords and monarchs who believe in their intrinsic superiority but the peasants, who throw their caps in the air. If we ask what group in Western societies occupies this position of untroubled self-regard supported by the general esteem of the people at large, I think the answer would be its capitalists, under their workaday title of businessmen. Individual figures in government may be revered, military leaders admired, but neither politicians nor generals put their own group's interests forward as those of the larger society. With due recognition given its well-publicized villains and its occasional bad repute—the counterpart of bad kings and outbreaks of antimonarchism—it must be conceded that the class of businessmen is the only group that naturally thinks of itself, and is generally thought of, as speaking for the social order as a whole. In this uncomplicated sense, business is the universal class of the regime of capitalism.

ALTHOUGH most businessmen would bridle at these terms, recognition of the regimelike character of capitalism and the "universality" of its business class seems to me indispensable in understanding the capacity of the system for withstanding critical assaults and for disarming political disaffection. People in business never think of themselves as the equivalents of kings or lords or commissars, for the very good reason that they are not. And the reason they are not is that capitalism is unique in history in having not one but two centers of authority, one built around the "economic" prerogatives of the business system, the other around the "political" prerogatives of the governmental system. In all other societies, from primitive to socialist, a single source of authority—village council, king, priesthood, party—makes both the determinations of war, law, and public ceremony, which we recognize as political, and the decisions on what shall be produced and how it shall be distributed, which we call economic. A seamless cloak of authority thus extends over the entire social structure, endowing every aspect of it with the aims of whatever group makes up its universal class. Under capitalism, this cloak is torn in two, and the realm of activities having to do with material life is removed from the reach of political authority. Capitalist governments still make fateful decisions of war and peace, or law and order, but are excluded from what is elsewhere a first prerogative of rulership—direct command over the material resources on which rulership must depend. When we look at the economic realm, we discover an even more astonishing constriction of authority. Capitalists, in whose name the system is organized, no longer possess the basic powers that accrue to persons of similar importance under earlier systems; unlike the most minor feudal lords, for instance, they cannot try, imprison, or forcibly muster "their" work forces, or enjoy the privileges of a legal code different from that applicable to other groups, much less promulgate laws or command military forces within their own bailiwicks. Thus, the two realms of authority help us understand why, unlike lords and kings and commissars, capitalists genuinely feel themselves to be without power.

It is not surprising that the establishment of two realms of authority sets the stage for what has always been and will always be the most difficult problem of capitalism—managing the relationship between the two realms. To judge by the talk that occasionally comes from the business community, that relationship is one of opposition and hostility; at times, one might think the government to be a foreign force that has temporarily occupied the capital, like the British in the War of 1812. I think it better to start from the opposite perspective—that ordinarily the government endorses the aims and objectives of the business community and bends a great deal of its efforts toward creating a framework within which business can operate smoothly. This business-oriented cast of mind is partly a consequence of the fact that the political realm, having surrendered authority over the workings of the economy, is now dependent on its smooth running to provide the wherewithal to carry out government programs, but on a deeper level it simply reflects the fact that the political realm and the economic realm are both parts of a single regime. Calvin Coolidge spoke the truth, however naïvely, when he said that "the business of America is business."

At the same time, it is obvious that the two realms live in uneasy coexistence. The objective of the economic realm is the organization of activity into whatever forms can produce a profit. The objectives of the political realm are two—the assertion of national sovereignty and the preservation of domestic tranquillity. In the normal course of events, the pursuit of economic life takes place within and offers no challenge to these *raisons d'état*, and, as a normal thing, the exercise of sovereignty and the cultivation of domestic peace support, and do not collide with, the overriding *raison d'entreprise*. But there are also built-in dissonances between the aims of the two realms. The aims of capital are as fragmented and individual as were the aims of the hundreds of feudal lords in the Middle Ages, each lord seeking his own aggrandizement, and no lord concerning himself much about the fate of feudalism. In similar fashion, each major corporation—not to mention the vast population of smaller businesses—is of necessity concerned with its own balance sheet, and is not in a position to affect, although it may worry about, the place of the nation in the world or the state of morale within the nation's borders. Government thus plays the role of the Holy Roman emperors who sought—on the whole, unsuccessfully—to defend and advance the cause of empire against its foes, including not least its own petty bickering, internal warfare, and social excesses. Governments of capitalist economies are also charged with the need to oversee, restrain, adjudicate, and correct tendencies of the economic realm that may arise from the uncoördinated or shortsighted or simply harmful operations of its individual members. These efforts may take such forms as Theodore Roosevelt's trust-busting campaign, the gradual growth of sentiment that resulted in the passage, in 1913, of the Federal Reserve Act, and Franklin Roosevelt's New Deal. Whether on narrowly focussed or broad issues, and quite regardless of which side is "right," this difference between the worm's-eye and the bird's-eye view introduces an inherent source of friction into the regime of capitalism.

LOOKING back, one sees that the boundary between the realms has moved in two directions. From the eleventh century, when the mercantile estate began to establish its place within the feudal hierarchy, through the seventeenth and eighteenth centuries, the authority of the economic realm expanded at the expense of that of the political realm. By 1776, "The Wealth of Nations" was able to delimit the proper economic reach of "the sovereign" to only three functions: "first, the duty of protecting the society from the violence and invasion of other independent societies; secondly, the duty of protecting, as far as possible, every member of the society from the injustice or oppression of every other member of it, or the duty of establishing an exact administration of justice; and, thirdly, the duty of erecting and maintaining certain public works and certain public institutions, which it can never be for the interest of any individual, or small number of individuals, to erect or maintain; because the profit could never repay the expense to any individual or small number of individuals, though it may frequently do much more than repay it to a great society."

Although it was certainly not Smith's intent, this minimalist prescription would actually permit a very large government sector—defense, the entire system of law and order, and the provision of what has come to be known as "infrastructure," including

(with Smith's explicit approval) public education. What is conspicuously missing from Smith's list is any license for government to carry on or regulate or otherwise become involved in the workings of the market system. Yet, as the examples of the two Roosevelts and the passage of the Federal Reserve Act illustrate, the boundary has moved in precisely that direction since Smith's time, starting with the English Factory Act of 1833, on whose inspectors' reports Marx was to rely heavily for his indictment of the factory system. Since then, of course, the boundaries have extended the reach of government into the economic realm both through the enactment of various entitlements to income, from workmen's compensation to social security in its various forms, and by the more or less official assumption of government responsibility for the over-all level of performance of the system—the latter perhaps first reaching its present-day form in the efforts of the New Deal to "pump up" the economy.

From the beginning, these reassertions of the ancient extent of the public realm have been fiercely debated. Conservative economists, fully as much as businessmen, have feared that the redrawing of the line in favor of the government would cause the goose to lay fewer golden eggs; liberals have feared that a failure to exercise public regulatory or supportive power would threaten the life of the goose. Although the terrain is still contested, I think it is by now abundantly clear that there exists no divinely, or even rationally, ordained division of responsibilities between the realms. At least in the post-Second World War era, the United States has tended to take a somewhat more hands-off attitude than have other capitalist nations, but it is difficult to draw lessons from a comparison of the two policies in practice. During the nineteen-seventies, it seemed that the European style, which featured a good deal of talk and some action toward "concerting" or even "planning" national action, was better suited to promoting economic growth and high employment than the American: European nations enjoyed almost twice the growth of the United States and suffered only about one-half its unemployment. Recent experience, however, has led to a different conclu-

sion. During the nineteen-eighties, United States growth outstripped European growth, and the American employment record—nineteen million jobs created in a decade—is the envy of the Common Market nations. In similar fashion, Great Britain, virtually the only strict constructionist across the Atlantic, seemed to be paying a high economic price for Margaret Thatcher's determination to dismantle the government-supported economy in the first years of her Prime Ministership, only to emerge in the last two years as the fastest-growing economy in Europe. On the other side of the fence is Japan, where the line of demarcation is drawn in a fashion that bewilders Western observers, blurring the government-enterprise border in ways that have led to its characterization as Japan, Incorporated.

This latitude of workable configurations does not mean, I should add, that it is still possible to relocate the economic-political boundary where Adam Smith placed it. The map has been redrawn in all capitalist nations, not just some, and although the specific elements of the terrain which are allowed to remain on one or the other side differ from one country to the next, all reflect a common enlargement of the political realm. This common movement suggests that the division of authority is affected by forces that override idiosyncrasies of individual place and history. One of these forces is surely the increasing power of industrial technology to puncture the protective mantle of the environment—a development that has moved all governments to intervene in the productive process to safeguard the human habitat against the disturbances caused by industrial processes and products. As an illustration, about five per cent of all state and local government employment in the United States exists just to cope with the automobile. A second force must be the growing urbanization of society. Cities have always been the seats of government, and the proportion of American citizens living in cities has increased from about a third in 1900 to over three-quarters today, a trend duplicated in all nations. Yet another force pushing for larger government has to be the increased concatenation of the economic realm itself. The economy of Adam Smith's day, with its many small farms and workshops, could be likened to a pile of sand, composed of innumerable small units of enterprise, each rubbing up against similar small units. Today's economy can best be compared to a girdered assemblage where miscalculations or shocks affect or threaten the entire system. Smith did not write about large-scale economic breakdowns, as Marx or Keynes did, because a sandpile economy does not manifest the instability of a girdered one.

Thus, a central cause of the century-long and universally apparent movement of the public-private boundary toward the side of government reflects the conservative political nature of capitalism much more than it does any emerging economic radicalism within it. Government extends its reach into the economic realm to cushion, restrain, or offset disruptions that emerge from the shuddering industrial machine in the basement. To the degree that the growing visibility and importance of government is due to these self-generated forces, the outlook is certainly for a continuation, and probably an extension, of the long historical trend toward the enlargement of the governmental realm. The disruptive power of technology, the complexity of urban life, the concatenation of the economy are all likely to increase—perhaps dramatically, in the case of technology—bringing with them the need for the government to mount more repair efforts, which usually get blamed after a while for creating the damage they are trying to repair.

THIS likely development would, however, be no more than an extension of a long-term trend in the division of authority. More significant is the growing encroachment of the economic realm upon the very core principle of the political realm, its sovereignty. Here the threatened salient lies along the boundary line that divides the international concerns of the economy and the state. Before the arrival of capitalism, there was an obvious conflict of interest along this salient between the merchants and the aristocrats—the precursors of the two realms to come. Medieval merchants bringing their packtrains across the face of Europe needed and sought the political protection of the rulers through whose domains they moved but were suspicious and fearful of those

rulers, the lords. The lords, similarly, needed and sought the marvellous objects brought by merchants from faraway lands, but were suspicious of a social group over which they held no rights of vassalage and who entered and left their domains in a manner that they were certainly not prepared to allow their own subjects to do. This tension between the border-blind view of merchantdom and the border-bound view of dukedom was lessened as the structure of capitalism gradually took shape, and in time the two realms acquired their symbiotic relationship. By the eighteenth century, the aims of government were generally conceived as congruent with those of the economic community and, by the nineteenth century, as properly subordinated to it—*raisons d'état* always excepted. Free trade was then everywhere defended as the logical extension into the world market of the competitive discipline of the domestic market—a process that would ultimately enrich, and therefore strengthen, the nation-states whose economies would be subjected to this Darwinian winnowing process.

None of the leading economists, then or later, seem to have remarked that competition at home produced depressed areas as well as boom regions, and that it might have similar effects on an international scale; and even those members of the underworld of economics—such as the early-twentieth-century English reformer John Hobson, who interpreted free trade as a weapon of the rich against the poor—agreed that the internationalization of economic relationships was unquestionably in the interests of the capitalist nations themselves. Hence no one perceived the international extension of the economic realm as a threat to political sovereignty. The reason, we can now see, was that the international economy was itself still in its formative stages. Enterprises were still mainly situated in and entirely identified with their mother countries. International finance linked stock exchanges, but modern international banking was still in its infancy—one travelled abroad with letters of credit. An enterprise in Hamburg or Dayton could not possibly exercise continuous supervision over production flows of manufacturing subsidiaries in Bangkok or Mexico

City, and, in fact, had no such subsidiaries. The enlargement of the international exchange of currencies to a level at which it exceeded by tenfold the entire value of the goods and services that crossed national boundaries was beyond the dreams of any banker and certainly beyond the technical capacities of the world's hand-operated banking system. The possibility that corporations in one country could clone themselves in the poorer regions, whence they would export automobiles, cassettes, high-density computer disks, and synthetic fabrics to their home markets was never discussed, because it was never remotely realistic.

All these developments are, of course, commonplaces of modern economic life, and a great deal of anxious attention is currently being paid to them. What is not so much discussed is that this movement represents a remarkable change in the complexion of capitalism itself, a change that threatens a considerable part—though, of course, not all—of the prerogatives of the political realm. Can a nation-state still effectively control its own currency, whatever its constitution may say, if currency flows into and out of its banks in volumes that vastly overshadow the size of "its own" money supply? Can it accurately assess the condition of its balance of trade if a significant fraction of its imports comes from its own companies situated abroad? Can the Darwinian process be counted on to strengthen national power if the outcome of the process is that companies situate their productive capacity outside the boundaries of the home country? I have avoided using American names and examples, because the questions apply to Germany and Switzerland as much as to the United States. The multinational corporation and the growth of a vast network of international finance affect the political independence of all capitalist governments. In the same way, the nascent transplantation of capitalism to parts of Asia and South America —symbolized in the meteoric rise of South Korea—affects the political hegemony that has until now belonged to the capitalisms of North America, Europe, and (more recently) Japan.

These deep-seated changes, present and latent, suggest that the boundaries of the two realms will be further readjusted in the foreseeable future, as the political realms within the older capitalist nations seek to protect their sovereignty against an unexpected threat from their own economic bases. In the emerging contest between the two realms—a contest in which the imperatives of expansion, efficiency, and profitable growth are pitted against those of inviolability, integrity, and independence—I will place my chips on the political side. The economy energizes people to work; the polity inspires them to work together. Men and women will not only salute a flag but fight and die for it—something they will not do for any corporation. The ultimate mobilizing power of capitalism lies in its political, not its economic, half, even though its dynamism and drive derive from the latter. The boundary of the realms is therefore very likely to move again toward an enlargement of state prerogatives with respect to the compartmentalization, quarantine, or buffering of the international reach of capital. The forms and the successes and failures of this reassertion of political prerogative cannot be foretold in particular, but the general movement can, I think, already be discerned under the name "protectionism."

IT must seem like a major oversight that I have left until now any discussion of the role of democracy within capitalism. I have done so for two reasons. The first is that capitalism, unlike all other major regimes in history, tolerates democracy but is not itself indissolubly dependent on it, as Nazi Germany, Fascist Italy, apartheid South Africa, and, until recently, dictatorial Chile amply illustrate. The second reason is that the democratic aspect of capitalism appears both as a source of strength and as a problem. The strength lies in the active involvement of citizens in the determination of their collective political life—a counterpart of their personal involvement in the achievement of their collective economic advancement. The problem is that this selfsame political involvement generates a tension within the larger regime, in that the economy kowtows to wealth and income but the polity bows to the general electorate. Because the distribution of wealth and income is highly skewed, the economic realm is

inherently a plutocracy, the eager servant of the rich, the deaf servant of the poor. Because the political realm is organized in democratic fashion, it caters to voters, and the vote of the millionaire counts for no more than that of the beggar. The conservative friends of democracy in every capitalist country have worried about the possibility that the masses might take advantage of their voting strength to undo the economic framework of inequality, but the shrewdest among them—starting with Adam Smith—have seen that the regime acquires political cohesion, because it is in "human nature" to admire one's superiors, not resent them.

Nonetheless, there is an inherent pulling apart in a social order composed of two realms—one built on the verticality of wealth, the other on the horizontality of democracy. In this remarkable joining of dissimilars, the political function of the governmental realm is not merely to protect, guide, and superintend the economic process but to prevent it from delegitimatizing itself with the voting public. This has been a motivation of the political sphere which has gained importance as democratic forces have gained strength. The history of every democratic capitalist nation is one of a widening provision of "entitlements," over the nearly universal opposition of business, because from the viewpoint of government these measures have seemed necessary to retain and strengthen the fealty of its citizens.

The political commitment to entitlements, especially in the United States and Great Britain, has waned in recent years, and what seems a fierce debate surrounds the question of whether it should move backward or forward. Nonetheless, the bone of contention is no longer the principle of entitlements but their reach and level, much as the quarrel over the government's responsibility to sustain the economy concerns ways and means rather than whether or not. I suspect, therefore, that political logic will tend to prevail over economic, which is to say that considerations of solidarity of the regime will take precedence over those of sheer efficiency. In all this, the touchstone remains whether the politico-economic system as a whole will work well

enough—that is, well enough to maintain the businessman in his position as the representative of the universal class. That depends, of course, not only on the severity of the economic contradictions that capitalism is certain to generate but also on the nonbusiness classes' enthusiasm for—or, at least, acquiescence in—the continued "universal" status of business values. At the risk of sounding banal, I do not see how one can answer the question other than by suggesting that there are likely to be successful and unsuccessful capitalisms, the former maintaining the "animal spirits" (as Keynes called them) of its economic life and the general liberties of its political realm, and the latter moving slowly or abruptly toward something like Schumpeter's anticipated managerial "socialism," only uglier. The characteristics that will sort out capitalisms into one or the other of these categories are apt to be institutional adaptability, ideological pragmatism, and common decency, the international distribution of all of which appears to be as uneven as the distribution of natural resources, although much, much more important.

Even such a relatively open-ended assessment leaves unasked the difficult question of whether capitalism could long continue, even in its most successful instances, if shattering explosions of technology or massive relocations of industrial power should alter the present technical and geographical framework of power. That is a question we can leave for our grandchildren. The question for our children is whether the capitalism in this country will be one of the successful examples. Given our lack of a national labor or employers' federation to work out a policy on wages and industrial management essential to the control of inflation, our timid and disorganized view of what government's guiding role might be, and our indifference, bordering on hostility, to the large and wretched underclass that has appeared in recent years, I do not see how one can offer bland assurances in answer. Yet candor leads me to recognize that the national performance has been adjudged good enough by the electorate. History is no doubt the final arbiter in these matters, but history does not vote.

AND, finally, what of socialism? As I said at the outset, I do not think that the triumph of capitalism means its assured long and happy life or that the defeat of socialism means its ignominious exit from history. The collapse of centralized planning shows that at this moment socialism has no plausible economic framework, but the word has always meant more than a system of economic organization. At its core, it has stood for a commitment to social goals that have seemed incompatible with, or at least unattainable under, capitalism—above all, the moral, not just the material, elevation of humankind. However battered that conception may be from the designation of bloody and cruel regimes as "socialist," the vision has retained its inspirational potential, just as that of Christianity has survived countless autos-da-fé and vicious persecutions. At a more down-to-earth level, the great question seems to be whether the still centralized economies can duplicate the remarkable coexistence of realms which has provided so much of the success of capitalism. As the Soviet Union, China, and Eastern Europe allow an increased autonomy to their managerial cadres and encourage the growth of entrepreneurial activity in the crevices of their economies, we find the ingredients of a new universal class; but if socialism is truly to make way for such a class, more will have to be ceded than the capacity for acting without consultation with the authorities. What is crucially at issue is whether socialism can accept a second republic within its own borders—a republic of economic affairs with its own rewards, punishments, imperatives, and ideology, without which the republic of political affairs seems unlikely to acquiesce in the all-important limitation of its powers.

Would this mean, in effect, the transformation of socialism into capitalism? This is to ask how closely capitalism, under its most democratic impulse, could approach socialism, under its most economically open arrangements. Sweden has always been the living example, real or slightly imaginary, of a system whose economic realm is unmistakably capitalist but whose political leaders have often declared their admiration for socialism, and sought—successfully, on the whole—to move toward its egalitarian standards. This raises the vision, once popular with political scientists and economists, of a historic "convergence" of systems that has grown increasingly less plausible in the light of the immense gulf between the performances of the two social orders. Perhaps the vision will again become a matter for serious consideration if the extraordinarily difficult movement of centralized socialism toward economic and political liberation is not derailed, and if the drift of capitalism toward a more responsible amalgam of economic freedom and political responsibility continues its slow historical advance. Mutterings of both right and left to the contrary, there is no evidence that at least some capitalisms could not progress in this direction. Whether that will be possible for centralized socialism we simply do not know. Meanwhile, for both sides the immediate aim is to create systems that will work well enough. Despite the triumph of capitalism, that is not a matter to be taken for granted, least of all by us.

INTERVIEW WITH MICHEL ROCARD

Ferdinando Adornato and Gabriele Invernizzi

The following interview with the Socialist Prime Minister of France has been excerpted from one conducted by Ferdinando Adornato and Gabriele Invernizzi that appeared in Verso il due mila #1: La nuova civiltà *(supplement to* L'Espresso, *March 18, 1990).*

F.A. & G.I. What has the word "left" meant for the twentieth century? Destruction or creation?

M.R. Creation. Always. By definition. The word "left" evokes two categories at the same time: aspirations, points of reference, ethical values; and then a system of rationalizations based on these values, that is, social prescriptions for the conduct of public action. At a time when some rationalizations—those that had become perverse—are changing profoundly, if not collapsing, it's necessary to remember that from an ethical point of view, nothing is changed. Even today, whoever says "left" is saying "the will to change, more justice, more equality, more democracy, more pluralism."

F.A. & G.I. So the bottom line seems positive to you?

M.R. Before thinking about bottom lines, it's necessary to examine the second meaning of the word "left"—what I call the system of rationalizations of left values. Underlying the system was the implicit and rather stupid hypothesis that in order to liberate man (who is fundamentally good) from the evils of capitalism, private property, profit, and competition, all that was needed was a political power not tied to those things. The opposite has been proven true. Today the end of this system of perverse rationalizations leaves the majority of left activists in the world without an identity—without that socialist identity based more on the rationaliza-

tions than on the initial values. So today we need a formidable effort of intellectual creation to reinvent a system of government rationalizations that respects all hopes but also accepts the fact that man is not necessarily good, but can be, just as he can be bad; that an economy functions only if it's competitive; and that we'll have more social justice only if we establish better rules for the market.

F.A. & G.I. But with the historical crisis of the communist systems, doesn't the utopian notion of new relations of equality and justice between men also disappear? Or do you think that it can be rewritten?

M.R. I can only say that human beings don't live without hopes and therefore there's a need for utopia. The horrible experiences of this century will leave us more lucid about human beings and their ambivalences. I, for example, no longer believe—if I ever did—in communitarian ideals. Perhaps new collective ideas will be found—I even think they're close at hand—but with the condition that they be better adapted to the circumstances of man as he is.

F.A. & G.I. Does the term "socialist society" still have meaning for you?

M.R. Institutionally, no. Among the one hundred sixty nations sitting in the United Nations, about eighty proclaim themselves socialist; and they go from Albania to Sweden, taking in China, the Soviet Union, and François Mitterrand's France along the way. On the ideological level, I've already told you what I think. In short, I don't believe in a reawakening of communism. I think rather that the intellectual work to elaborate the rules of a new public power that wants to assure more equality and less arbitrariness in a society where competition isn't negated—this will be the great challenge of the century's end.

Reprinted from *Dissent*, Winter 1991, pp. 31-33.

F.A. & G.I. What are the key ideas that can guide the left of the 1990s?

M.R. One day I tried to enumerate them, and I counted seven. [The first is] freedom. To come and go, to express one's own opinions, to join a union or a party, and so on—but also the freedom to buy and sell what one wants. Because it doesn't matter whether the seller is private, cooperative, or nationalized, the market is a constituent element of freedom. It's good for socialist discourse to make this truth its own. But doesn't the market amplify—one might object—all inequalities? In fact, it's necessary to place limits on the market. But a society without a market is without freedom.

F.A. & G.I. And the second?

M.R. Democracy. One might think that democracy is synonymous with freedom, but I want to refer with this word to the content of public power. And here I include pluralism, representative democracy, and a careful mix of direct democracy (such as referenda and the election of the head of state by citizens) and the indirect democracy of powers delegated to elected assemblies. I add that democracy is not a luxury reserved for rich countries. It's the condition of any lasting economic and social development.

F.A. & G.I. And the third idea?

M.R. The third idea is autonomy—in the sense of self-management and decentralization. Autonomy signifies that in the organization of public power what's needed is a system that permits every decision to be made in the most direct manner possible by those who will implement it and by those who will be affected by it. And also that the control of decisions be from below and not just from above. On the economic level, autonomy means struggle against monopolies and concentration, but this struggle can begin inside enterprises—with the discovery by workers that the valuation of an individual is not determined by salary and duties alone, but also by winning an area of responsibility. For this reason, autonomy is tied to the idea of self-management and decentralization.

F.A. & G.I. Value number four, Mr. Rocard?

M.R. I would call it domination of technologies. Today we are more victims than masters of the technological leap. This is true both in the automation of work—which is done brutally without taking into account the central idea of man—and in the field of biological experimentation. In the relations between man, matter, and life, the products of scientific research have progressed much faster than philosophical inquiry. Here also it's a question of reaffirming that, like the economy, science, too, must be at the service of man, and not vice versa.

F.A. & G.I. Now we're at five.

M.R. Solidarity—that is, the permanent will of public powers to assure above all else the nonmarginalization of all handicapped, of nature, health, economic development—and then a redistribution of income that takes into account the hierarchy of talents, more tiring types of work, and responsibilities. Today what a soccer player or television star earns provokes disorder and instills money values throughout society. One day, we must confront this problem seriously. But I don't think our Western societies—which were so afraid of collectivism and feel they've saved themselves from penury and the gulag thanks to market forces—are ready to reflect on this subject. It's too soon. I'm convinced, however, that if money continues to be an exclusive point of reference, it will definitively corrupt these societies.

F.A. & G.I. And what do you put in sixth place?

M.R. The supremacy of law. There's no civilization without law. Reaffirming this supremacy today becomes an absolute necessity because in the absence of international law, any state has the right to massacre its own people. Think of Pol Pot. The concept of the supremacy of law also holds for the economy. And here I'd like to underscore the great intellectual swindle I mentioned earlier. When speaking of civil liberties, no one imagines that included among them is the freedom to kill or to steal; and consequently one accepts the idea that there's no freedom without laws, a system of justice, police. When, however, one moves to the domain of economic exchanges between men, freedom is called the right to do anything—to trick, to sell below cost, to create economic concentrations . . . and every law, system of justice, or police that intervenes—even if only to control product quality—is decried as state planning, as entry into the gulag. All the same, there's no freedom without a market. So what's to be done? We must invent an international law that's also applicable to the economy.

F.A. & G.I. We're at number seven, the last.

M.R. Peace. This idea should induce us to find the solution to every conflict through negotiation and not force. I firmly believe this, and I've demonstrated it. In New Caledonia, the government preceding mine used gunfire; I negotiated peace.

F.A. & G.I. Do we stop here?

M.R. No. I want to add a point that's very important to me. These seven values I've listed aren't the exclusive property of the West. When transferred to the level of social organization, they're also the most effective means to assure the development of the Third World.

Translated from the Italian by Joanne Barkan

Squabbling German Greens Survey the Election Debacle

Serge Schmemann

Special to The New York Times

BONN, Dec. 6— The moderates accused the radicals of living by "rejection." The radicals attacked moderates as "undertakers," and for good measure blasted a newly arrived eastern German member as a "reactionary." Petra Kelly blasted them all as "mullahs of the party factions who have coagulated in dogmatism."

Beaten, battered and possibly destroyed by their drubbing in Sunday's election, the Greens were still at it, as if determined to go out with the same defiance, irreverence and chaos with which they first invaded the corridors of mainstream politics a decade ago.

Meeting in the environmentally sound conference room they had built in the Parliament building eight years ago, the 46 departing western German Green members of Parliament seemed agreed on only one point: that if the movement did survive, it could not avoid the schism that has all but paralyzed the Greens in recent years.

"The election result showed that the anti-party party project has failed," declared Wolfgang Ullmann, a pastor from Berlin who arrived in Bonn with the small group of eastern German Greens and civic-movement leaders to whom the mantle of left-wing protest now passes.

Only 3.9 Percent of Vote

In Sunday's election, the western German Greens mustered only 3.9 percent of the vote, less than the 5 percent needed to secure a seat in Parliament and far below the 8.3 percent they won in 1987. That meant that all 46 western German members of Parliament, and their staff of about 260, would have to vacate their parliamentary offices and lose much of their income this month.

The western Greens might have retained some seats if they had united before the elections with the eastern German Greens, since their combined vote would have nudged them over the 5 percent barrier. But because they were opposed in principle to the "colonialization" of the east, the Greens had postponed uniting their parties until after the election.

The eastern German coalition of Greens and civic movements—the remnants of New Forum and the other movements that arose during the 1989 uprisings—won 6.1 of the vote in the east, enough, under the special rules for this election, to claim eight seats in Parliament.

Whether the election really was the death knell of the Greens will become clear only at their next party congress in the spring, and before that they face elections in Hesse state on Jan 20. But the election defeat seemed to sever the last fragile links between the bitterly divided factions in the movement.

'Realos' vs. 'Fundis'

Leaders of the pragmatic "Realo" wing, led by Joschke Fischer, declared that only by engaging in active politics could the movement recover. "You cannot keep ignoring the laws of political physics and reduce yourself to non-representation," he declared as he proposed changes to move the Greens to a more established leadership.

From the radical "fundi" wing, whose members believed in keeping the Greens as a voice of radical opposition and permanent resistance, Jutta Ditfurth fired back that if the party went the way of conventional politics, she and her comrades would quit.

"If they come through with what they just proposed, then it's over, the Greens are dead," she declared to reporters outside the hall where Mr. Fischer had just finished a news conference. "This is really a news conference of undertakers."

Ms. Ditfurth rejected the notion that it was the public infighting that had damaged the movement. On the contrary, she declared, it was the realos' efforts to squelch debate that put people off. "The public loved the fights, against NATO, for social change," she said. "These were good fights. They raised consciousness."

Somewhere between the two, Miss Kelly, 42 years old and a founder of the movement, declared that the party had committed suicide through its internal struggles. "Each side keeps telling the other to go home, but when they leave the roof caves in," she said. "In the end the voters never learned about the good things we were still doing, because all the media tuned into was the fight."

Bickering Over Reunification

To outside commentators, the bickering that hurt the most came over German unity. Radical Greens rejected unity outright; others, including Miss Kelly, criticized it but accepted it; others supported it. In the end the party emerged without a position on the most fateful issue of the campaign.

At the same time, the Greens' original cause, the environment, became a standard plank of the mainstream parties, especially in the campaign of Oskar Lafontaine, the Social Democratic candidate.

Ultimately both the bickering and the loss of strong issues were less direct causes of the Greens' loss than symptoms of the movement's middle age, of its doomed efforts to perpetuate the heady resistance of the 1960's.

"We need a radical rejuvenation of our party," Mr. Fischer said. "The youth was our source of life. When we lost that, we lost the elections. The generation of the 1960's is now into parenthood and even grandparenthood."

Deputies Were Rotated

Ever seeking to combat institutionalization, the Greens experimented with constant rotation of parliamentary deputies, with fuzzy lines of command and an antipathy to party discipline. The best known of the Greens faded into the background because of the mandatory rotation.

The bulk of the party's losses were defections: 600,000 voters switched to the Social Democrats, 140,000 to the Christian Democrats. Equally painful, however, was that 270,000 former Green voters simply did not vote.

But however hard the blow, few Greens or political analysts were prepared to write off the movement. It was generally agreed that the year of German unity had the strong effect of pulling voters to the center, especially to those parties that had been most bullish on unity, the Christian Democrats and the Free Democrats.

EUROPE'S CHRISTIAN DEMOCRATS

Hello, Caesar, this is God

Much of Europe is run by Christian Democratic parties. Will they stay true to their religious roots, or become just another variety of the centre-right?

SINCE 1945 Christian Democracy has been Western Europe's most successful political movement. In Belgium, Holland, Luxembourg, West Germany, Austria, Switzerland and Italy, Christian Democrats have seldom been out of power. Yet many Christian Democratic parties today suffer, just as do Socialist and Communist ones, from doubts about their identity.

The idealists among them want to preserve the movement's original, Christian inspiration, which distinguishes it from liberalism or conservatism. The pragmatists, in contrast, argue that it should line up with European conservatives to confront the left. History seems to be moving the pragmatists' way. For the time being, though, Christian Democrats are a very different breed from conservatives such as Britain's Tories.

The movement springs from the nineteenth-century (and later) quarrels in mainland Europe between clerical parties and lay. What would today be broadly called the right was deeply divided. Clericals thought the church should be integrated into, and privileged within, the state; liberals that the two should be kept firmly apart. The church itself—essentially, the Catholic church—was happy to influence the mighty, but had little zeal for democratic politics of any sort, seeing democracy and the socialist parties that it bred as the road to atheism.

The aim of Luigi Sturzo, the Catholic priest who founded Europe's first Christian Democratic party, in Italy in 1919, was to reconcile Catholicism with democracy. His party was independent of the church and in favour of social reform. Similar parties were founded elsewhere in Europe and in Latin America. When fascism drove Sturzo into exile in 1924, he set up an international grouping in Paris. Among those active in it were an Italian aide, Alcide De Gasperi; a Frenchman, Robert Schuman; and a German, Konrad Adenauer. In the 1920s they talked of a common market and of European integration as a means of preventing further wars. In the 1950s these men were to achieve their dreams.

After the second world war, the Christian Democratic parties were refounded and immediately won elections. They had an obvious appeal in countries where Christian values had suffered from nazism and were now under threat from communism. Christian Democrats adopted from Jacques Maritain, a French philosopher, the principle of "personalism": the idea that an individual should fulfil his development through responsibility to other people, especially to the family and to the community. Personalists oppose both liberal individualism and socialist collectivism.

Christian Democrats took the rest of their doctrine from the social teaching of the Catholic church. They are thus set apart from conservatives by their principle of "solidarity"—the solidarity, that is, of all parts of society with each other. This means working to improve social conditions and, not least, accepting the role of trade unions. Most Christian Democratic parties (though not the West Germans) have strong trade-union wings. The European People's party (EPP—a get-together of the European Community's Christian Democratic parties) supports the EC's social action programme. Opposing class-consciousness, Christian Democrats claim to represent all social groups. They get votes from all, though relatively fewer among industrial workers.

Another principle, which the Christian Democrats accepted long before the Vatican did, is "subsidiarity": the notion that power should be decentralised as far as possible—but may be exercised at high, if need be even supranational, levels, when that makes sense. Thus Christian Democrats have always been federalists.

Christian Democratic theorists never got round to economics. But it was a Protestant member of West Germany's Christian Democratic Union (CDU), Ludwig Erhard, who dreamed up the "social market economy"—the free market with a social conscience. His success as West German finance minister during the 1950s helped persuade Christian Democrats elsewhere to rein in their interventionist instincts. This was, by the way, Protestantism's one clear contribution to Christian Democracy. The movement is dominated by Catholics, though 40% of CDU members are Protestant and the Dutch party is a union, formed in 1980, of one Catholic and two Protestant parties.

Decline and revival

The wave of secular liberalism in the 1960s both threatened the Christian Democratic parties and changed their character. The Catholic church, in the past a firm believer in its right to a privileged role in the state, came gradually closer to the liberal concept of their separation. In Italy the Vatican stopped offering direct advice to voters. Voters were listening less to it anyway. Church-going declined, while church views on matters such as contraception were widely disregarded.

The Christian Democratic parties were slow to catch up with such social trends. And though their leaders in the 1940s and 1950s mostly had been men of vision who took their ideals seriously, the new ones tended to be quite simply politicians, some of them pretty cynical politicians at that.

Christian Democracy's hold on power only just survived. As the table shows, in Belgium and Holland the Christian Democratic share of the vote dropped sharply during the 1960s. The fall was less sharp in West Germany. But the Social Democrats there got more votes in the 1972 election, for the first time, and kept the Christian Democrats out of government for the next ten years. France's Christian Democrats had won 28% of the vote in 1946, but later slid, under the weight of

From *The Economist*, March 17, 1990, pp. 17-19. Copyright © 1990 by The Economist. Reprinted by permission of The New York Times Syndicated Sales Service.

Gaullism, to 10–15%. In the 1970s they traded their independence for a place with Mr Valéry Giscard d'Estaing's centrists.

In Italy, where De Gasperi's party, Democrazia Cristiana, has been in government since 1944, its support held up, close to 40%, until the 1980s. The DC is expert at using its permanent hold on power in local government and in state industries to win votes. But it was on the losing side in the referendums on divorce and abortion, held in 1974 and 1981 respectively, and its vote fell to 33% in the 1983 parliamentary elections. In the 1984 Euro-elections it fell behind the Communists, for the first time ever.

Yet by the late 1980s the rot had stopped. Socialism, as a way of running the economy, has been largely discredited, and left-of-centre parties, little as they may have believed in it, have suffered. The pragmatism of power has helped Christian Democratic politicians to accept, in time, the liberal reforms that they disagree with. And voters care less about, say, abortion, than about jobs, wages and prices.

Party reform too contributed to the revival. The West German CDU, for instance, at one time did little more than run election campaigns. While in opposition, Mr Helmut Kohl supervised its transformation into a mass party, with a machine to rival that of the Social Democrats. Membership rose from 355,000 in 1971 to 734,000 in 1983. The CDU also adopted a popular new programme that combined lower taxation with welfare payments for mothers. In Italy, however, Mr Ciriaco De Mita, the DC party secretary since 1982, had less success. His attempt to shift authority from the competing factions to the party directorate was blocked by the old guard, who last year removed him first from his party post, then from the prime ministership, which he had held since April 1988.

Prose after poetry

For all its success at the polls, many Christian Democrats feel their movement has lost its way. Mr Fernand Herman, one of the most effective EPP members of the European Parliament, and a former Belgian economy minister, speaks for such people: "Christian Democracy has lost its soul and should go into opposition. The leaders now accept anything to stay in power, and they disregard our principles and traditions. They are not helping to renovate our doctrine. We were the first federalists, but now we focus too much on domestic politics, and leave it to socialists like Delors and Mitterrand to push forward European integration."

It is true that the movement has not produced any fresh political thinking since the 1940s, and that the current generation of leaders—Mr Ruud Lubbers (Holland), Mr Wilfried Martens (Belgium), Mr Alois Mock (Austria), Mr Giulio Andreotti and Mr Kohl—is one of technocrats and party managers rather than intellectuals and visionaries. Rightly, some think. "We are in a period of prose after the heroic age of poetry," says Mr Franco Maria Malfatti, a former president of the EC commission who now heads the

Holding the voters

Christian Democratic % of vote in lower-house parliamentary elections

	Belgium¹	Holland²	W Germany³	Austria⁴	Italy⁵
1945				49.8	
46	42.5	51.5			35.2
47					
48		53.4			48.5
49	43.5		31.0	44.0	
1950	47.5				
51					
52		48.9			
53			45.2	41.3	40.1
54	41.1				
55					
56		50.0		46.0	
57			50.2		
58	46.5				42.4
59		49.1		44.2	
1960					
61	41.5		45.3		
62				45.4	
63		49.2			38.2
64					
65	34.4		47.6		
66				48.3	
67		44.5			
68	31.8				39.0
69			46.1		
1970	30.1			44.7	
71		36.7		43.1	
72		31.3	44.9		38.7
73					
74	32.3				
75				42.9	
76			48.6		38.7
77	36.0	31.9			
78	36.1				
79				41.9	38.3
1980			44.5		
81	26.4	30.8			
82		29.4			
83			48.8	43.0	32.9
84					
85	29.2				
86		34.6		41.3	
87	27.5		44.3		34.3
88					
89		35.3			
1990					

1.Parti Social Chrétien (French) plus Christelijke Volkspartij (Flemish).
2.Christen-Democratisch Appel, formed 1980; till then, Katholieke Volkspartij plus (Protestant) Anti-Revolutionaire Partij and Christelijk Historische Unie, which formed it.
3.Christlich Demokratische Union plus (in Bavaria) Christlich Soziale Union.
4.Österreichische Volkspartei. 5. Partito della Democrazia Cristiana

Italian Christian Democrats' political bureau. "It's not a sin to win elections. We have the right and the responsibility to govern."

The argument between the idealists and the pragmatists will determine the future of Christian Democracy. Its more left-wing and/or more religious members think the movement should remain true to its origins, neither conservative, liberal nor socialist. The opposing camp, including most of the Germans, argues for a broader movement, more overtly right-wing and less Christian, that could cover the whole of Europe.

Sparks flew between these two camps in 1978, when a group of ten, mostly conservative, parties, including British Tories and French Gaullists, set up the European Democratic Union. To the horror of Italian and Benelux Christian Democrats, the CDU and the Austrian People's party also took part, while remaining in the European Union of Christian Democrats (first cousin of the EPP, but Europe-wide, not just EC-wide).

In the European Parliament, the need to compete with the left has already spurred the EPP to embrace Ireland's Fine Gael, Greece's New Democracy and, last year, the Spanish People's party, none of which has religious origins. But Christian Democracy's purists still carry some weight. After last year's European elections, British Conservative Euro-MPs applied to link with the EPP. Though the Germans were sympathetic, the Tories were told that their policies on EC integration, monetary union and the social charter made them unacceptable.

Holier than thou
The more Christian of Christian Democrats insist that religious inspiration could once again drive their movement. They rest their hopes on Eastern Europe, where 50 years of persecution have made the new or revived Christian political groups unashamedly forthright.

In the brief gap between liberation in 1945 and the imposition of Stalinism, Christian Democrats flourished in Poland and Hungary. In Poland they are now split between the re-established Labour party, the new National Christian party and Rural Solidarity. After the coming Hungarian elections, there is a chance that three Christian Democratic groupings will work together. Two of them, the Christian Democratic People's party and the Smallholders party, did well in the 1947 elections, while the third group is one of the strongest elements of Democratic Forum. A new Christian party is set to become a leading force in Slovakia. In Romania, the revived Peasants party has merged with a new Christian Democratic group.

Even in Western Europe, for all its secularisation, the Christian Democratic parties retain a firm religious base. Religion determines voting behaviour more than class does. In last year's Dutch elections, for instance, 85% of Christian Democrat voters described themselves as religious; for the Socialists, Liberals and Democrats '66, the figures were 55%, 40% and 25% respectively. In Italy in 1988, 30% of adults claimed to attend church at least once a week, but 50% of DC voters and 75% of delegates to the party's congress did so.

In Italy social and religious movements still play a big part in drumming up support for the DC. The Christian Democratic trade-union confederation claims 3m members. Comunione e Liberazione is a group of (a claimed) 100,000 religious activists who say they want to put Christ at the centre of life and society. It runs radio stations, businesses, publishing houses and "solidarity centres," which offer training for the unemployed; and an annual festival of political debate and entertainment at Rimini, the latest of which drew 700,000 people, most of them young.

For Mr Roberto Formigoni, Comunione e Liberazione's charismatic leader and a Euro-MP, "Faith means action. Other Christian Democrats have relegated faith to an abstract sentiment. While laicising the party, they've forgotten about the poor." This concern for the less fortunate did not stop Mr Formigoni being one of those who played a big part in bringing down the relatively laic but no less concerned Mr De Mita, and in restoring to the prime ministership the wily Mr Andreotti—one of the old guard, and a daily attender at mass.

The West German parties—the CDU and its Bavarian equivalent, the Christian Social Union (CSU)—represent the pragmatic pole of European Christian Democracy. The founders of the CDU included people who before 1933 had been liberals and conservatives, as well as Christian Democrats, and these mixed origins still mark its political complexion. The CDU and CSU do not always see eye to eye, but the differences are over policy—the Bavarians are more nationalist, and less keen on European integration, for instance—not about the place of religion in politics.

The West German parties think it inevitable that, in time, the EPP and the European Democratic Union, complete with its Gaullists and Tories, will merge. Projecting their own essentially bipolar politics on to Europe, they see socialism as the enemy. In Italy, Belgium and Holland, in contrast, Christian Democrats are used to working with socialists. Seeing themselves as centrist, they do not want to sink into the European centre-right.

Which way now?
Which of these tendencies will win? The continuing trend to a more secular society favours the Germans—and it seems unlikely to abate. The triumph of free-market economics makes it hard for Christian Democrats to maintain an economic policy distinct from that of conservatives. And the shift of Europe's left-wing parties towards the centre encourages some Christian Democrats to take a more right-of-centre line: they have to appear different.

Both the Italian and West German parties veered rightwards last year, mainly for their own internal reasons. In Italy the Communists' identity crisis helped to weaken Mr De Mita and his friends on the left of the DC, who would have accepted an alliance with the Communists. The now dominant centre factions prefer close links with the Socialist party. They feared that Mr De Mita's struggle against faction and patronage could endanger the DC's hold on power.

While the DC was purging Mr De Mita's leftish-leaning friends, the CDU in West Germany underwent similar surgery. Mr Kohl got rid of the powerful party secretary, Mr Heiner Geissler, and many of his followers. Mr Geissler's strategy had been to win votes from the centre-left. He had also been a fierce critic of the CSU's leader, Franz Josef Strauss. After Strauss's death in 1988, Mr Kohl feared that the CDU-CSU ticket would not look right-wing enough to get conservatives to bother to vote for it, nor to mask the far-right charms of the new Republican party.

The rightward shift of the German and Italian parties will encourage the EPP to become a broader centre-right grouping. Mr Thomas Jansen, its (German) secretary-general, used to think it should stay a purely Christian Democratic group. But last year he changed his mind: "The success of our link with the Spanish conservatives leaves Britain the only big EC country where we are not represented. In view of the new developments in Europe, it would be worrying if we kept the British out. We must try to persuade them to change their attitudes."

The coming intergovernmental conference on monetary union is likely to boost the powers of the European Parliament. The absence of the British from the EPP, which allows the left to dominate the parliament, will then matter more than it does now. The replacement of Mrs Margaret Thatcher as Tory leader, whenever it comes, will probably tilt the EPP towards opening its door. That would leave many Christian Democrats in Italy and the Benelux countries grumbling; for the founding fathers' vision of the movement would then be blurred beyond recognition.

EUROPE'S EXTREMES

JEFFREY GEDMIN

Jeffrey Gedmin is a research associate at the American Enterprise Institute.

ONE WEST GERMAN COMMUNIST SAW it all coming: "the betrayal of the working class," when one day the "class enemy" would be given "free rein to turn communists out of office through elections." From the time Mikhail Gorbachev began the implementation of his sweeping reforms in the Soviet Union in 1985, Stalinist-run communist parties in Portugal, France, and West Germany sensed that it was not only their comrades in Eastern Europe who would be in for rocky times but also their own parties. Even moderate "Eurocommunists" in Italy and Spain must have suspected that revolution in Mother Russia would ultimately spell upheaval in their ranks.

WHAT'S LEFT OF THE LEFT

Five years later, the evidence confirms their foreboding. While the Soviet-inspired demolition of communism in Eastern Europe has captured world attention, the nonruling communist parties in the West have not been far behind. Funding from Eastern Europe and the Soviet Union has dried up, membership has plummeted, and ideological disarray has left the few remaining faithful in tired confusion. Communism in Western Europe may soon be classified as a relic. That's the good news. But while Europe's communist left disappears, there are signs that a revitalizing extremist right may be waiting in the wings, ready to fill the vacuum in Europe's new politics.

Prelude to the Collapse

It would be unfair to give Mikhail Gorbachev all the credit for the demise of Western Europe's communist parties. In the mid-1970s, a thriving "Eurocommunism" threatened to transform the political landscape of much of Western Europe. But as democratic capitalism prospered and Marxian solutions to social and economic problems began gradually to lose

currency with left-wing constituencies across the continent, Western Europe's communist parties entered a phase of steady decline. The left in general has shifted in Europe. As Seymour Martin Lipset has documented, virtually all of Europe's social democratic parties shifted toward the center in the 1980s.

Between 1976 and 1986, the Italian communist party (PCI), the world's largest nonruling communist party, watched membership sink from 2 million to 1.65 million. In 1976, when the Italian communists made impressive gains in the national government (they secured 228 seats in the 630-seat Chamber—only 34 less than the Christian Democrats—and 116 seats in the 315-seat Senate—only 19 less than the Christian Democrats), the PCI could also boast of communist mayors in five large cities, including Rome and Naples. By the time Gorbachev had settled into power, over a quarter of the PCI's national support had evaporated, and Bologna was the only large city that still had a communist mayor.

In Spain in 1977, the communist party (PCE) managed to capture 9.4 percent of the national vote, expanding its portion to 10.8 percent in the second parliamentary elections, held in March 1979. But since that time, the party has been on the skids. Following a poor performance in the 1982 general election, the communists disintegrated into three factions. In 1986, an emaciated PCE was able to attain only 4.6 percent in the country's national election. Similar downward trends can be found for communist parties in pre-Gorbachev France and West Germany. Only Portugal's communist party (PCP)—the most Stalinist of Western Europe—was able to remain stable throughout the mid-1980s, consistently garnering around 15 percent of the Portuguese vote.

Over the last five years, Gorbachev's *"glastroika"* and popular revolution in Eastern Europe have plunged Western Europe's communist parties, Portugal's now included,

IS THE RIGHT ON THE RISE?

into the throes of a deep identity crisis, accelerating a process of decline leading to disintegration. Ironically, it has been the so-called moderate Eurocommunist parties in Italy and Spain, parties that appeared to have the most in common with Gorbachev's concept of communist "renewal," that have crumbled most quickly.

The Moderates: Spain and Italy

For more than two decades, communist parties in Spain and Italy have pursued a public position of "moderation" in their quest to participate in government. Following the Soviet invasion of Czechoslovakia in 1968, the Spanish communists labored to project their independence from Moscow. In his book *"Eurocommunismo" y Estado*, published in 1977, communist party boss Santiago Carillo went so far as to challenge the very nature of the Soviet Union's system of socialism—a view that earned him Moscow's condemnation for alleged collaboration with "the interests of imperialism."

Where the Spanish communists left off, their comrades in Italy tirelessly pushed forward. Embodying the Eurocommunist commitment to the parliamentary democratic process—a commitment opponents frequently referred to as a tactical position of "postponed totalitarianism"—the Italian communist party has come to resemble, at least on paper, something not far from the British Labour Party or West Germany's Social Democrats. Since the 1970s, the PCI has officially repudiated violence as a means of attaining power, rejected democratic centralism (running the party entirely from above), accepted limited market mechanisms, and even approved of Italy's membership in NATO. Such enlightened Marxism won for Italy's communists Gorbachev's praise as the "precursors of *perestroika*."

Perhaps uninspired by the Kremlin's own example, however, Italians responded with apathy in the 1987 elections, leaving the PCI with its most serious defeat in more than two decades and its third consecutive drop at the polls since 1976. Further demoralized by communism's collapse in Eastern Europe in 1989, nearly one-half of the 1.2 million Italians holding communist party membership cards had failed to renew their membership by the beginning of this year. In regional elections held this spring, the PCI limped home with its worst showing in more than 30 years.

In response to the PCI's collapsing ranks, general secretary Achille Ochetto has scrambled to revamp the party's image, proposing that the communists change their name and discard the party's hammer-and-sickle symbol.

To avoid further isolation of his party, Ochetto also proposes that the PCI join a broad coalition of the left that includes Bettino Craxi's Italian socialists (PSI).

Militant communists, fearing an unfavorable balance of forces, emphatically reject Ochetto's risky campaign to salvage something of their party, accusing the general secretary of a sell-out when he champions the union of "Marxist and liberal culture." Nevertheless, according to recent opinion polls, Ochetto's reformist course—a direction that could eventually reduce the PCI to extinction—has the support of nearly two-thirds of the current party membership.

If the PCI splinters, antireformers, who deplore what they see as the abandonment of the party's identity, may move to form a new communist organization. To be sure, the PCI's antireformers won't give up easily. As the *Wall Street Journal* reported earlier this year, old-guard communists in one small farming town in northern Italy were locked in battle with local citizens who had audaciously suggested that the larger-than-life bronze bust of Lenin gracing the town's square be taken down. But even if such "Cro Magnon communists" (so described by a PCI spokesman in Rome) band together, that tiny party of antireformers would pale in comparison to the significant Italian communist movement that was able to capture between a quarter and a third of the national vote since the war.

In Spain, the story has been much the same. The Spanish communists currently claim 83,000 members, a far cry from the peak of 200,000 members the party reported in 1977, two years after Francisco Franco's death. Although the Spanish communists insist they "will not renounce Marxism," ideological confusion among rank-and-file members stemming from communism's collapse in the East and the PCE's reported desire to move toward collaboration with the country's socialist party brought secretary general Julio Anguita to concede this year that the 68-year-old party has begun to dissolve. In March, Anguita fatalistically observed at a meeting of party *apparatchiks* that "within a year at most, we shall have to change [our] symbols and...name." In autonomous regions such as Navarra and La Rioja, the process is already under way; disillusioned proletarians have begun to detach the hammer-and-sickle from signs and party flags.

The Recalcitrants: France, Portugal, and West Germany

Staunch Stalinists, such as long-time French communist party boss Georges Marchais and Álvaro Cunhal, who has led the Portuguese

THE MODERATE EURO-COMMUNIST PARTIES ...THE PARTIES THAT APPEARED TO HAVE THE MOST IN COMMON WITH GORBACHEV'S CONCEPT OF COMMUNIST "RENEWAL," HAVE CRUMBLED MOST QUICKLY.

communist party for the last 48 years, have fought bitterly to keep *glasnost* from infecting their ranks.

Marchais still likes to maintain that he is "very close to Mikhail Gorbachev," despite the fact that Soviet publications like *Izvestia* have attacked the French communists for their unfashionable orthodoxy and intransigence. According to French press reports, the Soviet Embassy in Paris has even authorized active participation by its diplomats in meetings organized by opponents of the hard-liners.

In the 1986 and 1988 national legislative elections, the French communist party (PCF) captured 9.8 and 11.3 percent of the votes, respectively, roughly one-half of their support in the 1970s and their lowest totals since 1932. The beginnings of the PCF's current malaise can be traced at least in part to François Mitterrand's shrewd political manipulation of this domestic opponent.

In 1981, the PCF entered a coalition with Mitterrand's socialists in which the communists were able to obtain four ministries: civil service, transport, health, and education and vocational training. Caught in a trap undoubtedly laid by Mitterrand, the communists became partners in a government whose agenda they could not control but whose policies they were obliged to support. The last PCF minister left the Mitterrand government in the summer of 1984, leaving the French president to witness a prophecy come true. In 1972, Mitterrand, only two days after signing the Common Program with the PCF, had boasted that his party would "prove that out of five million communist electors, three million are quite capable of voting socialist."

Today, a frantic Marchais urges loyal supporters to fight on. The communist party boss decries reformers within the PCF's ranks as "liquidators" who, "duped" by events in Eastern Europe, "want us to stop being communists." But the liquidators appear to be gaining strength. Gorbachev enthusiasts, like French Central Committee member Charles Fiterman (who served as minister of transport and minister of state during the communist stint in the Mitterrand government), claim they have at least one-third of the PCF's membership on their side. The "restructurers" hope their own *perestroika* will engender a turnaround of the communists' declining fortunes.

If French communist reformers want a chance to save the party, however, they'll have to act quickly. Party statistics put current membership at 200,000 (compared to 710,000 claimed in 1985), but party insiders concede this figure may be doctored a little. Signatures on "humanitarian" petitions circulated at communist-sponsored rallies are frequently counted as PCF membership, and many old comrades, even the deceased, are still counted as vital members of the French communist movement. The Paris daily *Le Figaro* suggests that the number of actual PCF members may already have dwindled to 100,000.

In Portugal, 76-year-old hard-liner Cunhal has rejected the notion that the Portuguese communist party (PCP) be held responsible for the mistakes of others, insisting instead on what he calls the "solution of continuity." Facing sinking membership (199,000 currently claimed, with 28 percent having no regular ties to the PCP) and a decline in votes received in local elections (where the PCP is usually stronger than in national elections), the leadership clings to its Stalinist course. But party dissidents like Zita Seabra, who was one of a number of would-be reformers expelled from the party this year, continue to argue "in exile" for unlimited debate, acceptance of the multiparty system, and privatization of many of Portugal's means of production.

If Seabra and other reform-minded expellees prevail, it will likely signal the full-scale "social democratization" of Western Europe's most doctrinaire communist party. Meanwhile, a frail but militant Álvaro Cunhal digs in for a showdown that may never take place. Rumors are afloat that the general secretary's poor health, which was worsened by "deficient" treatment at a Moscow hospital in 1988, may soon force the PCP's fossilized Stalinist leader to step down.

Equally orthodox has been the leadership of West Germany's communist party (DKP), whose fate, it seems, was inextricably linked to Erich Honecker's Socialist Unity Party in East Berlin. During the course of East Germany's stunning popular revolution last fall, nearly 30,000 of West Germany's 58,000 communists turned in their membership cards. By Christmas, the DKP was forced to lay off the last of its estimated 500 paid employees. According to West German intelligence sources, the West German communists funded their activities with the 50–70 million West German marks ($29–41 million) they received each year from their comrades in East Berlin.

The West German communists never attained the success of communists elsewhere in Western Europe, receiving only 0.5 percent of the 1987 vote, for example. But support from East Berlin's regime allowed the DKP the opportunity to be at least a player in the Federal Republic's political system. Today, the handful of militants still remaining in the DKP struggle against further splintering and the absorption of their tiny party by the left wing of the Social Democratic Party (SPD) and the West German Greens.

As Western Europe's communist left

THE FRENCH COMMUNIST PARTY'S STATISTICS PUT CURRENT MEMBERSHIP AT 200,000 (COMPARED TO 710,000 CLAIMED IN 1985).... THE NUMBER OF ACTUAL PCF MEMBERS MAY ALREADY HAVE DWINDLED TO 100,000.

IN ITALY, SO MANY COMMUNISTS HAVE ALREADY JOINED THE COUNTRY'S TWO GREEN PARTIES THAT ITALIANS HAVE UNOFFICIALLY DUBBED THE GREENS THE "WATERMELONS"—GREEN ON THE OUTSIDE, RED ON THE INSIDE.

collapses, strident hold-outs from the Rhine to the Pyrenees, repulsed by the prospect of social democratization, may soon found new communist organizations whose size and influence are likely to remain modest for the foreseeable future. Other ex-communists may find a niche for themselves in lesser currents of militant environmentalism, radical feminism, or sundry other preoccupations of the left. In Italy, so many communists have already joined the country's two Green parties that Italians have unofficially dubbed the Greens the "Watermelons"—green on the outside, red on the inside.

In Britain, where the Communist Party has never exerted an overt influence on politics, the ranks and resources of the movement continue to flag. The Kremlin recently canceled half of its standing order for 12,000 copies of Britain's communist newspaper, the *Morning Star*, threatening the existence of the 23,500-circulation paper.

An Opening for the Extremist Right?

It seems premature to conclude, however, that the death of West European communism will spell the end of significant radical political movements in Europe. In the world of radicalism, psychology is infinitely more important than ideology. One might argue, for example, that for many Western communists, Marxist ideology has represented not just an alternative approach to organizing a society but also a defiant, antisocial act in itself. While there may be little space for political and social militancy on the left in the coming decade, there are already signs that in the very heart of Western Europe frustrated, alienated elements of European society have begun to find their expression in protest parties of the extreme right.

Extremist right-wing parties have been active in Italy, France, and West Germany for years. Italy's neofascist Italian Social Movement (MSI) was founded in 1946; Germany's National Democratic Party (NPD) in 1964. In France, Jean-Marie Le Pen's National Front, organized in 1972 on an anti-immigration program, was able to startle observers in 1984 by winning 10 of the 81 seats in the European Parliament. Nevertheless, the influence of extremist right-wing political parties has remained marginal. In Germany, the rise of Franz Schönhuber's *Republikaner*, a party some critics call neo-Nazi, could be the first sign of a change in this state of affairs.

Poor showings in two regional elections held this spring, together with the recent resignation of party chairman Franz Schönhuber, a former officer in Hitler's *Waffen-SS* (he became frustrated by the dominance

LIKE THE REPUPUB-LIKANER, LE PEN'S NATIONAL FRONT AND ITALY'S NEOFASCIST MSI ARE FUELED BY ANTI-IMMIGRATION SENTIMENT, OPPOSITION TO EUROPEAN UNIFICATION, AND IN SOME CASES, LATENT ANTI-AMERICANISM.

of "extremist functionaries" in the party), have taken some wind out of the *Republikaner*'s sails. But even if the *Republikaner* party falters, the *Republikaner* phenomenon shows signs of taking hold. With a platform that embodies a combination of ethnocentric nationalism, isolationism, and strong authoritarian tendencies, the *Republikaner* have reached a surprisingly diverse audience in West Germany. One-third of the party's current voters previously voted for the liberal SPD, and while the majority of *Republikaner* members are over the age of 50, according to party statistics nearly 70 percent of new recruits since January 1989 are under 30.

On the eve of German reunification, the *Republikaner* attempt to harness the anxiety of many Germans over their country's social and economic future. The *Republikaner* cast themselves as "the party of the little man," bent on protecting job security, providing affordable housing, and reinstating "law and order." But in doing so, the party aggressively exploits the issue of West Germany's 4.6 million immigrant workers, whose presence, according to the *Republikaner* platform, threatens the "property and social status of German citizens." The *Republikaner* have fared best in West Berlin—last year they captured 7.5 percent of the vote—where the foreign population is 10 percent of the city's two million total.

Winning 7.1 percent of the vote in the 1989 European parliamentary elections, the *Republikaner* believe—despite a drop in recent opinion polls—that they can attain the minimum 5 percent nationally required for representation in Bonn's *Bundestag* next December. And with an eye cast toward the first Pan-German elections, party activists have been exploring "fertile soil" in the present-day German Democratic Republic. In light of the multitude of socioeconomic problems East Germans will inevitably face in the process of reunification, it is conceivable that the *Republikaner* will do well in reaching a segment of East German society where, after 56 years of dictatorship, a residual authoritarian impulse may lead some frustrated voters to identify with the extremist *Republikaner* platform.

If the *Republikaner* manage to establish themselves at the national level, even if the party's support remained modest, Germany's system of proportional representation allows the opportunity for smaller parties to exert enormous influence. Rarely receiving more than 10 percent of the vote, for example, the Free Democrats have been able to serve in coalition governments in Bonn since the war, capturing important cabinet posts from economics to foreign affairs.

The prospects for right-wing extremists

in France and Italy appear favorable as well. Like the *Republikaner*, Le Pen's National Front and Italy's neofascist MSI are fueled by anti-immigration sentiment, opposition to European unification, and in some cases, latent anti-Americanism. In last year's European elections, the National Front received 11.7 percent of the vote, the Italian neofascists 5 percent.

In both countries, there is already some evidence that suggests the issue of "foreigners" is serving as a catalyst for the improved position of the extreme right. Italy's estimated 1.5 million non-European immigrants, convenient scapegoats for right-wing extremists in a country struggling with 11 percent unemployment, have been confronted by rising levels of isolated but well-organized racially motivated violence, according to Italian officials.

Italy's MSI, which received 5.9 percent of the last national vote in 1987, has undergone a process of political rehabilitation in recent years that may well place the extreme right-wing party in a position to profit from rising levels of racial conflict and an immigration debate that has only begun to heat up.

Perhaps no national party campaigns as vigorously on race as the extreme right-wing National Front. In France, where non-European immigrants represent 6.5 percent of the population (compared to 8 percent in West Germany and less than 3 percent in Italy), racial politics have been a source of tension for a number of years. With unemployment at 10 percent and many Frenchmen on edge over the economic threat—real or imagined—posed by German reunification, Le Pen has turned up the rhetoric, maintaining that his brand of racism is "French patriotism."

In May, the French National Assembly approved a bill, apparently aimed at Le Pen's National Front, that would bar anyone found guilty of inciting racial hatred from holding an elective office or a government job. (The bill also makes it a misdemeanor in France to engage in "revisionism"—the denial of the crimes of Nazi Germany. Le Pen was recently ordered by a French court to pay a fine for referring to the Nazi gas chambers as just a "detail in World War II history.") But this attempt to legislate morality is unlikely to fend off parties like the National Front in the long run if the preference of some voters indeed surges to the extreme right.

With 9.6 percent of the vote in 1988, France's system of majoritarian representation allowed Le Pen's party only a single deputy in the 577-seat National Assembly. But Le Pen's hate-mongering won him 14 percent of the vote in the 1988 presidential race, and this self-proclaimed protector of French interests will likely remain a force to be reckoned with.

It's ironic that in the aftermath of communism's collapse in the East, while so many observers have focused their attention on what some have called the specter of right-wing nationalism in the Soviet Union and Eastern Europe, racial conflict in Western Europe has begun to show signs of becoming less manageable than in the past. It's also true that the fragmented political landscapes of France and Italy have safely endured a certain amount of right-wing extremism since the war. Even in Germany, it remains to be seen whether the *Republikaner* can actually establish themselves as a national party with a future. But columnist Jim Hoagland is correct when he observed that Europe's new enemy is "the enemy within." With the scourge of communism disappearing in both East and West, Western Europe's democrats must hold the ship steady as the new Europe embarks on its course into the twenty-first century.

THERE ARE ALREADY SIGNS THAT IN THE VERY HEART OF WESTERN EUROPE FRUSTRATED, ALIENATED ELEMENTS OF EUROPEAN SOCIETY HAVE BEGUN TO FIND THEIR EXPRESSION IN PROTEST PARTIES OF THE EXTREME RIGHT.

WHAT WE KNOW ABOUT WOMEN VOTERS IN BRITAIN, FRANCE, AND WEST GERMANY

Nancy J. Walker

Nancy J. Walker is completing a doctoral dissertation at Oxford.

> *Whenever the consequences of women's suffrage have been studied, it would appear that women differ from men in their political behavior only in being somewhat more frequently apathetic, parochial, conservative, and sensitive to the personality, emotional, and aesthetic aspects of political life in electoral campaigns.*
>
> —Civic Culture, Almond and Verba, 1963

When *Civic Culture* was written, voting patterns and political attitudes showed women in Europe to be the more conservative—and more Conservative—of the two sexes. According to one popular saying of the time, if women had not been granted suffrage, the Labour party would have held office in Great Britain since the end of World War II. Further, in the early sixties "everyone" knew that women formed the base of support for the Christian parties on the continent. Two and a half decades later, we're about due for a new set of conclusions about gender and politics.

Great Expectations

German women fought for and won the right to vote in 1919. Propertied British women could go to the polls in 1920, but it was only in 1928 that universal suffrage was put on the books. And the nineteenth amendment to the American Constitution was signed into law in 1920. French women lagged behind their European and North American sisters, waiting until 1944 for the right to cast a ballot, partly because of strong opposition in the Senate. One anti-suffrage French senator quoted ancient authors to justify his position: "The woman of the Latin race does not think, does not feel, does not develop like the woman of Anglo-Saxon or Germanic races."

Women's entrance into the formal political sphere raised great hopes. They were expected to bring morality into politics and change the conduct of public life by waging battles against corruption, alcoholism, and even war.

Despite raised expectations, turnout among women was initially below that of men in all countries. It increased slowly but steadily with each election. After World War II the turnout gap was still evident, particularly in France, but it continued to narrow. Table 1 shows the percentage of men and women who've gone to the polls since the founding of the Federal Republic of Germany in 1949 and indicates the percentage of British men and women claiming to have voted, from 1964 to 1987. In both cases the gender difference decreased over time, becoming extremely small or disappearing by the mid-sixties. When controlled for age, the gender difference is much smaller among the young and over time has closed among the older age groups, as the older cohort has moved out of the electorate.

The Euro-barometre poll suggests that turnout

Table 1

TURNOUT BY GENDER WEST GERMANY, 1953-1987

	1953	1957	1961	1965	1969	1972	1976	1980	1983	1987
Men	88%	90%	89%	88%	88%	91%	91%	88%	89%	84%
Women	85	86	86	85	85	90	90	87	88	82
Difference	3	4	3	3	3	1	1	1	1	2

TURNOUT BY GENDER GREAT BRITAIN, 1964-1987

	1964	1966	1970	1974	1974	1979	1983	1987
Men	91%	85%	81%	89%	85%	85%	83%	
Women	87	83	82	87	85	86	84	
Difference	4	2	−1	2	0	−1	−1	0

Source: For Germany, Joachim Hofmann-Goettig (1953-1983), Representative Wahlstatistik (1987); For Great Britain, British Election Studies.

From *Public Opinion*, May/June 1988, pp. 49-52, 55. Copyright © 1988 by the American Enterprise Institute for Public Policy Research.

among French women is not quite as high as among British and German women, possibly because suffrage was granted in France so recently. As in Great Britain and Germany, younger French women are as likely to vote as younger men are.

Voting is only one measure of political participation, and by other gauges women in these three countries still lag behind the men, although the gaps are narrowing. Women are less likely than men to be members of a political party, less likely to give money to a party or candidate, and less likely to work for a political campaign. Among certain social groups, however—the upper and upper-middle classes in Britain, for example—women form the core of Conservative party workers. The Tory party could never manage to complete its mailings and canvassing without the aid of its loyal ladies.

Gender differences also persist in expressions of interest in politics and campaigns. In the early 1950s in Germany and France, women were two and a half times more likely than men to express *no* interest in politics—a majority of women in both countries. The gender difference was not quite so large in Great Britain. By the mid- to late sixties, about a third of all women—but only a fifth of the men—were uninterested in politics. The British gender gap narrowed in the late seventies, when both men and women plummeted into apathy, but even then women were more apathetic than men. This gender difference was always smaller among the younger and college-educated men and women in all three countries, but it persists today.

Talking about politics used to be a male prerogative, but this too has changed with the times. A 1959 question from *Civic Culture* and one from the Euro-barometre (1983) shows that the ratio of women to men who discuss politics has increased in both Great Britain and West Germany. In 1959 sixty German women for every one hundred German men discussed politics, but in 1983 it became ninety to one hundred. The number in Great Britain started out higher, with eighty-two women for one hundred men engaging in political conversations, and ninety-five British women for every one hundred men by 1983. Educated, working, younger women talk politics as often as men do in all three countries (see table 2).

If Political, Then Conservative?

Women were long thought to be apolitical, but if they were political then they were supposed to be conservative. Women's greater church attendance was one influence that led in this direction. But women's conservative inclinations seem to be changing.

In Great Britain the Conservative party's lead among women voters had disappeared in 1983, as shown in table 3. The Conservative lead declined during the late 1970s even among older voters (over sixty-five), virtually disappearing in the last two British elections. Younger voters, known to some as "Thatcher's

Table 2

INTEREST IN POLITICS
BY GENDER
GREAT BRITAIN, WEST GERMANY, FRANCE

| | Great Britain | | | |
	1959	1964	1974	1979
Not interested				
Men	31%	24%	28%	32%
Women	48	35	41	46

| | West Germany | | | |
	1952	1959	1965	1980
Men	18%	20%	6%	5%
Women	50	45	28	14

| | France | | |
	1953	1969	1978
Men	28%	34%	13%
Women	60	47	20

Source: *For Great Britain,* 1959: *Civic Culture* response was "Pay no attention to elections or politics"; 1964: British Election Survey, "Not much"; 1974 October: British Election Study, "Not much" plus "None at all"; 1979 British Election Study, same as 1974. *For West Germany,* 1952, 1965, and 1980: Allensbach Institute; for 1959: *Civic Culture.* For France, 1953, 1969, and 1978: Mossuz-Lavau/Sineau.

POLITICAL AND COMMUNITY PARTICIPATION
BY GENDER
GREAT BRITAIN, WEST GERMANY, FRANCE
(RATIO: WOMEN TO MEN)

| | Talk Politics | | Belong to Group | |
	1959	1983	1959	1983
Great Britain	.82	.95	.45	.78
West Germany	.60	.90	.36	.75
France		.98		.74

Source: For 1959, *Civic Culture*; for 1983, Euro-barometre, Men and Women of Europe.

children," display greater gender differences in voting, but in no persistent direction (see table 4). In some elections since 1964, the under twenty-five-year-old women were more likely than the youthful menfolk to support the Conservatives, in others they were more likely to throw their support to Labour. Since the Liberal/Social Democratic Alliance was formed in 1981, it seems that young women are slightly more inclined than young men to take the middle road, as both 1983 and 1987 election results suggest. In 1987 the MORI poll shows a huge lead for the Conservatives among

Table 3

PARTY VOTE BY GENDER
GREAT BRITAIN, 1964-1987

	1964	1966	1970	1974	1974	1979	1983	1987
Conservative								
Men	40%	36%	43%	37%	35%	45%	46%	43%
Women	43	40	48	39	37	49	45	43
Labour								
Men	47	54	48	42	45	38	30	32
Women	47	51	41	40	40	38	28	32
Liberal/SDP								
Men	12	9	7	17	16	15	23	23
Women	10	8	8	21	20	13	26	23

Note: Two elections were held in 1974.
Source: British Election Studies (1964-1983); Market & Opinion Research International (1987).

Thatcher's boys, but a lead for Labour among Thatcher's girls. It's too early for definitive statements, though.

Table 4

PARTY VOTE BY GENDER AND AGE
GREAT BRITAIN, 1964-1987

	1964	1966	1970	1974	1974	1979	1983	1987
65 years and over								
Conservative								
Men	48%	40%	45%	47%	46%	52%	50%	47%
Women	46	46	61	51	46	57	51	46
Labour								
Men	46	49	44	38	38	37	32	30
Women	44	50	30	34	37	32	26	33
Liberal/SDP								
Men	7	11	5	13	12	9	17	22
Women	9	4	8	14	16	10	21	20
Under 25 years								
Conservative								
Men	47	43	35	20	17	44	46	42
Women	33	33	40	30	32	36	40	31
Labour								
Men	45	50	51	39	53	38	33	37
Women	56	63	51	44	51	47	29	42
Liberal/SDP								
Men		7	12	28	23	23	19	19
Women		3	6	25	16	15	28	24

Source: See Table 2.

In the Federal Republic of Germany the right-of-center Christian Democratic party (CDU) used to boast a significantly higher percentage of women's votes than men's, but since the mid-1970s this lead has dwindled (see table 5). The left-of-center Social Democratic party (SPD) used to assume that more men than women voted for it, but since 1972 this is no longer the case, and the SPD is looking to younger women to provide its margin of victory in future elections. Men have always been slightly more likely to vote for the liberal-leaning Free Democrats (FDP), but the gender difference was never vast. The coming of the left-wing

Table 5

PARTY VOTE BY GENDER
WEST GERMANY, 1953-1987

	1953	1957	1961	1965	1969	1972	1976	1980	1983	1987
SPD										
Men	33%	36%	40%	44%	46%	47%	44%	43%	38%	39%
Women	28	29	33	36	40	46	43	44	39	38
CDU/CSU										
Men	39	45	40	42	41	43	47	44	48	43
Women	47	54	50	52	51	46	49	44	49	45
FDP										
Men	11	9	14	10	6	9	8	11	7	9
Women	10	7	12	9	5	8	8	11	6	8
Greens										
Men								2	6	8
Women								1	5	8

Note: Other parties not shown.
Source: Joachim Hofmann-Goettig (1953-1983); Representative Wahlstatistik (1987).

Greens into the Bundestag in 1983 certainly shook up German politics, but despite their excellent record on sexual equality, the Greens attract slightly fewer women than men.

The German gender difference in voting patterns is still somewhat evident today. Women over sixty did support the CDU in 1987 with much more fervor—and ballots—than older men did. But demographics may explain this as much as anything—there are many, many more women than men over sixty. The youthful vote in Germany started to diverge from the general pattern in 1972, with young women no more likely than young men to vote CDU, unlike the older generations. From 1972 until today, younger women cast more SPD ballots than young men. This margin shrank somewhat in 1987, to the dismay of the Social Democrats. The Greens drew their support heavily from the votes of "Kohl's children," with boys and girls in equal proportions (see table 6).

Table 6

PARTY VOTE BY GENDER AND AGE
WEST GERMANY, 1953-1987

	1953	1957	1961	1965	1969	1972	1976	1980	1983	1987
60 years and over										
SPD										
Men	30%	32%	36%	41%	42%	43%	42%	41%	40%	38%
Women	25	26	30	33	37	42	42	43	40	37
CDU/CSU										
Men	42	47	43	44	45	50	51	51	51	50
Women	51	57	54	56	56	52	53	49	54	54
FDP										
Men	11	8	13	10	6	7	6	7	7	8
Women	10	7	11	9	4	6	5	8	5	7
Greens										
Men									2	2
Women									1	2
Under 25 years*										
SPD										
Men	34	38	41	43	48	54	49	48	38	38
Women	29	31	35	37	45	55	50	50	41	39
CDU/CSU										
Men	41	46	43	46	40	35	40	36	42	37
Women	48	53	50	53	47	36	40	33	40	35
FDP										
Men	12	8	12	8	7	10	9	11	5	9
Women	10	7	12	8	6	9	9	12	5	8
Greens										
Men								5	14	15
Women								4	14	17

Note: * = under age 30 (1953-1969). Other parties not shown.
Source: See Table 4.

French trends were similar to those in Britain and Germany, with women forming the solid base of support for the Christian right and providing substantially fewer ballots than men to the French Communists. A decline in church attendance, coupled with an increase in college-educated and working women, helped diminish the gender differences on the right. Since Mitterrand came to power in 1981, the parties of the right no longer have a lead among women voters and are unlikely to regain it in this election.

Trends in the three countries suggest that the stereotype of the conservative and Christian woman voter no longer holds. Changes in age and family structure and work expectations, decline in church attendance, and new issues in the political marketplace have all contributed to the voting shift in the last twenty to thirty years. There is no reason to assume it will stop here in the late 1980s.

Wooing Women Voters

Once the political parties in Britain, France, and Germany realized that women voters were no longer more conservative than men voters, they changed their approach to capture the "women's vote." But the election of June 1987 in Britain and January 1987 in Germany saw the parties of the left making the same mistakes in interpreting these movements that the Democrats in the United States did in 1984. Attempts to woo women voters in France have evolved differently.

Under the conservative government of Valery Giscard d'Estaing, the French established a State Secretariat for the Concerns of Women as early as 1974, which was elevated to ministry status in 1978. The justification was that in post-1968 France, women were starting to become more active politically, making demands about equal rights, divorce, pro-choice legislation, and job opportunities.

At the time, analysts decided that women were going to make their voting decisions on women's issues and that the parties should respond in order to reap the benefits of women's votes. It is probably true that some women decided to support the Socialists in the 1970s and 1980s because of the party's more liberal position on divorce, abortion, and equal opportunity. But the left never persuaded some of the older and more conservative women (or men) to cross party lines because of these positions. The Socialists made appeals to young working women in 1981, a more receptive audience. There is some evidence that turnout among this group increased, to the benefit of the Socialists. This is the correct strategy—appeal to a group of women (or men) who have reasons, usually economic, to cast their ballots for one party or another.

During the most recent British election the Labour party promised to establish a Ministry for Women should they be elected to power. The theory behind the decision, in addition to the belief that a women's ministry should exist, was that it would bring in women's votes. The logic is dubious. The women (and men) who would support the idea of a Ministry for Women are likely Labour supporters anyway. The number of women who might switch from the Alliance to Labour because of this particular campaign promise was small at best (the number of men switching even smaller). In addition, the Labour party did not consider that the promise might lose votes for them among the older

(and more socially traditional) Labour supporters who might have felt that this contributed to the image of Labour as a party of special-interest groups.

The Labour party in Britain has a chance to pick up more votes among women, particularly white-collar workers and those in the helping professions. These women have been drawn to the more moderate but less traditional Alliance during the last two elections. Labour, in trying to modernize its image, could target these low-paid women by making the argument that the Labour party is best suited to serve their economic needs. The Labour party failed to make a pitch to older voters, mainly women, who are dependent on the welfare state for their livelihood. Mrs. Thatcher may be popular, but her party continues to make cuts in social services, not something older women support.

The German Social Democrats did not promise to elevate the women's section of the Ministry for Health, Family, Youth, and Women to a separate ministry. But in a postelection internal memo analyzing the 1987 campaign, they suggested that women's votes could provide the future margin of victory, noting that turnout among younger women had been particularly low in the contest. They discussed a need to promote women's issues as one key to the "women's vote." This might be somewhat successful for the women under thirty-five but would probably not be a big vote winner. The SPD realizes the stark generational difference in voting in the Federal Republic, but they don't go beyond that to note which issues are likely to matter to younger working women or older women who are dependent on social security.

Issue Differences

The expectation that women—as a bloc vote—would provide the margin of victory for the left is misguided. Women are no more a bloc vote than men are.

Men and women do tend to differ on some issues, even when age, religion, education, and labor force participation are factored out. Women on both sides of the Atlantic are in general less inclined to support government policies that involve the use of force, for example. They are more peace-minded than men on siting cruise missiles in Germany, stationing troops in Northern Ireland, and increasing the defense budget. National interest sometimes overtakes their objections, though: French men and women of the left and right are rather in favor of an independent *French* nuclear deterrent; British women are more inclined than British men to think *American* nuclear missiles are a threat to peace, but a majority of these same women join their compatriots in believing that *British* nuclear weapons increase their overall security.

In Britain during the last two elections, men and women alike saw unemployment as the most important problem facing the country. But women were less likely than men to identify national defense or international relations as the next most important issue. Rather, slightly more women felt that education and the National Health Service should be given greater government attention.

On women's issues such as abortion and equal rights, women as a whole are no more liberal than men. Older women are sometimes more conservative on these issues than are older men. Younger women are sometimes—but not often—more liberal than their contemporaries among men, as younger men today also support liberal abortion legislation and equal rights. The intensity of feeling about women's issues is higher among women, whether in strong support or strong opposition. With the abortion issue, for example, any gain a party makes in picking up a woman voter because of a liberal position on women's issues would probably be negated by comparable losses.

In addition to gender differences of opinion, the persistence of the "Don't Know Woman" is a curious phenomenon. On questions of economics, defense, international relations, and to some extent civil rights, women in these three countries are much more likely than men to answer "Don't Know" or "No Opinion." True in all three countries, the tendency is found in the United States as well. This gender difference is smaller

for highly educated women but does not go away entirely. On education, health policy, and local issues, the "Don't Know Woman" is less in evidence. And interestingly, on women's issues, particularly abortion questions, men give more frequent "Don't Knows" than women. Differing "Don't Knows" should provide additional clues to the political parties in attracting women and groups of men as voters.

The biggest change in the women's vote since *Civic Culture* was written a quarter century ago is that women now vote at a rate roughly comparable to the rate for men. They have made a more subtle shift away from predictable conservatism and toward a collection of issue concerns that is not substantially different from men's. This makes the political parties' task more difficult than if women voted as a bloc. For the parties to succeed, they're going to have to woo and win the women just as they do the men.

British data are taken from the British Election Studies, which started in the early sixties and are based on national samples of eligible voters. The British Election Studies asked respondents if they had voted, and while the resulting turnout rates are higher than the actual rate, we have no reason to believe that either men or women are more likely to exaggerate. German data, on the other hand, are actual representative election statistics. In some 200 representative constituencies, voters put their ballot papers into boxes according to age and gender, an unthinkable concept in the United States or Great Britain, but one that allows for highly accurate electoral analysis based on age and gender.

Women in parliament

Keeping a sense of disproportion

Western Europe's parliaments are still mainly men's clubs. Only one out of ten parliamentarians is a woman. Why?

They cannot buy contraceptives, divorce their husbands or have an abortion. And many men still think their place is in the home. Yet in the fiercely Catholic Irish republic, women won over 8% of the seats in last week's general election, twice the female representation in free-thinking, irreligious Britain.

At the top of Western Europe's women-in-politics league is Norway, where a third of parliamentarians—including the prime minister, Dr Gro Harlem Brundtland—are women (see chart on next page). But having a woman running a country does not necessarily help her sex to succeed. Mrs Thatcher has had no women in her cabinet during her seven years as Britain's prime minister. She presides over a parliament with the lowest share of female members of all West European countries except Greece. Dr Brundtland, by contrast, has given eight of her 18 cabinet posts to women.

What gives female politicians a better chance in Ireland and the Nordic countries? Proportional representation, for a start. In Britain's first-past-the-post voting system, parties have only one candidate in each constituency. Women are rarely chosen by party selection panels. When they are, it is often for unwinnable seats. At the most recent British election, 276 women stood for parliament, but only 23 got in—one fewer than in 1945, when only 87 women entered the race. In the previous, 1979, election only one female Conservative candidate—Mrs Thatcher herself—was standing in a safe seat. Yet academic studies in Britain suggest that people are not in principle against voting for female candidates.

Parties have less excuse to be sexist under proportional representation. If, as in Ireland, they have to offer voters a whole slate of candidates, they risk looking foolish—and losing votes—if they do not include at least one or two women. In

Iceland's 1983 general election, the all-female Women's Alliance got only 5% of its candidates returned to parliament, but its existence obliged the other political parties to field more women candidates too. Overnight, women's representation in the Althing rose from 3% to 15%.

Then there is the question of political will. The Norwegians have shown how easy it is to promote women in politics. In the Storting, 43% of the members from Dr Brundtland's Labour party are now women, a result of a decision taken three years ago at the party's congress to ensure that neither sex should have fewer than 40% of the candidates by the following election. The same commitment was given about office-holders: hence women's strength in the cabinet.

Europe's women, it seems, have a better chance of making it to parliament if their country is to the north, and their party to the left. After the West German election in January, the percentage of women in the Bundestag nearly doubled, to over 15%, thanks mainly to the efforts

of the Greens and the Social Democrats. Women occupy 24 of the Greens' 42 seats, and dominate most people's picture of it. Outside Germany, Petra Kelly is probably the best-known Green politician; inside the country, Jutta Ditfurth is catching up fast. The Greens have a policy of positive discrimination. They recently put up an all-female slate in the state election in Hamburg; because of or despite this (or neither), their share of the vote rose from 6.8% to 10.4%.

In a man's world

A fifth of Italy's Communist members of parliament are women, compared with only 2½% of the Christian Democratic ones. Britain's Labour party still refuses to adopt a quota system, but at least it runs training courses for women candidates, including advice on how to assert themselves in a man's world. In the European Parliament, the Greens and the Communists tie at the top of the women-among-members league with 20% each. Next comes the Socialist

Aren't we clever? says Thatcher to Brundtland

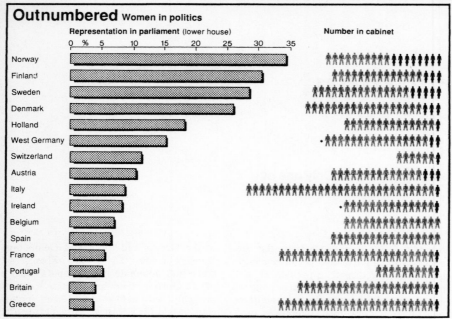

Outnumbered Women in politics

Representation in parliament (lower house)

Number in cabinet

*Outgoing cabinet

group, with 17%. The Christian Democrats and Conservatives have 12% and 14% respectively.

Countries with a small female representation in parliament seem to throw up women politicians with strong personalities. In Greece only 4% of parliamentary members are female, yet much of the West knows of Melina Mercouri, the minister for culture. In Britain a junior health minister, Mrs Edwina Currie, is rapidly making her mark. Not best known for tact, she claims that her sex is an advantage in parliament because she gets more attention.

In these countries, women need to be assertive to get on; if they reach cabinet level, the chances are that they will be surrounded by men and given posts associated with women, such as education or health. Melina Mercouri and Margaret Thatcher are good examples of tough women outnumbered by their male colleagues who have nevertheless burst out of the constraints. Simone Veil, once a formidable French minister for women, manages to combine resilience with popularity. She later made it to the presidency of the European Parliament. Less well-known, but on her way up, is Dr Michelle Barzach, France's minister for health, who is commonly described as "very clever".

Superior intelligence is the quality most often ascribed to female European politicians. Perhaps women still have to be better than men to succeed in politics.

Editor's note:

Students interested in the subject may wish to read Elizabeth Vallance's article, "Two Cheers for Equality: Women Candidates in the 1987 General Elections," *Parliamentary Affairs*, January 1988.

How the other half works

EUROPE'S WOMEN

The past two decades brought more paid jobs for Europe's women. But often the pay was poor and the job short-lived. The 1990s will need to adapt women better to the labour market—and the market better to them

NO LONGER do Britain's taxmen address their queries about a married woman's earnings to her husband. Spanish noblewomen have won a court decision—subject to appeal—that they, not a younger brother, can inherit a father's titles. The Anglican Church of Ireland has just ordained its first women priests. Italy last year got its first woman airline pilot. Europe's women are moving out of the home, into the workforce and into a semblance of equality.

Women in the European Community now, on average, have one fewer child apiece than 25 years ago. They have more freedom to work—and often more need to. As marriage has become less common, and divorce more so, the single-parent family, once a rarity, has become common. Most such families—more than 90% in Britain, for instance—are headed by women.

Equal-opportunities legislation made it more possible for women to work outside the home during the flush years of the early 1970s. Economic recession later made it more necessary. Women were 37% of the EC's civilian workforce in 1980, but around 40% by 1988. Among them, the Danes, followed by the British, are now, as for decades past, the most likely to have jobs. But the proportion of women who do so has risen markedly in other countries, such as Belgium and Portugal. Though Spanish women are still among the EC's least likely to work outside the home, one-third more of them do so now than in 1980.

Quantity, not quality

Women's share of employment has grown accordingly. Men lost almost 3m jobs in the EC between 1980 and 1987; women gained almost as many. This is not pure gain, however. It stems partly from the inevitable rundown of manufacturing jobs, typically done by men, and the rise in services, which employ almost three-quarters of Europe's working women. But it also reflects a strong growth in part-time and temporary working.

This kind of work suits employers looking for flexibility and lower costs. It suits some women, enabling them to combine paid work with child-care. But such jobs are often unskilled. They generally offer little training and no prospect of career advancement. The pay is usually low, lower than that, pro rata, for a full-time job, let alone a man's full-time job. In Britain, women in part-time manual work earn only half the basic hourly pay of male full-time workers, says that country's Equal Opportunities Commission.

Some 70% of the jobs created in the EC between 1983 and 1987 were part-time, says a report by the Centre for Research on European Women. Women hold most of them. In all, about 30% of the EC's working women (against 4% of men) work part-time: around 60% in Holland, 40-45% in Britain and Denmark, 25-30% in Belgium, France and West Germany, 10-15% elsewhere.

Women also have more than their fair share of other unusual work including temporary contracts, homeworking and helping (often unpaid) in family businesses. They are prominent in the black economy: sweated labour, the trade unions call some of this work, and often—in Italy's back-street shoemaking, for instance, or Britain's clothing sweat-shops—they are right.

So the gap between average women's and men's earnings is large. It has shrunk in all countries since the early 1970s and the EC directive on equal pay for equal work, but not so consistently since the early 1980s. Danish, French and Italian women manual workers are nearest to the hourly wages of their male counterparts; Irish and British women get only about 70% as much as men. Patchier figures on non-manual hourly earnings show a roughly similar pattern. The overall gap remains at least 25%, even without counting men's more frequent overtime.

Low pay is not the only disadvantage. In Ireland, anyone who works fewer than 18 hours a week is ineligible for maternity leave; about half of all EC countries require a minimum number of hours a week to qualify for equal, or any, social benefits. Temporary workers everywhere get no redundancy payments when their jobs end. Women also suffer more than their share of unemployment. Accounting for a bit more than two-fifths of the EC's workforce, they make up more than half of its unemployed. Unemployment among them is running about five percentage points above that of European men.

Slowly to the top

The pace at which women are storming male bastions is not exactly heady. About one-third of doctors in Britain, Denmark and, surprisingly, Portugal are women. But only 10% of Britain's senior corporate managers are, and fewer than 1% of executive directors. A senior Spanish scientist claims to be the only woman in the room as she travels Europe to discuss technological collaboration with her peers.

In two areas women are advancing faster than is generally thought. Between the extremes of Britain's buttoned-up Mrs Margaret Thatcher and Italy's bare-breasted parliamentarian Ms Ilona Staller, better known as the entertainer La Cicciolina, women are becoming visible in politics.

At or near the top, women are still rare. Mrs Thatcher apart, Gro Harlem Brundtland, briefly Norway's prime minister, is the only woman in Europe ever elected to lead her country. Only two of the 17 (appointed) members of the European Commission, Ms Vasso Papandreou and Mrs Christiane Scrivener, are women.

Yet women are working their way in. They won more seats than before in all but one of the national legislative elections in 1989. The gain was most dramatic in Spain, where two of the three leading parties established quotas for female candidates. Women make up 31% of Denmark's parliament and

25% of Holland's (taking its two chambers together). In contrast, they account for less than 7% of Britain's House of Commons or the French national assembly. Women won 19% of the seats in the European Parliament last year, a three-point rise.

There seem also to be more women entrepreneurs these days, though figures are uncertain. In Britain the number of self-employed women doubled during the 1980s, and one-third of them now employ other people. In West Germany it is estimated that one in every three new enterprises is set up by a woman; the French estimate is one in four. A fair for female entrepreneurs in Madrid last year was well attended.

Europe needs you

Women's work is attracting increasing attention for two good reasons. First, it is more than ever needed. Europe is running out of new young workers. Only in Ireland are women having enough babies to replace the population. By 2025 there could be about 2% fewer people in the EC than there are now.

The European Commission has calculated, for the first nine countries of the Community, that if labour-force participation kept to the 1985 pattern and demographic trends stayed the same, by 2000 the labour force in these countries would be shrinking by 300,000 a year. If something like this is not to happen, more women will have to work. Britain's labour force is expected to grow in the 1990s; women are likely to account for 90% of the net increase.

Secondly, even while more women workers are needed, their jobs are under threat as the EC moves toward a single market. This may in time bring more employment. But, as Miss Pauline Jackson, the author of an excellent report on what the 1992 programme will mean for women, points out, many women work in the industries

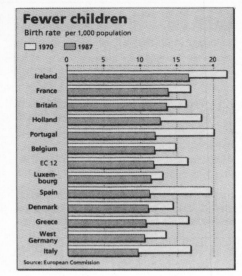

Fewer children

Birth rate per 1,000 population

that face the biggest shake-out from European integration, new technology, and low-wage competition from outside Europe.

Women make up 45% or more of employees in such industries as clothing, textiles and footwear, toys and photographic equipment. They are less numerous in other sensitive industries such as industrial and consumer electronics, but still fill the majority of the manual, assembly-line jobs. And if unemployment strikes, married women are even less free than are their husbands to move house in search of work.

Reshaping the job market

Women's interest groups and employment experts are shifting away from hammering home the message of legal equality to arguing for practical reforms to enable more women to work more productively.

Several governments are moving to ditch income-tax systems that bear relatively hard on a wife's earnings. Harder to solve are the unavoidable conflicts between employment policy and welfare policy. If a household—couple or single-parent—is receiving welfare benefits, these will often be cut if the woman goes out to earn extra money. Given the time and the extra costs, and the low wages that are the best many women can hope for, she may well ask why she should bother. Equally, the greater social protection that the EC's social charter recommends, and that some governments have already provided, for part-time or temporary workers is fine for those who already have such jobs; but it may well discourage employers from hiring more of this kind of worker.

Far the biggest obstacle to women's work, however, is the need for child-care. EC countries vary widely in the extent to which the state looks after children below school age. Mid-1980s figures from a 1988 study done for the European Commission show this, and its effects. In France, Belgium, Italy and Denmark, more than four-fifths of children aged three to five get at least some daytime care at the state's expense. Those are the countries where the most mothers of children under five work full-time: 45% of Danish mothers, 39% of Belgian, 38% of French and 34% of Italian. In Britain only about two-fifths of such children get any of this state care, and under 10% of the mothers concerned have full-time jobs.

Care for pre-school children is not the only need, however. Most schools' working day ends before that of a typical employer. So young children at least need to be looked after somehow in the afternoon, while their mother may still be at work.

Most countries are now taking some steps to improve the quantity and quality of child-care. In Spain, where state-financed nursery schools already look after two-thirds of all three-to-five-year-olds, a new education bill promises total coverage. Some of Holland's main cities have changed school hours, or added extra supervised activities, to bring them more into line with normal work days. The British government has just allowed employers to treat the cost of providing worksite creches as a business expense, while employees will not be taxed on the benefit. Several countries (though not Britain) allow parents a tax deduction for other forms of child-care costs.

The invention of statutory maternity leave (and in some countries paternity leave) has made it easier for women to have children and go back to work. All countries provide for maternity leave, variously defined and paid, though not for everyone. Spain,

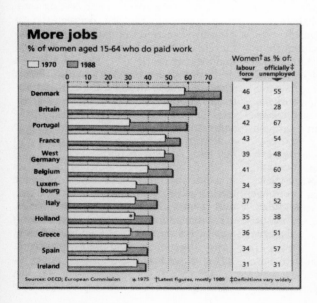

More jobs

% of women aged 15-64 who do paid work

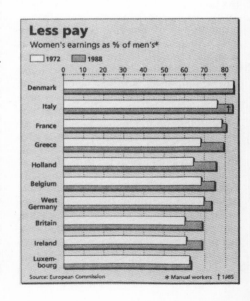

Less pay

Women's earnings as % of men's*

for example, has recently increased its leave to 16 weeks at full pay, and allows the father to take four weeks of it. Most countries, though not Britain or Ireland, also offer some sort of all-purpose parental leave.

Flexible working hours, for either parent, can make a big difference. This practice—"you work 36 hours a week, but, except for core times when you must be present, it is up to you which hours they are"—has increased in most countries, especially in the public sector. It is not a system that many commercial employers fancy. But it could do much to open jobs to women. And as more workers find themselves looking after old parents, flexibility will be of double value.

Even if all these practical difficulties can be overcome, many women still lack the skills to get into (or return to) good jobs. The trouble starts at school. In Greece and, to a lesser extent, Portugal, illiteracy among women is still seriously higher than among men. More widely, the issue is who studies what. The school-leaving age is the same everywhere for girls as for boys. And these days about as many young women as men get higher education too (though not in all countries: even in the mid-1980s women lagged behind in countries as advanced as West Germany, Holland and Britain). But boys are likelier than girls to study subjects that will help toward a skilled job. In Britain, boys were twice as likely as girls in the mid-1980s to sit "A-level" examinations (for 17-year-olds) in mathematics and almost four times as likely in physics.

France, Spain and others are trying to coax girls into school subjects, and then into professions, in which they are under-represented. In Britain and France government and business are working together to increase the number of women technicians and engineers. Greece, Spain and West Germany are among those that subsidise companies to recruit and train women. Dutch and British companies are setting up worksite nurseries. German companies including BASF and Audi have guaranteed re-employment to female workers who leave for domestic reasons, and encourage them to keep up their skills by standing in for absent colleagues meanwhile.

Counting the costs

Helping more women into better jobs at higher pay is all very well, but it will have its costs. These are more than financial. State-subsidised creches and nurseries will have to multiply in most countries, and to improve in all. Yet it is not only reactionaries who suspect that little children lose something by spending eight hours a day away from their mothers, however good the alternative. With divorce, drugs and delinquency on the rise, protecting the family unit must also deserve some priority.

The economic adjustment will not be easy. Women have been a convenient source of cheap labour for European employers. Their wages will have to rise. Few companies will have the nerve to take the opposite road to pay equality, real-wage cuts for men (though Marks & Spencer, a leading British retailer, is trying: while British prices soar, it recently announced a three-year (money) wage freeze for its warehouse jobs, typically held by men). So, in the short term, women may find they have won higher wages but have fewer jobs. Social protection for part-time and temporary workers could have the same effect.

A good deal will depend on attitudes in Brussels. The European Commission is likely to push hard now for practical changes in working conditions, as it did earlier for a legal framework to guarantee equal opportunities and pay. Spurred by an increasingly assertive and increasingly female European Parliament and, from September, by a new Brussels-based pan-European women's lobby, the commission has two instruments to hand.

It is now discussing plans for a new five-year (1991-95) action programme for equal opportunities. The social charter, vigorously pushed by Ms Papandreou and accepted, as a set of voluntary principles, by all heads of government except Mrs Thatcher at the Strasbourg summit last December, also touches on women's issues, and the commission's work programme to implement it makes these goals specific. High on the list are favourites, previously blocked, like a proposed directive on parental leave. A recommendation on child-care is among the suggested new initiatives.

The commission will have to tiptoe more carefully on these issues, though, than it has in the straight job-and-pay crusades of the past. Even among its own officials some question whether the EC has competence under the Treaty of Rome to prescribe in social matters such as child-care. The British government is sure it does not. Recommendations rather than directives may be the outcome.

In the end, it is Europe's governments and the societies they represent—especially the employers—who must make up their minds. How far, how fast and how expensively—for the costs will come before the gains do, and, as with most social advance, they will be enduring costs—are they prepared to act so that men and women can compete in Europe's labour market on equal terms? Or are they content to see that market go on giving most of the best jobs to men, while it increasingly divides women into those with a career and those scrabbling for an occasional piece of work?

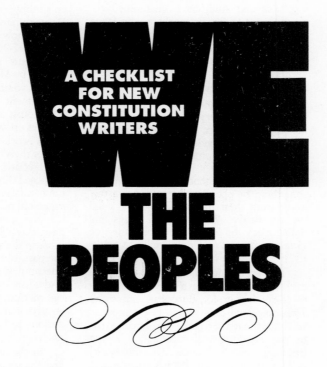

A CHECKLIST FOR NEW CONSTITUTION WRITERS

WE THE PEOPLES

ROBERT A. GOLDWIN

Robert A. Goldwin is a resident scholar at the American Enterprise Institute. He was director of AEI's Constitution Project. This article draws on the introductions of two of his books: Constitution Makers on Constitution Making *and* Forging Unity Out of Diversity.

AMERICANS ARE ACCUSTOMED to thinking of constitution writing as something done hundreds of years ago by bewigged gentlemen wearing frock coats, knee breeches, and white stockings, but for the rest of the world, constitution writing is very much an activity of the present day. The Constitution of the United States is now more than 200 years old, but a majority of the other constitutions in the world are less than 15 years old. That is, of the 160 or so written national constitutions, more than 80 have been adopted since 1975. This means that in the last few decades, on average, more than five new national constitutions have come into effect every year.

Some of these new constitutions are, of course, for new nations, but the surprising fact is that most were written for very old nations, such as Spain, Portugal, Turkey, and Greece. And now, in the old nations of Eastern Europe and possibly also in the Soviet Union or newly

independent parts of it, new constitutions are about to be written to replace outdated, one-party constitutions.

Those who are responsible for writing these new constitutions know they need assistance. As Professor Albert Blaustein of Rutgers University Law School recently reported, many East European legal experts "haven't seen a constitutional law book for 45 years." They need not proceed without advice, though, because there are so many still-active, experienced constitution writers in scores of nations around the world that have recently adopted new constitutions. There are also experts in international constitutional law in the United States and in many other nations who would be only too glad to offer their services.

Nonetheless, except perhaps for narrow technical matters, outsiders, however expert, are limited in the help they can provide. A successful constitution must be deeply rooted in the history and traditions of the nation and its people, and its writers need a clear sense of what is central to the way the nation is constituted. For millennia, East European nations have been battlegrounds for innumerable invasions, conquests, and consequent migrations. As a result, there is a great mixing of peoples who cannot be sorted out even by computer-guided drawing of borders. These peoples, who

From *The American Enterprise*, May/June 1990, pp. 70-75. Copyright © 1990, The American Enterprise Institute for Public Policy Research.

have no choice but to live side by side, are not necessarily able to love their neighbors. It seems as though everyone's grandfather was murdered by someone else's grandfather. As a result, most of these nations have diverse populations characterized by passionate hostilities. The constitutional task to make "one people"—to strengthen a sense of national unity by constitutional provisions—is a much greater concern for these nations.

Destructive Diversity

That all human beings are fundamentally equal is a central tenet of modern constitutionalism that is essential to all systems of political liberty. To assert that we are all equal means, necessarily, that we are all equally human, sharing one and the same human nature. This view is widely held and advanced, sometimes as fact, sometimes as aspiration, and denied or disputed for the most part by those who are thought to be benighted, or bigoted, or both. The universality of human nature, the oneness of humankind, is a vital element of modern democratic thought.

And yet, wherever we look in the world, we see mankind divided into tightly bound groups, set apart by racial, religious, language, or national differences. The bonds of loyalty these differences engender often override all other considerations, including even the obligations of national citizenship. Whether or not we are "all brothers and sisters under the skin," two indisputable, and indisputably linked, facts are evident everywhere: first, there is a natural, powerful fraternal bond among persons who share the same religion, or race, or language, or nationality; second, the same inclusive bond commonly has the effect of excluding those who are different, engendering hostility toward "outsiders."

In almost all countries with diverse populations—and almost all countries around the world do have significant diversity—we see, not the "domestic tranquillity" spoken of in the preamble to the Constitution of the United States, but domestic hostility between fellow citizens of the same nation-states: Protestants and Catholics in Northern Ireland, Muslims and Christians in Lebanon, Jews and Muslims in Israel, blacks and whites in the United States, Flemish and French speakers in Belgium, Armenians and Azerbaijanis in the Soviet Union, Serbs and Albanians in Yugoslavia, Greeks and Turks in Cyprus, Hausas and Ibos in Nigeria—and this list does not come close to being exhaustive. Given historic animosities in many countries of Eastern Europe, diversity presents a problem for their constitution makers.

Citizens who are members of groups significantly different from others of the population can reasonably have grave concerns: fear for their safety, concern that they will not be allowed to participate in the political, social, and economic life of the nation, and fear that they will be restricted in the practices that are characteristic of their special way of life. To address these fears, many constitutions have special provisions, usually addressed directly to groups by name, assuring them of participation in the national life and guaranteeing freedom of religion or use of language, or promising preferences in education or employment on the basis of nationality or race. The dilemma such provisions pose, however, is that they raise the differences within the population to a constitutional status and tend thereby to identify, emphasize, and perpetuate the divisions within society. Our own constitution is silent in this regard, aiming for unity by assimilation.

No Universal Formula

Years of study of constitutions confirm what common sense would suggest: that there is no universal formula for a successful constitution. A sound constitution for any nation has to be something of a reflection, although more than that, of the essence of a particular nation, and this is inescapably influenced by the character of each nation's people, or peoples, and their history.

Constitution writers may wish to make a break with their past, to make a completely fresh start, but they never have the luxury of a clean slate. They start with a population having certain characteristics (for example, homogeneous or diverse), an economy tied to its geographic characteristics (a maritime nation or landlocked), neighboring nations (peaceful or warlike) that cannot be moved or ignored, and a history that has shaped their understanding of themselves and their national aspirations. The constitution must reflect all of these elements of the nation, and the more it is in accord with these national characteristics, the better the constitution will be.

One day in Athens some years ago, while talking to a Greek judge who is also a constitutional scholar, I referred to the newness of the Greek constitution. He asked me what date I put on it, and I, somewhat surprised, said, "1975, of course." "Yes, I understand," he said, "but you could also say 1863." "But," I replied, "Greece has had nearly a dozen constitutions since then." "Yes," he said, "that's right, but they are always the same." He was exaggerating, of course, but not much. When Greece adopted its latest constitution, two

QUESTIONS FOR CONSTITUTION WRITERS

The Preliminaries

• How will delegates to the constitutional committee or constituent assembly be chosen? Will the new constitution be drafted by the legislative body or by a body chosen specifically for the purpose? If there is controversy about the method of selection, how and by whom will it be resolved?

• What will be the rules and procedures of the constitution-making body, once chosen, and how and by whom will controversies on this question be resolved?

Powers and Power Relationships

• What are the different branches of government, and what is their constitutional relationship? Are the executive and legislative branches separated or combined?

• Is there a single chief executive, or an executive cabinet, or some form of executive council? What are the executive powers, and how are they limited? Does the executive have some share in the legislative process: for instance, do laws require his signature; does he have veto power, the right to propose legislation? Does the executive have treaty-making powers, the power to declare war, command of the armed forces, law-enforcement powers, some degree of responsibility to appoint judges, power of executive pardon or clemency? Are police powers national, or is there some form of local authority? How are the executive departments established, and how and by whom are the department heads appointed and fired? How are executive salaries determined? How is the chief executive chosen, and what is the term of office?

• Is the head of state separate from the head of government, and if so, what is the role of the head of state? How is the head of state chosen? What is the term of office? If a monarch, what is the role of the crown? Does the head of state act to dissolve the legislature, call for new elections, name a new prime minister?

• Is the legislature unicameral or bicameral? What is the principle of representation, or is there more than one principle (for example, some legislators chosen on the basis of population, some by states or provinces)? What is the length of term for members? Under what conditions and by whom are new elections called? How are salaries of members determined and varied? Does the legislature have the power of the purse, taxing power, oversight powers, a role in executive and judicial appointments, budget-making powers, power over the monetary system, power to regulate domestic trade, foreign trade, a role in war making and treaty making, power to investigate and compel testimony, power to impeach executive and judicial officers? Do legislators have immunity from arrest? What are the conditions for dissolution of the legislature?

• What is the system of justice and law enforcement? What is the structure of the judicial system, and how and by whom is it established? In what ways, if any, are judges subject to legislative and executive controls? How independent are judges from executive and legislative control? How are judges appointed or elected and for what terms? Are judicial salaries protected? Do the courts of law have powers of judicial review of the constitutionality of legislative and executive actions, or is there a separate constitutional court?

• To whom are the powers assigned for the conduct of foreign policy? To what extent are they shared, and on the basis of what principle? Where is the power assigned to declare war and to make and ratify treaties?

• Are there powers to suspend the constitution in emergencies? If so, by whom and under what conditions? Are there protections against abuse of emergency powers?

• Are all public officials required to take an oath of office to uphold this constitution?

• To what extent are the executive, legislative, and judicial powers separated, and by what provisions are the separations maintained?

• Is the national government unitary or federal, and if the latter, what form of federalism? Whether unitary or federal, is it centralized or decentralized, or some combination?

• What are the limits of the powers of the government and of the various branches and officers, and by what means are the limits sustained?

---

issues were foremost, the roles of the armed forces and of the monarchy. However much Greek constitutions and regimes changed through the decades, these questions remained constant. There was not much leeway, not much discretion on many of the most important points. The same will be true for the nations of Eastern Europe.

Although there can be no universal formula for successful constitution writing—no canned answers that can be applied to any country in search of a new constitutional order—there are standard, universal questions that must be asked. A comprehensive list will include some questions that at first glance seem archaic or unnecessary to consider. Turkey or Portugal, for instance, did not have to dwell on the question of the role of the monarchy as Greece and Spain did, but considering how many modern nations are constitutional monarchies, it is not impossible that one or another East European nation might consider some form of constitutional monarchy before the turmoil is over.

Therefore, in the conviction that it is possible to develop a substantial, if not complete, list of the questions constitution writers must ask themselves in writing the constitution of any country, I offer this enumeration for guidance (see box above):

Elections and Political Parties

• By what methods are the various offices filled: direct popular election by universal suffrage or some indirect method; winner-take-all or some form of proportional representation? Which offices, if any, are not elective, and what is the method of appointment? Are there different methods of election or selection for different offices?

• What is the constitutional status of political parties, or is that left undetermined?

Nonpolitical Institutions

• What is the structure of the education system, and how is it supervised? Is the school system centralized, regional, local, or some combination? Are there provisions for ethnic, religious, or language schools? Are private schools allowed, and if so, what controls are imposed on them? Is the freedom of inquiry in university teaching and research protected?

• What are the provisions for the media? Are there government-owned, political party-owned, or privately owned newspapers, television channels, and radio stations? Are the media regu-

lated or licensed? What protections are there for freedom of the press, and how are abuses prevented?

• What is the constitutional status of the military? Who is the commander in chief of the armed forces? How much and what form of civilian control is there?

• What is the role of religion? Is there an established church, and one or more official religions? Are there church subsidies from public funds, and if so, are they on a basis of equality or are they preferential? Is there separation of church and state? Is freedom of religion protected and by what means?

Rights

• Is there a bill of rights? What protections are there for the rights of individuals: speech, press, religion, peaceable assembly, habeas corpus, public trial, and so on? Is there equality of all persons, or are there constitutional preferences based on race, religion, sex, nationality, or different levels of citizenship? Are the rights primarily political and legal, or are social and economic rights included? Are the rights provisions stated negatively or affirmatively? Is there a list of duties of citi-

zens listed, and if so, are the duties linked to rights? Are there protections of rights of aliens? What are the provisions for immigration and emigration? What is the status under the constitution of international declarations of rights? Are only the rights of individuals acknowledged, or are there also protections for the rights of religious, ethnic, racial, or regional groups?

• Are there different levels or kinds of citizenship; that is, are there qualifications or restrictions of voting rights, property rights, representation, access to education, or eligibility for public office based on race, sex, religion, language, or national origin? Do naturalized citizens have the same rights, privileges, and immunities as natural-born citizens? What are the naturalization provisions?

• Does the constitution specify any national or official languages? Are there provisions for schools, courts, government offices, churches, and other institutions to conduct their activities in languages other than the national or official ones?

The Economic System

• Does the constitution specify what kind of economic

system shall prevail (for instance, that this nation is a socialist democracy or that the means of production shall be owned privately)? Are there provisions for managing the economy, or is a market economy of private enterprise assumed? What is the status of private property? What is the status of banks, corporations, farms, other enterprises? What are the regulatory and licensing powers? Are there government monopolies and, if so, what kind? What are the copyright and patent provisions? Is there protection against impairing the obligation of contracts?

• What is the status of international law and international organizations in relation to national laws and institutions? What is the legal status of treaties and other international obligations?

Final Questions

• What is the amendment process? Is it designed to make amending the constitution easy or difficult? Does the amending process include the people as a whole, or is it limited to the legislature and other officials?

• What is the process for ratifying the constitution?

A Rare Activity

The frequency of constitution writing tells us two things. First, constitutions are very important, and great investments of time and effort are needed to write them; and second, it is very difficult, and rare, to write a constitution that lasts—which is why there have been so many of them.

A complete list—and this one surely has omissions—gives no assurance of finding the right answers in writing a constitution. But an enumeration such as this provides reassurance that major issues will not be overlooked.

It also reminds us what an extraordinary accomplishment our own 200-year-old Constitution is.

Making a constitution is a special political activity. It is possible only at certain extraordinary moments in a nation's history, and its success or failure can have profound and lasting consequences for a nation and its people. That is the challenge facing the constitution makers and the peoples of Eastern Europe.

Parliament and Congress:

Is the Grass Greener on the other side?

Gregory S. Mahler

Gregory Mahler is associate professor of political science at the University of Vermont in Burlington, and a member of the Canadian Studies Program there.

Aristotle long ago observed that man is a "political animal." He could have added that man, by his very nature, notes the political status of his neighbours and, very often, perceives their lot as being superior to his own. The old saying "the grass is greener on the other side of the fence" can be applied to politics and political structures as well as to other, more material, dimensions of the contemporary world.

Legislators are not immune from the very human tendency to see how others of their lot exist in their respective settings, and, sometimes, to look longingly at these other settings. When legislators do look around to see the conditions under which their peers operate in other countries, they occasionally decide they prefer the alternative legislative settings to their own.

Features which legislators admire or envy in the settings of their colleagues include such things as: the characteristics of political parties (their numbers, or degrees of party discipline), legislative committee systems, staff and services available to help legislators in their tasks, office facilities, libraries, and salaries. This essay will develop the "grass is greener" theme in relation to a dimension of the legislative world which is regularly a topic of conversation when legislators from a number of different jurisdictions meet: the ability or inability of legislatures to check and control the executive.

The Decline of Parliament

The theme of the "decline of parliament" has a long and well-studied history.[1] It generally refers to the gradual flow of true legislative power away from the legislative body in the direction of the executive. The executive does the real law-making — by actually drafting most legislation — and the legislature takes a more "passive" role by simply approving executive proposals.

Legislators are very concerned about their duties and powers and over the years have jealously guarded them when they have appeared to be threatened. In Canada (and indeed most parliamentary democracies in the world today), the majority of challenges to legislative power which develop no longer come from the ceremonial executive (the Crown), but from the political executive, the government of the day.

It can be argued that the ability to direct and influence public policy, is a "zero sum game" (i.e. there is only room for a limited amount of power and influence to be exercised in the political world and a growth in the relative power of the political executive must be at the expense of the power of the legislature). It follows, then, that if the legislature is concerned about maintaining its powers, concerned about protecting its powers from being diminished, it must be concerned about every attempt by the political executive to expand its powers.

Others contend that real "legislative power" cannot, and probably never did reside in the legislature. There was no "Golden Age" of Parliament. The true legislative role of parliament today is not (and in the past was not) to create legislation, but to scrutinize and ratify legislation introduced by the Government of the day. Although an occasional exception to this pattern of behavior may exist (with private members' bills, for example), the general rule is clear: the legislature today does not actively initiate legislation as its primary *raison d'être*.

Although parliamentarians may not be major initiators of legislation, studies have indicated a wide range of other functions.[2] Certainly one major role of the legislature is the "oversight" role, criticizing and checking the powers of the executive. The ultimate extension of this power is the ability of the legislature to terminate the term of office of the executive through a "no confidence" vote. Another role of the legislature involves communication and representation of constituency concerns. Yet another function involves the debating function, articulating the concerns of the public of the day.

Professor James Mallory has indicated the need to "be realistic about the role of Parliament in the Westminster system."[3] He cites Bernard Crick's classic work, *The Reform of Parliament*: "...the phrase 'Parliamentary control,' and talk about the 'decline of parliamentary control,' should not mislead anyone into asking for a situation in which governments can have their legislation changed or defeated, or their life terminated... Control means influence, not direct power; advice, not command; criticism, not obstruction; scrutiny, not initiation; and publicity, not secrecy."[4]

The fact that parliament may not be paramount in the creation and processing of legislation is no reason to condemn all aspects of parliamentary institutions. Nor should parliamentarians be convinced that legislative life is perfect in the presidential-congressional system. In fact, some American legislators look to their parliamentary brethren and sigh with envy at the attractiveness of certain aspects of parliamentary institutions.

Reprinted courtesy of *Canadian Parliamentary Review*, Winter 1985–86, pp. 19–21.

Desirability of a Congressional Model for Canada?

Many Canadian parliamentarians and students of parliament look upon presidential-congressional institutions of the United States as possessing the answers to most of their problems. The grass is sometimes seen as being greener on the other side of the border. The concepts of fixed legislative terms, less party discipline, and a greater general emphasis on the role and importance of individual legislators (which implies more office space and staff for individual legislators, among other things) are seen as standards to which Canadian legislators should aspire.

A perceived strength of the American congressional system is that legislators do not automatically "rubber stamp" approve executive proposals. They consider the president's suggestions, but feel free to make substitutions or modifications to the proposal, or even to reject it completely. Party discipline is relatively weak; there are regularly Republican legislators opposing a Republican president (and Democratic legislators supporting him), and vice versa. Against the need for discipline congressmen argue that their first duty is to either (a) their constituency, or (b) what is "right", rather than simply to party leaders telling them how to behave in the legislature. For example, in 1976 Jimmy Carter was elected President with large majorities of Democrats in both houses of Congress. One of Carter's major concerns was energy policy. He introduced legislative proposals (that is, he had congressional supporters introduce legislation, since the American president cannot introduce legislation on his own) dealing with energy policy, calling his proposals "the moral equivalent of war." In his speeches and public appearances he did everything he could to muster support for "his" legislation. Two years later when "his" legislation finally emerged from the legislative process, it could hardly be recognized as the proposals submitted in such emotional terms two years earlier.

The experience of President Carter was certainly not unique. Any number of examples of such incidents of legislative-executive non-cooperation can be cited in recent American political history, ranging from President Wilson's unsuccessful efforts to get the United States to join the League of Nations, through Ronald Reagan's contemporary battles with Congress over the size of the federal budget. The Carter experience was somewhat unusual by virtue of the fact that the same political party controlled both the executive and legislative branches of government, and cooperation still was not forthcoming. There have been many more examples of non-cooperation when one party has controlled the White House and another party has controlled one or both houses of Congress.

This lack of party discipline ostensibly enables the individual legislators to be concerned about the special concerns of their constituencies. This, they say, is more important than simply having to follow the orders of the party whip in the legislature. It is not any more unusual to find a Republican legislator from a farm state voting against a specific agricultural proposal of President Reagan on the grounds that the legislation in question is not good for his/her constituency, than to find Democratic legislators from the southwestern states who voted against President Carter's water policy proposals on the grounds that the proposals were not good for their constituencies.

Congressional legislators know that they have fixed terms in office — the President is simply not able to bring about early

elections — and they know that as long as they can keep their constituencies happy there is no need to be terribly concerned about opposing the President, even if he is the leader of their party. It may be nice to have the President on your side, but if you have a strong base of support "back home" you can survive without his help.

Are there any benefits to the public interest in the absence of party discipline? The major argument is that the legislature will independently consider the executive's proposals, rather than simply accepting the executive's ideas passively. This, it is claimed, allows for a multiplicity of interests, concerns, and perspectives to be represented in the legislature, and ostensibly results in "better" legislation.

In summary, American legislative institutions promote the role of the individual legislator. The fixed term gives legislators the security necessary for the performance of the functions they feel are important. The (relative) lack of party discipline enables legislators to act on the issues about which they are concerned. In terms of the various legislative functions mentioned above, congressmen appear to spend a great deal of their time in what has been termed the legislative aspect of the job: drafting legislation, debating, proposing amendments, and voting (on a more or less independent basis).

While many parliamentarians are impressed by the ability of individual American legislator to act on their own volition it is ironic that many congressional legislators look longingly at the legislative power relationships of their parliamentary bretheren. The grass, apparently, is greener on the *other* side of the border, too.

Desirability of a Parliamentary Model

The "decline of congressional power" is as popular a topic of conversation in Washington as "the decline of parliamentary power" in Ottawa or London. Over the last several decades American legislators have sensed that a great deal of legislative power has slipped from their collective grasp.[5] Many have decried this tendency and tried to stop, or reverse this flow of power away from the legislative branch and toward the executive.

One of the major themes in the writings of these congressional activists is an admiration for the parliamentary model's (perceived) power over the executive. Many American legislators see the president's veto power, combined with his fixed term in office, as a real flaw in the "balance of powers" of the system, leading to an inexorable increase in executive power at the expense of the legislature. They look at a number of parliamentary structures which they see as promoting democratic political behavior and increased executive responsibility to the legislature, including the ability to force the resignation of the executive through a non-confidence vote. The regular "question period" format which insures some degree of public executive accountability is also perceived as being very attractive .

Critics of the congressional system do not confine their criticism only to the growth of executive power. There are many who feel there is too much freedom in the congressional arena. To paraphrase the words of Bernard Crick cited earlier, advising has sometimes turned into issuing commands; and criticism has sometimes turned into obstruction. This is not to suggest that congressional legislators would support giving up their ability to initiate legislation, to amend executive proposals, or to vote in a manner which they (individually) deem proper. This does suggest, however, that even congressional legislators see that independence is a two-sided coin: one side involves individual legislative autonomy and input into the legislative process; the other side involves the incompatibility of complete independence with a British style of "Responsible Government".

In 1948 Hubert Humphrey, then mayor of Minneapolis, delivered an address at the nomination convention of the Democratic Party. In his comments he appealed for a "more responsible" two party system in the United States, a system with sufficient party discipline to have *meaningful* party labels, and to allow party platforms to become public policy.[6] Little progress has been made over the last thirty-seven years in this regard. In the abstract the concept of a *meaningful* two party system may be attractive; American legislators have not been as attracted to the necessary corollary of the concept: decreased legislative independence and increased party discipline.

While American Senators and Representatives are very jealous of executive encroachments upon their powers, there is some recognition that on occasion — usually depending upon individual legislators' views about the desirability of specific pieces of legislation — executive leadership, and perhaps party discipline, can serve a valuable function. Congressional legislators are, at times which correspond to their policy preferences, envious of parliamentary governnments' abilities to carry their programs into law because MPs elected under their party labels will act consistent with party whips' directions. They would be loath to give up their perceived high degrees of legislative freedom but many of them realize the cost of this freedom in this era of pressing social problems and complex legislation. Parliamentary style government is simply not possible without party discipline.

A Democratic Congressman supporting President Carter's energy policy proposals might have longed for an effective three-line whip to help to pass the energy policies in question. An opponent of those policy proposals would have argued, to the contrary, that the frustration of the president's proposals was a good illustration of the wisdom of the legislature tempering the error-ridden policy proposals of the president. Similarly, many conservative Republican supporters of President Reagan have condemned the ability of the Democratic House of Representatives to frustrate his economic policies. Opponents of those policies have argued, again, that the House of Representatives is doing an important job of representing public opinion and is exercising a valuable and important check on the misguided policies of the executive.

Some Concluding Observations

The parliamentary model has its strengths as well as its weaknesses. The individual legislator in a parliamentary system does not have as active a role in the actual legislative process as does his American counterparts, but it is not at all hard to imagine instances in which the emphasis on individual autonomy in the congressional system can be counterproductive because it delays much-needed legislative programs.

The problem, ultimately, is one of balance. Is it possible to have a responsible party system in the context of parliamentary democracy which can deliver on its promises to the public, and also to have a high degree of individual legislative autonomy in the legislative arena?

It is hard to imagine how those two concepts could coexist. The congressional and parliamentary models of legislative behavior have placed their respective emphases on two different priorities. The parliamentary model, with its responsible party system and its corresponding party discipline in the legislature, emphasizes efficient policy delivery, and the ability of an elected government to deliver on its promises. The congressional model, with its lack of party discipline and its emphasis on individual legislative autonomy, placed more emphasis on what can be called "consensual politics": it may take much more time for executive proposals to find their way into law, but (the argument goes) there is greater likelihood that what does, ultimately, emerge as law will be acceptable to a greater number of people than if government proposals were "automatically" approved by a pre-existing majority in the legislature acting "under the whip".

We cannot say that one type of legislature is "more effective" than the other. Each maximizes effectiveness in different aspects of the legislative function. Legislators in the congressional system, because of their greater legislative autonomy and weaker party discipline, are more effective at actually legislating than they are at exercising ultimate control over the executive. Legislators in the parliamentary system, although they may play more of a "ratifying" role in regard to legislation, do get legislation passed promptly; they also have an ultimate power over the life of the government of the day.

The appropriateness of both models must also be evaluated in light of the different history, political culture and objectives of the societies in which they operate. Perhaps the grass is just as green on both sides of the fence.

Notes

[1]There is substantial literature devoted to the general topic of "the decline of legislatures." Among the many sources which could be referred to in this area would be included the work of Gerhard Loewenberg. *Modern Parliaments: Change or Decline?* Chicago: Atherton. 1971; Gerhard Loewenberg and Samuel Patterson, *Comparing Legislatures*, Boston: Little, Brown, 1979; or Samuel Patterson and John Wahlke, eds., *Comparative Legislative Behavior: Frontiers of Research*, New York: John Wiley, 1972.

[2]A very common topic in studies of legislative behavior has to do with the various functions legislatures may be said to perform for the societies of which they are a part. For a discussion of the many functions attributed to legislatures in political science literature, see Gregory Mahler, *Comparative Politics: An Institutional and Cross-National Approach* (Cambridge, Ma.: Schenkman, 1983, pp. 56-61.

[3]J. R. Mallory, "Can Parliament Control the Regulatory Process?" *Canadian Parliamentary Review* Vol. 6 (no. 3, 1983) p. 6.

[4]Bernard Crick, *The Reform of Parliament*, London, 1968, p. 80.

[5]One very well written discussion of the decline of American congressional power in relation to the power of the president can be found in Ronald Moe, ed., *Congress and the President*, Pacific Palisades, Calif.: Goodyear Publishing Co., 1971.

[6]Subsequently a special report was published by the Committee on Political Parties of the American Political Science Association dealing with this problem. See "Toward a More Responsible Two-Party System," *American Political Science Review* Vol. 44 (no. 3, 1950), special supplement.

Presidents and Prime Ministers

Richard Rose

Richard Rose is professor of public policy at the University of Strathclyde in Glasgow, Scotland. An American, he has lived in Great Britain for many years and has been studying problems of political leadership in America and Europe for three decades. His books include Presidents and Prime Ministers; Managing Presidential Objectives; Understanding Big Government; *and, forthcoming from Chatham House,* The Post-Modern Presidency: The World Closes in on the White House.

The need to give direction to government is universal and persisting. Every country, from Egypt of the pharoahs to contemporary democracies, must maintain political institutions that enable a small group of politicians to make authoritative decisions that are binding on the whole of society. Within every system, one office is of first importance, whether it is called president, prime minister, führer, or dux.

There are diverse ways of organizing the direction of government, not only between democracies and authoritarian regimes, but also among democracies. Switzerland stands at one extreme, with collective direction provided by a federal council whose president rotates from year to year. At the other extreme are countries that claim to centralize authority, under a British-style parliamentary system or in an American or French presidential system, in which one person is directly elected to the supreme office of state.

To what extent are the differences in the formal attributes of office a reflection of substantive differences in how authority is exercised? To what extent do the imperatives of office—the need for electoral support, dependence upon civil servants for advice, and vulnerability to events—impose common responses in practice? Comparing the different methods of giving direction to government in the United States (presidential), Great Britain (prime ministerial and Cabinet), and France (presidential and prime ministerial) can help us understand whether other countries do it—that is, choose a national leader—in a way that is better.

To make comparisons requires concepts that can identify the common elements in different offices. Three concepts organize the comparisons I make: the career that leads to the top; the institutions and powers of government; and the scope for variation within a country, whether arising from events or personalities.

Career Leading to the Top

By definition, a president or prime minister is unrepresentative by being the occupant of a unique office. The diversity of outlooks and skills that can be attributed to white, university-educated males is inadequate to predict how people with the same social characteristics—a Carter or an Eisenhower; a Wilson or a Heath—will perform in office. Nor is it helpful to consider the recruitment of national leaders deductively, as a management consultant or personnel officer would, first identifying the skills required for the job and then evaluating candidates on the basis of a priori requirements. National leaders are not recruited by examination; they are self-selected, individuals whose driving ambitions, personal attributes, and, not least, good fortune, combine to win the highest public office.

To understand what leaders can do in office we need to compare the skills acquired in getting to the top with the skills required once there. The tasks that a president or prime minister must undertake are few but central: sustaining popular support through responsiveness to the electorate, and being effective in government. Success in office encourages electoral popularity, and electoral popularity is an asset in wielding influence within government.

The previous careers of presidents and prime ministers are significant, insofar as experience affects what they do in office—and what they do well. A politician who had spent many years concentrating upon campaigning to win popularity may continue to cultivate popularity in office. By contrast, a politician experienced in dealing with the problems of government from within may be better at dealing effectively with international and domestic problems.

Two relevant criteria for comparing the careers of national leaders are: previous experience of government, and previous experience of party and mass electoral politics. American presidents are outstanding in their experience of campaigning for mass support, whereas French presidents are outstanding for their prior knowledge of government from the inside. British prime ministers usually combine experience in both fields.

Thirteen of the fourteen Americans who have been nominated for president of the United States by the Democratic or Republican parties since 1945 had prior experience in running for major office, whether at the congressional, gubernatorial or presidential level. Campaigning for office makes a politician conscious of his or her need for popular approval. It also cultivates skill in dealing with the mass media. No American will be elected president who has not learned how to campaign across the continent, effectively and incessantly. Since selection as a presidential candidate is dependent upon winning primaries, a president must run twice: first to win the party nomination and then to win the White House. The effort required is shown by the fact that in 1985, three years before the presidential election, one Republican hopeful campaigned in twenty-four states, and a Democratic hopeful in thirty. Immediately after the 1986 congressional elections ended, the media started featuring stories about the 1988 campaign.

Campaigning is different from governing. Forcing ambitious politicians to concentrate upon crossing and recrossing America reduces the time available for learning about problems in Washington and the rest of the world. The typical postwar president has had no experience working within the executive branch. The way in which the federal government deals with foreign policy, or with problems of the economy is known, if at all, from the vantage point of a spectator. A president is likely to have had relatively brief experience in Congress. As John F. Kennedy's career illustrates, Congress is not treated as a

---

Looking presidential is not the same as acting like a president.

---

means of preparing to govern; it is a launching pad for a presidential campaign. The last three presidential elections have been won by individuals who could boast of having no experience in Washington. Jimmy Carter and Ronald Reagan were state governors, experienced at a job that gives no experience in foreign affairs or economic management.

A president who is experienced in campaigning can be expected to continue cultivating the media and seeking a high standing in the opinion polls. Ronald Reagan illustrates this approach. A president may even use campaigning as a substitute for coming to grips with government; Jimmy Carter abandoned Washington for the campaign trail when confronted with mid-term difficulties in 1978. But public relations expertise is only half the job; looking presidential is not the same as acting like a president.

A British prime minister, by contrast, enters office after decades in the House of Commons and years as a Cabinet minister. The average postwar prime minister had spent thirty-two years in Parliament before entering 10 Downing Street. Of that period, thirteen years had been spent as a Cabinet minister. Moreover, the prime minister has normally held the important policy posts of foreign secretary, chancellor of the exchequer or both. The average prime

minister has spent eight years in ministerial office, learning to handle foreign and/or economic problems. By contrast with the United States, no prime minister has had postwar experience in state or local government, and by contrast with France, none has been a civil servant since World War II.

The campaign experience of a British prime minister is very much affected by the centrality that politicians give Parliament. A politician seeks to make a mark in debate there. Even in an era of mass media, the elitist doctrine holds that success in the House of Commons produces positive evaluation by journalists and invitations to appear on television, where a politician can establish an image with the national electorate. Whereas an American presidential hopeful has a bottom-up strategy, concentrating upon winning votes in early primaries in Iowa and New Hampshire as a means of securing media attention, a British politician has a top-down approach, starting to campaign in Parliament.

Party is the surrogate for public opinion among British politicians, and with good reason. Success in the Commons is evaluated by a politician's party colleagues. Election to the party leadership is also determined by party colleagues. To become prime minister a politician does not need to win an election; he or she only needs to be elected party leader when the party has a parliamentary majority. Jim Callaghan and Sir Alec Douglas-Home each entered Downing Street this way and lost office in the first general election fought as prime minister.

The lesser importance of the mass electorate to British party leaders is illustrated by the fact that the average popularity rating of a prime minister is usually less than that of an American president. The monthly Gallup poll rating often shows the prime minister approved by less than half the electorate and trailing behind one or more leaders of the opposition.

In the Fifth French Republic, presidents and prime ministers have differed from American presidents, being very experienced in government, and relatively inexperienced in campaigning with the mass electorate. Only one president, François Mitterrand, has followed the British practice of making a political career based on Parliament. Since he was on the opposition side for the first two decades of the Fifth Republic, his experience of the problems of office was like that of a British opposition member of Parliament, and different from that of a minister. Giscard d'Estaing began as a high-flying civil servant and Charles de Gaulle, like Dwight Eisenhower, was schooled in bureaucratic infighting as a career soldier.

When nine different French prime ministers are examined, the significance of a civil service background becomes clear. Every prime minister except for Pierre Mauroy has been a civil servant first. It has been exceptional for a French prime minister to spend decades in Parliament before attaining that office. An Englishman would be surprised that a Raymond Barre or a Couve de Murville had not sat there before becoming prime minister. An American would be even more surprised by the experience that French leaders have had in the ministries as high civil servants, and particularly in dealing with foreign and economic affairs.

The traditional style of French campaigning is plebiscitary. One feature of this is that campaigning need not be incessant. Louis Napoleon is said to have compared elections with baptism: something it is necessary to do—but to do only once. The seven-year fixed term of the French president, about double the statutory life of many national leaders, is in the tradition of infrequent consultation with the electorate.

The French tradition of leadership is also ambivalent; a plebiscite is, after all, a mass mobilization. The weakness of parties, most notably on the Right, which has provided three of the four presidents of the Fifth Republic, encourages a personalistic style of campaigning. The use of the two-ballot method for the popular election of a president further encourages candidates to compete against each other as individuals, just as candidates for the presidential nomination compete against fellow-partisans in a primary. The persistence of divisions between Left and Right ensures any candidate successful in entering the second ballot a substantial bloc of votes, with or without a party endorsement.

On the two central criteria of political leadership, the relationship with the mass electorate, and knowledge of government, there are cross-national contrasts in the typical career. A British or French leader is likely to know far more about government than an American president, but an American politician is likely to be far more experienced in campaigning to win popular approval and elections.

Less for the President to Govern

Journalistic and historical accounts of government often focus on the person and office of the national leader. The American president is deemed to be very powerful because of the immense military force that he can command by comparison to a national leader in Great Britain or France. The power to drop a hydrogen bomb is frequently cited as a measure of the awesome power of an American president; but it is misleading, for no president has ever dropped a hydrogen bomb, and no president has used atomic weapons in more than forty years. Therefore, we must ask: What does an American president (and his European counterparts) do when not dropping a hydrogen bomb?

In an era of big government, a national leader is more a chief than an executive, for no individual can superintend, let alone carry out, the manifold tasks of government. A national leader does not need to make major choices about what government ought to do; he inherits a set of institutions that are committed—by law, by organization, by the professionalism of public employees, and by the expectations of voters—to appropriate a large amount of the country's resources in order to produce the program outputs of big government.

Whereas political leadership is readily personalized,

government is intrinsically impersonal. It consists of collective actions by organizations that operate according to impersonal laws. Even when providing benefits to individuals, such as education, health care, or pensions, the scale of a ministry or a large regional or local government is such as to make the institution appear impersonal.

Contemporary Western political systems are first of all governed by the rule of law rather than personal will. When government did few things and actions could be derived from prerogative powers, such as a declaration of war, there was more scope for the initiative of leaders. Today, the characteristic activities of government, accounting for most public expenditure and personnel, are statutory entitlements to benefits of the welfare state. They cannot be overturned by wish or will, as their tacit acceptance by such "antigovernment" politicians as Margaret Thatcher and Ronald Reagan demonstrates. Instead of the leader dominating government, government determines much that is done in the leader's name.

In a very real sense, the co-called power of a national leader depends upon actions that his government takes, whether or not this is desired by the leader. Instead of comparing the constitutional powers of leaders, we should compare the resources that are mobilized by the government for which a national leader is nominally responsible. The conventional measure of the size of government is public expenditure as a proportion of the gross national product. By this criterion, French or British government is more powerful than American government. Organization for Economic Cooperation and Development (OECD) statistics show that in 1984 French public expenditure accounted for 49 percent of the national product, British for 45 percent, and American for 37 percent. When attention is directed at central government, as distinct from all levels of government, the contrast is further emphasized. British and French central government collect almost two-fifths of the national product in tax revenue, whereas the American federal government collects only one-fifth.

When a national leader leads, others are meant to follow. The legitimacy of authority means that public employees should do what elected officials direct. In an era of big government, there are far more public employees at hand than in an era when the glory of the state was symbolized by a small number of people clustering around a royal court. Statistics of public employment again show British and French government as much more powerful than American government. Public employment in France accounts for 33 percent of all persons who work, more than Britain, with 31 percent. In the United States, public employment is much less, 18 percent.

The capacity of a national leader to direct public employees is much affected by whether or not such officials are actually employed by central government. France is most centralized, having three times as many public employees working in ministries as in regional or local government. If public enterprises are also reckoned as part of central government, France is even more centralized. In the United States and Great Britain, by contrast, the actual delivery of public services such as education and health is usually shipped out to lower tiers of a federal government, or to a complex of local and functional authorities. Delivering the everyday services of government is deemed beneath the dignity of national leaders in Great Britain. In the United States, central government is deemed too remote to be trusted with such programs as education or police powers.

When size of government is the measure, an American president appears weaker than a French or British leader. By international standards, the United States has a not so big government, for its claim on the national product and the national labor force is below the OECD average. Ronald Reagan is an extreme example of a president who is "antigovernment," but he is not the only example. In the past two decades, the United States has not lagged behind Europe in developing and expanding welfare state institutions that make government big. It has chosen to follow a different route, diverging from the European model of a mixed economy welfare state. Today, the president has very few large-scale program responsibilities, albeit they remain significant: defense and diplomacy, social security, and funding the federal deficit.

By contrast, even an "antigovernment" prime minister such as Margaret Thatcher finds herself presiding over a government that claims more than two-fifths of the national product in public expenditure. Ministers must answer, collectively and individually in the House of Commons, for all that is done under the authority of an Act of Parliament. In France, the division between president and prime minister makes it easier for the president of the republic to avoid direct entanglement in low status issues of service delivery, but the centralization of government necessarily involves the prime minister and his colleagues.

When attention is turned to the politics of government as distinct from public policies, all leaders have one thing in common, they are engaged in political management, balancing the interplay of forces within government, major economic interests, and public opinion generally. It is no derogation of a national leader's position to say that it has an important symbolic dimension, imposing a unifying and persuasive theme upon what government does. The theme may be relatively clear-cut, as in much of Margaret Thatcher's rhetoric. Or it may be vague and symbolic, as in much of the rhetoric of Charles de Gaulle. The comparative success of Ronald Reagan, an expert in manipulating vague symbols, as against Jimmy Carter, whose technocratic biases were far stronger than his presentational skills, is a reminder of the importance of a national political leader being able to communicate successfully to the nation.

In the United States and France, the president is both head of government and head of state. The latter role makes him president of all the people, just as the former role limits his representative character to governing in the name of a majority (but normally, less than 60 percent) of the voters. A British prime minister does not have the symbolic obligation to represent the country as a whole; the queen does that.

The institutions of government affect how political management is undertaken. The separate election of the president and the legislature in the United States and France create a situation of nominal independence, and bargaining from separate electoral bases. By contrast, the British prime minister is chosen by virtue of being leader of the largest party in the House of Commons. Management of Parliament is thus made much easier by the fact that the British prime minister can normally be assured of a majority of votes there.

An American president has a far more difficult task in managing government than do British and French counterparts. Congress really does determine whether bills become laws, by contrast to the executive domination of law and decree-making in Europe. Congressional powers of appropriation provide a basis for a roving scrutiny of what the executive branch does. There is hardly any bureau that is free from congressional scrutiny, and in many congressional influence may be as strong as presidential influence. By contrast, a French president has significant decree powers and most of the budget can be promulgated. A British prime minister can also invoke the Official Secrets Act and the doctrine of collective responsibility to insulate the effective (that is, the executive) side of government from the representative (that is, Parliament).

Party politics and electoral outcomes, which cannot be prescribed in a democratic constitution, affect the extent to which political management must be invested in persuasion. If management is defined as making an organization serve one's purpose, then Harry Truman gave the classic definition of management as persuasion: "I sit here all day trying to persuade people to do the things they ought to have sense enough to do without my persuading them. That's all the powers of the President amount to." Because both Democratic and Republican parties are loose coalitions, any president will have to invest much effort in persuading fellow partisans, rather than whipping them into line. Given different electoral bases, congressmen may vote their district, rather than their party label. When president and Congress are of opposite parties, then strong party ties weaken the president.

In Great Britain, party competition and election outcomes are expected to produce an absolute majority in the House of Commons for a single party. Given that the prime minister, as party leader, stands and falls with members of Parliament in votes in Parliament and at a general election, a high degree of party discipline is attainable. Given that the Conservative and Labor parties are themselves coalitions of differing factions and tendencies, party management is no easy task. But it is far easier than interparty management, a necessary condition of coalition government, including Continental European governments.

The Fifth Republic demonstrates that important constitutional features are contingent upon election outcomes. Inherent in the constitution of the Fifth Republic is a certain ambiguity about the relationship between president and prime minister. Each president has desired to make his office preeminent. The first three presidents had no difficulty in doing that, for they could rely upon the support of a majority of members of the National Assembly. Cooperation could not be coerced, but it could be relied upon to keep the prime minister subordinate.

Since the election of François Mitterrand in 1981, party has become an independent variable. Because the president's election in 1981 was paralleled by the election of a Left majority in the assembly, Mitterrand could adopt what J.E.S. Hayward describes in *Governing France* as a "Gaulist conception of his office." But after the victory of the Right in the 1986 Assembly election resulted in a non-Socialist being imposed as premier, Jacques Chirac, the president has had to accept a change of position, symbolized by the ambivalent term *cohabitation*.

Whether the criterion is government's size or the authority of the national leader vis-à-vis other politicians, the conclusion is the same: the political leaders of Great Britain and France can exercise more power than the president of the United States. The American presidency is a relatively weak office. America's population, economy, and military are not good measures of the power of the White House. Imagine what one would say if American institutions were transplanted, more or less wholesale, to some small European democracy. We would not think that such a country had a strong leader.

While differing notably in the separate election of a French president as against a parliamentary election of a British prime minister, both offices centralize authority within a state that is itself a major institution of society. As long as a French president has a majority in the National Assembly, then this office can have most influence within government, for ministers are unambiguously subordinate to the president. The linkage of a British prime minister's position with a parliamentary majority means that as long as a single party has a majority, a British politician is protected against the risks of cohabitation à la française or à la americaine.

Variations within Nations

An office sets parameters within which politicians can act, but the more or less formal stipulation of the rules and resources of an office cannot determine exactly what is done. Within these limits, the individual performance of a president or prime minister can be important. Events too are significant; everyday crises tend to frustrate any attempt to plan ahead, and major crises—a war or domestic disaster—can shift the parameters, reducing a politician's scope for action (for example, Watergate) or expanding it (for example, the mass mobilization that Churchill could lead after Dunkirk).

In the abstract language of social science, we can say that the actions of a national leader reflect the interaction of the powers of office, of events, and of personality. But in concrete situations, there is always an inclination to emphasize one or another of these terms. For purposes of exposition, I treat the significance of events and personality separately: each is but one variable in a multivariate outcome.

Social scientists and constitutional lawyers are inherently generalizers, whereas critical events are unique. For example, a study of the British prime ministership that ignored what could be done in wartime would omit an example of powers temporarily stretched to new limits. Similarly, a study of Winston Churchill's capacities must recognize that his personality prevented him from achieving the nation's highest office—until the debacle of 1940 thrust office upon him.

In the postwar era, the American presidency has been especially prone to shock events. Unpredictable and non-recurring events of importance include the outbreak of the Korean War in 1950, the assassination of President Kennedy in 1963, American involvement in the Vietnam War in the late 1960s, and the Watergate scandal, which led to President Nixon's resignation in 1974. One of the reasons for the positive popularity of Ronald Reagan has been that no disastrous event occurred in his presidency—at least until Irangate broke in November 1986.

The creation of the Fifth French Republic followed after events in Vietnam and in Algeria that undermined the authority and legitimacy of the government of the Fourth Republic. The events of May 1968 had a far greater impact in Paris than in any other European country. Whereas in 1958 events helped to create a republic with a president given substantial powers, in 1968 events were intended to reduce the authority of the state.

Great Britain has had relatively uneventful postwar government. Many causes of momentary excitement, such as the 1963 Profumo scandal that embarrassed

---

The French tradition of leadership is ambivalent.

Harold Macmillan, were trivial. The 1956 Suez war, which forced the resignation of Anthony Eden, did not lead to subsequent changes in the practice of the prime ministership, even though it was arguably a gross abuse of power vis-à-vis Cabinet colleagues and Parliament. The 1982 Falklands war called forth a mood of self-congratulation rather than a cry for institutional reform. The electoral boost it gave the prime minister was significant, but not eventful for the office.

The miner's strike, leading to a national three-day working week in the last days of the administration of Edward Heath in 1974, was perceived as a challenge to the authority of government. The prime minister called a general election seeking a popular mandate for his conduct of industrial relations. The mandate was withheld; so too was an endorsement of strikers. Characteristically, the events produced a reaction in favor of conciliation, for which Harold Wilson was particularly well suited at that stage of his career. Since 1979 the Thatcher administration has demonstrated that trade unions are not invincible. Hence, the 1974 crisis now appears as an aberration, rather than a critical conjuncture.

While personal factors are often extraneous to government, each individual incumbent has some scope for choice. Within a set of constraints imposed by office and events, a politician can choose what kind of a leader he or she would like to be. Such choices have political consequences. "Do what you can" is a prudential rule that is often overlooked in discussing what a president or prime minister does. The winnowing process by which one individual reaches the highest political office not only allows for variety, but sometimes invites it, for a challenger for office may win votes by being different from an incumbent.

Campaigning for office makes a politician conscious of a need for popular approval.

A president has a multiplicity of roles and a multiplicity of obligations. Many—as commander in chief of the armed forces, delivering a State of the Union message to Congress, and presenting a budget—are requirements of the office; but the capacity to do well in particular roles varies with the individual. For example, Lyndon Johnson was a superb manager of congressional relations, but had little or no feel for foreign affairs. By contrast, John F. Kennedy was interested in foreign affairs and defense and initially had little interest in domestic problems. Ronald Reagan is good at talking to people, whereas Jimmy Carter and Richard Nixon preferred to deal with problems on paper. Dwight D. Eisenhower brought to the office a national reputation as a hero that he protected by making unclear public statements. By contrast, Gerald Ford's public relations skills, while acceptable in a congressman, were inadequate to the demands of the contemporary presidency.

In Great Britain, Margaret Thatcher is atypical in her desire to govern, as well as preside over government. She applies her energy and intelligence to problems of government—and to telling her colleagues what to do about them. The fact that she wants to be *the* decision-maker for British government excites resentment among civil servants and Cabinet colleagues. This is not only a reaction to her forceful personality, but also an expression of surprise: other prime ministers did not want to be the chief decision-maker in government. In the case of an aging Winston Churchill from 1951-55, this could be explained on grounds of ill health. In the case of Anthony Eden, it could be explained by an ignorance of domestic politics.

The interesting prime ministers are those who chose not to be interventionists across a range of government activities. Both Harold Macmillan and Clement Attlee brought to Downing Street great experience of British government. But Attlee was ready to be simply a chairman of a Cabinet in which other ministers were capable and decisive. Macmillan chose to intervene very selectively on issues that he thought important and to leave others to get on with most matters. Labor leader Neil Kinnock, if he became prime minister, would adopt a noninterventionist role. This would be welcomed in reaction to Thatcher's dominating approach. It would be necesary because Kinnock knows very little about the problems and practice of British government. Unique among party leaders of the past half-century, he has never held office in government.

In France, the role of a president varies with personality. De Gaulle approached the presidency with a distinctive concept of the state as well as of politics. By contrast, Mitterrand draws upon his experience of many decades of being a parliamentarian and a republican. Pompidou was distinctive in playing two roles, first prime minister under de Gaulle, and subsequently president.

Differences between French prime ministers may in part reflect contrasting relationships with a president. As a member of a party different from the president, Chirac has partisan and personal incentives to be more assertive than does a prime minister of the same party. Premiers who enter office via the Assembly or local politics, like Chaban-Delmas and Mauroy, are likely to have different priorities than a premier who was first a technocrat, such as Raymond Barre.

Fluctuations in Leaders

The fluctuating effect upon leaders of multiple influences is shown by the monthly ratings of the popularity of presidents and prime ministers. If formal powers of office were all, then the popularity rating of each incumbent should be much the same. This is not the case. If the personal characteristics of a politician were all-important, then differences would occur between leaders, but each leader would receive a consistent rating during his or her term of office. In fact, the popularity of a national leader tends to go up and down during a term of office. Since personality is held constant, these fluctuations cannot be explained as a function of personal qualities. Since there is no consistent decline in popularity, the movement cannot be explained as a consequence of impossible expectations causing the public to turn against whoever initially wins its votes.

The most reasonable explanation of these fluctuations in popularity is that they are caused by events. They may be shock events, such as the threat of military action, or scandal in the leader's office. Alternatively, changes may reflect the accumulation of seemingly small events, most notably those that are reflected in the state of the economy, such as growth, unemployment, and inflation rates. A politician may not be responsible for such trends, but he or she expects to lose popularity when things appear to be going badly and to regain popularity when things are going well.

Through the decades, cyclical fluctuations can reflect an underlying long-term secular trend. In Europe a major secular trend is the declining national importance of international affairs. In the United States events in Iran or Central America remain of as much (or more) significance than events within the United States. In a multipolar world a president is involved in and more vulnerable to events in many places. By contrast, leaders of France and Great Britain have an influence limited to a continental scale, in a world in which international relations has become intercontinental. This shift is not necessarily a loss for heads of government in the European Community. In a world summit meeting, only one nation, the United States, has been first. Japan may seek to exercise political influence matching its growing economic power. The smaller scale of the European Community nations with narrower economic interests create conditions for frequent contact and useful meetings in the European arena which may bring them marginal advantages in world summit meetings too.

If the power of a national leader is measured, as Robert A. Dahl suggests in *Who Governs?*, by the capacity that such an individual has to influence events in the desired direction, then all national leaders are subject to seeing their power eroded as each nation becomes more dependent upon the joint product of the open international economy. This is as true of debtor nations such as the United States has become, as of nations with a positive trade balance. It is true of economies with a record of persisting growth, such as Germany, and of slow growth economies such as Great Britain.

A powerful national leader is very desirable only if one believes that the *Führerprinzip* is the most important principle in politics. The constitutions and politics of Western industrial nations reject this assumption. Each political system is full of constraints upon arbitrary rule, and sometimes of checks and balances that are obstacles to prompt, clear-cut decisions.

The balance between effective leadership and responsiveness varies among the United States, Great Britain, and France. A portion of that variation is organic, being prescribed in a national constitution. This is most evident in a comparison of the United States and Great Britain, but constitutions are variables, as the history of postwar France demonstrates. Many of the most important determinants of what a national leader does are a reflection of changing political circumstances, of trends and shock events, and of the aspirations and shortcomings of the individual in office.

With all her faults, she is my country still

The nation-state, that worldwide triumph of political, social and economic organisation, is barely 200 years old. It is also, many people now say, on its deathbed. They are wrong

THE signs of decay are everywhere. The Soviet Union, which was in part a heroic effort to unite many nationalities under one state, is cracking. French-speaking *Québécois* talk about parting company with the mainly-Anglophone rest of Canada. Hindus run riot in officially secular India, hinting that Indian-ness should be more closely identified with Hinduness. Yugoslavs argue violently over national differences so fine that Chicago neighbourhoods could become countries on the basis of them.

At the other end of the scale, Mrs Margaret Thatcher is toppled as prime minister partly because of her entrenched resistance to the idea of surrendering some British sovereignty to a prospective European currency and central bank. At the Uruguay round of talks in the General Agreement on Tariffs and Trade, countries negotiate about freeing trade in services, which would involve each of them admitting far more foreign people and foreign ways of doing business—quite a different matter from admitting mere foreign goods—into its territory. More bizarrely, America and Japan, in their bilateral trade talks, agree to snoop into each other's national habits, like savings rates and retail-distribution systems.

Even the meat-and-potatoes of the nation-state diet, the power to wage war, is no longer quite what it used to be. The struggle between George Bush and Saddam Hussein involved the American president in a complicated alliance-building exercise that has relied to a surprising degree on decision-making by the UN Security Council and the nation-state-smudging concept of collective security. Is that it for the nation-state?

First Italy, then Italians

If so, the world will not be losing some long-standing and deep expression of the nature of human society. In a fine recent book called "Nations and nationalism since 1780", Mr E.J. Hobsbawm shows that the nation-state, in any version that would be recognisable to twentieth-century man, is no older than the American constitution and the French revolution, both born in 1789.

Even nationality, in its modern sense, is surprisingly new. In most of Europe, until the nineteenth century, "nation" meant little more than "place of birth" or "where I come from". In Spain, which, together with Britain and France, is one of Europe's older and most natural nation-states, it was only in 1884 that the dictionary of the Royal Spanish Academy stopped referring to *nación* as "the aggregate of the inhabitants of a province, a country or a kingdom", or, just as good, "a foreigner". In that year the dictionary at last made the link that now sounds so inevitable: "the aggregate of the inhabitants of a country under the direction of a single government".

The nation-state, even national consciousness, is the result of a deliberate effort to mobilise economic and social resources in the pursuit of large political aims. This was obviously the case with the creation of Germany and Italy, neither of which had existed in even rudimentary form before the nineteenth century. ("We have made Italy," Massimo d'Azeglio said at the first sitting of the Italian parliament, "now we have to make Italians.") But the effort of the will is there, too, in the virulent, often racist, European and Japanese nationalisms of the years 1910-45. And it also characterises the great revolutionary states of the eighteenth century, the United States and France: especially America, whose nationhood has been defined almost entirely by acts of will rather than accidents of history. "Americans are those who wish to be," as Mr Hobsbawm puts it.

What man has created, particularly so recently, man can re-create, or even demolish. The medieval world was a world of local and personal allegiances, with great sway being held by often tiny places: city-states like Lübeck and Venice were global powers. The world could become such a place again in the twenty-first century—provided that the purposes which the nation-state has served for the past couple of centuries can now find a better servant.

What countries are for

Those purposes can be summarised under three or four headings. One is the organisation and use of social violence. Modern technology has brought this to an astonishing pitch of sophistication and destructiveness, but the tendency of human societies—or of the people whom they allow or choose to lead them—to try and exert power over others is deeply entrenched. If "national" defence and security are to be a thing of the past, something else will be needed to keep order between societies.

A second purpose of the nation-state has been to express a sense of political and social identity. It may be a very new-found identity, as Mr Hobsbawm's book argues, compared with family, local, religious, ethnic or linguistic attachments, but the awareness of being the citizen of a country does seem strong in much of the world. A closely

A different measure

Conventional and "ownership-based" trade balances, US (1986) and Japan (1983)

All figures $ billion

Exports			Less intra-company transfers		Plus local sales to foreign multinationals		Plus sales by home-owned multinationals abroad		Equals total "foreign sales"	
224	146		122	60	400	3	865	150	1,367	239
Imports			Less intra-company transfers		Plus local purchases from foreign multinationals		Plus purchases by home-owned multinationals abroad		Equals total "foreign purchases"	
368	114		190	65	617	58	558	90	1,353	197
Trade balance -144 42								Ownership-based trade balance		14	32

Source: DeAnne Julius

related function of the nation-state has been to legislate: to write and then execute the rules by which a society chooses to govern itself (and, not incidentally, to define the sort of society it is going to be).

The people who think the nation-state is fading do not often mention matters like law-making and identity; defence and security, too, still seem strongly rooted in the national system, despite alliances like NATO and whatever bigger role the United Nations wins as a result of the Gulf saga. But the one thing in which the nation-state's grip seems visibly to be loosening is the organisation of economic life.

One world, one economy

However much power over commerce and finance the newly rising states of the nineteenth century actually had—and this article will argue later on that it was not much—the leaders who built the early nation-states, from Hamilton in America to Bismarck in Germany to the Japanese in charge of the Meiji restoration, all wanted to use national economic activity to put muscle behind their political ambitions. Their modern counterparts do not find it so easy.

With information and money both as weightless as the electronic impulses that carry them down wires or beam them through space, a government's ability to shape business and financial decisions is limited. Companies and money alike are ever freer to move to wherever they find the best returns—which means that governments are being shorn of the power to set the economic rules within their borders, let alone outside them. France's President Mitterrand discovered this in 1982, when the markets forced him to reverse the socialist economic policies that his government had been elected to carry out.

World economic integration is being speeded up by growth in trade (trade in goods and services amounted to some $4 trillion in 1990, up 13-fold in real terms since 1950), financial flows, and the migration of people and companies. A look at companies alone suggests how quickly the world is being knitted together.

In the last three years of the 1980s, the flow of direct foreign investment measured in 1980 dollars was more than $100 billion a year, ten times as much as it had been in the first three years of the 1970s (again in 1980 dollars). Once installed, direct foreign investment begins changing economic calcula-

tions in ways that leave policymakers scratching their heads. Take the item that people have spent so much time worrying about in recent years, America's trade deficit.

By the book, the American deficit was $144 billion in 1986. But if, like Ms DeAnne Julius, the chief economist at Shell International Petroleum, you then take account of the activities of American-owned firms abroad and foreign-owned firms in America, you find that this huge deficit becomes a surplus of $14 billion (the two measures for Japan, whose companies have invested far less than America's in the outside world, are much closer, see the table). An "ownership-based" measure of American trade raises basic questions about how international transactions should be thought of. It certainly puts fears about American competitiveness in a sharply different light.

If "American" competitiveness means anything at all these days. Mr Kenichi Ohmae, who heads the Japan office of McKinsey, a management consultancy, has long argued that the nationality of companies is an irrelevance—and tried to prove it in a recent book book, "The Borderless World". Big firms, at least, have to operate in many different markets around the world and, if they are to succeed, have to behave like locals wherever they find themselves. They may be headquartered, or most of their shares owned, in one country, but employ more people and pay more taxes somewhere else. What can their "nationality" really count for?

Mr Michael Porter, a business professor at Harvard, produced a 900-page answer in 1990, called "The Competitive Advantage of Nations". Mr Porter says that a company's home determines much of its (and thus of the home's) competitiveness: education, industrial structure, consumer sophistication, and the fierceness of the competition at home. Two of his most interesting examples, though, are highly localised Italian industries, footwear and ceramic tiles. Italy again. Why not "The Competitive Advantage of Provinces and City-States"?

Thatcher, Delors and Macrae

The European Community's 1992 single-market experiment is testing many of these ideas. Optimists say that both Mrs Thatcher, who until she lost office was the nation-state's most outspoken defender in the debates, and Mr Jacques Delors, the

commission president who is the champion of a supranational Europe, are wrong about the way the EC is headed. Europe, they say, is going to be remade by a gradual competitive deregulation of its governments.

It could work like this. Even with a single European currency, individual countries will remain in charge of their own fiscal policies and most of the laws that regulate companies, professions, health standards and the like. Because the EC will be not only a free-trade zone, but also a place where people can move freely, along with services and the firms that provide them, some way will have to be found to allow, say, German lawyers to set up shop in Bordeaux.

One way would be to gather in rule-making powers to Brussels and Strasbourg. A likelier approach is for Community members to agree on a few minimum standards for rule-making ("lawyers cannot be licensed without at least two years of professional training") and then start giving full marks to the regulatory approvals of other members. That German lawyer, once the German authorities had pronounced him fit to practise law, could set up shop without further ado in Bordeaux—even though he had not satisfied the requirements France imposes on its own would-be lawyers.

This might lead to a gradual interweaving of Europe's economies and societies, while avoiding the Delorsian threat of supranational government. It would also start putting competitive pressure on member governments to run similar fiscal policies. With a single European currency, a British company that faced British corporate-tax rates substantially higher than those in France would have good reason to think that being incorporated in France was not a bad idea at all.

The idea that, once a certain level of economic integration is reached, the pressure on governments to pursue policies that will attract rather than repel people and companies can be applied far beyond the EC. Mr Norman Macrae, *The Economist*'s former deputy editor, wrote in a piece of futurology called "The 2024 Report" that in the second quarter of the next century the world will be run with a single currency under the control of Centrobank, a global central bank answerable to no politicians.

With people pretty much free to move where they want, local governments will be the ones that matter (and even they will not count for much). Tax rates long since hav-

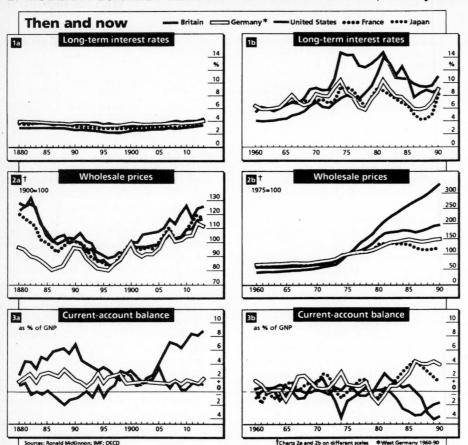

Sources: Ronald McKinnon; IMF; OECD

†Charts 2a and 2b on different scales *West Germany 1960-90

controlled little spending (10% of GNP or less), there were no quantitative barriers to trade and few to capital flows, and most countries had low or non-existent tariffs. The world was so tied together by trade and investment in the late nineteenth century that, despite the glorious years of growth in trade and GNP from 1950 to 1973, it took most countries nearly 70 years for merchandise trade as a proportion of their GNP to overtake the levels it had achieved in the years before the first world war.

The first lesson of these decades is that even a high degree of economic integration does not necessarily spell trouble for the nation-state. The gloomier lesson is that strong economic ties will not in themselves restrain countries bent on furthering other aims. The period of the gold standard ended with an appallingly destructive bout of nationalism that killed 75m people in the years 1914-45 and reduced the total GNP of the OECD countries by nearly 20% in 1929-32. Unless the nation-state fails to satisfy its other purposes as well—defence, social identification, rule-making—the global economy will not be in a position to pronounce its obituary.

Supra and infra, dubious twins

This might or might not be unfortunate. It all depends on what form of political and social organisation is best placed to make possible, worldwide, the kind of thing that chart 4 shows happened in the United States over the past 60 years. In 1929 the United States had large discrepancies in personal income from one region to another. Over the next seven decades they were practically eliminated. It is not too fanciful to believe that the technologies of production, information and communication have now entered a phase that would allow the same sort of convergence to happen worldwide by the year 2100.

This will come to pass only if the fewest possible restraints are placed on the movement of people, companies, money, goods, services and ideas. Letting these things find their right rates of return is what both raises and equalises incomes. The reason regional incomes could converge in the United States, once technology had become advanced enough, is that Americans enjoyed a single currency, and a set of laws and institutions that guaranteed them the right to move themselves and their property as they liked around their country.

The obvious analogy, on a global basis, is a world government. This is so implausible over the next century that it is not worth talking about. Besides, a world government is not necessary: the gold-standard years clearly showed that a great deal of freedom of movement is compatible with a strong system of independent states. The real question is about the size of the governing units, and the principles on which they operate.

ing been equalised by competitive pressure, public spending will amount to 10% or so of gross world product; and national defence spending, having proven its economic uselessness, will have been unilaterally abandoned, world order being secured by a small force under international control. Even welfare spending will be on its way to being equalised, which will at last finish off the nation-state.

It sounds like an appropriate end—except that this world, in many of its essentials, already existed once. It was called the nineteenth century.

The golden years

The years 1870-1913, when the world was on the gold standard as administered by the Bank of England, were a period of remarkable economic integration. Mr Ronald McKinnon, an economist at Stanford, has compared this period with the years 1960-88, the last 11 years of the dollar-dominated Bretton Woods system and the first 17 years of the floating-rate system. Some of his findings are shown in charts 1-3.

Because the gold standard was so rigid, and the rules were so widely adhered to (anybody who suspended convertibility, as the United States did during the civil war, felt compelled to return to the gold standard as soon as its crisis had passed), for all practical

purposes there was a single world currency. The first result was that long-term interest rates were low and uniform throughout the world, especially compared with the past 30 years (chart 1).

Second, price levels in the big economies were unstable, moving sharply up or down, but moving the same way everywhere; now they move only up, and at quite different rates in different countries (chart 2). Third, current accounts (and hence the flows of long-term capital) were volatile but were also, by modern standards, astonishingly large in relation to GNP (chart 3). In the decade before the first world war, Britain ran a current-account surplus that averaged 8% of GNP (and was investing that amount elsewhere in the world)—compared with a range of 2-4% for the West German and Japanese surpluses (and the American deficit) in the mid-1980s.

Immigration was freer in the nineteenth century. There were almost no restrictions on the movement of people, and move they did. In the 80 years beginning in 1845, 50m people, mostly Europeans, migrated to the western hemisphere: this in days when the world's population was less than a fifth of its present level. In the years 1900-13 alone, 10m Europeans left for the new world.

Long-term money and goods moved in larger relative volumes too. Governments

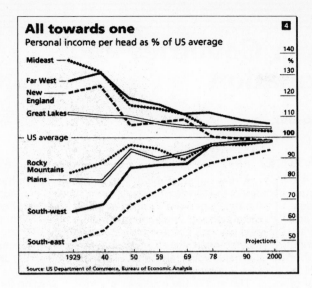

All towards one
Personal income per head as % of US average

Mideast
Far West
New England
Great Lakes
US average
Rocky Mountains
Plains
South-west
South-east

Projections

1929 40 50 59 69 78 90 2000

Source: US Department of Commerce, Bureau of Economic Analysis

These units are at least as much an expression of values, beliefs and experience as they are an instrument for making policies or delivering public services. Perhaps this is irrational. What made a true nation of America was a horribly bloody civil war which established, among other things, the principles that slavery is wrong even if most people in some places prefer it; and that, once those places had joined the United States, they could never leave it even if they democratically decided they wanted to.

Yet such things matter: they define whole societies. It therefore matters, too, who makes the laws and what the laws say, and who runs the public institutions. The link between a government and the society it governs needs to be a natural one. For the sake of peace and economic sense, it should also be a relaxed and tolerant one.

The nation-state has hardly been ideal at satisfying either of these aims. But would either supranationalism or infranationalism be any better? The trouble with supranationalism—which can be defined as the collection of several of today's largish and well-defined nation-states under a single government—is that it is hard to see how a true supranation could be put together. Not every state needs a civil war to forge its people's values. But every state does need something to make people feel comfortable with it and attached to it. The United States and Canada are more closely linked economically than many regions within America itself, and their recent free-trade agreement is drawing them closer together still. Yet the Canadians are fierce about wanting their own identity, their own government and their own country.

The likelier alternative is a breakdown of the nation-state into smaller units: call it infranationalism. A modern version of the pre-nineteenth-century world of unprej-

udiced local attachments sounds good, but that does not seem to be the direction in which today's nation-state unbuilders are pointing. The Soviet and Yugoslav break-ups, the revived religious fervor in India, even the language-based movement for Quebec's independence: they all are aiming towards states based not on tolerant and fairly open little countries, but on the blinkered view that what should hold people together is ethnic, religious or linguistic sameness.

This is a step backwards. Some homogeneous states work well (Japan and Korea being obvious examples). Most of the ones now being clamoured for are much likelier to end in bigotry, violence and protectionism. So where is the nation-state going to end up? In the short term, meaning the next few decades, in much the same place it now is. Some countries, like Yugoslavia or the Soviet Union, may disintegrate into near-warring ethnic or religious enclaves. Elsewhere, organisations like the EC, the GATT and the United Nations will continue to promote internationalism, and start becoming the scenes of a slow pooling of societies and sovereignties.

The basic unit, though, is going to remain the nation-state. Nothing else can govern whole societies without toppling, one way, into the infranationalist error of tribalism or, the other way, into the supranationalist sterility of rule by bureaucrats. If the world is lucky, the next era of nation-states will operate under a free-trading, fixed-exchange-rate (maybe even single-currency) regime. It will be liberal and open, with power more or less peacefully balanced. But most of the same flags will still be snapping on the poles outside the United Nations, and it will still be nations, and not something else, that are united.

Politics in a New Europe: Countries and a Continent in Transformation

- **The Shape of the New Europe (Articles 32–34)**
- **Growth of the European Community (Articles 35–36)**
- **European Institutions (Articles 37–38)**
- **Europe's International Role (Article 39)**
- **Post-Communist Central and Eastern Europe (Articles 40–42)**

The articles in this unit deal with some current topics of concern and controversy in European politics. On first sight, such issues may seem to vary erratically over time and place, but a student of comparative government will soon discover important patterns of continuity and similarity as well. Despite their separate national identities, the countries of Europe have some common cultural, economic, and social features that generate a number of comparable developments and issues in their politics. Moreover, they are increasingly linked together through a number of bilateral and multilateral treaties that have internationalized some policy areas ranging from certain aspects of economic and environmental affairs through civil liberties and social rights to tariff and defense policies.

All the articles in this section are devoted to one of two major developments that are bringing fundamental changes to the political map of the continent—the growing importance of the European Community, and the collapse of Communist rule in much of Central and Eastern Europe. Between the early 1970s and the mid-1980s, western industrial societies were beset by economic problems that brought an end to the unusually long period of rapidly growing prosperity that had followed World War II. The last half of the 1980s brought some improvement to the economic situation in most of Western Europe, partly as a result of favorable trade balances with the United States. Nevertheless, there are structural reasons why these countries no longer can take increased affluence for granted.

The economic downturn had come in the wake of sharp rises in the cost of energy, linked to successive hikes in the price of oil imposed by the Organization of Petroleum Exporting Countries (OPEC) after 1973. In the 1980s, OPEC lost much of its organizational bite, as its members began competing against each other by raising production and lowering prices rather than abiding by the opposite practices of a well-functioning cartel agreement. The resulting improvement for the consumers of oil helped the Western European economies recover, but as a whole they did not rebound to their earlier high growth rates. The short Gulf War did not seriously hamper the flow of Middle East oil, but it underscored the continuing vulnerability of Europe to external interruptions in its energy supply. Another important challenge to these affluent countries is the stiff competition from the new industrial countries (NICs) of East and South Asia, where productivity is high and labor costs remain lower than in Western Europe. The emergent Asian factor has probably contributed to the increased tempo of the European drive for economic integration.

Recent reports on the Western European economies tend to be far more upbeat, at least for the short and middle run, when compared to the ones of just a few years ago. Europessimism has been replaced by Europhoria, as some commentators put it. One major reason for the easing of the long recession, which plagued Western Europe until the mid-1980s, had very little to do with the attempts of those countries to revive their economies through fiscal or industrial policies. Instead, it resulted from the direct and indirect stimulatory effect exerted by the American upswing that had begun about two years earlier. The huge U.S. trade deficits could hardly continue indefinitely, of course.

A new sense of dynamism is closely tied to the implementation of the Single Europe Act, which sets December 31, 1992, as the date when the 12 nations of the European Community (EC) will become a single internal market. In addition, the end of the cold war has boosted the self-confidence of these countries, as they compare their own post-1945 records of achievement with the bankruptcy left behind by the Communist rulers of Central and Eastern Europe.

The end of the cold war is a mixed blessing for some critical observers. Thomas Risse-Kappen suggests that participants in the current debate in Europe can be divided into three general camps, defined by their different interpretations of the cold war and some closely linked assessments of the continent's prospects: The *realists* emphasize that international conflicts associated with the struggle for survival and advancement will continue and could become more dangerous after the end of the cold war; the *liberals*, by contrast, expect the collapse of communism to bring about a reduction of what they regard as ideologically rooted conflict; and the *institutionalists* challenge the assumptions of both, by emphasizing the need to maintain and expand an institutional framework that will encourage mutual crisis-management and cooperation among nations, whatever their geopolitical or ideological orientation. From this perspective, institutions matter a great deal, also at the international level.

The articles by Max Jakobson and Jochen Thies cannot be neatly classified according to the previous categories. But Jakobson does seem to make a cautiously optimistic and thus liberal assessment of Europe's future, now that the cold war division has come to an end. The German observer, Jochen Thies, is far more guarded in his analysis. He emphasizes and takes more seriously than many other observers that the political classes in Britain and France have reacted with consternation and growing concern to the possible change of direction by an enlarged and more powerful Germany. In his view, the British and French reactions will themselves be important in determining whether Germany decides to pursue its own *Ostpolitik* in post-cold war Europe. Thies could be called an institutionalist. He emphasizes the need for these three major countries to support European integration, not only for economic reasons but also as a means to tie a united Germany into the larger international framework.

The milestone year of 1992 is the theme of several of the articles in this unit. Robert J. McCartney explains the progress on the path toward a single internal market and provides a map that compares the 12 countries in terms of area, population, and economic productivity. Alexander MacLeod points out that the debate over whether to deepen or broaden the European Community is hardly an intellectual exercise, since a number of countries in both Western and Eastern Europe are eager to join. Neither author addresses the topic directly, but their articles would support a balanced view of Europe's future in which there is greater integration, but the nation-state has not yet become a museum piece. Implicitly, these and other authors included here reject the simplistic visions of a monolithic European Community. Instead they seem to anticipate a kind of pluralist maze. Checks and balances will come from an already apparent and possibly growing institutional diversity and political diffusion of power.

The European Parliament has been something of a political lightweight in the past. Voters in the member countries seem to have sensed this, for their rate of participation in the European elections of 1979, 1984, and 1989 was very low. But the European Parliament has been gaining in stature. Its partial veto over legislation passed by the Council of Ministers could develop into a co-legislative power shared with the Council. The relationship between Council and Parliament embodies the central dilemma of the Community, with the Council of Ministers representing the cooperation of associated sovereign member states and the European Parliament representing the beginning of a united European Government elected by the citizens of the Community.

Observers have contrasted two competitive ideas about the future shape of the EC, sometimes called the idealist and the nationalist visions. The former might also be called federal in its view of a future United States of Europe, while the latter clings to a more limited intergovernmental model of an association of sovereign states. De Gaulle advocated the intergovernmental position against the federal ideal of his countryman, Jean Monnet. Until recently, a similar contrast could be drawn between former Prime Minister Margaret Thatcher, who vigorously opposed European federalism, and Chancellor Helmut Kohl, who supported it. Not surprisingly, the French head of the community's executive commission, Jacques Delors, takes the latter view as well. But here too, there are changes, not least because of the changes brought about by the end of the cold war. Outside of Germany, at least, the nationalist position may become weakened by the prospects for a unification of that country, which West Europeans understandably wish to bind into a larger and stronger European framework. That is also the preferred scenario of Jochen Thies. Many Germans in leading positions support that view, but some observers have warned that there could be a new pull eastward on Germany as it pursues special opportunities for itself in the new markets of Central and Eastern Europe. The Gulf War presented something of an unexpected test to these theories. Elizabeth Pond reviews the consequences and comes to the counterintuitive conclusion that the conflict ended up giving the drive to unity a new impetus.

In the area of environmental protection, there would seem to be an obvious need for common and demanding standards, but they run up against strong economic interests in favor of lax standards that prevail in some countries and for some industries. The environmental problems in Western Europe are considerable, and many of them cannot be addressed effectively by a single country on its own. Even before the nuclear plant disaster at Chernobyl in the Soviet Union, the controversy over the use of atomic energy divided many West Europeans. It is a most difficult problem, at least for anyone who does not wish to return to a preindustrial economy, because the alternative sources now available (such as coal and oil) are themselves serious sources of pollution. It is interesting that the nuclear issue in many, but not all, countries has tended to reinforce the division between the Right and the Left.

One of the great themes in European politics in the 1990s will be the efforts geared to a political, economic, and social renewal of the countries in Central and Eastern Europe where Communists held a practical monopoly on power until 1989. For years to come, political scientists and historians will attempt to explain the major upheavals, as well as the reasons for our belated awareness that Communist rule was coming to an abrupt end.

It is already clear that the new Central and Eastern Europe is not going to begin with a clean slate. Not only have the four and

a half decades of Communist rule left a heavy economic and political mortgage behind, but the fledgling new democracies must also come to terms with an even older nationalist, anti-liberal, and anti-modern legacy. This grim tradition managed to survive, despite all official denials, during the many years of one-party rule. No longer repressed, it has come above ground and draws some strength from the present frustrations and dislocations. As Paul Lendvai emphasizes, liberal democracy will not be easily transplanted to these post-Communist countries.

Robert Kuttner reviews the economic catastrophe facing Central and Eastern Europe. This liberal American economist emphasizes that the problems are rooted in severe distortions brought about by central planning, but he foresees no easy transformation to a market economy. There are many theoretical writings and some historical experiences on the subject of moving from capitalism to socialism, but we have very little of either about the reverse process that is now facing post-Communist Europe. Kuttner's title ironically appropriates a classic Marxist phrase that consigned the allegedly obsolescent capitalist system to the dustbin of history. But he is clearly no purist advocate of laissez-faire in economic theory or practice. Some form of mixed economy is common in Western Europe, and it is precisely the flexibility and adaptability of modern capitalism that makes it attractive to many who have lived under state planning. A similar theme is suggested in John Lloyd's short essay. He points out that within the wide spectrum of possibilities offered by a market economy, the countries of Central and Eastern Europe must build their own pragmatic model to fit their own special contexts and needs. He discounts the talk about borrowing a western model, be it Scandinavian (for the high level of social protection), Spanish (for the successful transition from authoritarian government), or British (for the privatization of state-owned property).

There is an undeniable gloomy or hangover atmosphere in many of these accounts of post-Communist Europe. Some observers have talked about 1989–1990 as an *annus mirabilis* or year of miracles that has been supplanted by a year of misery or *annus miserabilis*. Some pessimists even forecast an *annus horribilis*, and it is clear that much will get worse before it gets better in the economic and social life of these countries. The political consequences could be very important, for social frustrations can now be freely articulated and represented in the political process. The transition from authoritarian or totalitarian politics to pluralist democratic forms will be neither easy nor automatic.

Looking Ahead: Challenge Questions

How do the realist, liberal, and institutional views of the cold war and Europe's future differ, and which do you find most persuasive?

What is the significance of the Single Europe Act? Will Western Europe reach its self-proclaimed goal of a free internal market by 1992?

Why will the French and British reaction to an enlarged and more powerful Germany be important in determining Europe's future?

What is the present importance of the European Parliament? Why can it not be called a truly legislative body for the Community?

What are some major reasons why many specialists on Eastern Europe failed to anticipate the major political upheavals of last year?

PREDICTING THE NEW EUROPE

While "realists" worry about anarchy,
"liberals" envision a peaceful continent.
European "institutionalists" say neither
peace nor chaos is at hand.

THOMAS RISSE-KAPPEN

Thomas Risse-Kappen, a German, is an assistant professor of government at Cornell University, Ithaca, New York. He is currently on leave at International Security Programs, Yale University. This is a shortened version of a chapter in a forthcoming book, World Security at Century's End, *edited by Michael Klare and Daniel Thomas.*

The end of the Cold War has kicked off a furious debate in academic and political circles about how the decades-long conflict was terminated, who won, and what the implications are for the future of Europe. The participants' positions and predictions depend largely on their assumptions about politics, international relations, and, ultimately, human nature. Despite the debate's sometimes esoteric nature, its outcome is bound to influence important governmental decisions in the months and years ahead.

To build on an idea put forward by Jack Snyder in a recent article in *International Security*, the most active debaters can be grouped into three general camps: the self-proclaimed "realists," the "liberals," and the "institutionalists." The "realists," generally speaking, think that peace was maintained in Europe after World War II by the U.S.-Soviet bipolar matchup and nuclear weapons; they worry that anarchy will dominate the continent's future. "Liberals" see the Cold War principally as a result of conflicting values and socioeconomic systems; they envision a Europe of peaceful liberal democracies. The "institutionalists" think that mutually reinforcing disputes and threats fueled the Cold War; they predict a further refinement of international institutions based upon the notion of common security.

The realists

The realist theory parsimoniously

From *The Bulletin of the Atomic Scientists*, October 1990, pp. 25-29. Copyright © 1990 by the Educational Foundation for Nuclear Science, 6042 South Kimbark, Chicago, IL 60637, USA. A one-year subscription is $30.

explains international relations as a self-help system in which states struggle to survive or improve their status by balancing the military and economic power of the other actors. Many realists believe that bipolar orders are more stable and peaceful than multipolar systems in which the actors more frequently shift alliances.

From this perspective the Cold War was the latest great power rivalry, a hegemonic conflict about global spheres of influence. Once the German attempt to establish world hegemony was thwarted in World War II, the U.S.-Soviet confrontation was inevitable, since they were the only two remaining great economic and military powers. The bipolar order was firmly in place in Europe by 1955, with West Germany entering NATO and East Germany joining the newly founded Warsaw Pact.

Realists such as John Lewis Gaddis argue that after centuries of great-power rivalries in Europe and two bloody world wars the Cold War finally established a "long peace" in Europe. The two superpowers maintained stability and prevented war for more than forty years. The peace was the result of a heavily armed confrontation: the integration of nuclear and conventional forces in Europe made any military conflict an unbearable risk.

How did this supposedly stable bipolar order collapse within the space of several months? The conventional wisdom of many policymakers and scholars is that Washington simply won the global power struggle with Moscow: "peace through strength" brought the Cold War to an end. A more sophisticated version of the argument follows Paul Kennedy's book, *The Rise and Fall of Great Powers*, and claims that the Soviets engaged in imperial overextension: the costs of maintaining the empire eventually outweighed the gains it brought. The burden of an empire which was not integrated into the world economy, of propping up authoritarian regimes which lacked popular support, and of pursuing a costly arms race with the West finally overwhelmed the already inefficient Soviet economy. Minor adjustments were no longer enough; Moscow's domestic and foreign policies needed drastic change.

Because they believe bipolar orders are stable, many realists, such as John Mearsheimer in his August 1990 article

in the *Atlantic*, offer a gloomy outlook on Europe's future. Without the predictability of behavior which is the only guarantee of stability in an anarchic world, Europe in the twenty-first century will revert to the conditions of the nineteenth century: conflicts, hostilities, and wars. Realists point to the ethnic and nationalist rivalries already reemerging in the Balkan states and the Soviet Union itself.

The consequences of a unified Germany raise special concerns. After all, one purpose of the two alliances was always to solve once and for all the "German question" that resulted in two world wars and the Holocaust against the Jews and other victims of Nazism. Even before unification, West Germany had emerged as the predominant economic power in the European Community. The West German Bundeswehr is one of the strongest, best-equipped, and best-trained conventional armies in Central Europe. Thus many fear that German unity could reestablish the country's hegemony in Europe. It might even lead to a resurgence of German militarism which caused so much bloodshed in the past. Finally, what will prevent a united Germany from acquiring nuclear weapons, the ultimate symbol of national sovereignty in the modern age?

This pessimistic view holds little hope for stability in a multipolar world. Without the Soviet threat, NATO, the guarantor of peace during the Cold War, will not survive and the United States will withdraw from Europe. Mearsheimer even goes so far as to argue that maintaining peace in the new Europe may require a modest spread of nuclear weapons to other countries, including a united Germany.

The liberals

A liberal interpretation of the Cold War and its end is so much at odds with the realist view that it seems as if the two groups are living in different worlds. Liberal theory posits a causal relationship between the internal political and economic organization of states and their external behavior. They maintain that liberal democracies behave peacefully and use force only if threatened—an argument that goes back to the eighteenth century German philosopher Immanuel Kant. Another version of the theory, ex-

pressed in the early twentieth century by Joseph Schumpeter, contends that the welfare orientation of modern capitalist societies reduces incentives for aggressive behavior in the world.

In this view, the Cold War was not so much about hegemonic rivalries as a result of the basic antagonism between liberal democracies and market capitalism on one side and authoritarian

> **How did the bipolar order collapse so quickly? Among realists the conventional wisdom is that Washington simply won the global power struggle with Moscow and the Cold War ended.**

regimes and centrally planned economies on the other. At the root was a basic disagreement about individual human rights. Liberals argue that the Soviet threat to Western Europe was not military power but the brutality with which Stalin imposed communist regimes on Eastern Europe. They find it hard to believe that the Cold War consensus to contain Soviet power would have emerged in the West if the Soviets had allowed East Europeans to choose their own domestic order and had not frequently intervened militarily in those countries to oppress popular opposition.

Liberals also disagree with realists about the benefits of the "long peace" of superpower confrontation. While the absence of major war in the northern hemisphere is an important achievement, given the history of this century, they believe the victims of the Cold War should not be overlooked. Millions of innocent civilians died in the so-called Third World when the superpowers took a stand against "imperialism" or "communism" in Korea, Vietnam,

Afghanistan, and elsewhere. And for millions of European and Soviet citizens who were deprived of basic human rights, the Berlin wall was the ugly symbol of the so-called long peace. Finally, billions of dollars were spent on an arms race which ruined the Soviet economy and kept the United States from addressing domestic and social needs. Liberals say peace should not be confused with the absence of war in one part of the world.

From this perspective, the collapse of the Soviet empire and the communist regimes in Eastern Europe is cause for joy. It was not the necessary result of imperial overextension but rather the effect of the inefficiency of a centrally planned economy, perpetuated for ideological reasons despite its adverse consequences. The Giereks, Kadars, Honeckers, Husaks, and Zhivkovs were kept in power only by Soviet tanks. The legitimacy of these regimes was constantly being undermined by the very presence of the West European democracies and their prosperity.

At the same time, the 1975 Helsinki accords of the Conference on Security and Cooperation in Europe (CSCE) established human rights as an international norm in Europe. Dissident groups emerging in Eastern Europe and the Soviet Union used the accords to legitimize their demands—an effort the West supported. A catalyst was all that was needed to transform the political systems [see "Eastern Europe: the Story the Media Missed," March 1990 *Bulletin*]. This explains, for liberals, the extraordinary speed and peacefulness of the transformation, once Gorbachev repudiated the Brezhnev Doctrine and made it clear that the Soviet Union would not use force to defend allied regimes. The exception of Romania only confirms the rule.

Liberals are optimistic about post–Cold War Europe—a view presented in its extreme, and therefore somewhat distorted, form by Francis Fukuyama in an article, "The End of History," which appeared last fall in *The National Interest*. Democracies have not gone to war against each other since 1815. The Western industrialized democracies have been by far the most peaceful region on the globe since 1945. The centuries-old hostility between France and Germany was turned into lasting friendship when Germany became a democracy. Post–Cold War Europe has nothing in common with Europe of the nineteenth century.

While realists point to Romania, Yugoslavia, and the Soviet southern republics to underline their arguments, liberals emphasize the relatively peaceful transition in Eastern Europe to democracy and independence from Moscow. Under the charismatic leadership of Václav Havel, the hostility of Czechs and Slovaks has been tempered and the two groups have been integrated into the new democracy. Poland has been remarkably stable despite a dramatic drop in living standards which would have provoked social turmoil in any Western democracy.

Finally, liberals argue that the united Germany of the twenty-first century will not turn into a *Reich* of the old style. Unification means simply that the democratic political, economic, and social institutions of the Federal Republic are being extended into former East Germany. Forty years of democracy in West Germany have firmly embedded liberal values in the population, while nationalist feelings are far less prominent than in other Western countries: the only nationalist outburst in Germany this year had nothing to do with unification; it was in response to the World Cup soccer victory. German leaders place high priority on cooperation with their Western and Eastern neighbors, a policy that enjoys overwhelming domestic support.

The sudden end of the Cold War, in the liberal view, does not represent the victory of Western containment strategy, or of the United States in its hegemonic rivalry with the Soviet Union. If anything, it is the triumph of liberal democracy and human rights, which is what the Cold War was ultimately about. The Soviets lost the competition over the most attractive political and economic system. As a result, real peace in a Europe "whole and free"— President George Bush's words—is now at hand.

The institutionalists

While liberals and realists are the main contestants in the U.S. debate, a third interpretation of the Cold War, its end, and the European future is more common among Europeans. The institutionalist perspective, as it may be called, challenges both realist and liberal assumptions, maintaining that tensions and international conflicts are not produced by deliberate aggression and sinister intention so much as by the escalation of crises in which all parties simply intend to defend themselves. Institutionalists see cooperation as an alternative to the vicious cycle of threats, counter-threats, and misperceptions—and international agreements and institutions create norms that foster cooperation. In other words, "common security"—a term coined by West German Social Democrats and made prominent by the 1982 Palme Report—is possible even between adversaries.

This perspective describes the Cold War as a mutually reinforcing process of threats, competing interests, and misperceptions. Stalinist ideology and Soviet behavior produced the threat perceptions which legitimized the Western strategy of containment and the enormous defense buildup in the aftermath of the Korean war. This in turn contributed to a climate of mutual hostility which endured throughout the 1950s and built up to the Cuban missile crisis of 1962. Skyrocketing defense expenditures in both the United States and Western Europe in the 1950s institutionalized the military, intelligence, economic, and bureaucratic apparatus which President Dwight Eisenhower called the military-industrial complex.

Institutionalists remind us, however, that during the Cold War there were also periods of détente leading to arms control efforts between the superpowers and in Europe. In 1967, NATO adopted the Harmel Report basing policies on deterrence and détente. The Helsinki Final Act of 1975 recognized the territorial and political status quo in Europe, affirmed human rights, and set a framework for political, economic, and humanitarian cooperation between the blocs. Détente also affected relations among countries in Eastern and Western Europe—most prominently in West Germany's *Ostpolitik* initiated in 1969.

A firm domestic consensus supported détente in many West European countries and even survived the deterioration of the superpower relationship after the Soviet intervention in Afghanistan and Ronald Reagan's election in 1980. The Conference on Security and Cooperation in Europe (CSCE), for example, was preserved largely through European efforts. New peace movements emerged in the early 1980s protesting the East-West arms race, and the level of public attention to security issues rose considerably. As a result, in late 1981 NATO proposed eliminating intermediate-range nuclear forces (INF).

When Mikhail Gorbachev reoriented Soviet foreign policy toward Western Europe and embraced the concept of common security, he quickly became the hero of many Europeans, particularly West Germans. The first result of the new détente was the Stockholm agreement on confidence-building measures in 1986, followed a year later by the INF Treaty which eliminated the U.S. Pershing IIs and Soviet SS-20s from Europe.

Realists and liberals usually overlook the European détente of the 1970s and the agreements and international institutions it put in place, such as the CSCE. Détente created an international climate favorable to domestic changes in the Warsaw Pact countries. It led to the emergence of concepts such as common security, which was meant in the West to gradually replace deterrence and which the new Soviet leadership later embraced. Thus while Gorbachev triggered the revolutions in Eastern Europe, the underlying causes go farther back than the events of the late 1980s.

Institutionalists question the liberal prediction of perpetual peace, because elements of the old realm coexist with the new order, at least during this transition period. Yet they believe that the crises predicted by some realists can be prevented or at least managed. But they warn that some cures for instability, such as allowing a united Germany to acquire nuclear weapons, might lead precisely to the kind of crises everybody wants to avoid.

Peace in Europe will not break out automatically, in this view. Efforts must be made to prevent instability, and institutions must be created or expanded to temper possible tensions. In *Europa 2000*, Dieter Senghaas provides a comprehensive outline for managing the transition period toward an extended Europe "whole and free," from Vladivostok to San Francisco.

These international institutions do not have to be created from scratch—they already exist, but they must adapt

to the new roles. The European Community (EC) is a forum for changes in economic policy, as the 12 member states will form a single market in 1992. The EC will also be the main instrument to keep a rein on the economic power of a united Germany and help rebuild the economies of the new Eastern Europe. In the security area, there is no reason why the Helsinki process should not be expanded and further institutionalized. A strengthened CSCE, with binding agreements among the members, could be the starting point for a future European peace order—one based on collective security arrangements guaranteed by the United States and the Soviet Union. It could serve as the forum for discussion of grievances on the German issue and other future conflicts. Besides preventing crises, CSCE can assist the process of democratization in Eastern Europe.

Most institutionalists also believe that NATO will continue to have a role in the new Europe, at least throughout the 1990s, but that its function will change drastically. NATO's priority will change from military containment of the Soviet Union to reassuring the Soviets of Western peaceful intentions. The Western alliance will also assume a major role in the demilitarization of Europe. Finally, NATO will continue to contain the military power of Germany, with U.S. troops stationed, in reduced numbers, in the western part of the country.

Whither Europe?

It is too early to tell which of these outlooks on the future of Europe will carry the day. Political scientists should be particularly wary of making predictions, since no one foresaw that the Soviet Union would stage a strategic withdrawal from Eastern Europe in 1989 or that the Cold War order would be undone so rapidly by the power of the people.

The Iraqi invasion of Kuwait seems, at first glance, to confirm the realists' prediction of increasing instability in the post–Cold War world. Policymakers are already using the invasion and the crisis which followed to prevent deep cuts in defense budgets. However, the bipolar order of the Cold War did nothing to prevent wars in the region during the past 40 years. In fact,

for reasons having much to do with the Cold War as well as with feelings about Iran, the Western powers, including the United States, supported Iraq's military buildup for years.

Nor would liberals and institutionalists describe the Middle East as a region destined for peace in the wake of the Cold War. Israel is the only liberal democracy in the region, and there are very few international institutions which might contain the aspirations of various Arab powers. These analysts would see the worldwide consensus against Iraq's invasion—not the invasion itself—as a result of the end of the Cold War. The revival of the United Nations Security Council as an instrument of international peacekeeping would have been impossible even two years ago.

Realists' views are confirmed neither by events in the Middle East nor by developments in Europe, where liberals and institutionalists are much closer to the reality of 1990. So far, the international arrangements favored by the institutionalists have adapted to the new situation remarkably well. The EC is speeding up the process of political integration and trying to keep the new democracies from being left behind. The first steps have already been taken to strengthen the CSCE—a summit will ratify the international arrangements for German unification; institutions for crisis prevention are in the making. NATO's London summit has gone far toward redefining the alliance's mission, reassuring the Soviets, and reducing the role of nuclear weapons in alliance strategy. The NATO decisions, along with Soviet withdrawals, mean that by 1992 or 1993, all land-based nuclear weapons will be removed from Central Europe.

Finally, German unification is proceeding in a nonthreatening way. The Germans have agreed to guarantee the current Polish borders and to limit their military power. They are continuing to enmesh themselves in international institutions such as NATO, the EC, and the CSCE.

The new Europe faces many problems, and the future of the Soviet Union is far from clear. But current developments suggest that a peace order can be built which prevents war, maintains stability, and guarantees human rights to all European citizens.

EURO FUTURE

*Germany uniting...the Soviet Union splitting...
both sharply affecting America, NATO, and the EC
as the electronic revolution changes everything
anyway. A front-line journalist sees tomorrow's
promise and pitfalls while pinpointing why
diplomats, spies, and journalists failed to
foresee what's happening now.*

Max Jakobson

The West has won the Cold War, yet the mood in Europe is one of apprehension and uncertainty. The Right has lost an enemy, the Left its illusions: Both feel disoriented. The emergence of a united Germany as the dominant power at the center of Europe casts a shadow over future prospects. The established international order has been shattered, as it was 120 years ago, when the birth of the first modern German Reich in 1871 moved Benjamin Disraeli to make one of his most memorable pronouncements on world affairs:

"Not a single principle in the management of our foreign affairs, accepted by all statesmen for guidance up to six months ago, any longer exists. There is not a diplomatic tradition which has not been swept away. You have a new world, new influences at work, new and unknown objects and dangers with which to cope, at present involved in that obscurity incident to novelty in such affairs."

Today, too, much of the conventional wisdom accumulated during half a century must be scrapped and many long-cherished political tenets reexamined. Yet "the obscurity incident to novelty" is dense.

The end of an era must mean the beginning of a new one, but so far no one has ventured to give the new one a name. The international community of political analysts and commentators views the future with understandable caution. It has been severely chastened by its collective failure to foresee the profound changes that have shaken the world in the latter part of the 1980s. Each successive dying spasm of the old order has been met with cries of incredulous astonishment: Unthinkable! Unimaginable!

None of us diplomats, journalists, scholars, or spies was able to draw the right conclusions from the mass of information available to all. No government can claim to have anticipated the change, let alone to have directed or controlled it. Indeed, political leaders have been inclined not to believe what they actually could see happening.

THE REASONS FOR FAILING

Before making a new attempt to peer into the future, it might be useful to analyze the reasons for this lack of foresight.

• Clearly, we were blinded by the façade of the totalitarian power structures: We believed they were invulnerable.

• We were overawed by the military capabilities of the superpowers and failed to assess them in a social and economic context.

• We counted missiles but discounted the influence of people like Lech Walesa, Andrei Sakharov, and Václav Havel—the real victors of the Cold War.

• We underrated the vitality of nationalism as a force stronger than ideological commitment.

• We underrated the vitality of nationalism as a force stronger than ideological commitment.

• Having resigned ourselves to what were called the political realities of the postwar status quo, we did not grasp in time that the fusion of generational change and the communications revolution would produce a political explosion within totalitarian systems.

• Most important, in my view, was our failure to see the social effects of the microelectronic revolution.

From *World Monitor,* December 1990, pp. 38-45. Copyright © 1990 by Max Jakobson.

On the Western side this last failure is an old story: one more example of the gap between the Two Cultures, to use C.P. Snow's phrase dramatizing how the literary establishment often fails to understand the sciences.

More surprising is that the Soviet side, to quote a recent report of the Soviet Foreign Ministry, "was very slow to respond to the strong and persistent signals of scientific and technological progress." Don't they read Karl Marx in Moscow? It was he, after all, who taught us to perceive the political implications of advances in the mode of production. What he wrote 150 years ago about the consequences of the first Industrial Revolution has a topical ring today.

The bourgeoisie, Marx wrote, "has accomplished wonders far surpassing Egyptian pyramids, Roman aqueducts and Gothic cathedrals. . . . The bourgeoisie has through its exploitation of the world market given a cosmopolitan character to production and consumption in every country. . . . All established national industries have been destroyed or are being destroyed. They are dislodged by new industries, whose introduction becomes a life and death question for all civilized nations. . . . In place of old local and national seclusion and self-sufficiency we have universal interdependence of nations. . . . The bourgeoisie draws all, even the most backward, nations into civilization. It will force all nations to use the same methods of production, unless they wish to perish. In other words it will create a world in its own image."

THE 19TH CENTURY OVER AGAIN

With a change of a word here and there, this text could well serve as an analysis of what is going on in the world today. As in the 19th century, the old order is undermined, not by any new political ideology or by an expansionist drive of an ambitious nation, but by scientific and technological developments. As access to information and the ability to use it have become the crucial factors in economic progress, the open societies, market economies—the bourgeoisie as Marx put it— have forged ahead; the closed societies, centrally planned economies, have been left behind.

Technology has triumphed over ideology, the Market has beaten Marx. According to one of the innumerable political jokes emanating from the Soviet Union, Karl Marx was given the chance to view the world as it is today and to address a global TV audience. His message was: "Proletarians of the world, forgive me!"

The manner in which Germany is being unified illustrates the character of the "new world, the new influences at work." The essential difference between 1871 and 1990 is that then unity was brought about by "blood and iron," as Chancellor Otto von Bismarck put it, while now the instrument of unification is the deutsche mark: a friendly takeover by a successful corporation of a smaller, almost bankrupt one. As a result, the world is witnessing the extraordinary spectacle of a state that has existed for forty years, a member of the UN, the leading industrial nation of the socialist camp and model member of the Warsaw Pact, being dismantled, brick by brick, and absorbed into the Federal Republic of Germany, the whole process to be completed in a matter of months and without a shot fired. Surely nothing like this has ever happened before in history.

This economic equivalent of German blitzkrieg has led to total victory for the West, unconditional surrender for the East. But it is a victory without victory parades. Who would

---

BISMARCK: A DIFFERENT BRAND OF UNITY

"My greatest ambition is to weld the Germans into a nation!"

Those words, with all their 1990s relevance, were uttered in the 1860s by Otto von Bismarck, the "Iron Chancellor" whose nickname applied not only to the way he pursued his ambition but also to his personal will (he once fought off a would-be assassin, holding him for the police despite having been shot).

Bismarck brought his chief goal to fruition. Before his term as prime minister (and later chancellor) there were 39 disparate German states. By 1890, when Kaiser Wilhelm II forced Bismarck into retirement, there was a German Empire stretching from Alsace and Lorraine in the west to eastern Prussia (now portions of Poland and the Soviet Union).

But historians inside and outside Germany advise against drawing parallels with today's unification. Yale's Paul Kennedy ("The Rise and Fall of the Great Powers"), for example, points out the critical difference between the new Germany, united by the people through a peaceful democratic action, and Bismarck's, forged by military conquest (Denmark in 1864, Austria in 1866, France in 1870) and diplomatic maneuvering. "Given the sentiments of the bulk of the German people," he recently wrote, "the only issue ought to be not 'unity or division?' but 'what kind of unity?' "

---

march in them anyway—the business managers, bankers, engineers, and other heroes of the market economy?

LIP SERVICE, AND THEN—POW!

There is no feeling of national triumph in West Germany, because unification is not really the product of West German national policy. True, every West German politician has paid lip service to the idea of unification: Germany will be united—one day. In the next century, former Chancellor Helmut Schmidt said only a year ago. To the people living today this was the same as saying never.

In practical terms the Federal Republic felt quite comfortable living in a divided Europe. Even after the fall of the Berlin Wall in November last year the action program put forward by Chancellor Helmut Kohl was still predicated on the continued existence of an East German state. It was the internal unraveling of the German Democratic Republic (GDR), rather than any deliberate government policy, that made unification inevitable. The decision was made in the streets, not in the chancelleries.

Thus unity fell into the lap of the German people like an

overripe fruit as a result of the collapse of the communist system throughout the eastern part of Europe and the worldwide advance of multiparty democracy and market economy. It is an event that can be understood only in an international context.

This may explain the lack of nationalist fervor in Germany itself. The East Germans are beginning to realize that freedom will mean more individual responsibility and risk. West Germans worry about what unification will cost them in terms of taxes and inflation.

It is characteristic of the state of opinion in West Germany that the Social Democratic opposition is making the cost of unity the central issue in the all-German elections this month. The famous victory achieved by the market economy may seem rather hollow if it can be said that it has bred a generation so lacking in idealism that it balks at making the economic sacrifices needed to integrate the Germans liberated from communist rule into the prosperous Federal Republic.

Is there no old-fashioned patriotism left? I asked a leading West German politician in Bonn. His answer was: not among the under-40s—that is, the majority of the West German population. Their loyalty is to the Federal Republic, which has given them political stability and unprecedented affluence.

WHO ARE WE NOW?

While the average German is concerned about his pocketbook, the intellectuals are engaged in an agonizing debate about national identity. In the more serious newspapers and periodicals, column after dense column is filled with earnest self-analysis. Having wrestled for decades with the Nazi legacy, German intellectuals now must confront the Stalinist past of the GDR.

The history of German unity is not a happy one, neither for the German people themselves nor for their neighbors. In the past thousand years the Germans have lived in a unitary state for only 74 (1871-1945), during which they experienced total defeat in two world wars as well as the ultimate horror of Nazi rule. Not surprisingly, thoughtful Germans ask themselves what will unity bring this time and what should be done to prevent new tragedies. Many answer by quoting Thomas Mann: Make Germany European rather than Europe German. But what this golden phrase means in practice remains to be seen.

REASSURING EUROPE

The sober German mood should be reassuring to the rest of Europe. Yet fears persist, on several different levels.

There is the obvious gut reaction conditioned by memories of Nazi aggression, the fear of the brutal Hun on the march.

There is the more sophisticated worry about German dominance in the business and financial world.

Among the political class in Britain and France, there is also an acute sense of loss of national prestige and status. Policymakers in these two former great powers naturally resent the prospect of playing second fiddle to Germany. The British feel their special relationship with the United States slipping away, while the French have discovered that the traditional Franco-Russian axis cannot be brought back to life. As both superpowers now court Germany, it is safe to assume that the political leaders of Britain and France will soon overcome their mutual dislike and join forces in order to create some counterweight to growing German influence.

Opinion polls reveal, however, that younger people in

Britain and France do not feel threatened by the unification of Germany. Indeed, the majority appears to welcome it. Is this due to the notorious lack of interest on the part of the younger generation, or is it the result of an internationalization of values and attitudes? Whatever the reason, the traditional game of power politics between the European nations no longer excites popular opinion.

WRONG ON MOSCOW TOO

But surely, it was argued until recently, the Soviets would not easily acquiesce in a unification of Germany. They could not be expected to give up the fruits of the victory achieved at such terrible cost in the Great Patriotic War without getting in return iron-clad guarantees against a renewal of German aggression. The marshals would simply not stand for it. And sure enough angry voices were raised in debates in the Supreme Soviet demanding to know who had "lost Eastern Europe and Germany," and President Mikhail Gorbachev was soon insisting on a neutralization of united Germany. The West geared itself for a long diplomatic battle.

But once again the experts were wrong. In mid-July, West German Chancellor Helmut Kohl met Gorbachev in the Russian's hometown, Stavropol, and struck a deal: Germany will be free to determine its own security policy—that is, to remain in NATO; Soviet troops will be withdrawn in four to five years.

Emotionally this may have been a painful concession. But rationally Gorbachev had no choice. He knew the West would not budge on the issue of German membership in NATO. In theory Gorbachev could have used the presence of 380,000 Soviet troops on German soil as a means of pressure. But this would have antagonized the West and cut the ground from under his grand strategy designed to integrate the Soviet Union, with Western assistance, into the world economy.

Gorbachev's handling of the German issue has been entirely consistent with his "new thinking" on the realities governing international relations at the present time. A report on Soviet foreign policy between 1985 and 1989, prepared by the Foreign Ministry for the Supreme Soviet and published in full in January this year, spells this out in plain terms:

"A dynamic economy based on new technologies, primarily electronics and information technology, is becoming a key source of influence in the world. Countries where traditional industries are predominant, especially those producing raw materials, are relegated to the role of involuntary tributaries of those whose might is based on investment in products of the human intellect."

NO FRONTIERS FOR NEWS

Clearly, the Soviet Union is a country relegated to such a subordinate role. And the report goes on:

"Global communications are giving rise to a single world information area. No frontiers can stop news or its interpretation from being transmitted immediately to any part of the earth. The information revolution has only just begun, yet its influence on the life of society and its every member is daily becoming more tangible. Attempts to shut out the rest of the world are particularly ineffective today, to say nothing of their unfavorable political consequences....The ideas of freedom and democracy, the supremacy of law and order, and freedom of choice are increasingly taking hold of peoples' thinking. Individuals and peoples who are now in a position to compare things are demanding conditions and a quality of life that technological progress can provide."

The conclusion drawn from this analysis is that "the very concept of national security" is changing:

"No nation can consider itself secure unless it commands a powerful, dynamic economy. More and more, it is economic, technological, and monetary factors that are at work as sources of political influence and of secure national interests, whereas huge arsenals that have swallowed so much effort and expenditure can provide no reasonable response to the challenges of today. Military means of procuring national security are objectively giving way to political and economic ones."

WHEN THE STOLZES HELP THE OBLOMOVS

In short, the security of the Soviet Union is not threatened by a united Germany or any other external power, but rather by the backwardness of its economy and society.

All energy must be concentrated on fighting the enemy within, personified by the fictional character Oblomov, the anti-hero of Ivan Goncharov's 19th-century novel of the same name, which has become a generic term for the inclination of the Russian people to argue all night about what should be done rather than doing it, to dream and plan rather than to work and act.

What makes Goncharov's novel particularly relevant today is that the only character who managed to inject some energy into the indolent Oblomov was his friend Stolz—a German, of course.

The relationship between Russians and Germans is long and complex. In the collective memory of the Russian people, beyond the hatred and fear engendered by the Nazi aggression, there is admiration and respect for the skills of the many Stolzes who have contributed to the development of Russia ever since the days of Peter the Great. Significantly, articles have appeared in the Soviet press recalling the practice of the 1920s, when thousands of foreign specialists, most of them German, were invited to work in Soviet enterprises. The emergence of a united Germany could thus be seen not as a threat but as a promise of an infusion of capital and know-how. There is, after all, no other nation that has both the resources and the self-interest to help the countries of Eastern Europe to lift themselves out of their present misery.

The German end of the Gorbachev-Kohl bargain has not been revealed in detail, but clearly it implies a strong commitment to helping Gorbachev overcome his formidable difficulties. This can be done in two ways. One is to agree to a sharp reduction in German military forces and other disarmament measures in order to strengthen Gorbachev's domestic political position against his conservative critics. The other is, of course, massive economic assistance. The West German government granted the Soviet Union considerable credits, actively lobbying among its allies to persuade them to take similar action.

Even without such an extra effort united Germany will have a greater stake in the Soviet economy than any other country. East Germany has been for decades the Soviet Union's biggest trading partner in the socialist group, while West Germany has the same position among capitalist countries.

A PURPOSE FOR NATO?

Every German politician is anxious to assure a visitor that the new relationship emerging between Germany and the Soviet

> ## IF AMERICAN TROOPS ARE NO LONGER NEEDED TO KEEP THE RUSSIANS OUT, THEY CAN HARDLY STAY ON JUST TO KEEP THE GERMANS DOWN.

Union will in no way weaken Germany's ties with the West. There is no reason to doubt the sincerity of such assurances. For, as far into the future as anyone can see, the Soviet Union will remain a crisis economy. It cannot become a major trading partner for Germany.

Yet, inevitably, unification will mean a shift in German political and economic interests. It could be described as a subtle redefinition of identity: The Federal Republic describes itself as a West European country, united Germany will be a European country.

The implications for the future of the European Community are profound. It is an institution constructed on the assumption that the division of Europe would be permanent. It cannot continue to develop along the old lines as if nothing had happened.

True, those who wish to make the EC into a political union of its present 12 member states—the French in particular—hope to accelerate the process in order to tie down the German giant, like Gulliver in the land of the Lilliputians, with innumerable little strings of common procedures.

But will the giant lie down and let himself be tied? It is more likely that German influence will work in favor of opening the European Community to new members, in the first place the neutral states comprising the European Free Trade Association, and later the countries liberated from communist rule. A more open community will mean less political cohesion, more diversity. But it will also mean that the community will finally catch up with its name and become a truly European, rather than merely West European, institution.

NATO, too, is a function of the division of Europe and now urgently in need of reconstruction. To Europeans, NATO stands for the presence of American forces on European soil, assuring the United States commitment to defend its allies. To Americans, it is the principal channel of United States political influence over European affairs. For as long as Soviet troops remain in Germany, no European government, either in the

3. POLITICS IN A NEW EUROPE: The Shape of the New Europe

West or in the East, is likely to question the need to maintain NATO as a guarantor of European stability.

But once the Soviet troops have been withdrawn, the strategic situation in Europe will be fundamentally altered. There will be no direct confrontation between the military forces of the two superpowers. The Warsaw Pact will have ceased to exist. Germany and the Soviet Union—perhaps one should say Russia—will be separated by a buffer zone of independent, Western-oriented states: Poland, Hungary, Czechoslovakia, Yugoslavia, possibly even Ukraine and the Baltic republics. What will then be the purpose of NATO?

It can no longer be the original purpose, which was defined by a witty British diplomat as "keeping the Russians out, the Americans in, and the Germans down." If American troops are no longer needed to keep the Russians out, they can hardly stay on simply to keep the Germans down.

WHAT WOULD BE SUICIDAL

Attempts to constrain a united Germany by external means would only lead to resentments among the Germans and friction between them and their neighbors. More effective and reliable constraints are inherent in the very structure of the German Federal Republic as it has evolved over the past 40 years.

As Václav Havel, the playwright president of Czechoslovakia, has put it, what matters is not how big Germany will be, but that it will remain a democratic society. Unlike the Weimar Republic, the democratic system of the Federal Republic has been a success. It has given the Germans a long period of political stability and economic prosperity. They are not likely to abandon a system that has worked so well.

The strength of the German economy brings political power but also a high degree of vulnerability. It can be maintained only in conditions of political stability at home and a peaceful evolution in Europe as a whole. In today's integrated world economy, Germany can continue its economic success only in conjunction with the success of neighbors and trading partners. To revert to an aggressive policy would be suicidal.

German unification—
opportunity or setback for Europe?

Jochen Thies

The treaty signed on 12 September in Moscow between the two German states and the victorious Allies of 1945 was not the result of a grand accord between all participants, but rather of a deal between West Germany and the two superpowers, the United States and the Soviet Union. This is clear both from the general pattern and the final communiqué of the 'two-plus-four' talks. Bonn was somewhere in the middle, courted by all sides and promoted by an American Administration which rose above backward-looking pettiness and treated Germany consistently as a European partner whose importance is bound to increase in the next decade. The actions of the Soviet Union were governed by similar considerations, although President Gorbachev's readiness to compromise was almost certainly motivated by his more short-term aims. After all, who, apart from the Germans, is at present prepared to help a country which is in the throes of dissolution? How much of this will actually come to anything remains to be seen. But German politicians would be well advised not to underestimate the intentions of the Soviet leaders, who are still trying to bind Germany more closely to the Soviet Union or, at least, to divert some of the capital and investment flows in their own direction. If this happens, the almost 80m inhabitants of the newly united Germany might one morning wake up and find themselves wedged in the middle, i.e., at a certain distance from the West as well.

Britain and France have not played a significant role in this process. The disappointment this has caused among German politicians will almost certainly be forgotten as soon as the West European integration process shows some results. But the reaction of Germany's small neighbours—a mixture of support for the Germans but also of worry lest some of the unhappy history of the first half of the twentieth century should repeat itself—was probably more honest. Predictably, perhaps, the greater the geographical distance from Germany, the more enthusiastic the reaction to its unification. It was therefore hardly surprising that the echo in Spain, Portugal, Italy and Greece, to mention only the members of the European Community that border on the Mediterranean, was particularly positive.

During the 1980s,[1] and most recently in the second volume of his memoirs,[2] the former West German Chancellor, Helmut Schmidt, advocated a political leadership role for France in Europe. Germany, Mr Schmidt argued, should remember its recent past, take a modest back seat and concentrate on keeping its economic policy on its present successful course. This thesis, which even at the moment of its conception seemed to fly in the face of history, has been proved wrong more than once by the events of the past year.

What Helmut Schmidt overlooked was not only Britain's continuing determination to play a prominent role in shaping European opinion, but also the fact that leading British and German politicians think far more alike than might be expected in the light of the special Franco-German understanding of the last 27 years. At the same time he—together with many other Germans—overestimated the determination of the French to assume a leadership role in Europe. Throughout their recent history, from Charles de Gaulle to François Mitterrand, the French have always shown a certain self-restraint, a wise awareness of their own limitations.[3] France as a country is deeply rooted in its history, and its political actions are guided by historical precedent and are therefore taken on a long-term basis. This is something which the Germans at present largely lack. They are more easily led by trends and fashions and consequently catch-phrases coined by a few opinion-formers. Vigorous debates, like those in political circles in London and Paris, are unknown. This explains the current French reticence: where—apart from the German Chancellor—are those great and true Europeans who will guarantee that Germany stays on course, i.e., in the Western camp, until the turn of the century and beyond?

Generally speaking, Germany's neighbours must view its economic dynamism with concern. This will become all the more apparent when, in the not too distant future, it leads to the expected enormous upsurge in economic activity in the five new *Länder*. One acute observer of the current German situation has perhaps managed to sum up the unspoken worries of the other countries: 'During the Second World War the Allies and the anti-Hitler coalition were united in their aim to cure the Germans of their obsession to expand their *Lebensraum* and to bring them back to European reality by reducing the size of Germany. By now the Germans have learnt their lesson, but in a way which the Allies, whose reasoning in 1942 was governed by strategic considerations, had not anticipated. Unable to gain access to additional living space and natural resources, the Germans grasped the one dimension whose borders cannot be guarded by armies and protected by strategic alliances—the dimension of time.'[4] It is almost tempting to add that this applies equally to that other big loser of the Second World War, Japan.

Whatever their reservations about German unification, the British have reacted quite differently from the French: the present Franco-German dialogue is characterised by dishonesty and ulterior motives on both sides, whereas the relations between the British and Germans are conducted in a rough but hearty atmosphere. And in the end London's reaction to German unification was the right one. Of course, Britain's entry into the European Monetary System does not mean that the members of its Tory government have suddenly become true Europeans, although this may change under Mrs Thatcher's successor, Mr John Major. What is clear, however, is that Britain no longer intends to remain aloof, that it wants to participate. France, on the other hand, is still in a state of shock and, with slightly childish resentment, has announced that within the next few years all its almost 50,000 soldiers will be pulled out of Germany. The only exception is the French-German brigade which took up its duties in October 1989. In the interest of Europe it is to be hoped that this is not President Mitterrand's last word on the matter. Here, too, Britain has behaved much more constructively. Although substantially reduced, its Rhine Army will remain in Germany, and London has no qualms about the creation of a multinational West European army or about stationing German soldiers on British soil.

During the 'two-plus-four' talks France and Britain found themselves, almost against their will, pushed into the role of spectators. Now, since the beginning of the Gulf crisis, they have been trying to regain some of the lost ground. There is very little

From *The World Today*, January 1991, pp. 8-11. *The World Today*, published by the Royal Institute of International Affairs.

evidence of concerted European action, for example, within the framework of the Western European Union (WEU), and all the more of the old superpower mentality. Britain is presenting itself to the Americans as a particularly reliable partner, much better suited to a 'partnership in leadership' than the less reliable Germans. After some initial hesitation France, too, has found its way to the Gulf, as have most of the other European NATO partners of the United States.

For the Germans, this is very embarrassing indeed. But the fault lies less with the Chancellor who—had the decision been left to him—would have sent troops to Saudi Arabia straight away, than with the tacit consensus among the political parties in Bonn during the heated weeks leading up to the Bundestag (lower house of the German Parliament) elections on 2 December. The consensus was that times like these are not the best to deal with unpleasant questions which are unlikely to bring domestic votes. However, the German arguments, which have never been particularly convincing, have, since the fall of the Berlin Wall and the end of the Cold War, lost all credibility. The German *Grundgesetz* (Basic Law) has never explicitly forbidden the stationing of German soldiers outside the NATO area. Bonn's problem is the interpretation of the Basic Law, which is nothing but a feeble compromise and should have been abandoned in 1987 at the latest, when the conflict between Iran and Iraq and the convoys sent by the West to protect its tankers could be seen as the first warning signs of the present Gulf crisis.

Now the Germans must pay for the delaying tactics of a generation which believed far too long that the memories of the Third Reich and the Second World War, as well as the continuing division of their country, would allow them to hang on to a policy which is basically nothing but opportunistic and selfish. It may be a lot to ask from German politicians of all parties, so soon after the elections to the first all-German Parliament, to pass the necessary amendments to the Basic Law which would help remove this self-inflicted German blockade. But just opening a small window to allow German soldiers to join the UN peace-keeping units will not be enough: any changes must also include legal provisions to enable German troops to join a future European army outside NATO territory, i.e., to operate within the framework of the Western Alliance and the WEU. Too narrow an interpretation of a potential German military involvement, which must never again be an isolated, national one, would quickly lead to renewed complications with the United States and with France and Britain. Here, too, France is to some extent justified in waiting for a German reaction. There can be no genuine West European commitment without the willingness to contribute towards the defence of that common interest. France—and other West European partners—have a much clearer understanding of the connection between political and military integration than the Germans.

The outcome of this debate in Germany is far from clear. In spite of his convincing election victory on 2 December, Chancellor Kohl will need the support of the Social Democratic Party (SPD) to amend the Basic Law, which requires a two-thirds majority. It remains to be seen whether, and to what extent, the lack of experience of the former East Germany in the field of foreign policy will make itself felt. It should be remembered that, even in the days of the Berlin Wall, the West German peace movement found a strong echo in the East. This may now lead to the emergence of a Protestant-oriented peace ethic, frequently inspired by clergymen, within a new political class. This is one of the reasons why Germany's partners will have to be very patient and leave the country alone so that it can find a new international role for itself. But time for this search is beginning to run out.

The West Germans were lucky that unification came when it did, at a point when the political leadership of the country consisted of men and women who, because of their childhood and wartime experiences, still had an all-German conscience. That is why, during the decisive months, there was a kind of unspoken spirit of solidarity across party lines. Names that come to mind, despite obvious weaknesses of timing, are those of the West German President, Richard von Weizsäcker, Chancellor Helmut Kohl, Willy Brandt and Hans-Jochen Vogel of the SPD, as well as the Free Democrats (FDP), Otto Graf Lambsdorff and Hans-Dietrich Genscher. Like the president of the FDP, Wolfgang Mischnick, Genscher was born in the former East Germany. There was no tangible contribution towards German unification from West German politicians aged between 40 and 50, whose colleagues in the East were streets ahead of them. The behaviour of the Greens in this context is best forgotten.

The role of the leading civil servants in Bonn as political advisers in this decisive phase in German history cannot be overemphasised. The percentage of people born in East and Central Germany and, above all, in Berlin at the level of Minister of State and Permanent Secretary is exceptionally high. Other areas where these personal factors have almost certainly played an important role since November 1989 are the print and electronic media.

All in all, the liberal-conservative camp cut the best figure during those vital months when assessing the situation and taking the necessary decisions. Also, one cannot help thinking that it was after all Konrad Adenauer's 'magnet theory' which was vindicated at the end of last year—even though its vindication only came several decades after its was launched in the late 1940s and early 1950s. But it should not be forgotten that in the final analysis it was Mikhail Gorbachev, Poland's trade union movement Solidarity and the hole in the Hungarian fence which brought about German reunification. There was no genuine revolution in the late autumn of 1989—and in retrospect this was not a bad thing. One of the reasons for the peaceful outcome in East Germany was probably the absence of a charismatic leader like Lech Walesa or Vaclav Havel to unite the masses in Leipzig and East Berlin, which is perhaps why the Soviet Union refrained from intervention. The Soviet President, Mikhail Gorbachev, never wanted German reunification. He did not want it five years ago, when he first embarked on his present reforms, nor did he want it in the autumn of 1989. But he did not try to stop the irreversible process whose beginnings coincided with the 40th anniversary of the East German state in October 1989.

Today it seems that Helmut Kohl has grown from a party politician into a statesman. Yet this Catholic politician from south-west Germany believed for a long time that the chances for a German reunification were minimal. As late as 1988 he dismissed as 'utter nonsense' an intra-party discussion, initiated by the backbenchers in the German Bundestag, which tried to put the German question on the agenda of East-West summits. Observers were, however, struck by the fact that the Chancellor listened to the discussion for a long time without intervening. Was he even then thinking of something else?

But then Kohl was well ahead of most other politicians in spotting the chances arising from the mass exodus of East German refugees for the German reunification process. Not even the sceptics among Germany's partners in the West could ignore the resulting dynamic developments, coupled with the growing danger of a gradual destabilisation of West Germany. However, nobody seemed to notice that after the East German elections on 18 March 1990, from which he emerged as the indirect winner, Kohl switched tactics and, both on the national and international level, began pushing for German reunification with great determination and speed.

Among Germany's neighbours, however, the initial joy at the fall of the Berlin Wall soon gave way to consternation and growing concern about a possible change of direction by an enlarged Germany. The political elites in France and Britain view the changes in Germany, Central and East Europe and the Soviet Union with particular concern. There can be no doubt that the international strategic position of the two nuclear powers has been diminished by the unification of the two Germanies. The geography of the continent has changed as well: it has moved in a north-easterly direction, pushing Britain and France—as national states—into a peripheral position.

It is to be hoped that, with the continuing progress of West European integration, Bonn will soon be able to forget the negative experiences of the last few months, when France and Britain tried temporarily if not to stop, at least to slow down the process of German unification. This barely concealed diplomatic game by the victorious Allies of 1945 might well have succeeded with a different Soviet leadership—but it made absolutely no impression on Mikhail Gorbachev. He placed everything resolutely on the German card, above all in order to survive in his own country, which is drifting towards chaos.

The United States adopted a similar stance and gave its unequivocal and, in contrast to the other three victorious powers, also its immediate support to the process of German unification. Only now do we begin to realise how serious George Bush was when, in Mainz during his European trip in May 1989, he referred to 'partners in leadership'.[5] The open question now is whether Paris and London will resign themselves to this unexpected loss of power and choose the path towards political, economic and military integration, or whether they will decide to hold on to their special nuclear role. If they hesitate too long they might end up with precisely the kind of Germany which nobody in Europe wants, not even the Germans in the East or the West. The Germans, although slightly Europe-weary, are prepared to cooperate with their partners, provided the government in Bonn is left free to lay on generous aid programmes for Eastern Europe.

The moment of decision for Europe will come within the next two to three years. Should France and Britain withdraw into 'splendid isolation'—which nobody in Germany can imagine—then they would literally force the Germans to pursue their own *Ostpolitik*. This would be the inevitable outcome if Germany receives no help in assisting the economic recovery of East Germany, Poland, Czechoslovakia, Hungary and other East European states, not to mention support of the Soviet Union. Basically even a united Germany leans towards the West, as the experiences of the 40 postwar years and the high level of German exports have shown. The volume of trade with Eastern Europe is generally vastly overrated. In the overall economy of Germany it plays a secondary role, and nobody wants to change that.

Even the sensational breakthrough achieved in the Gorbachev-Kohl talks in the Caucasus in July 1990 is unlikely to change this. Gorbachev is bound to place a high material price on German reunification. But this seems bearable compared to the possibility of integrating Germany militarily into NATO, which must be a welcome development for all Europeans. (This, incidentally, is a victory which the German Defence Minister, Gerhard Stoltenberg, scored over his adversary Genscher, the Foreign Minister, but was never given public credit for.)

What might jeopardise the German unification process is the time limit for the final withdrawal of the approximately 380,000 Soviet soldiers in East Germany, plus 120,000 family members and civilians: a period of three to four years is both too much and too little. It is by no means certain whether the East Germans are prepared to continue to exercise their long-tried patience in the face of these sometimes massive Soviet troop concentrations. According to official statistics military installations and exercise grounds cover about 20 per cent of the land area of East Germany. This must be added to the huge amount of disturbance caused by aircraft and military manoeuvres as well as environmental problems on a gigantic scale.

The growing instability in the Soviet Union aggravates these uncertainties. The entire western periphery of the country is in the process of severing its links with Moscow, and there are some doubts whether the Soviet Union, as a dependable partner of the West, can be 'saved' through assistance in various sectors. There are considerable differences of opinion on this issue, as demonstrated at the latest NATO summit in London and the economic summit in Houston. It goes without saying that, in view of its special position, Germany will have to do everything in its power to assist the Soviet Union in the transition from the last big colonial power in the world to some kind of Commonwealth. But that is a task which Germany cannot accomplish on its own. No one can say that the Soviet Union will not go the same way as the Ottoman Empire, which means the Europeans can expect a prolonged period of decline of their gigantic neighbour in the East.

There are a lot of question marks hanging over the developments in Eastern Europe in the next few years. Poland, in spite of so many hopes, will remain a problem, as will Romania. A change in the last Stalinist stronghold in Europe, Albania, could speed up the disintegration of the Yugoslav federation. These are all indications that Europe is facing a period of instability, with many chances for improvement, but also the risk to relapse into the era of overheated nationalism which it was supposed to have put behind it. It is unlikely that NATO and the Warsaw Pact could soon be replaced by the Conference on Security and Cooperation in Europe (CSCE) as a collective defence system. The experiences of the pre-1939 League of Nations, the helplessness of the United Nations in the critical moments of the post-1945 era are reason enough for scepticism. There is much to be said for tried and trusted arrangements like the Western defence alliance, which would not have to be transformed into a more political institution. That is something NATO has always been.

Helmut Kohl has emerged from the elections on 2 December a much stronger Chancellor. He is also more history-conscious than his predecessors, which might surprise many observers, and he will therefore ask himself what else he will have to do to consolidate the good fortune which made him Chancellor at the very moment when the Wall came down. Until that point he had more or less followed in the footsteps of his predecessors, pursuing basically the same course as Helmut Schmidt, both in domestic and foreign policy and also in defence policy, which had eventually brought about Schmidt's downfall. Perhaps Kohl believed more than any of his predecessors that the situation in Germany could change dramatically. He certainly realised the full implications of Hungary's decision at the end of August 1989 to open its borders to the East German refugees.

For Kohl this is new situation: to leave party politics still further behind and fight for recognition as an international statesman, a role in which he has been confirmed even by the critical left-liberal press and which will allow him to demonstrate an even stronger commitment to Europe. Like Charles de Gaulle, Kohl is able to think in a wider historical context without having so far been able to formulate his vision adequately. It could well be that this now gives him the courage to take the same chances in Europe which he took in the Caucasus with Mikhail Gorbachev when he bought East Germany from him for less than DM20bn.

A close examination of his recent statements shows that Kohl has set himself a limit of about four years within which he plans to advance the process of West European integration decisively. In this, incidentally, Kohl thinks along similar lines as the French and other EC partners: to strengthen the political, economic and military cooperation of the Twelve and, with the possible exception of Austria, to allow no new members to join the EC and, also, to keep a certain distance from Eastern Europe. It remains to be seen whether these wishes will come true or whether the collapse of the Soviet Union will pull our quiet Western Europe into the maelstrom of world politics. The coming over to the West of large masses of refugees would soon make a mockery of the sophisticated social security systems of the Western world.

Kohl, who can see these dangers, tries to stay on the path he has mapped out for himself—already a political leader within the Community without having been recognised as such by his fellow Germans. In the epoch-making negotiations confronting Europe in the coming weeks and months, his ability to compromise will certainly take him far—much further than any other German politician. For the Germans, therefore, there is a window of opportunity which by themselves they can hold ajar only for a limited period of time. It will require a willingness to compromise on the part of their European partners in order to make the most of this unique historical occasion, namely German unification as a consequence of the end of the Cold War and a still moderately intact Soviet superpower. They will all have to take risks, but perhaps these are easier to take in the knowledge that this is probably the last chance the Europeans will have.

NOTES

1. See 'Deutsch-französische Zusammenarbeit in der Sicherheitspolitik,' *Europea-Archiv* (Bonn), No 11/1987, pp. 302–12.

2. Helmut Schmidt, *Die Deutschen und ihre Nachbarn* (Berlin: Siedler Verlag, 1990).

3. See Ernst Weisenfeld, *Charles de Gaulle. Der Magier im Elysée* (Munich: C.H. Beck Verlag, 1990).

4. Lothar Baier, *Volk ohne Zeit. Essay über das eilige Vaterland* (Berlin: Klaus Wagenbach Verlag, 1990).

5. For the text of the speech, see *Europa-Archiv* (Bonn), No 12/1989, D pp. 356–61.

The United States of Europe

A bold plan progresses to put the 12 EC nations under one roof by 1992

Robert J. McCartney
Washington Post Foreign Service

BRUSSELS—In an ambitious effort to forge a more united Europe and compete better economically with the United States and Japan, 12 West European nations have approved nearly half of a revolutionary program to scrap barriers to travel, trade, employment and investment that have separated them for centuries.

The members of the European Community (EC) are seeking to create through negotiations something that has eluded statesmen and military conquerors since Charlemagne: a single European market, in which national boundaries would be no greater impediment to economic activity than state borders in the United States.

3. POLITICS IN A NEW EUROPE: Growth of European Community

Approved in principle four years ago, the project aims by the last day of 1992 to establish an identical economic environment for businessmen, workers and consumers across a giant region stretching from Scotland to Spain and from Portugal to Greece. With 322 million mostly middle-class consumers, it would be the developed world's largest single market.

The 12 EC governments have made significant progress on those parts of the program designed to harmonize industrial and technical standards and eliminate barriers to the free flow of money and financial services within the community. Of the 279 formal, legal directives by the EC Commission that form the core of the single-market program, 107 have now been adopted by the EC states. Tentative agreement has been reached on two dozen other directives, and some parts of the program already have taken effect.

Tough talks lie ahead, however, on those planks that call for abolition of customs and immigration checks at internal EC borders and the narrowing of tax policy differences among member states.

A major dispute also is brewing over proposals to create a single West European currency unit and a single EC central bank. Adoption of a single EC currency is not a part of the 1992 project but is viewed by many experts as a logical and perhaps vital step to be taken in the mid-1990s to ensure that the full benefits of the 1992 program are realized.

"We have completed about 45 percent of the program. Of course, that has been the easiest part of the project, and now we have to face the most difficult issues. But we have a very strong political commitment to meet the 1992 objective," says Michel Ayral, a senior planner for the 1992 project at the EC Commission in Brussels.

The program creates major opportunities for U.S. and other non-EC businessmen by making it easier to operate in Western Europe once they are established here. But it also poses big challenges for outsiders.

Non-European governments and businesses fear that the community will become a "fortress Europe," with free trade internally but new commercial barriers against non-EC members. Protectionist sentiment is particularly strong in France, Italy and Spain, and a showdown is expected between those countries and free-trade advocates Britain and West Germany.

Attempting to allay U.S. concerns, European officials indicate privately that any EC trade barriers after 1992 are likely to be aimed principally at Japan, which is viewed in Western Europe as a bigger trade threat than the United States.

But foreign firms are not the only ones worrying. Many West European companies that currently enjoy various degrees of state support fear that they may not survive the elimination or reduction of protectionist regulations and subsidies that have long sustained them.

"The single market will be able to fulfill the expectations placed in it only if, in European-wide competition, it is the efficient companies that win and not those that have easy access to state subsidies," says Alfred Herrhausen, chairman of West Germany's largest bank, Deutsche Bank AG.

The EC's planners acknowledge that the project will eliminate hundreds of thousands of jobs in the short term, as fresh competition drives inefficient firms out of business. Labor unions have expressed skepticism over the planners' argument that the plan, by stripping away regulations, will reduce company costs, spur economic growth and eventually create millions of new jobs. The unions also doubt claims that the new competitive environment will help hold down consumer prices.

The 1992 plan is explicitly designed to create a more dynamic economy in Western Europe, helping the EC compete more effectively with the United States and Japan.

"Behind the project is the feeling that a fragmented Europe would not be in the game anymore vis-à-vis the United States and Japan. The governments have become aware that their market base is too small," says Michel Petite, a senior staff official at the EC Commission, or executive body.

The EC's economic growth rates have consistently lagged behind those of the United States and Japan. EC leaders have worried that without major new steps to maintain the economic vitality of their industries, their countries would fall further behind in the international standings of the 1990s.

"The EC is trying to avoid being in the position of the bicycle, which falls down when it stops," says Paolo Cecchini, an adviser to the EC Commission.

The vision of a quantum leap in economic and social integration has generated an enthusiasm for West European unity unseen since the 1960s. The progress achieved so far has rekindled faith that Western Europe can make the necessary changes to avoid slipping behind other regions of the world.

West European companies already are scrambling to position themselves for what promises to be both a more open and a more competitive market. Companies have launched a wave of takeovers, similar to the one begun several years ago in the United States, to make sure they have an adequate presence throughout the EC.

West German banks, for instance, have bought smaller banks in Spain and in other EC nations where national regulations have made it difficult for foreigners to operate. Such regulations are now doomed under the 1992 plan.

British companies have staged numerous raids on firms based across the English Channel, with the aim of ensuring that they are well-positioned on the continent to take advantage of more open markets there after 1992. American, Japanese and other non-EC companies also are buying new subsidiaries in Europe, expanding current operations or otherwise preparing for the post-1992 world.

Everybody wants to preserve the rich diversity of cultures within the community, in which more than 10 languages are spoken. But, inevitably, the project appears destined to erode each nation's distinctiveness and speed up growth of a uniform West European lifestyle.

Some critics charge that the resulting lifestyle is likely to be similar to that of the United States. The 1992 plan, it is alleged, will accelerate the "Americanization" of Western Europe. Large-volume discount department stores and fast-food chains will find it easier to expand into sleepy farm areas in southern Spain and Italy.

In any case, by the end of 1992, if all goes according to the master plan, life in Europe will be much less regulated and national markets more integrated than ever before.

For instance, a Bavarian autoworker who always bought insurance from a West German company will find it much easier to shop around and perhaps get a cheaper policy from a British or Italian firm.

A Greek lawyer, eager to work for a Paris firm, will not be required to attend French law school. His diploma from an Athens university will be enough to qualify him.

Television sets, cement and baby rattles produced in, say, Spain will be made under safety and performance standards accepted by all 11 other EC states.

For most Americans, the most impressive part of the plan is likely to be the proposed abolition of border checks at internal EC frontiers. In theory, a vacationer touring Western Europe by car four years from now will breeze past abandoned immigration and customs booths when crossing from one EC state to another. After entering any of the 12 member countries, the vacationer should be able to visit the other 11 without having to show a passport or open a suitcase for inspection.

The abolition of such border checks is at the heart of the program and already has been approved in principle. Nevertheless, some governments are resisting it.

In particular, British Prime Minister Margaret Thatcher is skeptical that her country can keep out terrorists and other criminals without some form of immigration checks. Some EC officials believe that Britain may retain some border controls while the other 11 go ahead and scrap them.

The project represents a grand compromise between the EC's northern, wealthier countries such as West Germany and France, and its poorer, Mediterranean members, including Italy, Spain and Greece.

The better-off, northern countries hope to take advantage of the opening of the market to expand their business activities in southern Europe.

The less-developed, southern EC countries—while worried about penetration from the north—hope that the increased competition will give their economies a needed dose of dynamism. They also feel they must go along with the program or risk seeing themselves cut off from the most prosperous part of Europe.

In addition, the wealthier EC members have agreed to give tens of billions of dollars to the four poorest EC countries—Spain, Portugal, Greece and Ireland—to help finance structural investments designed to bring their economies up to the level of their better-off neighbors.

"It was recognized in the mid-1980s that what was needed was a comprehensive plan, so everybody benefited in some way and had a stake in the whole," says Adrian Fortescue, director of the EC Commission's general secretariat.

"It was also recognized that a time scale was needed, the discipline of a target date," he adds, explaining why the 1992 deadline was adopted.

The European Community, which was created by the Treaty of Rome in 1957, long ago abolished tariffs and other direct trade barriers within its borders. Now it intends to go a step further and get rid of all indirect or hidden hurdles that restrict commerce. Thousands of differences among the 12 members' industrial standards, commercial regulations and other laws and policies are to be eliminated.

Close to adoption, for example, is an EC-wide measure fixing the maximum permissible noise for lawnmowers. Any company that makes lawnmowers for one EC country is to be able to ship them to the 11 others without having to worry about making changes to satisfy differing national rules.

The plan will not abolish all economic differences within the community, however. Despite a harmonization of technical standards, for instance, at least three different kinds of electrical plugs will continue to be used in the EC. A study found it would cost $80 billion to adopt the same kind of plug throughout the community.

Each member country also will keep its own currency, although France, West Germany and some other members are pushing to adopt a single EC monetary unit sometime after 1992. Eight EC countries—all except Britain, Spain, Portugal and Greece—already have linked their currencies to one another within the European Monetary System.

The plan's architects at the Brussels-based EC Commission say that the plan will work only if there is a psychological leap of faith in the value of European union, an increase in the degree to which people identify themselves as "cit-

izens of Europe" rather than of their individual countries.

This shift in consciousness is needed in particular to make possible the abolition of border controls that is the plan's centerpiece.

"It's a question of confidence. The Danes, for instance, have to be convinced that Greek border checks on people entering the EC will be as good as those in Denmark," says Ayral, the commission planner.

The other major dispute threatening the plan concerns handling of value-added-taxes, which are roughly equivalent to sales taxes and are a major source of revenue for many EC members. The plan foresees abolishing the large bureaucracy that now collects such taxes at internal EC borders and bringing roughly into line the various tax rates of EC member states.

These tax collections now account for 90 percent of the paperwork at the borders. Internal EC border formalities as a whole cost about $45 billion, and the plan aims to abolish those costs and pass the savings on to EC companies to make them more competitive.

But France and some other countries are resisting the tax plan, partly to preserve their revenues and partly to preserve special, national tax breaks of various kinds.

In historical terms, the 1992 project represents a shift from the EC's expansionary phase in the 1970s and early 1980s to a period of consolidation. For about 15 years ending in the middle 1980s, the EC was preoccupied by the addition of new members—Britain, Ireland and Denmark in 1973, Greece in 1981 and Spain and Portugal in 1986.

"Enlargement became an excuse for paralysis," Fortescue says.

In addition, the EC was deeply divided throughout the 1970s and early 1980s by bitter disputes over its budget and agricultural policy. Chronic battles over these issues—especially between Britain and the rest of the community—fueled widespread cynicism throughout the EC.

Finally, the two oil shocks of the 1970s, and the recessions that followed, encouraged individual countries to erect subtle trade barriers of various kinds to protect their domestic industries during hard times.

By the mid-1980s, however, protectionist pressures were subsiding as the world economy recovered. The British cut a deal with the rest of the EC in 1984 on how to divide up many of the community's bills.

The stage then was set to move ahead and focus on making the enlarged EC more efficient. In January 1985, Jacques Delors, an ambitious Frenchman committed to the ideal of European unity, took over as EC Commission president and began looking for a theme for his stewardship.

Delors considered trying to push for increased cooperation within the EC on defense or monetary affairs. But he concluded that the EC member governments were not yet ready for major progress in those areas.

Instead, Delors settled on the idea of seeking to create a single, internal market. He drew up a now-famous white paper outlining the broad goals of what became the 1992 plan. The project's emphasis on making markets more competitive was inspired in part by the deregulation policies of the governments of Britain's Thatcher and President Ronald Reagan.

At an EC summit in June 1985, EC leaders approved the program in principle. EC Commission staff members in Brussels, nicknamed "Eurocrats," began drawing up the lengthy, detailed list of proposals to make the program a reality.

THE EUROPEAN COMMUNITY

BRITAIN
Population: 56.8 million   **GDP: $662.6 billion**
Prime Minister Margaret Thatcher fears that planned scrapping of border controls may make it harder to keep terrorists and other criminals out of the country.

IRELAND
Population: 3.5 million   **GDP: $29.1 billion**
One of the poorer Economic Community members, Dublin is to receive substantial economic adjustment aid under the 1992 plan. Ireland already gets large sums for training young workers.

DENMARK
Population: 5.1 million   **GDP: $101.4 billion**
Many Danes still favor leaving the EC. Denmark is pulled in two directions: toward fellow Scandinavians outside the EC and toward the continent and the Community.

NETHERLANDS
Population: 14.7 million   **GDP: $214.6 billion**
The Dutch expect to benefit greatly from the 1992 plan because of a strong presence in trucking and shipping—industries where costs should drop when customs controls are dismantled.

BELGIUM
Population: 9.9 million   **GDP: $138.5 billion**
As hosts of Western Europe's "capital" in Brussels, the EC Commission, or executive body, and its thousands of "Eurocrats," Belgians tend to benefit when the Community prospers.

LUXEMBOURG
Population: 0.4 million   **GDP: $6.2 billion**
This tiny grand duchy, the EC's smallest member, hopes that liberalization of banking rules will help it thrive as a financial center.

WEST GERMANY
Population: 60.1 million   **GDP: $1,118.8 billion**
Efficient manufacturers are looking forward to strong expansion southward. Highly regulated insurance industry here fears British and other competition.

NOTE: Population figures as of 1986, Gross Domestic Product figures as of 1987.

FRANCE
Population: 55.6 million   **GDP: $879.9 billion**
Of the major capitals, Paris is most enthusiastic about Western European integration. Outsiders see the French as too sympathetic to creation of a protectionist "Fortress Europe."

PORTUGAL
Population: 10.2 million   **GDP: $26.1 billion**
Lisbon hopes a combination of fresh competition and EC adjustment aid will give its economy a needed injection of dynamism.

SPAIN
Population: 38.7 million   **GDP: $288.0 billion**
Iberia expects to get a major influx of northern European manufacturing companies, banks and other firms that will take advantage of relatively low wages and underexploited markets.

ITALY
Population: 57.3 million   **GDP: $751.5 billion**
Some high-powered Italian entrepreneurs see great opportunity to move north after 1992. Others fear added competition will hurt Italy, already saddled with a staggering budget deficit and cumbersome bureaucracy.

GREECE
Population: 10.0 million   **GDP: $47.0 billion**
A backward administrative structure and less-developed economy are expected to make it difficult for Greeks to adjust to the post-1992 world.

EC TOTALS
Population: 322.3 million   **GDP: $4,263.7 billion**

UNITED STATES (for comparison)
Population: 241.6 million   **GDP: $4,435.8 billion**

COMPILED BY JAMES SCHWARTZ—THE WASHINGTON POST

One significant legal hurdle still remained. Throughout its history, the EC had required unanimous consent from its member governments to adopt any new EC legislation. That made it possible for any single country to block agreement and encouraged individual governments to blackmail the rest of the Community to get their way.

To ease the decision-making process, the EC in 1987 adopted the first major revision of its charter: the Treaty of Rome. No longer can a single nation veto an action.

Under a new, complicated voting formula, opposition from at least two large members, plus one or two small ones, is now needed to block a bill. Without that change, the 1992 program would be far behind schedule, EC officials say.

The 1992 project also was inspired by the worldwide shift in sentiment during the 1980s in favor of less government intervention and freer markets. But even socialist-led governments in France and Spain have been enthusiastic supporters of the 1992 project.

"It is revealing that governments of different ideological tendencies have backed the plan," says Petite, the senior EC staff official. "It simply reflects the fact that everybody, whatever their political background, felt the program was imperative for economic reasons."

Push Is On for

Wider European Community

Alexander MacLeod

Special to The Christian Science Monitor

LONDON

HOW large should the European Community – already a powerful grouping of 12 member-nations and a total population of 340 million – be allowed to become?

The question is fueling a growing debate as a list of applicants to join the EC continues to lengthen, and nonmembers in East and West Europe eye the advantages of joining what until now has been an exclusive "Euroclub."

The latest nation to knock on the EC's door is the small Mediterranean island of Malta (population 350,000). On July 16, it followed Cyprus, Austria, and Turkey in lodging a formal membership bid.

In doing so, it sharpened what for Jacques Delors, president of the Brussels-based European Commission (the EC's executive arm), was already a political dilemma.

"Mr. Delors," a Commission official said last week, "has to try to reconcile two imperatives that are currently gathering momentum: a wish by existing EC members to deepen their relationship before new members are admitted, and the desire of countries to join as early as possible."

The official said the line of EC aspirants was likely to grow in the next few years – but Delors held out little hope that a "yes" answer would be given to any but one or two of the applicants in the foreseeable future.

That view seems bound to become increasingly controversial as countries in Europe's two halves continue to adjust to the fading of the cold war and as the advantages of EC membership become more compelling.

William Wallace, deputy director of the Royal Institute of International Affairs here, and author of a new study, "The Transformation of Western Europe," called the Delors view "understandable but unsustainable."

"Admittedly, there is a lot of work to be done before the European single market comes into being in 1992, but after that happens, the EC is going to expand well beyond 15 nations in the next 10 years.

"I can envisage a Community of 20 or more nations, with a total population of over 400 million. The pressures will be too great for anyone to hold out against qualified nations determined to enter," Dr. Wallace said.

There is certainly evidence of a head of steam building up for a wider EC. In Scandinavia and Switzerland, there is quickening discussion of the issue. And Europe's former communist states are beginning to position themselves for EC membership in the next few years.

For example, on July 17 Jozef Antall, the Hungarian prime minister, said: "Our strategic aim is to obtain EC membership by 1995 – after Austria, no doubt, but before all the other countries of what used to be called Eastern Europe."

In January 1989, Delors, foreseeing a pileup of membership applications, tried to create a political buffer against at least some of them. He told the European Parliament in Strasbourg, France, that the 12 EC countries, plus the members of the European Free Trade Association (EFTA – Finland, Iceland, Norway, Sweden, Switzerland, and Austria) should enter a dialogue aimed at the creation of a "European Economic Space" (EES) which, starting in early 1993, could act as an 18-nation free trade zone.

Since then, however, political contacts between the EC and EFTA, aimed at producing the expanded grouping, have been going badly.

When the EFTA partners at a meeting in Gotenburg, Sweden, issued a statement on June 14 saying they would join the proposed zone only if they were given a seat at the top table in Brussels, Delors began backing away from his original proposal.

"We are not going to throw away the achievements of 30 years for a gamble that is not worth it," he said.

The tone of his remarks appeared to suggest that, in proposing the EES, Delors's real motive was to try to deflect the enthusiasm of the EFTA nations and any other country eager to join the

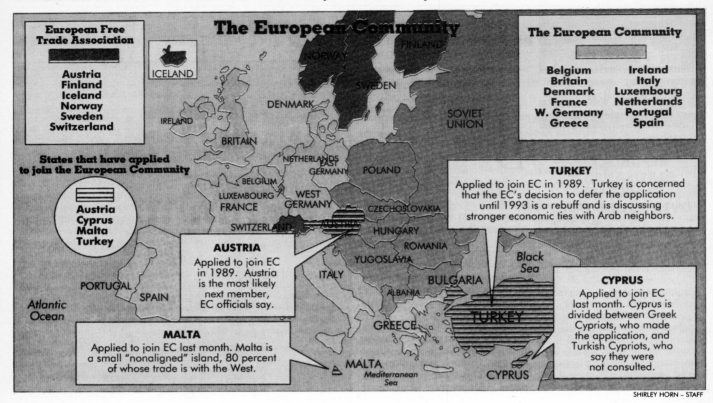

The European Community

European Free Trade Association

Austria
Finland
Iceland
Norway
Sweden
Switzerland

States that have applied to join the European Community

Austria
Cyprus
Malta
Turkey

The European Community

Belgium	Ireland
Britain	Italy
Denmark	Luxembourg
France	Netherlands
W. Germany	Portugal
Greece	Spain

TURKEY
Applied to join EC in 1989. Turkey is concerned that the EC's decision to defer the application until 1993 is a rebuff and is discussing stronger economic ties with Arab neighbors.

AUSTRIA
Applied to join EC in 1989. Austria is the most likely next member, EC officials say.

CYPRUS
Applied to join EC last month. Cyprus is divided between Greek Cypriots, who made the application, and Turkish Cypriots, who say they were not consulted.

MALTA
Applied to join EC last month. Malta is a small "nonaligned" island, 80 percent of whose trade is with the West.

SHIRLEY HORN – STAFF

EC or forge a close relationship with it.

An Austrian diplomat said: "Our impression is that he is merely buying time, and that is very discouraging. If the current contacts between the EC and EFTA get nowhere, which now seems likely, our partners in EFTA may have to join Austria in thinking in terms of straightforward applications to join the EC."

Wallace concurs. If the EC-EFTA talks fail to produce an agreement, he said, "there may be no alternative but for them to seek full EC membership. It would be extremely difficult to turn them down if they pressed hard."

In June, Delors's discouraging remarks roused Douglas Hurd, the British foreign secretary, to call for a more open-minded approach to new applications.

Mr. Hurd in June said: "It will be at least 1993 before new applications can be entertained. But after that I do not see how the Europe of the 12 can shut the door for any length of time against fully qualified European democ-racies which are anxious to join, whether they are now in EFTA or in Central Europe."

Inside the Berlaymont building, headquarters of the EC, Hurd's remarks provoked concern. The reaction, which was believed to reflect Delors's thinking, suggested that a clash will eventually occur between the Commission, determined to deepen the EC before it gains extra members, and those who would like to see the EC expand anyway.

Pascal Lamy, one of Delors's top officials, said that early and rapid expansion of the EC beyond the present membership would run the risk of "diluting" the Community and make it harder to take decisions.

Mr. Lamy said the EC might be able to expand its membership by another "two or three" members, "but not beyond." If membership went higher than 15, he said, the Community would become "unwieldy and diffuse."

Such views are also strongly held in the European Parliament. Lord Nicholas Bethell, a British member of the European Parliament (Euro-MP), said: "We may be able to accommodate Austria if it abandons its present neutral status in world affairs, but otherwise I do not see more than one or two members being added to the EC in the next 10 years."

Lord Bethell said he believed his view was shared by "a majority of Euro-MPs."

Lord Bethell noted that there has been growing resistance to Turkey being admitted to the EC, and that the application of Cy-

Even if East European countries are excluded on the grounds that they are not yet mature democracies, EC officials seem certain to come under heavy pressure to change their restrictive view of membership.

prus was likely to run into trouble, because the island remains divided between Greek and Turkish communities.

Even if East European countries are excluded for a while on the grounds that they are not yet mature democracies, as the Treaty of Rome (the EC's constitution) requires, Delors and his officials seem certain to come under heavy pressure to change their restrictive view of membership.

Public opinion in Scandinavia, where Denmark is already a member of the Community, indicates that more countries would like to line up on Delors's doorstep than he believes the EC can cope with.

In Norway, which in a referendum decided 18 years ago not to join the EC, an opinion poll earlier this year indicated that more Norwegians now favor membership in the EC than oppose it.

Finland, whose constitution requires it to be nonaligned, is also showing signs of a rethink. Last May, a Gallup poll suggested that 60 percent of Finns favored EC membership.

And in Sweden, argument is raging on future relations with the EC as well.

If William Wallace is right in believing that Delors will be unable to prevent the EFTA countries and others from joining the EC, the prospect of a grouping of as many as 18 or 20 countries becomes thinkable.

"It can easily be forgotten that the EC started with six members, and has since added as many again," he said.

Six EC Institutions

European Parliament

Credibility before democracy

How well are the European Community's institutions working? As 1992 approaches, the question matters more than ever. In the first of a series of articles, our Brussels correspondent looks at the European Parliament

A parliament without a real role provides a grand platform for politicians seeking to publicise purely local or even trivial issues. So it has often seemed with the European Parliament. The parliament has been given a modest but significant increase in power as part of the EEC's preparations for 1992. Will new power bring a new sense of responsibility?

The parliament is certainly taking itself

more seriously. Attendance at its plenary sessions in Strasbourg is up since the changes came into force in mid-1987. More than 300 of its 518 members regularly take part in the votes on single-market legislation. The pre-1987 average attendance at the monthly sittings was below 220.

Outsiders are paying attention too. Lobbyists are spending more time on Euro-MPs. This reflects a belief among their clients—multinational companies, non-EEC governments, pressure groups—that the parlia-

ment is playing a part, however modest, in 1992 decisions. Some big companies have teams of lobbyists devoted to influencing the course of EEC legislation. One American multinational had 20 people at last count, although their brief covers the other EEC institutions as well as the parliament.

The extra powers of the parliament are embodied in the Single European Act, which rearranged the responsibilities of the Community's various institutions: the Council of Ministers, the European Commission and the parliament. For the 518 Euro-MPs, this means a new power to amend draft laws on the 1992 project and a right of veto on international agreements concluded by the Community.

It is the commission that proposes new EEC laws. These nearly always require the approval of the council, whose members are ministers from the member-governments. Under the old procedure, the parliament could merely offer its opinion on the original draft; the commission and the council were free to ignore it. Now the parliament has a right of "second reading". The council's decision is no longer final but preliminary. Euro-MPs can either accept it or (with 260-plus votes) reject or amend it. The ministers then need a unanimous vote to overrule the parliament—unless the commission sides with them, in which case a majority vote is enough.

Since the new procedure came into force, the parliament has not rejected a draft directive outright. It has introduced nearly 1,000 amendments, of which 72% have been accepted by the commission and 42% adopted by the council. In this way, the par-

liament has modified laws on, for example, safety standards for toys.

The parliament also has power now to vet new international agreements concluded by the council. Under this power, it has approved updated versions of agreements with several Mediterranean countries, including Egypt, Israel, Tunisia and Algeria. It at first voted against the agreement with Israel, approving it only after Israel gave assurances that it would respect obligations concerning exports from the occupied territories.

The parliament's new powers come on top of those it already had: these include the right to sack the commission and joint responsibility with the council for fixing the EEC's annual budget. Budget rows between the two were an annual excitement until the procedure was clarified in 1987. The parliament has never dismissed the commission through a vote of censure, although it tried in 1976 and in 1977. The censure motions, by a British Conservative, the late Peter Kirk, and a French Gaullist, Mr Michel Cointat, were crushingly defeated.

Many Euro-MPs believe they will eventually have a bigger say in EEC decisions. They think the trend is for governments to take more decisions jointly in Brussels rather than in their own countries, and that this will mean that national parliaments are increasingly by-passed. Unless parliamentary power lost at national level is replaced at EEC level there will, they argue, be a "democratic deficit". They see the relationship between the council and the parliament developing into something like that between the two houses of a national legislature: the council as lower house, the parliament as upper house or senate.

For this dream to become reality, the European Assembly (its formal title) needs to sort out its own huge credibility deficit. It must prove it is more than a frivolous talk-

The right to differ

FROM OUR NORDIC CORRESPONDENT

THE United Nations thinks humans have rights, and asserts it in a declaration; so do the member-states of the Council of Europe and the signatories of the Helsinki Final Act. The people who teach law at Stockholm University disagree, and are trying to stop a colleague teaching students that such is the case.

Professor Jacob Sundberg teaches legal theory. His colleagues in the law faculty call it right-wing propaganda, lacking a "scientific basis". Swedish law schools have long been dominated by a theory called "legal positivism", which has formed generations of Swedish politicians and civil servants. It holds that people have just as many rights as the law of the land says they have, no more, no fewer; to argue that rights are "inherent", as Americans might say, or "natural", as Roman Catholic bishops maintain, is neither true nor false but meaningless.

This stark proposition is by no means confined to Swedish socialists, but it does suit them. If rights are what the state says they are, then the state can change them, and in a welfare state that must be good for welfare.

Professor Sundberg thinks this is wrong, and tells his students so. Some of them have complained. He says his accusers are left-wingers, eager to attack him not least because he is president of an international "commission of inquiry" into starvation in the Ukraine in the 1930s. European and American lawyers have spoken up for Professor Sundberg, among them Professor Alan Dershowitz of Harvard Law School.

ing shop for windbags from any of its nine political groups, ranging from the National Front to the Communists via the Greens.

Too often, Euro-MPs get involved in issues they know nothing about or can do nothing to change (or both). They must also guard against accusations of wasting money—study visits to sun-drenched re-

sorts are a current favourite. It seems that financial fiddling has been much reduced in recent years. But it was not so long ago that certain Euro-MPs were found to be claiming session expenses without being in Strasbourg. Others were involved in currency manipulations. Some enterprising deputies were known to camp on their office couches in order to pocket their hotel allowances.

EEC Council of Ministers
The powers that be

Our Brussels correspondent examines the European Community's dynamo in his second article on the EEC's institutions

Last year Mrs Margaret Thatcher pounced on Mr Jacques Delors, the European Commission's president, for predicting that within ten years 80% of EEC countries' social and economic legislation would be decided in Brussels. He says he was misunderstood. Mr Delors was not seeking more power for his commission and its 14,000 bureaucrats. He was just warning EEC governments that the creation of a seamless single market by the end of 1992 would force them to take

more decisions together instead of singly. The forum for doing this is the Council of Ministers, which consists of representatives of the 12 member-governments, not Mr Delors's non-elected civil service.

While Mrs Thatcher keenly mistrusts Mr Delors and his commission, she is quite taken by the council. So are most other EEC leaders. This is not surprising.

The council is at the apex of EEC power. It is also the point at which member-governments have the greatest influence on Community affairs. The commission drafts pro-

posals; the European Parliament chips in with opinions and amendments. But it is the council which decides what the Community is going (or not going) to do.

Project 1992 means more joint decisions by governments and so (in the phrase favoured by some EEC leaders but not by Mrs Thatcher) more "pooling of sovereignty" through the council. The Single European Act, which updated the EEC's founding Treaty of Rome, replaced unanimity with a majority vote for many decisions, to speed the single-market project along. All EEC governments agreed that the council should no longer be paralysed by the opposition of one or two members over minor matters.

The Single European Act took effect in July 1987. Since then the council has adopted nearly 100 pieces of legislation linked to the 1992 project. The average time for the council to approve a draft directive after it had been tabled by the commission used to be two years. Some decisions took a decade. Recently, directives have been getting through in less than a year.

For some things unanimity is still required. One of these is tax. This puts Britain in a strong position when it opposes the commission's ideas on value-added tax and its proposals for a withholding tax on interest payments on savings. Unanimity is also needed for agreements between the Community and other countries, and for legislation affecting workers' rights and the free movement of people.

Even where majority voting is meant to apply, any member-country which really wants to can probably still wield a veto. The Single European Act did not formally change the veto power, because it is not embodied in any legal text. The right of veto was merely spelt out in the so-called Luxembourg compromise of 1966 (which was General de Gaulle's price for staying in the EEC). The Luxembourg compromise states that the other governments will not overrule a country which opposes a piece of draft EEC legislation on the ground that a vital national interest is at stake.

The veto has been used sparingly over the years. It was scarcely needed when the council proceeded mainly by consensus, and the Luxembourg compromise has not been tested since the Single European Act came into force. The veto was last wielded—by West Germany—in June 1985, when the Bonn government blocked a price cut of 1% for its cereals farmers.

The blocking game

Before reaching for its veto, a member-state can do a lot to organise its opposition to a proposal under the majority-voting system. This is based on a weighted or "qualified" majority. The total number of votes in the council is 76. The four biggest countries—West Germany, Britain, France and Italy—have ten each. Spain has eight, Holland, Belgium, Greece and Portugal have five each, Ireland and Denmark three apiece, and Luxembourg two. It takes 54 votes to pass a law by "qualified majority". Together the big five can muster only 48; the other seven 28. So a coalition of the seven smaller members cannot outvote the five bigger ones. Nor can the big five impose their will on a reluctant seven.

The real game as the council gets into the more controversial bits of 1992 legislation will be less about forming majorities than about putting together blocking mi-

norities. With 23 votes against, a draft directive is thrown out. It takes only two of the big four countries plus any other (except Luxembourg, which is too small) to thwart a proposed law.

Consider how the game might work. At some time in the next two years the council will have to vote on ending national quotas on imports of Japanese cars. The toughest restrictions are imposed by Italy, Spain and France. If the commission seems too generous to Japan in its proposals, Italy and France will vote against them. Spain may hesitate; it is a base for Japanese investments in Europe and wants to attract more. So France and Italy would be looking around for another partner. This other country (Greece?, Portugal?) could choose to sell its support to France and Italy in return for a commitment by them to join it in blocking a piece of 1992 legislation it does not like. Since there are still 150-odd directives to go, the choice is wide.

So far, at the the half-way point in the 1992 project, fewer than half of the 285 necessary directives have been adopted. None has gone through since December. This is partly because of the way council business is run under its six-month presidencies. Each member-government (in alphabetical order in its own language) chairs the council in turn: Deutschland then Ellas last year, España to be followed by France in 1989. Britain will be in the chair for the six months up to the single-market deadline of December 31 1992. The presidencies make a special effort to get as many directives through by the end of their stint as possible. So decisions are bunched in June and December.

That is also when the European Council, more familiarly known as the EEC sum-

mit, takes place. These meetings (usually only two of them a year) of the EEC's heads of government tend to unblock some of the problems the lesser ministers have been unable to deal with. The European Council has no formal status in Community decision-taking: agreements reached there have to be formalised by the Council of Ministers. But its existence was at least acknowledged by the Single European Act.

Meet Poco and Coreper

So was the existence of Political Co-operation (Poco to initiates). This is the forum, hitherto informal, where EEC foreign ministers meet to discuss the co-ordination of foreign policy. Its best known production has been the formulation of a Community policy on the Middle East, although it has also fired off statements on Central America, Afghanistan, South Africa, Libya (and, this week, on Iran). Despite its new official status, Poco has not spawned a large bureaucracy. It has a tiny secretariat tucked away in a high-security wing of the council's headquarters at the Charlemagne building in Brussels.

Unlike a national government, the composition of the Council of Ministers changes with the subject being discussed. All told, there are more than a dozen different versions of the council. The senior squad are the foreign ministers, who meet once a month to discuss the main issues. They also keep an eye on the council's other incarnations. Farm and finance ministers have monthly sessions too. The former have hours of argument; the latter like to think of their sessions as discreet (and brief) gatherings of like-minded purse-holders. They have to loosen their collars and do without

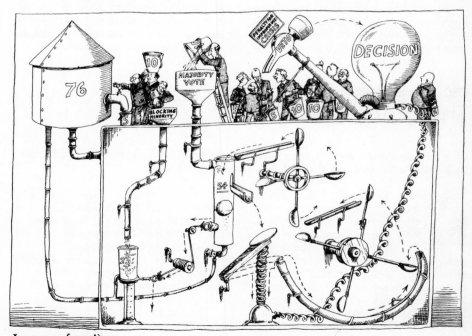

Jeux sans frontières

dinner when capital liberalisation or tax harmonisation is on the agenda. So-called specialist councils—of ministers of transport, the environment, industry and so on—meet less often, at three- or even six-month intervals.

Preparation for the council sessions, of which there are about 80 a year, is done mainly by the Committee of Permanent Representatives, commonly known by its French abbreviation, Coreper. Only the farm and finance councils are prepared by separate specialised committees. Coreper, consisting of the ambassadors of the 12 members, meets each week. The ambassadors negotiate on the commission's proposals until they can produce a text ready for ministerial approval or until they reach a point where the remaining problems can be sorted out only by the politicians.

The ambassadors themselves have little time for the trappings of their rank. Their reward lies elsewhere, in the proximity to power. It was said of one French permanent representative, Mr Jean-Marc Boegner, that he travelled to the foreign ministry in Paris every Wednesday to write its instructions to him for the next day's meeting of Coreper.

European Commission
The locomotive of 1992

In his third article on the European Community's institutions, our Brussels correspondent looks at its mighty bureaucracy

MR JACQUES DELORS and his 16 colleagues at the European Commission are the best-paid politicians in Europe, taking home more than $150,000 a year apiece after tax (and before perks). This is the financial reward for running the institution which is the heart, if not the soul, of the EEC. It is not just the salaries of the commissioners and the 12,000 people on their staff that are unmatched; the organisation itself is unique. It is both a civil service and the nearest thing the EEC has to an executive branch of government. The commission's job is to prepare and propose new policies and laws for the Community and to ensure that decisions, once taken, are carried out.

None of the commissioners is elected to his or her job, although some give up political posts at home to come to Brussels. They are nominated by their governments and then supposedly become thoroughly European by swearing an oath renouncing the defence of any national interests while at the commission. The European Parliament has long argued for the right to vet nominees, but governments have so far refused to let anyone else have a say. This may be just as well. Though most of the present commissioners would pass the John Tower test for sobriety and sexual behaviour, some of their predecessors would certainly have failed.

Commissioners take few big EEC decisions; those are the responsibility of the members of the national governments, who meet in the Council of Ministers. The commission has powers to act on its own in only two areas: competition policy and farming. It is trying to extend its direct authority to the liberalisation of telecommunications, under a little-used provision of Article 90 of the Treaty of Rome. But it now finds itself in the dock at the European Court of Justice, accused of exceeding its powers.

The commission's main role is as the instigator of EEC policy: the Council of Ministers can take decisions only on the basis of proposals submitted to it by the commission. No proposal means no policy.

Ministers are free to accept or reject the commission's proposals. They can modify them only by a unanimous vote; but usually the commission can be persuaded to amend its text if it detects the required majority emerging around something not too far removed from its draft.

The Single European Act, which simplified EEC decision-taking to help the 1992 project along, affects the council and parliament more directly than it does the commission. But it has made the commission bolder. A majority vote by member-states, instead of unanimity, is now enough to get many single-market decisions passed. If the commission reckons that a particular proposal will be opposed by, say, only Britain and West Germany, it can forget about their hostility and draft something palatable to the other ten. When unanimity was required, the commission had to submit drafts anodyne enough to be acceptable to all.

Rule of Delors
Voting within the commission as it draws up its proposals is based on one vote per commissioner. There is no weighting according to the size of their country of origin, as there is in the council. But size is taken care of to the extent that the five biggest EEC members—West Germany, France, Britain, Italy and Spain—each have two commissioners and the other seven only one apiece.

Not that commissioners are supposed to vote along national lines (remember that oath of independence). But old party allegiances and future patronage can influence a commissioner's attitude. Mr Delors himself is criticised by some of his colleagues at the moment for taking a line too favourable to the French on problems in the car industry. When commissioners do overcome national prejudices and pressures, they often get few thanks from those at home with the power of appointment. A former French commissioner, Mr Claude Cheysson, was accused of betraying France by the then prime minis-

Numbers of EEC officials			
Mid-1988	Directors-general*	"Grade A"	Total
W Germany	5	553	1,547
France	5	543	1,366
Italy	4	555	2,009
Britain	3	354	908
Spain	2	246	649
Holland	2	171	575
Belgium	1	419	3,044
Greece	1	139	468
Ireland	1	90	238
Portugal	1	90	318
Denmark	1	72	366
Luxembourg	1	52	382
Source: European Commission * or equivalent rank			

ter, Mr Jacques Chirac, for backing a draft commission proposal which went against French farming interests. Lord Cockfield, the main promoter of project 1992 in the previous commission, irritated Mrs Thatcher by his stance on tax harmonisation and was brought home by her last December as punishment.

Although not loved by colleagues, Mr Delors is the most effective president the commission has had over the past 20 years. Not since Walter Hallstein, its first head, has there been a strong president, or a strong commission. The commission seems to need a workaholic at its head if it is to act as the locomotive of the EEC, as the authors of the Rome treaty intended. Flunkies around Mr Delors like to address him as President Delors, as if running the commission were akin to governing the United States or France. Others are less kind. Mr Willy De Clercq, the easy-going Belgian in charge of external relations in the previous commission, describes Mr Delors's bullying of his colleagues as "intellectual terrorism".

Mr De Clercq, like Lord Cockfield and Mr Cheysson, was not renominated by his government to the commission which took over at the beginning of this year. Commissioners are appointed for a four-year term. The present lot are there until the end of 1992, the deadline for the creation of an EEC-wide single market. The president and six vice-presidents are named formally for terms of two years only. Mr Delors's mandate is up for renewal at the end of next year, which gives any government unhappy with his stewardship a chance to have him removed. No one yet has been thus vetoed.

The commission meets once a week, generally on a Wednesday. Individual commissioners submit their first drafts of EEC legislation for discussion by the full commission. These meetings are prepared by the heads of the commissioners' private offices, their *chefs de cabinet*. It takes skill to steer a proposal through the conflicting national and political interests of the commissioners. Woe betide a commissioner whose *chef* is unskilled in wheeling and dealing.

The *chefs*, some of them on short contracts like their bosses, are regarded as cowboys by some of the Commission's 22 (soon to be 23) directors-general. These are the people, with up to 30 years' service in Brussels, at the top of the EEC civil service. Each directorate-general is attached to one commissioner. The directors-general are in theory senior in rank to the *chefs* but are forced to deal with them as equals because the *chefs* control access to their common boss.

Promotion to the rank of director-general, or to lesser posts, depends only incidentally on ability. An internal survey published in a fit of *glasnost* last year showed that Eurocrats themselves listed the first criterion for promotion as whom you know rather than what you know. Member-governments carefully monitor promotions of their nationals within the commission.

Jobs for the big boys

The big members like to make sure that they get their share of the top jobs. The five largest member-states have bagged 19 out of 27 posts of director-general or equivalent rank; France and West Germany have done particularly well (see table). Some directorates-general are also considered to be at least partly under the influence of one nationality or another. The directorate-general for competition (DG IV in Brussels-speak) is considered a "German" department, while DG VI (farming) has a French tinge and DGs I (external relations) and XV (financial services) have tended towards Britishness.

Further down the hierarchy, the member-countries are more relaxed about the share-out of jobs. Luxembourg (population 360,000) has 52 "grade A" administrative posts, Britain (population 56m) only 354. If you count assistants, secretaries, drivers and so on, then Belgium—the host country—has more Eurocrats than France and West Germany combined.

Eurocrats do not have diplomatic status. They do have a few well-chosen perks—generous allowances and easy taxes—which leave them much better off than their national counterparts. But some people occasionally take a loss to serve on the commission. One of these is Mr Abel Matutes, the commissioner responsible for relations between the EEC and part of the third world. He has large banking and business interests in Spain. On arrival in Brussels, Mr Matutes was informed that all Eurocrats were allowed to buy their first car tax-free. "Can I buy a tax-free aircraft instead?" he asked. He was persuaded to settle for a car.

EEC institutions: European Court of Justice
Where the buck stops

In his fourth article on how the European Community works, our Brussels correspondent looks at its version of America's Supreme Court

THOSE who forget that the EEC and its structures are largely a French invention should visit the European Court of Justice in Luxembourg. The court, the final arbiter of EEC law, is inspired by the French Conseil d'Etat. The system of dividing the court into chambers, and the role of the advocates-general who assist the 13 judges, are derived from the French legal system.

The working language of the court is French, although cases can be heard in any of the nine EEC languages at the request of plaintiff or defendant. It is chiefly among wig-and-pen folk that French has resisted the claims of English for parity as a working language. The only other place where French still prevails is in the European Commission's press room in Brussels, the daily meeting place of more than 200 journalists from 50 countries, only a handful of whom are native French-speakers.

If the court's model is French, its functions are frequently compared to those of the United States Supreme Court. Just as the Supreme Court settles disputes in the federal structure of the United States, so the Court of Justice settles those in the EEC club. Its judgments are final; there is no further appeal. Wherever Eurorules have been set in Brussels, EEC law is national law for all Community countries. The court's task is to see that EEC law is properly applied throughout the Community.

Unlike the Supreme Court, its judgments have to be unanimous. There is no dissenting minority, at least outside the judges' private deliberating chamber. Also unlike the Supreme Court, it is the Community's only court, although one of its main functions is to give interpretations of EEC law to national courts which refer cases to Luxembourg for guidance.

A great part of the court's authority

comes from the fact that Community law prevails over national law where there is a conflict between the two. This principle was first established in 1964 in a seemingly minor case involving an Italian who refused to pay his electricity bill because he claimed the nationalisation of electricity distribution in Italy was against EEC rules. EEC members have no choice but to respect the rulings of the court: its powers are set out in the Treaty of Rome, which they have all accepted.

In this, the European Court of Justice differs from two other courts with which it is sometimes confused, the International Court of Justice in The Hague (the World Court) and the European Court of Human Rights in Strasbourg. EEC member-states cannot opt out of the European Court of Justice's jurisdiction, but they have no treaty obligation to accept rulings of the World Court or of the European Court of Human Rights, which was created by the Council of Europe. All Community countries are also members of the Council of Europe and have chosen to recognise the jurisdiction of its court in human-rights cases.

No member-country has refused to accept a ruling of the European Court of Justice on a large issue of principle. In some instances, however, they have dithered for a long time before complying. France delayed opening its market to imports of mutton and lamb from Britain to protect its own high-cost producers for several months after a court condemnation in 1979. Britain returned the compliment four years later by taking its time to put into practice a ruling that it should accept imports of long-life milk from the continent (mainly France).

When France delayed applying its ruling, the court came under pressure to issue a second condemnation under its emergency procedures. The court's refusal to do so was at first seized upon by some British commentators as evidence of the court bowing to political pressure. But its reasoning—that to issue a second ruling would devalue the validity of the first (and therefore the authority of the court)—was widely accepted as wise.

The same reasoning prevailed when the idea of penal sanctions to back up court decisions was rejected by EEC legal experts looking into reforms of the Treaty of Rome designed to help speed the 1992 project along. However, the reforms (in the shape of the 1987 Single European Act) did create a junior court to ease the workload in Luxembourg. This junior court, or Court of First Instance, will deal with minor cases and is due to begin work later this year.

Overworked and under Due

The creation of the new court is timely. The number of cases has steadily increased, to more than 350 a year. A judgment took nine months on average in 1975; that had doubled by 1985 and the average is now over 21

Hey, don't forget us

FROM OUR BRUSSELS CORRESPONDENT

A EUROQUIZ: name six institutions which help run the EEC. Answer: the European Commission, the Council of Ministers, the European Parliament, the Court of Justice, then there's . . . er. Stuck? Most people would be. In fact the Community does have two more institutions: the Court of Auditors and the Economic and Social Committee.

The Court of Auditors, based in Luxembourg like the Court of Justice, is the Community's financial watchdog. It checks all EEC revenue and spending and has uncovered many cases of mis-spent cash from the Community's annual budget of 40 billion ecus ($44 billion). These range from excessive expenses claims by commissioners, through money squandered on unsound aid projects in the third world, to massive frauds in the EEC farm fund. The vigilance of the 12 members of the court, hardly the most popular Eurocrats among their 20,000 colleagues, has led to some tightening of budgetary and financial procedures. Not

enough, say critics.

The 189 members of the Economic and Social Committee are altogether more harmless. They just offer opinions. The committee has the right under the Treaty of Rome to be consulted on certain draft legislation. Unlike the European Parliament it has no right of amendment, so its views have little formal impact on EEC decision-taking.

The committee, which meets once a month in Brussels, is made up of three groups: representatives of employers, of workers and of "various interests" (consumer groups, academics, farmers, the self-employed). The committee has to give its opinion on draft legislation on farming, transport, social policy and the Community's internal market. The president of the European Commission, Mr Jacques Delors, and the social-affairs commissioner, Mrs Vasso Papandreou, are trying to use the committee to gather support for the "social dimension" of the 1992 project. Most of the folk on the committee, who long to be taken more seriously, are delighted by the new attentiveness of the commission.

months. The biggest single category of cases, amazingly, has been staff disputes among Eurocrats, whose expatriate status means that they cannot take their complaints to any national court; these cases will henceforth go to the junior court.

The most important cases concern the respect (or otherwise) by EEC countries of their treaty obligations and—for private-sector companies—the application of Community competition and trade policy. American multinationals turn to the court if they feel the commission has fined them unfairly for breaches of EEC antitrust law. Japanese makers of ball-bearings and zip-fasteners have successfully appealed to the court when EEC governments have discriminated unfairly against their products. Nor are citizens' rights forgotten. Women take their grievances to the (all-male) Luxembourg court when they feel their rights to equal treatment under EEC rules are not respected.

The new rules resulting from the Single European Act and the 1992 project will add to the court's work. EEC legal experts complain privately that the act, which was drafted in less than six months, contains a number of ambiguities and even contradictions. The court will no doubt have to sort some of them out. It will also be called upon more and more by national courts for rulings on how they should apply the growing number of EEC rules. And it will have to arbitrate in cases where member-states contest some of the Community's new powers. Already governments are carefully checking each major item of 1992 legislation to see whether it requires a majority vote or a unanimous one in the Council of Ministers—or whether the EEC is competent to take the decision at all. Britain is being particularly vigilant.

But Britain gives the court less work than some of its partners. The British government has had fewer than 25 actions brought against it, compared with 150 against Italy, 80 against France and 75 against Belgium. Most of these are brought by the European Commission, which is responsible for the respect of EEC rules.

Although the 1992 project will make the court busier, other things will not change. Even before 1992 was thought of, the court took a number of famous decisions opening up national markets to products from other EEC states. While Eurocrats were still dreaming of Euroloafs, the court ruled that the West Germans could not keep out French crème de cassis merely because it did not conform to German standards. More recently it told the Germans not to ban foreign beer and the Italians French spaghetti just because they were different from the home product. Member-governments have complained in the past that the court has tended to have a bias in favour of the commission and against them, although they have been less critical in recent years.

This is partly because the court has been taking a more restricted view of its role. For a time it seemed to be pushing against the limits of its powers. Under Lord MacKenzie Stuart, a Scottish judge who was president from 1984 to 1988, the court grew more cautious. This approach is likely to continue under the new president, Mr Ole Due of Denmark.

To emphasise the court's independence from national governments, there is no relation (well, almost none) between the number of judges and the size of an EEC state, as there is for members of the commission. Each country has one judge, with a 13th member to ensure an uneven number. He is chosen on a rotating basis from among the five biggest Community countries.

Tackling the democratic deficit

EC institutions are seeking a wider mandate, report

David Buchan and Tim Dickson

The European Community's institutions are in for a serious jolting this year – from the sideways shock of absorbing East Germany, from the frontal impact of negotiations to achieve economic and monetary union (Emu), and from the hammering away of a Parliament in constant search of more clout.

The Strasbourg assembly will today overwhelmingly approve a report demanding new powers, including equal legislative standing with EC governments represented in the Council of Ministers and the right to elect the Brussels Commission.

East Germany poses far less of an institutional problem in joining the Community by merging with an existing member than it would by entering as the 13th state. West Germany has the same two seats in the Commission, 10 votes in the Council of Ministers and 81 seats in the Parliament as the three other largest EC states. Bonn says it will want no extra representation for a unified Germany. But even if it eventually does, accommodating such changes will be easy compared to the task of applying EC policies to businesses and people on East German territory.

Much more important is the assumption that flux in eastern Europe requires greater institutional solidity in western Europe. Behind this is the worry, as expressed by Prime Minister Wilfried Martens recently, about the EC "melting away under the warm glow of pan-Europeanism." This could be dismissed as predictable hand-wringing from the leader of a fervently federalist Belgium were it not for the fact that the sentiment is shared by most other EC governments. They feel that the chief geo-political contribution the Community can make to the new Europe is to strengthen its own institutions, the better to anchor united Germany.

Thus, the East is still acting as a catalyst in the Community debate on reform, even though people like Mr Jacques Delors, the European Commission president, and President Mitterrand of France lost their bid to use it as a pretext to bring forward the inter-governmental conference (IGC) on monetary union set to start at the end of this year. Mr Helmut Kohl, the West German Chancellor, told them he had to give priority to Emu between the two Germanys before tackling it among the Twelve. In fact, the very delay of the IGC simply serves the interests of those who want it to have the widest possible agenda.

In other ways, the link with developments in the East is still very much alive in minds of many EC institutional reformers. Mr David Martin, the British socialist whose report on sweeping new powers for the European Parliament was endorsed in Strasbourg this week, notes that the case for making Council of Ministers debates public is strengthened "because with democracy now in the East, the Council is the only body left in Europe which makes laws behind closed doors." He, and many others in the Parliament and the Commission, say the willingness of EC governments to dovetail their foreign policies towards the East, under the Commission's lead, shows that the Twelve can, and should, start pooling policy towards other parts of the world.

Well before the latest German events, proposals for institutional reform were flooding in, undammed by the prospect of the forthcoming IGC revising the Community's treaties. The biggest demands have been tabled by the Parliament which is calling for:
● Majority voting in the Council on all EC legislation, even matters like tax where the requirement for unanimity now gives individual states a veto.

● Co-decision for the Parliament, ensuring that legislation could only come into force if both the Council and the Parliament explicitly approved. The Parliament can now only make amendments which may be ignored by the Council.
● The Parliament to share in the Commission's right to initiate legislation.
● The right of the Parliament to elect the Commission's president.

Other solutions have been put forward to fill what has become known as the democratic deficit – a phrase designed to highlight a relative lack of control over EC policies and laws by Europe's elected representatives. From Mr Michael Heseltine, the Tory dissident who has been banging the pro-Europe drum in his bid for eventual power in the British Conservative party, has come the argument that this democratic deficit is best filled by giving national parliaments more control over EC policy. He has proposed giving Strasbourg an upper house, a Senate composed of representatives from national parliaments. This idea has some support from Mr Delors, though he is more concerned with efficiency than democracy in EC decision-making. The Commission president himself has suggested that governments should either give him and his fellow 16 commissioners more executive power or they should station ministers with the rank of deputy prime minister in Brussels as permanent, high-level managers of European business.

This debate is, however, running ahead of itself. When the 12 governments sit down to their conference, strictly speaking they alone will determine the agenda – not the Parliament, not Mr Delors and certainly not Mr Heseltine. Their immediate task will to be try to agree on moves towards economic and monetary union (Emu). This will have implications for EC institutions. Even the UK Government – which strongly opposes the Delors report's proposed European System of Central Banks – agrees. It objects that control of such a system would require a European finance ministry, even government – for which Europeans are not ready.

So far, there is little on the table in the way of strictly Emu-related institutional reform. The Delors committee report, now nearly a year old, suggested that the democratic accountability of a system of central banks might take the form of the Euro-bank reporting once a year to the European Parliament and EC heads of government. Despite its name, the Delors report is not (or at least not yet) official policy of the Commission, which is to due to issue a cost/benefit analysis of Emu to finance ministers this month and a report on institutional aspects to foreign ministers in May.

In fact, reckons one seasoned national diplomat in Brussels, "the final role of the Parliament may not in the end be very large in an Emu, because most people won't want it to control the Euro-bank." He argues that the only way to meet West Germany's particular concern about central banks being free of the vagaries of party political control is for a sharp distinction to be made between "control" and "accountability." Thus, the Euro-bank would be "accountable" in the sense of giving periodic account of its activities, to the Strasbourg assembly and EC finance ministers, but without being under their operational control.

It is also misleading, says this diplomat, to think that because there is more talk of the democratic deficit that the average European-in-the-street suddenly feels aggrieved about the lack of democracy in the Community. Rather, there are "two main vested interests – the Parliament and the Commission – which are permanently in favour of institutional reform," he says. "The democratic deficit is not an objectively observed truth, but more a slogan, a standard behind which these vested interests will march into battle."

None the less these vested interests may wrest some notable concessions from governments at the inter-governmental conference. They did so five years ago at the IGC that created the Single European Act. This time, the Commission and the Parliament may face a British Government which is

more opposed than ever to granting them more powers. In 1985 the Thatcher Government was lured into agreement on the Single Act by the prospect of getting the single market programme under way. Now, however, Mrs Thatcher is more isolated among the Twelve than ever, not only on Emu itself, but also on the issue of giving Strasbourg more clout. She is also more isolated inside her own country, if not party; in an extraordinary indication of Labour's new stance on Europe, last week the British Labour group backed the Martin report by 28 votes to eight.

Backing for reform is sure from many of the Community's Latin and smaller member states, among them Ireland and Italy who successively hold the EC presidency this year. Mr Kohl, at least until pan-German visions started to dance before his eyes, repeatedly said the current European Parliament should be the last to have its present powers and that the next Parliament should be elected in 1994 with new competences. A significant shift has also taken place in Denmark which hitherto has shared many of the British Government's reservations about the federalist drift in EC institutions, and in particular in Strasbourg. The Danish Folketing (parliament), traditionally even touchier than Westminster about its sovereignty, is now on record as welcoming the inter-governmental conference, provided it is widened beyond monetary union to allow majority Council voting – and consequent greater involvement of the European Parliament – in social and environmental policies.

Short of actually sitting in on the conference, the Parliament's hope is to at least help set the agenda by making it as wide as possible. Its Spanish socialist president, Mr Enrique Baron, has proposed to EC foreign ministers the holding of a pre-conference in May or June to discuss constitutional reform. Its federalist ally, the Commission, will certainly attend, and the Irish presidency will probably not be absent. But the steeper the Parliament pitches its demands, the more likely it is to arouse the jealousies of national parliaments, which must ultimately ratify any treaty changes. MEPs realise the danger. "The last thing we want to do is to make them hostile to what we propose," says Mr Martin. So, after hosting its IGC pre-conference, the Parliament proposes holding *assises* with national parliaments to keep

them informed and to canvass their support for reform.

Can MEPs win over MPs to their cause? Long-time federalists like British Tory MEP Bill Newton-Dunn believe so, arguing that far from taking power from national parliaments, Strasbourg is only fighting to regain powers of control lost by the separate legislatures of the Twelve. The latter, he says, "surrendered their powers when they first allowed their ministers to go to Brussels to make collectively-binding EC decisions." Arguably, the real undermining of national democratic control only came with the Single Act. Increased use of majority voting meant that even very tight national control of a minister's conduct in Brussels could be rendered pointless when that minister could be out-voted. Thus, all the talk at Westminster of improving the present derisory degree of effective scrutiny, let alone control, by the House of Commons may be rather moot, because logic now points to greater control at the EC level.

However, given that what Strasbourg is now demanding may be too much for national governments and parliaments to swallow, what about filling that democratic deficit by simply making debate in the Council public? It is hard to defend the fact that a body which plays the biggest part in passing legislation of increasing importance of a particularly entrenched kind (taking precedence over national law) and which is difficult to repeal (requiring EC, not national action) – operates in secret.

Briefings by EC Councils are quite enough for reporters, but this form of partial and filtered publicity is insufficient for businessmen, for whom the devil is often in the detail of EC legislation. It is also galling for national MPs who always have to learn second-hand about the laws they will shortly have to place on their national statute books.

The argument for letting the sunshine into the Council is that majority voting on many issues has changed the nature of the game; behind-the-scenes horse-trading is no longer so necessary to get ministers to abandon their vetos. But ministers and diplomats insist they must still have some privacy to search for the compromises that make the Community go round. This is clearly special pleading. But the political fact is that while most member states may feel uneasy about the present institutional arrangements the onus will be on the reformers to improve them.

After Gulf War, a drive toward European unity

Mideast situation made leaders shudder—and seek a united voice

Elizabeth Pond

Elizabeth Pond is Warburg Professor of International Relations at Simmons College and the author of a recent book on German unification, "After the Wall."

A funny thing happened to the Europeans on the way to the Gulf War. Their very disarray scared them into a drive toward future unity — among themselves, in the Western European Union, and with the United States, in the North Atlantic Treaty Organization.

This outcome is counterintuitive. Everyone knows that "out of area" crises divide the NATO alliance and drive "wedges" between the United States and Europe and between European allies themselves. And that the decline of the Soviet threat sounded the death knell for NATO. And that European integration and Atlantic alliance are not complementary but zero-sum competitive; they don't both profit simultaneously.

Indeed, Europe was divided as the war began. NATO did look peripheral. As one Benelux diplomat deftly expressed it, Europe showed itself to be an economic giant, a political dwarf and a military worm.

Quite naturally, pundits concluded that a backsliding "renationalization" of defense policy was the trend of the hour. All the brave talk about a European political union by the late '90s, with elements of a common foreign and even security policy, seemed to be so much rhetoric. NATO, it was thought, would be hollowed out, even if it survived.

But the funny things began to happen. Ironically, they had nothing to do with the *Realpolitik* of oil, and everything to do with the intangibles of psychology and politics.

Mitterrand's strategy

In France, President Francois Mitterrand used the gulf issue to outmaneuver the quasi-Gaullist wing of his Socialist Party — with the result that his Defense Minister Jean-Pierre Chevenement finally resigned. Mitterand's strategy in sending armed forces to the gulf — to forestall another "Yalta" in which the great powers minus France would carve up the postwar world — won out over the left's flirtation with Third World radicals.

In Britain, fledgling Prime Minister John Major — who had never invested the same amount of ego in a go-it-alone policy as his mentor Margaret Thatcher — looked beyond the Anglo-Saxon bond to announce, in Germany, that Britain's place is "at the very heart of Europe." And opposition leader Neil Kinnock, imitating Mitterrand, used the unpopularity of Saddam Hussein to isolate his pacifist wing and make the Labor Party more credible for the next election.

In Germany, Iraq's Scud attacks on Israel set off a wave of revulsion. Memories of the Holocaust suggested that in an imperfect world there might be another moral imperative to relativize the moral imperative of never going to war. The Germans began to question — only question, not yet challenge — their 45-year post-Hitler allergy to any resort to military power other than defense of the homeland. Prominent left peace activists such as balladeer Wolf Biermann and Green Party founding mother Petra Kelly urged that Saddam Hussein be stopped. It turned out in opinion polls that three-quarters of the population actually supported the American-led war effort.

In the midst of the turmoil, then, various Europeans looked at their blatant divergence over the gulf, and shuddered. They realized they would have precious little to say in determining the shape of the post-Cold War world unless they spoke with a united voice. They concluded at the same time that they must keep the Americans engaged in Europe, both to provide the kind of global leadership (as in the gulf) that no smaller democracy can, and to insure themselves against unpleasant surprises (as in Lithuania) from a collapsing but still-nuclear Soviet Union. They redoubled their efforts at cooperation, with each other and with the United States.

The upshot was that on the eve of the land war in Iraq the nine members of the Western European Union — all the members of the European Community, minus neutral Ireland, gun-shy Denmark and no longer gun-shy Greece, which now wants to join the WEU, but applied too late — resuscitated that on-again, off-again organization. Their general purpose is to curb their own centrifugal impulses by giving the WEU real clout for the first time in three decades and by forming a "bridge" between NATO and the EC. Their sensational hidden agenda — which European military sources are so far willing to talk about only privately and anonymously — is developing Western European forces for emergency deployment, should there be a request, to Eastern Europe. Their first concrete step in these directions will be to consolidate and move the split WEU headquarters from Paris and London to NATO's Brussels.

This latest WEU revival, following two

From *The Boston Globe*, March 31, 1991. Reprinted by permission.

ephemeral restarts in the 1980s, seeks to square two circles. First, it is drawing a fine distinction between "defense," which is to remain atomized, subject to sovereign national decisions as in the first weeks of the Gulf War, and broader "security," which is to be disciplined into a common European policy. Second, it is deliberately blurring the distinction between the British and French approaches to the WEU.

The British (along with the German Defense Ministry) want the WEU, at long last, to provide the "European pillar" to NATO that for 40 years the United States has been pleading for to match the American pillar. A relative increase in Europe's portion of "burden-sharing," they argue, would be easier to effect now, in a time of shrinking armies, than in the past — and such a gesture should help persuade the Americans to stay in Europe.

In this vision the WEU would eventually become a European "caucus" within NATO, coordinating but not cementing European views prior to NATO Council meetings. The currently no-tooth-all-tail WEU would acquire instant soldiers by unorthodox "double-hatting" with NATO. Multinational building-block units would be assembled in task forces of variable geometry and assigned either to NATO or the WEU as occasion arose.

Security arm?

By contrast, the French would like the WEU to become the security arm of the EC, excluding the Americans. Jacques Delors, president of the EC Commission, seemed to second this view in his surprise call a week ago for the EC to go beyond the original Treaty of Rome and adopt a common defense (and not just "security") policy as part of the vague "political union" members are currently negotiating. The French are ambivalent, however, since they want simply to reduce US influence and not to expel the Americans, who remain invaluable to them as a counterweight to the powerful Germans.

In fact, the French are still groping on several levels for the way out of their present identity crisis following German unification and its shattering of all the old premises of Gaullism. Mitterrand cannot yet bring himself to put French forces under foreign command in Europe or let German troops in multinational units be deployed in France. But Mitterrand's placing French troops under American operational command in the spectacularly successful gulf venture (with a smaller American unit tactfully subordinated to French officers) set a precedent that should make eventual multinational command in Europe less painful.

For its part, linchpin Germany has been advocating the animation of the WEU for months. Gemany itself will not be transformed from a consumer to a more active supplier of regional security, of course, unless Chancellor Helmut Kohl exercises uncharacteristic leadership in security issues. The one step he has taken in this direction is to ask for a constitutional amendment that would authorize use of the Bundeswehr not only in UN peacekeeping endeavors, but also in joint WEU operations.

To be sure, the skittish Social Democrats (and even more skittish East Germans) resist contributing their votes to the two-thirds parliamentary majority required to amend the constitution and let the Bundeswehr serve abroad in even peacekeeping missions. But German officials who seek a political role for Germany commensurate with its economic power now hope that a European framework can neutralize the objections of the many Germans who would mistrust a purely German wielding of power.

The United States is reacting to all the upheaval warily but positively. It gained a new appreciation of the value of the post-Cold War European alliance in providing NATO's vast supply dump and staging area for American force projection in the Middle East. It honors the role of the WEU in, if not really coordinating Europe's contributions, then at least lending an institutional aegis to out-of-Europe operations in a way that NATO could not. It relishes the implicit European sharing of more of Atlantic alliance burdens in the WEU revival, though it resists corollary European constraints on US decision-making.

Greater security integration in Europe will not be easy. But oddly enough, it looks far easier today than it did two months ago.

Eastern Europe I: liberalism vs. nationalism

Paul Lendvai

The Soviet bloc and the multinational Soviet Union itself are, in varying degrees, caught in a process of dissolution. From Berlin to Sofia, the entire political scene is being transformed at break-neck speed. From systemic change to the (so far at least) orderly withdrawal of Soviet troops from Czechoslovakia and Hungary, things are happening which until recently were thought unimaginable.

Books published only yesterday for the fortieth anniversary of East Germany in October 1989, depicting the supposedly stable coexistence of two German states and the great East German success story, have become mere wastepaper overnight. Today the European political agenda is headed by the question of whether and how the danger of a newly-burgeoning German nationalism can be averted.

'Nations abide, regimes decline,' wrote Raymond Aron a quarter of a century ago, at a time when most Western academics were ignoring the problem of nationalism, and 'political tourism', with leading politicians making frequent visits to the Eastern bloc, had placed this difficult question under a real taboo. We should not forget that the revised Party programme of the Communist Party of the Soviet Union (CPSU) in 1986 reads: 'The nationality question bequeathed to us by the past has been successfully solved in the Soviet Union.' In November 1987 Mikhail Gorbachev stated that the nationality question had essentially been solved. The violent unrest and pogroms in Azerbaijan, Armenia, Georgia, Uzbekistan and Kazakhstan and, also, the struggle of the Baltic states for independence, have made the nationality question the central problem of Soviet politics, and Gorbachev himself has openly acknowledged that it is 'the crucial issue for the Soviet state'.

Nationalism underestimated

The size and explosiveness of the nationality problem in the Soviet Union (Zbigniew Brzezinski, writing in *Foreign Affairs*, even speaks of a possible 'Lebanonisation' there) and the possible revival of nationalism in a united Germany are both factors being taken into account in the quest for a new pan-European security framework. Yet there is a frequent tendency to avoid or play down—maybe out of misplaced tact—a further dilemma, namely the rising tide of nationalism in Eastern Europe. However, it is precisely within and between the smaller East and South-East European states that there has been a build-up of national and socio-psychological tension so explosive that the interplay of nationalities could in places eclipse their desired move back towards Europe.

Adam Michnik, a former Polish dissident and now Editor-in-Chief of Solidarity's daily newspaper *Gazeta Wyborcza* and a member of the Sejm, has argued that to put forward 'social democracy or liberalism' as alternatives was fundamentally irrelevant in post-totalitarian Central Europe. According to Michnik, in these Central and East European states the conflict is not between 'capitalism' and 'socialism' or between 'Right' and 'Left', but rather between two paths, one democratic, pluralist and tolerant, the other nationalist, centralist and authoritarian.

It would be wrong to condemn outright the assertion of national identity and the transition from a Marxist-Leninist class concept (used to justify the brutal discrimination of millions) to a broad national consensus, seeing this only as the symptom of an infectious disease handed down from the past. Nationalism has many faces and is totally ambivalent. It can be a force for stability but also a revolutionary factor, sterile yet creative, reactionary but also progressive.

What may appear to the citizens of long-established Western nations as a disturbing relic of the past, and to the Americans as a spectre from the Dark Ages, has a very different significance for Central, East and Southern Europe. Most of these nations only attained sovereignty during the twentieth century. National feeling was their most important means of survival through centuries of foreign rule and the main instrument in the achievement of their independence.

That a damaged national consciousness can, in recovering, turn from a binding agent into dynamite and lead the inflamed masses into the abyss of totalitarian dictatorship, fired by the irrational emotions of nationalist zeal, was already foreseen by the Austrian writer Franz Grillparzer about 150 years ago. He wrote in his notebook the famous epigram, 'It is by way of nationality that humanity reaches bestiality'. In the pre-1941 period, the virulent nationalism of the dominant nations, set against a background of permanent economic crisis and 'middle-class panic', formed the breeding-ground for variously labelled anti-liberal and authoritarian regimes under Admiral Horthy in Hungary, Marshal Pilsudski in Poland, King Carol in Romania and King Boris in Bulgaria. Even in Czechoslovakia, the only functioning democracy in the interwar period, there was little regard for the problems of the Slavs, Germans and Hungarians.

Instead of idealising the prewar era, as has become fashionable in some quarters, we must be careful to note that the constantly recurring concept and ideology of a 'third way' or a 'third force' has in the twentieth century almost invariably worked against democracy, undermining it with illusory alternatives to the left and the right, downgrading it against supposedly more perfect social and political forms. The burden of the historical legacy of hatred, violence and mass killing gives national conflicts in this complex region an alarmingly explosive quality.

Yugoslavia is a particularly striking example of how deeply historical experience extends into individual family history for almost all inhabitants of the modern multinational state, and also how much it affects the problems of the present. The one-time 'Kingdom of the Serbs, Croats and Slovenes' collapsed in 1941 mainly as a result of open ethnic enmity pursued to breaking-point by Serbian supremacy. During the Second World War the Ustase (the extreme Croatian separatist movement), the notorious Serbian Cetniks and the Moslem militias managed between them to slaughter more of their fellow-Yugoslavs than all the German, Italian and other occupying forces with whom they alternately sided put together. Without taking into account this tragic past it is quite impossible to grasp the psychologically critical condition of Yugoslav society, especially the nationalistic hysteria in Serbia since 1988, seen by many outside observers as

From *The World Today*, July 1990, pp. 131-133. *The World Today*, published by The Royal Institute of International Affairs.

a decline into barbarism, and the bitterness of the long-oppressed Albanians who make up 90 per cent of the population in the crisis-torn province of Kosovo.

Yugoslavia is really a country without Yugoslavs, since the definition is a national and not a political one. The very intensity of the political, economic and socio-psychological conflicts between the dominant Serbs on the one hand and the Croats, the Slovenes and the Albanians on the other are a sign that in this part of the Balkans, the main division lies not between 'Left' and 'Right' but between nations and minorities, a fact that is taken for granted by those who really know Yugoslavia but continues to surprise many Western diplomats.

When a Slovene opposition newspaper not long ago proudly proclaimed 'Lithuania is our model', it was an unmistakeable indication of how strongly nationality disputes in the Soviet Union influence not only the so-called former satellite states but also non-aligned Yugoslavia. Conversely, Michnik rightly considers anti-Russian xenophobia as the greatest danger facing Poland, and nationalistic discord and anti-foreign movements as the most complex and dramatic problem confronting Central Europe.

The fact that the Soviet Union did not succeed in colonising Central and Eastern Europe and even at the height of its hegemony was unable to make the people conform to its brand of Marxism-Leninism, should not blind us to the enormous moral, intellectual and cultural damage which it inflicted on these countries. Their national character, their traditions and unique history, their way of life and their social code were thrown into an artificial melting-pot. National diversity was replaced by a regressive model of Soviet Communism. No sphere of life was safe from the process of homogenisation. It is often forgotten that the smaller nations of Eastern and South-Eastern Europe are only slowly and painfully recovering from the catastrophic effects of Soviet (and within the Soviet Union itself, Great Russian) domination. The extent of the damage and the degree of national renewal naturally differ from country to country. The deeply-rooted feeling of having been plundered, subjugated and kicked around for so long by a foreign superpower only became an openly decisive political factor in the period of revolution. The national self-determination of the small nations, expressed in their essentially defensive nationalism, has always formed the core of the resistance to the Soviet Union.

De-Sovietisation = Europeanisation?

The particular example of Yugoslavia and the numerous signs of re-emerging nationalism in Eastern Europe should, however, make us wary of the illusion that de-Sovietisation will lead automatically, as it were, to the Europeanisation of the small states. On the contrary, the transition is enormously difficult, hazardous and fraught with difficulty, not only on the political and economic level but also on the psychological and intellectual one.

Why? The frontier disputes and ethnic conflicts between the new states which are developing out of the collapse of the enormous empires in Central Europe and in the Balkans are the legacy of history. The decisions on political frontiers at the end of the First and Second World War were based not on the publicly proclaimed principles of ethnic frontiers but more often than not on power-political, strategic and other motives. Yet it is also true that the geographic distribution of ethnic groups and the traditional alliances in this region are so complicated that clear and satisfactory frontiers are impossible. Consequently, each country contains minorities, each of these feeling a sense of belonging to a different country. Even nationally homogeneous Poland faces not only the possible German threat to its Western frontier, but

also various frontier disputes with Lithuania, White Russia and the Ukraine.

To get a picture of the enormous complexity of unfulfilled territorial aspirations and nationality conflicts, one need only think of the acute conflict between Romania and Hungary concerning the treatment of the large, compact Hungarian minority in Transylvania; the Romanian claims to Bessarabia and Northern Bukovina in the Soviet Union and Dobruja in Bulgaria; the Albanian powder-keg within Yugoslavia and the dispute with Albania that is inseparably linked to it; Bulgarian ambitions in Macedonia; and the problem, aggravated in recent years, of the Turks in Bulgaria and the Moslems in Yugoslavia.

Problems suppressed under Soviet domination

Contrary to the theory, propounded by many American and German analysts, that Soviet domination prevented local conflicts, it actually exacerbated old conflicts and helped create new ones. After the Second World War the small nations were separated from each other still further and misunderstanding and mistrust among them grew. Behind the façade of a supposedly internationalist doctrine, the dual pressure of Soviet domination and Communist dictatorship created new barriers between the small states, without overcoming the old ones.

'In this Europe, which had created a world consciousness, a world civilisation and a world history, national consciousness, national cultures and national history remained the ultimate yardstick of thought and action, hopelessly inadequate and quite literally backward.' This is how the Swiss historian, Herbert Lüthy, summed up the task of establishing a united, free Europe after the Second World War.

It is only when one considers that the economic recovery, political stabilisation, successful cooperation and international understanding of the free part of Europe would not have been possible without a total change in spiritual climate and the availability of a liberal-democratic system, that one can grasp the full extent of the psychological and intellectual as well as economic devastation suffered by regions forced to vegetate for more than 40 years under Soviet domination.

The revolutionary process means an intellectual and moral 'zero hour' and an end to fictions such as that the concept of the nation or the taboo issue of anti-semitism had been overcome. Nationalism does not in fact simply mean resistance from below against the domination of a great power. For the very reason that history in the Danubian lands and in the Balkans, across the continually submerged regions of Central, East and South-East Europe, is shaped by small states, it is important to recall the unbroken tradition of small state imperialism, the mutually hostile nationalist movements and the horrifying efficacy of prejudices and hostile images nurtured over generations up to the present day.

The astonishingly rapid collapse of the totalitarian Leninist state structures, undermined from within and no longer shored up by fear of Soviet intervention, opened the way for the creation of states based on the rule of law, the separation of powers and an open society.

Culture shock of freedom

However, after decades spent within the Eastern bloc in isolation from one another and from the ideologically 'dangerous' West, the East European economies are a bizarre combination of a weakened but still dominant state sector and flourishing islands of unfettered, unregulated (and already to some extent foreign) speculative capitalism. The consequences of the destruction and persecution of the national elite are keenly felt. There are no entrepreneurs, no middle class and (except in Poland) no free farmers.

'What causes me anguish is not the sight of the empty supermarket shelves but the empty souls of the people,' a Bulgarian writer confessed recently. Though the political and economic, cultural and demographic conditions are totally different from region to region, the same general question arises: how will the people cope with the culture shock of freedom after so many years? How will the new Eastern Europe ride out the curve of increased expectations in the midst of a dramatic economic crisis?

The most important political and economic phenomenon is once again the growth of nationalism, often tied up with religion. The Catholic church in Poland, Croatia and (less militantly) in Czechoslovakia and Slovenia has been the chief protagonist of national self-assertion. Elsewhere, in Hungary and East Germany, in Romania and Bulgaria, the Catholic, Orthodox, Lutheran, Calvinist and Jewish communities were partly or in certain periods victims of their accommodation tactics. The great task of intellectual confrontation with church history and with individual complicity in the Communists' temporary success in imposing political and ideological conformity remains a continuing challenge facing the East Europeans in the future. Involvement in propaganda and other political activities on behalf of the totalitarian regime naturally went far beyond the church and is a problem besetting the whole of society, as Vaclav Havel said in his New Year speech and on later occasions.

Anti-semitism revived

A particularly tragic issue is the problem of anti-semitism, in connection with which two difficulties must be mentioned. First, since the end of the Second World War, with the exception of the Middle East, only in the countries of the so-called socialist bloc have the Jews been subjected to institutionalised discrimination and periodic persecution. Second, a campaign to counter anti-semitism and a really effective re-education movement was impossible east of the Elbe because the Communist regimes denied the existence of anti-semitism along with other social problems. The re-establishment of diplomatic relations with Israel by Hungary, Czechoslovakia and Poland is, therefore, a happy consequence of the revolution.

Meanwhile, however, there is a proliferation of open and covert, but nevertheless unmistakeable, anti-semitic activities, pronouncements and incidents in East Germany, Hungary, Poland and Romania, while the Soviet Union is a case by itself. The result of the Holocaust, the systematic destruction of the Jewish people during the Second World War, was that only 730,000 out of more than 5m Jews in Eastern Europe (excluding the Soviet Union) survived the Second World War. After several waves of emigration there remain altogether fewer than 150,000 Jews in East and South-Eastern Europe. The virulence of this 'anti-semitism without the Jews' is particularly disturbing since the intensity of racism, xenophobia and especially anti-semitism has always been a reliable indicator of the psychological and moral state of Eastern Europe. The Nazi reign of terror and its East European arms (the Arrow Cross in Hungary, the Iron Guard in Romania and so on) always drew strength from ideology or myths. The nationalism of the newly-emerging nation-states and the threatened minorities was from the outset a cover for a regressive, deeply anti-liberal and also, later, anti-modern tendency.

Dangers of a 'third way'

The nationalistic 'third way' of the Hungarian populists as well as for example the 'national democratic' stance of the advisers of Cardinal Glemp in Poland, inveighing against 'alien Western liberalism' and the 'ideological neutrality of the state', embody today, as in earlier times, the tendency towards exclusion and delimitation as opposed to cooperation and understanding. The fact that today there can still be different yardsticks for the rights of one's own nation and the rights of the foreign minority is shown in the case of Macedonia. On the one hand, tens of thousands of Macedonians, whose claim to their own national identity is disputed by Serbs and Bulgarians, demonstrate against the oppression of 200,000 of their kinsmen in Bulgaria. On the other hand, the new constitution of this constituent republic of Yugoslavia proclaims that from now on Macedonia is the nation-state of the Macedonian people only, thus excluding the Albanians and Turks who make up more than a quarter of the population in the same republic. Everywhere the legacy of convenient collective amnesia for a country's crimes both during the Second World War and before and after the Communist takeover weighs heavily. The victims of one type of totalitarianism should not be offset against those of another. Reflection on one's own history and achievements remains incomplete without reflection on one's own guilt. Self-critical national feeling must not be abused for the purpose of goading other nationalist tendencies.

'Patriotism good, nationalism bad'

The Czechoslovak President and foremost writer, Vaclav Havel, has with his open and moving admission of guilt concerning the brutal persecution of the Sudeten Germans in Czechoslovakia after 1945 shown the world how one should proceed in order to 'root out the foolishness of national pride' (Herder). The era when worthy patriotism would turn into evil nationalism directed against one's neighbours lies behind us, according to West German President Richard von Weizsäcker, speaking recently in Prague.

Have we really come so far? At almost the same time there were reports coming from Warsaw that just two months after the noteworthy visit of the West German Chancellor, Helmut Kohl, German-Polish relations were in pieces due to the unfortunate statements by Kohl on Poland's Western borders and the timing of German unification. 'The Romanian parties are sailing with the wind of nationalism and it is already about as easy to have a rational discussion with many Romanians about the Hungarian question as it is to debate Kosovo with the Serbs,' said one shrewd observer in Bucharest recently.

The nationalist movements in this part of the world are traditionally carried along by emotions and not by the pragmatism of *Realpolitik*. After the gross errors and the monstrous crimes of the last few decades the development of political awareness lags behind political upheaval. Only in the institutions and in the public arena of civil society can national and minority problems be taken up and outdated 'images of the enemy' broken down. Let us hope that this time the ghosts of an evil past will not fill the empty souls of the people, particularly the young generation. Therefore it is the duty of the West, which for the people of Central and Eastern Europe embodies not only the economic miracle but also the stance of liberal democracy, to sound a timely warning everywhere against the revival of aggressive nationalism and all that it implies.

THE DUSTBIN OF ECONOMICS

Robert Kuttner

Karl Marx wrote millions of words on the transition from capitalism to communism. He forgot to write word one about the transition from communism to capitalism. More surprising, though he saw all social reality as economically determined, Marx wrote virtually nothing on how economies would actually function under communism—how scarce resources would be allocated, prices set, wages determined, capital allocated. He simply defined private ownership out of existence, and the issue of scarcity neatly vanished.

Indeed, among the many astonishing findings in the ongoing autopsy of communism is how little attention Communists paid to economics. Although Russia's central planners attempt the staggering task of fixing some 15 million individual prices, one can read a shelf of Soviet economics textbooks without ever encountering Supply or Demand. Half the world's people have suffered greatly for this little theoretical glitch.

Eastern Europe's unanticipated struggle to build capitalism raises its own unanswered questions. Should the transition be abrupt or slow? Will the birth agony only add to decades of economic affliction suffered under communism, and give capitalism a bad name? Might there still be such a thing as a "middle way"?

As the East struggles to rebuild, the West is squabbling over the symbolic meaning of communism's fall, projecting onto it our own political conflicts over contending versions of capitalism. If Poland's Solidarity government is pursuing the "shock therapy" model, isn't this a proxy victory for Thatcherism? If Vaclav Havel is going more slowly and retaining some public ownership, shouldn't Western European social democrats take heart? No, and no. In Eastern Europe the ideological meanings of "left" and "right" have all but reversed, and so have the implications of certain policy choices. Most Eastern Europeans seem to want to end up with some form of social market economy—say, of the German variety. But wherever they want to go, the categories of dogma current in the West are not likely to help them get there. If ever there was a time to let Poland be Poland, that time is now.

As a problem of both economic theory and practical economic reconstruction, the transition from a command economy to a market economy is unprecedented. As such it presents an extraordinary laboratory for economists, international bankers, repentant ex-Marxists, and assorted capitalist carpetbaggers plying their trades—and the lab rats are real people, desperately hoping for something better than they had under communism. In modern history there have been other welcome transitions from crushingly tyrannical systems to democracies. But Hitler, Mussolini, and Tojo, as well as Verwoerd, Franco, and Pinochet, whatever their other crimes, did not kill capitalism within their borders. They turned a private economy to their own ends, but essentials such as labor markets, a functioning price system, commercial banks, privately owned enterprises, and an entrepreneurial class all remained. After World War II constitutions had to be written anew, but it was not necessary to reinvent Japanese or German capitalism from scratch.

By contrast, the nations of Eastern Europe, the USSR, and China may not have built communism—a good Marxist would insist that what they built was a travesty of communism—but they surely snuffed out capitalism. Thus, in Soviet-style economies prices were not real prices, because they reflected neither the real cost of production nor the real demand for the product. Wages were not real wages, because for the purchase of many ordinary goods and services the money earned was useless. Interest rates too were bogus, because they did not reflect the real cost of capital or the real return on competing investments. Gosplan economies had an unfortunate habit of producing millions of size ten left shoes, because fundamental forms of economic discipline had ceased to operate. The miracle is that these economies functioned at all.

Before turning to the practical dilemmas of converting these pathetic systems to market economies, or to mixed ones, it is worth lingering for a moment on a nearly forgotten, half-century-old debate about "market socialism." In the 1930s it began dawning on some smart socialists who had been "over into the future" that the future was not working all that well. The most notable proponent of this school was a cosmopolitan Pole, Oskar Lange, who worked at Harvard, Berkeley, Chicago, and London as well as Krakow before World War II, and at Warsaw for twenty years afterward. A socialist widely acquainted with the classics, an admirer of Schumpeter as well as of Stalin, Lange hoped to reconcile neoclassical economics with Communist social ideals, as well as to achieve a politics of peaceful coexistence. This endeavor, it turned out, was like squaring the circle.

Lange set out to refute the claim of Ludwig von Mises, Friedrich Hayek, and Lionel Robbins that socialism was theoretically and practically unrealizable. Lange hoped that a large state sector could coexist with small private enterprises, whose pricing and market discipline would keep the state sector honest. This, in effect, was the inverse of the Western social-democratic idea of "yardstick competition," in which public enterprises would serve as a check on private ones. He urged that state planners pay far more careful attention to prices as the crucial signaling devices necessary for an efficient allocation of resources. But despite Lange's technically ingenious ideas for permitting socialist ownership to coexist with roughly accurate pricing—by simulating markets or using trial-and-error price-setting—no Communist society ever succeeded in following anything remotely like his blueprint. This, as Marx might have said, was no accident.

In the late 1960s Hungary did attempt a bold series of economic reforms aimed at radical decentralization. This coincided with mild political liberalization, and was welcomed, even in the West, as "goulash communism." The specifics included far more autonomy for plant managers and greater worker involvement. Enterprises were empowered to make their own deals with each other; farmers were given freedom to sell to state trading companies or on an open market; and very small-scale private entrepreneurs were tolerated, eventually adding up to some 15 percent of total economic output. Though the reforms stimulated growth, Hungary's leading reform economists, such as Janos Kornai, gradually (and presciently) concluded that the Hungarian middle way was doomed. Paradoxically, in an essentially capitalist economy, like France's or Sweden's, some state ownership, some subsidy, some wage and price regulation are tolerable, even beneficial. But in a command economy prices are so badly distorted, and existing political elites so dependent on maintaining the distortions, that real market socialism cannot function until the bureaucracy is swept away. In short, economic counterrevolution requires political counterrevolution—a Marxian insight turned on its head.

The British economist Alec Nove, in *The Economics of Feasible Socialism*, quoted a Czech Communist asking plaintively: "Why is a capitalist monopoly so much more enterprising than a socialist monopoly?" The answer, of course, is that under capitalism even monopolies, to stay monopolies, have to keep on their toes.

As Kornai's thinking evolved, it became clearer to him that the real impossibility of "market socialism" was more political than economic; the truly inefficient monopoly was not of production, but of political power. Lange's market socialism might be possible in the-

ory, but to replicate the pricing decisions of markets, the managers of the Central Planning Board would need the wisdom and public-mindedness of a Platonic philosopher king—so why not just have markets in the first place? But this, as Kornai is the first to recognize, is easier said than done.

The first problem is the political one. As marketization is painfully proceeding, the dead hand of the past (a useful Marxian phrase) remains, in the form of the state bureaucracy. Moreover, although freedom of speech, and even convertibility of currency, can be proclaimed overnight, the conversion of enterprises to private ownership, the creation of an entrepreneurial class of managers, the sorting out of which enterprises deserve to survive and which belong in history's dustbin (Marx again) all take time. Thus, though marketization, paradoxically enough, needs to be planned, the leftover bureaucracy is unlikely to plan it competently.

A related question is which reforms can feasibly be accomplished with a big bang, and which ones must be done over time. At first some Western economists argued that privatization of enterprises should come first, while budget and currency reform should come more gradually. But this turned out to have it backward. The Harvard economist Jeffrey Sachs, who has helped guide Poland's Solidarity government (policy advice is the one thing that has been successfully privatized), has argued, rather in the spirit of Kornai, that the most basic task, the one that logically precedes the others, is price reform. Only by exposing Eastern Europe's economies to full competition from the West will it be possible to determine what its physical plant, its workers, its currency, and so on are actually "worth" on world markets, since local prices are so thoroughly distorted. Beginning January 1, 1990, the Solidarity government devalued the zloty and made it freely convertible. Government subsidies were curtailed. Trade with the West was liberalized. Private enterprise was allowed.

At first blush the "big bang" approach seems gratuitously harsh. If Western Europe could gradually deregulate and privatize in the early post-World War II era under Marshall Plan auspices, why impose a sudden shock cure in the East, except for reasons of ideological purism? This was certainly my early reaction. However, Sachs argues persuasively that the analogy is misleading in two key respects. First, because a market economy was basically intact in Western Europe, there was not the economic need to obliterate absurd price distortions at a stroke. Second, given either an unbroken democratic tradition (in the case of Britain) or a political clean slate (in the case of Germany and Italy), there was no ancien régime still living a bureaucratic afterlife to complicate or sabotage the process of reconstruction.

Yet the big bang solution, even for such basics as currency convertibility and price reform, has its limits. Political democracy in Poland, Hungary, and Czechoslovakia is still fragile, and it scarcely exists yet in Romania and Bulgaria. Governments brought to power on public expectations of economic as well as political liberalization are understandably reluctant to impose new austerities. Their double bind is excruciating. If they continue subsidizing ultimately uncompetitive industries, they only waste resources and defer a day of reckoning. On the other hand, if they instantly subject antiquated local industry to the full force of global competition, millions of workers are idled, the balance of payments worsens, and political stability is undermined.

In this respect, the West has been extremely short-sighted in its attitude toward both public aid for reconstruction and the collection of debt incurred by the old regime. The United States spent trillions of dollars to contain communism militarily. Yet we are spending virtually nothing to help its victims rejoin the capitalist camp—despite their new allegiance to our own idea of the good society.

Sachs and Kornai, though they have been embraced by free market triumphalists, are at heart what Thatcher might call wets. Sachs, though a thoroughly mainstream economist when it comes to stabilization policy, marketization, budget discipline, currency convertibility, and kindred cold bath remedies, is something of a radical on the subject of debt relief. In order to make stabilization economically bearable, he argues, much of the prior debt of Eastern Europe should be written off. This advice, which he has also given to Latin America, has not made him popular with international bankers.

Kornai also argues passionately, in his 1990 book *The Road to a Free Economy* and in conversation, that though budget reform and price reform can and should be accomplished quickly, privatization will necessarily take time. "I hate the phrase 'shock therapy,'" he told me. "We don't apply the therapy for the sake of the shock. The shock is an inevitable side effect. Budget stabilization, price decontrol, currency convertibility—these should be done quickly, after very careful preparation. If you protract the process, you just prolong the pain. But balancing supply and demand is an iterative process. You can't close down in one day all the factories that don't show a profit. On the question of property ownership, I'm against quick solutions. We need to encourage the evolution of real owners, and this takes time. You can wipe out an entrepreneurial class much faster than you can re-create one.

"That cannot be done in a big bang. Some state-owned enterprises are true dinosaurs; others are not. In Budapest, we had a state barbers' collective. State enterprises like that are not dinosaurs—they're entirely artificial creatures, like King Kong. The problem is what to do with them. Stabilization can be done in a single jump. Change of ownership takes time. You know, some American liberals objected to my book as a laissez-faire book. That is completely wrong. In Eastern Europe, we need a huge injection of market forces because we have had a hyperactive state. I wouldn't say the same thing if I were French or German."

Of the former Comecon countries, Poland has gone the furthest fastest, and is in better shape than it seems. In the short term, the result of its shock therapy was to increase unemployment. Overnight Poland became a society with plenty of goods on the shelves that few could afford to buy. However, the plain economic inefficiencies of the old system were so extreme that offsetting gains came relatively quickly. Official statistics indicating a 30 percent drop in Polish living standards were grossly exaggerated, since they were based on "wages" paid in an artificially valued currency that could not find many products to buy. Real living standards were roughly flat last year. Unemployment is about 8 percent—roughly at Western European levels. And with a more realistic exchange rate and a freely traded zloty, Polish wages are so low by international standards that many Polish products are actually competitive on world markets. Since mid-1990 Poland has been enjoying an export boom, and has a positive trade balance with the West.

Hungary, with a less self-confident government, began a more ambiguous liberalization program only last month, and still retains some controls on its currency. Last year a premature privatization backfired. Several of Hungary's few competitive enterprises were sold off at prices now held to have been too low. Czechoslovakia too has proceeded more cautiously. Interestingly, public opinion polls indicate much deeper pessimism about the immediate economic future in these two countries, where the cold bath has not yet begun, than in Poland. The Gallup organization reported that only 17 percent of Poles expect this year to be worse than last, compared with 78 percent of Czechoslovaks and 84 percent of Hungarians.

As a question of both economic philosophy and social engineering, the most intriguing issue by far is how to structure economic ownership in post-Communist Central Europe. In principle, most property belonged to "the people"—indivisibly. Now, suddenly, shares are being divided up. But how?

Each alternative has benefits and costs. One option is simply to auction off state property to the highest bidder, as Poland abortively attempted. The problem is that foreigners make off with the healthiest enterprises, and potentially salvageable state firms are shut down for lack of current buyers. A second option is what is termed "spontaneous privatization": the existing managers and/or workers are given ownership of the firm. The trouble here is that it leads to an indefensible distribution of windfall prizes or hardships, and rewards malefactors of the ancien régime who happen to be in place as managers.

The richest and ultimately most promising approach is to realize something of the original promise of socialism—by privatizing in a manner that broadly distributes ownership. This is as close as actual societies will ever come to acting out the philosopher John Rawls's thought experiment on how wealth might be justly divided in a hypothetical society. One possibility is simply to conceive of Hungary, Poland, or Czechoslovakia as giant mutual funds, and to hand out shares of stock in a basket of state-owned enterprises to all citizens. Unlike the alternative of giving enterprises to their employees, this would diversify risk as well as ownership. Unlike putting them up for bid, it would spread wealth. Over time, as the actual enterprises reorganized and the post-Communist economy stabilized, shares could be traded or individually owned. Sachs favors a broad distribution of shares to workers, households, and financial institutions, as well as some auctions. Kornai favors many roads to privatization, including joint stock companies, family firms, even coops. All over the former Soviet bloc, teams of experts are conjuring up variations on this theme of broad private ownership. It is, in my view at least, the single most hopeful social invention that could emerge from the wreckage of communism.

Of course, thus far we have been treating the easiest cases—countries where relatively democratic and stable political regimes already exist and where a Lech Walesa or a Vaclav Havel retains enough prestige to make hard decisions that will cause temporary adversity. In Yugoslavia, the risk of political disintegration is overwhelming attempted economic reforms. In Romania, Bulgaria, and Albania, genuine economic reformers are not yet in charge.

The former German Democratic Republic also presents a special case. In principle, things there should be easiest. These people, after all, are still Germans; they know how to make things. They also have the advantage, seemingly, of having been absorbed by West Germany, which instantly solved the problems of currency convertibility, property law, macroeconomic stabilization, and so on, as well as instantly transfusing many billions of deutsche marks. But East Germany is a disaster. By flooding the former GDR with hard deutsche marks, Bonn created a temporary consumer boom. However, with the end of price controls and subsidies, no consumer in East Germany wants to buy anything made in East Germany, since everything made in the West is better and cheaper. As a result, millions of East Germans who used to make cheap, second-rate stuff for the East German economy are now losing their jobs. East Germany has become the ultimate welfare economy. Ironically, by bringing East German workers into its own high-wage labor market, Bonn has denied its former Communist provinces the possibility of competing on the one basis available to the rest of the bloc: working for very low wages.

The most puzzling special case is China. Although events in Eastern Europe and the Soviet Union have proved once and for all that "market socialism" is an oxymoron, the Chinese have managed a series of ingenious reforms that have tolerated fairly sizable market institutions, and reaped economic benefits accordingly, while still remaining a totalitarian Communist state. Thus Chinese farmers are free, once they have met the state production quota, to produce whatever they can and sell it on the free market. Chinese entrepreneurs, operating Dickensian garment factories or electronics sweatshops with up to a hundred employees, can produce for world markets, in joint ventures with Western capital, and keep a big chunk of their profits. China seems to blend the inhuman faces of socialism and early capitalism beautifully—though political unrest may eventually force a clearer choice.

And in the mother of totalitarian socialist republics, the moment of glasnost and perestroika has come—and gone. Compared with the USSR, Eastern Europe has it easy. Russia seems proof positive that political revolution must be completed before economic revolution can move forward. But political revolution has stalled. Four months ago, after a brief window of possibility, the Shatalin 500-day plan toward marketization and kindred radical reforms were shelved. Gorbachev's regime lacks the legitimacy to extract sacrifice on behalf of an emerging market economy, while it is also losing power to make the existing command economy heed its commands. Production is falling, in part because suppliers are refusing to deliver product for worthless rubles, and local commissars can no longer enforce compliance with the Plan. As a result the economy is degenerating into a barter system. "The crisis consists precisely in the fact that the old is dying and the new cannot be born," a shrewd Marxist, Antonio Gramsci, wrote some fifty years ago. The Soviet Union is on the verge of political disintegration—and because the political repression that would be required to hold it together would also defeat economic reform, disintegration may now be its only real hope.

Communism has turned out to be a century-long detour from the nagging question that perplexed Marx and a great many non-Marxists as well: how to reconcile efficient production with a bearable society. Communism produced neither. The dilemma, however, persists, and the question now will be fought out on the terrain where it always belonged—among variations of a liberal, market society. The collapse of communism doesn't end the debate about the appropriate boundaries between state, market, and civil society, any more than it ended History. On the contrary, it allows a more serious debate to emerge, free from the grotesque distraction of totalitarian communism, which chronically upstaged and embarrassed democratic leftists—or should have.

Despite the collapse of communism, laissez-faire capitalism remains a system vulnerable to instability, as well as injustice. Its paladin, the United States of America, is not exactly free of economic problems. Capitalism itself depends on pre-capitalist or extra-capitalist values such as loyalty and community to anchor the stage on which the dynamic market plays. Otherwise, as Marx wrote, all that is solid melts into air. The complex task of domesticating market society remains. The third way, however, is not reform communism but reform capitalism.

John Lloyd examines the complex set of problems confronting the emerging democracies of eastern Europe

The dilemmas of freedom

"There is no linear development in eastern European history, but rather a Sisyphus-like labour of ups and downs, of building and wrecking, where little depends on one's own ingenuity and perseverance."
— Professor Jerzy Jedlicky, Institute of History, Warsaw; speech to Woodrow Wilson International Centre for Scholars, Washington, June 1990.

"The prospects for freedom are secure; but those for democracy remain uncertain."
— Bronislaw Geremek, Solidarity parliamentary leader; Gazeta Wyborcza, May 1990.

The drama of the eastern European countries in the past year is of peoples who have been brought face to face with the sober truth about themselves. Having liberated themselves, wholly or in part, from the loosened grasp of a decaying system, they are now left to discover what is left for them, and what they are capable of.

Freedom comes with a terrifying legacy of technical backwardness – locked into dependence on the Soviet Union and their own low-quality non-markets; of vast debt; of ecological catastrophe; of a dearth of democratic political culture; of a habit of inversion and dependency; of the unfreezing of old ethnic and national rivalries and demands. The cauterising effects of their crisis eats away at the initial prestige of their liberators – Mr Lech Walesa, Mr Vaclav Havel and others of lesser lustre. There are no answers, only ever-more-insistent questions. And the questions expose hopeless dilemmas, where standing still is impossible and movement in any direction blocked by poverty, stagnation or popular resistance.

Three main sets of problems identified both by their own political and intellectual élites and by those in the west, confront them. The most fundamental is their poverty. Put at its simplest, these countries do not offer much. None, outside of the Soviet Union, has precious raw materials. None makes much that is saleable in developed markets, beyond knick-knacks and booze.

Inward investment has been slow, prompting a growing impatience in east European ministries which play host to analysts, accountants, experts, academics and journalists – but make few big sales. The last month of this year has seen one of the biggest: the initial 31 per cent stake taken by Volkswagen of Germany in the Czechoslovak car company Skoda (growing to 70 per cent by 1995). But Skoda is the best of the region's car producers, and Czechoslovakia's relatively good roads and central position make it relatively attractive. Nobody is queuing up for the steel mills, heavy engineering plants, tank factories, for the nauseous chemical complexes, nor for the coal mines which still clank on like something out of Zola. The new political élites began by looking to booming, post-totalitarian Spain as their model: now they fear they may just about make the standard of Mexico.

The year which began with more or less common assent that there was no alternative to a rapid adoption of market practices ends with the larger parts of these economies as statist as ever. The sheer size of the task seems to enforce delay: they do not want wholly to sell out to foreigners – even if buyers were waiting – but the domestic market does not have enough capital. The only people who know anything about running things were in the old nomenklatura: the new governments do not want to reward them, but have little choice. There is little notion of value of assets, and little in the way of banking institutions to provide support.

Every time they ask the question: "Where do we go?" they are met by the famous Irish answer: "Don't start from here."

This year has marked the end of the beginning; the coming two or three years will be the eye of the storm. The latest forecasts from Morgan Stanley investment bank show national income crashing – down 3 per cent this year and 10 per cent next in Czechoslovakia; 5.5 per cent this year and 5 per cent next in Hungary; 20 per cent this year (but up 4 per cent next) in Poland; and down 7 per cent this year and 10 per cent next in the Soviet Union. The fall in industrial output and investments in these countries follow the income trends: and so do the unemployment totals – with drops in employment over the next two years of 7.5 per cent in Hungary, 8.3 per cent in Poland, 6.3 per cent in Czechoslovakia and 9.8 per cent in the USSR. At its peak in 1994 unemployment may rise to 12m in the east European countries and 47m in the Soviet Union.

There are vast reserve armies of labour which everyone desperately hopes will not become actual armies which could be mobilised by would-be dictators or mafiosi to fill vacuums already yawning beneath the feet of the politicians. Between the collapse of one all-encompassing ideological system and the lack of an alternative secular – or religious – order, lie 1,000 hatreds and feuds which only require mobilisation.

This throws up the next knot of problems: will the political structures be stable enough to provide a bulwark against the economic shocks, and be able to continue the economic transition? The year ends with government turmoil in Hungary, with some loss of the authority of Civic Forum in Czechoslovakia and with the election of the ambiguous figure of Mr Lech

Walesa as president in Poland; with continued stalemates in Bulgaria, Romania and Yugoslavia. Their common feature is only this: that none can rely on a bedrock of civil political culture which they can assume will tolerate reversals or, if they cannot, peacefully vote for an alternative.

In asking the east to become like the west, people in the west easily forget how much most of their government, most of the time, is about how to increase purchasing power. It is not about the core and inflammatory matters of nation, or ethnicity, nor the nature of the state itself. Nor, more practically, is there much concern for the loyalty of the bureaucracy, nor a problem of the competence of the state apparatus.

But the new governments of the east, which in their early days of office sometimes appeared blessed in their ability to write on clean sheets of paper, have discovered that the lack of these institutional constraints which channel and direct and often cramp government, is not so much a lack of unwanted constraint as a lack of needed institutions.

Mr Vaclav Klaus, the innovative Czechoslovak finance minister, says he has a mere handful of expert helpers who understand what he wishes to do. Mr Jacek Kuron, the Polish labour minister, has had to attempt to construct a chain of unemployment and social security offices from scratch, with neither domestic blueprints nor experienced staff. They are also faced with a unique problem: a relatively sophisticated people who have for some years now seen and admired western living standards on television, freed from the political restraints which kept them apart from the west, but who are now confronted with a barrier which was previously disguised: the just-as-effective economic barriers. The effect of this on the west has been to engender a certain shamefacedness, even guilt: for where it could properly, if rhetorically, make one with the masses oppressed under totalitarianism, it can do little for their oppression under poverty. But in the east, the effect may be murderous for the new politics.

Mr Gavril Popov, the mayor of Moscow, wrote in August of this year that in the new democracies emerging in eastern Europe and the Soviet Union, there were "contradictions" developing between the policies designed to lead to market relations (and thus greater inequalities than presently exist) on the one hand, and the people whose revolts ushered in the governments now instituting these policies.

"The masses long for fairness and economic equality. And the further the process of transformation goes, the more acute and the more glaring will be the gap between those aspirations and the economic realities . . . the interest (in economic transformation) is based not on an understanding of the new but on a hatred of the old — a destructive motive."

Mr Popov voices the central dilemma of the radicals in eastern Europe and the Soviet Union. It is easy to find, among even the bitterest critics of communism within its former citadels, men and women who fear the radical stratification of a society which (beneath the top layer of "them") was economically roughly equal, and in which workers could earn as much as the educated and the descendants of the old bourgeoisie.

It has been widely noted, in and out of these societies, how much envy, fiddling, black marketeering and frustration was bred by this imposed equality. Less stressed has been the concomitant sense of all being in the same boat. And even where this not also true, envy — and its active companion, levelling — now has huge supplies on which to feed, as the *nouveaux riches* of the east, operating usually in semi- or complete illegality, usually linked with and often drawn from the old nomenklatura, flaunt their wealth behind the padded wheels of their Mercedes.

This explains the continuing existence, and in many areas, growing strength, of the "discredited" trade unions. Neither in Poland nor in Hungary, nor in the Soviet Union, have these gone out of business: on the contrary, they act as a focus for what Popov has called a "left populism", and now, after decades of crushing independent action, they instigate and lead proletarian protest.

The last complex of problems concerns the west: what can it do? This past year has seen emerge, clearly, what is now the standard response: a wish, driven by fears of instability on the eastern borders of western Europe, to underpin the transition to democracy and the market — coupled with a reiteration of the doleful but inescapable injunction that the "return to Europe" on the part of the eastern European countries must be effected largely by these states themselves: that is, that the sacrifices necessary to achieving a transition must come out of their own peoples' skins. All the loose talk of adopting models — the Scandinavian (for its high level of social protection); the Spanish (for its transition from authoritarianism); the British (for its privatisations) — is now discredited. There are pointers and examples, but the odysseys of the east have no counterparts elsewhere: they will create their own "models".

Professor John Kenneth Galbraith — still the leading thinker of the left in the US — describes in a forthcoming book the neo-liberal economic policies of the past decade in the west as "the politics of comfort". This was a period in which the economic enfranchisement of a vast mass of lower-middle and working-class people fed through into political demands for lower taxes and for a lesser emphasis on welfare and public provision.

Just as the west Europeans recognise this new politics, and as their parties of left and right accommodate to it, so they are joined by Europeans whose politics are those of discomfort, anxiety and tremulous hope: a space in which, as Mr Bronislaw Geremek has observed, freedom seems to be possible but democracy is less so.

Those who claim that the west has an obligation to assist, speak cant. There was never either an explicit nor an implicit promise of assistance. No one with any responsibility said it would be easy. The spur for the west is self-interest: the self-interest in avoiding a flood of supplicant refugees, or of a new reaction and renewed military adventurism, especially in the Soviet Union: coupled with the convenience of seeing a market-democratic system, with common mechanisms and reflexes, extended, and so increasinf the likelihood that trade will grow and reducing the chance of war. Goodness, as that leading American theorist Mae West observed, has nothing to do with it.

This coming year will test how far the west can be enlightened in the pursuit of self-interest: a much deeper and more bitter test awaits the newly- or partly-free.

The Soviet Union and China: Two Communist Giants and the Dilemma of Reform

- The Erosion of the Soviet Union (Article 43)
- Russian Political Culture (Article 44)
- Soviet Upheaval (Articles 45–47)
- China (Articles 48–49)

In the 1970s it was common on both the political Left and Right to speak about a governing crisis in the industrial democracies, but careful observers did not overlook that Communist-ruled countries suffered from other and potentially far more serious governability problems. Still, these systems appeared to be under tight political control, and hardly anyone was prepared for their upheavals at the end of the next decade.

Looking back, it seems inevitable that at some point the Communist leaders would have had to acknowledge that their societies suffered from problems that could not be dismissed as simply minor setbacks on the road from socialism to communism. Yet it was only after 1985, when Mikhail Gorbachev became leader of the Soviet Union, that Moscow officially began to concede that Soviet reality suffered from problems of a deep-seated structural character.

It is this basic recognition that underlies some major Soviet reforms in both policy and ideology in recent years. In effect, Moscow appears to have given up crucial parts of what Robert Kaiser has called the great "Soviet pretense," namely the official belief in the inherent superiority of this system and its ultimate triumph over Western forms of government, society, and economy. One result has been an *authority crisis* that has undermined the ideological coherence and self-confidence of many Communist parties. Another consequence is the scuttling of much ideological dogma in favor of a new *pragmatism* that shows up in a willingness to borrow ideas that have worked in nonsocialist countries.

The effects have been most radical in the neighboring states of Central and Eastern Europe, where the great political upheaval of 1989–1990 resulted in the ruling Communists either abandoning power altogether or beginning to share it meaningfully with non-Communists. In effect, this was a revolution that brought an end to several of the party dictatorships that the Soviet Union had imposed on this region after World War II.

It must not be overlooked that Moscow played a crucial role in the final act of this drama, as it had at the beginning. As leader of the Soviet Union, Mikhail Gorbachev indicated that his government had abandoned the *Brezhnev doctrine,* according to which Moscow was committed to rescue any faltering Communist governments, if necessary by political and military intervention. This important foreign policy doctrine had received its name in 1968, when the Soviet Union stepped in to crush reform socialism in Czechoslovakia, but it had been practiced long before in East Germany (1953) and Hungary (1956). It later had served as justification for the Soviet intervention in Afghanistan in 1979, as well as insurance for the Polish Army when it took power and outlawed the Solidarity movement.

Gorbachev also seemed to encourage *reform* more directly, as when he warned hard-line East German rulers in October of 1989 that history punishes those who are tardy—in other words, those who fail to change in time. Such signals played an important function in triggering the breakup of the Communist hold on Central and Eastern Europe, even though that was hardly what Gorbachev had intended. In the case just cited, for example, he could hardly have foreseen that a month later the Berlin Wall would be opened, or that this would lead to a political dynamic that resulted in Germany's unification only a year later.

Unlike their counterparts in Central and Eastern Europe (with the notable exception of Yugoslavia), the ruling Communist parties in the Soviet Union and China came to power by their own efforts. Thus these regimes did not suffer from the special legitimacy problem of appearing to be a foreign product, imposed by an outside force. (Important exceptions to this generalization are many annexed regions, such as the three small Baltic countries and Tibet, where Communist rule is widely identified with the imperial domination of Moscow and Beijing respectively.) This circumstance may help explain why the Soviet and Chinese parties have not fully lost the will to rule. But both face some serious problems of governance.

Mikhail Gorbachev came to power in 1985 with a determination to reform and modernize his country. He soon recognized the need for a thorough *perestroika* or restructuring of the Soviet economy and he encouraged a relatively open discussion of some of the country's social and economic troubles. This policy of *glasnost* (openness) released a torrent of bottled-up grievances. The government made the new emphasis on accountability more credible when it acknowledged and condemned the brutalities of the Stalin era and the incompetence of the Brezhnev years. Before long, it even became possible to criticize publicly some hitherto sacrosanct Leninist positions.

Ironically, Gorbachev's troubles spring largely from some unwanted consequences of his own reform policies. Thus *glasnost* and democratization have allowed long-held resentments to surface, reflected in the surge of ethnic conflicts and nationalist tensions that now divide the Soviet people.

The task of building an overarching sense of common Soviet identity is complicated by the fact that many ethnic groups are not dispersed throughout the country, as in the United States. Instead, they form regionally dominant groups with their own cultures, languages, and territorial claims. In theory, an all-embracing identification with the Soviet Union could provide them with an additional or complementary sense of belonging. In reality, however, membership in separate and sometimes rival nationalities has been a hindrance to the development of a shared Soviet identity.

Gorbachev's other major problem is the rapid economic decline of his country. Reform of the economy had been the original reason for his other reforms. So far, however, Gorbachev has failed to deliver a comprehensive program and strategy for economic reform.

Political reform in the Soviet Union has gone much further, but it is still fraught with ambiguity, as the article by Lars Lih emphasizes. Between 1988 and late 1990, Gorbachev changed some central political institutions and brought about a major shift in the balance of power within the government, as well as between it and the Communist party. The possibility of a political backlash from the hard-liners, who now dominate the party, seems increasingly likely.

The main features of the institutional reform are as follows: A *Congress of People's Deputies,* with 2,250 members serving 5-year terms, has supreme power under the constitution. But it meets briefly only once or twice a year and probably will be important less for its own power than as the body for choosing the full-time legislature, called the *Supreme Soviet,* and the first chief executive or *president.* Only the president's initial election to a five-year term will be made by the Congress; thereafter it will be by popular vote for a maximum of two five-year terms. The president has considerable powers, of decree and repeal, and the office is roughly comparable to that of the strong presidency in France's Fifth Republic. Subject to confirmation by the Supreme Soviet, the president selects a premier, a cabinet, members of the Supreme Court and members of the Security Council, a new and possibly important body responsible for dealing with defense, security, emergencies, and the maintenance of domestic "stability, law, and order." Constitutional changes in 1990 also gave a stronger emphasis to the *federal* structure of the Soviet Union by providing for a *Federation Council* to coordinate between the central and republican as well as regional authorities "on matters affecting their interests." This anticipates a new treaty of union prepared by Gorbachev.

The Supreme Soviet consists of two chambers of equal standing. One of the two chambers, the Soviet or Council of the Union, reflects the population as a whole. It is drawn from the deputies elected on a constituency basis and from the public organizations, taking into account the number of people in each region or republic. The other chamber, the Soviet or Council of Nationalities, reflects the country's ethnic diversity. It is drawn from the deputies elected from the larger national-territorial constituencies and from the public organizations, according to a formula that will ensure representation for all ethnic groups large enough to have autonomous districts.

At the top of this new governmental structure, the Presidium of the Supreme Soviet can act on many matters when the Supreme Soviet is not in session. This is probably where real governmental power is located, insofar as it is now becoming separable from the party organization. The Presidium is headed by the chair of the Congress of People's Deputies—the new president—and will include his deputy as well as the chairs of the Soviet of the Union and the Soviet of Nationalities, the chairs of the Supreme Soviets from the country's 15 republics, and other high Soviet officials.

The political reforms have now gone even further by reducing the dominant role of the Communist party in public affairs. In a series of steps, Gorbachev has taken aim at the tradition of what was sometimes called dual government, in which the departments of the party's Central Committee used to fill a kind of quasi-state role by overseeing and frequently directing even the details of normal government operations. Gorbachev's plan appears to be that the party should occupy an important role in Soviet public life, but not an unrivaled or omnipresent one. By reducing its involvement in what are often administrative matters of government, he apparently expects it to focus more on the political work of developing theoretical perspectives, setting broad policy priorities, and providing popular leadership and support. Most important, the Soviet Union now has an embryonic multiparty system that could become a venue for further development toward genuine political pluralism in the Soviet Union.

But it can no longer be assumed that the Communist party of the Soviet Union will gracefully accept such a basic shift in the domestic balance of power. It has been surprisingly supportive, or at least tolerant, of Gorbachev's major reforms during most of his first five years in office. There are now unmistakable signs that the patience of some powerful groups and individuals within the party has reached its limit. Sometimes known as "hardliners," these critics have already applied a brake on some of the plans favored by reformers within and outside the party. They emphasize the existential primacy of restoring socialist order in the face of a looming chaos produced by social, economic, and ethnic problems. It is clear that they are uncomfortable with the political pluralism that has reduced the role of the Communist party. As a result, the coming year promises to be a very difficult one for the reform forces in the Soviet Union. It is indicative of their plight that Gorbachev's rival Boris Yeltsin and other reformers who have criticized Gorbachev for not going nearly far or quickly enough in the pursuit of change have begun to rally to his support as the lesser of evils.

China is the homeland of more than one-fifth of the world's population. Here Mao Zedong was able to lead the Communists to power in large part because he refused to follow the Russian model of revolution. Instead he devised a strategy for a prolonged armed struggle, which focused on mobilizing support in the countryside, rather than attempting to capture control of the few big cities with their industrial workers. Once the peasant-based Communist army had brought him into power, Mao continued to show an unorthodox bent in pursuing the socialist transformation of his country. His radical experiments imposed enormous psychic and physical costs on the millions of people caught up in the wrenching changes. Today specialists generally agree that his policies had catastrophic consequences for the country's development.

Mao died in 1976, and the radical left faction of the Chinese Communist party was removed from power in the same year. A reform-oriented leadership, headed by Deng Xiaoping, soon got busy undoing much of Mao's legacy in a series of policy changes designed to modernize the country. It put an end to the political campaigns to mobilize the masses. In their place came a domestic tranquility such as China had not known for over half a century. But the regime encountered a basic dilemma: it wished to maintain tight Leninist controls over politics and society while steering the country toward a relatively decontrolled market economy. When a new openness developed in Chinese society, comparable in some ways to the pluralism encouraged by Gorbachev's *glasnost* policy, it ran into determined opposition among more hard-line Communist leaders, especially after the spread of student demonstrations in early December of 1986.

In January 1987, Deng's heir apparent, Hu Yaobang, was driven to resignation in what observers evaluated to be a reassertion of tighter political controls over society, cultural life, and the economy. Toward the end of the year, however, Deng Xiaoping appointed another reformer, Zhao Ziyang, as heir to the political leadership of the vast country. Most observers at that point expected a continued relaxation of controls. This prospect has been crushed, at least for the time being. Zhao was purged in May 1989, and in the following month Deng ordered troops to crush student demonstrations for democracy in Beijing's Tiananmen Square. Hundreds of protesters were killed, and a period of brutal repression of political dissidents set in.

Looking Ahead: Challenge Questions

How does Gorbachev's assessment of his own country and its problems differ from that of his predecessors, and what consequences has he drawn for reform? What is meant by *glasnost*, *perestroika*, and democratization in the Soviet Union, and how has Gorbachev sought to implement them?

Do you see evidence that the members of the Soviet legislature are beginning to assert themselves as elected parliamentarians? How has the role of the Communist party been reduced under recent reforms in the Soviet Union?

Why are major economic and social reforms apparently more difficult to achieve in the Soviet Union than changes in the institutions of government? How does the Soviet Union differ from the United States as a multiethnic society, and why do its conflicts seem more difficult to resolve?

What were the aims of the student demonstrations in Tiananmen Square? How can the government's crackdown be understood as part of an overall reassertion of tighter controls on society? Discuss why, more than four decades after the founding of the People's Republic of China, its balance sheet is a very mixed one.

GORBACHEV'S GATHERING STORM

Michael Parks

Michael Parks, The Times' Moscow bureau chief,
won the Pulitzer Prize for international reporting in 1987.

It was past dusk on a late winter afternoon by the time Marina Kizilova got to Food Store No. 297 in suburban Moscow to buy a few pounds of potatoes on her way home from her job as a chemical engineer. She waited about 10 minutes in the slow-moving line, but just before her turn came, the store ran out. "*Nyet, nyet, nyet,*" the salesclerk said. "We have no more potatoes."

"I snapped—I just snapped," Kizilova says, recalling how she launched into an angry denunciation of President Mikhail S. Gorbachev, the Soviet government, the Communist Party, Marxism-Leninism, socialism, the party and government apparat and finally the store's employees, whom she suspected were hiding sacks of potatoes for themselves.

For her, this was not just another shortage, an extension of the chronic Soviet shortages of beef and pork, fish, sausage, cabbage, onions and carrots. Potatoes, as much as bread, are a staple of the Russian winter diet, and the housewife's perennial question of "What do I cook for dinner?" suddenly became, there in the gloomy dusk in front of that dingy, barren grocery, the much more serious problem of "How will my family live?"

As far as Marina Kizilova was concerned, when Food Store No. 297 ran out of potatoes, Gorbachev ran out of luck. "Curse as we might those dark days of [late president Leonid I.] Brezhnev, we never ran out of potatoes," she says. Kizilova has calmed down—she was hoarse for nearly a week after her diatribe—but her bitter fury at Gorbachev smolders. "When everyone else began to criticize him, oh, a year and a half or two ago, I defended him," says Kizilova, 49. "I had faith in him. But I've lost all that. After six years of *perestroika*, democratization and *glasnost*, nothing has improved, and everything is getting worse. Only a fool would hope now, only a fool."

As the Soviet Union emerges from winter, always its season of discontent, the mood across the country is one of hopelessness intensified by anger, of helplessness deepened by betrayal and, in the country's endless lines, of just plain hatred, all of it focused on Gorbachev. The man who was lauded around the world and awarded the Nobel Peace Prize for his reforms and the changes that they have worked in international relations is confronted at home by the prospect of total failure.

Radicals, conservatives and people in the street believe that *perestroika* destroyed a political and economic system that was functioning badly—but was at least *functioning*—when Gorbachev came to power and that he has failed to construct a better system as promised. Consequently, he faces three interlocking crises that, like a set of intricate equations, must be solved simultaneously if they are to be solved at all.

The Soviet economy is disintegrating far faster than even the most pessimistic analysts had forecast. This resource-rich nation is increasingly incapable of feeding, clothing or housing its 290 million people. At the same time, the political structure, dissolv when the Communist Party yielded its monopoly on power March, 1990, and replaced by weak, ineffectual new institution has all but collapsed.

Most cataclysmic of all, the Soviet Union is breaking up. T Baltic republics of Estonia, Latvia and Lithuania declared th independence a year ago, and Georgia is also likely to secede. the remaining regions, nationalism is growing, with the great challenge coming from the vast Russian republic, whose popu president, Boris N. Yeltsin, wants real power for the republics, ambition seconded by 70% of his republic's voters in unprecedented referendum conducted in March.

Gorbachev is determined to prevent further disintegration, f fear it could lead to massive upheavals and even civil war. But wi radicals clamoring for bolder reforms, conservatives demandi order and discontent flaring on the streets, he may have or months to pull his country out of its deepening crises or see l leadership and reforms consumed by them.

The strain is showing. No longer the buoyant optimist of two three years ago, Gorbachev is clearly tired and emotiona drained. His encounters with foreign leaders, Soviet lawmake and ordinary citizens lack his past energy; at a meeting with Briti Prime Minister John Major a few weeks ago, Gorbachev's fatig was all the more apparent as Major, 13 years his junior, showed t kind of zest for which Gorbachev was once famous. An Gorbachev's 60th birthday, on March 2, only prompted furth discussions of how long he can remain in power.

Massive rallies outside the Kremlin, some of the largest since t 1917 Bolshevik Revolution, have demanded that Gorbachev qu Yeltsin, his chief rival, has launched a campaign for his resignatio Posters on the street mock Gorbachev, and comedians in cabare tell off-color jokes about him.

"The May 1 demonstrations could turn into an uprising t year," predicts Andrei Kravchuk, an organizer of a ne independent trade union at a Moscow auto plant. "Last year," l says, "people just shouted 'Shame!' and whistled as they passed [Gorbachev and other leaders]; this year, it might take a division KGB troops to protect them. After years of Marxist rhetoric abo the 'fist of the proletariat,' these guys are about to feel it."

In late February, on the 73rd anniversary of the Red Arm 50,000 soldiers and policemen marched to the square just outsi the Kremlin, their heavy winter overcoats like battle armor as the moved in a phalanx through the streets of Moscow. Most middle-ranking officers, they were joined by their commanders– the defense minister, the interior minister and the head of t KGB. "There is anarchy in our country, and we understand th the army is the only stabilizing force," poet Mikhail Nozhkin to the rally. The warning to Gorbachev was clear: Either resto order, or the army will.

"Everyone feels every day that life is getting harder, the burde heavier and hope dimmer," says Otto Latsis, one of the country most respected economists. "At the same time, everyone wan someone to blame. So, some people blame the radicals, others th bureaucrats; some blame the party, others the black marketeer But Gorbachev stands out as the man who should have foreseen a and forestalled all. And so he gets the most blame."

I. Power Struggles

"Does the president's power extend beyond the Kremlin? Well, it all depends. . . ."

—A Gorbachev assistant

The imposing edifice known as the "White House" rises high on the embankment above the Moscow River. Built to house the proliferating bureaucracy of the Brezhnev era, the headquarters of the Russian Federation was once considered a vulgar joke—so much white marble hiding so much decay. Last spring, in a transformation emblematic of the vast changes in Soviet politics, it was taken over by Boris Yeltsin and his coalition of liberal and radical reformers, who had just won a majority of seats in the Russian Congress of People's Deputies.

Yeltsin, for many, has come to represent the future. His appeal stems directly from his break with the old Communist system. Ousted from the party's ruling Politburo in 1987, Yeltsin later won two stunning election victories and then last summer walked out of the Communist Party. His popularity has increased as Gorbachev's has declined. Reviled by most of the Soviet news media, bugged by the KGB and denounced by Gorbachev, Yeltsin gains simply by standing up to the Communist Party, attracting the reformers who, two or three years ago, were Gorbachev supporters.

Nearly a quarter-million people gathered outside the Kremlin March 10 to cheer Yeltsin's declaration of "war" on the Soviet leadership and his call for a united democratic front to challenge the Communist Party's stubborn hold on the government. Their chant of "Resign! Resign!" echoed off the Kremlin's red-brick walls. Gorbachev had long ago lost the support of radicals; now he was losing that of the middle class.

Most mornings at the Yeltsin White House, there's a long line of callers. "They are much like inventors with brilliant new gadgets, except these are ideas on how to move the country forward," says Ruslan Khasbulatov, a visionary but wily economist who serves as Yeltsin's vice president. "What they all have in common is the closed doors they are meeting in the central government."

While criticizing Gorbachev's slowness to put his pledges of economic reform into practice, Yeltsin's government is leading the way with privatization of state-owned enterprises, the distribution of land to farmers and a network of deals with other republics to replace the old state plans.

Yeltsin sees Gorbachev's end drawing closer. "Either democracy will be extinguished, or else we democrats will not merely survive but triumph this year," the burly Siberian told a recent rally.

Conservatives also sense Gorbachev's vulnerability, and with the backlash building against him, they have gained political muscle. They contend that Gorbachev's reforms started on the right foot—but then he decided in 1988 to break with socialism and its principles of common ownership and state planning. He compounded these mistakes, they say, by trying to hasten political and economic change without a clear, cohesive strategy.

"A civil war is beginning in this country," Col. Viktor Alksnis warned ominously one day between sessions of the Supreme Soviet, the country's legislature, where he and other conservatives increasingly shape policy. "A civil war in a nuclear state? Yes, it is quite possible. Even probable, I would say, unless strong measures are immediately taken to preserve the Soviet Union as a state and to preserve its political and economic system."

Known as the "black colonel" for his dark hair, leather jackets and penchant for political plotting, Alksnis, 40, was until a year ago an obscure air force engineer from Latvia. So great has been the resurgence of the right that Alksnis, a leader of the conservative parliamentary bloc Soyuz, now ranks as a major political figure.

It was a threat from Alksnis last November that forced the Kremlin showdowns between liberals and conservatives and confirmed the president's swing to the right. Gorbachev had lost the confidence of the armed forces, Alksnis declared, and Soyuz would give him no more than 30 days to correct his course.

In dramatic, late-night meetings, Gorbachev complied, according to liberal advisers who found themselves outnumbered. A tougher line was taken on law and order, the interior minister was fired, the military cracked down in the Baltics, conservatives were promoted to critical posts, and planned economic reforms, already scaled down, were modified further. By the end of the month, Gorbachev had confessed to a Moscow party meeting that he was "guilty before the working class" for mistakes made in *perestroika*. It was one of the biggest setbacks that liberals had suffered since Gorbachev came to power. Radicals argue that Gorbachev encouraged this conservative comeback by failing to accelerate reforms when they ran into opposition.

All of which Gorbachev acknowledges, blaming a "severe struggle for power" over the past year and a half and calling for support of his "centrism." But that path satisfies no one, for it seems like more dithering and drifting. Gorbachev, when pressed for an outline of his plans, can only reply vaguely. At a March forum of economists and social scientists, he blandly preached patience and asked for "constructive" advice.

II. A Pig-Iron Panic

"What people now see is what economists warned was coming—a systemic collapse."

—Political scientist Anatoly Butenko

Storage Subdepot No. 6 of the First Moscow Construction Trust had slumbered through most of the winter, snow covering the unused machinery as it awaited the mid-April thaw, when construction would resume. Suddenly on a Monday morning in March, two work crews arrived and, with a flourish of government orders, loaded almost everything metal onto waiting trucks and then hustled it off to the smelter.

The Soviet Union, the world's largest steel producer, was running out of pig iron, and the government had launched a nationwide drive to collect scrap metal to keep its steel mills in production. A worthy goal, but bizarre when one considers that, with a long list of fundamental reforms on its agenda, the government had made the scrap-metal drive its immediate priority.

The reason, as complex as it was simple, gave full evidence of the country's political as well as economic fragility. Angered by the government's failure to honor promises to improve their living conditions, more than 300,000 coal miners had gone on strike. The impact was almost immediate: The metallurgical industry began to shut down its furnaces, railways cut back their long-haul trains, and power plants reduced electricity supplied to factories in many cities.

Most worrisome, however, was the closure of steel plants, which feed the military-industrial complex. But with enough scrap metal, the plants could continue operating, satisfying the powerful military-industrial managers.

The pig-iron panic is just the latest in a series of pitiful, madcap measures to shore up an economy that, just two years ago, was estimated by the CIA to be the world's second largest. Today, it is collapsing at an accelerating speed, unchecked by attempts to halt its downward spiral.

Bread shortages are now routine in a country where bread is not only a staple but also a symbol of well-being. Despite a record grain harvest last autumn, the food shortage is now so serious that Vladimir Tikhonov, the country's leading agricultural economist, estimates that 40 million citizens, about 14% of the population, are gravely malnourished. Nearly half of the 240-million-ton grain harvest rotted for lack of transport and storage capacity, as did about 60% of the vegetable crop. The only dependable food supplies come from the West (including expensive grain from America), China and India.

The country's GNP is likely to decline by a staggering 11.6% this year, four times the rate of last year, and perhaps by as much as 16%, according to forecasts by the State Planning Committee. With steep drops in industrial production certain, store shelves will be virtually empty except for imports, and a poor harvest is feared because planting preparations during the winter were so disorganized.

Prominent political scientist Anatoly Butenko explains the hierarchy of hopelessness: "Farmers withhold their food from the market because the rubles they get buy nothing. Factories want to be paid in dollars or other goods for the same reason. Half the goods produced in this country now reach consumers through other than the regular wholesale-retail system. All this barter, in turn, reduces the production of steel, chemicals, machinery and parts, and that reduces the production of finished goods. And, given the centralization of our economy, problems in a key industry can bring the country to a sputtering halt."

III. Altered States

"The Soviet Union is a dying empire. None of us wants to die with it."
—Latvian President Anatolijs Gorbunovs

From Estonia, Latvia and Lithuania, from Armenia and Georgia beyond the Caucasus Mountains, from Moldava and the Ukraine, those republics that can are trying to secede; those that cannot are declaring "sovereignty" and rejecting control by the central government, some even threatening to print their own money. "How can you blame those who want to get out?" Nikolai Y. Petrakov, formerly Gorbachev's economic adviser, remarked last month. "Had we done a half-decent job on economic reforms and matched that with real autonomy and decentralization, we would not be locked in this showdown."

With conflicts under way in more than 10 regions and at least 26 nationalist militias carrying arms, the country's "Lebanization" has already begun, many believe. Deaths in ethnic clashes over the past three years number in the hundreds, but in the chaos the Interior Ministry has lost count. Lithuanians, like their neighbors in Estonia and Latvia, were determined that their secession, proclaimed a year ago after the first free elections in more than 50 years, would be peaceful. "We want no violence; it is not our way," says Algimantas Cekuolis, a leader of the Lithuanian nationalist movement Sajudis. But Soviet troops moved against Lithuanian activists early this year on Kremlin orders, killing 19. Lithuania, too, is now an armed camp.

The dissolution of the Soviet Union is very close, many fear. "We lost, if you will, our 'empire' in Eastern Europe, and that has hardened the resolve of our generals not to lose our 'internal empire,'" says Vitaly I. Goldansky, a leading scientist and member of the Congress of People's Deputies. "The situation is quite desperate as the separatist and nationalist pressures on Gorbachev bring counterpressures from the conservatives. The issue is much bigger than Lithuanian independence—we are talking about the viability of the Soviet state."

Making resolution of this crisis his first priority, Gorbachev warned in the Byelorussian capital of Minsk in March: "Disintegration and separation simply cannot, under any circumstances, happen in our country. If we start splitting, there will be . . . a dreadful war."

Gorbachev, encountering strong opposition in his efforts to fashion a new Union Treaty to bind the republics together, asked for a mandate from voters last month in the country's first national referendum. Despite the refusal of six republics to participate, he got the popular endorsement he wanted for a union that would be both "preserved" and "renewed." But the crisis has grown beyond the ability of a simple referendum to renew people's faith in the Soviet Union and Gorbachev's leadership.

IV. Lost Promises

"There are forces pushing us hard toward civil war."
—Mikhail S. Gorbachev

Another crisis is now upon the Soviet Union—a crisis of confidence. The optimism born with *perestroika* has given way to a conviction that nothing has changed—except for the worse.

Doomsday scenarios abound. The Soviet press speculates endlessly about military coups, ways that Gorbachev might be ousted by party hard-liners and conspiracies by "neo-Bolsheviks" to seize power. Conservatives see parts of the country breaking away, workers storming through the streets, the army splitting—and civil war looming. Liberals, too, fear civil war, with the government sending troops to subdue secessionist republics or put down strikes, as it has increasingly in the past three years. Any conflict could quickly overflow into Eastern Europe, it is said, and unleash a flood of millions of refugees across the continent. A dozen new nuclear powers could be created if breakaway republics took possession of the Red Army's weapons. The United States and its allies might feel compelled to intervene.

" 'Civil war' is a metaphor for a great political catastrophe," Alexander Tsipko, a leading political philosopher, explains. "It means tremendous upheaval across the country, it means famine and hunger and economic collapse, it means even foreign invasions again. 'Civil war' is like a prophecy of all the bad things that will happen to us if we do not find our way out of this crisis."

Proposed remedies vary with the analysis of what has gone wrong. Radical reformers, who last autumn proposed an accelerated, 500-day push to establish a market economy, argue that only such a campaign can free the country from the grip of the system built by dictator Josef V. Stalin. Conservatives, while accepting the need for further change, say the reforms must be based on socialist principles and carefully managed.

If the Communist Party still had its monopoly on power as the "vanguard of the proletariat," the old Politburo would make the decision in secret, and if it were wrong the men who made it might be purged or simply retired. But the old decision-making mechanism has been destroyed, and the fledgling democratic institutions are too weak and inexperienced to solve such momentous problems.

With the country spinning out of control, people and politicians alike turn to the comfort of folklore: the "good czar" solution. A figure of almost mythic proportions in Russian history, a good czar modernizes and Westernizes and yet preserves the national character; he rules with a firm hand, but justly and for the good of the nation. His power is absolute but used with restraint.

Gorbachev has zigzagged unpredictably and slowly, pressured on one side by liberals who still hope he will promote their reforms and on the other by conservatives who demand a "strong hand." There are alternatives to Gorbachev and his brand of "centrism"—such scenarios range from a military coup to a Yeltsin election victory—but each brings other, greater problems and fails to resolve the deeper crises. Even amid the present pessimism, even with the hatred seething in the lines of angry shoppers, Gorbachev remains, paradoxically, the Soviet Union's best hope for a modern-day "good czar."

THE RUSSIAN CHARACTER

Before he can reform the economy, Gorbachev must purge his country of its inbred escapism, lethargy and envy.

Hedrick Smith

Hedrick Smith has been both Moscow and Washington bureau chief for The New York Times. *This article is adapted from "The New Russians," to be published by Random House in December.*

One Saturday evening, when I was working late, alone, in a Moscow office, I heard a knock at the door. I couldn't imagine who it might be.

It was after 10, and even when I had come in at around 6 the building had been so deserted that I could hear my footsteps echoing in the corridor. The *dezhurnaya*, an elderly Russian woman working as the 24-hour watchman, had had to unlock the front door for me. She had emerged from the *dezhurnaya's* room, no bigger than a closet, in which was crammed a cot, small desk, clothes hooks, a hot plate. Each day, a different *dezhurnaya* was

on duty; I'd never seen this one before.

In Moscow, unexpected knocks at the door can bear ill tidings. I wondered who would be interrupting me at that hour in a locked office in a locked building.

When I opened the door, there stood the *dezhurnaya*, a rather tall woman in her 60's, erect and businesslike. I asked if there was some problem.

"No problem," she said and paused. "You've been working hard for a long time. You must be hungry. Would you like me to fix you a cup of tea?"

I was startled, not only because she and I were total strangers, but also because I have encountered many a *dezhurnaya*, and most have the mentality of a sentry—gruff, suspicious of aliens, protective of turf and accustomed to reducing human commerce to the inspection of a permit. I mumbled something like: "It's really not necessary. I hadn't realized it had gotten so late. I'll be leaving soon."

I was deep into my work

again and had almost forgotten her when she returned, not just with a cup of tea but with a whole tray of things: a large mug of tea, four small openfaced sandwiches, bologna topped with a slice of cucumber, a packet of tasty Polish biscuits. She said in clear but unpracticed English: "I put some strawberry preserves in your tea. We do it that way. Is that right? Is that how you say it, 'strawberry preserves'?"

Understanding that she must have sacrificed part of her own nighttime rations, I thanked her, invited her to sit down and said her English was quite correct. Not wanting to intrude, she stood by the doorway of our inner office as we talked.

I learned that she was a retired teacher, supplementing her tiny pension. When I told her my name and asked hers, she said, "My name is Anna Ivanovna." Only then did we shake hands, as properly acquainted. In return for her generosity, I gave her a book and some magazines to practice her English, and after that, when I

saw her, we would swap stories, comments, little gifts.

That first late-night encounter illustrates an endearing quality of Russians: their extraordinarily warm hospitality, their love of bestowing gifts on each other and on people whom they choose to befriend. To American travelers who have found Russians on the street to be brusque and impersonal, who have found Soviet officials to be cold and rigid and Soviet waiters exasperating in their imperious and surly indifference, this generous side of the Russian character often comes as a surprise.

But the Russian character is made up of both coldness and warmth. And it is the complexity of this character that complicates President Mikhail S. Gorbachev's drive to set up a law-governed state and plays havoc with even the most basic—and often faltering—steps that he is taking to raise the Soviet economy out of its morass. So, Gorbachev may have won the Nobel Peace Prize for his foreign policy, but

From *The New York Times Magazine*, October 28, 1990, pp. 31-32, 60, 62, 71. Adapted from *The New Russians* by Hedrick Smith. Copyright © 1990 by Hedrick Smith. Reprinted by permission of Random House, Inc.

at home his most fundamental problem is motivating his own people.

While the kind-hearted impulses of Russians and most other Soviet nationalities make private life tolerable, other less charitable qualities in the Russian character tend to make public life intractable and pose formidable obstacles to reform; their escapism, their-impracticality, their lackadaisical attitude toward work and their vicious envy of people who try to get ahead.

Westerners know, because Gorbachev has made it an issue, that an entrenched bureaucracy of party and Government officials—18 million strong by Gorbachev's count—has been blocking and sabotaging many reforms, clinging to power and privilege. What is far less understood in the West is that the mind-set of ordinary people is an equally forbidding obstacle to reform.

For the flip side of Russian generosity and sentimentality is Russian irresponsibility and impracticality.

"Russian mentality is not based on common sense," said the writer Tatyana Tolstaya. "It has nothing to do with common sense. Our thinking is not orderly, logical. In Western culture, European culture maybe, emotion is considered to be on a lower level than reason. But in Russia, no. It is bad to be rational, to be smart, clever, intelligent and so on. And to be emotional, warm, lovable, maybe spiritual, in the full meaning of that word—that is good."

"It is the Russian soul," the poet Andrei Voznesensky said one afternoon as we sat on a park bench. "In Russia, I think we have a love of literature, a so-called spiritual life. We can talk all day and all night long about all kinds of questions, immortal questions. That is the Russian style of thinking."

"I want our economy to be the same as in the West. I want our people to have a good quality of life, a good level, the same as in America, and technology as in Japan and America. But I am afraid to lose this Russian part of our soul, to lose our love of literature and . . . how to put it . . . our im-

practical character. Maybe too lazy, it is a minus, but it is a plus, too."

In this view, Russians are prone to escapism, whether it be the "lazy, dreamy" philosophizing of the intelligentsia, as Tolstaya put it, or the brutal, often self-destructive mass alcoholism of workers and peasants.

The system itself not only encourages, but nourishes, such behavior. The grim shortage of goods sends Russians seeking instant gratification. Why, if the future offers little hope, plan for the long term? Why not blow a month's salary on a birthday party?

Over the decades, the Soviet system has turned out regiments of result-oriented engineers, who now fill echelons of the Soviet Government and Communist Party, running city councils and party organizations at all levels. Yet even allowing for this group, who could roughly be compared to Western businessmen, Russians are not a career-driven people; their primary touchstones are not success, getting ahead, making deals, accumulating material possessions.

It is paradoxical that this should be so, given the relentless Soviet propaganda urging work and discipline as national values. But industriousness, discipline, efficiency do not rank high with most citizens. Years ago, I remember a Government economist describing where work stands on the Russian scale of values. "A man can be a good worker, but work is just a *thing*," he told me, "What really matters is his spirit, his relationship to others. If he is too scrupulous, too cold, people will dislike him. We have a word for that, its *sukhovaty*—dryish—but *sukhoi*—dry—is even worse. And finally *sukhar*—dry like a bread crust, no human touch at all—that is the worst."

Such admiration for human warmth is appealing, but Russians tend to slip over the line, turning commendable traits into a justification for avoiding responsibility and initiative, for a slack attitude toward work. If America is dominated by workaholic "Type A's," the

Soviet Union is mired in hard-to-motivate "Type B's."

Economists and political thinkers blame the Stalinist command economy and rigid central control for molding an obedient, passive labor force that is plagued by heavy absenteeism, idleness on the job, poor-quality work, low morale and serious alcoholism.

"Apathy, indifference, pilfering and a lack of respect for honest work have become rampant," said the reform economist Nikolai P. Shmelyov, "as has aggressive envy of those who earn a lot, even if they earn it honestly."

Gorbachev and his predecessor, Yuri V. Andropov, both recognized the slack Soviet work ethic as a national Achilles' heel, and they attacked it the moment they took office. Each began his tenure with a loudly trumpeted campaign to tighten work discipline, as well as to fight the indolent torpor of the Soviet working class and its companion disease, mass alcoholism. Andropov, the former K.G.B. chief, closed down liquor stores during working hours and even had his police agents chase workers out of the *banyas*, the communal Russian baths, notorious hideouts for workers playing hooky. In the *banyas*, people not only bathe, they also drink beer and eat salted fish and play cards or just while away the hours talking.

Soviet workers themselves have a saying that expresses their open cynicism: "They pretend to pay us and we pretend to work." Russians often make up for poor pay by stealing from the state. The common saying is "What belongs to everyone, belongs to no one, so why shouldn't it be mine?"

Pilfering is on a grand scale. Underground industries have operated on millions of rubles of pirated textile goods, entire warehouses of construction materials and equipment, fresh fruits and vegetables, lockers of meat. People love to swap jokes about such shenanigans. One of my favorite anecdotes is about a worker who leaves his factory one afternoon with a wheelbarrow, covered

with a piece of cloth. The guard at the gate, checking against thievery, lifts the cloth, looks underneath it and, finding the wheelbarrow empty, waves the worker on. The next day, the worker shows up again with a wheelbarrow covered with a cloth. Again the guard checks. Nothing underneath the cloth, so he lets the worker pass. A third day, it happens again — the wheelbarrow is still empty.

Finally, the guard bursts out, in utter frustration: "Look, comrade, you must be stealing something. What is it?"

"Wheelbarrows," the worker replies.

CYNICISM — AND SHEER fakery — pervade the system. Industrial managers and local party officials constantly deceive higher-ups about levels of output. When Gorbachev came into power, it was clear that practically everyone from the bottom up was cooking the books. In Uzbekistan, for example, investigators found that every year the entire republic had reported to Moscow one million tons of phantom cotton harvest; they covered the lie up with considerable bribery to keep officials quiet.

Perestroika, the restructuring of the nation, often gets lip service and a wry laugh. In one current joke, a man is demonstrating to another the meaning of perestroika. The first man has two pails. One pail is empty and the other is full of potatoes. He pours the potatoes from one pail into the other, very satisfied with what he is doing.

"But nothing has changed," objects the second man.

"Ah, yes," agrees the first, "but think what a noise it creates."

"PEOPLE ARE LOOKING for some external transformation to take place under perestroika, but perestroika is first of all internal," my friend Vladimir Pozner, the television commentator, remarked to me. "Perestroika has to happen in the mind. For it to work, people's outlooks have to change, and that happens as society changes. It's a push-pull, gradual process. It cannot be decreed."

Old habits die hard, even among supposedly reform-minded intellectuals. One morning I visited Vladimir Yadov, director of the Institute of Sociology in Moscow. The place was almost deserted, and as I sat down to talk with Yadov, I commented on the absence of people on a normal workday.

"This is what my driver calls 'bath day.'" He grinned, assuming I knew that people hid from work in the baths. "No one is around our institute except the director and a few of my assistants. Everyone else is away. No one is at work. Theoretically, this is library day, when they are all supposed to be at the library." He shrugged, assuming I understood that this was fiction. "Do you remember what Maxim Gorky told Lenin when Lenin asked Gorky why he did not want to come back from living abroad to work in Russia? Gorky told Lenin, 'You know, Vladimir Ilyich, at home in Russia they all go around and shake each other's hands and talk all the time and swap anecdotes. No one really works.' Well, that's how it is here on 'bath day.' They all go around and shake each others' hands and swap anecdotes."

O CCASIONALLY, I RAN into middle-aged officials and intellectuals who had begun to think that the casual Soviet attitude toward work took root during their youth, especially among the educated middle class, which allowed its children to develop an easy dependence on their parents.

Russians are soft on their children, spoiling them, trying to protect them from hardship; they keep them living at home after university and often support them financially during those years. The contrast with American young people is so striking that Soviet writers and journalists, reporting on travels across America, have been moved to send home detailed descriptions of the summer

jobs taken by American college students.

Soviet parents are both horrified and impressed to read about how middle-class American young people take jobs waiting on table, pumping gasoline, baby-sitting, digging ditches, serving fast food. They are horrified that well-heeled American parents coldly force their children to work to make money. To many Russians, that smacks of exploiting child labor. But they are impressed that American teen-agers show so much initiative and self-reliance.

On an all-day car trip through the farming regions of Yaroslavl province, a senior provincial party official named Igor Beshev fired questions at me about the jobs my children had taken and how I had persuaded them to go out and work.

His 20-year-old son was a university student, but he had never had a job. Like other Soviet young people, he had taken part in various work projects organized by the Komsomol, the youth wing of the Communist Party. Those activities, however, were not a step toward financial self-sufficiency.

"He's dependent on me," Beshev said. "He never earns any money. Of course, I expect he will have a good career when he finishes university. But I do not think he knows how to take care of himself. I'm trying to get him to find some job. But that's a big change, and it's very hard for him, for all of us."

Dependence on parents is a prelude to dependence on the state, which the Soviet system encourages. After graduation, university students are assigned jobs under *raspradeleniye* — literally, the "distribution" — which they must accept as a way of paying back the state for their education. Often, out of inertia or limited possibilities, they stick with those assigned jobs for many years, sometimes for the rest of their lives. In the countryside, villages are like old-fashioned company towns, dominated by the local state or col-

lective farm. The individual fits into the local hierarchy, which both supports him and checks his initiative.

Dependence is also nurtured by subsidies for the essentials of living — housing, food, health care, education. Soviet apartments are spartan and dreary by Western standards, but they are cheap. The rent for a one-room apartment can be as little as 15 rubles a month. Even a good-sized apartment of three rooms may be no more than 25 or 30 rubles a month, two or three days' pay. Health care is poor, but it's free — except for the bribes that people have to pay to get service. Education, even at the university level, is free. The staples of the diet — bread, milk, potatoes, cheese — are all subsidized, this year at a cost of about 96 billion rubles, about $155 billion.

The majority of Soviet workers clamor for greater efficiency, for more consumer goods, but they react violently to any proposal that could mean floating prices and an end to subsidies on consumer essentials. That is a potent deterrent to Gorbachev as he struggles with decisions on a free market; each time, he has backed off or watered down his plans as public complaints grew. His caution is in dramatic contrast to the boldness of the new Polish leaders, who have plunged headlong into free-market reforms, allowing price inflation.

"The Poles prefer high prices to empty counters," commented Nikolai Petrakov, Gorbachev's personal economic adviser. "In this country, all the opinion polls show quite the opposite. People accept rationing coupons and standing in line — especially during work time — but not price increases."

"We all shout in unison — including those who otherwise favor the market: 'Do not touch prices!'" observed a reform-minded economist, Otto Latsis. "This is the kind of 'market' we have imagined. Like a rose without thorns."

S OVIETS ALSO HAVE a widespread aversion to risk-taking. As a people, they are cautious and conservative. The specter of unemployment is terrifying, and Soviet society has little experience or infrastructure for dealing with it. By Government estimates, roughly three million people were thrown out of work from 1985 to 1989, and about 15 million more jobs will be eliminated by the end of the century. New jobs are developing in other sectors, including private enterprise hiding behind the euphemistic title of "co-operatives" — that is, group-owned businesses. The more daring workers, especially younger people, are giving this sector a try.

But most Soviet workers are reluctant to take the plunge. They would rather settle for a meager wage and miserable living standards — and continue to complain about these shortcomings — than quit their jobs and take the chance of shifting to a cooperative with an uncertain future.

"The masses expect change to come from the top," my friend Andrei Smirnov, the film maker, remarked over dinner one night. "They do not understand that real democracy, or real changes in the economy, must come from below. They resist the idea that we must change ourselves."

The habit of dependence on the state exists at all levels of Soviet society. Smirnov, head of the film makers' union for two critical years of adjustment in the late 1980's, described his union as a microcosm of Soviet responses to greater economic freedom.

"Everyone was enthusiastic about overthrowing the old dictatorial system," Smirnov said, "but our directors and producers are fearful of the new system of competition. If we have a choice between the free market and a guaranteed salary, the majority will pick a guaranteed salary. Those who can't compete on the market are unhappy at the prospect of being unemployed. Others who are more talented are unhappy because they think that studio directors will pick friends and favorites to make films, not the qualified people. They want the union to protect them and to go after the studio directors. The really good ones, who can work well in any situation, are unhappy with our poor technology and the bad system of financing in the country."

Rair Simonyan, head of industrial management at Moscow's prestigious Institute of International Relations and World Economics, reported similar reactions among industrial managers and even among his own efficiency experts.

"Everybody can tell you about the necessity for change, but when it relates to them, it's different," he told me. "I had trouble with my own people. Everybody said we need radical reforms. The first thing I tried to do was to cut our staff — 60 researchers is too many. But people were upset. They told me, 'You can't arrange these jobs purely on the basis of efficiency. You have to balance efficiency and social security. You cannot fire a man in his 50's with no job prospects or a woman with two children.' Even our industrial managers — to whom we are trying to give more autonomy from the state to decide their own production — they want the old system of being guaranteed their supplies. Often they will tell us, 'We need 100 percent state orders, so we will have no problem with material supplies.' "

ALEKSANDR N. YAKOVlev, who has long been Gorbachev's closest ally in the leadership, is an even more radical proponent of reform than Gorbachev. For him, psychological dependence on state paternalism leads to mass inertia, a Soviet habit of mind he calls the "most debilitating obstacle" to reform.

"Society is accustomed to freeloading, and not only in the material sense," Yakovlev explained during a long conversation one afternoon. "A person wants to be sure he'll get paid, even if he doesn't work. But also in politics, he wants to be sure that he'll be given instructions, orders, that people will explain, will show him what to do. In every sphere, this is a society of freeloading, of freeloading socialism.

"If we don't break through that, if a person doesn't accept some inner freedom and initiative and responsibility, if there is no self-governance in society in outlying districts, then nothing will happen."

"That means people taking real responsibility themselves," I interjected.

"And people don't feel like taking responsibility," he shot back. "Let someone else answer, but not me. That's also freeloading. And it has eaten into our pores and our life."

For the great mass of Soviet people, the years of unrelieved struggle against shortages of the most elementary of human needs have bred habits and attitudes that go against the grain of reform. Illicit profiteering is as pervasive as crab grass in a summer lawn; it's an almost universal defense mechanism that has been operating sub rosa for many years. Think of the worker stealing wheelbarrows and multiply him by a million. The pilfering causes many, even though they regularly benefit from underhanded dealings, to look on anyone who makes a profit as an illicit operator.

Beyond that, the competitive combat of daily shopping has fed a mean-spirited streak in the Soviet soul. For if Russians are justly known for their warmth within a trusted circle, and for their hospitality toward guests, they often show a churlish spite toward people outside their circle. The natural breeding ground for this attitude is the floating anger engendered by wretched circumstances. Russians are long-suffering people who can bear misery, so long as they see that others are sharing it. But let someone become better off — even if it is through his own honest labor — and the collective jealousy can be fierce.

Traveling around the country, I came to see the great mass of Soviet people as protagonists in what I call the culture of envy — corrosive animosity that took root under the czars in the deep-seated collectivism in Russian life and then was accentuated by Leninist ideology. Now, it has turned rancid under the misery of everyday living.

The Soviet ruling class, with cushy cars, clinics and country homes, is a natural enough target for the wrath of the little people. But what is ominous for Gorbachev's reforms is that this free-floating anger of the rank and file often settles on anyone who rises above the crowd. This hostility is a serious danger to the new entrepreneurs Gorbachev is trying to nurture. It is a deterrent to modest initiative among ordinary people in factories or on farms. It freezes the vast majority into the immobility of conforming to group attitudes.

From Valentin Bereshkov, a former Soviet diplomat, I heard of a farmer outside of Moscow whose horse and few cows were set free and whose barn was set afire by neighboring farm workers jealous of his modest prosperity. The Soviet press is full of stories about attacks on privately owned cooperative restaurants and other small service shops by people who resent seeing others do well. In debates at the Supreme Soviet, the most passionate arguments involve accusations that the free market will enable speculators to get rich by exploiting the working class.

Such antagonisms, of course, bear witness to the powerful influence of decades of Leninist indoctrination. For great masses of Soviet people, capitalism is still a dirty word; the fact that someone earns more, gets more is a violation of the egalitarian ideal of socialism. Tens of millions of citizens deeply mistrust the market, fearing they will be cheated and outsmarted. They see the profit motive as immoral. After all, in 1918 Lenin wrote: "We consider the land to be common property. But if I take a piece . . . for myself, cultivate twice as much grain as I need and sell the excess at a profit . . . am I really behaving like a Communist? No. I am behaving like an exploiter, like a proprietor."

But there is more than ideology at work here. There are class and collective instincts, born in the countryside of prerevolutionary Russia, embedded in the peasant psyche and often carried from the farm to the factory when peasants have migrated to the cities. This hostility toward those who rise above the herd reflects the collective ethic of the *obshchina*, the commune of villagers who in czarist times lived in a small huddle of homes, close by each other, not, as in the United States, in single homesteads dotted independently across the open plains. After serfdom was abolished in 1861, the peasantry banded together, working the land together. The peasant commune apportioned to each family strips of land to work, in different fields, some near the village, some off by the forest, distributed so that each family was assigned some good land and some not-so-good land. The *obshchina* decided when they would all plant, when they would all harvest and often how they would all work the fields. The villagers shared the bad weather. They planted the same crops. They grew accustomed to a common fate. And they reacted warily against anyone who tried to advance beyond his peers.

IN MY TRAVELS, VILLAGers often told me: Remember, the tallest blade of grass is the first to be cut down by the scythe. Lesson: Do not try to stand above the crowd, the collective.

Felicity Barringer, a former New York Times correspondent in Moscow, made the shrewd observation that "in America, it's a sin to be a loser, but if there's one sin in Soviet society, it's being a winner."

Dmitri Zakharov, anchor of the Friday night television show "Vzglyad," said: "In the West, if an American sees someone on TV with a shiny new car, he will think, 'Oh, maybe I can get that someday for myself.' But if a Russian sees that, he will think, 'This bastard with his car. I would like to kill him for living better than I do.' When Russians see a cooperative where people make a lot of money, they ask angrily, 'Why do those people make so much money?' Instead of making an effort to raise their own incomes, they want to close down the cooperative."

Anatoly A. Sobchak, the Mayor of Leningrad, told me: "Our people cannot endure seeing someone else earn more than they do. Our people want equal distribution of money, whether that means wealth or poverty. They are so jealous of other people that they want others to be worse off, if need be, to keep things equal. We have a story: God comes to a lucky Russian peasant one day and offers him any wish in the world. The peasant is excited and starts dreaming his fantasies. 'Just remember,' God says, 'whatever you choose, I will do twice as much for your neighbor as I do for you.' The peasant is stumped because he cannot bear to think of his neighbor being so much better off than he is, no matter how well off he becomes. Finally, he gets an idea and he tells God, 'Strike out one of my eyes and take out both eyes of my neighbor.'

"Changing that psychology is the hardest part of our economic reform. That psychology of intolerance toward others who make more money, no matter why, no matter whether they work harder, longer or better — that psychology is blocking economic reform."

Commenting on this problem, Vlad Pozner put a new twist on something I had noticed among Russians: the built-in caution of their daily greeting. "When two Americans meet, they ask each other, 'How are things?' and they tell each other, 'Fine,'" Pozner said. "An American will say 'fine' even if his mother died yesterday.

"By contrast, when two Soviets meet and ask each other how they are, they will say, 'Normal,' or 'So-so.' Even if things are good — especially if things are good! You don't want to tempt the devil. You don't want people to think things are great. Because they might be envious. And if they're envious, there's no telling what they might do."

This urge for leveling the fate of all, for sharing misfortune and spreading misery is what Nikolai Shmelyov, the radical economic reformer, has called the syndrome of "equal poverty for all."

"The blind, burning envy of your neighbor's success has become the most powerful brake on the ideas and practice of perestroika," Shmelyov told the Congress of People's Deputies in March. "Until we at least damp down this envy, the success of perestroika will always be in jeopardy."

Gorbachev himself has picked up this theme. Last April, he upbraided Soviet workers for lacking "a sense of responsibility" and for resisting wage reforms that would reward good work. Specifically, he warned that the culture of envy would snuff out any spark of initiative and daring and would cripple hopes of real economic progress.

"If we do not break out of this foolish system of wage leveling," he declared, "we will ruin everything that's alive in our people. We shall suffocate."

Soviet Politics: Breakdown or Renewal?

"To the tensions inherited from the past are added the frustrations engendered by today's economic and political crisis. The most obvious response is mutually destructive measures of self-protection. . . . It is the race between breakdown and renewal that will decide the fate of Soviet society."

LARS T. LIH

Lars T. Lih is the author of *Bread and Authority in Russia, 1914-1921* (Berkeley: University of California Press, 1990), and *Bolshevik Sowing Committees of 1920: Apotheosis of War Communism?* (Pittsburgh: University of Pittsburgh, Center for Russian and East European Studies, Carl Beck Papers, 1990).

IT is not easy to bring a picture of Soviet politics today into focus—like an optical illusion, it seems to shift even as we look at it. At one moment, we see a momentous renewal that is bringing a great country back into the mainstream of world civilization. In the next moment, we see a massive economic and political breakdown that threatens civil war.

One reason for this confusion is the pace of events. Several years ago Sovietologist Robert Tucker wrote that "history is on the move again in the Soviet Union"; today, history has been galloping at a frantic pace. Outside observers could not figure out the new rules of the game—but then, neither could the players themselves. Soviet politics seems to be a form of Bill Watterson's Calvinball, where the only rule is that the same rules are never used twice.

But perhaps the basic reason it is so difficult to achieve a focused picture is that the forces leading to renewal and breakdown are inextricably intertwined. The central question confronting Soviet politics today is whether the transition to a renewed society can be made without a collapse of civil order. The answer depends on the creative efforts of Soviet citizens.

The paradoxes of Soviet politics start with the Communist party. On the one hand, it is still the ruling party; on the other hand, the party clearly revealed itself in the course of the year to oppose the course set by the country's political leadership. To understand how this came about, we need to take a brief look at the historical role of the party.

The Soviet system is usually described as all-powerful. In reality, the system itself has been very weak. Basic state institutions like legislatures and the judiciary have had little independence, and even the bureaucracy has often been content to turn over local affairs to self-perpetuating elites. The party, which served as the rubber band that held this shambling structure together, provided an arena for conflict resolution, imposed a modicum of central priorities and allowed for emergency reactions to the constant stream of foul-ups.[1] (The party played a similar role in the economy. Under the facade of "central planning," the system was a patchwork of negotiation and improvisation conducted primarily through party channels.)*

This system may have had some excuse in earlier days when political unity was threatened from within and without, and the human resources for a competent bureaucracy were desperately scarce. But it is clearly incompatible with the Soviet reformers' vision of a market society, which requires first and foremost some predictability from the political system. The switchover to a new political system would be easy if the party were merely a self-serving elite that could easily be kicked out. Since the party as an institution made a vital contribution to holding the country together, however, the reformers' task was more challenging. If the party disintegrated before new structures were ready to take its place, the country might become ungovernable.

In Western society the process of separating church and state stretched over centuries. In the Soviet Union, the principal steps toward separating party and state took little over a year. It was only in the beginning of 1989 that there was any questioning of the role of the party in the Soviet press. Looking back, it can be seen that the first steps had already taken place in 1988, when President Mikhail Gorbachev announced plans for a new national legislature. This complicated two-tier structure began to operate in the spring of 1989 and immediately became the focus of political attention.

Parallel to the new role of the national legislature there was a gradual leaching of authority from party structures to state structures. At the top, the most vivid symbol of this process was Gorbachev himself, who defined himself more and more as head of state rather than as head of the party. In the spring of 1990, the new elective office of President was created. Although Gorbachev became the new Presi-

---

*For details on the economy, see the articles by Marshall I. Goldman, Karen Brooks and Judith McKinney in this issue.

dent only by vote of the national legislature, a commitment was made to a nationwide election after the first five-year term. Accusations at home and abroad about Gorbachev's grab for power missed entirely the revolutionary change in the source of his power.

As the state waxed, so the party waned. Traditional top party bodies like the Secretariat and then the Politburo began to meet less and less frequently. In the summer of 1990, the Politburo was transformed into an unwieldy institution whose main aim seemed to be to give a voice to the non-Russian republics. Gorbachev's top advisers, Aleksandr Yakovlev and Eduard Shevardnadze, simply left the Politburo on the assumption that their position in the new presidential Cabinet gave them a more secure base of authority.

This process was formalized in the spring of 1990 by the removal of Article 6 of the Soviet constitution, which guaranteed the Communist party's monopoly of power. The many alternative political parties that had been gestating at an embryonic stage now began to come forth openly. At lower levels, action was taken directly against the party's increasingly anachronistic privileged position within economic enterprises. For example, after striking miners announced that party committees added nothing to mining operations, they simply threw the committees out. The issue of the party presence in the military and in law enforcement agencies also moved to the center of the political agenda.

The anomalous position of the Communist party was on display at the twenty-eighth congress in July, 1990. Rarely has an organization so clearly had little use for the leader, and the leader so clearly had little use for the organization. After a week or so of criticism, Gorbachev told the congress:

> We must put an end to sectarian moods, put an end to this monopoly forever, erase its vestiges from the mind of party workers and all Communists. . . . Believe me, the party's success depends on whether it realizes that this is already a different society. Otherwise it will be pushed to the margin by other forces, and we shall lose ground.[2]

As yet, neither leader nor organization saw a better alternative; so Gorbachev consented to remain party leader as well as head of state, and the congress agreed to elect him. But like a marriage held together only by thoughts of the children and the house, there was no love in it.

At the twenty-eighth party congress, Aleksandr Yakovlev told the assembled delegates that the reform process would go on with the party or without it. Yegor Ligachev, the main defender of the party's traditional role, responded by asserting that the country was in great need of political stability and that perestroika would fail if a crippled party was not able to give it leadership. Ligachev had a point. The marginalization of the party contributed to a disintegration of central authority that threatened to make the country ungovernable. This disintegration took two main forms: regional independence and ideological intransigence.

The most vivid manifestations of regional independence were the secession movements in the non-Russian republics. But much of the power of these movements came from an underlying drive for protection from the consequences of a society-wide economic crisis. In 1917, when a similar process was going on, a politician remarked about regional separatism:

> What do they want? They want to remain intact in that sea of anarchy that is flooding the country; they want to save themselves, like an island.[3]

National identity provides an excellent basis for setting up these islands of order and deciding who gets in and who does not, but it is far from necessary. A basic plank in the platform of the reformers who took over the Leningrad city council in 1990 was to make Leningrad a "free economic zone."

The diffusion of authority to regional "popular fronts" and local reform coalitions can complicate the task of building a new society-wide authority. A large-scale opposition organization along the lines of Polish Solidarity would find it hard to survive in an environment of nationalism and other forms of separatism. Separatist searches for protection from economic crisis also accelerated the economic breakdown. One Soviet reformer argued that the strategy of economic sovereignty was no more than an invitation to economic civil war.[4] Even national identity, which might provide a secure basis for social unity in a few places like Lithuania or Armenia, would in most places lead to increased ethnic conflict. How could reform proceed in an atmosphere of mutual recrimination and frequent bloodshed?

Authority also disintegrated along the ideological spectrum. New parties ranged from monarchists to liberal democrats to Marxist fundamentalists. Ideological splintering could also be observed within the Communist party—an unprecedented development, since the counterpart of a ban on political organizations outside the party was a ban on independent factions within the party. Reformers joined together in the Democratic Platform and agonized aloud about whether or not the party was past hope. At most, the Democratic Platform was in, but not of, the party; and after the party congress the Democratic Platform became the nucleus of a new party. Party conservatives also found a new organizational form. Unlike all the other re-publics, the Russian republic never had a separate section of the Communist party. In 1990, a Russian Communist party (as opposed to the Communist party of the Soviet Union as a whole) was created and quickly became a bastion of hardliners.

POLITICS OF SUSPICION

It was not merely the many new organizations that created an obstacle to a broadly based authority; a polarization of attitudes also prevented compromise and cooperation. One form taken by this polarization can be called the politics of suspicion. Each side not only disagreed with its opponents but also accused them of sabotage and conspiracy. On the extreme right, groups like the notorious Pamyat (Memory Society) advanced anti-Semitic theories that accused the Jews (along with the Freemasons) of selling out the 1917 revolution or of responsibility for the revolution in the first place—it was not always clear which. Pamyat took to breaking up meetings of liberal intellectuals by force, thus adding nasty violence to an already strained situation. More commonsensical Soviet conservatives accused the post-glasnost Soviet media of being the Soviet equivalent of nattering nabobs of negativism (United States Vice President Spiro Agnew's description of the American press during the administration of President Richard Nixon).

The left's variant of the politics of suspicion was described by a new Russian word—*populizm*—that has more negative connotations than its American counterpart. The strategy of Soviet populism was to turn broad popular disgust with the failure of the system and the arrogance of the elite into an all-purpose accusation that "the apparatus" was responsible for every ill. The best symbols of Soviet populism were the ex-prosecutors Nikolai Ivanov and Telman Gdlyan. These two had been involved in anticorruption investigations during the Leonid Brezhnev era and had made plenty of enemies by their revelation of wrongdoing and their dubious, freewheeling methods. When the establishment turned on them, they responded by accusing Politburo member Yegor Ligachev and finally even Gorbachev of taking bribes. They could make these charges with impunity because their extremely wide popularity allowed them to become parliamentary deputies with legal immunity. A commission set up by the national legislature and headed by former dissident Roy Medvedev found their accusations to be unfounded, but any statement emanating from the elite had little or no credibility with the populists.

The destructive effects of the politics of suspicion were compounded by the politics of principle. In American political culture, politicians are expected to rise above principle and work with people with whom they strongly disagree in order to get the job done. In Soviet political culture, freedom is often seen as the chance to insist on principle and refuse even to shake the hand of one's opponent. Part of the contempt for the party apparatchik is aimed at the organization man required by any large bureaucracy. The Soviet intellectuals have lived so long without any power that opposition comes much more easily to them than support, and they are eager to denounce a leader who sells out his principles by cooperating with the other side.

AUTHORITY AND LEADERSHIP

The disintegration of authority and the possibility of political breakdown are dramatic occurrences that have caught the attention of outside observers. Many people both inside and outside Soviet society see no other outcome except the breakup of the Soviet Union, civil war or an authoritarian end to the chances for reform. But forces working in the opposite direction are laying the foundation for a new, broadly based authority. These positive forces are harder to discern and more ambivalent in their operation. Nonetheless, they exist and should be considered before analysts consign the Soviet Union to perdition.

Consider first three leaders of genuinely national significance: Mikhail Gorbachev, Boris Yeltsin and Yegor Ligachev. During the past year, the heart of Gorbachev's reform goals could be encapsulated in one word—the market—with all that this implies in terms of high productivity, the rule of law and openness to the world. People are less and less interested in whether or not such a goal can be described as "socialist." Several observers have noted that the word market (*rynok* in Russian) has acquired almost mystical connotations in the Soviet Union. To Soviet citizens, the market is such a symbol for contemporary world civilization that to achieve a market society will mean that the Soviet Union has rejoined the world. Above and beyond the economic perils and prospects promised by the actual market, the idea of the market has great integrative force because of the weight of the world consensus behind it. Gorbachev's other core value is his determination to move to his destination without letting the country fall into either civil war or national separatism.

According to the conservatives, Gorbachev is responsible for the parlous condition of Soviet society. He has destroyed everything that held the Soviet Union together: the moral power of the socialist ideal, patriotic pride in the country's past and its armed forces, the economic integration of the centralized economy and the political integration of the party-state. As one conservative is reported to have said, after Gorbachev is through, Russia will be no bigger than the blotch on Gorbachev's forehead.[5]

Many radicals dismiss Gorbachev as a has-been who has unleashed processes that go beyond the comprehension of someone trained in the old system. They resent the West's fascination with Gorbachev and argue that at best he is irrelevant to the real processes of reform. At worst, his fear of social disruption makes him temporize on reform and try vainly to buy off the conservatives. According to the radicals, Gorbachev remains in power only because the left and right ends of the political spectrum cancel each other out. But all the political initiative comes from the extremes and not from the dynamic center.

The Gorbachev loyalists retort that for all his caution, he always lands finally on the reformist side and in fact has carried out reforms of unprecedented scope. They argue that events like the Lithuanian impasse do not show Gorbachev's impotence but his strength: to date, no tanks have rumbled down the streets of Vilnius. The radicals should remember that Gorbachev is President of all the people and has responsibility to all Soviet citizens, including reactionaries.

LEADERSHIP PROBLEMS

As mentioned earlier, Gorbachev still prefers to build his authority on the basis of both state and party positions. The first Soviet leader to conclude that these two bases are incompatible was Boris Yeltsin. In July, 1990, when the twenty-eighth party congress tried to give Yeltsin a leadership post in the party, he announced that his office as elected head of the Russian republic precluded his submission to party discipline. He then walked out of the hall and out of the party.

Yeltsin rose to national prominence through party ranks, first as a provincial party boss and then, under Gorbachev, as party boss of Moscow. In the fall of 1987 an event occurred that seemed to mark the end of Yeltsin's career but was actually a new beginning. Yeltsin stood up at a Central Committee meeting and blasted the shortcomings of the reform program and the continuing privileges of the party elite. He was promptly removed from all leadership posts and subjected to an old-style ritual denunciation. Gorbachev offered Yeltsin a government post but warned him that he would not be allowed back into politics.

Meanwhile, Gorbachev was busy creating a situation in which he could no longer unilaterally determine who was or was not allowed to play a leadership role. In retrospect, Yeltsin's Central Committee speech can be seen as the first step in a transfer of loyalty from the elite above who appointed him to the electorate below who supported him. And the electorate responded enthusiastically to this transfer of loyalty, as shown by Yeltsin's election campaign in 1989 for the new national legislature. Despite, or rather because of, the opposition of the party apparatus, Yeltsin won in an overwhelming landslide. The same pattern was repeated at a higher level in the spring of 1990. By this time, Yeltsin had chosen to be a member of the legislature of the Russian republic rather than the national legislature. Here he ran for the equivalent of Gorbachev's presidential post at the republic level. Gorbachev personally intervened to persuade legislators to turn him down; it was revealing, however, that Gorbachev was unable to produce a credible candidate to oppose Yeltsin. Yeltsin's victory in this contest allowed him to leave the party altogether and to take the final step in transferring loyalty from party to people and from elite to electorate.

Not only Gorbachev but many intellectual leaders of the reform movement were suspicious of Yeltsin. They argued that he was long on populist mobilization of mass resentment but short on constructive programs. At the party congress, his heavy hint that party leaders might have to stand trial has made him popular with the Gdlyan–Ivanov constituency but has hardly contributed to a civilized political atmosphere. His insistence that reforms should not result in a drop in the living standard struck observers as a "read-my-lips" evasion of harsh realities.

In response, supporters pointed out that it is not the job of a political leader to devise concrete programs. Yeltsin in fact had surrounded himself with a brain trust of reformers who could work on that side of things. Yeltsin's contribution to the process of renewal was different: to provide basic reform goals with a mass base that intellectual reformers were unable to obtain. After leaving the party, Yeltsin was free to build up a nationwide alternative to the Communist party. Many Yeltsin supporters felt that the future of the reforms depended on whether Gorbachev and Yeltsin could put aside their differences and realize how much they actually had in common.

Yeltsin is often described as a demagogue, and there is much truth to this. But the original Greek meaning of demagogue was "leader of the people," and it was applied in the ancient Greek city-state to what was then a new Greek invention: a political leader whose power base came from the people rather than from a king or an aristocratic elite. In this sense of the word, history will undoubtedly honor Boris Yeltsin for being the Soviet Union's first demagogue.

Yegor Ligachev has also rejected Gorbachev's straddling act, but he has chosen to remain loyal to the party. Ligachev has been pictured as the man you love to hate in the reformist press, and this has had its effect on Western images. A more balanced view sees him as a man sincerely committed to the party as the only institution able to hold Soviet society together. But his very defense of the party in the new political environment has forced him to contradict his principles. In an effort to mobilize support for traditional party principles, Ligachev was forced to reach out to new types of organization like the United Workers Front and the Peasant Union.

All through 1989, Ligachev insisted that there were no fundamental divisions within the Politburo. He was soon thereafter involved in a public slinging match with fellow Politburo member Shevardnadze over responsibility for the decision to use troops in Tblisi, Georgia, in 1989. At the twenty-eighth party congress, Ligachev himself decided to run against Gorbachev's candidate for deputy party leader. Ligachev's defeat in this contest did not mean the end of his career, but it did mean the death of his effort to preserve the traditional style of leadership by the party.

COOPERATION FROM BELOW?

So far, discussion has focused on the role of national leaders, a topic on which world press attention has been centered. Just as important in the long run are efforts to create new forms of political cooperation at lower levels. These experiments are hard to find and even harder to evaluate, but their outcome will decide the fate of Soviet politics.

Often it is the disintegration of authority itself that leads to a creative response. The challenge posed by ideological polarization has led to an insistence on finding new forms of political culture that would end the traditional reliance on the image of the enemy and would allow civilized debate. At the party congress, Aleksandr Yakovlev eloquently called for an end to the civil war in people's thinking and to the atmosphere of suspicion created by the rule of Joseph Stalin. He emphasized that one precondition for this transformation was a new openness to the outside world.

One of the new parties built its political platform on the need for a new political tolerance. The Constitutional Democrats took their name from the main liberal party of prerevolutionary Russia. According to spokesmen at their founding congress, the aim of the party was to move to a civil society based on the market and the role of law, without turning the party apparatus and the many talented people who work there into enemies.

The regional diffusion of authority also created new risks and possibilities. One of the most striking developments of the year was the rise of reformist coalitions that came to dominate republican legisla-

tures, as well as city councils. In Moscow, the new reformist city council was headed by Gavriil Popov and in Leningrad by Anatoly Sobchak—two prominent reform spokesmen whose secure executive positions allowed them to follow Yeltsin's lead and to leave the party altogether. Less dramatic shifts in power also took place in provincial cities like Yaroslavl. This reanimation of previously moribund councils meant that local government might collapse and that feuding between the city councils and the entrenched party structures might bring basic services to a standstill. Much of the credit for avoiding this outcome must go to what Sovietologist Blair Ruble calls a new politics of compromise: people who previously only shouted at each other now had to sit down and work together.

Another risk created by the new regional self-assertiveness was the breaking of necessary links between regions—a situation that could degenerate into the economic civil war previously mentioned. In response, attempts were made to create a new sort of direct horizontal contact to replace the old link that was mediated through the center. Yeltsin's offer to establish trading ties between the Russian republic and Lithuania was only the most dramatic of these efforts.

A third risk was that reforms in one region would so far outstrip the rest of the country that a national market would become less viable. When the legislature of the Russian republic moved quickly to establish an independent monetary policy, there were fears that this would further weaken the ruble and perhaps even cause the Russian republic to print its own money. In response, legislators pointed out that only action from below would break the logjam of institutional reform at the center created by innumerable bureaucratic commissions and special interests. Regional self-assertion might tear the country apart, but it might also quicken the pace toward a common goal.[6]

A PARABLE

An episode that occurred in spring, 1990, will give us a concrete illustration of the complicated interaction between forces leading to breakdown and forces leading to revolutionary renewal.[7]

In May, when the Soviet government announced its long-awaited economic transition measures, the only item that caught the attention of the public was the proposal for a giant increase in the prices of staple goods. The response was a mass outbreak of panic buying and hoarding. This produced an intolerable strain on the Moscow retail system. In one store, ten tons of flour were sold in two hours. In order to save itself from the chaos surrounding it, the city authorities allowed only Moscow residents to make purchases.

This infuriated the surrounding localities. Under the centralized distribution system, Moscow has enormous privileges. This is tolerable to other regions only to the extent that people can visit Moscow — often called the Soviet Union's shopping center — to make their purchases. Now it looked as if Moscow was selfishly hoarding its privileges. The angry population demanded that food shipments to Moscow be cut off or rerouted to the empty shops of the suburbs. People in Moscow suspected darkly that "sausage passions" were being manipulated to discredit the new reformist city council.

But the situation also called forth creative efforts to bridge the ominous gap between city and hinterland. The new Moscow government tried to reassure the suburban population that it was a temporary measure and that not all stores were closed; it even offered to refuse the local products apportioned to the city by the State Planning Council. The situation also sparked a more intense search for long-term solutions that would end Moscow's anachronistic privileges. Some members of the Moscow city council demanded a quick transition to free market prices for Moscow goods as a way of opening the city permanently.

This episode reveals the forces at work in Soviet society today. To the tensions inherited from the past are added the frustrations engendered by today's economic and political crisis. The most obvious response is mutually destructive measures of self-protection. But the crisis can also galvanize constructive efforts to build new bridges between people. It is the race between breakdown and renewal that will decide the fate of Soviet society.

---

[1] A glimpse at how the party functioned can be found in Boris Yeltsin's *Against the Grain: An Autobiography* (New York: Summit Books, 1990).

[2] *The New York Times,* July 11, 1990.

[3] S.N. Prokopovich, cited in Lars T. Lih, *Bread and Authority in Russia, 1914–1921* (Berkeley: University of California Press, 1990), p. 117.

[4] Igor Klyamkin, *Ogonek,* no. 5 (January 27, 1990), pp. 5–8.

[5] For a presentation of the conservative case, see Aleksandr Prokhanov, "The Tragedy of Centralism," *Literaturnaya Rossiya,* January 5, 1990, excerpted in *Current Digest of the Soviet Press,* vol. 42, no. 4 (February 28, 1990).

[6] See the discussion by M. Berger in *Izvestia,* July 1, 1990.

[7] My account is based on material in *Moscow News,* nos. 22 (June 10, 1990) and 24 (June 24, 1990).

Gorbachev Lines Up New System

Daniel Sneider

Staff writer of The Christian Science Monitor

=====MOSCOW=====

MIKHAIL GORBA-CHEV'S vision of the Soviet state is virtually complete.

Through a process of constitutional amendments and presidential decrees, he has constructed a powerful presidential system, with the Soviet president at the core of a renewed federal state.

The decisions of the Congress of People's Deputies, which concluded its fourth meeting last week, completed a legislative process that began at the previous Congress session in March with the establishment of a presidency. Over the spring and summer, Mr. Gorbachev fleshed out that creation, adding the authority to rule through decree.

The latest constitutional changes simultaneously strengthened the presidency while offering the republics that make up the Soviet Union a place in the structure of power.

For some, Gorbachev has created a monster – a structure of legal authority that can lead, as Foreign Minister Eduard Shevardnadze warned dramatically, to a "dictatorship."

Gorbachev and his advisers argue that such fears are groundless.

"Without this, it is impossible either to stabilize the situation or reform the economy," presidential aide Georgy Shakhnazarov told the daily Rabochaya Tribuna on Saturday. "The president is strengthening his powers only in order to protect democracy and *perestroika* [restructuring], the cause of his whole life."

But even if Gorbachev "finds the resources to resist the cult traditions of socialism, where is the guarantee that his future successor will succeed in doing this?," asks liberal commentator Pavel Voshanov, writing yesterday in Komsomolskaya Pravda.

At the fourth Congress, Gorbachev got his way on virtually all the measures and changes he sought. The one exception was the narrow defeat of a proposal to create a Supreme State Inspectorate, a rather vaguely defined body that would ensure that the president's decrees and federal laws are carried out. This was seen as an attempt to infringe on republican authority.

But the constitutional changes give the president the authority to do this anyway. Article 133 of the Soviet Constitution now empowers the President's Cabinet to monitor the execution of presidential decrees and Soviet laws throughout "the entire territory of the USSR." Moreover, the president has the power to repeal any republican law or decree that he decides violates the Constitution or Soviet law.

Mr. Shakhnazarov argues that the main intent of the amendments is to restore the vertical structure of authority downward from the central government to local governments. This "has been disrupted by the confrontation between some republics and the union as a whole," he says.

Gorbachev has separately proposed his concept of a renewed federation in a proposed draft of a new treaty of union, which theoretically must be approved by all the republics. But a close look at the constitutional changes reveals that they encompass much of the contents of the union treaty.

In principle, the federal government will exercise its powers "together with republics." Practically, the only instrument for doing this is the Federation Council, which includes the heads of all the republics.

However, the constitutional amendments are vague about the Council's powers. Moreover, it includes the heads of some 28 autonomous republics and regions within the 15 republics as having a vote, making it large and potentially easily manipulated body.

Gorbachev revealed his view on the last day of the Congress, when he attacked the Russian Republic government for refusing to go along with his proposed 1991 central budget. "No one has rescinded nor has the right to abrogate the laws promulgated by the USSR. Proceeding from this, I will act as the President."

New Structure of Power in the Soviet Union

===== MOSCOW =====

THE Congress of People's Deputies, the Soviet Union's highest legislative body, passed a law on the organization of the Soviet state which extensively amends the Soviet Constitution. Those amendments extend, and in some cases alter, the amendments creating the presidency itself approved last March by the Congress. Together they create the following:

Basic structure of power. Under the previous Constitution, the Soviet Union was formally ruled by a parliamentary system in which the Supreme Soviet, or parliament, was the highest body, and the Council of Ministers, the Cabinet, was the executive authority directly responsible to the Supreme Soviet.

Now the highest executive is the president, who has a vast array of powers. The Council of Ministers has been converted into a Cabinet, directly responsible to the president. The Supreme Soviet's powers are not essentially changed, but the president and Cabinet can act independently on a wide range of issues.

The Soviet Union remains a federal state, composed of 15 union republics with 20 autonomous republics and 8 autonomous regions within them. All these are now represented in a Federation Council under the president.

The president. The president is to be directly elected by the population. He is the head of state, representing the country at home and abroad. He is commander in chief of the Soviet armed forces, with the power to declare war, martial law, or a state of emergency, as well as to introduce direct presidential rule in any region of the Soviet Union. He appoints the members of his Cabinet, the Security Council, the Supreme Court, and the Supreme Court of Arbitration, subject to approval of the Supreme Soviet.

The president and his Cabinet can issue decrees, which have the force of law. He can also repeal any decree or order of a Cabinet ministry or of a republican government which he decides contradicts the Soviet Constitution or laws. The parliament can repeal acts of the Cabinet on the same basis.

The vice president. The vice president is nominated by a president and elected together with him. His powers are decided by the president, whom he replaces in his absence or inability to exercise his duties.

The Cabinet. The Cabinet consists of a prime minister, his deputies, and ministers. The structure is to be determined later by the president with approval by the Supreme Soviet. Heads of union republics may participate in Cabinet meetings, with the right to vote. The Cabinet, acting on the basis of Soviet laws and the decrees of the president, can issue decrees and ordinances and monitor their execution throughout the territory of the Soviet Union.

Article 128 says the Cabinet is an executive agency of the Soviet Union and "subordinate to the USSR president." Article 130 says it is "responsible to the president and the Supreme Soviet." It reports on its work to the parliament at least once a year. The Cabinet may be forced to resign by a two-thirds vote of parliament.

The Security Council. This new body is responsible for defense, security (including economic and ecological), dealing with emergencies, and "ensuring stability, law, and order."

The Federation Council. Members consist of the president, vice president, presidents of all republics. Heads of autonomous republics and regions have the right to participate as voting members "on matters affecting their interests." On the basis of directives of the Congress of People's Deputies, the Council will coordinate between the central and republican authorities, monitor implementation of the union treaty, administer policies on the country's nationalities, ensure republican participation in "solving nationwide issues," and help solve inter-ethnic conflicts.

All decisions are made by two-thirds majority of votes.

– D. S.

THE GORBACHEV RECORD

The rise and fall of perestroika

The crackdown in the Baltic republics has dealt a body-blow to Mikhail Gorbachev's attempts to liberalise and democratise the Soviet Union. Where did it all go wrong, and why?

"COMRADE democrats . . . you have scattered. The reformers have gone to ground. Dictatorship is coming." Nobody can say he had not been warned. When the normally soft-spoken Soviet foreign minister, Edward Shevardnadze, announced his resignation in an emotional speech to the Soviet parliament last month, even he might not have guessed that the six-year odyssey of reform in the Soviet Union was to founder so abruptly, so soon.

Of the original team who set out on the venture, Mr Shevardnadze was one of the last to quit. Of those around Mr Gorbachev now, most have been chosen to confirm his own judgment, not to challenge it. Although on paper the most powerful president the Soviet Union has ever had, Mr Gorbachev has seen his political authority (as opposed to his military clout) dwindling alarmingly. The modern, apparently open-minded man who set out to remake the Soviet Union into a modern, open, competitive superpower now sits brooding in the Kremlin with only his troops to order about (and even they take violent liberties). He is either out of touch with or resentful of the changes that his reforms have brought. How did his endeavour founder?

Until recently, the conventional wisdom had it that of the three big reform projects—"new thinking" abroad and democracy and *perestroika* at home—Mr Gorbachev had two more or less down and only one to go (the economy was clearly going to be the hardest of the three). The optimism abroad about Mr Gorbachev's chances was always a bit overdone. Now the conventional thinkers must think again. Suddenly Mr Gorbachev's achievements look as uncertain as his failures are obvious.

The world as his mirror

This week's appointment of Alexander Bessmertnykh, an avowed "new thinker", as Mr Shevardnadze's replacement is a signal from the Kremlin that no foreign-policy reversal is intended. It is easy to see why. Leaving aside any financial or practical help that Mr Gorbachev may forfeit if he continues his crackdown, his authority at home would have evaporated all the faster, without the change in the image of the Soviet Union over these past six years, from marauding bear on the fringes of Europe to constructive partner in the post-cold-war world.

Above all, his decision after eight years of bloody and inconclusive war to pull the Soviet army out of Afghanistan pleased not only the Americans, who took it as an earnest of even bigger changes to come, but also many, if not quite all, of his own generals. For some time the value of Afghanistan as a place to test the mettle of Soviet soldiers and the reliability of their equipment had been outweighed by the damage being done to army morale by a dirty and unwinnable war. The casualties—officially 16,000 dead and 50,000 injured—had begun to take their toll on Soviet society, too.

A second valuable foreign-policy change was the reduction in "fraternal assistance" to the third world, from Central America to the Middle East, from Angola to Vietnam. Revealing the real cost of such assistance and weighing it against the meagre returns made it easier for the new thinkers in Moscow to argue against the old meddling. There was also a new political incentive: the greater influence that the Soviet Union was able to win where it could really work to Soviet advantage, in the political and financial councils of the West.

This shift from reliance on soldiers to reliance on diplomats had repercussions beyond the regular summits with world leaders that did so much to cast Mr Gorbachev as the thinking man's communist, both at home and abroad. It helped bury the hatchet with China, the Soviet Union's prickly neighbour with which it shares a long border. It also brought to life the United Nations. Without that change, the orchestration of world-wide condemnation of Iraq's invasion of Kuwait would have been impossible, even unthinkable.

But when it came to reassessing core Soviet security interests, the going was far harder. It was easy enough to defend the early agreement with America to abolish intermediate-range nuclear forces. The Soviet build-up of these weapons had provoked a western counter-deployment and had merely succeeded in exposing the Soviet Union to greater military threat. That was clear. Similarly, even the most bull-necked general can probably now see that piling up more and more longer-range nuclear missiles makes little sense either. So a new agreement on strategic nuclear weapons could be ready for signing at next month's Bush-Gorbachev summit, if it goes ahead.

Valiant and Nobel

But last November's agreement to reduce conventional forces in Europe was the last straw for conservatives in the army. Mr Gorbachev had long talked of "sufficiency" in defence. His announcement in December 1988 of a 500,000-man cut over two years in the then 5m-strong Soviet army brought gasps from the generals. Yet the intended reorganisation of the sprawling Soviet military establishment was welcomed by many younger officers. The rundown of the Soviet garrisons in Eastern Europe might have been welcomed too—except that it turned, a year later, into a disorderly rout as government after new government in the region politely but firmly asked the Soviet troops to get out.

For the Soviet Union's proud military brass and its harassed other ranks, the sting was that the governments doing the asking were in part the Kremlin's own creation. It was Mr Gorbachev's refusal to use force to halt the gathering democratisation of Eastern Europe in 1989 that allowed one thing on the streets to lead to another, and another, and another.

It won him the plaudits of the world and a Nobel peace prize, but was it a miscalculation? Yes, in that nobody around Mr Gorbachev or Mr Shevardnadze seems to have understood just how quickly the regimes in Eastern Europe would collapse, given a push. Yet the ultimate logic of Soviet policy during Eastern Europe's year of revolution had been understood in the Soviet foreign ministry, and at Communist Party headquarters, where it was bitterly contested.

It would have been easier for Mr Gorbachev had it all happened in slower motion. He may have hoped that he would not have had to accede to a united Germany until Europe as a whole had become less divided. And if he came to realise that the Warsaw Pact would inevitably collapse, NATO would surely, he must have thought, go too. He clearly had his doubts last year about a Germany united within NATO. But in the end the political facts spoke for themselves.

From ballot . . .

Both in foreign policy and on the home front, historians will see 1989 as the high-water mark of the great Gorbachev experiment—and the start of the ebb tide as the

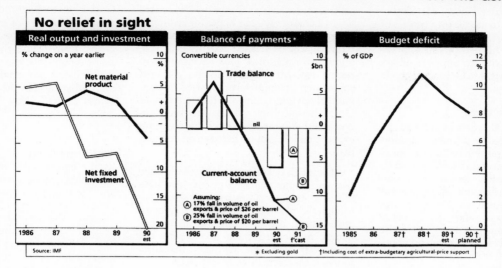

No relief in sight

Real output and investment

% change on a year earlier

Net material product

Net fixed investment

1986 87 88 89 90 est

Source: IMF

Balance of payments *

Convertible currencies $bn

Trade balance

nil

(A)

(B)

Current-account balance

(A)

(B)

Assuming:
(A) 17% fall in volume of oil exports & price of $26 per barrel
(B) 25% fall in volume of oil exports & price of $20 per barrel

1986 87 88 89 90 91 f'cast

* Excluding gold

Budget deficit

% of GDP

1985 86 87† 88† 89† 90† est planned

†Including cost of extra-budgetary agricultural-price support

wave of democracy that had been allowed to sweep through Eastern Europe now washed back through the Soviet Union. To most people at the time it did not seem that the backwash would really threaten the Gorbachev reforms. Mr Gorbachev seemed at his most daring.

When he had come to power in 1985 he had thought that he could work through the party-dominated bureaucracy to get his country moving again. The slogans were "acceleration", and *glasnost*. The press was freer to criticise poor management and to dig, gingerly at first, then more and more boldly, into the Communist Party's infamous past. Managers were encouraged to take the initiative, improve quality, reward efficient workers. For the first time some Soviet newspapers were worth the paper they were printed on. But the great bulk of the inefficient centrally administered system budged not one inch.

It took about 18 months for Mr Gorbachev to work out why. The Communist Party on which he was relying to push through change stood to lose most from it and was therefore resisting. Mr Gorbachev started plotting a shake-up of revolutionary proportions. At a special party gathering in the summer of 1988 he talked for the first time not of getting more out of the old system, but of "radical reform". Despite open hostility from some of the victims, the party's bureaucracy was to be cut. Party stalwarts were encouraged to stop interfering and to exercise their leading role in the privacy of their own offices. Later that year Mr Gorbachev announced what he called a "blowing up" of the old political system: freer elections, a full-time working parliament, more powers to the local councils (soviets).

The avowed aim of the changes was to shift power away from the bureaucracy and to limit the powers of the executive. To get his reforms going, Mr Gorbachev tried appealing over the heads of the bureaucrats to the Soviet people. He did eventually succeed

in stirring his sleepy country to life, but not where he would have liked—in the factories and on the farms. There his reforms still met massive indifference.

...to bullet

The year of Mr Gorbachev's first great political experiment was also the year that the Soviet empire at home literally blew up in his face. In his early days, before he realised quite what he was up against, Mr Gorbachev once referred to his reform experiment as a "revolution without shots". But in the past three years the outlying Soviet republics have seen some appalling violence. The worst atrocities have been committed not in clashes between the Soviet Union's ethnic minorities and the resented Russian majority, but in bloody battles between minorities: Armenians against Azerbaijanis in the bitter quarrel over the tiny enclave of Nagorno-Karabakh; Uzbeks against Meskhetian Turks over land rights, a bloody theme that runs throughout the patchwork of nationalities sprawled across Soviet Central Asia. The list runs on. It amounts to the Soviet Union having an incurable case of the splits.

Beyond the ethnic violence was a political challenge that has shaken Mr Gorbachev to his reforming core. As party conservatives never let him forget, it has been the political freedoms he granted which have helped channel political resentments into a direct threat to Kremlin rule. This has happened in the hitherto more peaceable republics, such as Lithuania, Latvia and Estonia, and also in the Ukraine and in Russia itself.

Last year Mr Gorbachev decided to reverse himself. The new democratic freedoms were to be balanced by increasing powers for himself as president—to direct the economy or declare martial law without consulting parliament. The danger in collecting too much power in one pair of hands was only too obvious from Soviet history. At the time, however, most people seemed less wor-

ried about a future dictator and more worried that Mr Gorbachev might be bumped off or elbowed aside. Indeed the Soviet parliament kept dumping more and more powers in his lap.

Anyway, political reform still seemed to be moving on quite briskly. The informal political groupings, from nationalist movements in the individual republics to the radical Inter-Regional Group of deputies in the parliament in Moscow, began to take on clearer shape. In 1989 there were said to be 60,000 of them throughout the Soviet Union. New laws were still being passed that stripped the Communist Party of its constitutional monopoly of power and provided for the formal registration of new political parties. Reformers took heart from the republican elections in the spring of last year and from the Communist Party congress in the summer. Ministers like Mr Shevardnadze and the then prime minister, Nikolai Ryzhkov, all withdrew from the party's Politburo so as to separate party from government.

Yet resistance was building up. The conservatives in the party were down after the congress (their standard bearer, Yegor Ligachev, had not even been elected to the new Central Committee), but not out. Mr Gorbachev carried the party congress, but the criticism increased. Mr Shevardnadze was accused of "losing" Eastern Europe. Mr Gorbachev was accused by a younger, more aggressive breed of communists in both party and army of all but losing the union.

Lithuania's declaration of independence last March was followed swiftly by declarations of either independence or "sovereignty" by the other republics. These were not just a personal challenge to Mr Gorbachev. They were a threat to the integrity of the Soviet state. Mr Gorbachev's proposed remedy—a new union treaty to redivide power between the centre and the republics—offered too little power to the republics and came too late to persuade at least the Baltic states to turn back. When he had been in a tight corner before, Mr Gorbachev had been able to use his own powers of persuasion to produce a compromise. Yet, in rushing through his new powers as president to try to cope with the uppity republics and silence his critics, Mr Gorbachev made a fatal tactical error.

All downhill from there

In the spring of 1990, when he still had the benefit of enough people's doubts, Mr Gorbachev could have put himself up for popular election as president and won. Instead he chose to have himself elected by an increasingly discredited parliament. Worse, he was not even an elected member of that—he was a Communist Party nominee. As the battle for the Soviet Union spilled over on to the streets, Mr Gorbachev could claim no popular mandate to support his authority. He was outshone both by the radicals, led by the Balts and the hugely popular president of the Russian republic, Boris Yeltsin, and by the old guard, led (in public at least) by Lieutenant-Colonel Viktor Alksnis, leader of the Soyuz group in parliament.

In the end, Mr Gorbachev had to side with one group or the other. He has chosen the hardliners, who have demanded and won the heads of prominent reformers, including both Vadim Bakatin, the former interior minister, who opposed the use of force against the republics, and later Mr Shevardnadze. The first casualty of Mr Gorbachev's shift has been his political reforms. Increasingly hardline statements from the defence minister, the KGB chief and Mr Gorbachev himself over the past three months have shown that he is prepared to see the new democratically elected republican parliaments and governments quashed in his determination to hold the union together.

But it is not just the awkward new political freedoms that Mr Gorbachev will sacrifice in a crackdown. His hopes for economic reform, the original reason for his political reforms, will be dashed too. Indeed, economic reformers now look increasingly to people like Mr Yeltsin. He has gathered round him an impressive team of market-minded advisers. Many of them are former Gorbachev acolytes fed up with their old boss's dithering in the search for the non-existent middle ground between market and plan.

For all his talk of reform, Mr Gorbachev has never quite managed to convince himself that state socialism will not work. Although he gave his approval for co-operatives (small private businesses in all but name), he hedged them about with too many restrictions. He instructed managers to make contracts directly with each other, instead of through the planners in Moscow, but then issued them with "priority" state orders that had to be filled first. Laws exist that might allow the break-up of collective farms and the sale of some state-owned factories; but local authorities have been given the power of virtual veto over them.

While shelves emptied and the economy plunged deeper into chaos (see chart on previous page), most of 1990 was spent wrangling over which reform plan—the radical Shatalin plan, the conservative Ryzhkov-Abalkin plan, or the compromise Aganbegyan plan—should be adopted. In the autumn Mr Gorbachev opted for a compromise that was too conservative for the comfort of many of his own advisers, who promptly deserted him. It was a fateful moment. The reformers lost heart and scattered. Mr Gorbachev has since governed autocratically—and increasingly erratically—by decree.

It might anyway have been too late. Mr Gorbachev took far too long merely to contemplate the sort of radical overhaul that might bring some economic order out of the chaos. Even before the crackdown in the Baltic republics, it was still not clear what he meant by his avowed determination to preserve what he calls the Soviet Union's "socialist choice". Now it may not matter anyway.

A reformer's end

By the end of 1990 Mr Gorbachev's two great challenges—a deteriorating economy and the threatened break-up of the Soviet Union—had rolled into one. Mr Gorbachev insists he will press ahead with reform and keep the union together. But he cannot do both. He had rejected the radical Shatalin plan partly because it handed over too much economic power to the republics, and with it inevitably a lot of political power too. The biggest challenge from the republics—from the Baltic states and from Mr Yeltsin's Russia—comes from those most determined to press ahead with economic reform.

But any reform, however modest, is unlikely to work at rifle-point. The cabal of army, KGB and party people determined to crack down on the errant republics wants to do more than uphold Soviet constitutional law. It also wants to restore economic "order"—a euphemism for killing reform.

In China, after the crackdown in Tiananmen Square, the hardliners failed to roll back the reforms very far because, after a decade of get-rich-quick licence in the countryside and in the powerful coastal provinces, too many people had a stake in prosperity. Not in the Soviet Union. All Mr Gorbachev has given the Soviet people these past six years is greater impoverishment and a string of broken promises. Not much to fall back on in the bad times ahead.

Ominous Embers From the Fire of 1989

Nicholas D. Kristof

Special to The New York Times

BEIJING, April 14—A silence has settled over China a year after a few fragile white flowers appeared at Tiananmen Square to encourage the student democracy movement, but it is an eerie calm and a potentially explosive one.

With a year's hindsight, the crushed movement of 1989 appears to fit neatly into the century-long pattern of student demonstrators opposing emperors, warlords and Communist Party leaders. The emperors and warlords were toppled, and the overarching question for the China of the 1990's is whether the hard-line Communist rulers will also fall.

"All the ingredients for an explosion are here," said a Western diplomat, reflecting a view commonly held by foreigners and Chinese, who speak of deep and sustained anger toward the Government.

"But that doesn't mean there will be an explosion," the diplomat added. "The scene could be quiet for a few years more."

It was exactly a year ago on Sunday that Hu Yaobang, the popular Communist Party leader who had been ousted in 1987 after nationwide student rallies for democracy, died of a heart attack, setting off a push for change that led to demonstrations in 100 cities. Students first brought white flowers, signifying mourning, to Tiananmen Square, the political focal point of the country. Soon hundreds of thousands of students and workers were filling the square to show support for hunger strikers and to hail the Goddess of Democracy, the statue that was the emblem of their hopes. Then, after weeks of threats, the army finally attacked on the night of June 3 and on June 4, turning submachine guns on the crowds and killing hundreds and wounding thousands.

The democracy movement was over, temporarily at least, and so was the decade-long perception of China as the pioneer of what was sometimes called "cuddly Communism." In the last year, the authorities have arrested thousands of dissidents, tightened regulations on study abroad, cracked down on the underground Christian church, and revived Maoist practices like the cult of adulation for the model soldier Lei Feng. (Indeed, part of the central triangle of Beijing University, which a year ago suddenly bloomed with angry posters, is now devoted to an official hagiography of Lei Feng.)

On the surface, last year's democratic conflagration has been extinguished. Yet the authorities acknowledge the existence of "unstable factors," and the young troops are clearly jittery as they patrol Tiananmen Square on motorcycles. And to talk with Chinese is to know that the movement still smolders, in veins deep beneath the surface, and that while the authorities can control it they may never eradicate it.

"Workers, intellectuals—almost everybody is against the Government now," said a middle-aged teacher who did not take part in the protests last year. "When you meet people and converse with them, it's taken for granted that they don't like the regime."

Asked whether he knew anybody who approved of the leadership, the teacher at first shook his head. Then he leaned forward triumphantly and added, "Oh, my sister's husband's father—he's different. He's an older man and he still believes what he reads in the newspapers here."

China has changed in many ways over the last decade, but basically it is governed as it always has been, the teacher said. "The situation itself hasn't changed so fundamentally," he said. "What has changed is our minds and our hearts."

Another man, in his 30's, was making a courtesy call on an elderly relative, a senior official, when the generational tensions exploded into harsh words. As the younger man relates the story, he criticized repression and his relative said in a rage: "That's the problem with you younger people. That's why we can't depend on your generation to take over the party from us."

The younger man retorted angrily: "And it's because of attitudes like yours that we all want to change the party."

This man and many intellectuals take heart in the success of democratic movements in Eastern Europe and in the collapse of authoritarian regimes in China's past. Another great convulsion of 20th-century China, the student protests of May 4, 1919, was also suppressed, through imprisonment rather than widespread killings. But it gave birth to a sweeping reassessment of Chinese culture and politics and led to the rise of the Communist Party.

3 Important Ways China Has Changed

Like the 1919 protests, those in 1989 may have been crushed by force, but they changed China. Conversations with Chinese intellectuals and workers, as well as with foreign diplomats and scholars, point to three fundamental changes that have reshaped Chinese politics and society.

The first is that democracy is an issue on people's minds in a way it never was before. It comes up constantly in political discussions. Last year's protests initially were as much about corruption and inflation as anything else. By the time the tanks rolled in, ordinary people were talking about the need for elections and a free press. What began mostly as an explosion of inarticulate discontent was channeled, by the reaction it encountered, into a full-fledged democracy movement. Of course, people are still vague about what they mean by democracy, but there is a broad consensus for deep political restructuring.

The second change brought about by last year's protests was that rulers and ruled alike came to see that the discontent was much broader than anyone had realized. There has been a revolution in perceptions: before, dissidents regarded themselves as a tiny and beleaguered faction facing an almost invincible behemoth; now, a common perspective is of a beleaguered Government surrounded by hordes of disgruntled citizens.

"Of course, I knew I was unhappy with the way things were run," an artist said. "But I thought it was only me or maybe just me and a small number like me. And then when the demonstrations began, I discovered that absolutely everyone felt the same way."

One consequence of this revolution in perceptions, particularly after the collapse of Communist regimes in Eastern Europe, is that the authorities are more intent than ever on tightening public security. Another consequence is that Prime Minister Li Peng and other hardliners are so consumed with maintaining domestic control that they have not focused much on international relations. Some critics of President Bush's policy toward China say that his conciliatory offerings are doomed to fail—or, more accurately, to be ignored—because the Chinese leaders now view foreign relations as peripheral to the central matter of political survival.

The third and perhaps most important legacy of the demonstrations is that the leadership, in handling the protests as it did, actually strengthened and expanded the opposition. A new vitriol burns in those who once were merely disdainful.

An international network of dissidents has been established to try to pressure China from without, just as Sun Yat-sen marshaled Chinese abroad to help bring down the Qing Dynasty in 1911 and 1912.

Such an opposition is new under Communism. When the protests began in China a year ago, they were not anti-Communist, as were those in Eastern Europe. Wuer Kaixi, the student leader, said last spring that he wanted to join the Communist Party, and some demonstrators carried banners reading, "We support the correct leadership of the Communist Party."

The Fire Next Time
May Claim the Party

While the 1989 protests did not begin with the intention of overthrowing Communism, many Chinese think the next ones will have that goal. One well-placed official, a man who had devoted his life to advancing the Communist Party, became active in the democracy movement in 1989, and in an interview not long before he was arrested he predicted with despondency that the ferocity of the crackdown would discredit the party and ultimately lead to its overthrow.

Like many Chinese of his generation, Hou Dejian, a 33-year-old pop singer, worries that while the students made every attempt to avoid violence in 1989, they may not be so scrupulous next time. Mr. Hou, who defected from Taiwan and thereby has a measure of protection, is the only dissident in China who remains as publicly outspoken as ever, and even he keeps a bag packed in case he is arrested.

"When Chinese heard that the Ceausescus had fallen in Romania, they were glad and they hoped that the same would happen to China's Ceausescus," Mr. Hou said. "But it would be worse here, much bloodier, and the situation would get out of control."

In interviews and in recent songs, which he is not allowed to sing in public, Mr. Hou calls for nonviolence and drives home the theme that there must be change and that if it is not granted peacefully it might be achieved violently.

Mr. Hou captures the impact of the new alienation created by the authoritarian policies: he says with a laugh that he was not a dissident before, but he is training to become one.

A Regime Besieged By New Alternatives

In many respects, the Communist Party's crisis today parallels the situation in China in the late 1970's, scholars say. The paramount leader, Deng Xiaoping, shares the fate of Chairman Mao Zedong in being unable to find a successor with whom he is entirely happy. Both men dismissed several heirs and settled on lesser-known candidates who lacked power bases. Mao chose Hua Guofeng, and Mr. Deng last year selected Jiang Zemin, a Soviet-trained engineer who had been leader of Shanghai. Mr. Hua lasted about two years after Mao's death in 1976; many Chinese think Mr. Jiang will be lucky to retain power on the second anniversary of Mr. Deng's death.

The Communist Party today, as at the end of the Maoist period, faces a crisis of legitimacy. Indeed, the situation may be worse today, because China has opened to the world and many Chinese

have a clear vision of an alternative: a free market and competitive democracy as exhibited by Taiwan. No less an authority than the People's Daily grumbled this week in a front-page commentary that "now there are some young people who are ignorant of party and government history, but who delight in discussing Taiwan-style 'freedom.' "

Virtually every opinion poll taken in China confirms the anecdotal impression of widespread discontent, particularly among urban residents. When 2,000 Shanghai university students were asked a few years ago why people joined the party, only 4 percent said it was because they believed in Communism; the main response was that a party card helps win promotions.

In another survey, in which 1,800 graduate students were polled in 1986 and 1987, not one reflected the official line that the views of Fang Lizhi, the dissident, "should be disdained."

Yet another survey, conducted in May in Beijing, during the protests, found that only 4 percent of those questioned were satisfied with the situation in China, and that only about 1 percent opposed the student movement. There are no polls to show trends since the crackdown in June, but the almost universal assessment is that opposition to the Government has increased.

A year ago a combination of factors—corruption, economic discontent, jockeying among leaders to succeed Mr. Deng, structural changes that weakened the state's control, and the party's declining legitimacy—provoked the democracy movement. Those factors remain in place and some are worse than ever: the economy is faltering and legitimacy has declined even further.

A Question of When And How, Not If

So if change is widely regarded as inevitable, how will it come? Two scenarios are common: renewed street demonstrations that topple the regime or change from within the Government.

The most common view among Chinese is that, barring the death of a leader, students will probably not return to the streets this year. "Security is too tight to hold protests," said a university student in Beijing. "It's too risky. This is a time for waiting."

Even if students do not take the lead, street protests could be started by laid-off factory workers, or by ethnic minorities in Inner Mongolia or in Xinjiang province in northwest China. Just in the last week, there have been sketchy reports of violent clashes around the Muslim city of Kashgar in the south of Xinjiang.

Yet while such protests are worrisome because they could arise anywhere—set off after a factory misses a payroll, for example, or after the murder or rape of a Muslim by a member of the Han majority—the Government could probably keep them from spreading nationally.

Like many China specialists, Andrew J. Nathan, a professor of political science at Columbia University, thinks change is most likely to come from above.

"The more likely scenario is that as the succession crisis matures, a faction within the leadership will use popular support to strengthen its own hand and give Li Peng the heave-ho," Professor Nathan said in a telephone interview from New York. Many Chinese agree, with some even predicting that if the situation seems stable, Mr. Deng will remove Prime Minister Li and push for further economic changes within about a year.

Professor Nathan suggested that once the leadership has been reshuffled, the new leaders may institute a measure of democracy to bolster their legitimacy. One factor that bodes in favor of democracy in China is that it could work in the interests of the leadership. While urban residents and especially intellectuals are deeply disgruntled, some 70 percent of China's population is made up of apolitical peasants. Even some dissidents think that the Communist Party could probably count on its organizational network to turn out the peasantry and win a reasonably free election. This is an option that Eastern Europe's leaders never had.

The parallel with the late Maoist period bolsters the view that change could come from within. It was raw political and military power, not popular uprisings, that ousted the Gang of Four in 1976 and that in the next few years chipped away at Hua Guofeng as chairman. Now, as then, it is difficult to tell what side anyone is on because the leaders all wear masks—sometimes layers of masks—to conceal their feelings.

Few officials have been purged, and the Politburo and Central Committee today are virtually the same as the ones endorsing liberalization just a year ago. Most of the Central Committee members were chosen not by the hard-liners but by their nemesis, Zhao Ziyang, the ousted party leader.

From abroad it may seem that China has been tugged back into a Cultural Revolution, but that perception is based on the storm of propagandistic oratory sweeping the nation. Beneath the ideological storm, life has changed much less than one might think. This is especially true in the countryside and in provincial cities, where the political squalls weaken as the distance from the capital increases.

"The surprising thing is how outspoken people are," a university professor said. "Back in the anti-rightist campaign in 1957, and in the Cultural Revolution, you didn't dare say anything because people would run to the leaders and report you. But now when you meet a colleague, the first thing you talk about is politics, and the party members are more critical than anyone else."

The hard-liners have tried to stifle their critics, but the instruments of repression are much less effective now than they were in the past. Ordinary Chinese did not turn in their neighbors to the police last year; they sheltered them. The dissident Chai Ling has just escaped from China after eight months on the run, and a student underground continues to operate quietly in Beijing with scores of active members. That would have been impossible a decade ago. Try as it might, China cannot be as totalitarian as it used to be.

CHINA
THE COMING CHANGES

Chong-Pin Lin

Chong-Pin Lin is Sun Yat-sen Professor of China studies, Georgetown University, and adjunct scholar, China Studies Program, American Enterprise Institute.

China will soon enter a new period of instability, the next episode in the cyclical economic pattern that began under Deng Xiaoping. For insights into the nature of this period and the positive developments likely to follow it, Western observers need to look carefully at the sequence of events in earlier cycles as well as the unique social and political factors now present. What emerges is a perspective on China's future that is very different from predictions made right after the Tiananmen Square bloodshed in June 1989.

At that time, two opposing views of China's political future took shape among China-watchers. A well-known Chinese dissident in exile at the time articulated one view: he said that a regime that had lost its legitimacy could not last more than a few days. His prediction missed the mark, but the rationale behind it—treating China as if it were a western democracy where legitimacy directly determines the continuation of the rule—persists. Others who shared this general viewpoint foresaw a recurrence of urban uprisings in China in the coming spring. Those taking the opposing view see the Chinese Communist Party (CCP) continuing to rule the country for at least another decade. For the time being, a modicum of stability has returned to the country.

China's post-Tiananmen economy has continued to benefit from a decade of reform. In the year tainted by the blood of Tiananmen, Sino-U.S. trade increased by 22 percent despite sanctions imposed by the United States and other Western nations. In the same year, China surpassed Taiwan as the world's number three textile exporter, and in the spring of this year China jumped to fifth position in the world in shipbuilding capacity.

The strong agricultural growth of the first part of the decade still had momentum in the late 1980s. China has seen two consecutive years of record summer harvests: last summer, right after Tiananmen, China produced 93 million tons of grain, up from 91 million in 1988. In 1990, not only did the 97-million-ton summer grain harvest break all previous records, but the projected 425-million-ton annual agricultural production is expected to do so as well.

Moreover, the two major causes for the Tiananmen unrest—hyperinflation and rampant corruption—seem to have abated. Inflation fell from 21 percent in 1988 to 17 percent in 1989. It is expected to be 5–8 percent in 1990. Just one and a half months after Tiananmen, the government launched an anti-corruption campaign. Twelve thousand Communist Party members were expelled by December 1989, and more were thrown out in 1990. People in China who believe in the good faith of the government see the expulsions as evidence of the government's sincere intention to address the problem of widespread corruption.

China's tourist industry, crippled by Tiananmen gunfire, has rebounded. In May 1990, for example, 10,000 foreign tourists visited Beijing, a 2-percent increase over the same period in 1989.

China launched a series of diplomatic offensives after Tiananmen that began to bear fruit by the fall of 1990. Amid an overall improvement in relations with other nations, Beijing established diplomatic ties with Saudi Arabia—once an anticommunist bastion—resumed formal relations with Indonesia after more than two decades, and paved the way for mutual recognition with Singapore and South Korea. Further, the Asian Olympic Games of 1990, held under the vigilant eyes of 650,000 security forces and agents (40 percent of the 1,697,000 spectators) in Beijing,

UNDER DENG XIAOPING, CHINA'S PARAMOUNT LEADER SINCE DECEMBER 1978, THE COUNTRY'S ECONOMIC CYCLES HAVE BECOME SHORTER AND MORE REGULAR, REPEATING EVERY FOUR YEARS.

From *The American Enterprise*, January/February 1991, pp. 18-25. Copyright © 1991, The American Enterprise Institute for Public Policy Research.

ALTHOUGH THE LEADERS IN BEIJING ARE TRYING TO KEEP ECONOMIC GROWTH AND THE INFLATION RATE WITHIN SAFE BOUNDS, THEY MAY VERY WELL LOSE CONTROL AGAIN.

came off calmly and without incident. The successful games seem to have dispelled the Tiananmen shadow, restoring people's confidence in the government while improving China's international image.

But stability has been won at a high price. The regime in Beijing was determined to achieve it and was willing to use force to that end. They silenced dissension and suppressed unrest by arrests, persecutions, and executions. Persistent purges against reformers brought about, among others, the expulsion from the Party of *People's Daily* Director Hu Jiwei 16 months after Tiananmen in October 1990. In September, Amnesty International spoke out against Beijing's record of executions—more than 720 people were put to death from January to August 1990.

The second view of China's future course—continued rule by the CCP—appears to be supported by the stabilizing factors just mentioned for two reasons: first, because no other viable political force exists in China today that can replace the CCP as the Communists supplanted the Nationalists in 1949; and second, because the Chinese people are averse to drastic change of political rule and fear chaos of the kind they experienced during the Cultural Revolution. But this perspective ignores the deep-rooted and widespread problems that lurk beneath the current appearance of stability. Among a myriad of problems facing Beijing, two destabilizing factors stand out: the fractured People's Liberation Army (PLA), and rising regional autonomy. These exist in a larger context of cyclical instability.

Cyclical Instability

Under Deng Xiaoping, China's paramount leader since December 1978, the country's economic cycles have become shorter and more regular, repeating every four years (see box, China's Economic Cycles, and figure). By late 1990, China's economy had undergone two years of relaxation (1987–1988) followed by two years of retrenchment (1989–1990) in the third cycle. If the pattern established under Deng continues, Beijing will soon relax its tight economic control and gradually phase out its austerity program. The results will possibly be rising economic growth and probably a soaring inflation rate by 1992.

By the fall of 1990, signs of relaxation in the general climate of economic austerity had begun to emerge as Beijing leaders felt both relieved at having achieved stability on the one hand and pressed by the need to revitalize their depressed economy—marked by low industrial growth, mounting inventories, and a rising budget deficit—on the other. In

mid-July 1990, China's hard-line gerontocrat Chen Yun publicly noted the "political, economic, and social stability" gained by "quelling the rebellion" at Tiananmen and by the "economic rectification" policy. At the end of July, Yuan Mu, the State Council spokesman, even brought up the "coastal development strategy," a plan that had been advocated by Zhao Ziyang in 1987 when he was premier but that had fallen out of favor. Meanwhile, Zhou Jiahua, who headed the National Planning Commission, publicly addressed the need to increase market activity and to stimulate the economy. On October 24, even Premier Li Peng, who had warned against the danger of economic relaxation, called for "deepening economic reform."

Interest rates had been lowered twice by August 1990 to loosen the availability of credit, and by November a series of steps had been taken to provide capital and raw materials to rural industry, relax restrictions on construction and spending on state enterprises, and raise the prices of coal, petroleum, water, electricity, bus fares, sugar and salt, rent, and tuition at certain city schools. Some of these moves had hitherto been considered responsible for overheating the economy and causing the hyperinflation China experienced in 1988. In July 1990, Finance Minister Wang Bingqian had advocated tightening both budget and credit to guard against economic "swelling." Adding to the inflationary potential for China's economy is the enormous and growing personal savings of the Chinese people. By fall of 1990, this reserve amounted to $150 billion, 40 percent of China's 1988 GNP of $368 billion. Once unleashed by a revived market, the accumulated savings could create tremendous demand and send inflation skyrocketing.

A more market-oriented economy, with higher growth rate and rising inflation, will almost certainly bring back corruption, widen income discrepancies, arouse popular resentment, and generate social unrest. All this had happened in the last economic cycle, before the 1989 Tiananmen incident. Although the leaders in Beijing are trying to keep economic growth and the inflation rate within safe bounds, they may very well lose control again. As long as Beijing remains "politically antirightist and economically antileftist"—a posture containing inherent contradictions that are difficult to alter while the conservative gerontocrats rule—the economic cycles described earlier will probably continue.

Since 1985, China has experienced inflation above 7 percent, and there have been more-frequent student demonstrations at intervals of one and a quarter to two and a half years—in September 1985, December 1986-January 1987, and April-June 1989. If the

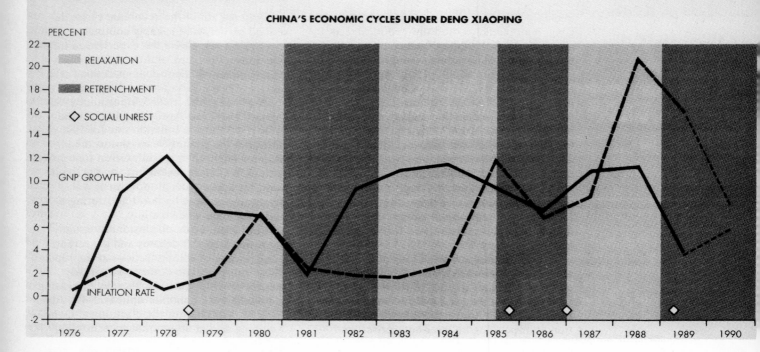

CHINA'S ECONOMIC CYCLES UNDER DENG XIAOPING

Sources: Robert Summers and Alan Heston, "A New Set of International Comparisons of Real Product and Prices" *Review of Income and Wealth,* Series 34:1 (March 1988); International Monetary Fund, *International Financial Statistics Yearbook 1990; Huagiao Ribao,* April 24, 1989; *Beijing Review,* June 4–10, 1990.

CHINA'S ECONOMIC CYCLES

Since 1978, China has gone through two complete cycles of economic relaxation and retrenchment, each lasting four years (see the figure above). The economy has just passed the fourth year of the third cycle.

In the figure, China's economic cycles under Deng Xiaoping are depicted using three key parameters: the gross national product (GNP) adjusted for inflation, the inflation rate derived from the consumer price index, and the alternations of Beijing's economic policy between relaxation (reform) and retrenchment (rectification).

A typical cycle began with the PRC leaders' deci-

sion to advance economic reforms by relaxing central controls. This occurred in 1978–1979, 1983, and late 1986. Relaxation accompanied by decentralization was then followed by rising GNP growth (1985–1986 and 1987–1988) and soaring inflation (1979–1980, 1984–1985, 1987–1988). The overheating of the economy compelled China's leadership to recentralize the economy-(1980–1981, 1986, 1988–1989). The effect of such policy changes was reduced inflation but also reduced GNP growth (1981, 1986, 1989). As the economy slowed, Beijing resumed a policy of economic liberalization, which started yet another cycle.

One exception here is the drop in GNP growth from

12.2 percent in 1978 to 7.1 percent in 1980 after relaxation began in December 1978. The reason may be that in 1978, Hua Guofeng —then simultaneous head of the Party, the armed forces, and the bureaucracy — pushed a high-growth economic policy with an emphasis on the mechanism of central planning rather than the forces of the marketplace. A record level of state investment, heavy foreign borrowing, and increases in urban wages boosted GNP growth without relaxed governmental controls over the economy. Lacking basic structural reforms, the forcibly escalated economic growth could not be sustained. Nonetheless, it settled at a respectable level above 7 percent in 1979 and

1980 after the policy of relaxation came into effect. In any event, the rising inflation in 1979–1980 was indicative of the decentralization that began in 1978.

The plummeting GNP growth and the drastic braking on inflation in 1989 also require further examination. Although the Tiananmen aftermath definitely contributed to cooling China's economy, the austerity program adopted in September 1988 caused economic slowdown even before the spring unrest of 1989. Thus, the model seems largely valid to date.

Chong-Pin Lin with Jeffrey Liang and Stephen Salerno

THE ARMY MAY NOT REMAIN MONOLITHIC OR BE A LOYAL INSTRUMENT OF THE DICTATORIAL RULERS IN THE NEXT UPHEAVAL FOR SEVERAL REASONS.

projected 8 percent inflation rate for 1990 rises further in the coming years, unrest among students might then spread. Given the cyclical pattern in China's recent history, the likelihood for a new student movement will drastically increase by late 1991, during a period of economic volatility.

In China, economic instability usually intensifies political debates and exacerbates power struggles among factions at the top. These can percolate down to an already restless urban population, thereby increasing the likelihood of another upheaval. On June 16, 1989, shortly after the crackdown, Deng Xiaoping said in an internal speech, "We must avoid endless quibbling over the problem of responsibility (for the Tiananmen incident) . . . stop all arguments for at least two years," because the major task at hand was to restore stability. With stability largely recovered, the chances for China's leaders to reopen the debate over the Tiananmen responsibility will likely rise, especially after mid–1991. This will be two years after the event and into a period of economic volatility.

Deng is now 86 years old, and rumored to be in declining health. His departure from the scene may trigger the onset of upheaval. However, even if he stays on, the next upheaval will occur as predicted by China's cycles of instability. Then, Deng's ability to maintain the loyalty of the PLA may be the key to whether or not Beijing can weather another political storm.

A Fractured Army

After the Tiananmen incident, PLA Major General Wu Jiamin wrote: *In 1949, I was a 17-year-old soldier. As we marched into Beiping [now Beijing] to liberate the people, there were flowers, ribbons, cheers, and smiling faces everywhere. I felt glorious and happy. Forty years later, as an army commander, I entered the city on the same route . . . . We were pursued, blocked, hit by bricks and soft-drink bottles, stared at, and cursed at . . . . Forty years ago, I came . . . under the Party leadership to seize power; this time . . . I came under the Party leadership to preserve power.*

The book *One Day Under Martial Law*, which contained the above and other passages unflattering to Beijing's hard-line leadership, was released by the PLA's official publisher in October 1989. It was banned in early 1990 by the Party. In September 1990, the Party banned another book released by the PLA, *White Snow, Red Blood*, and detained its author, Lieutenant Colonel Zhang Zhenglong, for "seriously exposing the dark sides of the Army."

These unusual episodes are symptoms of the fracturing of the army that once was the paragon of altruistic solidarity and the pillar of national unity. Despite the post-Tiananmen revival of political indoctrination in the PLA, the Army may not remain monolithic or be a loyal instrument of the dictatorial rulers in the next upheaval for several reasons.

Both horizontal and vertical fissures have developed in the PLA. The intellectual gap between the recruits from the countryside and the younger officers is widening. The quality of the former has deteriorated as their more-competent peers have decided not to join the Army, preferring to pursue more-lucrative careers—made possible by Deng's economic reforms. The quality of the younger officers, each with the equivalent of a college degree, has improved. A second horizontal gap occurs between the younger officers—more worldly and enlightened in outlook—and the senior veterans, whose ideas reflect the ideological straitjacket of the past.

Vertically, a fracture has grown between the generals Deng has commanded—in the Second Field Army during the Civil War (1946–1949) and in the 129th Division during the Sino-Japanese War (1937–1945)—and those without this connection. Since Deng emerged as paramount leader in December 1978, his former military associates have enjoyed greater opportunities for promotion. For example, in July 1988, when Deng as Central Military Commission (CMC) chairman reintroduced military ranks that had been abolished in the mid–1960s, he appointed eight Second Field Army soldiers among the 17 senior generals, a far larger number than from any other single Field Army. Those not so fortunate resented this favoritism. During the spring 1989 upheaval, seven generals who were veterans of the Long March joined in petitioning Deng not to send troops to Beijing. All were affiliated with the Third Field Army. This kind of dissension in the Chinese high command, rarely publicized, highlights underlying disunity.

Another vertical fracture that is still evident today developed among the Second Field Army generals themselves during the Tiananmen crisis. On one side were those sympathetic to the deposed reformer Party chief Zhao Ziyang and the demonstrating students. On the other side were those siding with the hard-line leaders Yang Shangkun, first vice chairman of the CMC, and his brother Yang Baibing, CMC general secretary. The post-Tiananmen ascendance of the "Yang family generals" has dimmed the future of those who sympathize with reformers: Defense Minister Qin Jiwei was passed over for promotion on the CMC in November 1989,

Beijing Military Region Commander Zhou Yibin was removed in May 1990, and the 38th Army Commander Xu Qinxian was reportedly imprisoned. During past political crises in the PRC, retired military leaders often functioned as "underground commanders" and were instrumental in the outcome of power struggles by persuading influential former subordinates to shift sides. The disgruntled reformers in the PLA, though stripped of official positions, can still have considerable impact in the next upheaval.

Furthermore, since 1983 the Army's expanded economic activities designed to compensate for the reduced defense budget (which have included such enterprises as manufacturing refrigerators, running hotels, producing cosmetics, and investing in real estate along the prosperous southeast coast) have provided partial financial self-sufficiency to the local military units, cultivated self-interest that is different at times from Beijing's, built personal networks with local nonmilitary elites, and spawned corruption. The military ethos of self-sacrifice and patriotism has been impaired as a result.

In the next upheaval, if Deng is alive, he may still rely on the PLA to suppress opposition, but his chances for success will be lower than in the past. The cost in blood will be higher. If he is gone, the historical pattern of complete submission by the PLA to the Party leadership may be broken, and violence may spread. No other leader in Beijing today can match the military prestige of Mao, who proved the correctness of his guerrilla strategy in the crucible of history, or Deng, who commanded successful military campaigns in the 1940s and was PLA chief of staff in the mid–1970s. In spring 1990, Jiang Zemin, Deng's heir apparent as both Party and CMC chairman, was not even invited to attend the ceremony launching China's fifth nuclear submarine. Meanwhile, the discontent in the PLA against the Yang family generals precludes the emergence of Yang Shangkun as the next ruler without precipitating a civil war. In either case, the probability of reduced central military authority after the next upheaval increases with time.

Rising Regional Autonomy

By January 1989, a saying had circulated widely through the country: "China now has 30 mountaintops and 2,000 'feudal lords'," referring to the increasingly independent provinces and counties. Beijing's rule over the provinces has been slipping, as has the reign of the provinces over the counties. During China's past decade of economic reform, local governments enjoyed increasing autonomy in economic decision making to maximize production under different local conditions. The results are increasing regional autonomy manifested in local defiance of higher authority, provincial protectionism, and intraregional cooperation that bypasses the central government.

"Those on top issue policies; those below invent counterpolicies" has become common wisdom. Deng Xiaoping has reiterated that local governments must obey orders from Beijing, according to the China News Agency in February 1988.

Take the increasingly inefficient tax-collection system for example. In 1979, 87 percent of a Shanghai citizen's income was paid to Beijing in taxes and redistributed to other localities; by 1987, the amount had shrunk to less than 20 percent. In 1988, the actual profits of locally controlled state enterprises rose by 21.3 percent, but the taxes they paid fell by 9.5 percent, according to *Jingji Ribao* (*Economics Daily*) in February 1989. According to a *New York Times* correspondent, city authorities were buying condominiums in Canada rather than funneling their earnings to Beijing in taxes. China-watchers began to use such terms as "economic warlordism" and "fiscal feudalism" to describe the new behavior.

Provinces are trying to protect their economic interests by restricting both the outflow of raw materials and the inflow of finished products. In central China, for example, patrols guarded the border of Sichuan to stop the outflow of raw silk. Meanwhile, the governments of the surrounding provinces attempted to defy the restriction by hiring well-paid mercenaries and even by deploying military vehicles. In recent times, Sichuan's "battle for raw silk" has occurred almost annually, while similar confrontations over wool, tobacco, hemp, and yams have taken place along other provincial borders in China, especially when there were serious shortages of raw materials. As the austerity program implemented in September 1988 started China's economy on a downturn, provinces began placing restrictions on the inflow of finished products—bicycles, color televisions, soft drinks, and so forth—from other provinces to protect local industry. By the summer of 1990, the government of Jilin province in the northeast had even officially banned importing beer from its neighbors, Liaoning and Heilonjiang provinces.

An additional aspect of China's rising regional autonomy is the growing cooperation among the provinces. The China News Agency reported in mid-June 1990 that funds to construct railroads along the east coast had been raised by neighboring provinces, with

DURING CHINA'S PAST DECADE OF ECONOMIC REFORM, LOCAL GOVERNMENTS ENJOYED INCREASING AUTONOMY IN ECONOMIC DECISION MAKING.

Beijing's approval but not its initiation. According to Hong Kong's Central News Agency in October 1990, Mainland economists have proposed creation of a South China Economic Union of five provinces (Guangdong, Guangxi, Hunan, Jiangxi, and Fujian) to stimulate the interprovincial flow of commodities, increase economic efficiency through cooperation, and strengthen regional economic bonds with the international market as well as with Hong Kong, Macao, and Taiwan.

China's rulers have tended to divide the immense country into regions having similar terrain, dialects, resources, and industries. When Mao conquered China in 1949, he ruled the country through six administrative regions. Beijing has divided its territories since 1985 into seven military regions and recently into seven economic regions, with the two seven-part systems largely overlapping. As a result of Dengist economic reform and expanded economic activities of the military regions, local political and military leaders have formed networks, sharing common interests. It is true that no other viable political force exists in China today that could replace the Chinese Communist Party. Yet it is also true that no one can prevent the CCP from gradually disintegrating because multiple power centers within the Party have emerged in the regions.

A Future Scenario

Examination of the two views of China's political future previously described gives rise to a third, a scenario that has four stages. First, the current post-Tiananmen stability will last one to two years because of the stabilizing factors described above.

The second stage will be a relatively short period of instability that will begin around 1992 as economic volatility induces social unrest and intensifies policy debates among the top leaders, who will become divided by political infighting cloaked in economic terms. A power struggle at the top may spark tumult among the urban population that the Party center will not be able to suppress without more bloodshed than in June 1989. However, widely shared aversion to the spreading chaos that characterized the disastrous Cultural Revolution will compel national and regional

leaders to convene and reach an accommodating arrangement. The result will be the rise of reformers and the further decline of central authority over the increasingly autonomous local governments. After that, although Party elites will continue to dominate the central and local governments, the influence of noncommunist elites will grow; both Marxism-Leninism-Maoism and the name of the Chinese Communist Party, if surviving at all, will become increasingly irrelevant.

The third stage, a relatively long period of robust economic development, will follow, facilitated by rising regional autonomy under a weakened central government. Economics will take command. A tendency for neighboring provinces to cooperate economically in competition with other regions will produce six to nine de facto political blocs in China under the nominal rule of a central government, with or without the name of federation. The active pursuit of external financial and technological assistance will lead to greater interaction (with or without the full supervision of the central government) among the regional blocs and with the outside world, especially Taiwan, Hong Kong, Singapore, Japan, the United States, and Europe. The socioeconomic and political ties between Taiwan and Mainland China as a whole will grow as Taipei deals with each regional bloc on a more-equal basis than it had previously with Beijing.

The fourth stage will be a period of integration. Among Taiwan, Hong Kong, and the regional blocs on the Mainland, living standards will begin to converge. The need for unified currency and other kinds of socioeconomic coordination among various Chinese-speaking entities will increase in the face of competition with global economic blocs. Socioeconomic cooperation will gradually lead to political integration of the Mainland, Taiwan, Hong Kong, and Macao under a more-democratic form of government demanded by an expanded middle class and an entrenched pluralistic society, both having developed in the previous period.

In Beijing, tourists will honor a monument erected years earlier in Tiananmen Square commemorating the event on June 4, 1989. In school, students will learn in history classes of the Chinese Communist Party.

The Third World: Diversity in Development

The Third World is an umbrella term for a disparate group of states, often called developing or less developed countries (LDCs). An important common thread among them is that they are not modern industrial societies. Otherwise these countries differ considerably in terms of history, present conditions, and prospects. Moreover, the designation *Third World* has been used so variously that it is dismissed by some critical observers, who charge that it is a category that is loaded with cognitive confusion and ideological symbolism but that has little or no analytical value. Their objections should at least make us cautious when speaking about the Third World.

Originally the term Third World referred to countries—many of them recently freed former colonies—that chose to remain nonaligned in the cold war confrontation between the First World (or Western bloc) and the Second World (or Communist bloc). In fact, the categories *first world* and *second world* have never been used widely, and they make increasingly little sense in view of the rapidly changing East-West relationship. But the derivative category Third World continues to be a handy, if imprecise and sometimes misleading, term of reference. It sometimes still carries the residual connotation of non-Western and non-Communist. Increasingly, however, the term is used to cover all largely non-industrial countries that are predominantly non-modern in their economic and social infrastructures. In that sense, there are also Communist-ruled countries that belong in the Third World, with China and its southeast Asian neighbors being prime examples.

Most of the Third World nations also share the problems of poverty and rapid population growth. However, their present economic situation and potential for development vary considerably, as a simple alphabetical juxtaposition of countries such as Angola and the Argentines, Bangladesh and Brazil, or Chad and China illustrates. An additional term, *fourth world*, has therefore been proposed to designate countries that are so desperately short of resources that they appear to have little or no prospect for a self-sustained economic improvement. Adding to the terminological inflation and confusion, the Third World countries are now often referred to collectively as the *South* and contrasted with the largely industrialized *North*, because most of them are located in the southern latitudes of the planet—in Latin America, Africa, Asia, and the Middle East.

It is just as important to remember that these countries also vary considerably in their sociocultural and political characteristics. Some of them have representative systems of governments, a few of which have a record of stability. Many are governed by authoritarian, often military-based regimes that espouse an ideologically promoted strategy of rapid economic development. Closer examination will sometimes reveal that the avowed determination of leaders to improve their societies may carry less substance than the determination to maintain and expand their own power and privilege. In any case, the politics of development or modernization in these countries vary enormously.

In studying the attempts by Third World countries to create institutions and policies that will promote their socioeconomic development, it is important not to leave out the international context. The political and intellectual leaders of these countries frequently draw upon some version of what is called *dependency theory* to explain their plight, often combining it with demands for special treatment or compensation of various kinds. Dependency theory is itself an outgrowth of the Marxist theory of imperialism, according to which advanced capitalist countries have established exploitative relationships toward the weaker economic systems of the Third World. The focus of such theories is on *external* reasons for a country's failure to generate self-sustained growth. They differ strikingly from more traditional explanations that give more emphasis to *internal* causes (whether sociocultural, political, environmental, or a combination of these).

In this anthology, David Landes reviews the differences between the state-oriented and market-oriented strategies of development. He finds that each approach has disappointed its advocates, and argues in favor of paying greater attention to the contextual or situational aspects of each case of development. Otherwise, developers overlook human factors that may bring their plans to naught. Landes also concludes that it is a major disadvantage to be a latecomer in modernization, despite some earlier exceptions to this rule (Japan, for example). It is far more difficult to catch up today.

Much attention has been given to the success of the new industrial countries or NICs, a small group of former Third World countries, in breaking the cycle of chronic poverty and low productivity. It is not at all clear what lessons we can draw from the impressive records of the four or five "tigers" or "dragons"— Singapore, Hong Kong, South Korea, Taiwan, and possibly Thailand or Malaysia.

Originally called the Group of 77, but now consisting of some 120 countries, the Third World states have banded together in the United Nations to promote whatever interests they may have in common. In their demand for a New International Economic Order, they have focused on promoting changes designed to improve their relative commercial position vis-à-vis the affluent industrialized nations of the North. Nevertheless, it would be a mistake to assume from these common efforts that there is a necessary identity of national interest among these countries or that they pursue complementary foreign policy goals.

Outside the United Nations, some of these same countries have tried to increase and control the price of industrially important primary exports through the building of cartel agreements among themselves, often to the detriment of other Third World nations. The most successful of these cartels, the Organization of Petroleum Exporting Countries (OPEC), was established in 1973 and reigned for almost a decade. Its cohesion has since eroded, resulting in drastic reductions in oil prices. While this development has been welcomed in the oil-importing industrial as well as developing countries, it left some oil-producing nations such as Mexico in economic disarray. Moreover, the need to find outlets for the huge amounts of petrodollars deposited by some oil producers in Western banks during the period of cartel-induced high prices led the financial institutions to make huge loans to many Third World nations, which the latter could not repay. The resulting economic, social, and political problems are particularly evident in Latin America.

The problems of poverty, hunger, and malnutrition are socially and politically explosive. In their fear of revolution and their opposition to meaningful social reform, the privileged classes often resort to brutal repression in an attempt to maintain a status quo favorable to themselves. In Latin America, this has led to a politicalization of many laypersons and clergy of the Roman Catholic Church, who demand social reforms in the name of liberation theology. For them, some variant of dependency theory fills a very practical ideological function by providing a relatively simple analytical and moral explanation of a complex reality. It also gives some strategic guidance for political activism to overcome this state of affairs. Their views on the inevitability of class struggle and their willingness to take a side have often clashed with Vatican policies.

The difficulty of establishing stable pluralistic democracies is another problem in Third World countries. Some authors have argued that Latin America's dominant political tradition is basically corporatist rather than competitively pluralist. They see centralized authoritarian governments, whether of the Left or Right, as reflections of this unitary bias of the political culture, and warn against expecting a pluralist development in most of the continent. From this perspective, the current trend toward democratization in much of Latin America may not last. Given the difficult challenges facing these new democracies, a return to authoritarian political responses cannot be ruled out. Of particular interest to Americans is the attempt by President Salinas of Mexico to move his country toward a more competitive form of market economics. His hesitance in moving from economic to political reform is understandable, since the latter would reduce the hegemony of his own party, the PRI, and give new outlets for protest in a time of socioeconomic dislocation. But critics of Salinas argue that his approach is too technocratic in its assumption that economic modernization can be accomplished without a basic change of the political system.

It is not possible within the confines of this anthology to explore thoroughly all areas of the Third World. However, the remaining selections will introduce you to complex problems that face many of these countries. Blaine Harden has no illusions about the major problems facing Africa—the most impoverished continent in the world. Yet in looking more closely at Nigeria, by far the most populous country in Africa, he discovers a learning curve in both economics and politics that gives reason to hope for progress.

South Africa faces an even more monumental task of introducing democracy in a multiracial society where the ruling white minority has never shared political or economic power with black Africans. Prime Minister de Klerk will be challenged from all sides as he attempts to implement reforms that go too far and too fast for a privileged minority, and not nearly far or quickly enough for many more who demand political equality and social improvement. It is clear, as Christopher Wren points out, that while formal equality can be achieved by scrapping the apartheid laws, the social and economic chasm that separates the races will need to be addressed if the changes are to have much meaning for the long suppressed majority. The politics of redistribution will be no simple or short-term task. Nevertheless, for the first time in decades, South Africa now offers hope for a major improvement in interracial relations.

The Middle East is another area of great interest to the student of comparative politics. Once again, it is not possible to cover all important aspects of this part of the world, but Robin Wright discusses a very important aspect in her article on an observable trend toward more moderate politics among active adherents of Islam. She sees a growing emphasis on working within the system.

The final two articles introduce another important region, namely the subcontinent of India. With its almost 800 million people, India is more populous than Latin America and Africa combined. It is deeply divided by ethnic and regional differences, and its external debt has lurched ahead of an otherwise impressive rate of economic growth. The potential for social and economic crisis looms over the country, but over 40 years after independence, India continues to disprove the forecast of political and economic disaster. In many ways, this subcontinent's development is impressive and deserves more attention than it normally receives. The first article briefly reviews the many problems that trouble the country, while the second suggests that India's solution may lie in developing a more decentralized, secular, and pluralist system of government.

Looking Ahead: Challenge Questions

Why is the term *Third World countries* of little analytical value? What have these countries in common, and how are they diverse? What is meant by the term *fourth world*?

How do explanations of Third World poverty and slow development differ in assigning responsibility for these conditions to external (foreign) and internal (domestic) factors? Why can theories of development be important in shaping strategies of modernization? What is the dependency theory, and why does it seem to have such a strong appeal in Latin America and some other Third World areas?

Why do economic development and democratic government run into such difficulties in most of Latin America? How has President Salinas revived the tradition of strong presidential leadership in Mexico? What are the basic features of his so-called *Salinastroika* in the economy policy area? What are the prospects for success in overhauling a stagnant economy and an anachronistic political system?

Why does a careful observer of Africa stress the diversity of the continent? How is the development of today's African states affected by strong cultural traditions and a history of colonial subjection? What are the prospects for a movement away from authoritarian rule toward democracy in the sub-Saharan parts of Africa?

How is Prime Minister de Klerk attempting to move away from the white supremacist legacy he has inherited? What obstacles will this *Pretoriastroika* run into? Why can the abolition of apartheid laws be only the beginning of reform?

How has India managed to maintain parliamentary democracy, given all the economic, social, and cultural conflicts that divide this multiethnic society? Why did the government of Prime Minister V. P. Sing fall in late 1990? What difficulties will the new government encounter in trying to preside over the unity and development of this vast country?

RICH COUNTRY, POOR COUNTRY

David Landes

DAVID LANDES is the author of *The Unbound Prometheus* (Cambridge University Press) and *Revolution in Time* (Harvard University Press).

In the beginning there was Smith, and Smith told us not to worry about economic growth. Left alone, people would sort things out, do what they do best, make appropriate choices to maximize return. The market would take care of the rest, rewarding reason and quickness and knowledge and punishing the opposite. All of this, moreover, would work to the general advantage, augmenting wealth and leading nations through a natural progression of stages from agriculture to industry to commerce. Long live the invisible hand!

For more than a century and a half following Smith's *Wealth of Nations* (another good reason to remember the year 1776), this confidence in the inevitability of material progress prevailed. It was one of the unspoken assumptions of a world caught in the wonder of science. There were, to be sure, places, times, and voices of discouragement. Malthus and Ricardo warned of limits on growth, of overpopulation and the "stationary state." It was not for nothing that economics was called the dismal science. But with the passage of time and the diffusion of new technologies through Europe and European offshoots overseas, such perils were seen as so remote and hypothetical as to be safely ignored.

Even the naysayers and rebels were caught up in the larger mood of optimism. There were no stronger believers in progress, for example, than the socialists, especially Karl Marx, Epigoni & Company, who proclaimed themselves scientific the better to color the religious character of their belief system. Even the most backward and poorest societies in the world would be swept up by the march of progress thanks to the intrusion of the front-runners. Marx deplored the abuses of imperialism, but he saw it as "objectively" progressive. In an oft-quoted passage on the British conquest of India, he noted that India had been conquered repeatedly by foreign masters, each of whom had simply renewed the plunder and exploitation of old. With the British, at least, India would be wrenched out of the changelessness of what he called the Asiatic mode of production and compelled into a process of modernization. British greed would make it so.

Two generations more of colonial experience were sufficient to disabuse socialists (and other observers) of this innocence. For one thing, the economic programs of imperialist nations were aimed at promoting the interests of the home country. They might also favor the development of their colonies—indeed, they usually did—but this was a byproduct and in any event a very different kind of development from that at home. For another, abuses and left-liberal politics made imperialism a dirty word. The South African ("Boer") war and the scandal of Belgian rule in the Congo provided material for outrage and votes. (The only damper on this combination of moral condemnation and political opposition was the awareness that the colonies sustained in various ways the jobs and wages of the proletariat at home, which is where all political charity begins. That is why the French Communist Party was long indifferent if not hostile to the movement for Algerian independence.)

This revision of Marx's (and Engels's) primitive optimism did not, however, signal abandonment of a fundamental confidence in the inevitability of progress. It simply meant that this progress, like socialism, would have to await the collapse of capitalist oppression. Liberation at home would be accompanied by liberation abroad, for obviously there could be no such thing as socialist imperialism. On the contrary, imperialism was a specific characteristic of capitalism, its "highest stage," to quote Lenin. And when freedom came, as it surely would and as it did after World War II, it would be followed by material development as the night the day.

This optimism was not confined to the political left. Center and right, it was the same. Two schools of thought held the field. Neoclassical economists saw no reason why the classical market mechanisms should not enable newly developing countries to follow the example of their industrialized precursors. One oft-cited model was the so-called staples theory or "vent for surplus": a country exports staples, usually primary products such as field crops or minerals; and the earnings will finance more balanced growth, in industry as well as in agriculture or mining.

This doctrine had been developed initially to explain Canada's path to high product and high income. The gains from a succession of export staples (furs in the

Reprinted from *The New Republic*, November 20, 1989, pp. 23-27. © 1989, The New Republic, Inc.

17th and 18th centuries, then timber in the late-18th and 19th, then grain and minerals in the 19th and 20th) had drawn people and capital and generated the earnings to make possible balanced growth in all sectors. It was subsequently applied to Australia (wool, meat, wheat, minerals), the United States (tobacco, cotton, wheat, minerals), and Sweden (timber, iron ore and semifinished bar iron, copper)—all of whom had done very well. And it could with equal plausibility be made to account for the transition of medieval England from a dependent primary producer (minerals and wool) to Europe's leading industrial nation.

The second school of thought has come to be known as development economics. The gist of this approach is that no one can afford to wait while natural market forces work their allegedly beneficent effects. They take too long, and they too often produce specialized economies that may follow their comparative advantage but are fearfully unbalanced and vulnerable to price shocks and the maneuvers of stronger trading partners. Witness the misfortunes of banana, cocoa, coffee, and other one- or two-crop republics. Even oil producers are not immune. If a country, then, wants to have a truly modern economy, versatile and technologically up to date, it has to go about it deliberately. It has to set goals, plan and facilitate action, control decisions, and manage performance.

This approach owed much to the state planning tradition developed by the Soviets, which still enjoyed prestige in the first postwar decades, but it was also readily compatible with the Keynesian economics that had been cultivated in free market countries struggling to pull out of the Great Depression. And it enjoyed the sanction of historical experience: as Alexander Gerschenkron argued in a seminal article of 1951, you don't have to be socialist to need the state. All the so-called follower countries, those European nations and offshoots that emulated the British Industrial Revolution, had to take special measures to catch up. They needed larger investments in capital for later vintages of equipment and plants, and they had to train their workers to a new discipline and higher technical standards.

The earliest followers, such as France, Belgium, Germany, and the United States, had been able to do this in large part with private resources, although the state did intervene to assist the costliest ventures. They had a long experience of their own in trade and industry, and their businessmen and property owners had accumulated sufficient capital to meet the needs of modernization.

Even so, it took special institutions to mobilize this wealth, and Gerschenkron, following an old tradition, stressed the role of so-called development banks as movers and facilitators of industrialization. Later developers, however, were too poor to do as much, and the state had to step in. Gerschenkron, a specialist in European and especially Russian economic history, took his example from czarist Russia and then the Soviet Union, beginning with Peter the Great and going up to the five-year plans of the 1930s, and emphasized the strain and cruelty of such efforts, which characteristically took the form of intense "spurts" followed by indispensable periods of respite. It should be noted here that Gerschenkron was in effect continuing the optimistic tradition that development is there to be had, so long as one uses a proper strategy. One has to mobilize capital and use it wisely; one has to acquire knowledge and know-how. But these are within reach and increasingly efficacious. Technology improves; knowledge advances. What's more, the late developer has the advantage of hindsight, which is always the best kind.

By this logic, the opportunity and potential gains of the leap to modernity increase over time: it pays to be late. The latecomers grow faster and maybe better than their predecessors: they buy state-of-the-art equipment; they move into heavy industry (in those days, coal and steel were the summum bonum of industrial capability). Gerschenkron took as his special examples Germany in the mid- and late-19th century and late-19th-century czarist Russia. Russia, Gerschenkron maintained, coming later, installed bigger and better equipment even than that used in German metallurgy. (He was wrong about that.)

He recognized that not every society is ready to make this leap: it takes awareness and preparation, in particular the liberation of productive energies held in check by bad institutions (in the Russian case, serfdom). In that regard he was at one with just about the entire economics profession, going all the way back to Adam Smith, who offers us among other things fascinating comments on the deleterious effect of bad political and social arrangements on Chinese economic performance. The leap might also require the mobilization of enthusiasm. This is the role of ideology.

In general the decades of the 1950s and '60s were sanguine years, marked by unprecedented rates of growth, a spectacular expansion of international trade, and an optimistic consensus, for different reasons, about the prospects of global economic development. And how could it not be so, since colonies were now free, and all that was needed was money and know-how? It was in this context that Walt Rostow brought out his *Stages of Economic Growth*, an almost biological model of development that envisaged a whole world maturing into a state of high consumption.

We have been disappointed since. Every year the World Bank publishes its "basic indicators"—statistics on economic and social performance of countries around the world. They are a record of success, but also of failure to the point of despair. They show the effects of natural and man-made disasters, of two oil shocks, of wars and revolutions, of freedom turned into political oppression. They show growth slowing even among the leaders, show some countries going backward while others limp in their aborted or interrupted flight; they testify to widespread famine and poverty, to a growing gap between rich and poor. One should not be systematically pessimistic, especially when some gains give reason for real satisfaction. Look at the life expectancy data. Or the growth rates of the quick economies of East Asia. Even so, the success of some merely highlights the failure of others. Africa is a heartbreaker. In sum, the easy confidence is gone. Economic development is not to be taken for granted. It is a hard business.

The failure of ambitious development programs in many Third World countries has inevitably led to a search for explanations. These typically fit the paradigm, in which we saw growth as natural and stagnation as an effect of non-economic interference and exploitation. Mainstream economists have had a field day denouncing the mismanagement and corruption of government planners and managers; the radicals have found their villain in capitalist greed. To be sure, formal colonialism has largely vanished, but it is argued that unequal economic ties and domination have survived the dissolution of political bonds. A copious and ferociously sectarian literature flourishes, much of it coming from a disappointed and frustrated Latin America, to explain this new "highest stage." This literature of neocolonialism, *dependencia*, unequal trade, and underdeveloping the developing countries has proved far more influential than the neoclassical market arguments about political incompetence—partly because neoclassical conservatives come across as scolds, partly because it is a lot easier for Third World countries to blame their ills on the outside than to look in the mirror.

Both these approaches, it should be noted, have maintained the paradigm. Both have assumed that development is natural, hence intrinsically easy; just give it a chance. The free marketeers take for granted that growth will bring about division of labor and specialization, with feedback gains in an upward cycle. And the planners assume that wanting and thinking can make it so. The material ingredients are all that is needed: land (resources), labor (bodies), and capital (money).

This has also been the position of the development planners and doers. These are variously economists, bankers, bureaucrats in national and international agencies, employees of philanthropic foundations. Their task is to make good things happen by injecting the ingredients. Put in money and ideas, send in technicians and designers, and the growth will take care of itself. For such doers, the classical paradigm is congenial as well as persuasive, for it assumes the homogeneity and sufficiency of these ingredients. Even labor: people may seem different, but for economists and people-movers, they are at bottom the same. They are rational optimizers and maximizers trying to get the most for the least, hence responsive to the right signals and opportunities; or they are like putty (economics jargon), made to be shaped at will. Even the most highly skilled or educated are in effect ready to hand because they can be hired, from elsewhere if necessary. Hence the expected efficacy of economic cookery.

In the period since the War, however, in addition to nagging and recurrent disappointment, two things have happened to shake these assumptions. One has been the "discovery" of the "residual" in the 1950s. This is the term economists have assigned to that part of growth apparently not accounted for by the conventional factors noted above. The very fact that these did not "explain" just about all of growth was in itself a big surprise, since the the conventional models (production functions) assumed an identity: growth was made up of, hence was, increase of land, labor, and capital. But even more surprising was the size of the unexplained category: on the basis of statistics drawn from national accounts (in itself a new branch of economics), the residual appeared to represent half or more of the growth of advanced economies in the modern period.

The first reaction of economists to the residual was to try to identify it. It was called technology, which seemed a reasonable explanation for productivity gains that increased product beyond what the conventional factors could account for. To be sure, technology is in itself a product of many inputs, in particular, of knowledge, skills, and enterprise. There remained the task, then, of explaining advances in technology—not only the invention of new ways of doing things but also their diffusion and application. Here the most popular line of analysis was to represent technological change as a response to growth and investment. Fast growth, for example, normally requires new equipment embodying more productive techniques. Another line emphasized changes in relative prices of the conventional factors. These will often enhance the reward to technological solutions: if labor gets more expensive, for example, perhaps because of a successful strike, it becomes that much more advantageous to build a machine to take its place. In this way, technology was tamed for economics—reduced to a buyable commodity available on demand as a response to needs and opportunities.

For some economists, though, the emphasis on technology seemed excessive. The problem, they felt, was not in the reality but in the counting. Why not shrink the residual? To do this, the conventional factors of production had to be redefined so as to take account of changes in quality as well as quantity. They were not homogeneous. They embodied improvements: labor became better educated and trained; machines got smarter; new raw materials worked better than old. If one weighted these factors for quality, one did reduce the residual by more than half, although it was not clear whether this was not simply a new bookkeeping convention.

In the meantime, the emphasis on quality and the abandonment of the homogeneity assumption necessarily raised the question of the human factor. If people are different . . . well, that makes the story of growth very different.

The issue came to the fore with the growing awareness of the spectacular rise of the Japanese economy to industrial pre-eminence, especially in some of the most advanced branches of manufacture. This was an achievement that no one would have dared predict in the aftermath of World War II. The Japanese economy was then in ruins, and the loss of empire left the country with little in the way of industrial raw materials. The prospect of recovery seemed small enough; the notion that Japan would soon compete successfully, even dominate, in such heavy industries as steel and motor vehicles was inconceivable.

Japan's performance since then has given rise to a new industry: that of explaining Japanese success. A small library of books and articles, some of them best sellers, have proposed to tell us the secret. For some, it lies in the venerable virtues: a high savings rate (thrift), hard work, good planning. For others, these are in themselves the manifestations of deeper characteristics of Japanese society and culture: the Japanese are different.

Over these same years, moreover, we have seen similar instances of ultrarapid growth elsewhere in East Asia—in Korea, Taiwan, Hong Kong, Singapore, the so-called little dragons—which raises similar questions about them and about East Asian societies in general. For a while, there was talk of rice-bowl cultures. My own preference was to speak of chopstick cultures, because I could see a direct link between the skills necessary to eat with chopsticks and to work with tweezers and similar implements at the fine tasks required by modern electronics manufacture. Some scholars are talking these days about Confucian culture. The assumption is that if all of this is happening in the same part of the world, an area that shares certain cultural characteristics, we ought to be able to find some common feature or features that have contributed to this result.

So we have looked, and it is clear that most efforts to understand and explain these developments include the human factor. What is more, by including attitudinal and cultural elements as well as levels of education and professional formation, these explanations introduce variables that are not only hard to measure, hence uncongenial to economists and planners, but hard to change and even harder to transfer. (Our individualistic Western societies, for example, may not be ready to emulate Japanese patterns of collective behavior, even in the glorious cause of industrial supremacy.) And this is indeed a major change in our intellectual apprehension of the process of development.

This brings me back to the problem of those Third World countries that have not done well. We have seen that the initial, conventional reactions to their and our disappointment have been to blame it on politics and power. And there is clearly much truth in that. But here too there has been an increased willingness to look at the influence of social and cultural variables. Not so much, of course, as with the high-growth countries. If one wants to impute success to such factors, no feelings will be hurt. But to attribute failure even in part to human shortcomings can be wounding. Some would say that such characterizations are intrinsically racist. And coming from the outside, from those who have "made it," they will almost inevitably smack of condescension—no way to phrase this sort of thing tactfully.

Even so, there is an implicit recognition of the human problem on the part of growing numbers of people in the less developed countries. It takes the form, interestingly enough, not of an effort to transform social structures and cultural patterns in the pursuit of modernization, but the reverse—a deliberate rejection of the values associated with industrialism, consumerism, and all the other preconditions and "rewards" of economic growth. Such economic refuseniks are as yet a small minority, drawn primarily from among religious fundamentalists and cultural conservatives (as in Iran and India). There may even be an element of sour grapes in this reaction. There is certainly pride. And yet I would be surprised were this movement to achieve more than temporary and local success—partly because most people prefer shoes and transistors to spiritual virtue, partly because modern technology is an important component of power, and power drives nations.

If, now, one admits the significance of this complex, relatively intractable human factor, what becomes of the effort to help the poor become richer, to spread the benefits of modern technology throughout the world, to narrow and even eliminate the gaps between haves and have-nots? Specifically, what is left of the comfort that latecomers could take in their lateness?

The answer has to be nuanced. On the one hand, the recent successes of the East Asian countries is evidence that it can pay to be late—if one possesses the social and human requisites. Lack of capital of its own will not prevent a thrifty, productive society from generating and attracting all the capital it needs, as we have seen in postwar Japan. Earlier colonial status and a history of imperial exploitation will not paralyze initiative, as it has not in Korea and Taiwan. Even the sophisticated technologies are not beyond reach.

On the other hand, today's would-be developers do seem to face greater problems than earlier followers did. For example:

(1) The very size of the gap is a discouragement. Even success looks like failure, because a large percentage gain on a small base is still smaller in absolute terms than a small gain on a large base. In real terms, then, even rapidly growing developers lose ground initially in terms of the difference between their income and that of the rich. This initial stage of relative deprivation, which easily translates into a sense of injustice, foments impatience and jealousy and contributes to the instability and inefficacy of government. (Students of revolution have long noted that trouble comes not from the depths of misery but from the appetite that grows with better eating.) It also encourages counterproductive ideology: Why should poor countries have to pay for knowledge? But if they will not pay for it, or even protect it, why should rich countries bring it to them?

(2) It is a fact of history that most developing countries are also new countries. They have young, untried institutions and administrative structures that fall far short of the tasks implicit in their ambitions for power and wealth. In many instances, they still have no firm identity, no sense of national purpose, no common

interest. On the contrary, they suffer the pains and aftereffects of colonial arrangements imposed without regard to reason or circumstances. Government is unstable or, even if enduring, essentially brittle. The regime may call itself democratic, but the people are subjects rather than citizens. As a result, whatever the economic gap that already separates many of these countries from the rich states, it is even bigger for the want of direction (in both senses) of the would-be followers.

(3) The new technologies are so esoteric and difficult as to be almost unlearnable, except for those who leave to study in advanced countries. This very process of study abroad is both gain and loss, for these students, once they have learned, are often reluctant to go home, if only because they can do much more with their knowledge abroad. Indeed, the better they have learned the more reluctant they are to return, because the gap is bigger between earnings potential abroad and at home.

The brain drain is further aggravated by the material, political, and cultural gap between the West and the Rest. How'ya gonna keep 'em down on the farm after they've seen Paree? Even in the straitened circumstances of the typical foreign student visitor, the living tends to be better in the rich countries, the social life more exciting, the politics more interesting and, very important, much safer. Most of the world's industrial nations are democracies, and students from Third World countries who learn and train there typically enjoy far more freedom than they know at home. To be sure, they also encounter the distance and hostility of racism, subtle and overt—though far more overt in such socialist countries as the Soviet Union and China than in most Western (capitalist) nations. (So much for progressive sentiment and indoctrination: socialists are entitled.) On balance, though, the university years build expectations that the home country is not able or willing to satisfy. Hence one more good reason not to go back.

(4) One should not overlook that category of difficulties that derive from "human nature." This includes among other things what economists have called the demonstration effect: seeing is wanting. For a variety of reasons related to communications technology, the poor people of the world are bombarded by testimonies of the material advantages enjoyed by others. They do not have to travel to learn these things: they see them in films and on television, hear of them on the radio and by word of mouth. The result is a sense of impoverishment and grievance (why they and not we?) and a great impatience.

Some of this hunger finds expression in fantasy, of which the most poignant examples are the cargo cults of the Pacific—magical cults that promised to summon back the American ships that had come during the war with their precious loads of goods and goodies. Some of it takes the form of exit: the massive migration since World War II, still under way in the face of all manner of political impediments, from poor places to rich. But in my opinion its most consequential effect has been the poisoning of development efforts in the direction of haste, waste, and corruption.

Does it pay to be late? On balance, no. This is not to say that today's latecomers are condemned to remain poor. Not at all. Many of them are growing faster than their predecessors and are substantially richer than they were a generation ago. But they are probably less happy. The very knowledge of difference and deprivation is something new. We have taught them that they are poor and given them to taste of the fruit of the tree of knowledge. It is a bitter fruit.

What is more, the earlier confidence that history is teleological, tending irresistibly toward industrialism and modernity, no longer seems tenable. Is it time for a paradigm shift? Suppose the process of economic development is not the destiny of all humankind. Suppose instead that what we are dealing with is a pool of candidates. Some are favored by circumstances; some are not. The ones most favored go first. Others follow. And as the pool is exhausted, the hard cases remain—not only because of the misfortunes and misdeeds of history, but because, for all manner of internal reasons, they do not take to these new ways. They don't like them; they don't want them; they are discouraged from learning them; if they learn them, they want out; etc. Perhaps what we are seeing now is simply that we're getting down to the hard cases.

Hard cases make bad economics and politics. We must and shall keep trying to help, as much for ourselves as for those we want to benefit. But we're going to have to choose our targets better and aim straighter. Otherwise the costs go up and the returns go down. The present Third World debt crisis is an excellent example of misconceived and misdirected assistance. That it is costing the lenders a fortune is as it should be. That most of the banker-statesmen who engaged in this rush to throw away money are still sitting in their lavish executive suites is proof that at a higher management level, what passes for statesmanship is more important than business acumen. To be sure, these statesmen may yet succeed, with the help of thoughtful economists, in getting the taxpayer to support the loss, in which case they will have proved once again one of my favorite cynicisms, namely, that capitalism is the privatization of gains and the socialization of losses. (That's not really fair: there are losers, but not usually banks.) They will also then be encouraged to lend again on the principle that some seed may fall on fertile ground.

There must be a better way to make money in and for poor countries. For starters, direct investment in competitive enterprise is probably better than giving to governments (if governments will let us). And if we want to give away money, we can do better by putting it into children (health and education) than into the pockets of parents and so-called leaders. If we can find some way to improve these human possibilities and prospects, we may not only overcome some of the penalties of lateness but reclaim some of its advantages. Better late than never.

SALINAS TAKES A GAMBLE

Robert A. Pastor

ROBERT A. PASTOR, professor of political science at Emory University, is co-author, with Jorge G. Castañeda, of *Limits to Friendship: The United States and Mexico* (Vintage). He was director of Latin American affairs at the National Security Council from 1977 to 1981.

Americans have been so transfixed by the fall of the Berlin Wall—and now riveted to the crisis in the Persian Gulf—that they have failed to notice the crumbling of the walls that have segmented Mexico and separated it from the United States. Yet Mexico's opening may be the more significant for us, in terms of infusing our economy and reshaping our society. Carlos Salinas de Gortari, challenging a long tradition of state control and anti-Americanism, is leading this change, transforming Mexico and U.S.-Mexican relations more profoundly than any Mexican president in this century.

Not yet one-third of the way through his term, he has moved decisively to arrest corrupt union bosses, financial speculators, drug traffickers, and repressive government officials, and has sold off state corporations, deregulated large sectors of the economy, lowered trade and investment barriers, and begun, grudgingly, to democratize. Yet his most daring gamble is his proposal for a free trade agreement with the United States, and he is ready to sell the idea in both countries. "In 1992," he told me, "the European Community will be the largest market in the world. The United States will be No. 2, but the U.S. and Mexico together could be No. 1." If President Bush fails to grasp the proposal, or if Mexico's economy does not improve or its political climate deteriorates—all real possibilities—Salinas's idea could become a historical footnote, and we might have to wait another generation for the next opportunity.

The twentieth century's first revolution was in Mexico, and it was cataclysmic. The Institutional Revolutionary Party (PRI), which eventually consolidated power, built a centralized state in which high tariff walls permitted miraculous growth and undemocratic political walls kept politics stable. But by the 1970s the Mexican revolution had grown decadent, becoming, in Carlos Fuen-

tes's words, "a fat lady who drives a Mercedes Benz." In the '80s, the debt crisis led to a decline in average wages by 40 percent, and inflation soared. By the 1988 election a political breach had opened in the previously impregnable PRI. One of its leaders, Cuahtemoc Cardenas, the son of the Mexican president who had nationalized the oil industry, left the party and challenged Salinas for the presidency and for the PRI's soul and legacy. Salinas was elected by a bare majority, though Cardenas charged fraud and refuses to accept defeat.

Like Mikhail Gorbachev, Salinas has not launched a second revolution or returned to the first: he is a post-revolutionary pragmatist. But unlike Gorbachev, Salinas opened the economy first, and he has been hesitant in opening the political system. This strategy might work better than Gorbachev's, whose economic reforms are now stuck because he cannot muster the necessary political support from his demoralized party and divided country. Salinas would probably prefer to postpone free elections until the economic reforms restart the economy, raise wages, and bring people back to the PRI. The pivotal questions are whether the economic reforms will work, and whether democracy will wait.

Salinas's first economic priority was to reduce his country's external debt. He assembled a first-rate economic team, and Mexico was the first to negotiate debt relief under Treasury Secretary Nicholas Brady's plan. External debt was reduced 20 percent, about $20 billion, which will result in savings of about $4 billion in debt service each year from 1990 to 1994. Mexico had hoped to reduce its debt much more, but this was sufficient to release some funds for investment.

The government then raised revenues 13.4 percent by enforcing the tax laws for the first time in Mexican history, and cut expenditures. The fiscal deficit shrunk from 11.7 percent of GDP in 1988 to 5.8 percent last year, and inflation plummeted from 160 percent in 1987 to 19.7 percent in 1989. Seventy percent of the state's corporations were privatized, and deregulation permitted businesses to respond to the market rather than to bureaucrats. Trade barriers were lowered so sharply that Mexico went from being one of the most protected markets in the world to a relatively open one. Manufacturing exports surged. Salinas also confronted the untouchables—privatizing the banks and revising the rules on foreign investment—and received surprisingly little criticism for it.

One year ago there was almost no confidence in the economy; today confidence is returning. In 1989 the rate of economic growth was 2.9 percent, the first real improvement since the onset of the debt crisis. The labor market is tighter than it has been in a decade, and capital, after moving north for years, has begun to return to Mexico. The stock market index doubled in the last year, a better performance than any other market in the world. In July *Forbes* magazine told American businessmen to "forget eastern Europe. The next great economic miracle will take place right on our borders." Mexico, it declared, had become "a revolution you can invest in."

Yet though expectations have improved, investment has not increased sufficiently to generate significant growth. Employment in manufacturing has grown, but not as fast as the labor force. Exports have expanded, but so have imports, and the peso may be overvalued. Agricultural production continues its descent while overall prices are starting to climb again. The oil price increase will help, but Mexico's new pragmatists are downplaying that as a panacea; they will not repeat their predecessors' oil-boom-and-bust mistake.

Paradoxically, the success of the economic changes may also depend on Cardenas. He stands astride a heterogeneous, leftist popular movement that he is trying, with limited success, to transform into a new Party of Democratic Revolution (PRD). He has criticized Salinas for "indiscriminately" lowering the economic walls and for not taking into account the social, political, and national security effects of those decisions. But he says if he becomes president, he would review the program on a "pragmatic" basis, not reverse it. Some businessmen believe Cardenas would return to the old state-led model, and there are many in the PRD who would like to do that. If the economy does not grow, their voices could prevail. Other businessmen, like Juan Elek, the former head of the Mexican-U.S. Private Sector Committee, believe Cardenas would modify—not reverse—current policy, but they also think Cardenas's popularity has already waned. The greatest threat, however, may come from Cardenas's followers, who could resort to violence if they feel their leader's path to power is blocked.

By leaving the PRI Cardenas turned a private internal discussion into a public debate, making opposition legitimate and democracy possible. Mexicans have stopped keeping secrets from themselves, and even from Americans. Yet there are still numerous obstacles in Mexico's path to democracy, the most important of which are the PRI's total control of the state and the reluctance by many in the PRI to risk their power for the uncertain results of a secret ballot. Salinas has promised to open the PRI's financial books to the opposition, but "the problem,"

complained Lucas de la Garza, a PRD leader who left the PRI, "is that you would have to audit the entire government budget to find all the funds that flow to the PRI."

The conservative National Action Party (PAN) has long complained of rigged elections, and when the PRI offered to negotiate a new electoral law with them, they leaped at the opportunity. The new law responds to most of PAN's concerns on registration, campaign finance, faster and more transparent counting and announcement of results, and a more balanced electoral commission. However, the PRD and one-third of PAN voted against the bill in the Chamber of Deputies because the electoral council is not independent of the government, and the PRI retains a majority of seats. Although an improvement on the past, the law does not go far enough to assure the opposition a fair shake.

Salinas's electoral record is better than his predecessors', though it is still uneven. In July 1989, for the first time since the revolution, an opposition party won a governorship—the PAN in Baja California. At the same time, the PRI stole elections from the PRD in Cardenas's home state of Michoacan. When his supporters seized the municipal palace, Cardenas called for restraint, and the army evacuated the buildings without a single death. Six months later Cardenas's party won municipal elections in Michoacan, but the PRI was accused of stealing an election in Iraupan from the PAN.

Local PRI officials are reluctant to lose power. Salinas would prefer to open the system gradually, but in the short term he will discipline his cadre only when the opposition leaves little choice. The PAN did that by covering Baja with its poll-watchers, and the PRD's reaction in July 1989 encouraged the PRI to accept its loss six months later.

On November 11 there will be local elections in 121 municipalities in the state of Mexico. The PRI did poorly in the state in 1988, and some recent polls suggest it could lose all of the twenty-five key towns, where 80 percent of the 12 million voters live. This would be difficult for the PRI to accept, but if these elections are rigged, the potential for violence in the state is quite real. And these are just a prelude for the August 1991 midterm elections for the Chamber of Deputies, one-half of the Senate, and seven governors, which will be the main test of Salinas's pledge to democratize the country. Unfortunately, he is in the awkward position of being credible only if the PRI loses.

One way to break out of this no-win situation would be to invite international observers. The Foreign Ministry describes elections as "the ultimate sovereign act," and the idea of letting foreigners, let alone Americans, judge elections gives them—the defenders of Mexico's virtue—paroxysms. Yet Cardenas, whose movement pretends to a higher nationalism than the PRI, has already broken Mexican tradition by criticizing his government in the United States, and told me he is prepared to invite international observers. If the next two elections are debacles, and the news media exaggerate the opposition's charges, then the PRI might begin to view observers as an escape from this predicament.

The most intrepid gamble of Salinas's presidency, and the one that has probably alienated some members of his party, has been to expand the boundaries of cooperation with the United States. "In the old days," Jesus Silva-Herzog, a minister of finance in the previous government, explained, "we PRIstas were taught that Uncle Sam and foreign investment were the problem. Now we are being told that they are the solutions."

Despite serious strains, particularly in the area of drug trafficking, the U.S.-Mexican relationship is as good as it has been for a very long time. The adeptness of U.S. Ambassador John Negroponte is one of the reasons, though he diplomatically offers three others: "excellent personal and substantive chemistry between Bush and Salinas; a good institutional relationship that includes regular meetings between numerous members of each Cabinet with their counterparts; and the growing importance of trade between the two countries."

Mexico is a more important trading partner for the United States than Germany, England, or France; it has been No. 3 behind Canada and Japan for most of the decade. It therefore seemed logical to formalize this relationship with a free-trade agreement, and Americans have regularly offered such proposals, undeterred by Mexico's lack of interest. A year ago Salinas dismissed this idea, saying that the unevenness of the two economies made it unrealistic. He says two developments led him to propose such an agreement in his meeting with Bush in Washington on June 10. "First, we opened the economy to reduce inflation." Now Mexico wants to secure access to the U.S. market. "Secondly, the changes in Europe and East Asia and an apparent reliance on blocs convinced me that we should also try to be part of an economic trading bloc with the United States and Canada. But," he insisted, "we do not want this bloc to be a fortress. We want it to strengthen our ability to be part of Asia, Europe, and especially Latin America."

Salinas needed new investments to move his economy, but he found Western Europe preoccupied by the East and Japan hesitant. The traditional Mexican strategy was to try to gain U.S. attention by feinting toward other regions, but Salinas reversed that. After proposing a trade agreement with Washington, he traveled to Japan, where he converted Japan's interest in a guaranteed U.S. market into $2 billion worth of commitments for new investments—equivalent to current Japanese investment in Mexico. Some Mexicans have raised questions about the details of the proposed agreement or about the style of the approach. Silva-Herzog quipped that "Mexico should have waited to be caressed first, before dropping its pants." But there was no serious criticism about whether to negotiate, and Mexican public opinion, for the moment, is in favor.

In Washington, Salinas encountered a cautious George Bush. In an ironic role reversal, Salinas proposed immediate negotiations, and Bush offered informal talks, with negotiations only after the completion in December of the GATT trade negotiations. The United States has a choice on how to negotiate this agreement. The special trade representative can deal with it in a routine way, squeezing the Mexicans point by point. As Mexico has a tradition of converting small problems with the United States into contests over sovereignty, this approach risks losing the whole enchilada. Or Bush can recognize that such an agreement is one of the nation's highest foreign policy priorities, requiring a long-term vision and a genuine bipartisan approach. As domestic opposition is likely to come from Democrats and labor, he should appoint a Democrat like Robert Strauss, Sol Linowitz, or Bruce Babbitt as the negotiator to report to him and to remain sensitive to the political ramifications in Mexico.

The first step is for both sides to remove the two most sensitive issues, oil and migration, from the agenda. Second, both should agree to phase in the reductions in trade barriers more gradually and less completely in Mexico than in the United States. Third, U.S. negotiators should concentrate on the largest issue—an agreement—and concede the smaller ones to permit Salinas to build a durable coalition in Mexico in favor of the agreement. Finally, borrowing the dispute-settlement mechanism and other elements of the Canadian agreement, negotiators should aim to complete the agreement in one year. If it takes longer, Mexicans could have second thoughts, and Americans could be distracted by possible political turmoil in Mexico.

The United States could ruin the agreement if it conditioned it on changes in the Mexican political system. The United States has a stake in those changes and should state clearly its preference for democracy over "stability" (a false choice anyway since Mexico will not be stable without democracy). But democracy is more likely to arrive in Mexico if the United States completes the agreement fast than if it conditions acceptance of an agreement on those changes, or worse, if it tried to interfere in Mexico's politics.

Bush also needs to demonstrate U.S. respect for Mexico's sovereignty. The involvement by the Drug Enforcement Administration in the kidnapping of a Mexican doctor, who was allegedly involved in the murder of a DEA agent, was illegal and wrong. While we broke the rules, the Mexicans followed them, requesting the arrest of two DEA agents who admitted in court their role in the kidnapping. The administration seems inclined to dismiss the case, but if we do that, we cannot expect Mexico to respond to our requests for cooperation or extradition.

The regional, hemispheric, and geopolitical implications of Salinas's proposal also argue for an immediate, positive response by the United States. North America has resources, energy, complementary labor skills, and a market of 350 million people. This is a formidable economic base. The fear of being locked out of a North American economic community is already beginning to generate interest in the rest of Latin America in a hemispheric-wide union. That interest was reinforced by Bush's speech on June 27 offering free-trade agreements to Latin America and by the fact that the most nationalistic country in the hemisphere, Mexico, has now proposed to tie its economic fate to the United States.

As Salinas suggested, neither a North American nor a Western Hemisphere community should be a fortress, but rather a platform for building a competitive edge. All of this starts in Mexico: if Mexico does not succeed in modernizing its economy and democratizing its politics, the United States cannot escape the consequences. Instability in Mexico would cause mas-

sive migration, capital flight, and radicalism. U.S. citizens and border states would be harmed. "U.S. unions," Salinas says, "will lose more jobs if Mexicans don't find them in Mexico." And the president will be pressured to solve Mexico's problems, though it will then be too late.

It is not too late now. Given Mexico's ultra-sensitivity, the United States is rarely invited to help Mexico develop. Salinas has taken a historic risk in proposing a way to do that while benefiting both countries. This is the time to reward a Mexican risk. President Bush has a momentous chance to reshape our most important and difficult relationship; he should not dawdle.

AFRICA'S GREAT BLACK HOPE

In a continent struggling for survival, Nigeria strives to learn from disaster and show the way out.

Blaine Harden

Blaine Harden, the Washington Post's bureau chief in Eastern Europe, wrote from sub-Saharan Africa for four years. He distilled this article from his book, "Africa: Dispatches from a Fragile Continent," © Blaine Harden, published October 1990 by W. W. Norton & Co.

AFRICA'S MOST POPULOUS country is its brightest hope. Nigeria is an odd place to find a silver lining. It is infamous, even among Nigerians, for being loud, dirty, violent, and corrupt. Its reputation is not unlike that of the United States at the end of the last century—and that is my point. In spite of its all-too-visible failings, I believe that Nigeria's mix of talent, resources, and gall will one day pull the country up out of Africa's own bleak social and economic category: the Nth World.

After coming to know Nigeria, I found myself more and more intolerant of a soft-focus stereotype of Africa that continues to captivate the West. The Oscar-winning movie "Out of Africa" was a paean to love lost among white colonialists. Time magazine devoted its most extensive African coverage of the 1980s—twenty pages of purple prose and color pictures—to an essay that rhapsodized about lions in the tall grass, sagacious pastoral warriors, and "miles and miles of bloody Africa."

This is anachronistic claptrap. Many Westerners have fixated on a self-glorifying illusion, a tranquilizing chimera that justifies ignorance of modern Africa while sanctifying the purchase of khaki pants at Banana Republic stores.

ELEPHANTS AND EXPORTS IN DECLINE

There are countless reasons to despair for Africa, by which I mean black Africa. In the 45 countries south of the Sahara and north of South Africa, at the end of the 1980s per capita income was lower than it was 30 years earlier. Seventy percent of the world's poorest nations are in black Africa.

Africa is the most successful producer of babies in recorded history and the world's least successful producer of food. Gains made in health and education in the 1960s have been lost in many parts of the continent to economic anemia and a population growth rate that is still accelerating. Central and Eastern Africa have emerged as the world epicenter of AIDS. The Sahara Desert creeps south and the Kalahari north, moving 100 miles closer each year as desertification and erosion spread. West African rain forests are rapidly being chopped down for hard currency. About half the 1.4 million elephants that roamed Africa in 1980 were killed by the end of the decade, shot and carved up by ivory poachers with automatic assault rifles and chain saws.

Africa's export earnings declined massively in the past decade. The foreign debt burden, relative to Africa's income, was the highest in the world. Interest payments bled away one of every three dollars Africans earned. The region became more

From *World Monitor*, August 1990, pp. 31-36, 39-41. Adapted from *Africa: Dispatches from a Fragile Continent* by Blaine Harden. Reprinted by permission of W. W. Norton & Co.

dependent on foreign assistance than any other part of the developing world. Outside investment dried up.

Yet there is more to modern Africa than a vast, flat plain of failure. A learning curve can be discerned. Governments have finally started to sift sense out of nonsense. They have, in the words of former Nigerian President Olusegun Obasanjo, begun "to accept that an unjust international order will not change simply because of the euphony of their own rhetoric..."

Many African leaders have stopped blaming their problems on the legacy of colonialism. They have openly admitted that their countries are bleeding from self-inflicted wounds. As in the Soviet Union and Eastern Europe, smothering state control is being lifted from the marketplace. Farmers in many reforming countries are being paid a decent price to grow food, and they responded in the later half of the 1980s with record crops. These tentative efforts have won the attention of rich countries, and Africa's share of world development aid has nearly doubled in recent years.

THE RUSSIANS ARE NOT COMING

For the first time in the post-independence era, the continent is no longer a chessboard in a global cold war. The Russians are no longer coming. Africa is not a region that the United States can win or lose to communism. It seems to have been tacitly agreed, by the Soviets and the Africans themselves, that communism is irrelevant and unworkable. In the last year of the 1980s, American-Soviet diplomatic cooperation laid the groundwork for South African withdrawal from Namibia. Soviet refusal to back endless civil war in Ethiopia has pressured the government there to make peace overtures to rebels (although the fighting continues).

More fundamentally, Africa's learning curve is etched into the everyday lives of human beings caught up in the fitful process of shifting from one set of rules to another. Hundreds of millions of Africans are lurching between an unworkable Western present and a collapsing African past. Their loyalties are stretched between predatory governments and disintegrating tribes, between arbitrary demands of dictators and incessant pleadings of relatives, between commandments of the Bible and obligations to the ancestors. At its heart, the great experiment in modernity that continues to rattle Africa goes on inside individuals, as they sort out new connections with their families, their tribes, and their countries.

Though continuously battered, African values endure. They are the primary reason why, beyond the sum of Africa's dismal statistics and behind two-dimensional images of famine victims on TV screens, the continent is not a hopeless or even sad place. It is a land where the bonds of family keep old people from feeling useless and guarantee that no child is an orphan, where religion is more about joy than guilt, where when you ask a man for

directions he will get in your car and ride with you to your destination—and insist on walking home.

The short, squalid history of independent black Africa is that of traditional cultures being forced and forcing themselves to accommodate Western ideas and technology. It has been a halting, confusing, demeaning process.

Nigeria—with its wealth, its huge pool of educated people, its aggressiveness—has invented itself at a higher velocity than the rest of black Africa. It certainly has not been any smoother, just faster.

Last year, three decades down the freedom road, Nigeria, as usual, was frantically falling apart. Africa's most populous nation was flailing about in exuberant desperation, struggling not to drown in its daily bath of chaos and self-flagellation, avarice and wild-eyed pride. The president, Ibrahim Babangida, a gap-toothed general with an endearing smile, was telling the assembled fat cats and stuffed shirts at the Oxford and Cambridge Club Annual Spring Lecture in Lagos that they—the privileged elite—were a major reason for the country's plight:

"You will, perhaps, agree that the worst features in the attitude of the Nigerian elite over the last three decades or more have included: factionalism, disruptive competition, extreme greed and selfishness, indolence and abandonment of the pursuit of excellence. Indeed, a companion cult of mediocrity—deep and pervasive—has developed and, with it, a continuous and, so to speak, universal search for excuses to avoid taking difficult decisions and confronting hard work, and a penchant for passing the buck."

Meantime, that is to say, in the last year of the 1980s, rioters exploded into the sewer-lined streets of Lagos, burning cars, looting supermarkets, trashing government offices. They were protesting something they called SAP, a four-year-old structural adjustment program which, by order of the unelected general with the endearing smile, was removing make-believe government subsidies and making every Nigerian (except a growing number of generals and selected members of the Oxford and Cambridge Club) miserable.

NO STOMACH FOR DOWNWARD MOBILITY

The young rioters, many of them college students, halted tens of thousands of cars and trucks at morning rush hour on Lagos freeways to hand out green leaves ripped from city shrubbery. The leaves betokened solidarity among the panicky middle class. They were symbols of an angry people with no stomach for the kind of downward mobility that the rest of black Africa passively accepts.

Hundreds of demonstrators seized the moment and gave the economic riots a peculiarly Nigerian twist. While denouncing SAP in the name of the downtrodden common man, they extorted cash from fellow sufferers stuck in traffic. Police shot about a hundred rioters and arrested 1,500 others before the trouble ebbed, and Lagos traffic accelerated to its normal maddening crawl.

Other pots boiled over. Nigeria was making a third run at democracy. The first try had foundered in 1966 because of incompetence, the second in 1983 because of greed.

President Babangida, having vowed to give power back to civilians, decided to ban all former politicians from taking part in the proposed "Third Republic" on the grounds that they were likely to be fools or thieves. If the "old breed" even joined a political party, the general decreed, they would spend five years in prison.

Even as things fall apart, pots boil over, signals cross, Nigerians somehow are managing to meld themselves into that most unusual of black African entities—a real nation. Against all odds, things come together.

Out of the Biafran war of the late 1960s, which was Africa's bloodiest tribal conflict, has come a lasting tribal peace—a feast of forgiveness remarkable in world history. Out of the berserk corruption of Nigeria's oil boom has come a gutty, sober-minded program of economic reform. Out of the two-time failure of democracy has emerged a moderate military regime that is orchestrating its own dissolution in favor of elective government. Out of six military coups, and after the assassination of three heads of state, Nigeria has wound up with an extraordinarily beneficent Big Man— President Ibrahim Babangida.

President Babangida has a more sophisticated economic mind than any other leader on the continent. He is a former tank commander and happens to be a nimble politician. While imposing a hated economic adjustment program on Africa's most disputatious people, he managed to remain personally popular. Most remarkable for an African Big Man, the general promised to step down in 1992 and the promise was believed.

REASONS FOR CONCERN

As the '90s began, there were no guarantees that any of Nigeria's gains would endure. There were sound reasons to fear catastrophe.

Like Sudan, Nigeria is rent by religion. It is divided north and south between Muslims and Christians, and economic hard times have ratcheted up religious tension.

Coups always threaten. Babangida sanctioned the execution of 10 military officers who conspired in 1986 to overthrow him. (He personally has been on the winning side in three coups, including the one that brought him to power in 1985.)

Nigerians deeply resent poverty. They have watched in disbelief and anger as their average annual income was sliced in half, from $670 to $300, in the past decade. The country slipped from low middle-income status to what it really is: a least developed country. The kind of strikes and economic riots that erupted in late 1980s will probably recur.

And yet Nigeria—horrible, ugly, boastful, coup-crazed, self-destructive, too hot Nigeria—is black Africa's principal prospect for a future that is something other than despotic, desperate, and dependent. If the world's poorest continent is going anywhere, Nigeria is likely to get there first. Two reasons are size and wealth.

The place is not a banana republic. One of every four Africans is a Nigerian. An estimated 114 million people lived in the country in 1989. The population is growing at a rate that is among the highest in the world. In less than 50 years, Nigeria will have at least 618 million people—close to the present population of all of Africa, more than double the population of the United States.

Besides sheer numbers, Nigeria has world-class wealth. The country's gross national product is bigger (in years when the world oil price is strong) than that of white-ruled South Africa and more than half that of all black Africa combined. It is the world's ninth largest oil producer and ranks fifth in natural gas reserves.

Below ground there are about 40 years worth of oil and a century worth of natural gas.

A UNIVERSITY-TRAINED ELITE

Above ground there is a wealth of well-trained and frighteningly ambitious humanity. There are an estimated 2 million university-trained professionals. They constitute the largest, best-trained, most acquisitive black elite on the continent.

Finally, many Nigerians have a penchant, indeed a mania, for self-criticism. They obsessively pick apart the failures of their leaders and of themselves. Titles of popular books by Nigerians include "Another Hope Betrayed," "The Trouble With Nigeria," and "Always a Loser—A Novel About Nigeria."

"It Wouldn't Be Nigerian If It Worked," howled a headline that typifies the Nigeria press, which is at once the best and most irresponsible, most boorish and brilliant in Africa. A letter to the New Nigerian newspaper by O. Gbola Ajao, a teacher at the College of Medicine in the city of Ibadan, said:

"Some years ago we were asking about developing a tourist industry in Nigeria. What a laugh! How will any foreigner in his right mind want to come for vacation in a place like Nigeria? Even those of us born there are always looking for one excuse or another to get out of the place."

The government in 1984 invented WAI—the War Against Indiscipline—which amounted to an official declaration that Nigerians are intolerably rude, messy, and violent. WAI posters were distributed throughout the country, urging people to queue in line, pick up their garbage, stop sleeping on duty, stop armed robbery, stop drug pushing, stop fighting, be nicer. Novelist Chinua Achebe upped the ante on national self-flagellation by writing:

"Nigeria is not a great country. It is one of the most disorderly nations in the world. It is one of the most corrupt, insensitive, inefficient places under the sun. It is one of the most expensive countries and one of those that give the least value for money. It is dirty, callous, noisy, ostentatious, dishonest and vulgar. In short, it is among the most unpleasant places on earth!"

DICTATORS ARE LAMPOONED

All true, and yet dictators—Big Men in the African mold—are not acceptable in Nigeria. They are lampooned in newspaper cartoons. They are overthrown. Babangida could not survive if he were to back away from his promise of a return to democracy.

Although they have badly botched it up when they achieve democratic rule, Nigerians refuse to settle for anything less. After 30 years of independence, civilians have been in power for 9 years, generals for 21, and the national consensus is that only democracy works.

Nigerians refuse to commit a corrosive crime common to most of black Africa—passive acceptance of tyranny. It is no accident that half the continent's newspapers, half its journalists, one-quarter of its published books, a Nobel laureate in literature, and a growing number of world-class novelists and poets are Nigerian.

"The worst sin on earth is the failure to think," writes Nigerian novelist and television producer Ken Saro-Wiwa. "It is thoughtlessness that has reduced Africa to beggardom, to famine, poverty and disease. The failure to use the creative imagination has reduced Africans to the status of mimic men and consumers of the products of others' imagination."

Nigerians foul up, but on their own initiative, not on other people's orders.

"Nigerians are not rational," Prince Tony Momoh, a wealthy businessman, influential traditional leader, and minister of information in Babangida's government, told me. "We would prefer to go hungry to being told what to do. I can't think of any other African country doing such an irrational thing. But there is more to a Nigerian than reasoning."

Nigerian pride careens off in self-deluding directions. There was talk, in the oil-boom years, of Nigeria's becoming a superpower. Until poverty nixed it, the country longed for a "black bomb." A former foreign minister, Bolaji Akenjemi, said in 1987 that "Nigeria has a sacred responsibility to challenge the racial monopoly of nuclear weapons."

Akenjemi, in another prideful vein, instructed Nigerian ambassadors around the world to open the doors of their embassies to all people of African origin. Expatriate Africans should come to view Nigeria in the same way that Jews view Jerusalem—as a shelter "for blacks in the diaspora," the foreign minister said.

He ordered his diplomatic corps never to hold an official dinner without reserving one-third of the guest list for Africans. Akenjemi either did not know or, more likely, did not care that most Africans view Nigerians as the loudest, most obnoxious people on earth. Akenjemi was sacked by Babangida for talking too much.

Like most other outsiders on their first trip to Lagos, when I got off the plane in 1985, I was scared. The city was hideous. It was like the post-nuclear-war backdrop for the movie "Road Warrior," only hotter, uglier, smellier.

I went to a Chinese restaurant where it proved impossible to order a meal for less than $100. Lagos was then the most expensive city in the world.

(The Union Bank of Switzerland surveyed 49 cities in 1985 and found that goods and services in Lagos cost more than anywhere else. The survey found that, exclusive of rent, it cost $2,010 a month to survive. That was $410 more than in New York City. Rent for a two-bedroom Lagos apartment was then $85,000 a year, three years payable in advance. All this changed dramatically with Babangida's economic reform. In 1988 Lagos ranked 71 on a list of the world's most expensive cities.)

WORLD'S MOST TWISTED ECONOMIC ORDER

Lagos was also part of the world's most twisted economic order. I sat one afternoon in a steamy back-alley saloon with a jet-lagged baby-clothes smuggler who was sipping iced palm wine.

"What I feel is better to fly with than anything else is baby wear," he told me, explaining his six trips a year to Taiwan. He explained the advantages of baby wear for a Nigerian trader: a profitable haul could be stuffed in a couple of suitcases. Customs inspectors at Lagos airport usually did not demand duty or bribes to clear booties and bibs. Nigerians would line up to pay 500% markups for baby clothes.

The key to the smuggler's existence was government price controls on air tickets and the grossly overvalued Nigerian currency, the naira. The smuggler bought naira on the black market with dollars, paying one-quarter price. He then bought air tickets with naira, paying about one-eighth the world real price. He flew first class, if he could get a ticket. Airlines reported "saturation bookings." One-tenth of the nation's discretionary income, $350 million a year, went for air tickets. The warped monetary system was driving economists around the bend.

"The government's overregulation of the economy is creating these opportunities for private gain at the expense of the society in general," complained Ishrat Hussein, a World Bank representative who had been sent to Lagos to do what then seemed impossible—persuade Nigerians to live within their means. "The traders are paying no taxes. There is no way local industry can compete with these imported goods. Consumers must pay outrageous prices. I call it private affluence, public squalor."

I went back to Nigeria four more times over the following four years. On each trip I escaped Lagos to travel to the north, east, and west of a country that is the size of California, Nevada, and Arizona combined.

Each time I returned to Nigeria, I confirmed that the impossible had occurred.

Nigerians stopped lying to themselves.

They struggled to retool the economy so it would run on what they actually earned, rather than on what they wished they earned.

The naira, for decades a symbol of Nigerian manhood, was devalued again and again.

A corrupt import licensing regime, which had spawned a parasitic elite of millionaires who did nothing but bribe bureaucrats, was scrapped.

Farm prices were increased, and agricultural production, after a 20-year nose dive, jumped sharply.

Africa's most ambitious program to sell off government-owned business was launched.

The baby-clothes smuggler was forced out of business.

Nigeria—a country that has been synonymous with all that was pompous, self-deceiving, and mindlessly extravagant in post-independence Africa—became in the later half of the 1980s an African model for free-market reform.

It was an impressive but agonizing adjustment.

Almost everyone was getting poorer. The price of the cassava-based staple food, which many Nigerians had long shunned as a poor man's food, jumped fourfold in two years. The middle class could not afford spare parts to fix cars. So it walked. Onetime high rollers who owned Mercedeses and BMWs swallowed their pride and entered the *kabukabu* trade, turning their onetime symbols of success into overcrowded taxis. Nigerians who used to shake their heads in disgust about reports of famine in Ethiopia were forced to live with hunger. College graduates were eating one meal a day. Hospitals around the country reported increasing malnutrition among children.

I talked to scores of Nigerians, middle class and poor, who found no point to their misery. "I do not understand what this is all about," the Rev. Ebenezer Okwuosa, pastor of a poor parish in the town of Uli in overcrowded eastern Nigeria, told me in 1988. Food and transport costs in Uli had doubled in just eight weeks. The minister asked me, "How can my government say there is no money?"

After the civil war of the 1960s, the second cleansing cataclysm that helped forge Nigeria into a nation had been an avalanche of money. Sudden hikes in the world price of oil in the 1970s and early '80s opened the floodgates, and $100 billion poured into the coffers of the Nigerian government in a decade. It was more money in less time than any black African nation had ever seen or was likely ever to see again. The cost of all that wealth (a typically Nigerian oxymoron) proved greater than the Biafran war. When the boom finally fizzled in the mid-1980s, the country had an $18 billion foreign debt. A generation was weaned on avarice. Corruption hypnotized the national psyche.

A LESSON LEARNED

Yet even money-mad Nigerians could not dispose of $100 billion without making a few socially useful purchases. In contracts laced with kickbacks, a vast highway system was built, along with more than 20 new universities. Primary school enrollment tripled. As recently as 1985, more than 100,000 Nigerian families were sending one or more children abroad to university. As greed lured Nigerians into cities, it broke down tribal and sectional differences. Ambitious men could not afford traditional hatreds. US economist Sayre P. Schatz, who analyzed Nigeria's situation, speculated that "pirate capitalism" in Nigeria helped speed "formation of a bourgeoisie that is truly national rather than regionally or tribally based."

The most important legacy of the oil boom was not what it bought, but what it taught. The squandering of Africa's greatest fortune sobered Nigerian leaders to the folly of too much government. It was a primer in the social cost of unbounded private greed when married to uncontrolled bureaucratic power. A new national Constitution, completed in 1989 as part of the preparations for the planned return to democratic rule, pointedly scaled back the role of the government. It deleted language describing Nigeria as a "welfare state" and excised clauses saying that Nigerians have a right to free primary, secondary, and adult education, and to free medical care.

The oil bust forced the country to cut its imports by two-thirds. Overstaffed government marketing agencies for cocoa and other cash crops were eliminated. Farmers began getting more money for their labor. All this, of course, is standard World Bank advice for sick African countries. But Nigeria turned to it not because it was ordered to do so, as have so many other African nations that go through the motions of reform in order to secure more loans. Humiliating experience—wasting a unique windfall that might have catapulted the country out of the third world—forced Nigeria to learn the hard way. The lesson seems to have stuck. In 1985, when I first went there, the country was a joke among economists who specialized in Africa. At the end of the decade, Tariq Husain, the World Bank representative in Lagos, told me that Nigeria was taking reform more seriously than any other country on the continent.

THIRD TRY AT CIVILIAN SELF-RULE

After Babangida seized power in a bloodless coup, as foreign debts mounted and oil revenues continued to shrink, it became clear that prideful opposition to reform would bankrupt and isolate the country. Unable to overcome nationalistic opposition to an International Monetary Fund loan, Babangida outwitted it. In one of the neatest economic maneuvers in African history, the general told the IMF that Nigeria did not want the loan. Then, as the country rejoiced in having told the IMF where to go, the military government implemented what

Babangida described as "our structural adjustment program produced by Nigerians for Nigerians." It was far stricter than what officials from the IMF or World Bank had dared demand, and it earned the country relatively generous rescheduling agreements with Western creditors.

An indomitable national spirit and a natural distaste for dictatorship, however, have not been enough—thus far—for Nigeria to lay the groundwork for a working democratic government. For the third run at civilian self-rule, in the hope that it might give democracy a better chance, Babangida's military regime had tried to phase in elected government, starting with local, then regional, then national elections.

At the same time, the general has attempted to treat his nation's social distemper with a government agency called the Directorate for Social Mobilization, or Mamser. It was supposed to do for politics what the defunct War Against Indiscipline was supposed to have done for garbage—clean it up. Babangida ordered Mamser to "eradicate all those features of our behavior in the past which have made our society a byword for disharmony, dishonesty, distrust, and disservice, and a haven for those who prefer to embrace and to promote in their conduct the least attractive traits in human nature."

To lure cynical, apathetic, and newly impoverished voters to attend a nationwide series of Mamser "political awareness" rallies, the military jazzed them up with performances from well-known Nigerian pop musicians. The military also invited local obas, chiefs, and emirs to come and speak their mind. The result was a political consciousness-raising exercise marked by unruly crowds, wildly contradictory speeches, and barechested musicians with dreadlocks, who made fun of pudgy generals and sang about how living in Nigeria was like "living in prison." The rallies proved less cures for social distemper than testimonials to it. Unimaginable or impermissible virtually everywhere else in black Africa, the rallies could have come off only in Nigeria.

I attended one such rally along with a gaggle of generals in combat fatigues; a handful of emirs in flowing white robes, turbans, and dark sunglasses; several hundred civil servants who had been let out of government offices to learn about honesty; and 15,000 or so pushy adolescents who were desperate to dance.

The generals, the traditional leaders, and the government workers sat in shaded bleachers. Everyone else stood (and sometimes fainted) in noontime heat.

A SINGER DENOUNCES WASTEFUL WAYS

Squads of "Mamser Youth," teen-agers employed and outfitted by the government to give an image of responsible political awareness, were deployed to help police with crowd control. They wore bright blue slacks, white sneakers, and T-shirts

urging "Be orderly," along with caps exhorting "Shun Waste and Vanity."

The chaos began when an insouciant reggae singer named Christy Essien jumped onto a stage erected in the middle of a vast asphalt military parade ground. In floppy camouflage fatigues, high-top Army boots, and a grass skirt, she gave the generals a mock salute. Then she rapped in pidgin about how voters should cheat the politicians who try to cheat them.

"If him bring you money, take am and chop. Make you no vote for am." ("If he tries to buy your vote, take the money and buy food. Then vote for someone else!")

This rally, one of scores held across the country in 1989, took place in Abuja, a new capital city planned in the mid-1970s when the country was stumble-down drunk with oil money.

As much as any other venue in Nigeria, the city was an apposite place to denounce the wasteful ways of the bad old politicians. Abuja has a 1,000-room, five-star Hilton Hotel with marble in every room, satellite-fed television, and imported gourmet chefs in the kitchen.

Several months after that rally in Abuja, in apparent disgust at the 30 political associations that his countrymen had come up with, General Babangida ordered the politicians to funnel their ambition into two political parties created by the military government: the National Republican Convention and the Social Democratic Party. "One a little to the right of center and one a little to the left."

At the time I wrote these words, it seemed doubtful, to say the least, that soldiers could forge the structures of an elected government by imposing them from above.

A CHIEF SPEAKS OUT

In any case, the only effective speaker at the prodemocracy rally in Abuja was a Nigerian who could not be bothered with democracy. His Royal Highness, Chief of Karibi, Alhaji Abubakar Mamman, waddled slowly to the speaker's platform, sheathed in layer upon layer of white muslin, turbaned, wearing gilded sandals, and carrying an ornately carved walking stick. The chief spoke slowly and with considerable precision. He addressed his remarks to the military government, as represented by the rotund senior military officer seated in front of him, Maj. Gen. Gado Nasko. Chief Mamman proceeded to tell General Nasko that the rally was a waste of time.

"Can we really embrace political awareness in this country at this time when hunger, illiteracy, and unemployment threaten us?" the chief asked, as the querulous crowd, for the first time, actually listened to a speaker. "What about the problems of armed robbery, train robbers, cocaine dealers, and others who have robbed us? After 29 years of independence, we have not gone far."

"Your assignment," the chief said, referring to the military government's crusade to instill disciplined democratic values in Nigerians, "is too much for you."

His Royal Highness returned to his seat amid deafening applause. At a rally intended to inculcate democratic awareness, an unelected hereditary ruler thrilled voters by arguing that such awareness was impossible. Self-rule was taking shape even as self-rule was being denounced. Nigeria, once again, was falling apart while coming together. Its future was confused and terrifying and limitless.

Whether in Nigeria or elsewhere, the Africans themselves are the only way to make sense of the news out of Africa. More than any other people on earth, their future is in jeopardy and they deserve the attention of the rest of us. It is premature, I think, to pass final judgment on their experiment. Scrawled on the tailgates of exhaust-belching trucks that rumble through the back roads of West Africa is a grass-roots admonition to those inclined to write the continent off. It says: "No condition is permanent."

South Africa's Constitutional Cry: Be Original

The nation is looking at many models of democracy as it prepares to give blacks a political voice. But in the end, it must come up with one that is its own.

Scott Kraft

Times staff writer

PRETORIA, South Africa—Ensconced in a tiny cubicle of a South African think tank, Barry de Villiers draws inspiration these days from the travails of America's Founding Fathers and the muggy summer of 1787.

"There were a number of times when it looked as if things would fall apart," the South African constitutional expert said recently, nodding toward an anecdotal book about the Philadelphia convention that he keeps on his desk.

"At one point, one of the leaders— an old, grayish gentleman—said: 'Either this convention is going to break down or we will have to pray to see if we can keep it together,' " De Villiers noted.

The delegates prayed and eventually emerged with what is today the world's oldest written constitution.

Like the American colonies in 1787, South Africa in 1990 is preparing to write a new constitution. That document will, for the first time in the country's history, give blacks a vote in national government and formally bind this ethnically and politically diverse population under one democratic banner.

Whatever South Africa's constitution looks like in the end, it will be one of a kind, the experts say.

"We can study other countries, but after that we have to develop something new," said De Villiers, who heads the 6-month-old Center for Constitutional Analysis at the Human Sciences Research Council in Pretoria. "That's the most important lesson from the American experiment: Be original."

The government predicts that full-blown constitutional negotiations could begin early next year, and an urgent hunt for governmental models has begun in board rooms, drawing rooms, think tanks, college classrooms, law offices and political party meetings across the country.

Hundreds of reports, pamphlets and books on possible constitutions have been produced. Dozens of constitutions, from Belgium's and Switzerland's to Fiji's and Canada's, are jammed onto computer disks for analysis. And some academics even are studying the chaotic behind-the-scenes process by which the United States and other countries drew up and ratified their constitutions.

The primary goal of this cottage industry is to find a system that will extend full voting rights to 27 million blacks, correct the economic imbalances created by 42 years of apartheid and also safeguard the civil rights of 5 million whites.

President Frederick W. de Klerk has promised the white electorate a separate referendum on any new constitution. But it also must be acceptable to blacks, who will make up the largest voting bloc when it comes up for ratification.

"THIS IS GOING TO BE A BUMPY ROAD, definitely. It would be naive to expect otherwise," said Margie Keeton, a member of the "Scenario Planning Team" at the giant business conglomerate, Anglo-American Corp.

Up to now, the government has been trying to persuade black and white opposition groups simply to accept its invitation to negotiate.

Nelson Mandela's African National Congress, which most analysts believe has the widest support among blacks, has tentatively agreed to participate, as have other black leaders, including Inkatha Freedom party chief Mangosuthu Gatsha Buthelezi.

Two left-wing black groups, the Pan-Africanist Congress and the Azanian People's Organization, and the right-wing white Conservative Party continue to hold out, and De Klerk said he will go ahead without them, if necessary.

But before even the preamble can be written, South Africa's competing political forces must agree on a negotiating forum.

The ANC wants a multiracial elec-

A Proposed Bill of Rights

The Broederbond (Brotherhood), the secret Afrikaner society that has heavily influenced the South African government's reform program, proposes to guarantee the following rights:

1. Life (although death penalty may be imposed in case of murder and high treason).
2. Human dignity and equality before the law.
3. A good name and reputation.
4. Spiritual and physical integrity.
5. Freedom from slavery.
6. Privacy.
7. Freedom of speech.
8. To freely carry out scientific research and to practice art if it doesn't infringe on accepted social norms.
9. Freedom of choice in education and training.
10. Integrity of the family, freedom of marriage.
11. To move freely within South Africa.
12. Guarantees against arbitrary refusal of a passport, exile, and prevention of emigration.
13. To engage freely in economic intercourse.
14. Private property.
15. To associate freely.
16. To freely form political parties.
17. To assemble peacefully, to hold demonstrations and present petitions.
18. Universal suffrage for those over the age of 18.
19. Free use of native language and free practice of culture and religion for all.
20. The use of one's mother tongue in courts of law.
21. Personal freedom and safety.
22. A maximum period of detention without charge of 48 hours.
23. A fair and public trial, to be regarded as innocent until proven guilty and to appeal a court's decision.
24. Guarantees against torture, assault, or cruel, inhuman or degrading treatment.
25. To seek a court ruling in civil disputes.
26. Due process in administrative proceedings.

The courts would be empowered to interpret the Bill of Rights, and they could only be amended or suspended by a three-quarters majority of all members of each house of Parliament or by a majority of all registered voters in a referendum.

---

tion to select an assembly to write the constitution. It also wants an interim government installed to watch over the country. The government has flatly refused both ANC demands but says it would be willing to grant black leaders a direct role in government during the negotiations.

MOST ANALYSTS BELIEVE THOSE DIFferences can be overcome, though, and that constitutional negotiations are imminent.

In the meantime, South Africa is bulging with suggested political alternatives:

• The Conservative Party favors the status quo—keeping South Africa and its major cities under white control and allowing blacks to govern only in the nominally independent "homelands."

• The *Oranje-Werkers Unie* (Orange Workers Union) wants to carve a large, irregularly shaped chunk out of the fertile and mineral-rich center of the country where whites already outnumber blacks, leaving the rest of South Africa to black majority rule.

• Seventy-five families who support Carel Boshoff's Afrikaner Volkswag (People's Guardian), a cultural movement, have already moved into what he envisions as a white homeland on rugged territory in the northern Cape Province.

• The Boer State Party wants to turn the clock back and reinstitute the boundaries of the white Boer republics that existed in the late 1800s, leaving a white nation covering about half the existing country and incorporating Johannesburg, Pretoria and the 2.5-million population township of Soweto.

• The Pan-Africanist Congress and the Azanian People's Organization reject power-sharing in favor of a socialist government, installed by a one-person, one-vote election, that would lift up the oppressed black masses and redistribute land from whites to blacks.

In between those extremes, however, are the ideas being considered by the most important players in the negotiating forum—the ruling National Party of president De Klerk, the multiracial ANC and the Zulu-based Inkatha party.

None of those parties has offered a constitutional blueprint, but each says it wants a unified South African state with multiple political parties, an independent judiciary and a bill of rights. Despite broad areas of agreement, though, the gulf between their visions of the future remains large.

The thinking of the National Party is evident in a detailed constitutional proposal drawn up recently by the Broederbond (Brotherhood), a secret Afrikaner think tank whose members include De Klerk and key members of his Cabinet. It offers an elaborate plan to give blacks full political participation while also protecting whites and other minorities.

Under that proposal, the country would be divided into 10 regions and governed by a two-chamber Parliament.

The 300-seat House of Representatives would be elected by all voters—black and white—on a common roll, with seats divided proportionally according to the number of votes collected by each political party. Decisions would require a simple majority.

The Senate would give 100 seats to senators chosen in regional elections and 10 seats each to officially registered "groups" that share a common language, culture or religion. Senate decisions would require a two-thirds majority.

Deadlocks between the two houses would be broken by an Advisory Council, nominated by the Senate, and a quarter-plus-one members of that council could veto any matter in dispute.

The Broederbond proposal includes a bill of rights, a ceremonial head of state and a Cabinet made up of representatives from the House, each region and each registered "group." The Cabinet would initiate legislation and make decisions by consensus.

For a government that until last year was trying to force blacks into ethnic homelands and take away their citizenship, the Broederbond proposal represents a radical change in thinking.

But it doesn't go nearly far enough for the ANC. ANC leaders argue that the Broederbond model would, in effect, maintain white veto power over important legislation.

"It's totally unworkable," said Albie Sachs, a white lawyer on the ANC's 20-member constitutional committee. "The government still has a long way to go to reach an acceptable democratic position. They don't want power-sharing; they want power division. It's hard for them to let go."

The ANC has not yet offered a constitutional model of its own, but its leaders favor a multi-party democracy with strong central control and a bill of rights, a rarity in Africa. The ANC contends that whites and other cultural, religious and language groups would be adequately protected by the bill of rights, enforced by an independent judiciary.

BUTHELEZI'S INKATHA, LIKE ITS BITTER rival the ANC, supports a black major-ity-rule government. But Inkatha says it's prepared to compromise to make sure that minorities are not dominated by an ANC-controlled government.

"The first step is to try to open people's minds and get them out of their straitjackets," said De Villiers, of the Center for Constitutional Analysis. "And since February [when the ANC was legalized], all the parties have been searching for clues. Not one has a rigid idea."

Several organizations, including the President's Council advisory group in Parliament and the independent Law Commission, have been drawing up proposals.

De Villiers' center, funded by Parliament, opened in May to dissect and computerize more than 30 of the world's constitutions and help all sides in the South African debate search for ways around the most contentious issues.

"For the moment, it's almost impossible to discuss group rights in South Africa, even though the principle has been used in many constitutions around the world," De Villiers said. "There's a very deeply ingrained suspicion [among blacks] about 'group protection.'"

The suspicion among whites, on the other hand, is that their civil rights will be trampled. That's why many are seeking some form of veto power in the new constitution. De Klerk must carefully consider their fears or risk losing white support for any new constitution.

However, "At the end of the day, if the government wants to entrench white privilege, it won't be able to get a new constitution," De Villiers warns.

Still, there is plenty of room for maneuvering, though, analysts say.

THE ANC AND OTHERS HAVE BEEN looking closely at the Swedish constitution, which gives cultural groups the right to go to court to test legislation that would infringe on their rights. South Africa could take the Swedish model a step further by allowing cultural groups, which would most likely be racially homogenous, to review and make recommendations on laws before they are passed.

Another suggestion has been a system of cantons, similar to those of Switzerland, that would create several hundred largely autonomous districts with a weak central government.

So far, both the ANC and the government agree that they can only resolve their constitutional differences by talking.

"We start with such a big gap of distrust between the main actors," said Gerrit Viljoen, the government minister of constitutional development. "It's only in the process of preliminary talks and negotiations that we can overcome that."

Sachs, of the ANC, says he wants a constitution under which "all South Africans feel comfortable. We want to reduce conflict, and the crucial thing is for people to start talking to each other."

The World

Apartheid's Laws Are Dismantled, But Not Its Cages

CHRISTOPHER S. WREN

CAPE TOWN

WHEN President F. W. de Klerk announced on Feb. 1 that he would scrap the basic laws underpinning South Africa's system of racial discrimination, he drew fresh acclaim from around the world. Yet apartheid was so intricately constructed over four decades and has created such economic disparity between blacks and whites that many South Africans might find their separate lives little changed by the reforms.

Moreover, President de Klerk's otherwise bold declaration was unaccompanied by any apology for the suffering inflicted upon so many for so long. Gerrit N. Viljoen, the Minister of Constitutional Development, told reporters "the reality of the diversity of South Africa should be accommodated in a non-discriminatory way," a deft recognition that disparities between whites and blacks cannot soon disappear.

Mr. de Klerk's critics suspect that after generations of white minority rule predicated on skin color and hair texture, the Government was shoring up white economic and social advantage under a less objectionable formula.

Mr. de Klerk's promise to bury the last apartheid laws marked the anniversary of a year that has brought momentous change to South Africa. Bans on the African National Congress and other anti-apartheid organizations were lifted, Nelson Mandela was freed and the Congress began talks with the Government aimed at opening the way to formal negotiations on a new constitution that would extend political rights to the black majority. Municipalities no longer can bar blacks from parks, swimming pools and toilets. Beaches and hospitals are open to all races.

The process has been confounded by violence that has perpetuated black suffering and deepened white fears of the change, though the peace accord reached last month between the leaders of the African National Congress and the rival Inkatha Freedom Party has raised hopes for an end to factional killing, which claimed some 3,700 victims in 1990.

Now Mr. de Klerk is scheduling the last three major apartheid laws for repeal before Parliament adjourns, probably in July. They are the Population Registration Act mandating a compulsory race classification that governs opportunities from birth to death, the Group Areas Act limiting where those outside the privileged white minority can live, and the Land Acts detailing what property, if any, they can own.

But those now covered under the Population Registration Act will retain their racial labels until there is a new constitution. Schoolchildren will continue to attend schools according to race. Young white men will still be called up for compulsory military service while their black peers must await the new constitution to be able to vote, or run for Parliament.

And apartheid has left so many blacks burdened with poverty and illiteracy that they will be hard put to use any new opportunities. "What is the use of repealing the Group Areas Act and Land Acts when the Government has given me no resources to take advantage of the situation?" Mr. Mandela asked journalists on Friday.

Government officials are wading through a morass of subsidiary legislation to identify references to race. There is uncertainty whether these statutes can be expunged with one overriding law or must be recast in hundreds of new ones once the Population Registration Act goes.

Moreover, Government ministers contend that not enough money is available to lift blacks up to the living standard long enjoyed by whites. Hernus J. Kriel, the Minister of Planning and Provincial Affairs, said the removal of the Group Areas Act would not solve the chronic shortage of black housing because most blacks could not afford to buy houses in white areas. Consequently, Mr. Kriel said, "economic forces will

Segregation's legal foundations are going; the economic chasm remains.

prevail and will decide where you live."

Strict housing codes will be kept to prevent blacks from crowding into white neighborhoods, although Mr.

Kriel said, "I want to make it very, very clear that this has got nothing to do with race." He predicted a growth in informal housing — a euphemism for squatter shanties — around cities.

The Government has no plans to return property taken from up to 3.5 million non-whites dispossessed from their homes under the Group Areas Act. Officials say it is futile to try to sort out what is past, but the omission has angered critics.

"The Government will have to investigate the question of reparation," said the Rev. Allan J. Hendrickse, the leader of the mixed-race Labor Party. "People suffered because of the Group Areas Act. People lost what they loved."

While white municipalities will be able to pool their resources with poorer neighboring black townships, it will be strictly voluntary, and, Mr. Kriel conceded, "there are not many advantages for white local authorities to join forces with black local authorities."

Indeed, many whites are likely to resent, if not obstruct, any concessions. Louis A. Pienaar, the Minister of National Education, expected classes in white schools to double in size. And while Mr. Mandela, among other critics, has called upon the Government to spend as much money educating a black child as a white one, instead of barely a quarter, Piet Clase, the minister overseeing white education, said that this would mean allocating 40 percent of the Government budget to education and that no nation could afford this.

The right-wing Conservative Party, which walked out on Mr. de Klerk's Feb. 1 speech, hopes the repeal of the racial laws will increase the opposition party's support among whites. "They never believed that what has happened would happen," said Pieter Mulder, a Conservative Member of Parliament. "So they're quite angry out there."

Islam's New Political Face

"Islam has proved to be a dynamic and energetic force at a time when the world is awash with new political formulations. From India's Kashmir to the Soviet Union's Asian republics, Islam has become an increasingly important political idiom."

ROBIN WRIGHT

Robin Wright, a former Middle East correspondent, researched this article on a grant from the John D. and Catherine T. MacArthur Foundation. She is the author of *Sacred Rage: The Wrath of Militant Islam* (New York: Simon and Schuster, 1985), and *In the Name of God: The Khomeini Decade* (New York: Simon and Schuster, 1989).

DURING the 1980's, activist Islam became synonymous in the Western mind with political extremism, terrorism, hostage ordeals and suicide bombings. As the decade came to a close, the Islamic resurgence began a new phase; Islamic movements began to participate in the political system instead of opposing it. Increasingly, the Iranian model has been shunned and the fanatics' bullets have been forsaken for the ballot box. While pockets of virulent militancy remain, notably in Lebanon and the Israeli-occupied territories, developments in North Africa and the Arab heartland indicate that Islam and democracy may not be incompatible.

The two most striking examples of this change occurred in Jordan and Algeria. In both countries, the first open elections in more than two decades led to stunning victories by local Islamic fundamentalist parties. The fundamentalists campaigned using a one-line slogan that is now the rallying cry of a host of disparate Muslim groups in the region: "Islam is the solution."

In Jordan, King Hussein allowed the country's first national elections in 22 years in November, 1989. In the contest for a new Parliament, members of the moderate Muslim Brotherhood and independent Islamic candidates won 34 of the 80 seats. Local elections in 1990 were also won by Islamists, while young Islamic candidates won more than 90 percent of the votes for a student body at the University of Jordan in mid-1990.

In June, 1990, the Islamic Salvation Front (FIS) won an upset victory in Algeria's first multiparty election since independence from France 28 years earlier. The fundamentalist party captured 32 of the 48 regional assemblies and 55 percent of the 1,541 municipal councils. In Algiers, the FIS won all 34 municipal council seats. The ruling National Liberation Front (FLN), which had dominated local and national politics since 1962, came in a poor second, winning 14 regional assemblies and 32 percent of the municipal councils; independents and a Berber party took the rest. In all of Algeria's major cities, the FLN was overwhelmed by the fundamentalist FIS. Not since the 1979 Iranian revolution had an Islamic party's victory been so decisive. And never before had Islam so overwhelmingly routed a long-dominant power by democratic means.

The decisive Islamic electoral victories in Algeria's municipal and regional elections and Jordan's national elections represented a shift from the vengeful Islamic convulsions—among both Sunni and Shiite activists—witnessed in Iran's revolution and the takeover of Saudi Arabia's Grand Mosque in 1979, in the assassination of Egyptian President Anwar Sadat in 1981 and in Lebanese extremism since 1982.

These election results seem to confirm a trend that first emerged in Egypt in 1987, when the Muslim Brotherhood (in coalition with the Wafd party, since the Brotherhood was officially outlawed) became the largest opposition force in the National Assembly. The elections in three different political systems—a monarchy, a socialist state and a pro-Western country inching toward democracy—demonstrated that Islamists can work within the system and adhere to the rules of the new political game. "The Algerian elections have proven that Islamist movements in our region need not be 'Khomeinist,' " commented Ghassan Tueni, editor of

Lebanon's *An-Nahar* and a former United Nations (UN) envoy, in mid-1990. "Islamist movements are capable of being absorbed into the political mainstream."[1]

ISLAM'S POLITICAL APPEAL

Islam's victories, of course, have not happened in a vacuum. In Algeria, secular parties boycotted the local elections, demanding that national elections should have been held first. That left the FIS with a distinct edge.

Islam's appeal has grown because of economic hardship, political failure, social turmoil or a combination of all three. These are the very reasons that Middle east governments have begun to experiment with pluralism and democracy. In Algeria, the FIS won in part because of the failure of a revolutionary party, the FLN, that just three decades ago captured the imagination of struggling nations around the world by battling the powerful French army for independence. In the past decade, Algeria has been plagued with strikes and riots over issues ranging from chronic housing shortages and land policies to education issues. During the last round of riots, which occurred in October, 1988, an estimated 400 people died.

The Muslim demands for change are no different than the demands in East Europe. In a country with an unemployment rate of at least 25 percent, people want jobs. In Algiers, where the legendary Casbah is teeming with several times more people than it can hold, people want housing. With a $26-billion foreign debt, Algeria has had limited funds to address the country's economic problems; almost 70 percent of its oil revenues have been spent paying off the debt instead of funding local development. In many of the municipalities where the FIS won, the local governments were effectively bankrupt. Algerians were voting as much against an inefficient system as for Islam. The day the election results were announced, the continuing discontent with economic conditions was as visible as ever: gas station attendants on strike, causing long lines of angry motorists; a newspaper strike; and a boycott by garbage collectors, creating piles of garbage on streets throughout Algiers.

"The depth of frustration and anger is causing the kind of fundamentalism that you see making inroads into the middle classes and upper classes and people who ordinarily should not be fundamentalists," said Kamal Abu Jaber, a Jordanian political analyst and historian.

When do people turn to [new] ideology? Whether it's in America or here or France, they turn to ideology when they are in trouble. And the Arab Muslims are in trouble. Every idea they have had has been either condemned or swatted or frustrated.[2]

So far, however, Islam has not proved that it has all the promised solutions. Despite its motto, the FIS's campaign noticeably lacked specific cures for Algeria's structural problems. But the FIS did mobilize its followers. In response to the garbage strike, bearded men dressed in coarse cotton galibeyah robes, the traditional Algerian dress, collected the slimy piles of refuse with their bare hands.

In Egypt, Islam is also seen as providing alternatives to inadequate or inefficient government services and high-priced private institutions. Various local Islamic societies have established hundreds of clinics and schools with first-rate services at marginal or no cost. The same has been true in Jordan, although on a much smaller scale.

One of the most striking examples of the "Islamic alternative" cultivating a potent political following has been among Israel's Arab population. In a little-noticed local election in Umm el-Fahm, the second largest Arab town inside Israel, the Islamic bloc won 75 percent of the vote in February, 1989, replacing a Communist administration that had dominated local politics for 15 years. Two popular fundamentalist clerics were elected mayor and deputy mayor of the town of 27,000 in Israel's northern Galilee. The upset followed almost a decade in which fundamentalists had mobilized volunteers and appealed for private donations to organize services — from day-care centers to soccer leagues and local construction projects — that the Communist government had been unable to provide.

Sheik Raed Salah, Umm el-Fahm's Islamic mayor, explained the Islamic bloc's election success. "It wasn't what we said as much as because of the things we had already done. We had been working for ten years, changing people's view of Islam and carrying out a whole range of social projects. That's why people voted for us." A poll conducted in mid-1990 revealed that if the Islamic bloc went national, it would win at least 11 percent of the Arab vote throughout Israel — and thus two seats in the Knesset. Sheik Salah claimed the Islamic bloc could capture between three and six seats.[3]

AN ORGANIZED FORCE

Islamic movements have also made headway in the Middle East because of the undeveloped political system in newly democratizing regimes; they are the only groups sufficiently organized to move quickly to fill the political vacuum. In Jordan, the Muslim Brotherhood's victory was at least partly due to the fact it was the only "party" allowed to function, mainly as a social movement, before the election. Most other political groupings had not mobilized publicly and new parties had not yet been allowed to register. Indeed, Jordan's election took an unusual course: elections first, then working out the details for implementing pluralism, including registering parties.

Islamic groups have been successful as political systems have opened up in the Middle East for three reasons. First, Islam, the only major monotheistic religion that includes a set of rules to govern a state as well as a set of spiritual beliefs, is a familiar idiom that requires no ideological education or explanation.

Second, Muslim groups also have a network for communication through the mosques and Islamic societies. Third, in many nations, including Egypt, Tunisia, Jordan (and even in Israel's occupied territories), Islam was actually encouraged or cultivated by governments beginning in the 1970's to counter leftist, Marxist or Palestinian nationalist movements. Two decades later, Islam had taken deep root. And, when the political dikes were finally opened, the Islamists flooded the system.

The risky gambles by the leaders of Algeria, Jordan and Egypt amounted to a new approach in dealing with Islam: including fundamentalists rather than confronting them and co-opting the Islamic ground swell by forcing its leaders and followers to share the burden of solving staggering domestic problems. The cost-benefit ratio of the alternative—attempting to check the Islamic tide—appeared to be too costly.

The consequences of trying to suppress Islamic tendencies was evident in Tunisia during its local elections in June, 1990. After fundamentalists running as independents won 12 percent of the vote in the 1989 legislative elections, the government banned the Islamic Renaissance party and six other opposition groups from running again. The Renaissance party, Tunisia's largest opposition group, has been considered among the most moderate Islamic parties in the Middle East.[4] It has not called for the implementation of Islamic law as the basis for governing the state and has pledged to protect women's rights, including their choice of dress and their right to work or to initiate divorce. On the eve of the election, the Renaissance party's exiled leader, Rachid Ghannouchi, pledged, "It is neither moral nor possible to demand freedom for ourselves when we are persecuted and [then] refuse it to others when we are in a position of strength."[5] Ghannouchi later publicly repeated his pledge at a conference on Islam and democracy in Algiers.

With the Renaissance party and several other opposition groups banned during the 1990 election, the ruling Constitutional Democratic Rally won 99 percent of the vote—according to the government. Both European and American officials, however, said the tally was hardly representative of a country that was also witnessing strong Islamic political fervor. Western envoys estimated that Muslim candidates could win between 25 and 30 percent of the vote in a fully free election. The overwhelming victory for the party of President Zine el-Abedine Ben Ali was also partly due to the boycott of the election by all other major opposition parties on the grounds that the country's leaders had too much control over the process and that the opposition did not stand a fair chance.

In the short term, the Tunisian government may have secured its hold on power. However, the election undermined President Ben Ali's claim that he was opening up Tunisia to democracy. It also increased the possibility of future confrontation or even violence between the government and the suppressed opposition. Ghannouchi predicted that

> the government's intransigence will lead to bloodshed unless Ben Ali follows through on pledges made in 1988 to recognize the aspirations of youth, to open the media to real freedom, to allow a genuine multiparty system and to allow the Islamic party and other opposition forces to be legal. Instead of following through on these pledges, the government has begun to openly harrass us.[6]

Recent food riots and campus demonstrations involving Islamists bear out Ghannouchi's prediction.

Indeed, the most militant strains of Islam are in areas where Muslim movements have been suppressed or where grievances have not been addressed, notably in Israel's occupied territories. Since the outbreak of the intifada in 1987, fundamentalists have become increasingly important political forces. The two main Islamic groups are the Islamic Resistance Movement (Hamas) and Islamic Jihad. Both underground groups call for the restoration of mandatory Palestine as a national homeland and publicly reject international initiatives on exchanging land for peace. Both have their strongest support in the Gaza Strip, although Hamas, an offshoot of the Muslim Brotherhood, has gained significant ground in the West Bank.

Three factors in 1990 appeared almost certain to increase the appeal of Islamic activism: the deadlock in the five-point plan put forward by United States Secretary of State James Baker 3d;[7] the indefinite suspension of United States talks with the Palestine Liberation Organization (PLO) after a foiled seaborne attack on Israel in May, 1990, by the radical PLO faction headed by Abu Abbas; and the death of 21 Palestinians in the October, 1990, clash between Palestinian protesters and Israeli police on the Temple Mount in Jerusalem.

While the PLO retained majority support among Palestinians, Hamas appeared to be gaining ground. In elections for the United Nations Relief and Works Agency staff council in the Gaza Strip in mid-1990, Hamas won 15 of 27 seats. Its election success and its claims of growing appeal in the West Bank and Gaza, particularly among the young, emboldened Hamas in mid-1990 to demand between 40 and 50 percent of the seats on the Palestine National Council, the PLO's parliament-in-exile, as a precondition for joining the PLO. Among its other demands were the PLO's rejection of any resolution short of the full return of mandatory Palestine; a return to the military struggle in the form of jihad, or holy war, to liberate Palestine; and retraction of all recent concessions, including recognition of Israel's right to exist. The PLO rejected the demands.[8] In the absence of a settlement on a Palestinian homeland, many Palestinian analysts predict that Islam's appeal may deepen.

THE REVIVAL'S SHIFT

One of the major shifts in the Islamic revival is evident in the cases cited so far: each case involves members of the mainstream Sunni sect, not the Shia, Islam's so-called second sect, which dominated the headlines throughout the 1980's. Indeed, Shiite activism has been less visible than at any time in recent years.

In Lebanon, the pro-Iranian Hezbullah (Party of God) remained a disproportionately strong militia force. But it was constantly challenged militarily and often defeated by Amal, the largely secular Shiite movement, and further kept in check by Syrian forces deployed in Lebanon. Furthermore, Iran cut back its financial assistance to Hezbullah leaders by as much as 90 percent. In the spring of 1990, Islamic Jihad, a cell under the Hezbullah umbrella, released the first two American hostages it had been holding since 1985. Three remaining British hostages were expected to be released soon. The surrender of General Michel Aoun, the Maronite Christian army commander, and the end of his mutiny against the government in October, 1990, also increased hopes that all militias would be disarmed or at least weakened.

The shift in Hezbullah's fortunes was tied largely to Teheran, where Iran's leadership had begun charting a more pragmatic course after the death of Ayatollah Ruhollah Khomeini. The pressures of chronic economic troubles, stalled war reconstruction totaling at least $350 billion and the devastation caused by the earthquake in 1990 led President Ali Akbar Hashemi Rafsanjani to hasten moves toward reestablishing relations with other countries, including Western nations. Despite the furor over Ayatollah Khomeini's call for the death of British author Salman Rushdie for his "blasphemous" treatment of Islam and the prophet Mohammed in *The Satanic Verses*,* London and Teheran reestablished diplomatic relations in the fall of 1990.

---

*New York: Viking, 1988.

And the first visit by a World Bank delegation to Teheran since the 1979 revolution resulted in a $300-million loan to Iran. Iran's brand of Islamic revolution appeared, at least on the surface, to be settling down.

In another shift from the earlier bursts of Islamic activism, by 1990 many of the movements were focusing primarily on either domestic agendas or regional issues; the anti-Western rhetoric and extremist campaigns against Western targets had noticeably diminished. However, that trend was abruptly interrupted by Iraq's invasion of Kuwait on August 2, 1990. The deployment of more than 20 foreign armies and navies in the Persian Gulf region shifted attention to the issue of Western intervention in Islamic lands—specifically Saudi Arabia, considered the "Guardian of Islam" because the two most important Muslim shrines are in Mecca and Medina. The growth and direction of the Islamic movement will depend on how the fundamentalists react to the confrontation in the desert sands.

In a blatant attempt to widen his base of support after several UN resolutions left him diplomatically and economically isolated, Iraqi President Saddam Hussein began depicting himself as a pious Muslim and the confrontation in the Gulf as a holy war against foreign intruders and infidels. "Arabs and Muslims are called to liberate the tomb of the prophet from capture by the unbelievers and Jews," he said in reference to Saudi Arabia, where American and other foreign armies were deployed.

Iraqi television also began broadcasting the five daily calls to prayer, a practice common in other Muslim nations but long abandoned in Baghdad. A new genealogy of the Iraqi leader's family revealed that he was descended from the prophet Mohammed, while a pro-Iraqi paper in occupied Kuwait claimed the exiled ruling al-Sabah family was descended from Christian Crusaders and the Saudi royal family was of Jewish ancestry.

Few fundamentalists initially seemed convinced or swayed by President Hussein's born-again appeal. Saddam Hussein has long been the leader of one of the most secular and socialist regimes in the region. Indeed, he gained most of his external support during the eight-year war with Iran because his regime was prepared to stop the Islamic revolution in Iran. Baghdad also had a long record of persecuting fundamentalists and executing their leaders, particularly those from the country's majority Shiite community. But many Islamists were attracted by the Iraqi leader's position on three issues: a Palestinian homeland as a precondition to ending the Gulf crisis; the "injustice" of Arab oil being provided to the West on a preferential basis while poorer Arab nations were suffering from enormous debts, rising unemployment and economic stagnation; and the intervention of foreign forces.

The anguish felt by Muslims over the sight of an Islamic nation—Saudi Arabia—depending on foreign forces to defend itself against a brethren state became a main source of debate. The Western intervention struck deep into the soul of the Islamic world, renewing fears of recolonialization and ending the fledgling attempts to restore Muslim and Arab dignity through an Islamic revival. The conflicting points of view were played out at Friday prayer sermons throughout the Middle East.

In Amman, where Iraq already had strong support among frustrated Jordanians and Palestinians, Sheik Abdel Moneim Abu Zant gave a fiery sermon in August lambasting the United States and other Western countries. "They only believe in materialism. Oil has now become the property of God," he told an overflowing crowd of worshipers. "So what will you do with the will of God, Mr. Bush? You cannot exercise your veto against the words of God." Sheik Abu Zant also referred to the United States leader as "empty-headed, pork-eating President Bush" and predicted that he would leave the White House "as a cripple in a wheelchair."[9] Many leading members of the Muslim Brotherhood in Jordan, which has been supported and financed by Saudi Arabia, eventually rallied to Iraq's side.

In contrast, on the same Friday in Cairo, Sheik Ibrahim Galhoum told worshipers:

> I call on all Muslims to stand by the dishonored Kuwaitis. Were the struggle between Iraq and an infidel country, we would hope Iraq would be victorious. . . . But in this case, what can I ask of God? I cannot pray that the Iraqis will be victorious over Muslims, so what I pray for is Saddam's senses to come back to him.[10]

Most analysts predicted that the debate would continue as long as the confrontation remained a standoff. But the prospect of a full-scale military clash between Iraq and the multinational force assembled in the Gulf sparked fears that even moderate Islamists might end up condemning the West.

CONTINUED ACTIVISM

Analysts in the region seemed to agree that Islamic activism will be a major feature of regional politics into the twenty-first century. "In the next two to three decades, Islam is the new wave of the future," predicted Abu Jaber, the Jordanian political analyst.[11] "As long as we are suffering economically and politically in the third world, God will be the solution," added Egyptian analyst Ahmed Fakr.[12] "For the next five years there is no alternative to the fundamentalist movement in Algeria,"

commented Ammar Ben Hemmer, editorial writer for the FLN's paper. "The only thing we have to do is make sure that Islam does not turn to fundamentalist militancy because in this country Islam has always been a tolerant religion."[13]

Others suggested that religious activism is only a phase in the historic transition to a new era. Said Saad Eddin Ibrahim, a sociologist at the American University of Cairo:

> While Islamic activism will be on the rise for the next ten years, until the democratization process is completed, even now I think the extreme fanatic, violent wing is subsiding. The early results show that even when Islamic activists gain power and in fact exercise it, they will not necessarily fare much better than the liberals before them, or the socialists before them or the nationalists before them. They will make their mistakes. Maybe they will achieve something in the beginning just by the force of their enthusiasm and dedication, but there is always a limit for achieving [with only] that kind of dedication or devotion.[14]

At present, however, Islam has proved to be a dynamic and energetic force at a time when the world is awash with new political formulations. From India's Kashmir to the Soviet Union's Asian republics, Islam has become an increasingly important political idiom.

---

[1]Ghassan Tueni, "Algeria Is Infectious," in *An-Nahar,* June 18, 1990, as translated in the journal *Middle East International,* July 6, 1990.

[2]Kamal Abu Jaber, interview with author, Amman, May, 1990.

[3]Jackson Diehl, "Moslems Clean Up Israeli Arab Town," *Washington Post,* July 17, 1990.

[4]The Renaissance party is the name of the former Islamic Tendency Movement, which dropped the religious reference as a concession to the government in exchange for a pledge that the party would be allowed to register—a pledge that was not fulfilled.

[5]Rachid Gannouchi, three interviews with author, Washington, D.C., 1989 and 1990.

[6]Ibid.

[7]For a discussion of Baker's plan, see the article on Israel by Alan Dowty on p. 17 of this issue.

[8]"Islam Ascendant: Jordan, the West Bank and Gaza," by Robert Satloff in *Islamic Fundamentalism in the Levant* (Washington, D.C.: Washington Institute of Near East Policy, 1990).

[9]Nora Boustany, "A Fiery Warning to Americans, A Plea to Saddam," *Washington Post,* August 26, 1990.

[10]William Claiborne, " 'Allah Will Bring Vengeance,' Iraqi President Told," *Washington Post,* August 26, 1990.

[11]Jaber interview, op. cit.

[12]Ahmed Fakr, interview with author, Cairo, May, 1990.

[13]Youssef M. Ibrahim, "Militant Muslims Grow Stronger as Algeria's Economy Weakens," *The New York Times,* July 25, 1990.

[14]Saad Eddin Ibrahim, interview with author, Cairo, May, 1990.

Israel: The Deadlock Persists

"Iraq's attack on Kuwait in August, 1990, simplified short-term problems for the new Israeli government, but posed very serious long-term issues that will clearly outlast the government even if it survives until the next elections in late 1992."

ALAN DOWTY

Professor of Government and International Studies, University of Notre Dame

Alan Dowty is a research associate at the University of Haifa (Israel). He is currently working on a study of the roots and functioning of the Israeli political system.

THE crisis that erupted in the Persian Gulf in August, 1990, came as a reprieve to an Israeli government that had been anticipating a period of intense internal and external pressure to break the diplomatic stalemate on Israeli-Palestinian issues. This government—a narrow coalition of right-wing and religious parties led by the Likud party's Yitzhak Shamir—had itself been established only two months earlier, following the collapse of the national unity government that had been established after the 1988 elections (and that succeeded an earlier national unity government that had managed to hold together for four years after the 1984 elections). But while the Iraqi invasion of Kuwait provided some temporary short-term relief to Israeli policymakers, it raised some disturbing long-term implications for Israel and did nothing to resolve the basic problem of Israeli politics: the persistence of a fairly even balance between opposing views on key foreign policy issues, which is embodied in a political deadlock that has guaranteed immobility.

The deadlock in Israeli politics can be traced back to 1984, and in some sense to the "upheaval" in the 1977 elections, when Likud ended almost a half century of domination by the Labor party and its predecessors in Israel and the pre-independence Jewish community in Palestine. The traditional position of the Labor party and its allies was, and is, to accept the partition of Palestine in principle and to regard the future of those parts of mandatory Palestine occupied by Israel in the 1967 Six-Day War (the West Bank—or Judea and Samaria in Israeli terminology—and the Gaza Strip) as subject to negotiation. In practice, this has been interpreted as "a willingness for territorial compromise": certain territories considered vital for security reasons would be retained and Jewish settlement would be limited to these areas. However, the bulk of the territory, and especially the Arab-populated areas, would be returned to Jordanian rule, possibly as a Jordanian-Palestinian federation, or as an Israeli-Jordanian condominium, in return for a permanent peace treaty.

Likud's position was and is a continuation of the historic position of its constituent Herut party, whose former leader, Menachem Begin, was Prime Minister from 1977 to 1983. In Likud's view, Israel has a claim to Judea and Samaria (Greater Israel) on both historic and security grounds, and should act to realize this claim.* The area west of the Jordan River should not be redivided, no "foreign sovereignty" should be reintroduced in the area, and there should be no restriction on Jewish settlement anywhere in the historic homeland. Arabs in the occupied territories should be offered autonomy as individuals, but should express their national identity in the framework of an existing Arab state (especially Jordan, seen as a basically "Palestinian" state). The peace process is thus conceived as a negotiation between Israel and these Arab states on the basis of existing lines of demarcation.

Behind these opposing conceptions, there is a fair degree of consensus in Israel on certain basic issues: both major parties (and most of the Israeli public) oppose the creation of an independent Palestinian state between Israel and Jordan, and both oppose recognition of and negotiation with the Palestine

---

*Editor's note: Greater Israel, which includes the territory now under Israeli control in Judea and Samaria, refers to the whole of the biblical land of Israel.

Liberation Organization (PLO) as now constituted and represented (although some Israelis are willing to promise a positive response to a future PLO that is reformed and moderated). Likud, like Labor, also favors the continuation of the "temporary" legal status of military occupation in the West Bank and Gaza, since immediate annexation (a course favored only by small groups on the right) would at once pose the question of the civil rights of the Arab inhabitants who still comprise about 95 percent of the population there, despite 20 years of Jewish settlement. Nevertheless, the gap in approaches to Arab-Israeli diplomacy has prevented the development of a coherent foreign policy during periods when the two parties shared power, and Likud's opposition in principle to Israeli withdrawal from the occupied territories has stymied diplomacy based on this quid pro quo (land for peace)—the only position in which Arab interlocutors have been interested—during its periods of dominance in the government. At the same time, the question of the future of the occupied territories has become the defining issue of Israeli politics.

Part of the problem has been the evenness of the balance between the two major parties. Some long-term trends underlay Likud's success in 1977 and since: the assertion of Sephardic voters (those from Afro-Asian backgrounds) who were alienated from the Labor establishment and more in tune with Likud's hawkishness; the decline of Labor Zionist ideology as a vital force in Israeli life; and the passing of a generation of charismatic Labor leaders (especially David Ben-Gurion) who had symbolized national rebirth. Nevertheless, by the time of the 1984 elections, it was widely expected that the pendulum would swing back to Labor. The unpopularity of the 1984 Lebanese war and the continuing Israeli occupation there, an economic crisis in which inflation reached well into three-digit figures, and the resignation of the colorful Begin as standard-bearer all seemed to indicate a break in the deadlock in Labor's favor.

However, this was not to be. In defiance of expectations, the 1984 elections produced a balance so delicate that Labor and Likud were forced to embark on an era of power-sharing and mutual veto, rotating the prime ministership within the framework of a national unity government. Despite repeated threats of collapse, this rickety structure actually outlasted its term of office.

In part, this could be attributed to the inability of either bloc to form a government on its own and the unwillingness of key parties, at crucial junctures, to face new elections. But it also represented recognition of the need for unity in addressing the country's economic crisis, a task that could not be accomplished unless both Labor and Likud were will-

ing to share the onus of instituting the tough and unpopular measures required. This was accomplished through a sweeping economic stabilization program that successfully reduced inflation from triple digits to low double digits through cuts in government spending, price controls and wage restraints (within a short period of time, real earning power dropped by as much as 30 percent).

These measures aggravated two growing problems in Israeli society: the deterioration of public services in areas like health care and education, and the threat of economic collapse in the agricultural sector (the kibbutz and moshav movements). Nevertheless, the stabilization program was considered a success. Although it did not overcome the basic pressures on the Israeli economy, the program restored some semblance of balance, with the annual rate of inflation running at "only" 18 percent in late 1990.

FOREIGN POLICY

On foreign policy issues, however, the national unity government was stalemated by the opposing approaches of its components. No major diplomatic initiative could gain the support of both Labor and Likud; in early 1987, Shamir (recently rotated to the prime ministership) blocked the effort of Labor leader and newly rotated Foreign Minister Shimon Peres to convene an international conference that would sponsor talks between Israel and a joint Jordanian-Palestinian delegation. The paralysis in foreign policy seemed to be the price most Israelis were willing to pay in return for government unity on economic and other domestic matters. It was also a luxury they could afford so long as they also believed that no credible Palestinian negotiating partner committed to coexistence with Israel had yet emerged. In the mid-1980's, international conditions were also favorable to inaction: the Iran-Iraq war preoccupied much of the Arab world, and Israel was not faced with any crucial decisions on foreign policy issues.

These conditions changed, however, with the onset of sustained Arab unrest (the intifada, or uprising) in the occupied territories beginning at the end of 1987. The intifada posed a sharp challenge that the country's deadlocked political system was ill-equipped to handle. In this context, the scheduled elections of November 1, 1988, like those of 1984, were a potential turning point that in the end turned nowhere. Again the two major parties offered the electorate their opposing conceptions for dealing with Palestinian issues, and again the electorate responded by dividing its allegiance almost evenly between the two camps.

Likud had a slight edge in postelection bargaining, however, because the balance was held by a reinvigorated religious bloc holding 18 of the 120 Knesset (Parliament) seats. Some of the religious parties were closer to Likud's position on foreign policy and defense, and none of them were likely to sit in a government with some of Labor's secular leftist partners. As a result, the Labor party was forced to agree to a national unity government on less than equal terms, with Shamir projected to remain as Prime Minister for the full four-year term of office.

Basic disagreement over foreign policy still deadlocked the government, despite Shamir's stronger position. This became more critical after December, 1988, when PLO leader Yasir Arafat made his highly publicized declaration renouncing terrorism and calling for a negotiated peace based on the coexistence of Israel and a Palestinian state. This statement changed the rules of the diplomatic game, leading to the opening of direct contact between the United States and the PLO, and increasing pressure on Israel for something other than the standard negative response.

It was also clear by this time that the intifada and other developments were having a contradictory impact on Israeli opinion; while the public continued to favor severe measures against violence in the occupied territories, there was also a slight but measurable shift in a dovish direction on some key long-term questions in Arab-Israeli relations. For example, a poll in March, 1989, showed a 58 percent majority in favor of talks with the PLO if it explicitly recognized Israel and ceased all terrorist activity (only 18 percent regarded Arafat's December statement as adequate for this purpose).[1] Another study carried out in early 1989 showed that 27 percent of those who voted for Likud and other right-wing parties in 1988 favored a compromise based on withdrawal from the occupied territories in return for peace—indicating less than full acceptance of Likud's opposition to withdrawal and the possibility of a mobilizable majority in Israel for territorial compromise.[2]

Under growing pressure, in May, 1989, Israel put forward a proposal that has dominated the diplomatic agenda ever since. Shamir proposed free elections in the West Bank and Gaza to choose Palestinian representatives who would then negotiate with Israel over terms for autonomy and other long-term arrangements in the occupied territories. Although Shamir was later forced by his own party to add conditions that made this proposal less attractive, by early 1990 the mediation efforts of the United States and Egypt had narrowed the gap in terms of holding discussions between Palestinian representatives and Israel regarding such elections. Still unresolved were Israeli demands for an end to violence in the occupied territories before such

discussions, the role of the PLO (as well as the inclusion of East Jerusalem residents and West Bank deportees) in the Palestinian delegation, and PLO insistence that eventual Palestinian statehood should also be on the agenda.

THE GOVERNMENT CRISIS OF 1990

By early 1990, mounting pressure for the resolution of these remaining points made it clear that the foreign policy immobility of the 1980's could no longer continue. By this time, Shamir was under increasing fire both from the right (with a threatened split within his own party) and from the left, and he added to his difficulties by tying the issue of Soviet Jewish immigration to the need to retain control of the occupied territories (few Soviet Jews actually settled in the territories, and linking these two previously unlinked issues only increased pressures and strains from abroad). Labor threatened to break up the national unity government unless the government accepted a pending United States compromise proposal on Israeli-Palestinian talks. Finally, in March, Labor party leader (and Finance Minister) Peres succeeded in bringing down the government on a vote of no confidence, presumably on the issue of Palestinian negotiations but with the help of a religious party dissatisfied for other reasons with Shamir and Likud.

Bringing down the government, however, did not mean that Peres was in a position to offer a viable alternative. After long and involved negotiations, he was ultimately unable to attract enough of the religious bloc to form a government. The mandate was returned to Shamir, who, after equally protracted and intricate maneuvering, was finally able to form a government with a bare majority in early June. This government, marking the end of five and a half years of power-sharing by the two major blocs, was basically a Likud government backed by three smaller parties to the right of Likud and by three of the four religious parties. Shamir remained as Prime Minister; David Levy, the leading representative of Likud's Sephardic constituency, took over the foreign ministry while remaining as Deputy Prime Minister; and two other Likud leaders returned to posts they had filled in the past: Moshe Arens as defense minister and Yitzhak Modai as finance minister. The controversial Ariel Sharon, blocked once more from returning to the Defense Ministry from which he had been ousted after the Lebanese war, nevertheless was given the Cabinet portfolio of minister of construction and housing.

The prolonged hiatus between the fall of the government and the formation of its successor occasioned a considerable amount of public criticism and discontent. For almost three months, the political scene was dominated by the unedifying spectacle of unprecedented political haggling; at one point, a smaller party even demanded the quashing of criminal proceedings against one of its members as a condition for joining the government. Coalitions stitched together at great effort were torn apart by the defections of one or two members, while the intervention of ultraorthodox rabbis, whose influence over their followers was often decisive, stirred feelings of outrage among Israel's secular majority (one such rabbi, an anti-Zionist leader living in Brooklyn who refuses even to visit Israel, was largely responsible for Peres's failure to achieve a majority). The result was the reemergence of strong sentiment for electoral reform, with calls for modifications in Israel's strict proportional representation system that would curtail the power of smaller parties. The proposal for direct election of the Prime Minister attracted the most attention. But once a government had been formed (and once the Gulf crisis brought new concerns), the fate of the projected reforms was again left up to the Knesset, the body that was itself the target of the demands.

The concern over what appeared to be the growing power of the religious community was also unlikely to find an early resolution. This concern was hardly new, but it had reached a new peak after the religious parties had won 18 seats in the 1988 Knesset elections, with the ultraorthodox parties accounting for 13 of those seats (contrasted with the 6 they had won in 1984). Other observers pointed out, however, that the bargaining power of the religious parties was basically a function of the close division between the two major blocs that has prevailed since 1981 and that the 15 percent of the Knesset held by the religious parties is roughly proportional to the percentage of religious (meaning Orthodox in Israeli terms) voters in the country. In addition, surveys on religious identification continued to show a long-term trend toward secularization in Israeli society, despite the greater visibility of religion and the strong political leverage of religious parties in a closely balanced political system.[3]

The new government committed itself to the vigorous pursuit of Shamir's peace initiative of May, 1989, which it sees as a step in implementing the Camp David accords of 1978; these accords would establish an autonomous regime for the Arab population of the West Bank and Gaza.[4] While the Camp David accords envisioned this regime as a transitional phase, Shamir and his new government regarded autonomy as the final resolution of the West Bank and Gaza issue. Under pressure from its smaller right-wing allies (one of which is committed to the "transfer" of Arabs from the occupied territories), the coalition agreement for the government also promised a renewed push for Jewish settlement in Judea and Samaria; such efforts had been slowed down during the period of the grand coalitions with Labor.

SOVIET JEWISH IMMIGRATION

Even before the Iraqi crisis, the new government's attention was greatly distracted by the issue of Soviet Jewish immigration. By mid-1990, the number of Soviet immigrants had reached an unprecedented level as a result of the liberalization of Soviet policies, renewed anti-Semitism in the Soviet Union (also, paradoxically, a result of liberalization) and the imposition of stricter limits on the number of Soviet refugees accepted by the United States. As the problems of housing and other matters of absorption became critical, the Cabinet turned to Housing Minister Sharon—a man with a reputation for overcoming obstacles, whatever they may be—to act on an emergency basis in dealing with the influx. One of Sharon's first steps was to try to remove the issue from partisan politics and international complications by announcing that Soviet Jews would not be settled in the occupied territories, implicitly reversing Shamir's earlier linkage of the two issues.

Projections that the new "hard-line" government would adopt harsher policies toward the intifada proved initially to be unfounded. In general, the level of violence in the occupied territories had been declining, and in recent months more casualties had been caused by the "intrafada" (intra-Arab violence) than were inflicted by the Israeli army. Defense Minister Arens instituted changes designed to lower the profile of the Israeli presence still further, and the initial result was a lowering of Arab casualties.

On October 8, however, this trend was dramatically reversed by a clash in Jerusalem that left at least 21 Palestinians dead. It was not clear that this incident resulted from changed Israeli policy; the casualties were inflicted by the border police rather than the army, and the government appointed a commission to investigate the causes of the tragedy. But the resulting increase in tensions, reinforced by strong Palestinian support on the street for Iraqi President Saddam Hussein, made it hazardous to predict the future direction of events.

Iraq's attack on Kuwait in August, 1990, simplified short-term problems for the new Israeli government, but presented very serious long-term issues that will clearly outlast the government even if it survives until the next elections in late 1992. Shamir, Levy, Arens and the rest of Likud's leadership had been braced for what, by all signs, would have been a serious effort to revive the "Baker Plan" for Israeli-Palestinian negotiations on terms that Likud would have had trouble accepting. In a widely publicized speech in October, 1989, before the chief pro-Israel lobbying group in the United States, United States Secretary of State James Baker 3d had already served notice that proposals for a "Greater Israel" should be discarded, and that the United States would expect the cooperation of the Shamir government in carrying out what had begun as the Shamir initiative.** While the collapse of the national unity government in March put all this on hold for a while, the administration of United States President George Bush had let it be known in many ways that the United States State Department expected the diplomatic process to move forward once a new Israeli government was formed, be it a government of the left or the right.

But Saddam Hussein took the heat off for the foreseeable future. So long as the crisis in the Gulf was playing itself out, United States diplomacy could not focus for any length of time on other Middle East problems. In addition, the pro-Iraqi stance taken by PLO leaders further distanced them from Washington; the United States-PLO dialogue had been broken off anyway in June, after the failure of Arafat and the official PLO leadership to dissociate themselves convincingly from the perpetrators of a failed attack on Israeli beaches near Tel Aviv in May, 1990. The crisis aggravated the PLO's problems by splitting it between a membership largely sympathetic to Saddam and sources of funding that are largely dependent on the governments of the Gulf area threatened (and in Kuwait's case, dispossessed) by that same man. From the perspective of a Likud government to which any PLO problem is a blessing, this was also welcomed.

In addition, while Israel was ordered to keep a very low profile in the Gulf crisis, events there inevitably strengthened the hands of those who stress Israel's strategic value to Western interests in the region. The value of pre-positioning military supplies, the calls for strategic coordination and the impetus behind programs like the joint development of the Arrow antitactical ballistic missile were all reinforced. Years of claims about the extent of Israel's security needs, the likelihood of unprovoked attacks and the wisdom of preventive measures like the bombing of Iraq's nuclear reactor near Baghdad in 1981 (condemned by the United States government at the time) stood to be vindicated.

On the other hand, Iraq had put together a standing army roughly twice the size of Israel's totally mobilized forces, and it possessed large stockpiles of chemical weapons and missiles capable of reaching any part of Israel. The fear that Iraq would convert the crisis into an Arab-Israeli confrontation, even without a retreat from Kuwait, was reinforced by Saddam Hussein's transparent efforts to do exactly that, by linking the two conflicts. In threatening to move against any Iraqi presence in Jordan, Israel also essentially gave Hussein an option to ignite an Arab-Israeli confrontation at a moment of his choosing. It was assumed that Saddam, though clearly willing to run large risks, would shrink from setting off a two-front war that he would almost certainly lose. But the fears in Israel remained, as seen in widespread apprehension about the risk of chemical warfare and public demands (to which the government ultimately acceded) that gas masks be distributed free to the entire Israeli population.

However, a greater concern for Israelis is the possibility that Iraq will successfully extricate itself from Kuwait with its government and armed forces still intact. In this case, the specter of a wounded but still powerful Iraq, looking for a cause with which to rally the Arab world to its side the next time around, is taken very seriously. It has even led knowledgeable Israelis to speculate that, under such circumstances, Israel would be forced to unveil its nuclear deterrent in order to neutralize — publicly and effectively — the weapons of mass destruction in Iraqi hands. The Iraqis might also acquire their own nuclear weapons, despite the best efforts of "unilateral arms control" carried out by hostile states. A nuclearized Middle East is not a prospect that most Israelis view with equanimity, which is why Israel has kept its own nuclear capabilities in the basement and has proposed a broad regional nonproliferation pact with effective enforcement (not to be confused with the Nuclear Nonproliferation Treaty to which Iraq and most other states already subscribe).

Even if Iraq is humbled, Israelis have to consider the long-term implications of the new United States military and political relationship with Arab countries, as expressed in the proposed massive arms sale to Saudi Arabia. Apart from the threat this might pose to the "qualitative edge" that Israel seeks to maintain, the feedback of such close cooperation into United States Middle East policy is cause for concern. Foreign Minister Levy visited Washington in September, 1990, in order to seek reassurances that arms shipments to Arab countries would be matched by an upgrading of future military aid to Israel.

Finally, the Gulf crisis dealt a harsh blow to dovish opinion in Israel among those seeking to promote a dialogue with Palestinians and with the

---

**Editor's note: Baker proposed a five-point plan that calls for: a comprehensive settlement based on UN resolutions 242 and 338; direct negotiations; a transitional period between negotiation and the final settlement; neither permanent Israel control of the territories nor an independent Palestinian state; and self-government for Palestinians in the West Bank and Gaza.

PLO itself. In the last few years, this body of opinion had drawn encouragement from Arafat's apparent recognition of Israel's right to exist and his denunciation of terrorism in December, 1988. While most Israelis considered these statements insufficient to qualify Arafat as a negotiating partner, a small majority in various surveys indicated willingness in principle to negotiate with a peaceful PLO. Some had drawn back because of incidents like the May, 1990, beach attack, but there was a widespread perception that the gap was, indeed, beginning to narrow. The fervent support given by Palestinians to the "military solution" espoused by Saddam Hussein has led, however, to a declaration of disillusionment by many on the Israeli left who had promoted the idea of dialogue.

When the dust from the Gulf crisis settles, there will be a fresh start in Arab-Israeli diplomacy. It is not clear how far the entire process will have been set back by events in the Gulf and from what point it will have to make this start.

[1] *The New York Times,* April 2, 1989.

[2] Elihu Katz, "Hawkish Majority, but Dovish Trend," *Jerusalem Post,* February 10, 1989.

[3] See the evidence collected in Alan Dowty, "Jewish Political Traditions and Contemporary Israeli Politics," *Jewish Political Studies Review,* vol. 2, nos. 3–4 (fall, 1990).

[4] The Camp David accords were signed in 1978 by United States President Jimmy Carter, Israeli Prime Minister Menachem Begin and Egyptian President Anwar Sadat at Camp David, Maryland. The accords established a framework that would lead to the "full autonomy" of the Arab inhabitants of the West Bank and Gaza Strip after a five-year transitional period.

Turmoil erodes the Nehru legacy

Democracy in India is being sorely tested by communal unrest, political instability and separatist movements. **David Housego** reports

As caste and religious violence have rolled across India in recent weeks, many Indians have had that uncomfortable sense of living through a period of social upheaval without precedent in their country's post-independence history.

Few had ever imagined that students would take despair to the point of setting fire to themselves in protest against Prime Minister V P Singh's programme for reserving public sector jobs for the lower castes. Nor had they imagined a collapse of discipline among the police that would enable Hindu militants to storm the disputed 400-year-old mosque at Ayodhya and hoist their saffron flags on the domes. Hindu extremists claim the site is the birthplace of the god Lord Rama. Ayodhya has become the focus of renewed Hindu-Moslem clashes which have claimed several hundred lives across India in recent weeks.

Both events point to the unleashing of forces which the government is unsure how to control and which are carrying India into uncharted waters. Also indicative of the uncertainties is the political confusion in Delhi as Mr Singh's administration lives out its last days amid manoeuvrings by every conceivable combination of party and faction to form a successor government. What does seem clear is that the "old order" – the India of Nehru's vision with its priorities on maintaining a secular, democratic and unified national framework – is facing its most serious challenge since India became independent in 1947.

Some of the familiar landmarks are now being eroded. After the bloodshed of partition and the creation of a separate Moslem Pakistan, Nehru promised to Moslems who remained in India the security and equality of opportunity of a secular state. But with the rise of Hindu fundamentalism – exemplified by the seizure of the Ayodhya mosque last week – and with some senior politicians speaking fearfully of the county as in danger of tumbling into religious civil war, Moslem confidence has been shaken.

The student suicides reflect the anxieties of the upper castes over a social revolution which could ultimately wrench from them the dominance of senior government jobs – and the influence and patronage that goes with this – that they have enjoyed since independence.

The lower castes have become increasingly aware of their electoral power and are using strength in numbers to increase their access to jobs and resources. These so-called "backward castes" – mostly farmers, rural labourers and artisans – account for an estimated 52 per cent of the population and the Scheduled Castes (untouchables or Harijans) for a further 22 per cent. Their leaders are dismissive of the Nehru emphasis on industrialisation and want the priorities shifted to the rural areas and to job creation programmes in the villages.

Other traditional assumptions are also being questioned.

● Separatist movements in three border states – Kashmir, Punjab and Assam – are overstretching the security forces in maintaining the unity of the country as never before.

● In the management of the economy India's reputation for caution is also being undermined. Through a combination of loosening the reins domestically and of the unexpected external blow that came with the Gulf crisis (loss of remittances and higher oil prices), India faces as bleak a picture of high external debt, widening balance of payments and fiscal deficits and accelerating inflation as it has ever confronted.

● India's record of stable democratic government is also being tested by the continuing prospect of fragile coalition rule in Delhi and by the increasingly systematic use of violence by political parties, caste groups, regional movements and interest lobbies who see no other way to promote their interests.

These elements alone add up to a picture of a nation in turmoil. But this does not begin to convey the complexity of the situation for India is also experiencing several other upheavals that feed on each other:

● There has been a sharp surge in demand for western-style consumer goods with the growth of a middle class market of 150m-200m.

● There is a small entrepreneurial "revolution" under way with companies better managed, expanding faster and producing record profits.

● There is also an agrarian revolution taking place in the north – with the increase of farmers' incomes in part responsible for their demands for greater political power.

This effervescence is evocatively captured in the sub-title – "A million mutinies now" – of V S Naipaul's new book on India.

India is a vast country with so many differences of region, religion, culture and language that there has always been an uneasy balance between the pressures of unity and disintegration. The emperor Akbar at the height of the Mughal empire provided a unified administration and judiciary. By the 18th century the imperial capital at Delhi had been reduced to one of many competing power centres.

Britain also established a unified

rule over India. But it left the subcontinent divided with the creation of the Moslem state of Pakistan. Yet even within the newly independent India, the autonomy enjoyed by princely Hindu and Moslem states such as Hyderabad and Mysore gave the country the character of a federation.

Nehru's goal was to weld this untidy mass into a nation state committed to modernisation and industrial development. The cornerstones of his vision were a democratic system that recognised the country's pluralism: a secular state that provided protection for Moslems and other minorities, thus demonstrating that the creation of Pakistan

The 'old order' — the India of Nehru's vision with its priorities on maintaining a secular, democratic and unified national framework — is facing its most serious challenge since independence

had been a mistake; and an emphasis on national unity and integrity to forestall further separatist movements and divisions of caste and religion.

The instrument for this nation building process was the Congress party. Congress had established itself as a mass movement during the independence struggle. After independence it became an umbrella organisation bringing different castes, regions, and religions into its fold.

But strains soon developed. Regional and linguistic movements in Tamil Nadu and the Punjab tugged at the nation's unity. In the southern states the lower castes pushed the upper castes from power in a revolution which is still little known. In the 1960s and 1970s the challenges were greater. The Congress party, split under Mrs Indira Gandhi, became a vehicle for dispensing jobs and patronage and disintegrated as a mass organisation. Faced with economic stagnation in the 1960s, Mrs Gandhi turned to populism to win votes. After nationalising the banks, she launched an election campaign in 1971 on the slogan of *"garibi hatao"* (remove poverty). But govern-

ment and state institutions fell into disrepute because economic performance failed to meet the expectations aroused.

Mr Rajiv Gandhi, taking over power in 1984 after his mother's assassination by Sikh extremists, accelerated these changes, liberalising the economy, encouraging competition and relaxing controls that had for long hampered industrial expansion. During Mr Gandhi's period of office, India recorded its highest rates of economic growth since independence. But rapid growth further widened the disparities between rural and urban areas—and the uncertainties that accompanied accelerating change have helped unleash the forces that are now gripping India.

India has often defied its Cassandras. But many observers in Delhi feel that the combined challenges of caste and communal violence, political instability, separatist insurgencies and external debt and fiscal deficits pose a greater threat than any since independence. They are also challenges to which there is no quick solution.

Hindu militancy has increased rapidly to a point where the creation of a Hindu state becomes a possibility. Shortly before independence, fundamentalists tried to destroy the concept of a secular state by assassinating Mahatma Gandhi—its most courageous supporter.

Mrs Gandhi was the first prime minister to compromise India's secular tradition when she encouraged Hindu militancy against Sikh separatism in the early 1980s. Revivalism since then has been bolstered by the continuing Sikh insurgency in the Punjab and by the Moslem separatist movement in Kashmir.

Hindu fundamentalists have never forgiven Moslems for the division of the subcontinent and the creation of Pakistan. They claim that Hindus are now treated as "second class citizens" in their own country, while Moslems are favoured—in the name of protecting minorities—by being allowed their own personal law, their own educational institutions and by a government that backs their cause in the Ayodhya controversy.

In recent weeks, the revivalists have made strategic gains. Their campaign to build a temple at Ayodhya has encouraged the growth of a mass movement that stretches across castes and through most leading states. The tem-

ple has been projected as a symbol of Hindu unity.

The Hindus' other success has been to exploit student and urban middle class opposition to Mr Singh's job reservation programme for the poorer castes. Accusing him of dividing India on caste lines, they projected themselves as defenders of Hindu unity.

The lower castes' challenge to the dominance of the upper castes' administration of the country has a long history that has only come to fruition in the past 20 years. It has its roots in traditional friction between rural and urban India, and the hatred of Brahmins and other higher castes by the lower castes.

Ram Manohar Lohia, a charismatic agrarian anarchist, was the first politician to recognise in the 1950s the potential electoral strength of the lower castes. Lohia condemned Nehru's policy of industrialisation as impoverishing the rural areas. He is still regarded as a "prophet" by many of the Janata Dal leaders in Mr Singh's coalition government.

Since 1967 the backward castes have made significant political gains in state elections in the north and in national elections. But their principal goal of securing jobs in the central government as a lever of prestige and patronage eluded them until Mr Singh announced his programme of reserving 27 per cent of jobs in public service for the backward castes.

Mr Singh's intention was to accelerate the shift in the social balance of power that was taking place in the north and to build a new electoral alliance. The threat his policy posed to the higher castes—many of them poor and without jobs—was shown by the despair of students who set themselves ablaze.

The "old order" is also under threat from the insurgency movements around India's borders. In Kashmir more than 1,000 people have been killed in the first nine months of this year. In the Punjab, the death toll is running at 200-300 a month.

There is a widespread fear among politicians in Delhi that a general election held now would bring to boiling point the castle, religious and regional tensions that have been unleashed. Yet without elections there is no prospect of a government obtaining the stable majority needed to tackle problems that are now tearing India apart.

Just Changing the Guard Can't Save India from Asphyxiation

■ **Democracy:** To survive, it needs a looser confederation, with more authority given to the constituent states

JOYDEEP BHATTACHARYA

Joydeep Bhattacharya is a Ph.D candidate in International Relations at the University of Pennsylvania and a pre-doctoral fellow at the Foreign Policy Research Institute, Philadelphia.

War in the Persian Gulf and turmoil in the Soviet Union monopolize today's news, but what about tomorrow's headlines? India's troubles make for a good candidate.

India is going through grave internal turmoil, the potential magnitude of which could severely destabilize international security. Recurring violence testifies to the alarming plight of the world's largest democracy. There are three related aspects to the crisis: the ascendancy of religious fundamentalism, the rise of separatist movements and the steady erosion in the legitimacy of the institutions of government. Together, they threaten the secular and pluralist lifeline of the political system, crippling its democratic foundations.

Until very recently, Indian democracy had been based on securing the rights of its many ethnic and religious groups by secular guarantees written into the constitution. The intention was clearly to avoid a repetition of the Hindu-Muslim genocide produced by the "divide-and-rule" policy of British imperialism, which led to the bloody partition of the subcontinent into India and Pakistan in 1947. The system that resulted, however, was extremely cumbersome. Charismatic leaders like Jawaharlal Nehru and Mahatma Gandhi managed to hold it together by the force of their personalities, and, time and again, this nation of millions confounded pundits at home and abroad by abiding by that secular framework.

The current crisis threatens the very roots of that tradition. It has a long genealogy, dating back to the viciously divisive process of religious polarization begun in the late 1970s in Punjab. Today, that unhappy region, once lauded as the granary of the Green Revolution, has been joined by its northern neighbor, the idyllic valley of Kashmir, as tragic testimony to the inefficacy of the Indian politicians who succeeded Gandhi and Nehru. As the current prime minister, Chandra Shekhar, proves as inadequate as his immediate predecessor, V.P. Singh, in dealing with the continuing violence, the problem clearly goes beyond the policies of any specific administration. It lies at the heart of Indian democracy and is one of a singular lack of correspondence between nation and state in the Indian union.

This condition bears an eerie parallel with current events in the Soviet Union. In both countries, a centralized state infrastructure is struggling to cope with the increasingly strident demands of the constituent nationalities. In India, religious conflict further vitiates the problem: in

From *The Los Angeles Times Magazine*, February 12, 1991, p. B7. Reprinted by permission.

Punjab and Kashmir, the minority population of Hindus is pitted against the majority Sikhs and Muslims; in the rest of the country, the majority Hindus besiege minorities, especially Muslims, in a rising tide of Hindu fundamentalism. Unlike the Soviet dictatorship, however, India cannot resort to authoritarian means to restore order. Former Prime Minister Indira Gandhi lost political credibility by trying that in the mid-1970s by declaring a state of political "emergency." Few politicians today want to repeat that experiment. Meanwhile, the system stagnates.

For most of India's post-independence history, the Nehru family ruled the country. However, Nehru's daughter and heir-apparent, Indira Gandhi, and her son and successor, Rajiv, governed with decreasing degrees of efficiency and credibility. In fact, it was Mrs. Gandhi's cynical manipulation of regional politics that encouraged the rise of rabid Sikh fundamentalism in Punjab. In opening that Pandora's box, however, she eventually paid with her life, gunned down by an outraged Sikh bodyguard in 1984.

The years that followed have witnessed an astonishing pandering by politicians to reactionary religious movements, resulting in the sectarian and caste-based politics so anathemic to Nehru's cosmopolitan legacy. Political issues have been trivialized and reduced to violent struggles centering around the repossession of temples and mosques. Meanwhile, years of economic hardship and broken political promises have increasingly built up support for Hindu fundamentalists who attack the constitutional protection of minorities as responsible for every problem ranging from unemployment to poverty. They promise to make it very different in a "Hindu nation." The irony is that this movement is led by organizations that claim direct descent from the very extremists who assassinated Mahatma Gandhi, the father of the secular ideal.

Is there a political solution? The answer must be a qualified affirmative. Under current conditions, divisive crises undermining stability will recur with progressively vicious predictability, making it imperative to restore the original logic of Indian democracy: inalienable liberty and equality of all citizens irrespective of caste and creed. This is possible only by altering the structure of the system. The hierarchical center-state relationship that prevails at present, with disproportionate power enjoyed by the central government at New Delhi, has proved asphyxiating. It must be shelved. India needs a looser confederation, with more decision-making authority given to the constituent states, thereby more faithfully reflecting dichotomies. A mere change of guard in New Delhi will not solve the problem. Neither will repeated reshufflings of the same pack of power-hungry politicians.

The hope for India lies in a decentralized secular and pluralist system that recognizes the divisions in society and instead of seeking to suppress them by force, seeks strength from that diversity through a system of political checks and balances.

The choice is clear. India's demography demands a secular political system. The alternative, both domestic and international, is too appalling to contemplate: a nation of nearly 1 billion led by an insular and reactionary Hindu regime, defining its policies in a pattern of clear confrontation with an increasingly fundamentalist Islamic world.

Appendix

BY THE NUMBERS
David Berg, Kelley Dock, and Harmon Zeigler
The University of Puget Sound

	United States	United Kingdom	West* Germany	France	Japan
DEMOGRAPHICS					
Area (1,000 Square Kilometers)	9373	245	249	547	378
1990 Population (Millions)	250.3	57.1	61.2	56.5	123.8
Life Expectancy at Birth (1988)	75	75.3	75.8	75.9	79.1
% of Population Over Age 65	20	19	26	22	20
Percent Increase (1980–2023)	130	40	38	75	131
% of Population Living in Cities Over 500,000	77	55	45	34	42
1987 Birth Rate per 1,000	16	13	10	14	11
1989 Infant Mortality per 1,000 Live Births	10	9	8	8	6
% Teen Age Birth Rate	50	29	8	15	4
Heterogeneity Scale (1 = Least, 20 = Most)	12	12	6	9	4
Divorces per 1,000 Marriages	22	14	6	4	3
Index of Social Progress Ranking	5	3	1	2	4
Economist "Nirvana" Rank	8	9	2	1	4
UN Quality of Life Score Rank	.961 (17)	.970 (10)	.967 (11)	.974 (8)	.996 (1)
Suicides/100,000 pop.	12.4	18.6	17	21.8	21.1
Youth Suicide Rate; Male per 100,000	21	10	17	15.5	12
Murders/100,000	7.91	1.37	4.41	4.63	1.47
Rapes/100,000	35.7	2.7	9.7	5.2	1.6
Robberies/100,000	205	45	46	109	2
Drug Offenses/100,000	320.11	10.07	103.78	52.51	1.60
Serious Assaults/100,000	290.21	219.69	107.55	70.01	19.58
Prison Population (per 1,000)	43	10	8	8	5
Abortions/1000 Women of Childbearing Age	139	12	8	15	84
Out of Wedlock Births as a % of All Births	29	19	8	18	2
Food Consumed as a % of All Consumption	11	14.5	17.6	17.9	19.9
Alcohol Consumed as a % of All Consumption	1.4	2.0	3.3	2.0	1.3
Cigarettes Smoked per Person per Year	2,285	1,695	1,910	1,680	2,515
Television Sets/1,000	798	333	373	394	580
Newspapers/1,000	268	414	350	212	585
Cars/1,000	580	330	450	410	250
Persons per Car	1.8	2.9	2.2	2.6	4.2
Kilometers per Person per Day in Cars	52	21	23	21	8
Kilometers per Person per Day in Bus or Train	1	4	5	6	10
1989 Living Costs (New York = 100)	New York 100	London 95	Bonn 101	Paris 90	Tokyo 126
Days in Standard School Year	180	192	240	185	243
International Math Test Scores; High School	52	55	59	58	65
Science Achievement Scores	25	80	91	71	92
College Enrollment/1,000	57	22	30	30	30
Female College Enrollment (College Pop./ Females 20–24)	5	1.5	2.5	3	0.5

*West German figures are used due to lack of effective relevant statistics for a unified Germany.

	United States	United Kingdom	West Germany	France	Japan
Status of Women (100 = Highest)	82.5	74.5	76	76	68.5
Females as a % of Civilian Employment	44.8	42.4	39	41.6	39.6
Date of Women's Suffrage	1920	1928	1919	1944	1947
Date of First Woman in Cabinet	1933	1929	1961	1947	1989
ECONOMICS					
1987 GNP per Capita	$18,413	$11,718	$18,471	$17,061	$19,322
GNP Growth Rate (1965–1987)	1.5%	1.7%	2.5%	2.7%	4.2%
1991 GNP Growth Rate (Projected)	2.5%	1.9%	3.1%	2.8%	4.3%
Inflation Rate (1980–1987)	4.3%	5.7%	2.9%	7.7%	1.4%
Unemployment Rate	6.1%	8.9%	5.5%	8.9%	2.3%
Trade Balance (Billions)	− 173.7	− 23.3	65.9	− 10.0	80.7
Public Debt as a % of GNP	30%	39%	23.8%	26.6%	24.6%
Economic Stability World Rank	10	21	7	11	1
Income Distribution —top 20% —bottom 20%	1980 39.9% 5.3%	1979 39.7% 7.0%	1978 39.5% 7.9%	1975 42.4% 5.5%	1979 37.5% 8.7%
Proportion of Income Distribution Due to Government Efforts	14%	22%	4%	9%	13%
Top Personal Income Tax Rates	28%	40%	53%	57%	50%
% of GDP Collected as Taxes	31%	38%	40%	43%	30%
% of GDP Spent on Education	6.8%	5.2%	4.6%	5.8%	5.6%
% of GDP Spent on Health	11.1%	6.2%	8.1%	8.5%	6.7%
% of GNP Spent on Defense	6.6%	5.3%	3.2%	4.1%	1.0%
Public Health Spending as a % of Total Health Spending	40.8%	86.2%	78.1%	79.2%	72.9%
% of 1987 Budget Spent on Housing, Social Security, and Welfare	31.3%	31.6%	33%	38.5%	22%
Central Govt. Total Expenditure as a % of GNP (1987)	23.3%	38.9%	30.1%	45.1%	17.4%
% of Economy Under Govt. Ownership	32%	48%	36%	54%	31%
Total Foreign Aid as % of GNP	2.1%	3.0%	3.8%	7.1%	3.0%
Inflows of Foreign Investment as % of GNP	28.2	7.6	0.9	3.0	0.2
Personal Savings Rate (% of Disposable Income)	4.5%	1%	12.2%	14.9%	16.4%
Investment Spending (% of GNP)	18%	16%	21%	21%	29%
Interest Rate for Borrowing on Equipment and Machinery	11.2%	9.2%	7.0%	8.1%	7.2%
Non-Defense Research & Development Spending as % of GNP	1.8%	2.3%	2.6%	2.3%	2.8%
GNP per Capita Adjusted by Purchasing Power Parities	$18,200	$12,000	$13,300	$13,000	$13,000
Net Domestic Purchasing Power (Japan = 100)	200	154	225	135	100
Net Hourly Earnings	$10.70	$9.00	$8.00	$9.00	$6.60
% of Payroll Taxed for All Social Security	7.15	9.0	17.75	14.81	10.95
Working Hours per Week	39	36.5	40	40.5	47
Holidays per Year	13	24.1	29.5	28.2	16.1
% of Population Active in Labor Unions	15%	38%	34%	17%	22%
Strike Days Lost per 1,000 Workers	180.2	79.3	1.4	26.8	4.3
Productivity (GDP Output per Hour)	132.4	148.1	132.4	141.2	170.5
Productivity Growth (Growth in GDP Output per Hour '79–'89)	1.09%	2.95%	1.88%	3.24%	3.06%
Govt. Employees (% of Work Force)	8.1%	13.2%	8.6%	12.1%	4.4%
Energy Consumption (Kilos per Capita)	9,489	5,363	5,829	3,831	3,625
Nuclear Electricity (% of Total Production)	19.5%	19.3%	34%	69.9%	23.4%

	United States	United Kingdom	West Germany	France	Japan
Annual Oil Consumption in Gallons	1,067	462	567	508	622
% of Oil Use Met by Imports	37	0	95	96	100
1987 Carbon Emissions from Fossil Fuels (Tons per Capita)	5.03	2.73	2.98	1.70	2.12
POLITICS					
Government Sponsored Bills Enacted (% of Laws)	33%	97%	87%	82%	77%
Average Turnout in National Elections	52	77	87	74	73
Yearly Salaries for Members of Lower House	$120,700	$50,800	$63,800	$78,250	$102,600

ELECTIONS

United States

*1988 Presidential Election Popular Vote/House and Congress Popular Vote

George Bush (Republican)   53.4%/45.5%
Michael Dukakis (Democrat)   45.7%/53.3%

*1990 Party Composition of Congress

	Republican	Democrat
Senate	43	57
House of Representatives	166	269

*Number of women holding cabinet level positions: 1

United Kingdom

*1987 House of Commons Elections Popular Vote/Seats Won

Conservatives   42.3%/376
Labour   30.8%/229
Liberal/SDP Alliance   22.8%/22

*Number of women holding cabinet level positions: 0

Germany

(First All-German election since World War II)
December 2, 1990, All-German Bundestag Election
Popular Vote/Seats Won

Christian Democrats/Christian Social Union   48.2%/319
Social Democrats   33.5%/239
Free Democrats   11.0%/79
Greens (west)   3.9%/24
Alliance '90 (east)   1.2%/8
Democratic Socialists   2.4%/17

*Number of women holding cabinet level positions: 3

France

*1988 Presidential Election Popular Vote

François Mitterrand (Socialist)   54.02%
Jacques Chirac (Gaullist)   45.98%

*1988 Party Composition of the French National Assembly

Socialists and Allies   275
Gaullists   130
Independent Republicans (UDF)   90
Centrists (UDC)   41
Communists   27
National Front   1
No party   10

*Number of women holding cabinet level positions: 5

Japan

*1989 Party Composition of the House of Representatives

Liberal Democratic Party   293
Japan Socialist Party   83
Komeito   54
Japanese Communist Party   26
Democratic Socialist Party   26
United Social Democratic Party   4

*Number of women holding cabinet level positions: 0 (2 women dismissed in February 1990)

German Social Union (DSU), 32, 36, 38
Germany: 134, 135, 136, 203; federalism
in, 45–48, 49–50; and France, 59–60,
62, 66; and Green party, 90–91; and
Gulf War, 39, 159, 160; and
immigration, 11–12; national elections
in, 35–40; reuniting of, 8, 9–10, 29–34,
139–142, 167; and Soviet Union, 137;
see also, East Germany; West
Germany
Ghannouchi, Rachid, 225
Giscard d'Estaing, Valéry, 51, 52, 53, 56,
57, 61, 66, 103, 118
Gorbachev, Mikhail, 136, 139, 140, 141,
172, 174, 175, 180–181, 182, 183,
186–187, 188–190
Greece: 13, 105, 106; constitution of,
111–112; and European Community,
144, 145, 146, 152, 154
Green party: and German national
election, 90–91; West German, 31, 32,
36, 38, 102, 104
Group Areas Act, 221, 222
Guildford Four, 27, 28

Hamas, 225–226
Havel, Vaclav, 37
Heath, Edward, 117, 121
Helsinki agreement, 151
Hezbullah, 226
Hindus, 234, 235, 236–237
Holland: Christian Democratic party in,
92, 93, 94; and European Community,
146, 152, 154
Hong Kong, 72, 205
Hungary, 94, 162, 163, 165, 166–167, 168
Hussein, Saddam, 159, 226, 231, 232

Iceland: 105; and European Community,
147
immigration: 11–13; and France, 12, 59,
63, 66; and right-wing movements, 98,
99; of Soviet Jews into Israel, 230–232
India, 204, 206, 234–235, 236–237
inflation, in China, 194, 195–197
infranationalism, 126–127
Inkatha Freedom party, 218, 220
Institutional Revolutionary Party (PRI),
207, 208
institutionalists, view of changes in
Europe by, 132–133
inter-governmental conference (IGC), 157,
158
International Monetary Fund, and Nigeria,
215–216
Iran, 123, 152, 205, 226
Iraq, 226–227
Ireland: 11, 105, 106; in European
Community, 145, 146, 152, 154, 158;
see also, Northern Ireland
Irish Republican Army (IRA), 11, 15, 27–28
Islam, political side of, 223–227
Islamic Jihad, 225, 226
Islamic Renaissance party, 225
Islamic Salvation Front (FIS), 223, 224
Israel: 151, 163, 224; politics in, 228–233
Italian Social Movement, 98, 99
Italy: 86, 105, 106; Christian Democratic
party in, 92, 93, 94; Communist party
in, 95, 96; and European Community,
144, 145, 146, 152, 153, 154, 156, 158;
and immigration, 12–13

Japan: 84, 85, 123, 204–205; and
European Community, 144, 152, 156;
national character of, 74–75; politics
in, 69–73, 76–77
job reservation program, for poorer castes
in India, 234, 235
Jordan, 223, 224, 225, 228
justice, British, and Northern Ireland,
27–28

Kennedy, John F., 118, 121, 122
Keynes, John Maynard, 80, 81, 82, 85, 86,
203
Khomeini, Ayatollah Ruhollah, 226
Kinnock, Neil, 16, 123
Kohl, Helmut, 9, 10, 29, 31, 33, 34, 35,
36–37, 38, 39, 40, 41, 42, 44, 50, 59,
62, 140, 141, 160, 163
Korea: 205; see also, South Korea

Labor Party, in Israel, 229, 230
Labour Party, British, 14, 15, 16–17, 18,
19, 21, 25, 100, 102, 103, 105, 120, 122
LaFontaine, Oskar, 31, 38
Land Acts, of South Africa, 221
Latvia, 172, 189
Le Pen, Jean-Marie, 56, 63, 66, 98, 99
League of Nations, 71, 115
Lebanon, 226
legal postivism, 151
Li Peng, 192, 193
Liberal Democratic party, Japanese, 69,
70, 72, 76–77
liberals, view of changes in Europe by,
131–132
Liberal/Social Democratic Alliance,
Britain's, 101, 102, 103
Libya, 152
Ligachev, Yegor, 182, 183–184
Lithuania, 172, 174, 189
local community charge, 15, 25
Luxembourg, and European Community,
146

Macedonia, 163
Major, John, 11, 23–24, 159
"malaise français, le," and French
national identity, 65–66
Mamman, Alhaji Abubakar, 216–217
Mamser, 216
Mandela, Nelson, 218, 221, 222
market socialism, 165, 167
Marxism: 206; vs. capitalism, 80, 81, 82,
83, 85; French, 54, 55
Mexico, economic and political reform in,
207–210
Middle East: 133, 152; Islamic politics in,
223–227; and Israel, 228–233; see
also, individual countries
Mitsotakis, Constantine, 13
Mitterrand, François, 51, 52, 53, 55, 57,
59–60, 61, 62, 65, 66, 102, 118, 121,
122, 159, 160
Morocco, 54
Muslim Brotherhood, 223
Muslims: 213, 234, 235, 236–237; see
also, Islam

Nakasone, Yasuhiro, 70, 71, 76
National Action Party (PAN), 208
National Assembly, of France, 53
National Front party, 56, 59, 63, 66, 98,
99

National Liberation Front (FLN), 223, 224
National Party, of South Africa, 219
nationalism: 124, 134; and Eastern
Europe, 161–162, 163; French, 63, 64,
65; in Soviet Union, 181
nation-state, 64, 124–127
NATO, see North Atlantic Treaty
Organization
Nehru, Jawaharal, 234, 235, 236, 237
Netherlands, see Holland
Nigeria, 211–217
North Atlantic Treaty Organization (NATO),
8, 33, 61, 131, 133, 137–138, 140, 141,
159, 160
Northern Ireland, 11, 27–28, 103
Norway, and European Community, 11,
147, 149
nuclear weapons, 102, 119

Oder-Neisse line, and Germany and
Poland, 10, 31
Official Secrets Act, 120
Orange Workers Union, 219
Organization for Economic Cooperation
and Development, 81, 119, 120

Pakistan, 234
Palestine, 225–226, 228–229, 230, 231,
232–233
Palestine Liberation Organization (PLO),
225–226, 228–229, 230, 232, 233
Pamyat, 182
Pan-Africanist Congress, 218, 219
Pares, Shimon, 229, 230, 231
parliament: 117, 118, 120; vs. Congress,
114–116; European, 150, 151; women
in, 105–106
Party of Democratic Revolution (PRD),
208
Party of Democratic Socialism, 31, 35, 36,
38
People's Guardian, 219
People's Liberation Army (PLA), 195, 197,
198
People's Republic of China (PRC), see
China
perestroika, 172, 173, 174, 176, 188
Persian Gulf War, 39, 159–160, 228,
232–233
Poland, 10, 31, 94, 162, 163, 164, 165,
166–167, 168
Political Cooperation (Poco), in European
Community, 152–153
poll tax, 15, 25
Pompidou, Georges, 51, 53, 123
Population Registration Act, 221
populism, in Soviet Union, 182
Portugal: 106; communism in, 96–97; in
European Community, 109, 110, 111,
128, 130
presidents: authority of French, 62–63; vs.
prime ministers, 117–123; and new
Soviet system, 186–187
Presowitz, Clyde, on Japan, 69–73
prime minsters, vs. presidents, 117–123
privatization, 15–16, 52, 57, 206, 215
proportional representation, in European
political systems, 105
protectionism, and European Community,
144, 146

Credits/ Acknowledgments

Cover design by Charles Vitelli

1. Country Studies
Facing overview—The Christian Science Monitor photo by R. Norman Matheny.

2. Modern Pluralist Democracies
Facing overview—WHO photo by E. Mandelmann.

3. Politics in a New Europe
Facing overview—The Dushkin Publishing Group, Inc.

4. Soviet Union and China
Facing overview—Soviet Mission to the United Nations, Novasti photo by Yelin.

5. Third World
Facing overview—United Nations photo by B. Cirone.

ANNUAL EDITIONS ARTICLE REVIEW FORM

■ NAME: _____ DATE: _____

■ TITLE AND NUMBER OF ARTICLE: _____

■ BRIEFLY STATE THE MAIN IDEA OF THIS ARTICLE: _____

_____

_____

_____

_____

■ LIST THREE IMPORTANT FACTS THAT THE AUTHOR USES TO SUPPORT THE MAIN IDEA:

_____

_____

_____

_____

_____

_____

■ WHAT INFORMATION OR IDEAS DISCUSSED IN THIS ARTICLE ARE ALSO DISCUSSED IN YOUR
TEXTBOOK OR OTHER READING YOU HAVE DONE? LIST THE TEXTBOOK CHAPTERS AND PAGE
NUMBERS:

_____

_____

_____

_____

_____

_____

_____

■ LIST ANY EXAMPLES OF BIAS OR FAULTY REASONING THAT YOU FOUND IN THE ARTICLE:

_____

_____

_____

_____

_____

■ LIST ANY NEW TERMS/CONCEPTS THAT WERE DISCUSSED IN THE ARTICLE AND WRITE A
SHORT DEFINITION:

_____

_____

_____

_____

_____

_____

*Your instructor may require you to use this Annual Editions Article Review Form in any number of ways:
for articles that are assigned, for extra credit, as a tool to assist in developing assigned papers, or simply
for your own reference. Even if it is not required, we encourage you to photocopy and use this page;
you'll find that reflecting on the articles will greatly enhance the information from your text.

We Want Your Advice

ANNUAL EDITIONS: COMPARATIVE POLITICS 91/92
Article Rating Form

Here is an opportunity for you to have direct input into the next revision of this volume. We would like you to rate each of the 58 articles listed below, using the following scale:

1. **Excellent: should definitely be retained**
2. **Above average: should probably be retained**
3. **Below average: should probably be deleted**
4. **Poor: should definitely be deleted**

Your ratings will play a vital part in the next revision. So please mail this prepaid form to us just as soon as you complete it.
Thanks for your help!

Annual Editions revisions depend on two major opinion sources: one is our Advisory Board, listed in the front of this volume, which works with us in scanning the thousands of articles published in the public press each year; the other is you—the person actually using the book. Please help us and the users of the next edition by completing the prepaid article rating form on this page and returning it to us. Thank you.

Rating	Article
	1. 1990: A Europe Transformed
	2. British Politics in the Post-Collectivist Era
	3. Margaret Thatcher—Brought Down by Her Own Strengths
	4. John Major: More Than a Tedious Talent
	5. The Scots Who Want to Be Alone
	6. History as Plague: Two Islands Struggle to Recover
	7. Reunited Germany
	8. German Elections and National Unity in 1990
	9. The East German Disaster
	10. Some Thoughts on Federalism and the Federal Republic
	11. New Federalists
	12. France's Fifth Republic: Sure-Footed
	13. The End of French Exceptionalism
	14. France Faces the New Europe
	15. France Questions Its Identity as It Sinks Into 'Le Malaise'
	16. Quiet Revolt in the Corridors of Power
	17. The Real Japan
	18. The Two Faces of Japan: Most of What You've Heard Is True
	19. Giving Hostages to Electoral Fortune
	20. Reflections: The Triumph of Capitalism
	21. Interview With Michel Rocard
	22. Squabbling German Greens Survey the Election Debacle
	23. Europe's Christian Democrats: Hello, Caesar, This Is God
	24. Europe's Extremes
	25. What We Know About Women Voters in Britain, France, and West Germany
	26. Women in Parliament: Keeping a Sense of Disproportion
	27. Europe's Women: How the Other Half Works
	28. We the Peoples: A Checklist for New Constitution Writers

Rating	Article
	29. Parliament and Congress: Is the Grass Greener on the Other Side?
	30. Presidents and Prime Ministers
	31. With All Her Faults, She Is My Country Still
	32. Predicting the New Europe
	33. Euro Future
	34. German Unification—Opportunity or Setback for Europe?
	35. The United States of Europe
	36. Push Is On for Wider European Community
	37. Six EC Institutions
	38. Tackling the Democratic Deficit
	39. After Gulf War, A Drive Toward European Unity
	40. Eastern Europe I: Liberalism vs. Nationalism
	41. The Dustbin of Economics
	42. The Dilemmas of Freedom
	43. Gorbachev's Gathering Storm
	44. The Russian Character
	45. Soviet Politics: Breakdown or Renewal?
	46. Gorbachev Lines Up New System
	47. The Gorbachev Record: The Rise and Fall of Perestroika
	48. Ominous Embers From the Fire of 1989
	49. China: The Coming Changes
	50. Rich Country, Poor Country
	51. Salinas Takes a Gamble
	52. Africa's Great Black Hope
	53. South Africa's Constitutional Cry: Be Original
	54. Apartheid's Laws Are Dismantled, But Not Its Cages
	55. Islam's New Political Face
	56. Israel: The Deadlock Persists
	57. Turmoil Erodes the Nehru Legacy
	58. Just Changing the Guard Can't Save India From Asphyxiation

(Continued on next page)

ABOUT YOU

Name_____ Date_____

Are you a teacher? ☐   Or student? ☐

Your School Name _____

Department _____

Address _____

City _____ State _____ Zip _____

School Telephone # _____

YOUR COMMENTS ARE IMPORTANT TO US!

Please fill in the following information:

For which course did you use this book? _____

Did you use a text with this Annual Edition?   ☐ yes   ☐ no

The title of the text? _____

What are your general reactions to the Annual Editions concept?

Have you read any particular articles recently that you think should be included in the next edition?

Are there any articles you feel should be replaced in the next edition? Why?

Are there other areas that you feel would utilize an Annual Edition?

May we contact you for editorial input?

May we quote you from above?